Reader in the Academic Library

edited by

Michael M. Reynolds

NCR MICROCARD® EDITIONS

901 TWENTY-SIXTH STREET, N.W., WASHINGTON, D. C. 20037, 202/333-6393

INDUSTRIAL PRODUCTS DIVISION, THE NATIONAL CASH REGISTER COMPANY

Published *Readers* in the series are:

Reader in Library Administration. 1969.
Paul Wasserman and Mary Lee Bundy.

Reader in Research Methods for Librarianship. 1970.
Mary Lee Bundy and Paul Wasserman.

Reader Series
In Library and Information Science

Forword

Unlike many other academic disciplines, librarianship has not yet begun to exploit the contributions of the several disciplines toward the study of its own issues. Yet the literature abounds with material germane to its concerns. Too frequently the task of identifying, correlating, and bringing together material from innumerable sources is burdensome, time consuming or simply impossible. For a field whose stock in trade is organizing knowledge, it is clear that the job of synthesizing the most essential contributions from the elusive sources in which they are contained is overdue. This then is the rationale for the series, *Readers in Library and Information Science.*

The *Readers in Library and Information Science* will include books concerned with various broad aspects of the field's interests. Each volume will be prepared by a recognized student of the topic covered, and the content will embrace material from the many different sources from the traditional literature of librarianship as well as from outside the field in which the most salient contributions have appeared. The objectives of the series will be to bring together in convenient form the key elements required for a current and comprehensive view of the subject matter. In this way it is hoped that the core of knowledge, essential as the intellectual basis for study and understanding, will be drawn into focus and thereby contribute to the furtherance of professional education and professional practice in the field.

Paul Wasserman
Series Editor

Contents

Introduction

I
THE ACADEMIC ENVIRONMENT

II
THE LIBRARY IN ACADEMIA

III
ADMINISTERING THE LIBRARY

IV
FINANCING THE LIBRARY

V
THE STRUCTURE OF THE LIBRARY

VI
THE MANAGEMENT OF THE LIBRARY

Personnel

The Collection

Housing the Library

Library Cooperation

The Library Performing

VII
THE ACADEMIC LIBRARY TOMORROW

Introduction

For several years prior to the time I accepted the assignment of assembling a collection on academic library administration, I was becoming increasingly aware that the behavioral problems inside and outside the library with which I was confronted as an academic library administrator were those facing others; that these problems would become even more difficult of solution by future academic librarians; and that it would be useful to publish such a volume.

Not too long ago an academic library administrator was reasonably effective if that person had a moderately good humanistic background and a pleasant life style, and had mastered a relatively defined body of library principles and vocational skills. For the college librarian an interest in another discipline might have proven additionally helpful, while for the university librarian knowledge of antique books was extremely useful. But the differences were largely in degree and less in kind.

This situation — of questionable value academically — no longer exists. The accelerating increase in information, the demands of information users, and the increased competition for resources are only a few of the more demonstrable factors which have challenged the very existence of academic librarianship. For the academic librarian, Miss Zulieka Dobson's little bag of tricks is no longer enough.

This collection of readings is an attempt to make available a body of analytical and descriptive information which can provide an understanding of a particular and evolving institution of our time, the academic library. While there is certainly no shortage of literature on the academic library, much of this takes the form of a display of some operational innovation — probably no longer used; a tribute to the perfection of a technique abstracted from a procedure within a process of dubious relevance; or a historical description of a particular library that managed to be removed from societal contacts. Consequently, it was this editor's conviction that the graduate and advanced undergraduate student might profit from a text which presented the academic library both as a part of a larger social process and as an institution and process which is itself subject to analysis, research and experimentation. There has been no attempt to avoid issues or controversy; nor has there been an attempt to suggest solutions. Instead, by a careful selection of readings it was intended to illustrate problems representative of the nature of higher education and of library administration, to expose the issues in contention, and to suggest that solutions lie in comprehending a particular reality and the means to affect it.

This volume, therefore, is less an encyclopedic guide for the academic librarian than it is an attempt to provide the basis for this comprehension. Academic librarians must be aware of the substantive nature of the uncertainty and controversy existing within their profession; academic librarians must extend their educational experience to include contributions by experts in many other disciplines rather than merely proclaim shibboleths incapable of examination; and academic librarians must recognize the realities which can make possible the definition, interpretation, and contribution of librarianship within the educational process. Certainly not all of this can be accomplished within one collection, but a beginning can be attempted.

The introductions to each of the major sections and the commentaries which are prefatory to each selection were provided as continuity for the reader. They were not meant to explain the selection, nor to predispose the reader.

I would like to express my thanks to the authors and publishers who generously agreed to the reprinting of their work in this volume.

College Park, Maryland   M.M.R.
September, 1969   ix

I
THE ACADEMIC ENVIRONMENT

Higher education was never, nor is it now, a static whole. Rather it is constantly in a state of change, its diverse institutions evolving to meet new interpretations of reality. While it is committed to a particular–knowledge–higher education lacks a single plan of action and must instead be examined holistically. The academic librarian must accept the idealism of this commitment to knowledge and be, at the same time, a realist. He must proceed logically in his own system, accepting the limitations placed on that system by the differences inherent in the society, institution, and machinery which provide the basis for his activity. He must, at the same time as he accepts the limitations, be prepared to examine higher education as he would any other phenomenon in order that he may better relate the library to it and provide advocacy for the library. In this section some of the significant forces in educational administration are examined in their societal environments.

Higher Education As An Institution

by John D. Millett

As an ongoing effort by society to perform a unique function, higher education has become institutionalized. Today it reflects the major characteristics of the dominant coeval institutions with which it shared a historical continuum. Yet higher education, if it is to carry out its unique function effectively, must function with the possibility that it will be a change agent. To do this it must maintain an organizational arrangement that will not inhibit success. The academic librarian accordingly must not find in artificial or restrictive managerial conveniences ends in themselves but rather must establish fundamental relationships that will relate the library as a sub-institution directly to the mission of higher education.

Higher education is a unique institution in Western society generally and in the United States in particular. It is customary to speak of higher education as having three primary purposes: instruction, research, and public service. Actually, the public service referred to is vitally related to instruction and research, involving dissemination of knowledge on a continuing basis or the performance of activities essential to instruction. It might more appropriately be said that higher education seeks to preserve, transmit, and advance knowledge.

This is a peculiar purpose—peculiar in that it is served only by higher education. It might be mentioned that institutions of society—the family, the economy, the church, the government, and others—tend to be differentiated one from another not just in structure but more importantly in function. No two serve the same purpose. The identifying characteristic of a social institution is its particular objective which marks it off from any other institution. So it is with higher education. It serves a peculiar purpose, and hence is a unique or identifiable institution.

Knowledge is a precious and illusive thing. Bacon long ago described knowledge itself as power. So it is: the power to guide action, to make one person and one group and one nation superior to others, to influence the life and well-being of others. Knowledge of how to produce and distribute goods, how to guide and direct others, how to protect and advance

the public weal, how to undertake the pursuit of personal satisfaction—such knowledge is much in demand today as in ages past. But knowledge is not easy to identify or to discover. Knowledge seldom seems complete; it always seems to present new challenges.

Higher education has made its province the realm of knowledge. This knowledge may be inherently valuable for its own sake, for the satisfaction it brings to the individual who seeks to escape ignorance and superstition. This knowledge may be useful in solving human problems from health to production, from justice to unemployment. Knowledge for its own sake and for use—knowledge is what higher education would impart.

As an institution with this special purpose—to preserve, transmit, and advance knowledge—higher education has over the years evolved in an amazing way. It has seemed at times to be a part of other social institutions or to take on their peculiar characteristics of operation. Higher education has at times appeared to be a religious institution. At times it has appeared to be a part of the market place where goods and services are produced and distributed. At other times it is an eleemosynary institution, a part of a system of voluntary support by which society seeks to meet its obligations to help others with a generous and benevolent hand. And yet higher education is none of these institutions in fact. It has been closely allied with other institutions in history. It behaves in patterns reminiscent of

SOURCE: Reprinted from John D. Millett, *The Academic Community* (New York: McGraw-Hill Book Company, 1962), Chapter 2, "Higher Education as an Institution," pp. 33-64, by permission of the publisher and the author.

other institutions. Through all these similarities, it remains apart, peculiar, different, custodian through the ages of the higher learning.

HIGHER EDUCATION AS
A RELIGIOUS INSTITUTION

In its origins in the medieval world, higher education was clerical, and some of the medieval customs and costumes survive to this day as a reminder of religious beginnings. The university of the Middle Ages, from which in direct descent our colleges and universities of today have evolved, was an outgrowth of cathedral schools and monasteries.[1] As universities emerged early in the twelfth century, they were something more than an ecclesiastical agency. The student body and the masters (the teachers and scholars) were regarded as clerks, as part of the great body of churchmen of the time. Yet these persons were not necessarily members of religious orders. And while the university functioned under the general oversight of ecclesiastical authority, conflict between the two was not unknown.

To a considerable degree, society in Western Europe in the Middle Ages was either feudal or clerical. At the base of feudal society was the serf or peasant, for all practical purposes tied to his land. At the apex of this hierarchy was the Roman Emperor, at least in theory, and in practice a king or other ruler of a large area. The medieval town with its merchant and craft guilds impaired the symmetry of this social system. The clerical world, on the other hand, centering in a supposedly universal church, was at least a structure based upon individual ability, thanks to the rule of celibacy. It was quite natural that in such a bifurcated society the university should find itself primarily allied with the church.

The educated clerk became a teacher, an ecclesiastical official, the member of a religious order, or in time a civil servant. A considerable career was open to his ambition and effort, but this was true primarily because of his clerical status. If high officials of the church became even more nationalistic than the kings they served, their rise to positions of political power was made possible in large degree because of their clerical—that is, their educated—background.

With all its disruption of the political, social, and economic fabric of the sixteenth century, the Reformation brought likewise its changes in the position of the university. Luther was highly critical of universities as he knew them, but

Protestant states found it convenient to continue them under their own direction. The international characteristic of many universities, such as the one at Paris, suffered under the division of Europe into two warring religious camps. And a new orthodoxy was expected of the universities. Yet fundamentally the university was still thought of as an appendage of the church, or closely allied to it, even when the church as in England and certain German states was no longer Roman Catholic.

The college as it was transplanted to colonial America from England in the seventeenth century still had a decidedly religious bias. Harvard was established in 1636 in large part, according to the well-known statement of Puritan principles, "to advance learning and perpetuate it to posterity; dreading to leave an illiterate ministry to the churches, when our present ministers shall lie in the dust." Other colleges were founded in the eighteenth century for similar purposes. Yet these colleges in the New World were more than religious seminaries, even as were the universities of Western Europe. Moreover, Protestant society, in the process of struggling toward religious toleration and freedom, was providing a widening role for higher education. Still in the first decades of the nineteenth century in the United States most American colleges, as Professor Hofstadter has pointed out, "were not only religious, in the broad sense, but actually under denominational control and under the leadership of clerical presidents." [2]

The period after the Civil War in the United States witnessed a great transformation from the age of the college to the age of the university.[3] It was a process accompanied by a growing secularization of higher education. The higher learning and religious faith knew at best an uneasy truce; at worst, they engaged in bitter and fruitless warfare. In 100 years the ties of higher education and religion in the United States have largely been severed. Yet the relationship has by no means been completely ended. The two institutions continue to share common concerns and to seek a basic unity in which knowledge and faith realize complementary rather than competing contributions to man's life.

The role of the church in higher education in the United States is by no means negligible. A recent listing of some 2,000 colleges and universities by the Office of Education indicates that nearly 800 of these remain "related" to a religious denomination, of which nearly 500 are related to Protestant denominations and nearly 300 to the Roman Catholic Church. To be sure, close to 80 of these are entirely devoted to education in theology. Yet nine-tenths of the total number are engaged in liberal and professional programs of higher education.

"Related to a religious denomination" is a difficult term to define. In the instance of most colleges and universities related to Protestant denominations, other than theological seminaries, "related to" means that some church body officially elects all or a substantial part of the trustees. In addition, in varying amounts the parent church body, usually on an area or regional basis, may contribute some direct financial support to the operation of these colleges and universities. In the instance of Roman Catholic colleges, "related to" means usually that a religious order of the Catholic Church has established and operates a college or university in a particular community. Ordinarily such colleges and universities receive no direct financial support from and have few if any formal ties to the diocese of the area. On the other hand, a goodly part of the support of such colleges and universities comes from the contributed services of teaching members of the order, and necessarily the order retains substantial authority of direction over the work of the college or university.

Even so, it is possible in many instances involving Protestant, Jewish, and Roman Catholic colleges and universities to exaggerate the degree of external church control. Such church authority as exists is apt to be exercised with considerable moderation. Thus, trustees elected by a Protestant conference or synod may in effect be self-perpetuating. And a religious order of the Roman Catholic Church may leave extensive discretion in academic matters to the administrative officers and faculty of the individual college or university.

Furthermore, many so-called "nondenominational" colleges and universities may operate a school of theology and otherwise maintain close working relationships with one or more religious denominations. And it is not uncommon for public colleges and universities to have a department of religion or of religious education and to provide informal discussions of religious subjects.

The institution of higher education as it is known in the United States has not entirely escaped from its clerical origins. Nor is there reason to believe that it necessarily should. Even as in the medieval university, a concern with theology and the philosophy, art, and literature of religion remains a continuing and important cultural preoccupation of higher education.

Yet in spite of this long association, our colleges and universities in the twentieth century do not belong to any church in any real sense. Colleges and universities belong to the world of knowledge. A church-related college opens its doors to students of all religious denominations; no religious test is applied for admission. While some formal study in religion may be required of the student who is a communicant of the church to which the college or university is related, this requirement is not usually applied to other students. The objective of a college or university is not to be religious but to be intellectual in a rigorous, determined way. No college or university can survive upon faith. It must conserve, transmit, and advance knowledge.

HIGHER EDUCATION AS A WELFARE INSTITUTION

The university of the Middle Ages and of later times was an object of charity. Kings and princes, noblemen and merchants provided endowments which built great buildings and which provided operating income. Because of its religious connection, the university was an appropriate recipient of benevolence. It was blessed to give to the medieval university, just as today it is comforting to contribute to our colleges and universities.

The college and university became an eleemosynary agency for a simple reason. If young men who came from the lower gentry and the yeoman class of society were to be educated, their education had to be subsidized. It is interesting to realize that nearly one thousand years ago higher education was not thought of as the privilege of nobility and wealth but as the province of persons of talent, wherever in society these might be found. Undoubtedly, the children of serfs were ignored, as well as the progeny of the medieval slums. But youth of lesser social status and younger sons of nobility might be destined for clerical careers, and once within the confines of the university it was talent which rose to the top.

Such a system of education open to youth of varied status was possible only through the subsidy of the university. Great churchmen joined great lords in contributing to the support of universities.

The practice was so widespread as to become part of an accepted way of finance, continuing until this very day.

As we have noted, social mobility was at one time possible only within the clerical order. There were occasional exceptions through military prowess. As cities prospered and brought new classes into existence, more opportunity for individual achievement occurred. Higher education remained an avenue of advancement. This was noticeable in the English university of Protestant times, in the seventeenth and eighteenth centuries, as well as in the universities in Catholic nations of the same period.

The American college inherited the welfare tradition. In the Colonies, colleges were early established to provide opportunity for youth of varied social backgrounds to qualify for religious, legal, and other professions. One colonial college was even intended as a missionary enterprise to the Indians. In the early Republic, colleges under private and state sponsorship dotted the frontier, promoting educational opportunity in a society which gave special importance to self-confidence, equality, and local autonomy. In such an atmosphere the means of education were to be forever encouraged.

In order for youth of ability to have equal access to higher education, regardless of economic or social status, some special provision had to be made to find ways in which young people might attend college at small personal cost. One method was to raise funds through gifts with which to build facilities and with which to defray current operating costs. In this way higher education took on the special characteristics of a welfare institution.

Since the time of its medieval origins, the institution of higher education has always been economically poor. Its object has not been to make money but to lose money. Our colleges and universities have remained in the category of a charitable undertaking. This fact is indicated by several situations. One is the philanthropic nature of much of the financial support of higher education. Another characteristic is the tax-exempt status enjoyed by colleges and universities. Still another factor is the customary description of higher education as a "nonprofit" enterprise.

Today philanthropy is practiced on a sizable scale in the United States. It is estimated that as much as 8 billion dollars is contributed annually by various individuals, corporations, and private foundations to charitable and educational purposes.[4] Of this total, approximately 16 percent goes to education: schools, colleges, and universities.

The welfare nature of higher education is peculiarly important in the United States because of the substantial number of students enrolled in colleges and universities functioning under private sponsorship. If we except the junior colleges, we find today that about 45 percent of all students attend privately sponsored colleges and universities. The publicly sponsored colleges and universities—mostly operating under state financing—would be seriously pressed to accept a substantially larger proportion of students. Furthermore, the existence of colleges and universities under private sponsorship may set standards of excellence and freedom which are useful indeed for the publicly sponsored colleges and universities. For these and other reasons, there is considerable effort expended in the United States to preserve and strengthen the status of that segment of higher education functioning under private sponsorship.

The continuance of privately sponsored colleges and universities depends in large measure upon adequate gift support. In this sense the welfare characteristic of higher education remains important.

Even in the instance of state-sponsored colleges and universities, private gift support on a welfare basis has its usefulness. Many buildings have been provided by voluntary giving. The maintenance of student aid programs, the encouragement of certain kinds of research, and the enrichment of instructional programs may depend in considerable degree upon gifts from individuals and private foundations. The publicly sponsored college or university in the United States is by no means 100 percent publicly financed. In many instances state tax funds may provide no more than one-third of total current operating expenditures. The remaining income may be derived from student charges, federal government research and other grants, various charges, and philanthropy.

Both privately and publicly sponsored colleges and universities are eager to expand their gift income. They thus acknowledge their kinship to a voluntary welfare institution.

HIGHER EDUCATION AS AN ECONOMIC INSTITUTION

In one sense every institution of society is economic; it must have some method of earning income if it is to survive in a system of specialized production. In our society we know only three principal methods of economic survival. One method is for a person or group of persons to sell a product or service to other individuals or groups. This is the prevailing concept of the market place in the economy of the American people. The individual obtains his personal income by the sale of his services on this same market. A second method is to obtain economic support through a tax upon the market or upon individuals in a society. This is the way in which government operates. A third method is for an individual or group to receive gifts on a voluntary basis from other persons.

To the extent that higher education receives gifts for its financial support it is a welfare institution. To the extent that higher education receives tax support it is an agency of government. To the extent that higher education sells a product or a service it is part of the economic institution in our society which operates through the market place.[5]

In recent years there have been several studies of the "economics" of higher education in terms of various sources of income and various objects of expenditure.[6] Only certain selected items of this economic analysis need be mentioned here. Higher education as an institution is concerned about the resources required to provide the quantity and quality of educational service needed by the American society. These needs are determined in accordance with cultural tradition and current social policy. A society requires a certain quality and quantity of education in order to provide a given proportion of youth with higher education in varying degrees of specialization and depth. In the light of these educational objectives, the needs for economic resources are calculated. The needs come first. How to obtain the resources to meet these needs is a second consideration.

A different kind of economic analysis has been undertaken by Prof. Theodore W. Schultz.[7] It is concerned with the impact of education in general and higher education in particular upon the total economic activity of American society. Professor Schultz looks upon education as a human investment. He holds that there are fruits of education which consist of improvements in the capacity of people to produce economic wealth. The health of a working population, the technological skill of a working force, the availability of finance capital— all these factors play a large part in determining the economic output or gross national product of a society. Moreover, all these factors are enhanced by education in general and higher education in particular. To the degree that higher education contributes through knowledge to increased economic output it has advanced the economic growth of a society. Professor Schultz argues that education is an investment in human capital just as a factory is an investment in physical plant capital.

Professor Schultz estimates that in 1956 nearly 29 billion dollars was expended in all forms of educational endeavor, of which about one-third represented the economic resources employed by higher education. This outlay included an allowance for income which students forego by being enrolled in education rather than in the labor force. At the same time, Professor Schultz estimates that the investment return to the individual upon the cost of his higher education as a result of increased earnings above those of a high school education may be around 9 percent. He also argues that a goodly portion of increased economic output in our society must be attributed to this investment in human capital; it cannot all be attributed to investment in physical plant.

Professor Schultz does not suggest that the investment return of higher education necessarily implies a particularly desirable method of financing. It may still be desirable to obtain income in the three principal ways known to our society. On the other hand, Prof. Seymour E. Harris insists, primarily upon the grounds of expediency, that an increasingly larger share of the total resources needed by higher education must be charged to the individual student. In effect, this is an argument that higher education should become more of an economic institution, pricing its product (educational service) at a level to meet costs (needed resources).

Professor Harris points out that about 25 percent of the educational and general income of higher education was obtained from charges to students in 1958, and he estimates that about 40 percent of such income will be provided from student charges by 1970.[8] As of 1960 the total current operating expenditures of higher education were probably 5.5 to 6 billion dollars. It seems likely that nearly 40 percent of this total amount was derived from student charges, since almost all auxiliary service income results from charges to students.

If we were to consider certain research activities as being in the nature of services rendered for a charge to the federal government, we would probably find that well over 50 percent of all income for higher education at the present time resembles "earned" income. Although the motivation of a desire for profit is lacking in higher education, it seems fairly obvious that in substantial degree higher education as an institution is taking on characteristics of the market economy. There may be a trend indeed in this direction, not from desire or intent but from necessity.

It must be remembered that the figures cited here pertain to higher education as a whole and do not differentiate between state, local, and federal government sponsored colleges and universities on the one hand and privately sponsored colleges and universities on the other hand. It is probable that the trend toward behavior as an enterprise allied to a market economy is even more pronounced among the privately sponsored colleges and universities than among the publicly sponsored colleges and universities.

HIGHER EDUCATION AS A PART OF GOVERNMENT

The state became interested in higher education almost as early as the church. There are documents indicating imperial concern with universities and their students in the twelfth century, not too long after the universities began to emerge from their cathedral school and monastic origins. In the next three centuries there were several instances of imperial and kingly charters to new universities. And many of the universities founded under church auspices soon enjoyed noble patronage.

It was natural for the state to concern itself with higher education. At best there was ever an uneasy truce between spiritual and temporal power in medieval society. The state could not afford to permit the education of its clerks to fall entirely into church hands and hope to maintain the substance of its claim to jurisdiction over the immediate life of man. In order to obtain some balance of power in the earthly struggle of churchmen and statesmen, the state had to extend its interest to higher education. It is an interest which has never waned.

The governmental interests of our nation in the realm of higher education today are largely twofold. Government has an interest in the education of our citizenry. A democratic society presupposes wide-scale educational attainment among the people. A democratic society furthermore seeks to promote an elite of talent rather than an aristocracy of status and wealth. Our government is concerned to promote social mobility, and no means to this end is of more

importance than education, including higher education. Government is also concerned to promote economic well-being, and education is an important means here as well. Secondly, and more recently, higher education is a stake in the cold war. In the struggle for world domination between Russia and the United States, higher education has a vital part in enlarging the resources of strength. To be indifferent to higher education is to be indifferent to our national security.

There is no need here to trace the history of governmental concern with higher education in the United States. It was evident in colonial days in the support given to supposedly "private" colleges. It was evident in the Northwest Ordinance of 1787. The new states joining the Union after 1789 were encouraged to create seminaries of learning and were given land grants to help finance their operations. In 1862 the federal government provided further land-grant assistance to colleges or universities set up in the various states to give instruction, among other subjects, in agriculture and the mechanic arts. But the principal support for higher education has come from state governments themselves, primarily through state-sponsored universities. Local governments have established universities in only a few instances, although some 250 junior colleges operate through local school districts or other special arrangements. The federal government has confined its direct chartering of universities under federal sponsorship to military academies, Howard University, and one or two others.

Government has assisted the privately sponsored colleges and universities by exempting their property used for educational purposes from the general property tax, on occasion by exempting them from state sales taxes, and by exempting gifts from federal and state income taxes. In a few instances, state governments have directly or indirectly channeled tax funds to privately sponsored colleges and universities.

Both government support and government encouragement of higher education have expressed a public interest in providing educational opportunity for youth. To have a portion of our citizenry educated in colleges and universities has become increasingly important over the years. This fact is clearly evident in the ever larger percentage of youth enrolling in our colleges and universities from 1900 to 1960.

In the past twenty years, however, a new dimension has been added to government interest in higher education. This concern began with World War II when above all else the federal government looked to American universities for assistance in research and development activities. The atomic bomb was only the most spectacular achievement of this partnership; it was by no means the only important accomplishment. After the war, federal government research support to American universities continued, and in the past decade this support has steadily expanded until today it reaches almost 1 billion dollars a year. Moreover, the research assistance is made directly to universities regardless of whether they are publicly or privately sponsored.

In 1950 the federal government's housing laws were amended to make colleges and universities, public and private, eligible to borrow funds for dormitories and related facilities. After a change in the interest rate formula in 1955, considerable use began to be made of this program. More recently, through the National Defense Act of 1958 a whole new array of activities of public and private colleges and universities became recipients of federal government financial assistance.

These and other governmental actions, both current and proposed, have developed primarily because of the importance of higher education to the national security of the United States. Nor does this importance seem likely to diminish in the years ahead. On the contrary, governmental financial assistance to colleges and universities to educate needed talents and to perform vital research will unquestionably grow.

In state governments, the cost of this assistance has necessarily increased as state universities have expanded in enrollment, in the quality and level of educational programs undertaken, and in public service. With this enlarged cost has come a greater concern with the administrative operation of universities. Legal activities, the appointment of personnel, budget and other financial practices, the procurement of supplies, and the construction of buildings have come more and more under the supervision and control of various state agencies, such as the attorney general, the civil service commission, the state auditor, the state purchasing office, the state public works department, and the state budget office. Presumably all this supervision has been desirable in order to improve the efficiency of operation at state universities.

This tendency to make the state university simply another administrative agency of govern-

ment had gone so far that during the 1950's many state university presidents and boards of trustees began to protest. One result of this effort was the publication in 1959 of a study and a declaration by a group of prominent citizens interested in state universities demanding a greater concern for the autonomy of the state university.[9]

For the institution of higher education as a whole in the United States, about 50 percent of educational income and about 35 percent of all current operating income are being provided by government. In terms of social purpose, our national security, and financial support, higher education has begun to assume more and more the appearance of an agency of government.

HIGHER EDUCATION AS A UNIQUE INSTITUTION

It is readily evident that higher education possesses attributes of religion, private welfare, economic enterprise, and government administration. In terms of both tradition and current operating practice, higher education resembles other institutions and agencies of society. Yet higher education is not to be equated with any of these. Rather, our colleges and universities constitute a unique institution different from any other.

The peculiar institutional characteristics of higher education derive from the peculiar objective which the institution exists to serve: to preserve, transmit, and advance knowledge. The pursuit of this objective gives to higher education its partial resemblance to religion, welfare, the economy, and government. There are religious, welfare, economic, and governmental interests in the performance of our colleges and universities. Higher education is still unusual.

What gives higher education its unique status is its relation to society at large. The objective of higher education—the preservation, transmission, and advancement of knowledge—implies not just a belief in the importance of knowledge. There is, as well, a more practical goal: to enable individuals to develop their talents for the service of others. The use of knowledge by young persons of educated ability may ever be a threat to those who already hold and exercise power in society.

Education is a dangerous business. It is committed to change. It expects first of all to change individuals by augmenting their store of knowledge and by developing their ability to reason. Beyond this, the educated person may become an instrument of social change. By the discovery and utilization of knowledge in biology and medicine, we may conquer disease; by the discovery and utilization of knowledge in the physical sciences and engineering, we may create great new stores of material wealth, as well as great new instruments of military destruction. Higher education may be used in infinite ways to seek improvement in the social, economic, political, and voluntary patterns of human behavior. Creative change is the province of a higher education which is a part of society rather than an escape from it.

Higher education by its activity appears to threaten the positions of leadership in the established institutions of society. Higher education may question the ways and means by which men produce goods and services, the ways and means by which men live together, the ways and means by which men govern themselves and others, the ways and means by which men express their ultimate concern for the Ultimate. Higher education may declare that what is thought to be knowledge is no more than folklore and convention. Higher education is indispensable to any concept of material, biological, and spiritual progress, and at the same time it is a threat to the present power structure of society.

In many countries for many centuries, universities have been centers of social disturbance. In more recent years the issues have ranged from theories such as that of Darwin concerning natural selection which seems to refute the literal explanation of man's creation given in the Bible to theories such as that of Keynes concerning the equilibrium of a market economy in modern capitalism which seems to refute the idea of a "natural law" of economic behavior.

The essence of the objective to preserve; transmit, and advance knowledge is ever to question and ever to challenge the accepted ways of society. A democratic society devoted to the dignity of the individual and to the welfare of all should and does find this questioning tolerable. Even so, the institutions of economic, political, and social power in a democratic society may succumb on occasion to the practice of intolerance or even of tyranny. In an authoritarian society the status of higher education is precarious indeed. This fact is surely evident in the deplorable state of the study of the social sciences and the humanities in Russia.

The whole concern in the United States and in the Western world with academic freedom is an effort to acknowledge the unique relationship between higher education and society. Higher education is dangerous. It carries with it at all times the possibility that it may upset an existing power structure in society. It carries with it at all times the possibility that individuals and institutions in society may have to accept new ideas and new ways of behavior. The truth which higher education perpetuates and expands is never final but only tentative. At least this is the faith of scholars today.

A concept and practice of academic freedom have been necessary in Western society in order to provide maximum opportunity for the university to fulfill its mission in society.[10] Without a concept and practice of academic freedom, the institution of higher education cannot function fully or effectively. At the same time it seems clear that only in a free society can academic freedom hope to flourish with any vigor or reality.

In the United States it is sometimes said that the problem of academic freedom became real only with the emergence of the university after the Civil War. Prior to that time the American college had a relatively narrow and static curriculum. Then with the birth of the university in which graduate study and research became major preoccupations, there was an explosion of knowledge. The expansion which has taken place in the past 100 years is great indeed, and now we are concerned to increase the rate of advancement through enlarged expenditures for research. In any event, when knowledge is considered dynamic, and when the rate of growth in knowledge is to be speeded in the national interest, then academic freedom is essential.

The freedom which higher education seeks is noninterference from government and from various groups in society in the exploration of new knowledge and in the discussion of the present state of knowledge in each field of academic interest. Colleges and universities do not seek to propagate knowledge outside their own walls, but the use made of knowledge occurs largely outside the institution of higher education itself.

In our society no wall separates the university from the world of everyday affairs. This is desirable, since the problems of current concern give additional meaning to the pursuit of knowledge, and knowledge illuminates the amelioration of problems. The student who is persuaded of new intellectual truth may as a practitioner of his profession seek to apply what he has learned. Business leaders interested in economic and technological growth may find it profitable to make use of new ideas generated in the university world. Political leaders may seek advice and assistance from scholars. In such ways as these, knowledge is carried into human affairs. Higher education as an institution generates knowledge. Individuals and other institutions must decide how to use it.

HIGHER EDUCATION AND ORGANIZATION

The peculiar institutional character and tradition of higher education are reflected in its organization. The purpose of such organization is to provide effective means for preserving, transmitting, and advancing knowledge. This purpose in turn requires a process whereby a certain degree of insulation may be realized between colleges and universities on the one hand and government and society on the other.

I purposefully speak of government and society as distinct. It is one of the basic propositions of a democratic society and polity that there is a difference between society and government. In a totalitarian society, government is everything; family, church, economy, voluntary association must serve the ends of the state and have no goals not approved by the state. In a democratic society, government is one of several social institutions, important but not dominant. In the United States we have not only a pluralism of social institutions but a pluralism of groups and of agencies within each institution.

In the realm of higher education in the United States there is no such thing as a system of colleges and universities in any cohesive, unified sense. We have no ministry of higher education in the federal government, and do not desire one. There has been some effort to create in effect ministries of higher education in the fifty states, although this attempt has been resisted by state-sponsored colleges and universities. At least the result of this effort would be fifty ministries, not one. Furthermore, of approximately 1,200 degree-granting colleges, professional schools, and universities in our country, some 800 operate as privately rather than publicly sponsored agencies.

Thus the institution of higher education in the United States has no central organizational structure but a wide variety of individual operating units. Such interrelationship as does exist is voluntary and usually extends to cooperation in limited areas of common concern without impairing the fundamental self-responsibility of each college and university.

A good deal of attention might be given to the subject of interrelationship between a college or university and society. A college or university cannot isolate itself from the society of which it is a part. As an institution, higher education is responsive to the influences of religion, philanthropy, the economy, and government. Drawing financial support from these various elements of society, higher education cannot very well ignore them. The world is very much with those who labor in the cause of higher education.

In this discussion I am much more concerned to dwell upon the internal organization of an individual college or university. There are two reasons for this. First, I believe there is more general misunderstanding about the subject of internal organization than about almost any other aspect of the American college or university. Moreover, this misunderstanding is just as widespread inside our colleges and universities as outside. Secondly, the attempt to insulate the college and university from the social passions of the moment has found its principal method one of internal organization.

For reasons already outlined, higher education has desired to avoid the manifestations of strong social authority from other institutions. In America absolute authority is as abhorrent in higher education as it is in the church, the economy, and the government. A pluralism of units of higher education, as I have just commented, is one of the fundamental procedures for avoiding such absolute authority.

At the same time, in terms of their own internal organization our colleges and universities have sought arrangements which would equally reflect this concern to avoid absolute authority. In this endeavor the colleges and universities have built up a practice of community as the fundamental basis of organization. This essay seeks to explain this practice of community.

Within the agencies of other institutions, such as particular religious denominations, particular business enterprises, and particular administrative agencies of government, the principle of a hierarchy of authority centering in a council or an administrator may be satisfactory. Within the agencies of higher education the principle of hierarchy with authority centering in a board or a single administrator is not satisfactory. It is not satisfactory in terms of the objective of higher education to preserve, transmit, and advance knowledge while enjoying a degree of insulation from social pressure outside the institution of higher education itself.

The principle of hierarchy applied to the internal organization of a college or university would permit an absolute authority to gain control of the individual unit. If the board were to exercise absolute authority over the operations of a college or university, then control of the board would achieve control of the college or university. Such control may be desirable in certain types of operations. For example, we cannot have political responsibility for governmental bureaucracy without control of the permanent officials by the instruments of government: legislative, executive, and judiciary. We cannot have maximum efficiency in industrial production without control of the activities of each component group contributing to the productive output. Such considerations as these are not operative in the instance of a college or university. The institutional and social role of colleges and universities is different, and the method of operation is different.

Instead of being organized upon the principle of a hierarchy of authority, our colleges and universities are organized internally upon the principle of a community of authority. Power is shared by four different constituent groups in the academic entity. These groups are faculty, students, alumni, and administration. Each group possesses substantial power. Such power might be used for self-destruction. In practice, the power of each constituent group is brought together in a community of authority which enables each college and university to pursue its noble purpose.

The goal of the academic community is to provide an *environment* of learning, not a *product* of learning. Knowledge is acquired by individuals. It is not an object to be built and used like an automobile, a piece of furniture, a house, or a pencil. To be sure, knowledge is divided into many fields with a great deal of specialization. There are specializations in techniques of study and research, such as aesthetics, historical and archaeological inquiry, the collection of empirical data, statistical and mathematical computation, laboratory experimentation, logical deduction and inference, the formulation of hypotheses, and conceptualization.

The scholar and the student have distinct but interrelated roles. The one preserves and transmits knowledge; the other absorbs. But there is the stimulus of interaction in the process of learning, and this may occur also in the conduct of research. The scholar has a high degree of commitment to the cause of education. The student is apt to be more concerned about the practical uses of knowledge.

The scholar and student labor as individuals. The goal of education is realized in individuals. It is conceivable that the learning process could be carried on with just one scholar and one student. Or one scholar could pursue his efforts alone, as might a single student. The college and university provide the convenience and even the necessity of scholarly association; they provide economies of common endeavor.

One final observation may be important. When we study the institution of government, we quickly perceive that in our country there is a sharing of power between central and state governments and a sharing of power between legislative, executive, and judicial branches. This is not a hierarchy of power but a sharing. If there is any hierarchy of power, it is within administrative agencies functioning under the supervision and control of these three branches of government.

The institution of government in America has avoided a hierarchy of power. Why then should we assume that other institutions would seek such a hierarchy? Within the institution of higher education, hierarchy of power has been avoided by a pluralism of agencies. But the avoidance of a concentration of power goes even further than this. Within each agency—that is, each college and university—there is an attempt in practice to avoid a hierarchy of power.

Community of power rather than a hierarchy of power is the organizational basis of American colleges and universities.

FOOTNOTES

[1]Scholars will, of course, know Hastings Rashdall, *The Universities of Europe in the Middle Ages,* edited by F. M. Powicke and A. B. Emden (New York: Oxford University Press, 1936). This is the second edition of the great three-volume work originally published in 1895.

[2]Richard Hofstadter, "The Development of Higher Education in America," in Hofstadter and C. DeWitt Hardy, *The Development and Scope of Higher Education in the United States* (New York: Columbia University Press, 1952), p. 9.

[3]The designations are those employed by Professor Hofstadter, *ibid.*

[4]*Giving U.S.A.,* 1961 edition (New York: American Association of Fund-Raising Counsel, Inc.).

[5]Obviously, I have ignored the process whereby income for current expenditure or capital formation is obtained by borrowing from others. I have also omitted the practice whereby government may obtain income by the simple though usually dangerous process of making (printing) money for its own use.

[6]Among many articles and books on this subject, I would refer here particularly to Dexter M. Keezer, ed., *Financing Higher Education,* 1960-70 (New York: McGraw-Hill Book Company, Inc., 1959); and Seymour E. Harris, ed., *Higher Education in the United States: The Economic Problems* (Cambridge, Mass.: Harvard University Press, 1960).

[7]Theodore W. Schultz, "Education and Economic Growth," in *Social Forces Influencing American Education – 1961,* Sixtieth Yearbook of the National Society for the Study of Education (Chicago: University of Chicago Press, 1961), p. 46.

[8]See his "Financing of Higher Education: Broad Issues," in Keezer, *op. cit.,* p. 36.

[9]Committee on Government and Higher Education, *The Efficiency of Freedom* (Baltimore: Johns Hopkins Press, 1959); and Malcolm Moos and Francis E. Rourke, *The Campus and the State* (Baltimore: Johns Hopkins Press, 1959). Dr. Milton S. Eisenhower, president of the Johns Hopkins University, served as chairman of the Committee.

[10]See Russell Kirk, *Academic Freedom* (Chicago: Henry Regnery Company, 1955); Robert M. MacIver, *Academic Freedom in Our Time* (New York: Columbia University Press, 1955); and Richard Hofstadter and Walter P. Metzger, *The Development of Academic Freedom in the United States* (New York: Columbia University Press, 1955).

ABOUT THE AUTHOR

—**John D. Millett**, Chancellor, Ohio Board of Regents; President, Miami University, 1953-1964; Ph.D., 1938, Columbia University. His academic training is in political science and in public administration and he has taught in these areas. His major research interests are in governmental planning, the management of public agencies, and the administration of institutions of higher education.

The Idea of a Multiversity

by Clark Kerr

In this chapter, an academic administrator analyzes both the forces that shaped the modern American university and its present characteristics. The author is concerned, in large part, with the multiversity, but much of what is said is germane to the whole spectrum of types of institutional and organizational elements comprising higher education: the diversity of educational interests and the resultant conflict, the competition for power, and the role of the chief academic officer. Since the academic librarian is identified with the administrative structure and, in fact, identifies with the school administration, he should recognize the difficulty of obtaining consensus on the library's role in this milieu.

The university started as a single community—a community of masters and students. It may even be said to have had a soul in the sense of a central animating principle. Today the large American university is, rather, a whole series of communities and activities held together by a common name, a common governing board, and related purposes. This great transformation is regretted by some, accepted by many, gloried in, as yet, by few. But it should be understood by all.

The university of today can perhaps be understood, in part, by comparing it with what it once was—with the academic cloister of Cardinal Newman, with the research organism of Abraham Flexner. Those are the ideal types from which it has derived, ideal types which still constitute the illusions of some of its inhabitants. The modern American university, however, is not Oxford nor is it Berlin; it is a new type of institution in the world. As a new type of institution, it is not really private and it is not really public; it is neither entirely of the world nor entirely apart from it. It is unique.

"The Idea of a University" was, perhaps, never so well expressed as by Cardinal Newman when engaged in founding the University of Dublin a little over a century ago.[1] His views reflected the Oxford of his day whence he had come. A university, wrote Cardinal Newman, is "the high protecting power of all knowledge and science, of fact and principle, of inquiry and discovery, of experiment and speculation; it maps out the territory of the intellect, and sees that . . . there is neither encroachment nor surrender on any side." He favored "liberal knowledge," and said that "useful knowledge" was a "deal of trash."

Newman was particularly fighting the ghost of Bacon who some 250 years before had condemned "a kind of adoration of the mind . . . by means whereof men have withdrawn themselves too much from the contemplation of nature, and the observations of experience, and have tumbled up and down in their own reason and conceits." Bacon believed that knowledge should be for the benefit and use of men, that it should "not be as a courtesan, for pleasure and vanity only, or as a bond-woman, to acquire and gain to her master's use; but as a spouse, for generation, fruit and comfort."[2]

To this Newman replied that, "Knowledge is capable of being its own end. Such is the constitution of the human mind, that any kind of knowledge, if it really be such, is its own reward." And in a sharp jab at Bacon he said: "The Philosophy of Utility, you will say, Gentlemen, has at least done its work; and I grant it—it aimed low, but it has fulfilled its aim." Newman felt that other institutions should carry on research, for "If its object were scientific and philosophical discovery, I do not see why a University should have any students"—an observation sardonically echoed by today's students who often think their professors are not interested in them at all but only in research. A University training, said Newman, "aims at raising the intellectual tone of society, at cultivating the public mind, at purifying the national taste, at supplying true principles to popular enthusiasm and fixed aims to popular

SOURCE: Reprinted from Clark Kerr, *The Uses of the University* (Cambridge, Mass.: Harvard University Press, 1963), Chapter 1, "The Idea of a Multiversity," pp. 1-45, by permission of the publisher and the author.

aspirations, at giving enlargement and sobriety to the ideas of the age, at facilitating the exercise of political powers, and refining the intercourse of private life." It prepares a man "to fill any post with credit, and to master any subject with facility."

This beautiful world was being shattered forever even as it was being so beautifully portrayed. By 1852, when Newman wrote, the German universities were becoming the new model. The democractic and industrial and scientific revolutions were all well underway in the western world. The gentleman "at home in any society" was soon to be at home in none. Science was beginning to take the place of moral philosophy, research the place of teaching.

"The Idea of a Modern University," to use Flexner's phrase,[3] was already being born. "A University," said Flexner in 1930, "is not outside, but inside the general social fabric of a given era . . . It is not something apart, something historic, something that yields as little as possible to forces and influences that are more or less new. It is on the contrary . . . an expression of the age, as well as an influence operating upon both present and future."

It was clear by 1930 that "Universities have changed profoundly—and commonly in the direction of the social evolution of which they are part." This evolution had brought departments into universities, and still new departments; institutes and ever more institutes; created vast research libraries; turned the philosopher on his log into a researcher in his laboratory or the library stacks; taken medicine out of the hands of the profession and put it into the hands of the scientists; and much more. Instead of the individual student, there were the needs of society; instead of Newman's eternal "truths in the natural order," there was discovery of the new; instead of the generalist, there was the specialist. The university became, in the words of Flexner, "an institution consciously devoted to the pursuit of knowledge, the solution of problems, the critical appreciation of achievement and the training of men at a really high level." No longer could a single individual "master any subject"—Newman's universal liberal man was gone forever.

But as Flexner was writing of the "Modern University," it, in turn, was ceasing to exist. The Berlin of Humboldt was being violated just as Berlin had violated the soul of Oxford. The universities were becoming too many things. Flexner himself complained that they were "secondary schools, vocational schools, teacher-training schools, research centers, 'uplift' agencies, businesses—these and other things simultaneously." They engaged in "incredible absurdities," "a host of inconsequential things." They "needlessly cheapened, vulgarized and mechanized themselves." Worst of all, they became " 'service stations' for the general public."

Even Harvard. "It is clear," calculated Flexner, "that of Harvard's total expenditures not more than one-eighth is devoted to the *central* university disciplines at the level at which a university ought to be conducted." He wondered: "Who has forced Harvard into this false path? No one. It does as it pleases; and this sort of thing pleases." It obviously did not please Flexner. He wanted Harvard to disown the Graduate School of Business and let it become, if it had to survive at all, the "Boston School of Business." He would also have banished all Schools of Journalism and Home Economics, football, correspondence courses, and much else.

It was not only Harvard and other American universities, but also London. Flexner asked "in what sense the University of London is a university at all." It was only "a federation."

By 1930, American universities had moved a long way from Flexner's "Modern University" where "The heart of a university is a graduate school of arts and sciences, the solidly professional schools (mainly, in America, medicine and law) and certain research institutes." They were becoming less and less like a "genuine university," by which Flexner meant "an organism, characterized by highness and definiteness of aim, unity of spirit and purpose." The "Modern University" was as nearly dead in 1930 when Flexner wrote about it, as the old Oxford was in 1852 when Newman idealized it. History moves faster than the observer's pen. Neither the ancient classics and theology nor the German philosophers and scientists could set the tone for the really modern university—the multiversity.

"The Idea of a Multiversity" has no bard to sing its praises; no prophet to proclaim its vision; no guardian to protect its sanctity. It has its critics, its detractors, its transgressors. It also has its barkers selling its wares to all who will listen—and many do. But it also has its reality rooted in the logic of history. It is an imperative rather than a reasoned choice among elegant alternatives.

President Nathan Pusey wrote in his latest annual report to the members of the Harvard Board of Overseers that the average date of graduation of the present Board members was 1924; and much has happened to Harvard since 1924. Half of the buildings are new. The faculty has grown five-fold, the budget nearly fifteen-fold. "One can find almost anywhere one looks similar examples of the effect wrought in the curriculum and in the nature of the contemporary university by widening international awareness, advancing knowledge, and increasingly sophisticated methods of research . . . Asia and Africa, radio telescopes, masers and lasers and devices for interplanetary exploration unimagined in 1924—these and other developments have effected such enormous changes in the intellectual orientation and aspiration of the contemporary university as to have made the university we knew as students now seem a strangely underdeveloped, indeed a very simple and an almost unconcerned kind of institution. And the pace of change continues."[4]

Not only at Harvard. The University of California last year had operating expenditures from all sources of nearly half a billion dollars, with almost another 100 million for construction; a total employment of over 40,000 people, more than IBM and in a far greater variety of endeavors; operations in over a hundred locations, counting campuses, experiment stations, agricultural and urban extension centers, and projects abroad involving more than fifty countries; nearly 10,000 courses in its catalogues; some form of contact with nearly every industry, nearly every level of government, nearly every person in its region. Vast amounts of expensive equipment were serviced and maintained. Over 4,000 babies were born in its hospitals. It is the world's largest purveyor of white mice. It will soon have the world's largest primate colony. It will soon also have 100,000 students—30,000 of them at the graduate level; yet much less than one third of its expenditures are directly related to teaching. It already has nearly 200,000 students in extension courses—including one out of every three lawyers and one out of every six doctors in the state. And Harvard and California are illustrative of many more.

Newman's "Idea of a University" still has its devotees—chiefly the humanists and the generalists and the undergraduates. Flexner's "Idea of a Modern University" still has its supporters—chiefly the scientists and the specialists and the graduate students. "The Idea of a Multiversity" has its practitioners—chiefly the administrators, who now number many of the faculty among them, and the leadership groups in society at large. The controversies are still around in the faculty clubs and the student coffee houses; and the models of Oxford and Berlin and modern Harvard all animate segments of what was once a "community of masters and students" with a single vision of its nature and purpose. These several competing visions of true purpose, each relating to a different layer of history, a different web of forces, cause much of the malaise in the university communities of today. The university is so many things to so many different people that it must, of necessity, be partially at war with itself.

How did the multiversity happen? No man created it; in fact, no man visualized it. It has been a long time coming about and it has a long way to go. What is its history? How is it governed? What is life like within it? What is its justification? Does it have a future?

THE STRANDS OF HISTORY

The multiversity draws on many strands of history. To the extent that its origins can be identified, they can be traced to the Greeks. But there were several traditions even then. Plato had his Academy devoted to truth largely for its own sake, but also truth for the philosophers who were to be kings. The Sophists, whom Plato detested so much that he gave them an evil aura persisting to this day, had their schools too. These schools taught rhetoric and other useful skills—they were more interested in attainable success in life than they were in the unattainable truth. The Pythagoreans were concerned, among other things, with mathematics and astronomy. The modern academician likes to trace his intellectual forebears to the groves of Academe; but the modern university with its professional schools and scientific institutes might look equally to the Sophists and the Pythagoreans. The humanists, the professionals, and the scientists all have their roots in ancient times. The "Two Cultures" or the "Three Cultures" are almost as old as culture itself.

Despite its Greek precursors, however, the university is, as Hastings Rashdall wrote, "a distinctly medieval institution."[5] In the Middle Ages it developed many of the features that prevail today—a name and a central location, masters with a degree of autonomy, students, a system of lectures, a procedure for examinations and degrees, and even an administrative structure with its "faculties." Salerno in medicine, Bologna in law, and Paris in theology and philosophy were the great pacesetters. The university came to be a center for the professions, for the study of the classics, for theological and philosophical disputes.

Oxford and Cambridge, growing out of Paris, developed in their distinctive ways with their particular emphasis on the residential college instead of the separate faculties as the primary unit.

By the end of the eighteenth century the European universities had long since become oligarchies, rigid in their subject matter, centers of reaction in their societies—opposed, in large part, to the Reformation, unsympathetic to the spirit of creativity of the Renaissance, antagonistic to the new science. There was something almost splendid in their disdain for contemporary events. They stood like castles without windows, profoundly introverted. But the tides of change can cut very deep. In France the universities were swept away by the Revolution, as they almost had been in England at the time of Cromwell.

It was in Germany that the rebirth of the university took place. Halle had dropped teaching exclusively in Latin in 1693; Göttingen had started the teaching of history in 1736; but it was the establishment of Berlin by Wilhelm von Humboldt in 1809 from his vantage point in the Prussian Ministry that was the dramatic event. The emphasis was on philosophy and science, on research, on graduate instruction, on the freedom of professors and students *(Lehrfreiheit* and *Lernfreiheit).* The department was created, and the institute. The professor was established as a great figure within and without the university. The Berlin plan spread rapidly throughout Germany, which was then entering a period of industrialization and intense nationalism following the shock of the defeat at the hands of Napoleon. The university carried with it two great new forces: science and nationalism. It is true that the German university system later bogged down through its uncritical reliance on the great professorial figure who ruled for life over his department and institute, and that it could be subverted by Hitler because ot its total dependence on the state. But this does not vitiate the fact that the German university in the nineteenth century was one of the vigorous new institutions in the world.

In 1809 when Berlin was founded, the United States already had a number of colleges developed on the model of the colleges at Oxford and Cambridge. They concentrated on Calvinism for the would-be preacher and classics for the young gentleman. Benjamin Franklin had had other ideas for the University of Pennsylvania, then the College of Philadelphia, in the 1750's.[6] Reflecting Locke, he wanted "a *more useful* culture

of young minds." He was interested in training people for agriculture and commerce; in exploring science. Education should "serve mankind." These ideas were not to take root for another century. Drawing on the French enlightenment, Jefferson started the University of Virginia with a broad curriculum including mathematics and science, and with the electives that Eliot was to make so famous at Harvard half a century later. He put great emphasis on a library—an almost revolutionary idea at the time. Again the application of the ideas was to be long delayed.

The real line of development for the modern American university began with Professor George Ticknor at Harvard in 1825. He tried to reform Harvard on the model of Göttingen where he had studied, and found that reforming Harvard must wait for an Eliot with forty years and the powers of the presidency at his disposal. Yale at the time was the great center of reaction—its famous faculty report of 1828 was a ringing proclamation to do nothing, or at least nothing that had not always been done at Yale or by God.[7] Francis Wayland at Brown in the 1850's made a great fight for the German system, including a program of electives, as did Henry Tappan at Michigan—both without success.

Then the breakthrough came. Daniel Coit Gilman, disenchanted with the then grim prospects at California, became the first president of the new university of Johns Hopkins in 1876. The institution began as a graduate school with an emphasis on research. For Flexner, Gilman was the great hero-figure—and Johns Hopkins "the most stimulating influence that higher education in America had ever known." Charles W. Eliot at Harvard followed the Gilman breakthrough and Harvard during his period (1869 to 1909) placed great emphasis on the graduate school, the professional school, and research—it became a university. But Eliot made his own particular contribution by establishing the elective system permitting students to choose their own courses of study. Others quickly followed—Andrew Dickson White at Cornell, James B. Angell at Michigan, Frederick Barnard at Columbia, William W. Folwell at Minnesota, David Starr Jordan at Stanford, William Rainey Harper at Chicago, Charles K. Adams at Wisconsin, Benjamin Ide Wheeler at California. The state universities, just then expanding, followed the Hopkins idea. Yale and Princeton trailed behind.

The Hopkins idea brought with it the graduate school with exceptionally high academic standards in what was still a rather new and raw citilization; the renovation of professional education, particularly in medicine; the establishment of the preeminent influence of the department; the creation of research institutes and centers, of university presses and learned journals and the "academic ladder"; and also the great proliferation of courses. If students were to be free to choose their courses (one aspect of the *Lernfreiheit* of the early nineteenth-century German university), then professors were free to offer their wares (as *Lehrfreiheit,* the other great slogan of the developing German universities of a century and a half ago, essentially assured). The elective system, however, came more to serve the professors than the students for whom it was first intended, for it meant that the curriculum was no longer controlled by educational policy as the Yale faculty in 1828 had insisted that it should be. Each professor had his own interests, each professor wanted the status of having his own special course, each professor got his own course—and university catalogues came to include 3,000 or more of them. There was, of course, as a result of the new research, more knowledge to spread over the 3,000 courses; otherwise the situation would have been impossible. In any event, freedom for the student to choose became freedom for the professor to invent; and the professor's love of specialization has become the students' hate of fragmentation. A kind of bizarre version of academic laissez-faire has emerged. The student, unlike Adam Smith's idealized buyer, *must* consume—usually at the rate of fifteen hours a week. The modern university was born.

Along with the Hopkins experiment came the land grant movement—and these two influences turned out to be more compatible than might at first appear. The one was Prussian, the other American; one elitist, the other democractic; one academically pure, the other sullied by contact with the soil and the machine. The one looked to Kant and Hegel, the other to Franklin, Jefferson, and Lincoln. But they both served an industrializing nation and they both did it through research and the training of technical competence. Two strands of history were woven together in the modern American university. Michigan became a German-style university and Harvard a land grant type of institution, without the land.

The land grant movement brought schools of agriculture and engineering (in Germany relegated to the *Technische Hochschulen*), of home economics and business administration; opened the doors of universities to the children of farmers and workers, as well as of the middle and upper classes; introduced agricultural experiment stations and service bureaus. Allan Nevins in commenting on the Morrill Act of 1862 said: "The law annexed wide neglected areas to the domain of instruction. Widening the gates of opportunity, it made democracy freer, more adaptable and more kinetic."[8]

A major new departure in the land grant movement came before World War I when the land grant universities extended their activities beyond their campus boundaries. "The Wisconsin Idea" came to flower under the progressivism of the first Roosevelt and the first La Follette. The University of Wisconsin, particularly during the presidency of Charles Van Hise (1903 to 1918), entered the legislative halls in Madison with reform programs, supported the trade union movement through John R. Commons, developed agricultural and urban extension as never before. The university served the whole state. Other state universities did likewise. Even private universities, like Chicago and Columbia, developed important extension programs.

New contacts with the community were created. University athletics became, particularly in the 1920's, a form of public entertainment, which is not unknown even in the 1960's, even in the Ivy League. Once started, university spectator sports could not be killed even by the worst of teams or the best of de-emphasis; and few universities seriously sought after either.

A counterrevolution against these developments was occasionally waged. A. Lawrence Lowell at Harvard (1909 to 1934) emphasized the undergraduate houses and concentration of course work, as against the graduate work and electives of Eliot. It is a commentary not just on Harvard but also on the modern American university that Eliot and Lowell could look in opposite directions and the same institution could follow them both and glory in it. Universities have a unique capacity for riding off in all directions and still staying in the same place, as Harvard has so decisively demonstrated. At Chicago, long after Lowell, Robert M. Hutchins tried to take the university back to Cardinal Newman, to Thomas Aquinas, and to Plato and Aristotle. He succeeded in reviving the philosophic dialogue he loves so well and practices so expertly; but Chicago went on being a modern American university.

Out of the counterreformation, however, came a great new emphasis on student life—particularly undergraduate. Earnest attempts were made to create American counterparts of Oxford and Cambridge; residence halls, student unions, intramural playfields, undergraduate libraries, counseling centers sprang up in many places during the thirties, forties, and fifties. This was a long way from the pure German model, which had provided the student with only the professor and the classroom, and which had led Tappan to abolish dormitories at Michigan. British influence was back, as it was also with the introduction of honors programs, tutorials, independent study.

Out of all these fragments, experiments, and conflicts a kind of unlikely consensus has been reached. Undergraduate life seeks to follow the British, who have done the best with it, and an historical line that goes back to Plato; the humanists often find their sympathies here. Graduate life and research follow the Germans, who once did best with them, and an historical line that goes back to Pythagoras; the scientists lend their support to all this. The "lesser" professions (lesser than law and medicine) and the service activities follow the American pattern, since the Americans have been best at them, and an historical line that goes back to the Sophists; the social scientists are most likely to be sympathetic. Lowell found his greatest interest in the first, Eliot in the second, and James Bryant Conant (1934 to 1954) in the third line of development and in the synthesis. The resulting combination does not seem plausible but it has given America a remarkably effective educational institution. A university anywhere can aim no higher than to be as British as possible for the sake of the undergraduates, as German as possible for the sake of the graduates and the research personnel, as American as possible for the sake of the public at large—and as confused as possible for the sake of the preservation of the whole uneasy balance.

THE GOVERNANCE OF THE MULTIVERSITY

The multiversity is an inconsistent institution. It is not one community but several—the community of the undergraduate and the community of the graduate; the community of the humanist, the community of the social scientist, and the community of the scientist; the communities of the professional schools; the community of all the nonacademic personnel; the community of the administrators. Its edges are fuzzy—it reaches out to alumni, legislators, farmers, businessmen, who are all related to one or more of these internal communities. As an institution, it looks far into the past and far into the future, and is often at odds with the present. It serves society almost slavishly—a society it also criticizes, some times unmercifully. Devoted to equality of opportunity, it is itself a class society. A community, like the medieval communities of masters and students, should have common interests; in the multiversity, they are quite varied, even conflicting. A community should have a soul, a single animating principle; the multiversity has several—some of them quite good, although there is much debate on which souls really deserve salvation.

The multiversity is a name. This means a great deal more than it sounds as though it might. The name of the institution stands for a certain standard of performance, a certain degree of respect, a certain historical legacy, a characteristic quality of spirit. This is of the utmost importance to faculty and to students, to the government agencies and the industries with which the institution deals. Protection and enhancement of the prestige of the name are central to the multiversity. How good is its reputation, what John J. Corson calls its "institutional character"? [7]

Flexner thought of a university as an "organism." In an organism, the parts and the whole are inextricably bound together. Not so the multiversity—many parts can be added and subtracted with little effect on the whole or even little notice taken or any blood spilled. It is more a mechanism—a series of processes producing a series of results—a mechanism held together by administrative rules and powered by money.

Hutchins once described the modern university as a series of separate schools and departments held together by a central heating system. In an area where heating is less important and the automobile more, I have sometimes thought of it as a series of individual faculty entrepreneurs held together by a common grievance over parking.

It is, also, a system of government like a city, or a city state: the city state of the multiversity. It may be inconsistent but it must be governed—not as the guild it once was, but as a complex entity with greatly fractionalized power. There are several competitors for this power.

The Students

The students had all the power once; that was in Bologna. Their guilds ran the university and dominated the masters. And the students were tougher on the masters than the masters have ever been on the students. The Bologna pattern had an impact on Salamanca and Spain generally and then in Latin America, where students to this day are usually found in the top governing councils. Their impact is generally more to lower than to raise academic standards although there are exceptions such as Buenos Aires after Peron under the leadership of Risieri Frondizi. Students also involve the university as an institution in the national political controversies of the moment.

Jefferson tried a system of student self-government in the 1820's but quickly abandoned it when all the professors tendered their resignations. He favored self-government by both students and faculty, but never discovered how both could have it at the same time—nor has anybody else. Although José Ortega y Gassett, in addressing the student federation at the University of Madrid, was willing to turn over the entire "mission of the university" to the students, he neglected to comment on faculty reaction.[10]

As part of the "Wisconsin idea" before World War I, there was quite a wave of creation of student governments. They found their power in the area of extracurricular activities, where it has remained. Their extracurricular programs helped broaden student life in such diverse fields as debating, theatrical productions, literary magazines.

Students do have considerable strictly academic influence, however, quite beyond that with which they are usually credited. The system of electives gives them a chance to help determine in which areas and disciplines a university will grow. Their choices, as consumers, guide university expansion and contraction, and this process is far superior to a more rigid guild system of producer determination as in medicine where quotas are traditional. Also students, by their patronage, designate the university teachers. The faculty may, in fact, appoint the faculty, but within this faculty group the students choose the real teachers. In a large university a quarter of the faculty may be selected by the students to do half or more of the actual teaching; the students also "select" ten percent or more to do almost none at all.

The Faculty

The guilds of masters organized and ran the University of Paris, and later they did the same at Oxford and Cambridge. Faculty control at Oxford and Cambridge, through the colleges, has remained stronger than anywhere else over the centuries, but even there it has been greatly diminished in recent times.

In the United States, the first great grant of power to the faculty of a major university was at Yale when Jeremiah Day was president (1817 to 1846). It was during the Day regime that the Yale faculty report of 1828 was issued. Harvard has had, by contrast, as McGeorge Bundy has said in his inimitable style, "a tradition of quite high-handed and centralized executive behavior—and it has not suffered, in balance, as a consequence."[11]

Faculties generally in the United States and the British Commonwealth, some earlier and some later, have achieved authority over admissions, approval of courses, examinations, and granting of degrees—all handled in a rather routine fashion from the point of view of the faculty as a whole. They have also achieved considerable influence over faculty appointments and academic freedom, which are not handled routinely. Faculty control and influence in these areas are essential to the proper conduct of academic life. Once the elective system was established, educational policy became less important to the faculty, although, as at Harvard under Lowell, the elective system was modified to call for general rules on concentration and distribution of work. Since Harvard adopted its program for general education in 1945[12] and Hutchins left Chicago, there has been remarkably little faculty discussion of general educational policy. By contrast, there has been a great deal in England, particularly in the "new universities," where faculty discussion of educational policy has been very lively, and faculty influence, as a consequence, substantial.

Organized faculty control or influence over the general direction of growth of the American multiversity has been quite small, as illustrated by the development of the federal grant university. Individual faculty influence, however, has been quite substantial, even determinative, in the expanding areas of institutes and research grants. Still it is a long way from Paris at the time of Abelard.

Public Authority

"Public" authority is a very mixed entity of emperiors and popes, ministers of education, grants committees, trustees, and Royal Commissions. But almost everywhere, regardless of the origin of the system, there has come to be a public authority. Even in the Middle Ages, emperors and popes, dukes, cardinals, and city councils came to authorize or establish the universities to make them legitimate—the guild alone was not enough. When Henry VIII had trouble about a wife it shook Oxford and Cambridge to the core.

In modern times, Napoleon was the first to seize control of a university system. He completely reorganized it and made it part of the nationally administered educational system of France, as it remains to this day. He separated off research activities and special training institutions for teachers, engineers, and so forth. The universities became a series of loosely related professional schools. Not until the 1890's were the universities brought back together as meaningful entities and a measure of faculty control restored. Soviet Russia has followed the French pattern with even greater state control.

In Germany, the state governments traditionally have controlled the universities in great detail. So also has the government in Italy. In Latin America a degree of formal autonomy from the government has either been retained or attained, although informal reality usually contradicts the theory.

Even in Great Britain, the "public" has moved in on the faculties. Royal Commissions have helped modernize Oxford and Cambridge. The Redbrick and Scottish universities and London either have had from the beginning or acquired governing boards of a mixed nature, including lay members representative of public authority. Since 1919, and particularly since World War II, the University Grants Committee has made its influence felt in a less and less gentle and more and more effective way.

The lay board has been the distinctive American device for "public" authority in connection with universities, although the device was used in Holland in the late sixteenth century. Beyond the lay board in the state universities are the state department of finance and the governor and the legislature with a tendency toward increasingly detailed review.

Richard Hofstadter has made the interesting observation that the first lay board and the first effective concept of academic freedom developed in Holland at the same time; and that academic freedom has never been inherited from some Golden Age of the past but has instead been imported from the institutions of the surrounding society.[13]

Through all these devices, public influences have been asserted in university affairs. Public influence has increased as much in Paris as student influence has declined in Bologna. Everywhere, with the decreasing exception of Oxford and Cambridge, the ultimate authority lies in the "public" domain; everywhere, with a few exceptions, it is fortunately not exercised in an ultimate fashion. We have, however, come a long way from the guilds of masters, the guilds of students, the guilds of masters and students. The location of power has generally moved from inside to outside the original community of masters and students. The nature of the multiversity makes it inevitable that this historical transfer will not be reversed in any significant fashion, although the multiversity does permit the growth of subcultures which can be relatively autonomous and can have an impact on the totality.

The distribution of power is of great importance. In Germany it came to be lodged too completely in the figure of the full professor at one end and the minister of education at the other; in Oxford and Cambridge, at one time, in an oligarchy of professors; in the United States, during a substantial period, almost exclusively in the president; in Latin America, too often, in the students within and the politicians without.

Influences—External and Semi-External

Beyond the formal structure of power, as lodged in students, faculty, administration, or "public" instrumentalities, lie the sources of informal influence. The American system is particularly sensitive to the pressures of its many particular publics. Continental and British universities are less intertwined with their surrounding societies than the American and thus more inward-looking and self-contained. When "the borders of the campus are the boundaries of our state," the lines dividing what is internal from what is external become quite blurred; taking the campus to the state brings the state to the campus. In the so-called "private" universities, alumni, donors, foundations, the federal agencies, the professional and business communities bulk large among the semi-external influences; and in the so-called "public" universities, the agricultural, trade union, and public school communities are likely to be added to the list, and also a more searching press. The multiversity has many "publics" with many interests; and by the very nature of the multiversity many of these interests are quite legitimate and others are quite frivolous.

The Administration

The original medieval universities had at the

start nothing that could be identified as a separate administration, but one quickly developed. The guild of masters or students selected a rector; and later there were deans of the faculties. At Oxford and Cambridge, there came to be the masters of the colleges. In more modern times in France, Germany, and Italy, the rector has come to stand between the faculty and the minister of education, closer to the minister of education in France and closer to the faculty in Germany; internally he has served principally as chairman of the council of deans where deans still retain substantial authority as in France and Italy. In Germany the full professor, chairman of his department, director of his institute, is a figure of commanding authority.

Even in England, even in Oxford and Cambridge, the central administration is attaining more influence—the vice chancellorship can no longer be rotated casually among the masters. The vice chancellor now must deal with the university grants committee and the vice chancellors of the other universities. The university itself is a much more important unit with its research laboratories, central library, its lecturers in specialized subjects; the college is much less self-contained than it was. All of this has created something of a crisis in the administration of Oxford and Cambridge where administrators once were not to be seen or heard and the work was accomplished by a handful of clerks working in a Dickensian office. Oxbridge is becoming more like the Redbricks. London is *sui generis*.

The general rule is that the administration everywhere becomes, by force of circumstances if not by choice, a more prominent feature of the university. As the institution becomes larger, administration becomes more formalized and separated as a distinct function; as the institution becomes more complex, the role of administration becomes more central in integrating it; as it becomes more related to the once external world, the administration assumes the burdens of these relationships. The managerial revolution has been going on also in the university.

MULTIVERSITY PRESIDENT, GIANT OR MEDIATOR-INITIATOR?

It is sometimes said that the American multiversity president is a two-faced character. This is not so. If he were, he could not survive. He is a many-faced character, in the sense that he must face in many directions at once while contriving to turn his back on no important group.

In this he is different in degree from his counterparts of rectors and vice chancellors, since they face in fewer directions because their institutions have fewer doors and windows to the outside world. The difference, however, is not one of kind. And intensities of relationships vary greatly; the rector of a Latin American university, from this point of view, may well have the most trying task of all, though he is less intertwined in a range of relationships than the North American university president.

The university president in the United States is expected to be a friend of the students, a colleague of the faculty, a good fellow with the alumni, a sound administrator with the trustees, a good speaker with the public, an astute bargainer with the foundations and the federal agencies, a politician with the state legislature, a friend of industry, labor, and agriculture, a persuasive diplomat with donors, a champion of education generally, a supporter of the professions (particularly law and medicine), a spokesman to the press, a scholar in his own right, a public servant at the state and national levels, a devotee of opera and football equally, a decent human being, a good husband and father, an active member of a church. Above all he must enjoy traveling in airplanes, eating his meals in public, and attending public ceremonies. No one can be all of these things. Some succeed at being none.

He should be firm, yet gentle; sensitive to others, insensitive to himself; look to the past and the future, yet be firmly planted in the present; both visionary and sound; affable, yet reflective; know the value of a dollar and realize that ideas cannot be bought; inspiring in his visions yet cautious in what he does; a man of principle yet able to make a deal; a man with broad perspective who will follow the details conscientiously; a good American but ready to criticize the status quo fearlessly; a seeker of truth where the truth may not hurt too much; a source of public policy pronouncements when they do not reflect on his own institution. He should sound like a mouse at home and look like a lion abroad. He is one of the marginal men in a democratic society—of whom there are many others—on the margin of many groups, many ideas, many endeavors, many characteristics. He is a marginal man but at the very center of the total process.

Who is he really?

To Flexner, he was a hero-figure, "a daring pioneer" who filled an "impossible post" yet some of his accomplishments were "little short of miraculous"; thus the "forceful president"—the Gilman, the Eliot, the Harper. The necessary revolutions came from on high. There should be Giants in the Groves. To Thorstein Veblen he was a "Captain of Erudition,"[14] and Veblen did not think well of captains. To Upton Sinclair, the university president was "the most universal faker and most variegated prevaricator that has yet appeared in the civilized world."[15]

To the faculty, he is usually not a hero-figure. Hutchins observed that the faculty really "prefer anarchy to any form of government"[16]—particularly the presidential form.

The issue is whether the president should be "leader" or "officeholder," as Hutchins phrased it; "educator" or "caretaker," as Harold W. Dodds[17] stated it; "creator" or "inheritor," as Frederick Rudolph[18] saw it; "initiator" as viewed by James L. Morrill[19] or consensus-seeker as viewed by John D. Millett;[20] the wielder of power or the persuader, as visualized by Henry M. Wriston,[21] "pump" or "bottleneck" as categorized by Eric Ashby.[22]

The case for leadership has been strongly put by Hutchins. A university needs a purpose, "a vision of the end." If it is to have a "vision," the president must identify it; and, without vision, there is "aimlessness" and the "vast chaos of the American university." "The administrator must accept a special responsibility for the discussion, clarification, definition and proclamation of this end." He must be a "troublemaker, for every change in education is a change in the habits of some members of the faculty." For all this he needs the great "moral virtues" of "courage," "fortitude," "justice," and "prudence." In looking for administrators who really thought and wrote about the "end" of their institution, Hutchins particularly identified Marcus Aurelius as the great prototype.[23] Lowell, too, believed a president should have a "plan" and that although the faculty was "entitled to propose changes," the plan should not basically be subject to interference. He also had the rather quaint idea that the president should "never feel hurried" or "work . . . under pressure."[24]

There were such leaders in higher education. Hutchins was one. Lowell was another; and so was Eliot. When Eliot was asked by a faculty member of the medical school how it could be after eighty years of managing its own affairs the faculty had to accommodate to so many changes, he could answer, "There is a new

president."[25] Even in Oxford, of all places, as it belatedly adapted to the new world of scholarship, Benjamin Jowett as Master of Balliol could set as his rule: "Never retract, never explain. Get it done and let them howl."[26] Lord Bryce could comment in his *American Commonwealth* on the great authority of the president in the American university, on his "almost monarchical position."[27]

But the day of the monarchs has passed—the day when Benjamin Ide Wheeler could ride his white horse across the Berkeley campus or Nicholas Murray Butler rule from Morningside Heights. Flexner rather sadly recorded that "the day of the excessively autocratic is . . . over. He has done a great service . . ." Paul Lazarsfeld could observe the "academic power vacuum" that resulted—leadership no longer taken by the president nor assumed by the faculty, with the result of little "institutional development."[28] Hutchins was the last of the giants in the sense that he was the last of the university presidents who really tried to change his institution and higher education in any fundamental way. Instead of the not always so agreeable autocracy, there is now the usually benevolent bureaucracy, as in so much of the rest of the world. Instead of the Captain of Erudition or even David Riesman's "staff sergeant," there is the Captain of the Bureaucracy who is sometimes a galley slave on his own ship; and "no great revolutionary figure is likely to appear."[29]

The role of giant was never a happy one. Hutchins concluded that the administrator has many ways to lose, and no way to win, and came to acknowledge that patience, which he once called a "delusion and a snare," was also a virtue. "It is one thing to get things done. It is another to make them last." The experience of Tappan at Michigan was typical of many, as Angell later saw it: "Tappan was the largest figure of a man that ever appeared on the Michigan campus. And he was stung to death by gnats."[30]

The giant was seldom popular with the faculty and was often bitterly opposed, as in the "revolution" against Wheeler at California. And faculty government gained strength as faculties gained distinction. The experiences of Tappan, Wheeler, Hutchins, even Thomas Jefferson, are part of the lore of the university presidency. So are those of Wayland, who resigned from Brown in frustration after vainly trying something new, Woodrow Wilson with all his battles over innovations at Princeton, and many others.

Moreover the university has changed; it has become bigger and more complex, more tensed with checks and balances. As Rudolph saw it, there came to be "a delicate balance of interests, a polite tug of war, a blending of emphases." The presidency was "an office fraught with so many perils, shot through with so many ambiguities, an office that was many things to many men."[31] There are more elements to conciliate, fewer in a position to be led. The university has become the multiversity and the nature of the presidency has followed this change.

Also, the times have changed. The giants were innovators during a wave of innovation, to use the terms of Joseph Schumpeter drawn from another context. The American university required vast renovation to meet the needs of the changing and growing nation. As Eliot said in his inaugural address, "The University must accommodate itself promptly to significant changes in the character of the people for whom it exists." The title of Wilson's inaugural address was, "Princeton for the Nation's Service." They and others helped take what had been denominational colleges and turn them into modern national universities. They were not inventors—the Germans did the inventing—but they came along at a stage in history when massive innovation was the order of the day. The giants today, when found at all, are more likely to be in a few of the old Latin American universities undergoing modernization or the new British universities in the midst of an intense discussion of educational policy.

The giants had performed "a great service," but gentler hands were needed. University administration reverted to the more standard British model of "government by consent and after consultation."[32] There is a "kind of lawlessness"[33] in any large university with many separate sources of initiative and power; and the task is to keep this lawlessness within reasonable bounds. The president must seek "consensus" in a situation when there is a "struggle for power" among groups that share it.[34] "The president must use power economically, and persuasion to the fullest extent."[35] As Allan Nevins sees it, "The sharpest strain on growth lies not in finding the teachers, but expert administrators," and the new type of president required by the large universities "will be a coordinator rather than a creative leader . . . an expert executive, a tactful moderator . . ."[36]

Academic government has taken the form of the Guild, as in the colleges of Oxford and Cambridge until recent times; of the Manor, as in

Columbia under Butler; and of the United Nations, as in the modern multiversity. There are several "nations" of students, of faculty, of alumni, of trustees, of public groups. Each has its territory, its jurisdiction, its form of government. Each can declare war on the others; some have the power of veto. Each can settle its own problems by a majority vote, but altogether they form no single constituency. It is a pluralistic society with multiple cultures. Coexistence is more likely than unity. Peace is one priority item, progress another.

The president in the multiversity is leader, educator, creator, initiator, wielder of power, pump; he is *also* officeholder, caretaker, inheritor, consensus-seeker, persuader, bottleneck. But he is mostly a mediator.

The first task of the mediator is peace—how he may "the Two-and-Seventy jarring Sects confute." Peace within the student body, the faculty, the trustees; and peace between and among them. Peace between the "Two Cultures" and the "Three Cultures" and their subcultures; among all the ideas competing for support. Peace between the internal environment of the academic community and the external society that surrounds and sometimes almost engulfs it. But peace has its attributes. There is the "workable compromise" of the day that resolves the current problem. Beyond this lies the effective solution that enhances the long-run distinction and character of the institution. In seeking it, there are some things that should not be compromised, like freedom and quality— then the mediator needs to become the gladiator. The dividing lines between these two roles may not be as clear as crystal, but they are at least as fragile.

The second task is progress; institutional and personal survival are not enough. A multiversity is inherently a conservative institution but with radical functions. There are so many groups with a legitimate interest in the status quo, so many veto groups; yet the university must serve a knowledge explosion and a population explosion simultaneously. The president becomes the central mediator among the values of the past, the prospects for the future, and the realities of the present. He is the mediator among groups and institutions moving at different rates of speed and sometimes in different directions; a carrier of change—as infectious and sometimes as feared as a "Typhoid Mary." He is not an innovator for the sake of innovation, but he must be sensitive to the fruitful innovation. He has no new and bold "vision of the end." He is driven more by necessity than by voices in the air. "Innovation" may be the historical "measurement of success," the great characterizing feature of the "giants of the past";[37] but innovations sometimes succeed best when they have no obvious author. Lowell once observed that a president "cannot both do things and get credit for them"—that he should not "cackle like a hen that laid an egg."

The ends are already given—the preservation of the eternal truths, the creation of new knowledge, the improvement of service wherever truth and knowledge of high order may serve the needs of man. The ends are there; the means must be ever improved in a competitive dynamic environment. There is no single "end" to be discovered; there are several ends and many groups to be served.

The quality of the mediation is subject to judgment on two grounds, the keeping of the peace and the furthering of progress—the resolution of inter-personal and inter-group warfare, and the reconciliation of the tug of the anchor to the past with the pull of the Holy Grail of the future. Unfortunately peace and progress are more frequently enemies than friends; and since, in the long run, progress is more important than peace to a university, the effective mediator must, at times, sacrifice peace to progress. The ultimate test is whether the mediation permits progress to be made fast enough and in the right directions, whether the needed innovations take precedence over the conservatism of the institution. Mediators, though less dramatic than giants, are not a homogenized group; they only look that way.

They also appear to some people to be doing very little of consequence. Yet their role is absolutely essential if carried out constructively. They serve something of the function of the clerk of the meeting for the Quakers—the person who keeps the business moving, draws forth ideas, seeks the "sense of the meeting." David Riesman has suggested the term "evocator." The techniques must be those of the mediator; but to the techniques may also be added the goals of the innovator. The essence of the role, when adequately performed, is perhaps best conveyed by the term "mediator-initiator."

Power is not necessary to the task, though there must be a consciousness of power. The president must police its use by the constituent groups, so that none will have too much or too little or use it too unwisely. To make the multiversity work really effectively, the moderates need to be in control of each power center and there needs to be an attitude of tolerance between and among the power centers, with few territorial ambitions. When the extremists get in control of the students, the faculty, or the trustees with class warfare concepts, then the "delicate balance of interests" becomes an actual war.

The usual axiom is that power should be commensurate with responsibility, but, for the president, the *opportunity to persuade* should be commensurate with the responsibility. He must have ready access to each center of power, a fair chance in each forum of opinion, a chance to paint reality in place of illusion and to argue the cause of reason as he sees it.

Not all presidents seek to be constructive mediators amid their complexities. One famous president of a New York university succeeded in being at home only five months in five years. Some find it more pleasant to attend meetings, visit projects abroad, even give lectures at other universities; and at home they attend ceremonial functions, go to the local clubs, and allow the winds of controversy to swirl past them. Others look for "visions." But more presidents are in the control tower helping the real pilots make their landings without crashes, even in the fog.

Hutchins wrote of the four moral virtues for a university president. I should like to suggest a slightly different three—judgment, courage, and fortitude—but the greatest of these is fortitude since others have so little charity. The mediator, whether in government or industry or labor relations or domestic quarrels, is always subject to some abuse. He wins few clear-cut victories; he must aim more at avoiding the worst than seizing the best. He must find satisfaction is being *equally* distasteful to each of his constituencies; he must reconcile himself to the harsh reality that successes are shrouded in silence while failures are spotlighted in notoriety. The president of the multiversity must be content to hold its constituent elements loosely together and to move the whole enterprise another foot ahead in what often seems an unequal race with history.

LIFE IN THE MULTIVERSITY

The "Idea of a University" was a village with its priests. The "Idea of a Modern University" was a town—a one-industry town—with its intellectual oligarchy. "The Idea of a Multiversity" is a city of infinite variety. Some get lost in the city; some rise to the top within it; most fashion their lives within one of its many subcultures. There is less sense of community than in the village but also less sense of confinement. There is less sense of purpose than within the town but there are more ways to excel. There are also more refuges of anonymity—both for the creative person and the drifter. As against the village and the town, the "city" is more like the totality of civilization as it has evolved and more an integral part of it; and movement to and from the surrounding society has been greatly accelerated. As in a city, there are many separate endeavors under a single rule of law.

The students in the "city" are older, more likely to be married, more vocationally oriented, more drawn from all classes and races than the students in the village;[38] and they find themselves in a most intensely competitive atmosphere. They identify less with the total community and more with its subgroups. Burton R. Clark and Martin Trow have a particularly interesting typology of these subcultures: the "collegiate" of the fraternities and sororities and the athletes and activities majors; the "academic" of the serious students; the "vocational" of the students seeking training for specific jobs; and the "nonconformist" of the political activists, the aggressive intellectuals, and the bohemians.[39] These subcultures are not mutually exclusive, and some of the fascinating pageantry of the multiversity is found in their interaction one on another.

The multiversity is a confusing place for the student. He has problems of establishing his identity and sense of security within it. But it offers him a vast range of choices, enough literally to stagger the mind. In this range of choices he encounters the opportunities and the dilemmas of freedom. The casualty rate is high. The walking wounded are many. *Lernfreiheit*— the freedom of the student to pick and choose, to stay or to move on—is triumphant.

Life has changed also for the faculty member. The multiversity is in the main stream of events. To the teacher and the researcher have been added the consultant and the administrator. Teaching is less central than it once was for most faculty members; research has become more important. This has given rise to what has been called the "non-teacher"[40]—"the higher a man's standing, the less he has to do with students"—and to a threefold class structure of what used to be "the faculty": those who only do research, those who

only teach (and they are largely in an auxiliary role), and those who still do some of both. In one university I know, the proportions at the Ph.D. level or its equivalent are roughly one researcher to two teachers to four who do both.

Consulting work and other sources of additional income have given rise to what is called the "affluent professor," a category that does include some but by no means all of the faculty. Additionally, many faculty members, with their research assistants and teaching assistants, their departments and institutes, have become administrators. A professor's life has become, it is said, "a rat race of business and activity, managing contracts and projects, guiding teams and assistants, bossing crews of technicians, making numerous trips, sitting on committees for government agencies, and engaging in other distractions necessary to keep the whole frenetic business from collapse."[41]

The intellectual world has been fractionalized as interests have become much more diverse; and there are fewer common topics of conversation at the faculty clubs. Faculty government has become more cumbersome, more the avocation of active minorities; and there are real questions whether it can work effectively on a large scale, whether it can agree on more than preservation of the status quo. Faculty members are less members of the particular university and more colleagues within their national academic discipline groups.

But there are many compensations. "The American professoriate" is no longer, as Flexner once called it, "a proletariat." Salaries and status have risen considerably. The faculty member is more a fully participating member of society, rather than a creature on the periphery; some are at the very center of national and world events. Research opportunities have been enormously increased. The faculty member within the big mechanism and with all his opportunities has a new sense of independence from the domination of the administration or his colleagues; much administration has been effectively decentralized to the level of the individual professor. In particular, he has a choice of roles and mixtures of roles to suit his taste as never before. He need not leave the Groves for the Acropolis unless he wishes; but he can, if he wishes. He may even become, as some have, essentially a professional man with his home office and basic retainer on the campus of the multiversity but with his clients scattered from coast to coast. He can also even remain the professor of old, as many do. There are several patterns of life from which to choose. So the professor too has greater freedom. *Lehrfreiheit,* in the old German sense of the freedom of the professor to do as he pleases, also is triumphant.

What is the justification of the modern American multiversity? History is one answer. Consistency with the surrounding society is another. Beyond that, it has few peers in the preservation and dissemination and examination of the eternal truths; no living peers in the search for new knowledge; and no peers in all history among institutions of higher learning in serving so many of the segments of an advancing civilization. Inconsistent internally as an institution, it is consistently productive. Torn by change, it has the stability of

freedom. Though it has not a single soul to call its own, its members pay their devotions to truth.

The multiversity in America is perhaps best seen at work, adapting and growing, as it responded to the massive impact of federal programs beginning with World War II. A vast transformation has taken place without a revolution, for a time almost without notice being taken. The multiversity has demonstrated how adaptive it can be to new opportunities for creativity; how responsive to money; how eagerly it can play a new and useful role; how fast it can change while pretending that nothing has happened at all; how fast it can neglect some of its ancient virtues . . .

FOOTNOTES

[1] John Henry Cardinal Newman, *The Idea of a University* (New York: Longmans Green and Co., 1947). The quotations used here are from pp. 129, 91, xxvii, 157.

[2] Francis Bacon, "The Advancement of Learning," *Essays, Advance of Learning, New Atlantic and Other Places* (New York: Odyssey Press, Inc., 1937), pp. 214-215.

[3] Abraham Flexner, *Universities: American, English, German* (New York: Oxford University Press, 1930). The quotations are from pp. 3, 4, 42, 179, 132, 25, 44-45, 197, 193, 231, 235, 197 (again), 178-179.

[4] Harvard University, *The President's Report, 1961-62,* p. 3.

[5] Hastings Rashdall, *The Universities of Europe in the Middle Ages* (3 vols., 1895, ed. F. M. Powicke and A. B. Emden, Oxford: Clarendon Press, 1936), III, 358.

[6] Benjamin Franklin, *Proposals Relating to the Education of Youth in Pennsylvania* (Philadelphia, 1749).

[7] *Reports of the Course of Instruction in Yale College by a Committee of the Corporation and the Academical Faculty* (New Haven, Conn.: Hezekiah Howe, 1828).

[8] Allan Nevins, *The State Universities and Democracy* (Urbana: University of Illinois Press, 1962), p. vi.

[9] John J. Corson, *Governance of Colleges and Universities* (New York: McGraw-Hill, 1960), pp. 175–179.

[10] José Ortega y Gassett, *The Mission of the University* (London: Kegan Paul, Trench, Trubner and Co., Ltd., 1946), p. 56.

[11] McGeorge Bundy, "Of Winds and Windmills: Free Universities and Public Policy," in Charles G. Dobbins, ed., *Higher Education and the Federal Government, Programs and Problems* (Washington, D.C.: American Council on Education, 1963), p. 93.

[12] *General Education in a Free Society,* Report of the Harvard Committee with an Introduction by James Bryant Conant (Cambridge, Mass.: Harvard University Press, 1945).

[13] Richard Hofstadter and Walter P. Metzger, *The Development of Academic Freedom in the United States* (New York: Columbia University Press, 1955), pp. 71, 61.

[14] Thorstein Veblen, *The Higher Learning in America* (Stanford, Calif.: Academic Reprints, 1954), p. 85.

[15] Upton Sinclair, *The Goose-Step: A Study of American Education* (Pasadena: John Regan & Co., 1923), pp. 382-384.

[16] Robert Maynard Hutchins, *Freedom, Education and The Fund: Essays and Addresses, 1946-1956* (New York: Meridian Books, 1956), pp. 167-196.

[17] Harold W. Dodds, *The Academic President—Educator or Caretaker?* (New York: McGraw-Hill, 1962).

[18] Frederick Rudolph, *The American College and University: A History* (New York: Alfred A. Knopf, 1962), p. 492.

[19] James Lewis Morrill, *The Ongoing State University* (Minneapolis: University of Minnesota Press, 1960), p. 48.

[20] John D. Millett, *The Academic Community: An Essay on Organization* (New York: McGraw-Hill, 1962), p. 259.

[21] Henry M. Wriston, *Academic Procession: Reflections of a College President* (New York: Columbia University Press, 1959), p. 172.

[22] Eric Ashby, "The Administrator: Bottleneck or Pump?" *Daedalus,* Spring 1962, pp. 264-278.

[23] Hutchins, pp. 177, 169.

[24] A. Lawrence Lowell, *What a University President Has Learned* (New York: Macmillan, 1938), pp. 12, 19.

[25] Rudolph, p. 291.

[26] James Morris, "Is Oxford Out of This World?" *Horizon,* January 1963, p. 86.

[27] James Bryce, *The American Commonwealth,* new edition (New York: Macmillan, 1914), II, 718-719.

[28] Paul F. Lazarsfeld, "The Sociology of Empirical Social Research," *American Sociological Review,* December 1962, pp. 751-767.

[29] David Riesman, *Constraint and Variety in American Education* (Garden City, N.Y.: Doubleday, 1958), pp. 30-32.

[30]Ernest Earnest, *Academic Procession* (Indianapolis: Bobbs-Merrill, 1953), p. 74.

[31]Rudolph, p. 423.

[32]Eric Ashby, "Self-Government in Modern British Universities," *Science and Freedom,* December 1956, p. 10.

[33]Theodore Caplow and Reece J. McGee, *The Academic Marketplace* (New York: Basic Books, 1958), p. 206.

[34]Millett, p. 224.

[35]Wriston, p. 172.

[36]Nevins, pp. 118-119.

[37]Dodds, p. 43.

[38]W. Max Wise, *They Come For the Best of Reasons—College Students Today* (Washington, D.C.: American Council on Education, 1958).

[39]Burton R. Clark and Martin Trow, *Determinants of College Student Subculture,* unpublished manuscript, Center for the Study of Higher Education, University of California, Berkeley, 1963.

[40]Robert Bendiner, "The Non-Teacher," *Horizon,* September 1962, p. 14.

[41]Merle A. Tuve, "Is Science Too Big for the Scientist?" *Saturday Review,* June 6, 1959, p. 49.

ABOUT THE AUTHOR

—**Clark Kerr,** Chairman and Executive Director, Commission on the Future of Education; Professor of Economics and Business Administration, University of California; Ph.D., 1939, University of California. His major research interests are in industrialization, industrial relations, labor economics, and higher education.

Structure, Function and Co-ordination

California Liaison Committee of the University of California and the State Board of Education

This academic plan is an attempt to find a reasonable solution to the difficulties of providing an adequate educational experience, to reduce the competition among academic institutions, and to facilitate decision-making for the agencies concerned with policy determination and resource allocation. It provides tangible insights into the process of categorization apparently necessary in academic administration. As a formal document the academic plan assumes a power which has immediate relevance to the provision of library services. In responding to the contradictions of a plan by its nature restrictive of academic programs–and the demands of the academic environment for unlimited materials and services–the academic librarian must be prepared to affect the determinations, as well as to accept the facts of academic dissatisfactions.

The task of the Survey Team has been to obtain a formula that will seek two objectives. First, it must guard the state and state funds against unwarranted expansion and unhealthy competition among the segments of public higher education. Second, it must provide abundant collegiate opportunities for qualified young people and give the segments and institutions enough freedom to furnish the diverse higher educational services needed by the state.

Although structure, function, and co-ordination are each sufficiently important to warrant a separate chapter, they are discussed together because of their intimate interrelationship. As the Survey proceeded, it became obvious that no one of the three problems could be settled alone; the solution of each required determinations for the other two. Long negotiations and extensive consultation produced a delicately balanced consensus among the three segments. The agreement that has been reached is essentially a "compact"; it must be fostered and refined, and care must be exercised that modifications do not emasculate it.

A "package" acceptable to all segments required compromises. Frank recognition of the needs and desires of each segment and of relative priorities among them was an essential starting point. The junior colleges sought fuller recognition of their role and a mechanism to arrest the projected decline in their proportion of lower division students. The state colleges wanted "the efficiency of freedom" to manage their own affairs, the authority to enter the research field, and a potential role in graduate education beyond the master's level. The University wanted to expand in proportion to the growth of the state and was concerned lest changes undermine its quality standards for graduate and professional education and jeopardize its premier role in advanced training and research. All segments, plus the independent colleges and universities and the general public, have an obvious stake in setting up a co-ordinating agency to collect facts and figures, to check compliance with agreements, and to act as a "watchdog" in preventing duplication and in assuring optimum utilization of facilities and maximum quality at minimum cost.

THE QUEST FOR PROPER ORGANIZATION

The machinery for governing state-supported higher education in California has been about as diverse as could be conceived. The junior colleges, although regulated by state law and financed in part by state funds, have been highly decentralized and have answered primarily to the local districts that created them and provide most of

SOURCE: Reprinted from California Liaison Committee of the Regents of the University of California and the State Board of Education, *A Master Plan for Higher Education in California, 1960-1975* (Sacramento: California State Department of Education, 1960), Chapter 3, "Structure, Function, and Co-ordination," pp. 27-44.

their support. The state colleges have been subject to some direct control by several state agencies to the extent that many functions that are normally in the province of a governing board have been in the hands of officers in other departments of government. The structure of the University of California has long been marked by two characteristics: substantial autonomy from direct state controls and centralization of administrative authority on state-wide rather than on local campus levels.

Considerable diversity in organizational pattern would remain even if each segment were assigned an "ideal" internal mechanism. Nevertheless, many common characteristics and requirements of the three segments suggest a need for more similarity in structure and procedures. Each requires, in differing degrees, the efficiency and quality control that a central administration can give and also the local initiative and community orientation that are hallmarks of well-conceived decentralization.

Underlying much of the following exposition on the government of higher education is a conviction, shared by all members of the Survey Team, that educational policy ought to be free from political interference and external controls. This conviction has been effectively stated in the report of the Committee on Government and Higher Education as follows:

> . . . effective, responsible management of the academic institution is more likely to result from giving authority to strong, able boards of lay trustees than by scattering managerial responsibility among various agencies of state government. Boards of trustees should of course have not only responsibility but accountability as well.[1]

Junior Colleges

The junior colleges have been, and ought to be, community based and locally controlled. However, they are part of the public school system; they exercise a state function; and they are financed with substantial amounts of state funds. Consequently, general goals and standards should be set forth in the Education Code so that the state has authority to enforce the legal provisions pertaining to them.

No real reduction of local autonomy is proposed by the Survey Team; however, it does suggest setting up uniform rules to cover several matters in which school districts previously have adopted their own procedures. For example, these sugges-

tions include the definition of legal residence for nonresident tuition purposes and the standardization of probation and dismissal practices. The local board should remain the governing body, with the decided balance of control.

A majority of the Survey Team believes that most junior colleges should be operated by boards of their own rather than by unified or high school district boards. The chances of obtaining a faculty of college caliber, students of maturity, and added collegiate prestige appear to be greater when junior colleges are operated by junior college boards.

Although local authorities have been permitted very largely to control their activities, the junior colleges could use somewhat more attention than they have been receiving from the state agencies that are charged by law with making rules and regulations for them. If relieved of responsibilities for the State College System, as the Survey Team recommends, both the State Board of Education and the Superintendent of Public Instruction should have opportunity to give additional attention and positive leadership to this large and important segment of higher education.

State Colleges

With regard to their control, the state colleges have occupied a middle ground between that of the decentralized control of junior colleges and the centralized control of the University of California. Authority over them has been fragmented, with most of it nominally vested in the Superintendent of Public Instruction and the State Board of Education. However, much control has been exercised also by the Department of Finance, the Public Works Board, the State Personnel Board, the Division of Architecture, and other agencies. The Legislature itself commonly has taken the initiative in establishing new colleges and locating them. Lacking a governing board that can give them undivided attention or that has full power over them, the state colleges have received a large measure of their leadership from their presidents.

In the opinion of the Survey Team, the state colleges should be placed under the control of a governing board and should be centrally administered by a chief executive officer who would have real authority but be responsible to the board. The board should be an independent one, created by a constitutional amendment that clearly spells out the division of labor among the public segments of higher education and provides co-ordinating machinery through which all segments could consult and settle jurisdictional questions.

The state colleges have been most in need of freedom from detailed and sometimes conflicting state administrative controls. With the creation of an independent governing board and the appointment of a state-wide executive officer, the State College System would be "tooled up" to accept the responsibility that comes with authority. The degree of autonomy should be substantial, but substantial autonomy in no way implies that the Legislature or the Governor should abdicate their ultimate control over the level of support. The new board should have full responsibility for funds appropriated to the system and for its internal policies. Reports should be made by the board, and it should be subject to post-audit of its financial transactions. Line-item, pre-audit, and other detailed fiscal controls by the State Department of Finance should be terminated; full fiscal authority should be vested in the governing board. Doing so would not necessarily mean greater expenditures but would mean rather that the money would be spent for purposes educators deem the most essential.

To carry out recommended changes will require more centralization in the state college state-wide administration. A central staff of business and academic officers must be assigned such tasks as setting standards of performance and checking compliance. The initial complement of additional state-wide personnel probably need not exceed the full-time equivalent (FTE) of those in various departments now providing services to the state colleges. But the power and responsibility must rest with the governing board, which should be comparable in autonomy, composition, and terms of office to The Regents of the University.

University of California

The University traditionally has been both autonomous and centralized. Its autonomy derives from the State Constitution, which makes it "a public trust" and vests its government in The Regents. Much of its distinction has been made possible, in the opinion of the Survey Team, by the independence and stability that come from its autonomous position and the long terms of the appointive Regents. The ex officio membership of the Governor, Lieutenant-Governor, and

Speaker provides a built-in co-ordination with the executive and legislative branches of government.

Designed to conduct the affairs of a single institution, the University administration adapted rather slowly to fit the changed circumstances that followed establishment of new campuses in various sections of the state. Chief campus officers, now called chancellors on general campuses, were given added authority and status, and decentralization of business and fiscal operations has proceeded rapidly since 1958. The Academic Senate, to which The Regents have delegated responsibility for important educational matters, has set up divisional units on each general campus, still retaining sectional machinery in northern and southern California, and recently has expanded its state-wide organization for purposes of co-ordination.

The Survey Team has been careful not to recommend any changes that might encourage tampering with the constitutional autonomy of the University. Article IX, Section 9 of the State Constitution must be preserved; chipping away at the foundations on which the quality of the University rests should not be countenanced. Inside the University, however, much remains to be done to achieve proper administrative balance between the central whole and the operating campuses. Individual campuses need a larger measure of initiative in operations; officers with state-wide responsibility should not have administrative line controls over local campus functions. Final authority over University policies and operation rests with The Regents and the President, as it should, but University operation will benefit from appropriate division of labor between the state-wide offices and the local offices. Increasingly, the state-wide administration should be charged with developing central policy, setting budgetary standards, and co-ordinating programs.

Conclusions on Structure

After the first months of consideration, the Survey Team concluded that three major possibilities for restructuring the state higher education deserved more thorough consideration: (1) a single governing board for both the state colleges and the University; (2) a superboard over the governing boards; and (3) two separate but parallel autonomous governing boards. For reasons given in the following paragraphs, the first two were rejected and the third adopted.

Initially, a good deal of attention was given

to the possibility of placing both the University and the state colleges under a single governing board. Throughout the study some members of the Survey Team have insisted that they would advocate a one-board plan unless the differentiation of function could be spelled out in some secure form. Other members of the Survey Team preferred stronger coordination plans rather than a single governing board.

The one-board plan was the chief alternative to the separate but parallel boards that was suggested in the December 18, 1959, joint meeting of The Regents and the State Board of Education when the "compact" was finally approved. At no time, however, did a specific version or draft of a single-board plan receive wide acceptance. Some University people undoubtedly thought of The Regents as the one board—perhaps slightly enlarged. Some state college people anticipated a wholly new board, with no carry-over members. Most proponents assumed that the constitutional autonomy of The Regents would extend to the single board.

The one-board plan was abandoned because it might result in (1) loss of the benefits of countervailing power and lead to concentration of enormous authority in a single board; (2) opening up the possibility of a leveling effect, without net gain and perhaps with some net loss in over-all distinction of the institutions involved; (3) lessening the amount of attention board members could devote to a given problem because of their responsibility being spread over such a huge system, making the board in effect legislative rather than governing; (4) neglect of some aspects of higher education; and (5) leaving the junior colleges out of the co-ordination.

As an alternative to a single governing board, a superboard standing above the existing governing boards in matters of common concern was given consideration. Such a board of higher education might follow the Texas or Oklahoma patterns. Lyman A. Glenny, in *Autonomy of Public Colleges: The Challenge of Co-ordination,*[2] reports that nearly all systems of co-ordination established since 1950 are of the multiboard, co-ordinating agency type, with co-ordination provided by a superboard. In practice, he found that this type of co-ordination does not afford individual institutions more initiative and freedom than do statewide governing boards.

Circumstances peculiar to California make the superboard difficult to establish here. The University of California has autonomy guaranteed under Article IX, Section 9, of the State Constitution. A superboard could not be established over The Regents without constitutional amendment. The Survey Team agreed that the status of the University should not be tampered with and, moreover, that a constitutional change opposed by one segment was unlikely to be adopted.

Having weighed these circumstances and other disadvantages of the first two plans, the Survey Team in October, 1959, put aside these plans and turned its attention to putting together a "package" that would achieve the optimum educational service to the state. The fact became increasingly obvious that the majority on one and perhaps both boards would oppose a one governing board plan. The risks to University independence, if Article IX, Section 9, of the State Constitution came up for amendment, appeared very great.

Then came the breakthrough of early December, 1959, when, for the first time, representatives of the state colleges and the University were able to agree on the general terms of a compact designed to settle the outstanding problems of machinery of government, division of labor, and co-ordination. The text of that agreement, as subsequently approved by the State Board of Education and The Regents of the University, appears in the recommendations at the end of this chapter.

The Survey Team, having presided over the formulation of this compact, supports it unanimously and vigorously. It has enormous advantages over the existing situation, which is marked by undue competition, fragmented responsibility, unnecessary duplication, and lack of co-ordination. An unprecedented number of young people are just about to reach college age; demands will be made for huge amounts of funds for operations and capital outlay. The Survey Team is convinced that if this compact is put into effect it will engender efficient and economical operation of all three segments of public higher education. California simply must put its higher educational house in order.

THE FUNCTIONS OF THE SEGMENTS

The values of division of labor are widely recognized—in the home, in the labor force, and among the nations of the world. They received at least implied recognition in higher education when California in its first years of statehood provided for both a state university and a state normal school. Until after World War I, few jurisdictional questions arose among the University, the teacher-training institutions, and the junior colleges that made their appearance beginning in 1907.

Initially, the University provided all state-supported higher edcational services except teacher training, which it shared with the normal schools. The University long demonstrated a reluctance to launch general campuses in other parts of the state, even though it made the decision to expand into a second metropolitan area in 1919, when The Regents accepted the Legislature's offer to transfer the Los Angeles Normal School.

Meanwhile the normal schools—later the state teachers colleges, and still later the state colleges, paralleling developments in other states—expanded in numbers, in enrollments, and in curricular offerings. They added to teacher training both vocational-occupational education and general liberal education. After World War II they expanded enormously, with new colleges, broader curricula, and graduate work through the master's degree. Despite stress on functional differentiation, the undergraduate programs of the state colleges and the University appeared increasingly similar.

The junior colleges also grew rapidly. From the beginning they recognized dual purposes—transfer and terminal. The late William Henry Snyder, a pioneer in the junior college movement, once stated its aims:

> The junior college is generally conceded to have two rather distinct functions. One of these is to duplicate the curricula of the first two years of the university ... The other is to be of service to that great group of high school graduates who feel that they have not the time, money, or academic desire to spend four more years in study.[3]

By the time of the Strayer study, the problem of division of labor among the public segments was becoming acute. The report stated one principle of differential functions:

> The vocational or occupational level for which training is provided by these [state college] curricula lies between the level that can be supplied by the two-year training of the junior colleges and the professional schools of the University.[4]

The staff of the *Restudy,* convinced that the principle of differentiation was sound, recommended:

> ... that the junior colleges continue to take particular responsibility for technical curriculums, the state colleges for occupational curriculums, and the University of California for graduate and professional education and research.[5]

Both studies recognized that many similarities of function would occur. All three segments, for example, share general education at the lower division level, and both the state colleges and the University engage in teacher training. Indeed, the similarities are often more striking than the differences.

In practice, differentiation of functions has been difficult to enforce. In 1953 substantial agreement was reached on the division of engineering education between the state colleges and the University, but by 1959 it was honored in the breach as well as in the observance. Reasons for the breakdown are numerous. Agreements were often thought to be one-sided, imposed by the University on the state colleges. Some people argue that static arrangements are unsuitable for dynamic situations imposed by the changing needs of society. Some agreements or understandings made by the two boards have been nullified by legislative action or by a particular institution.

The problem of functions was referred to the Joint Advisory Committee[6] in March, 1959, three months before the Survey Team came into being. After the Survey was launched, the team asked the Joint Advisory Committee to continue its work on the problem. Its report, entitled "Public Higher Education in California, Functions of the Junior Colleges, State Colleges, and the University of California," was completed October 13, 1959. The Joint Advisory Committee was unable to reach agreement on the most controversial issue: the proposal to permit the state colleges to award the doctorate. It finally proposed the appointment of a commission to study the need for additional college teachers and the best ways to meet the need.

Utilizing the Joint Advisory Committee statement, the Survey Team formulated a briefer statement of functions for inclusion in the proposed constitutional amendment on structure, function, and co-ordination. As recommended by the Survey Team and approved in principle by the Liaison Committee, and by the State Board of Education and The Regents in joint session on December 18, 1959, the functions are as follows: (These also appear as a part of the proposed constitutional amendment at the end of this chapter).

> Said public junior colleges shall offer instruction through but not beyond the 13th and 14th grade level, including but not limited to one or more of the following: (a) standard collegiate courses for transfer to higher institutions; (b) vocational-technical

fields leading to employment, and (c) general or liberal arts courses. Studies in each field may lead to the Associate in Arts or Associate in Science degree . . .

The state colleges shall have as their primary function the provision of instruction in the liberal arts and sciences and in professions and applied fields which require more than two years of collegiate education, and teacher education, both for undergraduate students and graduate students through the master's degree. The doctoral degree may be awarded jointly with the University of California, as hereinafter provided. Faculty research, using facilities provided for an consistent with the primary function of the state colleges, is authorized . . .

The University shall provide instruction in the liberal arts and sciences, and in the professions, including teacher education, and shall have exclusive jurisdiction over training for the professions (including but not by way of limitation)[7] dentistry, law, medicine, veterinary medicine, and graduate architecture. The University shall have the sole authority in public higher education to award the doctor's degree in all fields of learning, except that it may agree with the state colleges to award joint doctoral degrees in selected fields. The University shall be the primary state-supported academic agency for research, and The Regents shall make reasonable provision for the use of its library and research facilities by qualified members of the faculties of other higher educational institutions, public and private.

Writing a statement of functions into the Constitution will bring about real advantages. Not only will the differentiation of functions have the force of law, but also the difficulty of amendment will give a new area of stability to public higher education. Enforcement, the weakest link in the old liaison machinery, can be achieved by legal processes. The knotty problem of the doctorate is settled without denying participation to the state colleges, yet providing assurance that high standards will prevail. Sharing of library and research facilities can augment scholarly production and assure fuller use of cultural assets without great extra cost to the state. Inclusion in the Constitution of a definition of functions should help greatly in eliminating duplication and provide a standard that can be used by each segment to judge which of its programs are marginal or peripheral to its functions.

If this statement of functions is written into the Constitution, the question arises as to whether the boards should adopt additional and more detailed ones, such as the one prepared by the Joint Advisory Committee. The Survey Team approved with some amendments the greater part of the Joint Advisory Committee statement, and favorable action was taken on the recommended version

by the Liaison Committee on December 17, 1959. (This statement on functions as amended by the Survey Team appears in Appendix II to this report.) The statement was removed from the agenda of the joint boards on December 18. The team suggests that the Joint Advisory Committee report be referred by the Liaison Committee to the new Co-ordinating Council when it is established and that the section of the report entitled "Extension Programs and Adult Education" be referred by the Committee to the State Advisory Committee on Adult Education.

THE MACHINERY OF CO-ORDINATION

The Liaison Committee since 1945 has had a remarkable record of agreements reached, but the fact is increasingly obvious that enforcement will require more sanctions than are available at present. If the demands of the state for rational development and maximum economy in higher education are to be met, the co-ordinating agency will require considerable influence.

Early in its work the Survey Team's attention was called to an opinion of the Legislative Counsel (Kleps to Donahoe, August 27, 1959, No. 239), which indicated that a strong co-ordinating body could not be established by statute, even though The Regents consented. Proceeding on the assumption that a constitutional amendment is unlikely to pass if opposed by any one segment, the team then undertook to work out the composition of a co-ordinating agency that would be acceptable to all segments.

Assuming that the state colleges and the University would be represented through two separate governing boards, the team gave attention to appropriate representation of the junior colleges and the independent institutions. The State Board of Education will continue to be the chief state policy body concerned with the junior colleges; however, the junior colleges are primarily locally based and their most authentic spokesmen are from associations composed of local board members and administrators, not state agencies. Independent higher education is also difficult to represent, for its organizations are private associations. The team recognized the justice of participation by junior colleges and independent institutions, particularly when decisions affecting them are being made, but found no simple way to arrange representation and voting privileges.

From the beginning considerable sentiment existed for an agency of co-ordination with "public" members not connected with any segment of higher education. States with strong co-ordinating boards (New Mexico, Oklahoma, and Texas) are composed exclusively of "public" members, appointed by the Governor. Two recently organized agencies have part "public" (Wisconsin, four of fifteen, Utah six of nine) and part segmental. The pattern of voluntary co-ordination in Ohio, Indiana, and California is to have all members drawn from or chosen by the segments.[8]

After careful consideration, the Survey Team decided to recommend a body composed exclusively of segmental representatives in order to assure informed members. Lay representation predominates at the governing board level, and the majority of the proposed Co-ordinating Council probably would consist of laymen representing boards. Experience of the Survey Team has shown that authentic representatives of the several segments quickly penetrate to the heart of higher educational problems. The problems of co-ordination require a degree of expertness that someone new to higher education is unlikely to have or soon acquire.

Having decided to recommend a Co-ordinating Council of 12 (three each from the junior colleges, the state colleges, the University, and independent institutions), the team faced the problem of voting. To relieve the junior colleges and the independent institutions of the unenviable role of casting deciding ballots in matters pertaining only to the state colleges and the University, the team determined that several types of questions would be decided on different bases. All members would vote on all questions, and all votes would be recorded; on the selection or dismissal of a director of the staff of the Council, all votes would count with eight of the 12 being required for effective action. Effective action on a matter pertaining to junior colleges would require the affirmative vote of five (including two junior college representatives) of the nine junior college, state college, and University representatives. Effective action on state college and University matters would require the affirmative vote of four of the six state college and University members. Procedural matters would be determined by rule of the Council.[9] Figure 2 shows graphically this co-ordination structure.

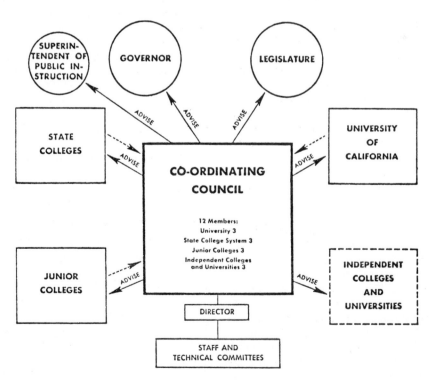

FIGURE 2
Recommended Co-ordination Structure

The proposed Co-ordinating Council will have advisory functions to review operating budget and capital outlay requests, to interpret functional differentiation on programs, to study new facilities and programs, and to advise The Regents, the State College Trustees, the Governor, the Legislature, and other appropriate state officials regarding these matters. It will have a director and technical staff, and it will have power to require data from the public institutions. Its effectiveness and its influence with the governing boards, the Governor, the Legislature, and the public will flow from its mastery of the problems of higher education. If the Council, along with its staff, performs well, confidence in its recommendations and their rate of acceptance will be high. The Survey Team places high reliance on the impartial directorship and staff and in the persuasiveness of the facts and figures that will be assembled by them.

THE PROPOSED
CONSTITUTIONAL AMENDMENT

The kernel of the Survey's proposals on structure, function, and co-ordination is contained in the proposed constitutional amendment. The basic agreement, approved in principle by the State Board of Education and The Regents at their joint meeting of December 18, 1959, is of fundamental importance both to the future of public higher education and to the fiscal solvency of the state. Although it contains some details, particularly on co-ordination, that under ordinary circumstances might not be included there, the Survey Team advises embodying the basic plan in the Constitution. Adoption of an amendment that includes the provisions here recommended will lay the basis for orderly development of public higher education for decades to come.

As stated at the outset of this chapter, the plan is a "package" of interrelated items. If substantive amendments are made that are not agreeable to the parties to the compact, the amended instrument should be dropped by mutual consent. The team cannot advise on appropriate strategy to be employed in proposing the constitutional amendment or in obtaining its ratification. If the Governor puts the matter on a special session call, it can be considered by the Legislature in 1960.[10] If it is not placed on a call or if the Legislature fails to approve a satisfactory constitutional amendment, consideration might be given to proposing the plan through the initiative process.

The text that follows is not in final form for submission to the Legislature or to the electorate. A perfected draft must come from the segments' attorneys and from the Legislative Counsel. The recommendations that follow, however, do contain the essence of what is thought to be a reasonable and viable proposition.

RECOMMENDATIONS

It is recommended that:

1. An amendment be proposed to add a new section to Article IX of the State Constitution providing that public higher education shall consist of the junior colleges, the State College System, and the University of California. Each shall strive for excellence in its sphere, as assigned in this section.

2. The junior colleges shall be governed by local boards selected for the purpose from each district maintaining one or more junior colleges. The State Board of Education shall prescribe minimum standards for the formation and operation of junior colleges and shall exercise general supervision over said junior colleges, as prescribed by law. Said public junior colleges shall offer instruction through but not beyond the fourteenth grade level including, but not limited to, one or more of the following: (a) standard collegiate courses for transfer to higher institutions, (b) vocational-technical fields leading to employment, and (c) general, or liberal arts courses. Studies in these fields may lead to the Associate in Arts or Associate in Science degree. Nothing in this section shall be construed as altering the status of the junior college as part of the Public School System as defined elsewhere in the Constitution.

3. The State College System:

   a. Shall constitute a public trust, to be administered by a body corporate known as "The Trustees of the State College System of California" with number, term of appointment, and powers closely paralleling those of The Regents.

   b. The board shall consist of five ex officio members: the Governor, the Lieutenant Governor, the Speaker of the Assembly, the Superintendent of Public Instruction, and the chief executive officer of the State College System; and 16 appointive members appointed by the Governor for terms of 16 years. The chief executive officer of the State College System shall also sit with The Regents in an advisory capacity, and the President of the University of California shall sit with the Trustees in an advisory capacity. The members of the State Board of Education shall serve ex officio as first Trustees, being replaced by regular appointees at the expiration of their respective terms.

c. The state colleges shall have as their primary function the provision of instruction in the liberal arts and sciences and in professions and applied fields which require more than two years of collegiate education and teacher education, both for undergraduate students and graduate students through the master's degree. The doctoral degree may be awarded jointly with the University of California, as hereinafter provided. Faculty research, using facilities provided for and consistent with the primary function of the state colleges, is authorized.

4. The University of California shall be governed by The Regents as provided in Section 9 of Article IX, of the Constitution. The University shall provide instruction in the liberal arts and sciences and in the professions, including teacher education, and shall have exclusive jurisdiction over training for the professions [including but not by way of limitation],[11] dentistry, law, medicine, veterinary medicine, and graduate architecture. The University shall have the sole authority in public higher education to award the doctor's degree in all fields of learning, *except that* it may agree with the state colleges to award joint doctoral degrees in selected fields. The University shall be the primary state-supported academic agency for research, and The Regents shall make reasonable provision for the use of its library and research facilities by qualified members of the faculties of other higher educational institutions, public and private.

5. An advisory body, the Co-ordinating Council for Higher Education:

a. Shall consist of 12 members, three representatives each from the University, the State College System, the junior colleges, and the independent colleges and universities. The University and the State College

System each shall be represented by its chief executive officer and two board members appointed by the boards. The junior colleges shall be represented by (1) a member of the State Board of Education or its chief executive officer, (2) a representative of the local governing boards, and (3) a representative of the local junior college administrators. The independent colleges and universities shall be represented as determined by agreement of the chief executive officers of the University and the State College System, in consultation with the association or associations of private higher educational institutions. All votes shall be recorded, but effective action shall require an affirmative vote of four of the six University and state college representatives; except that on junior college matters the junior college representatives shall have effective votes; and on the appointment and removal of a director of the Council all 12 shall be effective.

b. A director of the staff for the Co-ordinating Council shall be appointed by a vote of eight of the 12 Council members, and may be removed by a vote of eight members of the Council. He shall appoint such staff as the Council authorizes.

c. The Co-ordinating Council shall have the following functions, advisory to the governing boards and appropriate state officials:

(1) Review of the annual budget and capital outlay requests of the University and the State College System and presentation to the Governor of comments on the general level of support sought.

(2) Interpretation of the functional differentiation among the publicly supported institutions provided in this section; and in accordance with the primary functions for each system as set forth above, advise The Regents and The Trustees on programs appropriate to each system.

(3) Development of plans for the orderly growth of higher education and making of recommendations to the governing boards on the need for and location of new facilities and programs.

d. The Council shall have power to require the public institutions of higher education to

submit data on costs, selection and retention of students, enrollments, capacities,

and other matters pertinent to effective
planning and co-ordination.

FOOTNOTES

[1]"The Efficiency of Freedom." *Report of the Committee on Government and Higher Education.* Milton S. Eisenhower, Chairman. (Baltimore: Johns Hopkins Press, 1959), p. vi.

[2]Lyman A. Glenny, *Autonomy of Public Colleges: The Challenge of Co-ordination.* (New York: McGraw-Hill Book Co., 1959), p. 264.

[3]*A New Type of College Training: An Illustrated Symposium of the Los Angeles Junior College Semi-professional Curricula.* (Los Angeles: Los Angeles Junior College, 1932), p. 5.

[4]Monroe E. Deutsch, Aubrey A. Douglass, and George D. Strayer. *A Report of the Survey of the Needs of California in Higher Education.* (Berkeley: University of California Press, 1948), p. 26.

[5]T. R. McConnell, T. C. Holy, and H. H. Semans, *A Restudy of the Needs of California in Higher Education.* (Sacramento: California State Department of Education, 1955), p. 89.

[6]On recommendation of the Liaison Committee the State Board of Education at its meeting on December 17, 1958, and The Regents of the University at their meeting on December 19, 1958, approved the creation of the Joint Advisory Committee, which consists of four representatives each of the junior colleges, the state colleges, and the University of California. The Committee is advisory to the Superintendent of Public Instruction, the President of the University, and the Joint Staff for the Liaison Committee.

[7]The draft of the proposed constitutional amendment, by mutual agreement, omits the phrase "including but not by way of limitation."

[8]For a careful analysis of co-ordinating plans, see Layman A. Glenny, *Autonomy of Public Colleges: The Challenge of Coordination.* (New York: McGraw-Hill Book Co.), 1959.

[9]This is not specifically stated in the approved recommendations; here the Survey report attempts to clarify the recommendations.

[10]See Appendix I for actions by the special session of the 1960 Legislature on the recommendations in this report which require legislative action.

[11]A later draft omitted by mutual agreement the phrase "including but not by way of limitation."

The Chicago Campus

by Edward C. Banfield

The concern for higher education extends beyond that of the students, faculty, and academic administrations. This case study examines the effect of social, political, and economic conflict factors on the academic decision-making process. For many academic decisions, the stakes are too high to be made primarily on an educationally sound or a technically correct basis. In much the same way the library may be too important as a symbol and resource to groups within the academic community, to be left to the expertise of the librarian.

For several years there had been agitation to establish a branch of the University of Illinois in Chicago. The main campus was at Urbana-Champaign, in the central part of the state, 130 miles south of Chicago. It had been placed there, in 1868, on the assumption that its students (there were fifty of them then) would come mainly from nearby farms and villages to study agriculture and the mechanic arts. When the veterans flooded in at the end of the Second World War, however, the University was offering 3,000 courses, and half of its 25,000 students came from Chicago and other parts of Cook County. In 1946 it established a temporary branch at Navy Pier, a decommissioned naval training center on Lake Michigan about half a mile from Chicago's central business district, which was attended by 3,800 students. The Navy Pier branch would have to be temporary (the University had only a three-year lease), and its facilities were so limited that only the first two years of the four-year curriculum could be offered. Before very long, students and faculty began a lively campaign to persuade the state legislature to make the branch permanent and to give it a four-year curriculum and a suitable campus.

It was an uphill fight. The private colleges and universities in and around Chicago were, to say the least, cool to the idea. Actually, an expanded curriculum at a University of Illinois branch would not have seriously hurt most of them. (Northwestern University and the University of Chicago were in a different price class and took relatively few of their students from Chicago anyway. DePaul and Loyola, the Catholic colleges, were somewhat more vulnerable. Roosevelt College, the only one which depended entirely upon commuters, was most vulnerable, but it was also of little consequence politically.) Nevertheless, for a time they opposed the establishment of any permanent branch of the University of Illinois in Chicago, and they finally agreed to it only on condition that it give a two-year, not a four-year, course.

The most powerful opponent of the branch, however, was the University of Illinois itself. The administrators at Urbana-Champaign believed that the parent campus would always be the principal one and that, unless the resources for expansion were virtually unlimited, the best thing would be to maintain Urbana-Champaign at a high level rather than divide the resources in such a way that neither campus would be first-rate. As it looked to some Chicago eyes, however, Urbana-Champaign was simply selfish, jealous, and fearful that it would eventually be overpowered by competition from the branch. The dean of the Navy Pier branch, Charles C. Caveny, an ardent advocate of a permanent, four-year branch, found himself a minority of one at meetings of the University administration. "From top to bottom," he told an interviewer, "the administrators at Urbana-Champaign were afraid they would become a whistle-stop. I was poison ivy."

Some alumni, having perhaps a sentimental attachment to the campus they had known, were opposed to a "skyscraper" campus in downtown Chicago. A few leading spirits among them were very much against anything that might give the University the reputation of being a "poor boy's

SOURCE: Reprinted from Edward C. Banfield, *Political Influence* (Glencoe, Ill.: Free Press, 1961), Chapter 6, "The Chicago Campus," pp. 159-189, by permission of the publisher and the author.

college" or, above all, a "Negro's college." A city campus, they may have thought, would be too near the Black Belt.

Merchants and other business interests in Urbana and Champaign were also much opposed to a Chicago branch. They had long benefited from the University's presence and its constant expansion, and they were in the habit of using their influence to further its development: for many years they had blocked construction of dormitories in Urbana-Champaign (renting rooms was profitable), they had delayed organization of a co-operative bookstore and of co-operative restaurants (selling books and meals was also profitable), and they had been instrumental, some said, in getting the University to raise its fees $20 a semester in order to build facilities, including a $7,500,000 basketball arena, for high school basketball tournaments and other events that attracted business to Urbana-Champaign.

A four-year branch in Chicago, some people thought, would pose a fundamental threat to Urbana-Champaign. The Chicago metropolitan area was growing fast, and a recent reapportionment had given it control of the House of Representatives. The metropolitan area representatives would probably not be solid in their support of the Chicago branch, but, even so, Urbana-Champaign would have to compete with Chicago for appropriations. And if Chicago joined forces with Southern Illinois University, at Carbondale, which had its own small but dependable bloc of votes in the General Assembly, Urbana-Champaign might find itself third in line when the appropriations were handed out. Some prophets gleefully said that eventually the Chicago branch would have a better football team than the old alma mater. This, they playfully affected to believe, was what worried Urbana-Champaign most.

Against this view, it could be argued that the Board of Trustees of the University, not the legislature, would allocate funds between the campuses and that, consequently, there was no danger of competition. It was true that the legislature had always accepted the recommendations of the trustees. There was, however, no way of knowing that it would always do so in the future. And, of course, a split along Chicago-downstate lines might appear within the Board of Trustees itself. The board consisted of nine persons elected on the major party tickets, and two who were ex officio.

Its members were unsalaried, but the position offered good opportunities for public service and for self-advertisement, and there were always prominent people who wanted it. Nominations were made in the party conventions rather than in primaries, and the parties almost always accepted the recommendations of the Alumni Association. As a rule the Republicans controlled the board, as they did the rest of the state government, but there was always the possibility (realized in 1958) that the Democrats would win a majority. If that happened, Chicago might have a good deal to say in the affairs of the University.

In 1948 the University prepared an "inventory of needs" which totaled $100 million without providing anything for Chicago. In 1953, however, there was a change in the University's administration. An interim president, Lloyd Morey, who had been on the staff of the University for forty years, most recently as comptroller, made energetic efforts to get something built in Chicago. His successor, David Dodds Henry, who became permanent president in 1955, although believeing that the Urbana-Champaign's essential needs should be met first, favored expansion at both Urbana-Champaign and Chicago. The 1960 potential enrollment would be 38,000, he estimated soon after taking office; students should be allowed to go to whichever campus they preferred, and it was likely that 23,000 would want to go to Urbana-Champaign and 15,000 to Chicago.

By 1955 the administrators at Urbana-Champaign seemed to have become reconciled to the inevitability of a four-year Chicago branch. The proponents of the branch, however, felt that the University's intentions could not be trusted. Public promises did not necessarily mean that action was seriously intended. On the contrary (the proponents thought), the University was likely to postpone the evil day as long as possible. "The development of opinion in Urbana-Champaign," Dean Caveny told an interviewer in 1958, "has been from apathy to resentment to acceptance. But they still don't put me on the budget committee, although I am the senior academic officer of the Chicago campus."

The University, together with the allied local interests of Champaign and Urbana, was a powerful force in the legislature. Three of the most powerful legislators came from its district. These—all Republicans—were: Senator Everett

R. Peters, chairman of the Illinois Budgetary Commission and chairman of the Senate Committee on Committees; Representative Ora D. Dillavou, chairman of the House Appropriations Committee and, therefore, a member of the Budgetary Commission; and Representative Charles W. Clabaugh, chairman of the Illinois School Problems Commission. All three depended in some ways upon the University and were often its spokesmen. But the University was also dependent upon them. Senator Peters, the most powerful of the three, was said to regard President Henry as a "carpetbagger." "Who the hell is he to tell me how to run the University," he once said to a fellow senator. His remark may have been made in a moment of pique and perhaps should not be taken seriously. One close and reliable observer, at any rate, was of the opinion that Peters generally accepted the policy line of the University. There was no doubt, however, that he could exercise a great deal of influence upon the administration of the University if he chose to do so.

Although it depended greatly upon these three, the University was not unmindful of the other legislators. It gave each of them four season passes to football games, and every two years it wined and dined them lavishly on a two-day "tour" of the University in May, the season when important bills were coming out of the committees. According to a Chicago legislator, the University used these occasions to extol its Urbana-Champaign campus and to lobby against the proposed Chicago branch—"brainwashing," this ingrate called his entertainment. Under the title of Assistant to the President, the University kept a lobbyist whom Peters amiably called his "errand boy."

Despite all the opposition, the proposal for a permanent campus and a four-year curriculum gained ground. This was largely due to the efforts of a few Chicago legislators who worked hard to get it accepted by the others. One of these was Representative Paul J. Randolph, in whose district Navy Pier was located. Very few of Randolph's constituents cared one way or another about the branch campus. His interest in the issue, one who knew him well surmised, could be explained by the fact that the Chicago *Tribune* warmly favored a Chicago branch. Randolph, it was said, was generally very responsive to the wishes of the *Tribune*.

At any rate, Randolph had, in 1949, introduced a bill requiring construction of a permanent campus in Chicago. When it came up for passage,

Governor Adlai Stevenson called him in and told him that he would be obliged to veto the bill unless it were amended by the addition of the words "as soon as feasible." With this change, it passed with only two contrary votes in the House and with none in the Senate. In 1953, Randolph tried again. He introduced a resolution to establish a legislative commission to study the need for a permanent branch. In 1955, the commission reported: a permanent branch should be established at once. Randolph then introduced a bill to appropriate $4 million to get it under way. His bill was beaten because Cook County Democrats, acting on orders from above, failed to vote for it. The private colleges in Chicago, insiders said, had beaten the bill.

Randolph's efforts were somewhat handicapped because the University had not selected a site for the proposed campus. Why make an appropriation, some legislators asked, before the University was ready to spend the money? The next move was up to the University. If it wanted to go ahead without delay, it would have to find a site before the legislature met again.

From a formal standpoint at least, the site would be chosen by the Board of Trustees. Of the elected members, one was a big businessman, one a wealthy Chicago lawyer, one a Chicago milk company executive, two were downstate lawyers, one was a Peoria insurance agent, one was a well-to-do Chicago housewife, and one was a farmer's wife. The board worked harmoniously and without factionalism. Its decisions were always unanimous.

The most influential member of the board, and the chairman of the site selection committee, was the big businessman. This was Wayne A. Johnston, president of the Illinois Central Railroad, a blustering, assertive man whose word carried much weight with the other trustees partly, perhaps, because of his manner but partly also because of his experience in the management of large affairs. The Illinois Central line passed through Champaign on its way between Chicago and New Orleans (it was an Illinois Central agent, in fact, who had fixed the location of the campus in the first place), and the railroad profited from the traffic the University created. At first, Johnston had opposed the establishment of a four-year campus in Chicago. He was, a former trustee who knew him well told an interviewer, incapable of seeing merit in anything that might adversely affect his railroad. (Once, when the Illinois football team was to play in the Rose Bowl, he insisted that it go there by Illinois Central, although doing so meant a tiresome detour via New Orleans.) Johnston, many thought, would be unwilling to lose the fares of the thousands of students and visitors who had to travel between Chicago and Urbana-Champaign. Difficult as it may have been for him, he had, however, come to believe that a four-year branch should be built in Chicago. Even so, he was not an easy man for the proponents to deal with. He was single-minded, stubborn, and autocratic. "There is only one monarch left—the railroad president," a University official remarked to an interviewer early in 1958. "Johnston's resigned now to the idea that there is need of a Chicago campus, but he thinks the Board of Trustees should do as it damn pleases."

The second most influential member of the board was probably Cushman Bissell, the wealthy Chicago lawyer. He was also a member of the site selection committee.

The other member of the site selection committee was the Chicago housewife, Mrs. Frances B. Watkins. Being a woman and having no special knowledge of business matters, particular weight was not attached to her views. Unlike most of the other trustees, she was a Democrat.

Bissell and Mrs. Watkins were Catholics. They might, therefore, be expected to take a sympathetic view of the problems of De Paul and Loyola, the Catholic colleges that would have to compete with a Chicago branch of the University.

Although not technically a member of the site selection committee, the chairman of the board, Park Livingston, played a part in its deliberations. He was the vice-president of a Chicago milk distributing company and was serving his ninth one-year term as chairman of the board. A resident of a western suburb of Chicago, he had always enjoyed politics. In college he had been president of his senior class; afterward, he had been state director of the Young Republicans of Illinois and an unsuccessful candidate for the Republican nomination for governor and then for United States senator. Those who knew him said that being a trustee was a step on the political ladder for him.

Although the selection of a site, like all important matters, would be discussed at length by the full board, it was likely that the board would accept any recommendation made by the site selection committee and Livingston.

Such a recommendation, however, would have to take into account the views of President Henry. This was so because the President was liked and respected by the board members and because they felt that he was in a better position than they to decide what was good for the University. There was, however, an additional reason why his influence was great. A few years earlier the University had been rocked to its foundations by a struggle between Livingston and a former president which had ended in the president's resignation. It had taken two years to find a suitable replacement, and in this time the University's prestige had been at a low ebb. If Henry, the new president, were also to leave after a row with the trustees, the loss of standing to the University might be irreparable. He, therefore, had the upper hand in dealing with the trustees; if his wishes were disregarded he might leave, and he was, for all practical purposes, irreplaceable.

When he came on the scene in 1955, President Henry found that some beginnings had been made toward the selection of a site. The interim president, Morey, had appointed a faculty-administration Committee on Future Development to advise him—and, through him, the trustees—with regard to the proposed Chicago branch. The Committee soon recommended establishing a four-year campus and suggested five possible sites. Its preferred site was adjacent to the West Side Medical Center, a vast development which included the Cook County Hospital, the University of Illinois Medical School, and in which Dr. Karl A. Meyer played a prominent part. Meyer, a former president of the University's Board of Trustees, had gone to some trouble to persuade the Committee to recommend this site. From his standpoint, there were great advantages in having the University adjacent to the Medical Center: for one thing, it would be a barrier against the surrounding slum.

Another possibility suggested by the Committee was Thatcher Woods, one of the many public forest preserves in the western suburbs. Announcement that Thatcher Woods was under consideration brought an immediate protest from the superintendent of the County Forest Preserve District. Thatcher Woods, this official told the press, would not be available under any circumstances: it was one of the most beautiful of the preserves; besides, it was the policy of the district, and indeed its legal obligation, to retain all lands in its possession.

A little later, the Committee was reorganized

and Dean Caveny made its chairman. The re-organized Committee decided on a new and more thorough survey of site possibilities. For this it recommended, and the President and Board of Trustees approved, employment of a firm of consultants, the Real Estate Research Corporation. One of the biggest and best known firms of its kind in the United States, the Real Estate Re-search Corporation was run by James C. Downs, an economic analyst and businessman whose technical and public relations skills were much admired and whose judgment was much respected by the Chicago business community and by Mayor Daley. Downs was one of the University's most prominent alumni.

Downs had little to do personally with the site selection process. One of his employees, John Ducey, a former director of planning for the Chicago Housing Authority, did most of the work. Ducey met frequently with the Committee to discuss its requirements and to formulate a long list of criteria that would have to be taken into account in the selection of a site. Five of the criteria were "minima": a site which did not meet all of these would be rejected out of hand. The others were of "general desirability": sites which met the minima would then be rated on the basis of these other criteria.

The minima had to do with availability, size, and accessibility. At least half of a site would have to be "buildable" by July, 1959. A site would have to be large enough for efficient operation—140 acres was the lower limit—and there would have to be the possibility of expan-sion later if necessary. A site would have to be within ten miles of the estimated future student potential in Cook and DuPage counties. More precisely, it would have to be accessible by public transportation from the homes of at least 50 percent of the student potential, with a maximum fare of fifty cents for a one-way trip.

This last criterion—accessibility—in effect ex-cluded both the northern and the southern sides of the city from consideration. Neither North-western nor the University of Chicago would have to be provoked by the prospect of a too-near neighbor. Had they seen fit to do so, the planners could have framed this criterion so as to exclude the western suburbs as well: to do this it would only have been necessary to require that two-thirds of the student body be no more than three-quarters of an hour away by public trans-portation.

From a political standpoint, it was probably good strategy to exclude the northern and southern sides of the city and to include the western suburbs, but political judgments did not enter into the criteria. The Real Estate Research Corporation viewed the problem as a purely technical one. "We had no initial bias," Downs told an interviewer afterward. "We didn't know anything about the University, which I think was the ideal situation. The only attitude we had was that convenience is a major factor in American life." In location studies for shopping centers, banks, and other businesses, the Corporation had often used atti-tude surveys and various statistical indices of con-venience. The problem in locating a campus was essentially the same as that in locating a shopping center, the only difference being that the "cus-tomer" was a student. The student's convenience was to be the determining factor. As Downs explained:

> Convenience means a lot of things. It means cost out of pocket, or cost in time, anxiety or transpor-tation. It means physical fatigue. The cost of driv-ing three blocks downtown is greater than the cost of driving three blocks in the country. All costs are constantly being appraised by people who are doing something: your wife will estimate the cost of a shopping sortie in relation to the rewards. If she is going after a dress the rewards will be greater and she will expend more. And if she is going after hose she will not expend as much.
>
> For the students, the cost is the same every day. For them there are two cost elements—money and time.

Given any area—the city of Chicago, Greater Chicago, or Illinois—it was possible, Downs be-lieved, for his organization to find by purely tech-nical means the precise location at which conven-ience (the ratio of rewards to costs) would be maximized. This, in Downs' terminology, was the "idealized" location. There might be a political reason against using the idealized location after it was found, but that was another matter and one entirely beyond his concern as a technician. But even if there was a strong likelihood that the idealized location could not be used, there was, Downs believed, much justification for finding it anyway, for without it one could not estimate the value of what was being sacrificed to political con-siderations. As he told an interviewer:

> If we wanted to locate a bank, we'd establish an idealized location. If we couldn't locate it there, *we'd know it.* Now you may not be able to locate the University at the best site but you ought to know where it should be so that you can estimate the costs.

I think that is the reason the University engaged us. They wanted an idealized site.

As I look at it, the ultimate decision is a political decision. This decision will in practical essence be arrived at by the Mayor and Governor. I think the study is valuable to them. That's the reason I don't say, "Why do you bother to hire us?" When the Mayor and Governor sit down to resolve the question the study will be just as valuable to them as a study for a bank is to the bankers.

The process by which the planners established the technical criteria for an "idealized" location of the University campus was essentially as follows: They plotted on a map the residences of all Navy Pier students and of all Chicago-area undergraduates at Urbana-Champaign. It appeared from the map that most of those who lived less than 55 minutes away from Navy Pier went there, whereas most of those who lived more than 65 minutes from Navy Pier went to Urbana-Champaign. Sixty minutes, therefore, seemed to be a reasonable and workable standard. About 25 percent of the Navy Pier students drove cars to school. In the normal course of events this proportion would probably increase to 40 percent by 1970. Students with cars could travel greater distances in 60 minutes than students who used public transportation. Adding the number who would have cars to the number who would be willing to spend abnormal amounts of time in travel, the planners concluded that a campus would serve its purpose satisfactorily even if only half of the potential student body could reach it in less than an hour by public transportation.

When the criteria had been established to everyone's satisfaction, the Real Estate Research Corporation was asked to recommend the site which met them best. After an examination of fifty possibilities, the planners concluded that the best was an artificial island to be built in Lake Michigan opposite the central business district. It would be expensive to build ($3.25 a foot), and it might not be completed before the deadline. However, it had an advantage which Ducey (whose background, incidentally, was in real estate, not architecture or city planning) seemed to find decisive: it would provide the greatest "dramatic potentiality." Indeed, a campus there, his report said, "could very easily become the most famous in the nation."

When Downs, the chairman of the board of Real Estate Research, learned that his staff recommended the island site, he was skeptical. Before there could be any construction in the Lake, it would be necessary, he pointed out, to get permission from the Army Corps of Engineers; this would not be easy and might be impossible. Moreover, the Lake Front was sacred by tradition. Any proposal to build anything there was sure to provoke controversy. The staff, however, insisted that the island would make the best site for the University and that it was feasible. Downs, although still doubtful, decided not to overrule the staff.

That the branch campus might become the most famous in the nation—or even in the state of Illinois—was exactly what would arouse the fiercest opposition in Urbana-Champaign. When the Board of Trustees met to consider the site recommendation, some of its downstate members were critical. The island would cost about $20 million. Surely, some of them said, it should be possible to find a site for much less than that. ("That is $20 million less for us," the Urbana-Champaign people were saying to each other, according to one of the proponents of the Chicago branch.) At the initiative of the trustees, the Real Estate Research Corporation was asked to suggest three or four alternative possibilities.

According to his later recollection, Dean Caveny suggested to Ducey that he take a look at Miller Meadows, a county forest preserve in a western suburb. Ducey could not remember any such suggestion from the Dean. Miller Meadows, he thought, came to his attention in the course of a systematic survey of all site possibilities within the area indicated by the criteria. It would not have been necessary to call it to his attention, he said; he would have considered it as a matter of routine.

In any case, when the Real Estate Research Corporation made its alternative recommendations, Miller Meadows was at the top of the list. The great advantages of the site, the new report said, were two. It lay in the path of the future growth of metropolitan population, and it was relatively cheap—29 cents a foot, or $3 million dollars. It was reasonably accessible (55.4 percent of the student potential were within one hour's travel by public transportation), although not as accessible as certain central city sites. The Cook County Forest Preserve District had rented part of it to local farmers in order to prepare the land for eventual development for recreation. Another part was occupied by the District's central garage, shops, and warehouses; these facilities, the District said, could not be moved and would have to be replaced. According to the District, the area had unique value because ot its great spaciousness and its accessibility to the west side of Chicago and to the most populous suburbs. For these reasons, the District considered it irreplaceable.

Miller Meadows had one defect which, if the minimal criteria were rigidly applied, might have excluded it from consideration altogether: it was not easily available and it might not be available at all. "The Forest Preserve District," the Real Estate Research Corporation said in its report, "has been historically hostile to such requests. The fact that its attitude has not changed is evident from the District's refusal to furnish us even with factual information relative to sites analyzed in this study." Open opposition from the District, the report said, must be anticipated and counted as a disadvantage of the site.

In order for the site to be considered at least 50 percent "buildable" by July, 1959, it had to be assumed that the University would be extraordinarily successful in influencing the District or that it could readily persuade the General Assembly to let it take the land in condemnation proceedings. Neither assumption was very plausible.

Organized in 1915, the District was one of the accomplishments of the "city beautiful" movement in which Daniel Burnham and others were pioneers. Early in the century, prominent bankers, merchants, and professional people—most of them ardent conservationists who took walks in the woods on Saturdays—persuaded the politicians to put twenty thousand acres on the western edge of the city into preserves which would be kept in their natural state. The Commercial Club's famous Plan of Chicago anticipated the eventual sale of tracts, here and there, to rich men whose estates, protected by the remaining preserves from encroachments, would form an elegant and aristocratic greenbelt around the city.

After the District was organized, the civic leaders turned their attention to other things. Soon a strong smell of corruption arose. Politicians and their friends were buying up land for resale to the District. Organizations with political pull—American Legion posts, Polish-American clubs, volunteer firemen—were demanding and getting special privileges in the use of the land. When the *Tribune* threatened an expose, Anton Cermak, the Democratic boss, promised to give control of the District to the civic leaders themselves.

Under a plan of reorganization adopted in 1926, an Advisory Committee of nine prominent citizens was created. It had no legal powers, but Cermak agreed that it was to recommend policies and plans for land acquisition and management. From a formal standpoint, control of the District remained in the hands of a Board of Forest Preserve Commissioners. These were to be the elected commissioners of Cook County wearing, so to speak, other hats. Having a set of politicians act at one moment as Commissioners of Cook County and at the next as Commissioners of a legally separate Forest Preserve District might seem like a needless complication to some, but Cermak and the civic leaders agreed that it would be well to keep the affairs of the District, which were to be under the watchful eyes of the civic leaders, separate from the affairs of the County, which were to be left with the politicians.

The arrangement worked well. On the nomination of the Advisory Committee, the commissioners employed Charles G. Sauers, a professional park administrator, as general superintendent of the District. In 1957 Sauers had been on the job twenty-eight years, and the District comprised 44,000 acres. In all those years the commissioners never once overruled the Advisory Committee, and, of scores of attempts to take land from the District, the committee had successfully resisted all but two. In these cases it did not oppose the taking of twenty acres by a high school district.

The Advisory Committee had its way because it was useful to the politicians and because it consisted of powerful and determined men. In 1957 the chairman was Edward Eagle Brown, a benign but stubborn old gentleman who was chairman of the board of the First National Bank of Chicago. Others on the committee were prominent businessmen (including Chester R. Davis, senior vice-president of the Chicago Title and Trust Company, and Gilbert H. Scribner, Jr., the realtor who was president of the Civic Federation) and conservationists. In theory, the Advisory Committee was chosen by the commissioners. In practice, it was self-selected, for the commissioners never failed to take its advice.

Brown, the chairman of the Advisory Committee, was kept advised by Sauers, the professional manager, and nothing of importance was done without his knowledge and consent. About four times a year, the full Committee met for lunch at the Mid-day Club in Chicago to pass on plans for land acquisition and to consider other policy matters. Between meetings, the Committee's affairs were managed by its chairman and those he chose to consult.

Brown and Sauers managed the District in a pre-emptory, perhaps sometimes even a waspish, manner. They had no patience with special pleaders. As one of their published reports said: "All employees are thoroughly inoculated with policy standards. Any suggested change or deviation is carefully analyzed. That which is deemed inimical to public interest is resisted with firmness and resolution."

In 1957 the president of the elected board of commissioners was Daniel Ryan. The relationship between him and Brown was symbiotic. Since the District was fated not to be a source of political patronage or "gravy," Ryan, like Cermak before him, was happy to let the civic leaders run it and to take responsibility for it. "The politicians welcome us as a help to relieve pressure," Brown once told an interviewer. "The Advisory Committee is of such stature that no one can attack it. It does what it wants. That way the heat is taken off the politicians." But if Brown and the civic leaders were useful to Ryan, he was indispensable to them, for he and he alone could get money from the taxpayers and authority from the legislature.

The banker-civic leader, the politician, and the professional administrator, having worked together intimately and successfully for many years, understood each other well enough so that they acted as one. Ryan, Sauers thought, had a deep and sincere attachment to the forest preserves (one preserve was named for his father, an immigrant who became president of the County Board) and could be depended upon to fight for them, come what might. Whether he felt such an attachment or not, Ryan had good reason to rely upon the advice of Brown and Sauers and to give them strong backing. Doing so would mean trouble-free tenure for him. Not doing so would mean a hornet's nest of protest, some loss of confidence in him by good government-minded voters, and perhaps, eventually, embarrassment.

Johnston, the railroad president who headed the trustee's site selection committee, was oblivious to the Real Estate Research Corporation's warning that Miller Meadows would be hard to get. (He later insisted to an interviewer that no such warning had ever been given, but he added that he would have ignored it if it had.) He was used to getting what was hard to get. "Johnston thinks that if you know the right fellow and swing the right club, that's it," one who worked with him in the site selection matter said afterward.

In this case "the right fellow" was Ryan, the president of the County Forest Preserve Board. Ryan blandly assured Johnston that he had no objection to selling Miller Meadows to the University—provided that the Advisory Committee agreed. Johnston then talked to Brown, the Advisory Committee chairman, and got a flat and unqualified "no." But Johnston did not take that for an answer. "You old. . . . . . ," he told Brown good-humoredly, "you're on the wrong side of the fence.".

Livingston, the president of the Board of Trustees, then tried his hand with Brown. Brown's bank, the First National, was one of the main depositories of the University, and one of its officers was the University treasurer. This was the kind of a connection which might be expected to produce co-operation. But Brown was quite indifferent to the University's business claims upon him.

Johnston supposed that it was only Brown's stubbornness that stood in the University's way. However, Chester R. Davis, who was both a former trustee and a member of the Advisory Committee, assured Johnston that this was not the case. The Advisory Committee was unanimous, Davis told him, and if Ryan overruled it, all of the committee members would resign in protest.

Despite these warnings, the trustees, the president, and the faculty-administration Committee on Future Development unanimously agreed to try for Miller Meadows. In May, 1955, the University took the press on a tour of Miller Meadows and announced that this was the site it favored. The Advisory Committee at once made a formal recommendation against the University's request, and this recommendation was unanimously accepted by Ryan and the other commissioners of the Forest Preserve District.

It was Sauers, the administrator of the District, who wrote and signed the letter setting forth the grounds for its refusal. However, he consulted Brown about the line to be taken and even about the details of wording.

Sauers and Brown ignored the fact that the University was offering to pay the District the market value of the land and so, in effect, to replace Miller Meadows with another equally valuable tract. They took the position that the University's was just one more in a long series of attempts to encroach upon public resources. That the University's purpose was also a public one and that it was at least as important as conservation and recreation made no difference. Any attempt to take "the people's land" was "morally reprehensible," especially an attempt by another public agency.

Sauers wrote: "The proposal to seize Miller Meadows area for the University of Illinois is opportunistic and an easy out at the expense of all Cook County people. If a Chicago Branch is needed, also there is needed on the part of the University the courage and principle to achieve the purpose without resort to destruction of existing and hard won values."

Yielding to the request, Sauers went on to say, would establish a precedent which would endanger all forest preserve holdings. (This was not quite true; a precedent already existed in the few acres which a high school district had been allowed to take.) It would cost the District $1,500,000 to provide warehouses and machinery sheds to replace those at Miller Meadows. And, in any case, Miller Meadows was irreplaceable because of its strategic location and great size. "There is not the ethical right to take this area, that through hundreds of years will be needed and enjoyed by our country-starved people. The purpose of the proponents for conversion is one of opportunism— in hope of securing a site cheaply and easily at the expense of the foresightedness and courage of the Forest Preserve District and at the sacrifice of accessibility, so important to a Chicago campus."

In private, Sauers conceded that Miller Meadows would make a very good site for the University. But that, he added, was beside the point. "We're very conservative here. It's not our business to give land to the University. It would be just like selling our land for gas stations. There isn't an inch of land we hold that isn't valuable for public purposes. Even if nobody ever sets foot on the land, we must still hold it."

Sauers and Brown expected the trustees to take their case to the legislature. Accordingly, Sauers wrote to all of the Cook County legislative leaders, warning them to be on guard against a surprise attempt to amend a routine bill so as to give Miller Meadows to the University.

No such attempt was made, however, Johnston and Livingston did not even discuss their plans with Representative Randolph, who had done so much to promote a Chicago branch, or, apparently, with any of the other legislators who were interested in the matter. Without the help of Randolph and the other sponsors of the branch campus, there was not the slightest possibility that the legislature would take Miller Meadows from the District and give it to the University or, indeed, that any provision at all would be made for a Chicago campus.

The trustees' failure to press the matter in the legislature was particularly surprising because the Forest Preserve District happened at that time to be asking the legislature to authorize it to enlarge its holdings. That the District wanted something from the legislature gave the trustees a strategic advantage: they could have the University's friends in the legislature hold up the District's bill until the District came to terms with Johnston and Livingston. The trustees failed to take advantage of their opportunity, however, and the session ended with Miller Meadows never having been discussed.

After the legislative session, the trustees reiterated their desire for Miller Meadows, and Sauers and Brown, speaking sometimes through Ryan, reiterated their opposition. Finally, the secretary of the trustees wrote Brown, asking for a joint meeting of the trustees and the Advisory Committee members. Brown flatly refused. The trustees renewed their request. They were disappointed, their secretary wrote, that representatives of one public body should refuse to meet with those of another. Brown had the secretary of the Advisory Committee write an indignant refusal. "We question the propriety and ethics of the proposal . . . ," the letter said.

When the legislature met again, in the winter of 1957, it was plain that if the University was to get Miller Meadows, it would have to be by action of the legislature. Randolph and other legislators who had been trying for years to get a branch campus established expected that the trustees would come to them early in the session for advice and assistance. The trustees had asked the Budgetary Commission for $3 million to start the Chicago branch, but the Governor, acting on the advice of the Commission chairman, Senator Peters (whose district, it will be remembered, included Urbana-Champaign), reduced the amount to $1 million on the grounds that the trustees, not having fixed upon a site, were unready to spend more. Randolph intended to introduce a bill to appropriate $4 million. When he did not hear from the trustees, he took the initiative by telephoning Livingston to tell him what he planned to do. Livingston asked him to hold off for a week and said he would call him back then. However, he did not call back. Randolph called Livingston twice and left his number, but Livingston did not return the call.

At the end of March, Randolph introduced a bill to appropriate $4 million for a permanent, centrally located campus "in the city of Chicago."

The bill had 93 sponsors—4 more than the number of votes needed to pass it in the House. Robert E. Cherry, a Democrat, introduced a bill in the Senate which in effect called for quick action somewhere, and another Chicago Democrat, Representative James P. Loukas, introduced a resolution to establish a House committee to consult the trustees and assist them in finding a site. Loukas, who was a newcomer to the legislature, took the advice of old-timers who said that the resolution would have a better chance if he "dealt the Senate in" by making the committee a joint one. He did so, but although his resolution was quickly passed in the House, 95 to 27, it never reached the committee stage in the Senate. Senator Peters, acting, some thought, for the trustees, had it killed.

Randolph, Cherry, and Loukas all preferred downtown Chicago to Miller Meadows as a location for the branch. Their bills were not intended to rule out Miller Meadows or to override the trustees, however. The important thing, in their eyes, was to get the permanent branch established promptly. If action could be had faster by building in the suburbs than by building in Chicago, they were willing, as their subsequent behavior proved, to accept a suburban site.

The trustees, however, seemed to think that the Chicago legislators were their natural enemies. Before the session had advanced very far, the feeling was mutual. The trustees, a Chicago representative told a newspaper reporter, were "arrogant and smug—too powerful."

The trustees had chosen Miller Meadows precisely because it would be hard to get, Randolph and some other Chicago legislators finally concluded. They had chosen it because they were secretly determined to prevent the establishment of any branch at all, or at least to delay it as long as possible, and because they wanted to create a prolonged and finally fruitless controversy as a delaying tactic. Randolph and others publicly charged the trustees with "stalling." A parent-teacher association at Navy Pier passed a resolution accusing them of insincerity and bad faith.

This theory was plausible. It would explain why the trustees had not pressed their advantage in the last legislature and why they did not take Randolph or other leading legislators into their confidence in this one. It would explain, too, their failure to ask for an adequate appropriation and to propose legislation enabling them to take Miller Meadows from the Forest Preserve District.

One could offer various "explanations" of why this or that member of the board wanted to delay—Johnston because he wanted the traffic between Champaign and Chicago for his railroad, Bissell and Mrs. Watkins because they wanted to protect the Catholic colleges from competition, Livingston because he wanted to make political capital downstate while seeming to promote the welfare of the western suburb in which he lived, the downstate trustees because they were jealous of Chicago, and so on. But these explanations were, at best, no more than plausible, and many well-informed people put no stock in them at all. "The trustees and the administration," a former high official of the university commented privately, "have been faced with very great problems in this matter, internally and externally. Whether they faced those as aggressively and courageously as they might have done is of course a matter of opinion. Whether they moved as rapidly as they might may be questioned. But that does not necessarily mean lack of interest or presence of dubious motives."

The "dubious motive" theory derived its plausibility—such plausibility as it had—partly from the difficulty of explaining the trustees' behavior on other grounds. If they were sincere in wanting a site in the western suburbs near Maywood, why had they not chosen a privately owned tract which could be quickly acquired under the power of eminent domain? Very early in the site selection process an alumni committee headed by Chester R. Davis had unofficially recommended such a site, one which, it happened, almost adjoined Miller Meadows. Moreover, the Real Estate Research Corporation had listed as one of several recommended sites the Riverside Golf Course, only two hundred yards from Miller Meadows. The golf course would cost about the same as Miller Meadows, and it was virtually as accessible (50.3 percent of the potential students would be within an hour's distance of it by public transportation, as against 55.4 percent for Miller Meadows—an insignificant difference, considering the margin of error in the population projections), but it had the great advantage (an advantage only if the trustees were sincere, of course!) of being readily available.

There were other theories privately offered to explain the trustees' behavior. One was they wanted to locate the branch so that it would not become a Negro or a "poor boys" college. When an interviewer asked a trustee about this, he replied: "Miller would not bring in Negroes. My dear man, they just don't go to college. There are only a few large Negro colleges. They haven't got the desire, ambition, intelligence, the capacity. Why, look at how few there are out there at your University of Chicago. . . ."

Some suspected that the trustees' real reason for insisting upon a suburban site was to avoid opposition from the private colleges, which (according to this theory) were up in arms against any threat of competition for night-school students. The trouble with this explanation was that the University of Illinois had never offered night classes, and, besides, none of the private colleges or universities regarded that kind of business as anything but a nuisance.

Neither the anti-Negro theory nor the night-school theory explained why the trustees did not take the Riverside golf course when they found that they could not get Miller Meadow without a fight. The golf course would have served either of these purposes just as well as Miller Meadows would.

Another explanation would account for the trustees' insistence upon Miller Meadows. It was an ugly one, and there was nothing to support it, but this did not prevent it from being offered in private. The Illinois Central had a railroad siding at Miller Meadows. Johnston, some said, was insisting upon Miller Meadows to get business for his railroad and to appreciate the value of its land. Even darker possibilities were suggested. "Why don't you check the options that certain trustees hold in the Miller Meadows area?" some Republican representatives asked a Chicago newspaper man. One representative was said to have evidence of something amiss and to have been dissuaded at the last minute from bringing it to the floor of the House. No one who knew how things had sometimes been done in Chicago could rule out these possibilities entirely. Such gossip, however, was always spreading through the corridors, the hotel lobbies, and the bars of Springfield. The legislature produced it as a by-product, as a sawmill produces sawdust, and no one attached much importance to it.

There was an explanation which would fit the known facts better and which was inherently more plausible. This was that the University president, Henry, having had previous experience in the administration of two downtown campuses, Wayne, in Detroit, and New York University, strongly believed that the atmosphere of a big city would not be conducive to the best undergraduate life. Henry, consequently, favored a suburban site, and the trustees backed him because they agreed with him and because they felt that in such a matter he should have a free hand.

This would not explain the University's failure to accept the Riverside Golf Course. But for that, too, a plausible explanation could be offered. Miller Meadows was a more desirable site than Riverside Golf Course because it was larger. That was enough for Johnston, who was a railroad president and used to having his own way. If it was the better site, he wanted it for his University. And he expected to get it, no matter what.

With the full support of Brown and the other members of the Advisory Committee, Sauers, the administrator of the Forest Preserve District, led a lively campaign to arouse public opinion against the University's plan to take Miller Meadows.

Ryan, the president of the Forest Preserve Commissioners, was a powerful first line of defense. The University could not possibly put him under such pressure as to compel him to yield. Nevertheless, it would make it easier for him to resist if he could claim that public opinion favored the Forest Preserve. Sauers and an assistant, Roland Eisenbeis, accordingly went to work to generate expressions of public support that would strengthen Ryan's hand and—if that should prove necessary—his resolution.

There was no danger that the Board of Commissioners would overrule Ryan, but there was danger that the legislature might overrule the Board. This could only happen with the consent of Governor Stratton. Sauers and Eisenbeis therefore bombarded the Governor and key members of the legislature, as well as Ryan himself, with appeals to save Miller Meadows from the University.

Sauers and Eisenbeis made speeches to Rotary clubs, garden clubs, Izaak Walton leagues, YMCA's, Boy and Girl Scouts, and community-improvement associations throughout the suburbs. They sent out mimeographed letters on the official letterhead of the District to conservationists, to the many associations which held their annual picnics in the preserves, to school teachers, and to many others. They inspired editorials in the Chicago and suburban press; a Chicago *Tribune* editorial writer was particularly close to them, and the *Tribune* carried four editorials in support of the District. When a newspaper said anything favorable to the University's proposal, Sauers and Eisenbeis saw to it that the editor received a volley of protests.

Sauers' letters, the phrasing of which was

approved by Brown, went right to the point. A typical one, addressed to "Dear Citizen and Group Member," read:

> These recreational lands should remain in the hands of the people. They should not be allowed to be broken up for the benefit of a few at the expense of the public. If this should take place, none of your park systems would be safe from unwarranted grabs. You must protect what is yours.
>
> Will you bring this matter before your organization and consider it in the light of public good? We ask that you formally resolve against the taking of forest preserve lands by the University of Illinois or any other body. We also ask that you advise President Daniel Ryan of the Board of Forest Preserve Commissioners, County Building, Chicago, and Governor William Stratton at the State Capitol in Springfield.

Sauers and Eisenbeis gave special attention to the towns near Miller Meadows. If the people of these places could be convinced that the University would be an undesirable neighbor, the forest preserve would win some powerful allies, for the legislature was not likely to put the campus in the suburbs if the suburban representatives did not want it there. In a letter to the president and trustees of the village of Riverside, Sauers wrote:

> For ninety percent of the village residents nothing is to be gained by more congested streets or by increased populations. Inherent in an increase in population are incessant demands to meet the needs for more apartment houses, traffic control, schools and adequate law enforcement. To meet these demands will require each village to assume a larger financial burden and with this will go the loss of those values that make suburban life so pleasant and desirable.

Some village people were fearful that a campus would bring Negroes. Sauers did not allude to this possibility in so many words, but he came very close to it: "Demands for residential facilities for the large corps of service employees necessary to maintain and clean buildings and grounds would be expensive. Then, too, in the future, nearby housing developments might be sought by or for attending students."

In its controversy with the trustees, the District labored under a handicap. Whereas the trustees were fortified with the "impartial" and "expert" report of the Real Estate Research Corporation, the District had nothing of the kind. Without a "purely factual" report of its own, the District's case might seem like special pleading. At this juncture, Charles DeLeuw, of DeLeuw Cather Company, a large firm of management engineers,

telephoned Sauers and offered to make a site selection study as a public service at the nominal fee of $1,000. Sauers quickly accepted. The DeLeuw Cather report found, not surprisingly, that a site near the West Side Medical Center was much to be preferred over Miller Meadows. It would be nearer to the potential students, and to cultural institutions, would afford greater opportunities for part-time employment for students, and would facilitate urban redevelopment. "Chlorophyll and running water are important to college students," the Chicago *Tribune* remarked approvingly, "but time, money, educational opportunities, and civic realism are more important."

The District's effort to arouse public opinion seemed to be highly successful. Hundreds of people sent Sauers copies of letters they had written to Ryan, the Governor, and others. "We have them licked," Sauers wrote Ryan in March, 1957. "Hold fast to your present position . . . that you have no alternative except to abide by the recommendation of the Advisory Committee. I fervently hope that you will maintain this stand."

Some forces in the suburbs, however, were mustering in the University's behalf. Louis Nelson, an official of a Maywood bank, got the suburban chambers of commerce to organize in support of the Miller Meadows site. Several high school principals and other public officials spoke out in favor of it. Although certain localities, fearing Negroes, were set against having a campus nearby, it was clear, in the spring of 1957, that most suburban politicians favored one. Sauers and Eisenbeis, although they had done their cause much good, had not succeeded in arousing the suburbs against the University.

In the spring of 1957, the legislature had before it two bills—Randolph's in the House and Cherry's in the Senate—which required the trustees to establish a branch campus *in the city of Chicago.*

Cherry knew that his bill could not be passed without the help of the suburban senators, and when one of them, Senator Ozinga, told him that unless it were amended to substitute "Cook County" for "the city of Chicago" not a single suburbanite would vote for it, he accepted the change. He was confident that the bill would be amended in the House; accepting Ozinga's amendment was merely a maneuver to get it under way.

Senator Peters, the tough and powerful spokesman of the Urbana-Champaign interests, opposed Cherry's bill. There was, he said, no need of a four-year branch in the Chicago area. There were already six colleges and universities there, and not one of them was operating at capacity. To duplicate in Chicago the Urbana-Champaign facilities would cost $275 million. Eventually, there would be need for this expenditure, but at present the existing two-year branch at Navy Pier should suffice.

Korshak, a Chicago Democrat, took the floor to assure Peters and other downstaters, half seriously, that a Chicago branch "would not jeopardize the integrity of the football team at Urbana."

Cherry's bill passed the Senate, 35 to 18.

A few days later, Peters approached Korshak to ask him to vote against a proposal by Southern Illinois University to establish an engineering school. If Korshak changed his vote, Southern Illinois' bill would come out of committee. Peters wanted to prevent that because an engineering school at Carbondale would compete with the one at Urbana-Champaign. Korshak, who had independently come to the conclusion that an engineering school was not needed at Carbondale, told Peters he could be counted upon. In return, he said, he hoped that when the Chicago branch campus came before the Senate again, Peters would "forget the football team." Peters promised he would.

In the House, meanwhile, something similar had happened. When Randolph's bill came before the Appropriations Committee, a member from a western suburb offered an amendment directing the trustees to build a branch in Chicago "or in the environs thereof." Randolph much preferred a downtown site, but he needed the support of the suburbanites and therefore agreed to the amendment. In his opinion, the most important thing was to get the branch under way; the question of location was secondary, and, anyway, the amendment did not exclude Chicago as a possibility.

Another leading Chicago Republican, Pollack, vigorously opposed the amendment to Randolph's bill. Pollack had introduced a bill in the previous session to locate the branch on a particular site in his ward. His bill had never got out of committee. Pollack emphasized that this time he was not recommending any particular site but that he was determined the branch should be in Chicago.

Pollack's views were especially important because he was the majority whip. Randolph's bill was not an administration measure; consequently, as Pollack himself explained to the House, he was not acting in his official capacity. Even so, his position was not exactly that of an ordinary member.

Livingston and Johnston, the trustees, came before the appropriations committee to justify their choice of Miller Meadows. A downtown site, Johnston explained, would take valuable property from the tax rolls and would increase traffic congestion. It would be hard to expand on a downtown site if the need arose; the necessity of finding relocation housing for the people displaced from the site would mean delay; and high-rise construction would be expensive. On the other hand, a suburban location would offer pleasant living conditions for faculty members and would be easily accessible to students. If the branch were at Miller Meadows, there would be no encroaching land uses in the future. The University, Johnston said, expected to pay the Forest Preserve District a fair price for the land or to find it another tract as good or better for its purposes.

Randolph, Pollack, and other Chicago representatives who had expected to be consulted had an opportunity now to tell the trustees what they thought of them.

"You have been stalling on this," Randolph told Johnston. "Unless something happens soon there's going to be a separate four-year state university in Chicago with a separate board of trustees."

Elroy C. Sandquist, also a Republican of Chicago, asked Livingston:

"You found out eight months ago that you couldn't have Miller Meadows and you're still stuck with it. Is that right?"

"That's one way of putting it," Livingston replied.

"It'll be another two years before anything is done for a Chicago campus," Sandquist shouted. "Don't try to kid this committee."

Sauers also appeared before the committee. He said that the trustees' proposal to take Miller Meadows was "an unethical encroachment on another public body."

A downstate Republican, acting on his own initiative and without consultation with the trustees, then introduced an amendment which would empower the trustees to take Miller Meadows by right of eminent domain. A Chicago Republican said that if this amendment were accepted the bill would surely be defeated by Chicago votes; he moved that the amendment be tabled. His motion lost, but when the amendment was put to a vote, it also lost.

Finally, the Committee accepted an amendment requiring construction in the city of Chicago "or the environs thereof."

The next week, when the bill came to the floor of the House, the debate centered on the amendment. Pollack and others argued that the word "environs" was much too indefinite and that the trustees were likely to use it as an excuse for insisting on Miller Meadows and, thereby, to delay matters further. Randolph, on the other hand, was willing to accept the amendment. "All we want is action," he told the House.

Representative Harewood, a Negro Democrat from Chicago, wanted the branch to be in Chicago. It should not be a country club, he said. Students should be able to ride a streetcar to school; poor boys and girls couldn't afford automobiles. But another Negro from Chicago, Robinson, a Republican, took a contrary view. The experts, he said, referring to the University authorities, should be free to do what they thought best. A Chicago alderman, Vito Marzullo, who was present to lobby in behalf of the City Council, came on the floor and told Robinson— somewhat irately, Robinson thought—that he was betraying the Negroes by not insisting upon a downtown site. (Marzullo was one of several lobbyists who, being former representatives, had the privilege of the floor.) Robinson begged to differ. "The South Side Negro," he told an interviewer afterward, "doesn't go to college just to prepare for a job; going is part of the status pattern. The middle-class Negro is the one who goes to college, and he goes as an expression of his drive upward in the status pattern. Most Negroes who would go to the University probably have their own cars and would go regardless of location."

Downstaters sat back in amusement while the Chicago area representatives quarreled. It was the downstaters who would finally decide, for they held the balance of power. "You downstaters should be suspicious of a suburban site," a Chicagoan warned them. "There would be marching bands and football teams at a suburban branch."

When the vote was taken, the amendment adding the words "or in the environs thereof" lost, 55 to 100. The bill then passed the House, 116 to 18.

Now that the Senate had passed a bill directing the trustees to establish a branch in Cook County and the House had passed one directing them to establish it in the city of Chicago, a conference committee consisting of two members of each house was appointed to recommend a settlement of the difference. The House conferees were both prepared to insist upon "the city of Chicago." Senator Cherry, who was one of the Senate conferees, preferred that wording also. But the other Senate conferee, Ozinga, would not agree to a unanimous report unless the crucial words read "Cook County." If it were not unanimous, the report would probably not be accepted and both bills would die. It was only a day or two until adjournment, and controversial matters were likely to be dropped by the wayside.

Randolph urged Cherry to withdraw his Senate bill. If Randolph's bill were the only one in the field, the conference problem would not arise.

Cherry refused. He thought there was a good chance of getting his bill adopted.

Finally, the conferees yielded to Ozinga and reported in favor of "Cook County." However, the House, energetically led by Pollack, refused to accept the report. The conferees met again and, this time, produced a "city of Chicago" report which was immediately and overwhelmingly accepted in the House. The bill reached the Senate only ten minutes before adjournment *sine die.* When the roll was called, Senator Peters, the Urbana-Champaign leader who had promised Korshak that he could forget the football team if Korshak would vote against Southern Illinois University's engineering school, did not vote. Instead, he signaled Ozinga and a number of other Republican friends, who left the floor as the vote was being taken. The report failed to get enough votes for passage, and a minute or two later the legislature adjourned.

Supporters of the Randolph bill felt that Cherry was responsible for what had happened. Cherry, they said, hated to see Randolph get the credit for the bill: that was the real reason why he had refused to withdraw his own bill.

Nonsense, Cherry told an interviewer later. The reason he had not withdrawn his bill was that he had expected it to pass. It was Peters who killed it, and those who had taken up so much time discussing it had given him the opportunity. "Frankly," Cherry said, "I don't think the amendment made any difference at all. I don't think Senator Peters wanted a branch in Chicago, in Cook County, or anywhere else."

It was Pollack, others said, who was responsible for the bill's failure: if he had really wanted to get the branch under way, he would have agreed, as did Randolph and Cherry, to a wording that

the suburbanites would support. Not so, Pollack told an interviewer. The Senate leaders had agreed to accept the House's wording, and it was only because of an oversight in the last-minute rush that it failed to pass. Cherry was amused at this interpretation. It was not by oversight, he said, that Peters, although remaining on the floor, failed to vote or that Ozinga and his friends left the floor when the voting began.

The downstaters were amused. John W. Lewis, the genial farmer who was majority leader in the House, chuckled, some weeks later, when he recalled what had happened. "The Chicago people were like the dog that saw his bone reflected in the water when he crossed a bridge," Lewis said. "He dropped it by trying to get more. It just shows about human nature."

If the trustees really meant to "stall," they had been entirely successful. It would be two years before the legislature met again. And then the same thing was likely to happen all over again; with downstate help the suburbanites would always be strong enough to check the Chicagoans, without, however, being strong enough to get the branch for themselves. Those who wanted delay— if, indeed, there were any who did—had reason to hope that if the suburbanites eventually retired from the fray, two sets of Chicagoans would enter the lists and fight each other to a draw. One set of Chicagoans wanted the campus located near the West Side Medical Center. These included Dr. Karl A. Meyer, head of the Cook County Hospital; the Sears-Roebuck Company, whose main plant was affected by the deterioration of

the neighborhood; and Raymond Hilliard, head of the County Welfare Department, who believed the campus should be situated so as to eliminate the city's worst skid-row district and who, with an architect friend, had gone to the trouble of preparing perspective drawings and supporting statements in the hope that his boss, Ryan, the president of the County Board, would enter the controversy.

Another group favored a near-South Side site. This was a railway yard which would be made available through the consolidation of several terminals. Many businessmen thought that to interpose the University campus between the South Side slum and the central business district would be a great boon to real estate values: it would give the downtown area a southern "anchor" comparable to the northern one that the Fort Dearborn Project was intended to provide. Holman Pettibone, the head of the Central Area Committee, began to take an interest in the University's site selection problem when it became clear that the railroad terminal consolidation would be consummated.

Unless Governor Stratton and Mayor Daley intervened, the struggles between Chicago and the suburbs and between the west and the south sides of Chicago might go on indefinitely. Anticipating the argument to come, the trustees, early in 1958, employed the Real Estate Research Corporation to make another study of site possibilities. "I want someone to back up the recommendations I am going to make," Johnston told the press. "I want an unbiased viewpoint."

ABOUT THE AUTHOR

—**Edward C. Banfield**, Henry Lee Shattuck Professor of Urban Government, Harvard University; Ph.D., 1952, University of Chicago. He teaches public administration and urban government and problems. His current research is in the problems of the cities.

Academic Tensions

by Ben Euwema

The modern institution of higher education is a community of diverse interests. Each sees academia as a reflection of what it itself understands to be significant: a community of scholars, a complex business operation, a learning instrument. As the position of each is not clear to and accepted by the other members of the community—as this article makes apparent—conflict is inevitable. The academic librarian finds himself representing each group in discussions affecting the library and, in time, becomes counsel for the library rather than for the administration, the student body, or the faculty.

It is clear that one characteristic phenomenon of American higher education these days is a growing tension in the relationships of faculty and administration. As might be expected, the situation tends to be more serious and tangible in our larger institutions, although it is certainly not entirely unknown in the smaller ones. It is not unlike the relationship which existed between the secular clergy and the regular clergy in the Middle Ages.

The growing tension is indicated by the large number of dissatisfied faculty members and administrative officers and by the statements, constantly reiterated on both sides, to the effect that "they don't really understand us." Members of the administrative staff blame the faculty for modes of behavior and attitudes which are simply professional characteristics, whereas members of the faculty accuse the administration for actions which are clearly beyond the responsibility or capability of that group.

By and large, the chief administration complaint is that certain members of the faculty do not take their responsibilities seriously enough—advising, for example; attendance upon classes and general departmental and university functions; and so on. On the other hand, the members of the faculty feel that the administration is responsible for low salaries, insufficient office space, and inadequate facilities; furthermore, the administration is accused of not appreciating the nature of the university, of being too responsive to public pressures, and of stressing quantity instead of quality.

We can admit, at the outset, that some of these strictures are deserved, at least in some places and at certain times. However, the mutual recriminations are, at least to a degree, neurotic; and we should look for causes.

There are actually a fairly large number of causes for the phenomenon. Of these, perhaps the most obvious one is simple misunderstanding. When the faculty and the administration are at odds, sometimes the difficulty may reside in the fact that no one is quite certain as to who are the faculty and who are the administration. Obviously, the professor of Sanskrit (who is not also a department head) is a member of the faculty; the president (unless he is also a professor) is a member of the administrative group. But what of the department heads? the registrar? the academic deans?

When someone blames "the administration" for encouraging, or permitting, low academic standards, whom does he actually have in mind? It is all very vague. All we can certainly know is that the speaker is blaming someone other than himself. On the other hand, when a dean says that the faculty attitude toward teaching is "frivolous and unprofessional," whom exactly does *he* refer to? Certainly, one hopes, not to every classroom teacher. It is more likely that he is referring to a particular instructor whom he has reprimanded recently for laxity in class attendance.

These are perhaps relatively minor causes of tension in themselves, but they become serious as soon as we begin, first, to generalize about them and, second, to act upon them. Whereas the logical leap from one instance to a universal judgment will earn the student in Logic A a failing grade, his elders (unfortunately) need

SOURCE: Reprinted from Ben Euwema, "Academic Tensions," *Educational Record* 42: 187-193 (1961), by permission of the publisher and the author.

pay no such automatic penalty for their logical confusion.

A second cause of the difficulty is—let's face it—the regrettable fact that, by and large, the faculty and the administrators turn their worst faces toward each other. Like incompatible marriage partners, they inevitably bring out the worst in each other. Here is an example so familiar as to be recognizable to any member of a university family.

The business manager will have reason to meet the university's ranking Egyptologist, in any official way, only when the latter is embroiled with the campus police. Last week, for example, the business manager's office sent around a notice requesting everyone to refrain from parking in Lot Q for two days in order to give Plant Operations a chance to remove the snow. The Egyptologist never reads his mail, or very seldom; and so he simply will never see the notice. He will, of course, be the first to complain if the snow is not removed; nevertheless, he will park as usual in Lot Q, also (as usual) straddling two stalls. Even so, no one can adequately describe his fury when he finds a police sticker under his windshield wipers. The business manager to whom he complains can hardly avoid the conclusion that the Egyptologist is not entirely bright.

He is, of course, quite wrong; for the Egyptologist is a genuinely distinguished scholar and one of the true ornaments of the university. Next week the shoe will be on the other foot: the scholar will meet the business manager at a reception. Forgetting his pique, he will refer conversationally to a recent archaeological expedition, only to be appalled at the business manager's epic ignorance of the whole business. What is even worse, the business manager will actually seem not to be embarrassed by his ignorance.

Now they are both able and devoted servants of the university; each is, in his own way, extremely valuable to the whole enterprise. And yet neither understands or appreciates the other. Each thinks the other unreasonable and unintelligent. The business manager generalizes on the basis of his own slight experience; so does the Egyptologist.

A consequence of this phenomenon is the sort of professional parochialism or myopia with which we are all familiar. The professor often does not know what the administrative officer is supposed to do, nor does the administrative officer always fully realize what it means to be a professor.

The professor should know that a large, complex university simply cannot manage itself in a light-hearted medieval fashion. Most American universities are engaged in a number of highly complex and bewilderingly different ventures. For instance, the university must provide food and lodging for six thousand students. The living and dining facilities must first be financed, then built, and then operated with a very small margin of profit or with no profit at all. A doctor's degree in topology or in ancient history hardly prepares a man to operate or criticize a hotel business of such magnitude. Furthermore, the university has a campus of five hundred acres, studded with 100 millions of dollars worth of buildings—classrooms, laboratories, offices, and the like. These buildings have to be planned, financed, built; and then heated, lit, and ventilated. The grass must be planted, fertilized, and cut; sidewalks must be maintained; water and sewage disposal must be provided. Meanwhile, someone must register the students, keep their records, and arrange for their transfers or graduation; someone else must pay the faculty, administer the institution's finances, and keep books on the whole enterprise.

And so it goes. It is, of course, easy enough to complain about the proliferation of administrators and the burgeoning of bureaucracies. Parkinson is always relevant, and it is fashionable to be quite arch about Parkinson's Law at the faculty reception. Nevertheless, the nature of an academic institution becomes daily more complicated. To cite only one other rather simple example: When I began to teach in 1928, I received annually ten pay checks, each for $200; the total was my $2,000 salary. There was not a single "withholding." Today, on the other hand, there are deductions for retirement, health insurance, "major medical" insurance, life insurance, income tax (federal), income tax (municipal), social security, and perhaps a few others. Someone has the task of computing all these sums, allocating them properly, reporting the allocations, and writing the (reduced) checks. What a single clerk did in 1928 now requires an office full of clerks and a battery of IBM machines. We may all regret the growing complication of academia, but none of us can reverse an irresistible trend.

Nevertheless, older members of the faculty are always harking back to the "good old days," when one clerk in the registrar's office enrolled every student in the institution and when the president's secretary signed the entire payroll once a month. Admittedly these were, in many respects, good old days indeed; but we can no more recapture them than we can rediscover our youth. And it is often a nostalgia for youth which invests the good old days with their glamour.

Certainly the most important development in university organization during the last half century is the growing isolation of the administrative officers from the members of the faculty. In the good old days, the president of the university knew personally almost all permanent members of the faculty; upon occasion he visited them in their offices and he saw them in his office from time to time; every member of the faculty participated regularly at the monthly faculty meeting at which the president presided; and every member of the university community attended certain social functions.

Of course, these things are no longer possible of achievement. It is possible for a man to become acquainted with a group of two or three hundred; it is impossible with a group of two or three thousand. Furthermore, the faculty has grown to be highly mobile, particularly since 1945. The president would now have to get to know not ten times as many individuals, but actually twelve or fifteen times as many.

The isolation of the two groups is, of course, automatically responsible for a great many misunderstandings. When you see a man periodically and know him personally, you are willing to give him the benefit of the doubt on the occasions when you feel he is acting unwisely. When, however, you see a person very rarely, if at all, what you hear about him at a cocktail party or read about him in the newspapers becomes "monstrous," "stupid," and "irresponsible."

This, at least partially, accounts for the administrator who feels that all faculty members are lazy and irresponsible and for the professor who feels that all administrative officers are anti-intellectual penny pinchers.

The misunderstanding arising from these conditions is partly responsible for the growing faculty-administration tension. But there are, of course, many other causes. One of them is a misunderstanding of the functions of the faculty, by both the administration and the faculty itself.

Because so many university officials are constantly engaged in conducting rather complex business enterprises, they run the danger of viewing the university as primarily a business operation. No error could possibly be more serious. It may be necessary to operate the university's housing facilities somewhat as though they were part of a hotel business; even here, of course, there is one very significant difference: the university should not, or dare not either, earn a profit. However, to operate an academic department on "a sound business basis" would simply be to convict the department head of bad management.

In an academic enterprise, quality is everything. A good teacher—a really good one— cannot possibly be overpaid: it is impossible to put a monetary value on the sort of liberalizing of the human spirit that a really fine teacher can help to produce. Conversely, a poor teacher cannot possibly be paid too little: to pay him anything at all is to be guilty of an inexcusable overpayment.

The ordinary standards of the business community simply do not apply to the faculty. There is, for example, the matter of office. There is, for example, the matter of office hours. Here is Professor X, who spends eight hours a day, forty hours a week, in his office and classroom. You can set your clock by his schedule. Professor Y attends his classes and then disappears into the library stacks for the rest of the day. Professor Z divides his time equally between his classroom, his home office, and the library. Who is the most faithful and effective member of the faculty? The answer would seem to be easy enough; but actually there is no way of telling on the basis of the evidence given. What I have said about each of them may be interesting but it is actually irrelevant.

Professor X may be a "harmless drudge"— really, of course, if a "drudge," then most harmfull Professor Y may, after twenty years, write a book which, like *Das Kapital* or *Gulliver's Travels,* will enter into the common heritage of our culture. Professor Z may be a good, conscientious journeyman. The point about X, Y, and Z is simply that their real contributions to the university and to society cannot be described in any purely quantitative terms.

Therefore, in any "real" sense, these men cannot be administered, supervised, or directed. They can merely be coordinated or led. This is a hard lesson for a man trained in industry to learn. Alas, many so-called educational administrators never learn it; and so, inevitably, they fail. They may hope to gain the cheap bauble of efficiency only to lose the pearl of great price.

It must also be said that the confusion as to the proper role of the faculty is not clarified by the repetition of pious cliches on the part of faculty members themselves. "The university," we are constantly being told, "is a community of scholars." This is about as accurate as Carlyle's assertion that the university is "a collection of books." It is true, a university cannot exist without scholars or books; but to equate scholars and books with the university is about as meaningful as defining a man as a "concourse of atoms."

The university cannot exist without scholars, but neither can a modern university exist without buildings, laboratories, and hosts of dedicated bureaucrats, minor and major. A university needs some sort of legal status, certain machinery for bringing scholars and disciples into a "community." And a good university has a deep commitment to certain institutional goals.

A flourishing and healthy university also must provide for diversity within the community of scholars, disciples, and bureaucrats. As this diversity deepens, the sense of community may all but disappear. (One such crisis has been eloquently described recently by C. P. Snow.[1]) Nevertheless, the sense of community remains a highly desirable goal and—if American higher education is to reach its full potential—fundamentally necessary.

What it comes to, then, is that the complex American university requires for its effective operation several differently oriented groups of people. I shall list the most important of these:

The Trustees

These are public-spirited men and women whose primary responsibility it is to select the university president, review the institution's fiscal policies and practice, help the president keep the university operating in conformity with its charter, and, in general, promote the welfare of the institution in every possible way. The trustee is jealous of the university's reputation for academic freedom, academic excellence, and fiscal soundness. He renders his most important service when he helps to find an able president and a few generous millionaires.

The President

The modern university president may have to play a number of different roles, or he may select one role and concentrate mainly on it. That is to say, the president may be in turn the chief "promoter" of the institution, its chief fiscal officer, the leader of its research and instructional programs, the buffer between the institution and the legislature or alumni or general public, a national leader in higher education, or any single one of these or a combination of these.

The presidency of a modern, complex university is an awesome post. It requires a very rare combination of skills: scholarship, business acumen, salesmanship, diplomacy, and that indefinable aura of leadership without which everything else will be ineffectual. Because it is in the nature of his position to operate on many different fronts, the president constantly runs the danger of being misunderstood. And because he is desperately busy almost all the time, he must depend a great deal upon his assistants. It is a very fortunate—and rare—university president who will find in his assistants that curious combination of selflessness and expertness without which they will either overplay or underplay their roles—and thus fail to serve him and the institution most effectively.

The Business Office

Here again one is aware of a curious dualism. The chief business officer of the university must operate, in a businesslike fashion, an institution that is actually about as businesslike as marriage or the church. The basic efficiencies of big business must be understood and adapted to an institution which exists neither in order to gain the whole world nor to lose its own soul. At the same time, however, the business officers of the university must resist the impulse towards philanthropy—even though ultimately they know that the university exists to serve the most philanthropic of all purposes.

More important, for our purpose, is the fact that the business manager will have to deal with the general business community as well as with the faculty; with certain trustees who feel it immoral to do anything without making a profit, as well as with some students who feel that the world owes them everything. And somehow whatever is done—however "commercial"—must assist in the achievement of the university's spiritual objectives. Therefore, for example, it will not be enough merely to house the students in dormitory-hotels; it will be essential to house them in educational and educative communities so that one member of the group may have the benefit of interaction with others of the group, and so that even here the spiritual objectives of the university may be served.

The Student Body

Note that we are using here a curiously biological term. For when we say *student body*, we imply an organic wholeness. Like many other academic phrases, this one is highly idealistic in denotation; nevertheless, now and again, in our better institutions, the ideal is approximated.

The individual student, who helps to form the "body," to complicate matters somewhat more, is half boy and half man. He will never achieve maturity unless he is treated as an adult; but he is, in fact, neither infant nor adult, but something in between. The same confusions that befuddle his elders in the university community disturb him. On the one hand, his task is made much more difficult than theirs because, as a student and an adolescent, he must survey the whole of creation and make up his mind about it; on the other hand, he must earn a living in the world as at present constituted. He must be *in* his time but not always exactly *of* it. A university education worthy of the name should permit him to see, as from the perspective of an enormous distance, the machinations of men and nations as well as the stately procession of the stars. And yet even this very disinterestedness must be instilled and encouraged by men and women of the faculty who are themselves wage-earners, citizens, fathers, mothers, voters, taxpayers, members of minority groups, churches, and political parties—who are alternately wise, foolish, credulous, skeptical, happy, despondent, objective, and highly "engaged."

Of course, the student's confusion stems from a noble source: the disparity, increasingly obvious to him, between the *is* and the *ought,* the factual and the ideal. Alas, too soon, he will learn to accept the universe as it is; but, until the day of this unhappy capitulation, he will not be easy to live with.

He will discover, in the high-flown language of the catalogue, certain statements of intent which he will measure against the university's actual accomplishment. He will rail at the natural human frailties of his professors, and he will assume axiomatically that the business office exists to bedevil him and to earn inordinate profits at his expense.

The Faculty

It is my point that all of the elements of the university community are essential to the success of the enterprise. Among these, certainly the one completely indispensable group is the faculty. There is at least that much truth in the ancient cliché—"the university is a community of scholars." In academia, as in Orwell, all are equal, but the faculty is more equal than the others.

The effective member of the faculty is not a tradesman or a mere jobholder. It is possible for a man to work as a salesman or as a plumber for 40 hours a week; during the remaining 128 hours he may completely forget about his job. This is not true of the professor. He "professes" 168 hours a week—all the time, in fact. He lives a certain kind of life because he is, in the first instance, a certain kind of person. He is, first and foremost and all the time, a scholar; and it must be said that a scholar has certain unique attributes. He sees, with exceptional clarity, the principles of his own specialty, but not necessarily those of any other scholar. This fact always disturbs the conscientious student and the members of the administration. They expect a chemist to be sophisticated about chemistry, of course; and so he is. But they also expect him to be sophisticated about ceramic technology or Greek literature; and, very often, he is not. The extreme concentration that expertness in a specific discipline demands may militate against a sympathetic appreciation of all other disciplines. The professor's narcissist complex must be clearly understood so that the proper allowances may be made. In a general faculty discussion of course requirements, therefore, the professor of physics will tend to be just about as objective about physics as the judge of a beauty contest whose beloved is one of the contestants.

However, without this imbalance, the professor will never be worth his salt. He is engaged in order to profess his subject—not everyone else's. The corrective, if one is necessary, comes from the interaction of various specialists, one with the other. A faculty, viewed in this light, is similar to the Congress: a congeries of pressure groups, each representing his own interest but each willing, if necessary, to compromise with the others. This is merely to say that democratic procedures are essential to the successful operation of a university faculty.

It is almost unnecessary to add that, without complete freedom of thought and expression, the faculty member cannot hope to play his proper role in the university community. This is especially so since, on the whole, members of the faculty tend to be rather more timid than other members of society. Academia is still partly a cloister; and some of us chose to become academicians out of a desire to escape the rough-and-tumble of the outside world. (It does not weaken my argument to note that often the tranquility one looks for in academic life is an illusion!) Therefore, it is often possible to cow a professor very easily; as a matter of fact, sometimes he is afraid of what he *thinks* the trustees or the president thinks he thinks. He must constantly be reassured that his own mature, considered judgments, because they are based on sound scholarship, are of great importance to society and should, under no conditions, be suppressed or modified. One of the chief duties of the administrative officers of the university is to see that the professor speaks out boldly and clearly on important matters.

The mere recognition of a few causes of faculty-administration tension and an indication of the true functions of each group will not, of course, appreciably lessen the tension; but they may help. If everyone recognizes what everyone else is expected to contribute to the university community, he may not therefore love his fellow men more; but he may learn to respect them. In this instance, that is just as good.

FOOTNOTES

[1] Snow, C. P., *The Two Cultures and the Scientific Revolution* (New York: Cambridge University Press, 1960).

ABOUT THE AUTHOR

—**Ben Euwema,** Professor of English, Pennsylvania State University; Ph.D., 1934, University of Chicago. Dr. Euwema has served several terms as an academic administrator, including the Deanship, College of Liberal Arts, Pennsylvania State University, 1946-1964. He is now teaching and doing research in Victorian literature.

II
THE LIBRARY IN ACADEMIA

Higher education is an entity, however differing the expressions of its critics and conformists as to its particular mission. Within it the desire to provide particular types of educational experience and to facilitate access to this experience has resulted in another entity—the library. In organizing itself operationally, the academic library has developed traditions which have successfully achieved for it an existence somewhat removed from its academic relevance. In turn, the academic librarian, in the certainty of his speculations on the nature of the library, interprets the library's role on the basis of higher education's implicit and explicit acceptance of these conventions. Confronted with the lack of educational definition, the complexity of higher education, and his less-than-direct involvement with the institution's teaching, research, and service functions, the library administrator finds the subsequent result of this process of abstraction—a separate organization—to be the base from which he can most easily determine the responses the library will make. He can easily be caught between his concept of the library as having a separate and distinct existence and the library as a creature of educational purposes, and he has responded with ambiguities and obscurities. Academic librarianship must not be accepted as an outing to be taken within the structure of a discrete profession but rather as an exploration which will necessitate a constant examination of the possible directions to be taken, a willingness to accept uncertainty and risk, and an ability to make reasoned accommodations to changes in educational conditions.

The Library in the American College

by William Warner Bishop

This overview describes the academic library in both its simple and its complex nature. As an integral part of the academic community, the library is directly affected by institutional changes. If the academic librarian cannot influence the fundamental direction of change, he should nevertheless attempt to find the means to make the library responsive to the academic program and to articulate how this might be achieved.

The publication of this first *Yearbook* devoted to American college, university and reference libraries seems to offer to librarians of such institutions a chance to take stock of their functions and their opportunities. This article will attempt a brief statement of both from the point of view of one in the thick of daily pressure from the demands of service in a very busy library. Complete detachment can hardly be expected under these circumstances, but then complete and utter philosophic detachment is seldom found in viewing contemporary processes or events. Melvil Dewey once reprinted an encyclopedia article "On Libraries" with the subtitle, "By a librarian, for librarians." This subtitle exactly expresses the viewpoint of the present writer in this paper.

It is well to remind ourselves once in a while that the American college and the American university are distinctly native growths. They bear slight resemblance today to the transplanted college set up at Cambridge in New England in the seventeenth century, or to those English successors of the seventeenth century colleges and universities now flourishing on their own soil. Cambridge University of today with its residential Colleges manned by fellows, tutors and professors, its Schools, its university organization, its Members of Parliament, its government by the votes of Masters of Arts, and its grants from the British Treasury is amazingly unlike Harvard University. The latter (in common with other American universities) has developed from the single college *not* into a group of many colleges and a loose university organization, but into one huge undergraduate college, a Graduate School, and many professional schools of law, medicine, engineering, business administration, theology, and even dentistry, administered by a small self-perpetuating Corporation through a very complex system of officers. The growth of most American universities and colleges has been along similar lines involving intricate organization, professional schools, and a governing body other than the teaching staff, whether called trustees or (in most state universities) regents. And the numbers both of colleges and universities, and of students enrolled in them, have become portentous.

One factor all of these, both the English prototype and its complex American successors, have in common—the library. But here also there has been a diverse development. The Oxford colleges all had their libraries before Sir Thomas Bodley set up his Library for the University—and they still have them to the lasting benefit of the undergraduates and dons resident therein. The American university libraries have, in most instances, grown out of the single library of the college. Separate libraries for professional and technical schools have grown up side by side with the college-university library. But just as we have not generally developed the residential and teaching colleges as units within the university, so we have seldom had both the smaller residential college library and the university library to boot. A certain direct and intimate relation to smaller groups of students possible in the English college library has therefore up to the present time been almost wholly lacking in our American practice. In this, as in so many other things, we have had to act with larger units, to face, if not mass production, at least mass service. And we have been almost crushed by the pressure of numbers and the amazingly rapid growth of our

SOURCE: Reprinted from William Warner Bishop, "The Library in the American College," in Association of College and Research Libraries, *College and Reference Library Yearbook, No. 1* (Chicago: American Library Association, 1929), pp. 1-12, by permission of the publisher.

colleges and our libraries. There was a time—we can all remember it—when colleges were eager and proud because of rapid growth; when the mounting totals seemed a sure sign of strength. Happily, that day of complacency has passed. But the actual numbers with which we have to deal are still our most serious educational problem, whether in college, secondary school or primary grades. We count in America our colleges by hundreds and our students by tens of thousands. The pressure of numbers on the libraries is very real and very cruel. We must serve so many that too often both our books and our people are not enough.

The third decade of the twentieth century has been a time of sincere searching of heart in college circles. The colleges have been questioned and surveyed and tested and measured. Experts and laymen alike have examined us and given us confusing verdicts and worse remedies. We have been told very sharply that we need humanizing and vivifying and standardizing and regulating. The only thing which we have not been told to do by journalists and experts— equally deadly physicians, some of us think—is to close our doors. There has grown up—along with the literature of abuse—a very valuable and serious group of studies about the work of the American colleges and universities, much of it quite recent, and giving promise of better things to come. The Association of American Universities and the sister Association of American Colleges have shown real leadership and constructive thinking about the problems of higher education. In most of these studies the libraries of those institutions have come in for a rather small share. At least one important study—the "Works Report"—has been devoted almost wholly to university libraries. But we lack any comprehensive and searching survey of college library conditions, and, more important, any such standards either of service or of books as are almost universally accepted for collegiate work in the various subjects of instruction. No college can fall far below grade in its work in chemistry, for example, without sharp comment and criticism alike from friends and rivals. But many colleges are giving students and faculties a low grade of library service without much comment from anyone.

The cost of all education has been mounting with a speed which has brought much unfavorable criticism of late years. There are not wanting signs of impatience and resentment on the part of heavy tax-payers. One result of this restlessness under high expense has been an insistence on careful accounting, sound business organization, and real budgeting alike of educational and financial projects. It is perhaps not without significance that the introduction of sound business systems into college and university finance has largely come about within the past three decades. In the change in business methods that has come about, to the great advantage of administration, librarians have too often found themselves without proper means of supporting their claims to a larger share of the college funds. There has resulted from this situation a flood of correspondence and of questionnaires which has been eloquent testimony to an absence of commonly accepted standards of library service, of costs, of nomenclature and of function. The American Library Association Committee on Library Revenues has in vain sought data which would enable it to formulate a satisfactory statement as to a proper income for college libraries. Other committees have recently busied themselves with the problems of college library personnel. The *Survey of Libraries in the United States* published as part of the Fiftieth Anniversary Publications of the A. L. A. has produced some quite unsatisfying figures and statements of practice from a large number of college and university libraries. The *Survey* gives an admittedly incomplete picture. But out of our very reluctance to accept it as final or satisfactory may yet arise far better statements of practice and some workable standards of costs of service and of the character of book collections.

Most of our universities have undergraduate arts-colleges at their core. But few of these arts-colleges in universities have separate libraries designed for the needs of undergraduates. The university librarian must see to it that his libraries serve the needs of undergraduates, of candidates for master's and doctor's degrees, of the research work of professors, and the demands of professional instruction in law, medicine, engineering and other branches as well. From the standpoint of the university librarian the librarian of the isolated college has a comparatively simple task. There is often in the university library a real struggle to reconcile needs which are not alone diverse but frequently conflicting. It is absolutely necessary to differentiate between various classes of readers and their diverse requirements. Precisely so far as money and organization permit this differentiation in service and in book stocks is success probable, and indeed attainable. This has been instinctively felt by the law schools. It is no accident that most of their libraries in universities are not administered by the librarian who directs the more general library gathered for undergraduates and (of late years) for graduate students. Whether the law-school libraries have gained or lost by this change is a moot question on which much might be said. It is perhaps worth while to point out the real significance of this separation—the conviction that law students require a peculiar service of their own sort of books. Whether the present tendency to recognize the importance of "border-line" subjects will grow into effective protest against this splitting up of the book resources of the university is an interesting line of conjecture as to future development. No matter what changes time may bring, the principle of direct and specialized service to different groups of readers is likely to become more and more the basis of college and university library organization. This does not necessarily involve a weakening of centralized administrative control, but quite the contrary. Even in the separate colleges, specialized library service is likely to develop. In universities it is a basic principle. And in the most progressive public libraries it has been recognized as fundamental for the last forty years.

Not only do we have college libraries and university libraries (many of which resemble the public library "systems"), but there has arisen in the last thirty years a group of libraries of teachers' colleges which has become formidable in numbers. These libraries are likewise increasing greatly in size and importance. They have complex problems resembling but not identical with those of both the college and university libraries. Many librarians in the older normal schools and the newer teachers' colleges have dignified our profession and have contributed largely toward the growth of libraries in general and the esteem in which they are held. These teachers' college libraries present opportunities denied to the librarians of many colleges, chiefly because they are supported by taxation and their incomes are surely growing in size. By reason of their extension services and of the alumni of the teachers' colleges their librarians have many opportunities of influencing public opinion regarding libraries and library practice. Unhampered (in many cases) by traditional methods, nomenclature and practices, they have great opportunities of experimentation, especially in direct service to students, adapting the practices of readers' advisers of the public libraries to suit an older and more definitely trained clientele. Many of them control directly high school libraries and libraries for children in experimental schools under the teachers' college. We may confidently expect most interesting developments from these libraries in the next decade.

There are numerous other sorts of libraries attached to isolated institutions of higher learning, such as those of technical colleges, theological schools, schools of medicine and of dentistry. All of them come within the purview of this *Yearbook*. Many of them are struggling with problems identical with those of the colleges. Their librarians will profit by study of and acquaintance with those problems and by close association with their colleagues in college library work.

Finally, there are the libraries of junior colleges— an increasing host, and as yet with but scanty resources of their own. They present acute problems both for their own librarians, for their faculties and students, and for those colleges and universities which are asked to accredit their graduates seeking admission to upper classes. Many of them are but additions to high schools, still dependent on the high school library, and on special service from the local public library. Their very number and their popularity demand a careful study of the library service they can and should render. It is not too much to say that at present the junior college libraries as a group seem to fall far short of efficiency either in service or in books. This deficiency is one of the most serious counts against the junior college as it now exists. If junior colleges are to be admitted to full academic fellowship, they must look to their libraries at once. Their opportunity through good libraries to perform a real educational service is unquestioned.

The Works report on *College and University Library Problems,* (more particularly its statistical tables), brings out very clearly certain marked changes in university libraries in recent years, changes in which the college libraries have shared in some measure. Perhaps nothing is more noticeable in these tables than the persistent evidence of growth both in size of the libraries, in their annual cost and in the variety and extent of service rendered. Certain of our university libraries rank high in number of volumes—indeed after the Library of Congress and the New York Public Library, Harvard stands a firm third, with Yale, Columbia, Chicago and others taking commanding rank among the large libraries of the country. In number of volumes, in buildings and in service the American university libraries will compare favorably with or indeed surpass those of any other country, although they labor as a group under certain inherent disadvantages, chiefly the continental sweep of the country which separates them so as not to permit immediate access to such huge reservoirs of books as are found in London, Paris, Berlin and Vienna. Our research workers have now at their disposal a body of printed materials far in excess of that available even twenty years since. Inter-library loans and the photostat have vastly enlarged the available resources of scholarship and have tended to counterbalance the obstacle of distance between important collections. Along with this growth in volume has necessarily come an increase in appropriations, both actual and proportional. Accompanying larger budgets has come greater responsibility, more definite recognition of the professional status of the librarian and his staff, even though there is much room for clearer understanding of both the responsibilities of the librarian and the position of his force in the academic community. No one can study the statistics in the Works report without noting these obvious increases of numbers, of money expended, of professional opportunity.

No figures, however, can reveal the more subtle and vital changes in the character of the collections of books in both university and college libraries. Numbers of volumes mean very little in weighing the value of a library either for instruction or for research. The quality of the book-selection which has gone on during the last thirty years is what really counts, and as a rule it has been high, thanks to the active cooperation of faculties and librarians. The number and kind of special collections which have come to the university libraries of late years have been remarkable. Though far from wholly adequate for research purposes— recalling our frequently unsuccessful efforts of the past fifteen years to locate books and journals needed in investigation—our university libraries as a class may be said to have stocked themselves with at least the fundamentally needed works. They have reached the stage where specialization in given lines is clearly indicated as the next step. That means cooperative buying and division of the fields of acquisition. And this problem—so thoroughly sensed by librarians—needs to be brought home to university faculties and trustees for effective solution.

Specialization in service is likewise clearly indicated as another imminent step. That service to undergraduates is at present barely adequate in our university libraries is a well known fact. Want-ing the residential college library, we have here and there tried to develop special collections for undergraduates. The Linonian and Brothers Library at Yale is an example, unfortunately not as yet typical. Here the smaller independent college library, if well supported, has a great advantage over the university library. It can establish intimate and unrestricted relations between books and students by giving students direct access to the greater part of its books. Nothing in the entire college course is likely to prove of more lasting benefit. It would pay every university having a library of 300,000 volumes or more to establish a separate arts-college library under the general library administration. Such a library would have perhaps thirty to fifty thousand volumes on open shelves and would have several copies of its more interesting books, allowing free circulation. Required reading and research should be equally absent from such an undergraduate library. Better still would be good libraries for reading and consultation in separate residential colleges, from which students could take books to their rooms. The bane of our present system is the necessity for trying to do all things under one roof and in one library. Departmental libraries are no aid in solving the problem—they exist for the convenience of specialists, not for the education of undergraduates. "Browsing rooms" from which books may not be drawn are but slight help toward forming an ingrained habit of reading.

One may truly remark that the ideals of service in our university and college libraries have changed— and for the better. The older generation of college librarians had but small means for doing their work. They did it on the whole very well indeed. But that modern spirit of community service which marks the American librarian demands far larger funds than the college or the university libraries have ever had until very recent years. The "library movement" in America had many distinguished university and college librarians among its earlier exponents. In the huge development of the nineties and after, the academic librarians bore a lesser part, chiefly because of their more narrow resources and more restricted fields. The third decade of the twentieth century finds them fully imbued with the "library spirit," and securing results which promise a far higher grade of service than in earlier days. It is not too much to say that the immediate future shows promise of a happy combination of public library ideals of direct service to individuals with those more exacting demands of scholarly service to collegiate groups and to faculties.

In the November, 1928, number of the *Bulletin* of the Association of American Colleges I tried to set forth briefly some conceptions of the contribution of the college library to teaching. It may be better to refer here to this article than to attempt to elaborate its chief contentions. Suffice it to say that the college library cannot and does not exist apart from the work of teaching. Such other functions as it performs—and they are many—are merely incidental to its work of assisting in instruction. Its chief services are two—aid to class teaching, enlarging and strengthening the work of the teacher; and the development of a habit of intelligent reading in generations of students. To perform these two tasks well is the chief aim of library method, of technique, of administration. All other purposes are secondary to these two in the college library. To carry them out intelligently demands librarians themselves familiar with the problems of college teaching and with the methods of introducing students to the world of interesting books, sometimes but imperfectly revealed by the work of organized classes. Of course university and reference libraries add the provision and organization of the means of research to their more strictly academic duties.

It would be most profitable to make a survey of our college libraries, not with any purpose of gathering statistics, but solely to see for ourselves how far our organization and our methods have enabled us to meet well these two primary functions of the college library.

We should have to scan our shelves—do they contain the books really needed and desirable in successful teaching of the subjects in the curriculum? Are they so fresh, modern and stimulating as to attract students to read them by their very appearance? We should also have to test our technical methods—are our catalogs and our arrangement of books designed to help in teaching collegiate subjects? Our organization must come under a searching test—is it flexible and strong enough to perform its difficult task of interpreting the library to students in cooperation with the faculty? And has our staff been chosen and trained with the two major ends of the college library in view? Perhaps the librarians who read these lines will be moved to put down on paper their own candid answers to these (and other) questions. It will not be necessary to publish the results of this type of self-survey—they will be reflected in service.

One of the most delicate and difficult questions confronting college and university librarians is that of their own professional status. They are working and will continue to work in a highly organized community, burdened (and strengthened) with traditions, proud of its own standards, properly jealous of academic status. Into this academic fellowship no one has been admitted (until recent years) save those actually teaching classes, and those only by stated degrees, advancing slowly (on the whole) from instructor to assistant professor, to associate professor, to professor. So long as collegiate organization remained simple and numbers few, there was no need to disturb the serene and serried ranks of the academic hierarchy by any non-professorial persons. But with the growth of institutions of higher learning, and especially with the growth of their libraries and the increasingly constant dependence of the work of teaching on the proper functioning of these libraries, the trained librarian has not only come on the scene, but he has become a necessary part of the academic organization. With him (or her) now stand many other persons without whose services the work of a modern college or university could not go on for a day. In many places the librarians and other non-teaching officers are already as well paid as are the teachers of the same length of service. But as yet the status of the library staff in the academic community is not on the whole well determined.

In countries where academic rank is fixed by government regulations, librarians of universities and their staffs have a definite status, a place in the governmental scheme of things. In America there is the greatest variety. It is perfectly patent that librarians are daily more and more necessary to the teaching work of colleges and universities, especially as their libraries grow in size and complexity of organization. It is simple enough—as many institutions have done—to give definite academic (professorial) standing to different grades in the library service. Local social conditions may be made smoother and much heartburning saved by this process. But it does not solve the problem. Librarians in colleges and universities have yet to make for themselves so unmistakable a place in the daily work of those institutions that recognition of the value and standing of their services will come of itself as a reward. The colleges and universities will likewise have to come to an understanding of the real value of the work of the non-teaching members of their staffs. The present uncertainty and confusion will one day give way to clearer conceptions of the work of the librarian and its place in college life. But now it is beyond question true that strong men in library work sometimes avoid the college libraries just because of this matter of academic status. It is equally true that the long professional training required of aspirants for professorships has as yet but seldom been demanded of librarians. Indeed until very recently there have been no opportunities for professional training in librarianship comparable with those offered to candidates for higher degrees in arts and philosophy. This question of academic standing is likely then to vex librarians and college administrators for some time to come. Patience and hard work are the only remedies for a situation not wholly unfortunate if it puts the librarians on their mettle to justify their existence by their service alike to students and faculties.

One rather practical result of the growth of libraries in colleges has been a very decided enlargement of their personnel. In 1892, when I graduated from Michigan, the entire professional staff of the University Library—then about 90,000 volumes in size—consisted of four men and one woman, with half a dozen student assistants. There were but half a dozen undergraduate courses requiring collateral reading. There were two seminar rooms for graduate students. Today that small library has grown to eight times the size in 1892 and the staff to 107 full-time librarians, while the public service is carried on in eight reading rooms in the main library and ten places outside it. The university is about six times as large in students as in 1892 and the summer session has been added to the nine months of the academic year. Similar (and greater) growth has been taking place all over the country. This growth of course implies not only far larger numbers working for the library but necessarily also very marked differentiation in grades of work and in the preparation necessary to perform it well. This condition is now reflected in our customary division into professional, sub-professional and clerical grades of service. It may be well to utter a word of caution against too rigid division and classification of personnel. Obviously education can never be a negligible factor in a college librarian or library assistant. But experience counts in library work far more than is often recognized. And adaptability to library work, a flair for successful

service, is more to be sought for than academic credits even in university library work. Our sticklers for degrees and for formal training—more power to them!—must not cut us off from the possibility of rewarding merit and discovering unexpected capacity in those exceptions that prove the rules.

One last and most important consideration—the library building. No one has yet solved the college library building problem—nor that of the university library building. We have had some very notable advances in the past two decades, and it is perfectly evident that our library buildings are becoming more and more adapted to college library needs as we build more of them. But too many of them merely copy some other building. There is room for a detailed and careful study of college library buildings in the light of the most modern college library service. It is plain that the problems of college and university library buildings are very different. Progress is likely to be made just so far as specific needs are kept in mind, and those needs are fully as much educational as bibliothecal. It would be very easy to plan a library building solely for the librarian's convenience. It is very hard to plan for storage, for records, for direct use by large numbers, for special service to classroom instruction, for the research work of professors and advanced students. There is need for a sound book on college library buildings fully illustrated with floor plans and sections drawn to a uniform scale.

There are not wanting signs that the problems of the library in the American college are engaging the attention of many others besides their librarians. This is a most welcome and happy condition. If this paper has any point, it lies in a clear recognition of the fact that the college library is not an end in itself. It exists in and for the college. If all those who make up the college community—not omitting the student body—are thinking about the college library, we are likely to see its real problems solved and its work advanced. The library is sure to play an increasing part in college life—unless the progress of invention renders books in their traditional form completely obsolete. Barring that possibility—and it exists—the college librarian has an increasing burden and responsibility. His is the opportunity. Will he seize it?

ABOUT THE AUTHOR

—**William Warner Bishop,** (d. 1955), Librarian, University of Michigan, 1915-1941; M.A., 1893, University of Michigan. His major interests were in collection development and in the education of librarians.

The Library

by Peter Sammartino

In this chapter Peter Sammartino, the chancellor of a university with multiple campuses, describes the role and function of the academic library. While librarians may view this analysis as simplistic, compounded even more by the complexities of managing separate, often competing operations, it is a commentary based on responsible experience as an academic administrator. The necessity for academic librarians to involve themselves meaningfully in the academic process is certainly indicated by what is said and what is not said in this statement.

The library is probably one of the most important elements in the organization of a multiple campus institution. It is possible to have one large central library for the use of all campuses, if the campuses were near each other with subsidiary libraries in the branches. In most cases, there necessarily has to be a separate library for each campus. Although the second alternative is more expensive, the formation of individual libraries has been very successful and, in the long run, more practical at Fairleigh Dickinson University.

One would have to admit that to operate several libraries is more expensive than having one large library. For one thing, there are necessarily duplicates of the greater part of the reference volumes, although most of the larger libraries have to supply duplicates and triplicates of these same works anyway. Furthermore, in many universities, there are departmental libraries for special segments of the institution such as the school of education, the school of business management, or the school of engineering. The idea of breaking up a large library is not necessarily wrong or unheard of; it is just more costly since items cannot be as readily shared when departmental usage overlaps. For control, additional staffing is also required.

There are some advantages in having separate libraries, each one of which is more intimate and friendly. Each one also is tailored to the character and tone of the particular campus. Libraries need not be massive in feeling. The stacks can be as cavernous as necessary, but libraries should be personal. With the great increase of students predicted for the next few years, huge reading rooms are necessary to accommodate thousands of people. Yet coziness may be obtained by the use of muted colors and interspersed lounge areas. Although a room may need to seat hundreds of students, it still can be as inviting as the reading room of a social club.

In coequal libraries, the budget is determined according to the needs of each library. In the beginning, a new library needs more reference tools, back numbers of periodicals, and then later, indices to make periodicals meaningful, and last, multiple copies of many books for circulation. Many basic books are out of print and thus cost more, by and large. Sometimes special expenses are incurred during a certain year. For instance, in one institution, after several years, a large proportion of the budget had to be assigned to indices many of which were out of print and costly. Library usage of periodicals had reached a point which required their immediate purchase.

One question which is difficult to answer is whether there should be central purchasing of books. Each institution has to solve this problem in the light of its own situation. At first, it might seem unquestionably cheaper to order all books from a central campus. But there is a great drawback: the process takes that much longer, both in accumulating orders and reshipping books received at a central depot. In one institution with two campuses, a list of books ordered by an instructor took so long in going through the various steps from one campus to another and then back again that by the time the books were available to the students, the instructor had gone and the course was no longer taught.

Where books are ordered directly by the cam-

SOURCE: Reprinted from Peter Sammartino, *Multiple Campuses* (Rutherford, N.J.: Fairleigh Dickinson University Press, 1964), Chapter 5, "The Library," pp. 37-43, by permission of the author.

pus and received and processed immediately, more efficient service is bound to take place. The argument for central purchasing is that a better contract with the book company can result. Actually, the companies involved should be willing to set up a better contract on greater volume, and the factor that should count is the total yearly order whether it comes from one campus or more.

Another problem in a new library is the choice of a qualified library director. He must be not only an excellent reference librarian, but also have administrative talents. He must be a good business manager with a mind for supervision of meticulous detail. In addition to these, he must also be a curator. There have been many excellent librarians who simply could not cope with staff discipline, student discipline, statistical records, business management, deans and faculty members.

Modern library practice tends towards departmental secretaries or clerks, but staffing of a new library should be from the quality aspect in order to avoid costly mistakes. Because of the very nature of the subject matter, typists and certainly all circulation people should have a college background or be certified librarians, since initial guidance and reference work emanates from the charge desk to the reference librarian at a university library. Just pleasant people as order clerks may possibly run a public library order entry department, but the technical services department of a college or university library requires hourly decisions of a professional nature. Although seemingly typist clerks, all members of this department need college backgrounds to enable them to select the best sources for purchase. With the growth of the department, typist clerks can be added for filing and directed work, and pages can be taught accessioning.

Photocopying and microfilming are of greater importance in a multiple campus institution, especially where back numbers may be on the older campus. Today, when entire collections of manuscripts and important ancient books are available in microfilm, there is more opportunity to split the building of these collections among various campuses if restricted budgets are a factor. If these materials are located on another campus, there is no reason why the student cannot in special research go to the books. Where the campus is too far away, this is, of course, impossible, but if campuses are within twenty or thirty miles, it will not do the student any harm to drive to the other library and spend the day there.

In the interest of efficiency, microfilming of the accession book can be done yearly in the records office of the university at a low cost, if done when the student records are being microfilmed. Microfilms should be kept outside of the library in a fireproof safe which is the latest insurance practice.

Rarely used volumes and very expensive works pose another problem. These volumes are usually ordered for only one campus. However, there is a union catalog arrangement so that each campus library has a card for the other libraries. In this way, each campus knows exactly what is available in the university as a whole. Daily intralibrary loans insures that a book from another campus can be received within twenty-four hours. Request calls made at a designated expedient time eliminate nuisance phoning. When a certain volume has three or more calls necessitating a loan from another campus, it is surely an indication that the volume should be ordered by the requesting campus.

In multiple campus libraries, flexibility in transferring entire collections is easy if courses in entirety are transferred. This saves money for other things. Catalog and shelf cards are removed and sent on with books for quick adjustment to the campus receiving the books, but if the transfer is a temporary measure, a semester loan is adequate for handling.

Each campus can select its own specialty. All cannot offer depth in Robert Frost, Shakespeare, Browning, state history or specific science. Diversification brings great value and meaning to the total joint collection. It is in a multiple campus institution that the faculty participation in building a library has to be most carefully integrated. The horizontal administration, that is, a dean or chairman who has responsibility for two or more campuses, can use the strengths of faculty members in gradually creating libraries on new campuses. The dean or chairman has an opportunity to spot aberrations, since comparisons of order lists are possible. If a faculty member on one campus has two or three titles to suggest for a certain course and a faculty member on another campus has a list of a hundred titles for the same course, something is wrong somewhere. Is the first institution making good use of the library? Is the second institution just putting volumes in the stacks and not seeing that they are used? This type of situation can be analyzed by the dean or chairman, thus helping to build useful collections at each campus.

In conclusion, libraries have to be used judiciously. To fill them with students who are doing nothing else but their textbook assignments is not fulfilling the true purposes of a library. Building up statistics by artificial, meaningless, and picayune assignments in a great many books is a prostitution of the attempt to encourage scholarly work. The guiding principle should be that the good things on one campus be used to advantage in stimulating another campus.

ABOUT THE AUTHOR

—**Peter Sammartino** is Chancellor, Fairleigh Dickinson University; Ph.D., 1931, New York University. His subject interests are French and education.

Librarian, Administrator, and Professor: Implications of Changing College Social Structures

by Charles E. Bidwell

This study examines the current and developing ambiguities of higher education as evidenced in the diverse ends it pursues, and explores the different administrative, organizational, and professional responses that result. As a major resource the library is too important to remain solely the province of the library administrator, external to the ongoing struggle between administrative centralization and the particular segments of the pluralistic academic environment. For the academic librarian this phenomenon requires a re-examination of his traditional role, as well as considerable professional concern about the ramifications of this struggle for the effectiveness of the information gathering process.

As late as 1870, higher education in the United States formed a relatively undifferentiated system of simply-structured units. But this system soon was to be transformed in a great wave of innovation. Only a year before had the first class at Cornell been admitted. Cornell was a radical and eminently successful experiment that in its electric conception and structure forecast the practical vocationalism of the land-grant movement, the devotion to graduate scholarship of a Chicago or Hopkins, and the internal diversity of the state universities.

1870 marked the close of an era in which the liberal arts colleges had been ascendent. These schools with varying degrees of success offered to all of their students a uniform classical and mathematical curriculum of Renaissance origin.[1] They were small and communal; in 1870 the average college had ten professors and just under 100 students.[2] The professors ranged widely over the curriculum, and the president himself offered the capstone senior course on moral and intellectual philosophy. While these colleges by no means were sanctuaries of privilege, neither were the students impoverished, and, as most were recruited locally, they were homogeneous in interests and background.

If college libraries by 1870 were faring better than they had before the Civil War, when the student forensic societies built book collections richer and more accessible than those the colleges possessed, they still reflected the undifferentiated curriculum and rather rigid mode of teaching.[3] One is startled to read that in the 1860's Daniel Coit Gilman resigned as the librarian of the Sheffield School at Yale because he could not obtain an assistant and had himself to light the library stove each morning.[4]

However sterile and impecunious these colleges may have been and however strong the religious motives that guided them, they were the guardians and agents of the humanistic ideal of liberal education; they sought to produce men both morally responsible and cultivated. In 1870 the liberal ideal, with the college, dominated American higher education. But as the Cornell experiment foretold, this ideal very soon was to be reduced to no more than coordinate status by two quite different conceptions of the higher learning: the university ideal of specialized, creative scholarship in the arts and sciences, and the populistic ideal of the usefulness of knowledge.

By 1900, the former found expression in the

SOURCE: Reprinted from Charles E. Bidwell, "Librarian, Administrator, and Professor: Implications of Changing College Social Structures," in Dan Bergen and E. D. Duryea, eds., *Libraries and the College Climate of Learning* (Syracuse: Syracuse University Program in Higher Education of the School of Education and the School of Library Science, 1964), pp. 61-80, by permission of the publisher and the author.

new graduate universities; the latter in the land-grant colleges, the flowering of professional and technical education, and in programs of university extension. Moreover, in perhaps the most distinctive contribution of this turbulent period, the state universities followed Cornell's lead, developing as "collections of disparate agencies"—these agencies variously devoted to liberal teaching, to graduate scholarship, and to the application and diffusion of knowledge.[5]

In point of fact internal differentiation was as much a part of the development of the graduate universities and liberal arts colleges as of the big state schools. The graduate universities became major centers for professional training not only in the old learned professions, but in such fields as business, home economics, engineering, and social service. As Rudolph notes, the universities raised the vocations to the status of professions.[6] Such men as William Rainey Harper were pioneers of university extension, to the horror of the purist, Abraham Flexner.[7] An undergraduate division was present from the beginning on the university campus as a feeder for the graduate school.

As for the colleges, the more lively and eminent were rapidly evolving into universities, some like Harvard forging a synthesis of graduate and undergraduate curricula, others like Yale trying to build a graduate program atop a still-pristine college of liberal arts. Throughout the ranks of the colleges, the classical baccalaureate curriculum was replaced by a range of departments and courses that introduced a more diversified and specialized faculty and also worked to break the hold of piety upon these schools, replacing it with a secular spirit of intellectual curiosity.

THE GROWTH OF A PLURALISTIC SYSTEM OF HIGHER EDUCATION

By the early years of this century, American higher education formed a truly pluralistic system of autonomous units. These units had differing interests, goals, and clienteles and claimed legitimacy by appealing variously to the liberal, university, and populist ideals. Moreover, each of the units within this system itself incorporated diverse structures, programs, and personnel. The succeeding years witnessed the elaboration of this pattern. Two sets of processes appear to have been primarily responsible. One of these has been the differentiation of knowledge itself. Knowledge specialization formed the base for the disruption of the classical curriculum and continues to find structural expression in the strengthening and multiplication of the academic disciplines and of subfields within them.

The second set of processes has resulted in the appearance of new sources of students and of new clients anxious to use the knowledge created and guarded by academic men. As Martin Trow reminds us, lacking a centralized means for establishing priorities and, one might add, enjoying access to multiple sources of philanthropic and government funds, American higher education has been especially responsive to external demands and sensitive to new opportunities.[8] The cultural pluralism of American society, the pressures of an expanding and mobile population, and the technical and vocational requirements of an industrial-bureaucratic social order have been mirrored readily by the entrepreneurial and pluralist growth of new kinds of colleges and new programs in the universities.

In adapting to these processes, the universities have been expansionist and incorporative. As the disciplines have specialized, the universities have not become differentiated with respect to one another, but have all alike embraced an increasingly fine division of academic labor and now mirror one another in their intent to "cover everything," at least in the arts and sciences and major professional fields.

At the same time, they have been hospitable to the most diverse functions and activities, providing services to wide-ranging public and private clienteles. Here the universities differ more from one another, according to local or regional opportunities for entrepreneurship and their differing ability to draw clients in this or that field. As entrepreneurs of service, the state universities traditionally have led the way, finding it at once easier to justify such action on a populistic basis and more difficult to resist local demands from politically significant directions. The University of Minnesota provides an apt example of this multifunctional diversity. It includes undergraduate and graduate schools of arts and sciences, professional, engineering and agricultural schools, elaborate extension services, a program for dental hygienists, another for practical nurses, a third for morticians, and a two-year college of general studies open to persons not regularly admittable to the university.

Now as the national interest places the federal government more centrally among the clients of the universities, scientific eminence more than political vulnerability opens them to grants and contracts, so that the great universities spew out new laboratories and institutes, while fretting over soft money in the budget and over professorial independence.

The universities also have been hospitable to new breeds of students. As industrial growth and mobility have raised aspirations and incomes among groups for whom higher education had been neither desired nor possible, the universities with growing rigor (aided, as President Gilman foresaw, by extensive programs of student aid) have admitted and retained students of diverse backgrounds principally on the criterion of merit—especially promise for and, later, performance in graduate study.

At the same time, among the colleges, the tendency has been to respond either to the populist dynamic, in the form of "open door" state and city colleges and junior colleges or to the liberal ideal, now translated into preparation of the able within an expanded and specialized arts and sciences curriculum. Thus the colleges, unlike the universities, have been differentiating with respect to one another, and this is reflected particularly in their varying degrees of selectivity and of internal curricular and structural specialization. Nonetheless even the selective schools have remained single-function organizations, sharing with the mass colleges a central emphasis on undergraduate instruction.

In another way, both universities and colleges have come to differ. Groups that have not found a comfortable place within the embracing arms of this already pluralistic system of higher education could set up separate academic shops. This path has been followed, for example, by the advocates of education for women and Negroes, by the Protestant fundamentalists, the Catholics, and the Jews. Thus a parochial pluralism, of sponsorship and of student and faculty recruitment, crosscuts those patterns dominant throughout higher education, tending to arrest or accelerate certain lines of change. Catholic colleges, for example, have remained more centered on the classical curriculum and less receptive to science, Catholic universities less tightly linked to the world of academic specialization.

The transformation of American higher education toward pluralism and specialization has had profound consequences for the academic library; indeed, because of its centrality to teaching and scholarship in all the disciplines, the library is particularly sensitive to shifting academic goals and structures and to the strains such changes

induce. Thus the appearance of the graduate faculty at the center of the university has been accompanied by the provision of a research library on every university campus. However singular the eminence of the Library of Congress or the New York Public Library, it is chiefly the universities that have provided for the United States a far-flung network of research libraries, readily accessible and of surprisingly uniform strength. Moreover, with the incorporative nature of the universities, these libraries, mirroring their university sponsors, have evolved as comprehensive rather than specialized collections. Consequently university libraries have been funded and controlled primarily as centralized agencies of the university.

These characteristics have generated certain distinctive problems of university librarianship. Although the chief task of the university librarian is to build and maintain a collection at once deep and wideranging—itself a taxing matter of budget-stretching and competition with numerous peers for scarce material—he must provide as well bibliographic service for the other major activities of the university. Since the scholarly collections come first, he must contrive within the frame of the research library to serve, for example, the study and reading needs of undergraduates and the geographically scattered activities of university extension. One gathers that university librarians have come to no generally satisfactory solution to either problem.[9]

Within the realm of scholarship itself, as the disciplines have become more specialized, the styles of scholarly work have grown more disparate, so that the librarian must mediate quite different faculty demands upon the collection—e.g., the scientists who want extensive journal collections close to their laboratories, in contrast to the historians who seem to want the local library to have everything in print. Moreover, disciplinary specialization tends to generate a parochial view by faculty, whose departmental and disciplinary interests tend to displace a concern for the general welfare of the university. Such faculty look to the library with an eye to maximizing the strength of collections in their own fields, to the provision of services specialized along disciplinary lines, and to some measure of departmental control not only over accessions but over the full range of library services.

These faculty pressures for specialization and plural control contest with the librarian's concern for general coordination, balance, and economy. In his role as mediator, the librarian must keep an eye on the general interests of the university and strive for a reasonable allocation of his resources among the several library functions and subject-matter fields. At the same time he must try not to alienate the various faculty groups, who after all are his chief clients, important sources of bibliographic guidance, and at least potentially important political allies within the university.

One must conclude from the perennial anxiety of librarians over their relations with university presidents and deans that they lack political power vis-a-vis these administrators.[10] This may throw the librarian into an alliance with the faculty who perhaps can get for the library what the librarian himself cannot obtain, but it must be at best an uneasy alliance in view of the often parochial motives of the faculty and the danger that in this way the librarian will be coopted by his faculty clients.

In any event, the librarian more than the professor is dependent on the university administrator. Libraries are notoriously expensive and difficult to finance, and the librarian seldom can recruit his own money. Moreover the librarian lacks such external support as is provided to the professor by his disciplinary affiliation. Hence the librarian is especially vulnerable to the administrator's power to appoint and to the bargaining power provided by his general budget control. In addition it may be that as librarians strive to meet diverse demands for service to scholars and undertake to span the university's functions, their budget requests and calls for administrative support represent the quintessence of pervasive strains and conflicts within the university. Thus in the administrator's eyes, the librarian and the library may do little more than exacerbate his problems.

In the selective colleges, the difficulties of librarianship tend to mirror those characteristic of the universities. The departmentalization of the faculty and curriculum and the increasing involvement of students in preparation for graduate study open the college library to similar demands for specialized service and to the question of serving persons who follow differing scholarly styles. In these colleges, however, teaching remains the primary task, so that the librarian's uncertainty centers not so much on how to serve instructional needs within a research frame, but how to build a collection and a library staff that can serve instruction that verges on research. This uncertainty has most often been expressed as discussion of the optimal size of college libraries, but it seems in fact to

center on determining what bibliographic tools undergraduate researchers will need, how these needs will differ from field to field, and how they may be accommodated within the necessarily limited budget of a college.[11]

The faculties of such schools are by no means divorced from productive scholarship and are becoming less so as faculty specialization becomes more refined. Since college libraries cannot be comprehensive, the librarian often must confront faculty demands for materials useful only in a narrow field of research—demands that are hard to resist but tax slender resources and lead to serious discontinuities in the collection.[12]

Finally, college libraries, like the colleges themselves, have evolved in two distinct directions. In contrast to the library of the selective college, the mass college library has developed essentially as a collection to serve instruction, the aim of which is not the stimulation of inquiry but the orderly communication of content in set courses. Staffed by a faculty for whom the instructional role dominates, the mass college does not generate the divergent bibliographic demands characteristic of the more selective schools. Hence the library can remain largely a reserve collection of texts and teaching materials, bolstered by a small reference section, and organized simply so as to be readily accessible to a relatively unsophisticated student body. The librarian in such a college is not likely to be either mediator or subject specialist, but instead a clerk whose work centers on routines of book ordering, organizing, and locating within a frame set for him by the college curriculum.

THE DECLINE OF PLURALISM: ELITE VS. MASS EDUCATION

As a response, therefore, to the pluralism and specialization of higher education, three varieties of academic libraries have evolved, each related in a distinctive way to student and faculty clients and administrative control. But pluralism in the system of American higher education seems to be on the wane, as the distinction between higher education for the mass and for an intellectual elite grows sharper and the lines of cleavage crosscutting these categories more blurred. One may expect, in turn, important changes in libraries—in their internal structure and organizational placement.

There appear to be two principal forces for the separation of mass and elite education: the continuing differentiation of knowledge and the diffusion and intensification of college attendance as a valued goal.

The consequences of the differentiation of knowledge are socially pervasive. First, as propositions and data become more systematically ordered and centered on more numerous but more narrowly defined events, the possibility of the rational control of human affairs (i.e., the provision of a basis for predictable action) is extended. In turn the differentiation and technical up-grading of occupational roles accelerates. Consequently there forms a stratum of para-professional occupations that lack the traditional status of professional work but have a systematic and complex knowledge base. Such roles are explicitly technical in content and recruitment criteria; they demand knowledge-ability and sophisticated competence. Moreover as this stratum grows, it displaces lower-level occupations; witness the recent, rapid growth of tertiary occupations at the expense of those in the primary and secondary sectors of the labor force.[13]

Second, the differentiation of knowledge has a catalytic effect on knowledge itself; it increases the necessity for systematic codification as the number of facts, ideas, and potential relationships increases. For similar reasons, it fosters discovery (although it may alter the nature of discovery as the scholar's view narrows) and encourages innovation in applying knowledge.

Certain consequences of these closely-related trends appear at once: (1) growing numbers of technical occupations that require training beyond high school, (2) a closer link between the creation and application of knowledge, (3) a growing number of occupations (many non-academic) devoted to producing and disseminating knowledge, (4) a new impetus to the specialization of scholarship and research, coupled with more complex and powerful disciplinary organizations nationally and on the campus, (5) increasing scope and demand for research as the main function of the universities and selective colleges, (6) an opening of fields of practical application to an increasing number of academic disciplines, and (7) a tendency for knowledge-production and diffusion to be centered where they can be supported properly (in academia in the universities and wealthier private colleges where facilities and funds are concentrated and where there is a growing clientele eager and able to pay for the direct application of the fruits of research).

While these forces are at work, American higher education is in one sense becoming thoroughly democratized. The view of college attendance not as a privilege but as a natural right appears to cross the major boundaries of class, ethnicity, race, religion, and region that divide American society.[14] Despite Parsons' dictum that the assurance of four years of college separates the upper from the lower middle classes, it now seems true that many groups have raised their levels of expectation from the high school to the college diploma and will demand for their children access to some kind of college.[15] To be sure, college-going rates continue to differ markedly with social class and race, and to some extent according to other social divisions, but the contribution to these differences of variability in college-going intentions is declining.

As the goal of college attendance spreads, levels of ambition also are rising among those students from families already habituated to the idea of college. With the technical upgrading of work, increased levels of education are required of each generation, if to do no more than maintain parental occupational status.[16] This generational discontinuity no doubt contributes to the diffusion of the college-attendance aim, but, at least as important, it presses those students who would in any case attend college to aspire to some form of graduate training and to follow an undergraduate curriculum sufficiently specialized to prepare adequately for graduate work. For example, if one compares the educational plans of those Harvard undergraduates today who are intent on business careers with comparable students of the 1940's, he is struck by the indifference of the latter to the vocational relevance of their studies and the rarity of those who planned to go beyond the A.B. But the present-day students almost uniformly aim for business school and prefer a major that they think will fit them for business training.[17]

Thus demand for college education is created in new places and at new levels. Whatever the background of the potential student this demand is increasingly focused on specialized, vocationally-relevant courses of study—on the one hand as terminal preparation for work, on the other as prologue to graduate study. As a consequence of the entrepreneurial quality of American higher education, one would expect to see increasing numbers of college admissions, rising probabilities of college attendance, and a reinforcement of the specializing impetus of the differentiation of knowledge.

There are indeed growing numbers: 3,610,000 resident college students in 1960; 2,659,000 in 1950; 1,101,000 in 1930, and; 238,000 in 1900.[18] Thus the rate of college admissions is increasing much more rapidly than the size of the age cohorts from which the students are drawn.[19] But over the half-century from 1900 to 1950 in the United States, the probability of attending college after graduating from high school remained remarkably stable, varying between 40 and 50 percent despite war, depression, population growth, and the G. I. Bill.[20] The larger and larger size of the under-graduate population reflects instead the decay of the high school as a selective agency; 81 percent of the 16 and 17 year-olds were in school in 1960, in contrast to 43 percent in 1910.[21]

This pattern of college attendance appears to reflect heightened selectivity by colleges and universities along ability lines, with some expansion in size especially among the publicly supported schools. Without such expansion, the probability of moving from high school to college would have declined drastically. Certain schools, particularly among the universities and traditionally selective colleges, have established a policy of stable size and heightened selectivity. Many other colleges and universities that hitherto have not been as selective as they wished can now raise their admissions standards. At the same time they can increase markedly the number of their under-graduates, for the pool of able applicants from which to draw is growing very large.

The University of Illinois, to take but one of many examples, has just opened a four-year branch in Chicago that increases the university's undergraduate capacity by some 4,200 under-graduate places, or 23 percent. At the same time, the university has announced that it will accept at Chicago no applicant who stood below the upper-fourth of his high school class, at its main Urbana campus no one below the top third. A year ago the respective cutting points were the top third and top half.[22]

Thus the universities and selective colleges can expand to meet rising demand, while at the least maintaining their admissions standards. Such schools, moreover, are those most likely to attract students interested either in scholarly careers or in preparation for professional training. This tendency simply makes it easier for the universities to get on with their work; thus the state universities generally are freed from bothersome concern with a mass student body. In the selective colleges, the consequences are more dramatic: reinforcement of the tendency toward a specialized curriculum and faculty, toward research inquiry as an instructional technique, and toward close integration with the university graduate and profes-

sional schools. The terminal A.B. will become less and less common among these colleges.

The ability of these schools to become more selective rests as much with the expansion of mass education as with growing numbers of able applicants. The extension of "open-door" colleges and junior colleges, with regional and local orbits of recruitment, appears to be accelerating steadily and in time is likely to raise the probability of college attendance. The mass colleges serve to siphon off the pressure of numbers from the elite schools and to provide places for high school graduates (whether newly or traditionally imbued with college) whose performance is outrun by ambition.

Such schools will become devoted especially to preparation for middle-level technical occupations—those demanding some specialized training, but without the complexity or innovative quality for which a university background is required. Offering terminal education and, one suspects, drawing their faculties increasingly from the secondary schools and from the fallout of the graduate schools, the mass colleges will look less and less like their elite brethren. Moreover they will have only tenuous links to the universities.

The foregoing observations suggest the development in the United States of two distinct and largely nonoverlapping systems of higher education: one research-centered, multifunctional, and intellectually-elitist, the other instruction-centered, serving a mass student body as its one proper task. In the elite system, one should observe: (1) an increasingly tight linkage between the colleges and universities as undergraduate and graduate training become successive stages in the student's career, (2) a faculty turned toward productive scholarship and the cosmopolitan colleague group of discipline, and (3) a curriculum specialized along narrowing disciplinary lines.

In the mass system, one should encounter (1) a tight linkage between the colleges and the technical vocations, (2) a curriculum specialized according to vocational rather than disciplinary divisions, and (3) a faculty bound closely into the instructional role, local colleague relations, and local school interests.

One would expect the students in these two systems to differ from one another not so much in status characteristics as in ability and academic performance. Those in the selective system should display growing uniformity in the upper levels of aptitude and achievement; those in the mass system should range widely along both dimensions.

CONSEQUENCES FOR THE MASS COLLEGES AND THEIR LIBRARIES

In line with the polarization of higher education the mass colleges should sharpen their present characteristics. Moreover these schools, tightly bound into local communities, should rarely develop more than local orbits of recruitment and alumnus placement. Consequently they will remain unknown and uncompetitive, isolated by these orbits from one another and from a national or even regional audience.

The administrators of such schools therefore should find themselves preoccupied by local foreign relations: maintaining and increasing access to public funds and political good-will, mending fences with potential employers of graduates and with the local public that votes and supplies new students. Internal administration, given the single-function, undifferentiated structure of these schools, will tend toward centralization and hierarchy, relying heavily on the shared but parochial interests of the faculty as a means of control.

All this suggests that the libraries of mass colleges will continue essentially as service agencies, administered almost as part of the plant, and tied closely in their collections and bibliographic organization to immediate course offerings. Librarianship in such colleges seems unlikely to develop either as a powerful office or as a highly professionalized task. The clerical components of the job should continue to bulk large.

At the same time, the more alert of the mass colleges are especially likely to adopt the latest innovations in "instructional media" (e.g., television, films, and graphics), all in elaborate electronic guises. Print then will become one among many media, partly supplanted in budget and in use by these expensive and intriguing newcomers. This event will tend to demean the status of the librarian. He will find himself working side by side with sub-professional electronics technicians, all alike serving the needs of instruction and, very probably, all ranked alike as the subordinates of an organizationally powerful "director of media services."

THE COMPETITIVE INTEGRATION OF THE ELITE SYSTEM

In contrast to the mass schools, the elite system and its libraries already are undergoing marked structural changes. These changes center on the tendency for competition between schools and departments to become the integrating principal of the elite system of its component colleges and universities. As these changes proceed, the selective colleges should come to resemble the universities more and more. There will of course be lags and limits in this convergence, but the following discussion will not distinguish between the college and university units of the elite system.

Perhaps the most important trend in this system is heightened organizational diversity and specialization. In this, the departments (or such functionally equivalent units as teaching and research institutes and interdepartmental committees) become the functional and administrative centers of the elite schools. In turn the organizational structures of these schools segment along department-discipline lines, their authority and incentive systems decentralize radically, and the central administrator indeed becomes a mediator, as Clark Kerr suggests.[23]

Why should this be so? First, there is the disciplinary specialization of the curriculum that will bring both graduate and undergraduate instruction firmly within departmental control, whatever the costs in cross-department articulation. Undergraduate as well as graduate students will come under the departmental wing.

Second, the burgeoning number of client-serving activities of the elite schools (and the financial resources they generate) come to rest more in departmental hands, less in special extension units, for they involve consultation with "pure" scientists and scholars while these academic men become more prone to involvement in action programs and knowledge application.

Third, the departments assume a central place in attracting research grants and contracts because of their expertise and reputation in the specialized fields, their participation in the communication nets of the disciplines, and their ease of access to agencies interested in supporting research in the specialty. To be sure, individual faculty entrepreneurs may do a great deal of this work, but they are likely to remain to a significant degree integrated into the departmental structure.

Fourth, the departments emerge as the chief structural and ideological links between individual faculty members and the employing school. There is no need here to rehearse the many commentaries on the cosmopolitan proclivities of professors or the organizationally centrifugal pull of discipline-centered scholarship.[24] With the central point of these commentaries, one can have little quarrel. For present purposes, it is necessary only to note that the disciplines form for their members consensually based communities and control the chief incentive system for scholarly activity. This is a system of judgmental competition in which the criteria are agreed upon (in most disciplines involving both quality and priority of innovation). Within this community personal eminence is universally desired and is obtained on the basis of evaluations by national or international colleague groups.

Consequently the university or college does not itself incorporate the incentive system to which its scholars most readily respond—it can attract or retain (and involve in instructional and other "non-scholarly" activities) young men mainly to the extent that it can provide them with a setting that will foster the excellent and abundant scholarship that will win eminence for them—and older men only to the extent that the setting suits their reputations. To structure such settings, the school must try to provide good colleagues, good graduate students, and such facilities as time, access to data, computers, laboratories, and libraries. In this effort the department has a dual function. Departmental colleagues alone can assess accurately a scholarly reputation; the department controls how the resources for scholarly work are allocated among its members.

To this there are, of course, exceptions. Some professors may have enough resource control individually to withdraw effectively from the department. The central administration, moreover, retains significant budget control, control of appointments, and administers facilities too massive or expensive for departmental incorporation—among which the library has been notable.

The picture of the elite school that emerges is of an organization that is internally diverse or pluralistic—a cluster of semiautonomous departments forming multifunctional complexes specialized by subject-matter. These departments have important access to external funds and serve as major centers of internal control as they mediate between local faculty and the cosmopolitan disciplines. As a result, the administration of these schools should itself differentiate along disciplinary lines and become embedded in the departments. Thus department chairmen and their senior colleagues will largely determine day-to-day operations and even long-range policies as these bear upon departmental affairs.

In this connection, it is important to note that departments as well as individual scholars are involved in judgmental competition within the disciplines. Thus a prime motive of a department chairman is to make his department as eminent as possible, so that he strives to gain maximum

scholarly resources for his own faculty—for example, prestigefull colleagues, light teaching loads, numerous assistants, and specialized library collections. From the point of view of the general interests of the school, this outlook tends to be disruptive and parochial. It leads the various departments into political competition and at times open conflict as each tries to maximize its own interests: money, access to university-administered facilities, and central administrative support for departmental activities.

Since interdepartment competition must always threaten the general welfare of the school, it becomes a prime task of the central administration to mediate departmental claims for support and resources in the interest of a balanced allocation that will distribute across the departments sufficient funds and facilities to hold the loyalties of each chairman and to enable him in turn to hold the loyalties of his faculty.

These internal characteristics of the elite schools have major consequences for the nature of the elite system itself. There is no sign that the incorporative nature of the universities is lessening; indeed the selective colleges behave similarly. Few elite schools find it desirable or possible to follow Princeton in building excellence within a limited domain. As a result, the elite schools, because of their comprehensive similarity to one another, form a system that is itself integrated through the competitive ranking, both academic and popular, of its units. It seems reasonable to expect that this competition will grow more intense as it becomes possible for growing numbers of schools, having entered the elite system, to claim eminence. Indeed as faculty become more cosmopolitan, it seems harder for a very few great universities to attract all of the best scholars in all of the major fields. AAUP statistics suggest that the range of salaries within the elite system is narrowing.[25] Moreover, the granting of doctorates, in the 1920's monopolized by the eminent private universities, now is spread quite evenly among the graduate schools; and, although the half dozen universities that were clearly eminent in the 20's and 30's have maintained their reputations, they now have been joined by another dozen from which, in prestige, they are not readily distinguished.[26]

In this interschool competition, there is no single set of judges, and the criteria of judgment differ. The university has many publics: parents, employers, legislators, alumni, philanthropists, and the diverse world of scholarship itself. Under these circumstances the judges tend to abdicate active evaluation, especially as disciplinary specialization makes this task increasingly esoteric and the varied activities of the elite schools impossible to translate into common terms. Thus the judges tend to accept the evaluations of departmental excellence made within the various disciplines, aggregated into some generalized ranking of school quality—for instance, the Keniston rankings based on disciplinary consensus. Or such rankings may be approximated by attending to presumed correlates of the disciplinary rankings—eminence of graduates, size of endowment, or number of library volumes, for example.

Hence resources for scholarship, and thus for prestige enhancement, have as important a place in the foreign relations as in the internal management of elite schools. Faculty recruitment and retention hinge to a great extent upon the prestige-reputations of the departments.[27] At the same time, to create and maintain a suitable image of quality and in this way maximize the school's legitimate claim to inputs of resources, the administrator must bank heavily upon the eminence of the faculty currently in residence. Moreover, prestige must be maintained uniformly across the departments, so that successful internal mediation benefits interschool as well as interdepartment relations.

Given the prestige calculus, administrators of elite schools are placed in a manipulative-dependent relation to external allocators of resources: the foundations, government agencies, philanthropists, alumni, and disciplinary organizations. The administrator's strategy is to reap great gains in input without relinquishing essential control over internal policy. Long an art in the state universities, this strategy now finds numbers of able practitioners in the private schools as well, as their sources of support diversify and endowment incomes shrink.

The manipulative-dependent relation to resource allocators is accompanied by a keen sensitivity to the claims and strategies of competing schools. Because they become acutely sensitive to the continuing threat that their competitive positions will decline, the competitors tend to hoard prestige resources. The greater the resource bank upon which an administrator can draw, the more viable his role as mediator within his school and the greater his advantage in interschool competition. He then can afford to take risks.

Hence the administrative stance toward resources for scholarship should grow increasingly retentive, occurring as an attempt to gain autonomous control of as much and as many of these resources as possible. From this phenomenon, one can derive the proposition that elite schools will cooperate with one another only when the venture promises greater local control over prestige (i.e., research) resources than otherwise would be the case. The most immediate example is the regional nuclear research laboratory that makes available to several schools facilities that none alone possibly could muster.

CONSEQUENCES FOR LIBRARIES WITHIN THE ELITE SYSTEM

The libraries of the universities and more selective colleges have in recent years been noted for their innovations in library cooperation far more radical than participation in Library of Congress programs. As these enterprises have involved the development of complementary, specialized collections (e.g., the Farmington Plan) or central, independent collections open to participating libraries (e.g., the Midwest Inter-library Center), they reveal the cosmopolitan stance of the elite academic librarians. These ventures weigh more heavily the long-run interests of national bibliography than the parochial interests of the participating schools; few of them have enjoyed unqualified success.[28]

The direction in which the elite system now is moving suggests a rising failure rate. Recall that the library's universal relevance for scholarship and teaching and comprehensive collection make it more or less central to the work of all departments in an elite school and that its great cost and unattractiveness to donors place general control of the library necessarily in the central administration.

Also recall that whatever the cosmopolitan proclivities of the academic librarian, he is inextricably bound into the local school, lacking an external system of peer-controlled judgmental competition. His career typically is local, so that he must respond especially to the incentives (often polar in direction) of administrative and faculty approbation.

The library, organizationally central and locally vulnerable, should become increasingly central as an administrative tool, both in foreign relations and internal control, as the elite system advances toward competitive integration. A fine library collection is, of course, a major resource for faculty in residence, and also in many disciplines an important drawing card in faculty recruitment. Moreover, in and of itself a large or well-known library contributes to the school's prestige.

Consequently academic administrators are likely to be more interested in the library than they have been in the past—more willing to provide funds and at the same time more exacting in their expectations for performance. The head librarian may be encouraged to plan a new building, may command an augmented budget, and may find the library the object of a drive for funds.

But administrative interest in the library will remain locally centered, since it is the comprehensiveness and depth of the collection in one's own library and its accessibility to one's own faculty that matter. Thus the general proposition that interschool cooperation is a function of gain for local interests will apply fully to interlibrary projects. If such projects involve specialization or relinquishment of holdings, and thus appear to lower the local fund of prestige resources, they may expect strong, defeating administrative opposition. Hence, one looks forward to intensified library competition and reinforcement of the local comprehensive library precisely because elite schools will grow more incorporative and competitive.

At the same time, not all elite schools will in fact be able to maintain outstanding, independent collections, less so as the number of competitors grows. As a result one should observe administrative support for those forms of library cooperation pointing toward improved local access to major collections. One thinks in particular of technological innovations in information storage and retrieval and in photoduplication, coupled with greater reliance upon the great national collections (and perhaps cooperative regional libraries) as communication centers.

Such ventures can be justified as extending local service and at the same time making it less necessary for faculty to travel to foreign libraries—at times an activity dangerously revealing of local shortcomings to a mobile and sought-after professor. If this trend does develop, interschool competition may have the paradoxical effect of producing a more tightly-knit national bibliographic system.

While administrators may be expected to conserve general control over their libraries, the administrative stance here as elsewhere is likely to be mediating, insuring chiefly that some reasonable balance in allocating library resources is maintained.[29] In other respects control should devolve to the departments. Indeed a fully centralized library will run counter to the dominant pluralistic structure of the elite schools. The administration of the library, like that of the parent

school, should become not only decentralized but structurally differentiated along disciplinary lines. The chief interest of the administrator, after all, is in making the library as responsive as possible to the demands of his faculty, while the departmental proclivity, to the extent that print is important to the faculty, will be to compete actively for maximum access to library resources and for branch units organized to suit the distinctive scholarly style.

Hence, within the limits set by the administrator's mediating role, there may develop something of an administrative-departmental coalition, pressing the library for discipline-specialized collections and services and, despite the cost, for decentralized facilities. Indeed, in view of the growing strength of departmental administration, the president or dean may find it unwise to insist too strenuously upon his formal prerogatives in setting library policies.

It may then become increasingly difficult for librarians to follow systematic, long-run plans for collection building except as these parallel faculty interests (although case of access to other collections may provide some defense against particularistic faculty requests). Moreover, especially in view of the growing strength and significance of the departments as centers of authority and control, the librarian may find that departmental intervention into library affairs, pressing toward departmentally administered branch libraries, will become more frequent and difficult to withstand, especially if there is little support for central library autonomy from the central administration.

These pressures should further a marked differentiation of the library in its collections, physical arrangements, and internal structure. Thus libraries fully responsive to distinctive styles of research will find it necessary to maintain several catalogues, differently ordered; to keep materials physically segregated at least in part on a disciplinary basis, so that their organization can be differentiated; to provide specialized reference and accessions staffs manned by librarians trained in one or a few related scholarly specialities; and to open these specialized staffs to active collaboration with department faculties in setting policies governing accessions and reader services.

Thus the centrality of the library to scholarship and the logic of disciplinary specialization together will work in the elite schools toward the structural and physical decentralization of the library, beyond the effects of generalized administrative decentralization. That library staffs will evolve as scholarly specialists—social scientists, biologists, or humanists—as much as librarians, itself suggest a commonality of interest with the cognate faculty that should exert a strong decentralizing force.

Consequently library staff members should come to have less in common with one another than with their faculty clients, while those clients will come to exercise significant control over the branch libraries that these specialists staff. If so, then the internal politics of the library should come more and more to resemble the internal politics of the parent school, as the relation between the head librarian and his specialist staff is attenuated and the bibliographic interests of the branch staff and departments converge. The head librarian under these conditions will find himself mediating competing demands not, as before, external to the library, but now coming from the branch librarians as intralibrary spokesmen for the bibliographic interests of their own scholarly fields. At the same time he will be drawn more tightly into the central administration as a servant of the university's general welfare.

Thus in the elite system of higher education—in the universities and selective colleges—some of the endemic problems of academic librarianship will be swept away; for example, the indifference of the faculty or the marginal status of the librarian. Others, such as the strain between local and cosmopolitan bibliographic interests, will grow more severe. Still others, especially the political centrality of the library, will be novel creations. But in the elite sector of American higher education, if not among the mass colleges, the old saw that the library is the heart of the university will have a truer ring.

FOOTNOTES

[1]Frederick Rudolph, *The American College and University* (New York: Knopf, 1962), pp. 115, 130-135, 221-33.

[2]U. S. Bureau of the Census, *Historical Statistics of the United States, Colonial Times to 1957* (Washington, D. C.: Government Printing Office, 1960), pp. 210-211.

[3]Rudolph, op. cit., pp. 122, 143-6.

[4]Abraham Flexner, Universities: *American, English, German* (New York: Oxford, 1930), p. 76.

[5]Rudolph, op. cit., p. 333.

[6]Ibid., pp. 339-40.

[7]Flexner, op. cit.

[8]Martin Trow, "The Democratization of Higher Education in America," mimeographed.

[9]Cf. the various papers in H. H. Fussler (ed.), *The Functions of the Library in the Modern College* (Chicago: University of Chicago Graduate Library School, 1954).

[10]Cf. Paul H. Buck, *Libraries and Universities* (Cambridge, Mass.: Belknap Press, 1964).

[11]Cf. Fussler, op. cit.

[12]Newton F. McKeon, "The Nature of the College-Library Book Collection," in Fussler, ibid., pp. 48-61.

[13]John K. Folger and Charles B. Naum, "Trends in Education in Relation to the Occupational Structure," *Sociology of Education,* 38 (1964), 26 (Table 2).

[14]Trow, op. cit.

[15]Talcott Parsons, *Essays in Sociological Theory* (rev. ed., Glencoe, Ill.: The Free Press, 1954) p. 433.

[16]Talcott Parsons, "The School Class as a Social System," *Harvard Educational Review,* 29 (1959), 312.

[17]Unpublished data collected by the author in 1961, from interviews and examination of College records.

[18]1900 and 1950 data are from U. S. Bureau of the Census, op. cit.; 1960 data are from U. S. Office of Education, *Opening (Fall) Enrollment in Higher Education, 1961 Institutional Data* (Washington, D. C.: Government Printing Office, 1961), p. 1.

[19]From 1900 to 1960 the age group 18-22 increased from 7,416,688 to 11,326,588, an increase of 52.7 per cent. The per cent increase in college enrollment for the same period was 1,518 per cent. Source of population data: *12th U. S., Census, 1900: Population,* Vol. II, Part II, p. xxxvi, *18th U. S. Census of Population,* Vol. I, Part I, pp. 1-349.

[20]James A. Davis, "Higher Education: Selection and Opportunity," *School Review,* 71 (1963), 252 (Table 2).

[21]Davis, op. cit., 250.

[22]Data supplied by the Public Information Office of the University of Illinois, Congress Circle campus.

[23]Clark Kerr, *The Uses of the University* (Cambridge, Mass: Harvard University Press, 1963).

[24]Cf. Logan Wilson, *The Academic Man* (New York: Oxford, 1942); Theodore Caplow and Reece McGee, *The Academic Marketplace* (New York: Basic Books, 1958); A. W. Gouldner, "Cosmopolitans and Locals: Toward an Analysis of Latent Social Roles," *Administrative Science Quarterly,* 2 (1957-58), 281-306, 444-480.

[25]"The Economic Status of the Profession," AAUP *Bulletin,* 50 (1964), 139-184.

[26]Bernard Berelson, *Graduate Education in the United States* (New York: McGraw-Hill, 1960), pp. 98, 280.

[27]Caplow and McGee, op. cit.

[28]Ralph T. Esterquist, "Cooperation in Library Services," in Lester Asheim (ed.), *Persistent Issues in American Librarianship* (Chicago: University of Chicago Graduate Library School, 1961), pp. 71-89.

[29]With the following discussion, compare Richard L. Meier, "Communications Overload: Proposals from the Study of a University Library," *Administrative Science Quarterly*, 7 (1963), 521-544.

ABOUT THE AUTHOR

—**Charles E. Bidwell,** Associate Professor of Education, University of Chicago; Ph.D., 1956, University of Chicago. Currently he is teaching sociology of education and doing research on the effects of academic organization on the socializing of undergraduate programs. His major research interests are the sociology of higher education and the organizational analysis of schools.

The Teaching Library and the Development of Independent Study

Swarthmore College Special Committee on Library Policy

While the academic library represents higher education's ideal of independent intellectual fulfillment, the reality of the library as a warehouse falls short of this mark. The Special Committee on Library Policy illustrates the possibilities of realizing the ends of a liberal arts education through the utilization of the academic library as a major resource for information in the problem solving process. The alternative roles for the library described in the report clearly suggest for the librarian fundamental differences in relating it to the educational experience.

Discussion over library policies may polarize around two widely disparate, mutually contradictory conceptions of what a college library should be. At one extreme there are those who argue that libraries should be passive repositories, existing to store and circulate the raw materials which teachers assign students. In such a system, the responsibilities of the librarian are exclusively administrative: to ensure efficiency in the acquisition, storage, retrieval, distribution and return of library materials. The analogue of such a library is a warehouse, with its custodian. At the other extreme is the idea of the "library-college," according to which the library and the college become coterminous and indistinguishable, following the design of the library more than that of the conventional college. With the library as the matrix of all educational activity, other facilities of the college—courses, curriculum and faculty— serve as ancillary devices, to facilitate training in the use of the library as a problem-solving instrument. The responsibilities of the librarian then resemble those of a dean of the college. Such a system lends itself readily to the use of automated instruction, independent study, and inter-disciplinary teaching and learning, while the potential of the library is extended to its theoretical limit.

The first, warehouse, concept has the authority of custom to support it; we know it works. Librarians over the past century have solved many of the organizational problems arising from the rapid increases in scholarly publication and in college population, and teachers are generally confident in their selection and disposition of library materials for instructional use. On the other hand, under the warehouse concept important library resources (such as the reference services) are wasted, and students graduate without having learned to use the library with any sophistication, without having gained the technical skill which, together with critical thought, will allow them to develop independent intellectual lives.

The second, library-college, concept is attractive stylistically for its apparent modernity, efficiency and dynamism, and educationally for its combination of practicality (the teaching of useful research skills) and nobility of purpose (the development of the habit of independent study). It is at present, however, still only an idea, offering more promise than proof. In fact, the persistent difficulties experienced in library-college experiments suggest a certain unnaturalness of this particular realignment of the faculty and the library.

Is some sort of faculty-library realignment necessary? All studies of the subject have demonstrated that students cannot be taught to use the library well unless that training takes place in the context of their normal course assignments. This evidence reveals that the faculty must assume the responsibility for teaching the use of the library,

SOURCE: Reprinted from Swarthmore College Special Committee on Library Policy, "Report," in Swarthmore College Commission on Educational Policy, *Critique of a College* (Swarthmore, Pa.: 1967), Chapter 1, "The Teaching Library," pp. 337-345, and Chapter 2, "The Development of Independent Study," pp. 347-353, by permission of the publisher.

and yet this practice involves difficulties. For one, teachers are generally less concerned with how a student locates materials in the library than with what he does with them after they are found. Therefore, teachers rarely make challenging library assignments, choosing to perform the reference work themselves in order to "save the students' time"; and when library assignments are made, the teacher's lack of enthusiasm is conveyed to his students, who respond accordingly.

A fundamental reason for these cross-purposes between the library and the faculty is that each represents a different institutional organization of scholarship. The university faculty organization was established primarily for instructional purposes, the library organization primarily for purposes of record and research. Teachers may regard these fundamentally different institutions as educationally incompatible or complementary, depending on their attitudes toward their own responsibilities.

Most college teachers do not consider library training to be an important part of their teaching responsibilities. Having acquired their own research skills primarily in connection with their professional apprenticeship, they regard such training as appropriate only to the graduate schools. This practice has two significant results: students who do not go on to graduate school never acquire sophisticated library training, and those who do attend graduate schools acquire such skills only in their professional fields. It may be asked whether these results are salutary, particularly in relation to liberal education.

For the student who does not go on to graduate school, this neglect of library training in his undergraduate years will foreshorten his intellectual growth in later life. Without teachers at his elbow to select books for him, he will find it difficult to exploit library resources—the most important single means of inquiry—and it is safe to say that the chance of his carrying on independent study at levels of greater maturity, in those circumstances, will be small. Similarly, for the student who goes on to graduate school and learns to use the library in his professional field, neglect of undergraduate library training will narrow his scholarly competence to that field. In both cases, failure to teach the use of the library as part of a liberal education discourages the students' development of sophisticated intellectual lives coincidental with the broad range of their liberal studies. If the primary purpose of a liberal education is to teach students how to teach themselves—how to ask and answer, by scholarly means, questions of importance to themselves—then the neglect of library training in college diminishes his ability to maintain whatever liberal education is achieved there.

In this perspective, it seems that undergraduate education proceeding exclusively according to the university, discipline-oriented, approach to learning can only accomplish half its task of preparing students for independent intellectual activity as adults. It is to a liberal arts college's interest, therefore, that the faculty should consider the two systems of learning—their own and the library's—as educationally complementary and compatible and as equally important aspects of their teaching responsibilities. The question is not whether, but how, libraries and faculties should work together in liberal education.

For this purpose, the warehouse library policy is inadequate, for it neglects to allow, much less to require, students to enter actively into the library's approaches to organized learning. The library-college, at the opposite extreme, seems to place so much emphasis on the library that the faculty suffers excessive neglect or de-emphasis. This dilemma prompts the consideration of a possible third alternative which would preserve the integrity of the faculty, discipline-oriented, system, while ensuring the equal importance of the library and its organization—an alternative, that is, which would lie somewhere between the two extremes outlined above.

A model which, with some modification, might prove adaptable to this purpose is the kind of library training most of the faculty received in graduate schools. Operating in conjunction with a university research library, graduate students acquire bibliographic skills from necessity, in departmental bibliography courses, or in the process of fulfilling other curricular requirements, with the assistance of instructors in their departments or, occasionally, of library personnel. The interplay between the faculty and library systems works well in graduate training, because graduate students come to depend increasingly on the library as they cut loose from their dependence on courses and devote more of their study time to reading and research, on an increasingly independent basis. The development of productive interplay between the discipline-oriented and library systems of learning may occur most naturally with the growth of independence from courses of assigned reading to self-motivated and self-formulated programs of study, in which research in the various disciplines uses the library's organization of learning for the successful solution of problems.

This does not mean that colleges should move toward the kind of specialized and professionally-directed studies now found in graduate schools; it merely suggests that the mode of library training common to graduate schools, familiar to the experience of nearly every member of a college faculty, can promote effective interplay between the library and disciplinary systems. The search for a viable college library policy now narrows itself to finding a means of adapting that mode of training to the curriculum and institution of the liberal arts college.

The first prerequisite of library training in liberal education is that it should apply across the entire range of each student's liberal studies, and not, as in the graduate schools, be confined to one specialized area. It should work, then, in conjunction with every department of the college, so that a student would actually be prepared, upon graduation, to continue building on and even increasing the breadth of his intellectual interests.

How would this program affect the kinds of courses now offered in colleges? In two ways: teachers would try to incorporate, within their present syllabi, assignments which would call upon students gradually to increase their skills in the use of the library as an elaborate research instrument; and the curriculum as a whole would be directed explicitly toward the development of heuristic competence and self-confidence in each student, presumably requiring students to demonstrate their capability in this realm as a prerequisite to graduation. This general subject will be discussed further in the next Chapter.

Will this increased emphasis on library training, especially if it involves more independent study, require significant changes in the normal college library itself? It will, and it is the purpose of this Report to describe them. For now, let it suffice simply to indicate in general what kind of library would be needed for such a program, and what would be its relation to, and advantages for, the liberal arts college as a whole.

There are considerable risks involved in simply grafting a library program onto existing faculty responsibilities. If the program is lightweight, it tends to fade away in a short time. If the program is too heavy, it tends to overwhelm the discipline-oriented system, justifiably arousing faculty resentment. If the library, however, undertakes to assist the faculty in such a program, assuming a significant portion of the additional teaching responsibility and compensating for the balance through expanded services, a successful interplay between the two systems may be achieved.

This collaboration would not mean simply that the library would contribute traditional orientation courses to bibliographic training. Such courses are notoriously tedious, irrelevant, and ineffectual. The kind of teaching the library itself can perform lies rather in the area of tactfully applying the library system to the development of liberal intellectual competence, which is the avowed purpose of the discipline-oriented system. This effort would be undertaken cooperatively with the faculty, in a curriculum which embraced and emphasized both systems.

There is, therefore, as a moderate alternative to the polar policies of the warehouse concept and the library-college: the concept of the teaching library. The teaching library should be understood as having three main functions: 1) to assist the faculty in its teaching; 2) to teach students directly how to use the library; and 3) to serve students as they teach themselves. In each of these roles the library would demonstrate the relevance of its organization of learning to the disciplinary system, the utility and benefits of their interplay, in both teaching and learning. It would fulfill these roles by offering a rich and carefully-selected collection, bibliographically organized and physically deployed as to encourage either casual, leisurely exploration, or rigorous systematic search, under the unobtrusive guidance of a professional staff dedicated to teaching with books.

ASSISTING FACULTY TEACHING

The assistance of faculty teaching, through the provision of materials assigned to students, is traditional even under the warehouse concept of libraries. With the teaching library, however, a much more comprehensive assistance is envisioned, involving greater exploitation of printed materials in courses, as well as the provision of materials used in the preparation of courses and in faculty research.

Though most teachers would agree that, for purposes of purveying information, printed materials are more efficient than lectures, few courses fully exploit this fact. Modern reproductive techniques invite local publication and dissemination of a wider variety of printed materials, more accurately tailored to meet local needs, than has been generally appreciated. Even beyond the purveyance of information, books and articles may be used more fully than they frequently are, for example, in the exemplification of completed scholarship. The assignment of entire scholarly works, to be studied and re-studied, tested and savored at the student's own time and speed, can accomplish certain ends particularly in teaching scholarly method, for which the live performance is relatively unsatisfactory. A college is not well-served when teachers spend time and effort doing things which printed materials could do equally well, or better, any more than it would be if books were used where teachers alone can perform what is desired, as may be the case in certain library-college situations. For greatest effectiveness within a college, a balance must be achieved in allocating to books and teachers those functions which each does best. The determination of a proper balance can only be left to each individual teacher, in connection with his own work.

The provision of materials with which teachers prepare courses is now feasible for many college libraries, and it should be considered an obligation of the strongest colleges. The time, money, effort and inconvenience of having to travel off-campus to prepare courses, hinder a college's efforts to attract a strong faculty. Moreover, the materials with which courses are prepared can also be of use to the better students, who therefore deserve to have them. If there was once a necessity for stocking a library almost exclusively for student use, it no longer exists.

Since the fruits of research often enrich teaching, in both the increased alertness of the teacher-scholar and in the content of his courses, a college which prides itself on the quality of its teaching must maintain a considerable number of working scholars on its faculty. While colleges cannot afford the degree of aid and comfort to research that has become common at better universities, a good college can provide substantial assistance through the library. Not only is the library indispensible to faculty research, but it is probably the most economical channel for a college's support. Compared to costly machinery, staffs of research assistants, grants for publication and the like, library materials, especially in the humanities and social studies, offer greater common utility per dollar spent and, whether through student reading or through instruction, are more likely to contribute to the teaching program of the college. Moreover, the conspicuous use of the library by the college faculty is a part of that teaching-by-example which is desirable, and the sharing of the library between students and teachers undoubtedly enhances the sense of participation in a community of scholars, which most colleges consider beneficial to their students.

TEACHING DIRECTLY

In its second function—teaching students directly how to use the library system of learning—the teaching library asserts itself as an important partner, with the faculty, in the educational offering of the college. Though the initiative rests with the faculty, who must direct their students' increasing reliance on the library, the library itself can train students to find materials which will help them answer the questions they bring to it. This direct teaching will require a larger staff than is customary, including teaching-librarians representing the several divisions of disciplines, who may assist students personally in bibliographical searches; it will also require an extension of library services in order to manifest the various tools which are part of the library's equipment. By this process, the library system can operate much as the faculty does, even to the extent of exercising some initiative in student programs. Just as the faculty sends students to the library, so also will the library send students back to the faculty. It will reveal through its different categories of materials (by subject, authorship, time and place) alternative approaches to these same materials. For example, a student approaching Max Weber's *The Protestant Ethic and the Spirit of Capitalism* from a sociology course might be referred to the disciplines of economics, history or religious studies by his having seen the book shelved with materials pertaining to subjects treated more specifically in those disciplines. By browsing and extensive bibliographic searching, the subtle and intricate interplay between the subject- and discipline-oriented systems may be made more stimulating to further inquiry and thus more beneficial to all concerned. It is hoped that the dialectical process which results will demonstrate to students the limitations as well as the strengths of both systems and will contribute, more than either would by itself, to the liberality of their education.

The necessity of adding to the staff and services of the normal library, if it would be made into a teaching library, derives from the facts that without these supplements the library program is too burdensome to the faculty and hence is impermanent and that a sink-or-swim policy of sending students to the library almost always produces more sinkers than swimmers. The library itself must be strengthened to support an effective library program, so that the faculty will view it as a useful supplement to their efforts and not simply as another addition to their already-heavy teaching load.

The successful demonstration of the library's competence and potential should produce in a student who first discovers it a sense of exhilaration and personal power, as he discovers that linguistic, geographic and historical boundaries may readily be crossed in his pursuit of inquiry. It would be to the program's benefit if this student were encouraged to indulge his excitement, for purposes of persuasion and the strengthening of his conviction in the discovery. Broad bibliographic investigation, though it may not all contribute substantially to the solution of a particular problem, should be allowed and encouraged simply for the delight it may afford a student.

SERVING STUDENT SELF-INSTRUCTION

The third main function of the teaching library is fulfilled after students have attained reasonable proficiency in using the library in the various fields of their liberal studies. The student should now be able to use library resources in truly independent study. Whether he is reading extensively to inform himself on a given subject or conducting intensive research, his use of the library under varying degrees of faculty supervision can replace more conventional instruction.

Nor should the services of the teaching library stop with the curriculum. It should contain a wealth of materials, attractively presented and arranged, which will stimulate the free indulgence of curiosity in recreational or informal reading. Here also the library can teach the versatility of its bibliographic systems by bringing to the attention of the college community ways in which library materials can be used to increase and develop the amenities of life.

The expression "teaching library" is intended, therefore, to suggest the full range of possible teaching capabilities of a college library. The distinction between what is predominantly a teaching library and what is predominantly a research library depends more on the relative sizes of the respective libraries themselves and of the communities they serve, than on the kinds of service they provide. While the research library generally serves and requires the support of a large university and is designed primarily for advanced research and professional training, the teaching library finds its home in the college, is designed primarily for undergraduate education in the liberal arts, and supports the teaching and scholarship of the college faculty. Both libraries have active reference divisions; but whereas that of the research library serves scholars who are already trained in bibliographic methods, that of the teaching library must be larger, relative to the size of its community, and useful in a variety of teaching capabilities. Thus any small college library is not necessarily a teaching library, and any university library must take special measures in order to serve its undergraduate-college constituency in the full sense of the teaching library described above.

How does the teaching library affect the liberal arts college as a whole? First, the teaching library is only an institution. Teaching is a personal enterprise, which institutions can only help or hinder, and not create or prevent by themselves. The kind of teaching which the teaching library encourages will only be as productive as are the students, teachers and library staff in their use of it. As an institution, however, it can provide the external conditions under which superior liberal education can flourish. By directing students to the tools of learning and by inviting the faculty to develop students' skill at inquiry, the teaching library encourages concentration on the fundamental aspects of education in the liberal arts.

Second, while the quality of teaching at a college depends primarily on the faculty, the scope of its accumulated expertise must be narrower than it would be at a larger institution. However, a college can attempt to achieve comprehensive coverage of the universe of learning through its library and a curriculum which allows a student to follow his curiosity even if it ranges beyond the limits of regular course offerings. By these means, a college can compete with multiversities for the most energetic students, who may wish not to foreclose study of recondite subjects by matriculating at a smaller, more narrowly oriented, institution. For such students, indeed, the college might offer the added incentives of the opportunity for greater independence of study, as well as the possibility of closer personal guidance in a community of scholars. It may even be that only with a teaching library can a college offer the combination of a comprehensive scope and a community of scholars, and, what may be as important, exposure to the community of learning which that combination may encourage.

Third, the teaching library should strengthen the appeal of the small college for teacher-scholars, by providing a situation in which the energies and abilities of a teacher are concentrated on those aspects of teaching which he alone can do well, in which students are expected and trained to assume an increasing responsibility for their own development and in which the teacher's research is considered an integral aspect of his teaching preparation and supported as such. Such a college would prove most attractive to precisely those individuals from whom it would most benefit: scholars who appreciate the reciprocal benefits which an exciting teaching environment confers upon scholarship and who produce scholarly works which are educationally sensitive and effective.

It must be admitted that the development and maintenance of a teaching library will cost more than would a warehouse library. But in view of the educational advantages, to both students and faculty, the relative economics of the teaching library should be considered. Both the library and the faculty will be used more efficiently. Moreover, the quality of the library may be more readily maintained, at lower cost, than any other major facility of the college. About two-thirds of the annual budget of a good library—that portion spent for purchasing materials and paying that part of the staff which acquires and organizes them for use—is really a capital investment, each increment adding to the utility of the collection for many years. It is not necessary to pay a book yearly for its services, and it will not be lured away by an attractive offer from another institution.

The remainder of this Report will attempt systematically to describe an ideal teaching library. Naturally, the immediate reference is to Swarthmore College, though much of what is said may apply equally well to similar institutions. Probably no college in America now has such a library. Excellence in teaching, however, is a traditional goal at Swarthmore, and the College has developed, particularly in recent years, a library which will provide a sound base for future growth. The teaching library outlined below is not something which may simply be bought tomorrow; it will take, especially its educational functions, years to develop. What is offered here is an ideal. It is to be hoped that the faculty, administration, and

Board of Managers will respond in kind to the conviction that Swarthmore, in the years to come, should strive for an excellent, and possibly even a great, teaching library.

THE DEVELOPMENT OF INDEPENDENT STUDY

It has already been argued that one of the major goals of liberal arts education is to develop the student's ability to think and inquire for himself so that he may better continue self-education after graduation. It is clear that the forms of instruction normally conveyed by the phrase "independent study" are not the only avenue to this goal, but the position of this Report is that true independence can be more effectively attained by assigning the library a major role in the instructional program and permitting the student ample opportunity to instruct himself through reading and investigation.

The direct confrontation of the student with the literature of his subject, his personal evaluation and analysis of this literature, and his submission of his conclusions to the criticism of his instructor, have long proved effective in developing intellectual maturity and self-reliance at British universities and American graduate schools. This experience strongly indicates that to the degree burden of instruction is shifted from the classroom to the student's self-instruction, there is a liberating effect on the student, who becomes freer to exercise his choice and discrimination, and on the instructor, who becomes less involved in the purveyance of information and more concerned with the development of curiosity and judgment. There should be a wide variety of instructional formats for the student, but certainly independent study should constitute a significant part of his education. This Chapter, then, will suggest ways in which the faculty can apply this fundamental method to learning situations in order to develop the student's capacity for independent study.

The goal of independent study is by no means foreign to Swarthmore College. It was prominent in the initiation of the Honors Program, which was founded on the belief that "the best and only true education is self-education," and has continued to be among the professed objectives of the institution. There are strong indications, however, that many students pass their undergraduate years at the College without any substantial experience of independent learning. Responses to questionnaires from both faculty and students indicate that in both introductory and advanced courses, the major portion of reading was assigned in textbooks.

In all types of courses, the faculty indicated that only a small minority of reading was from materials discovered by the student himself. In elementary courses, half the faculty members reporting on their assignments stated that 100 percent of the reading came from textbooks. In advanced courses, the faculty indicated that in most instances, 50 percent of the reading came from textbooks and the bulk of the remainder from prescribed titles on reserve. In Honors Seminars, faculty responses revealed that most reading was either from reserve titles or from optional reading lists.

As might be expected in light of the above responses, students reported heavy use of the library as a study hall for reading textbooks and assigned readings and confessed a lack of familiarity with library materials from bibliographic aids to microfilm. No other issue elicited from students as much written comment and suggestion. It was frequently stated that greater emphasis and explanation from the faculty in this regard would be helpful and that more printed guides and handbooks as well as a more substantial and effective program of instruction in the use of the library should be provided.

This picture of student library use was borne out by the responses to questions on the purpose of the library. While the students indicated a strong need for greater sophistication in the use of the library, the faculty indicated that the chief function of the library was to provide assigned and optional readings named by the instructor. Only a small minority reported that they made assignments which forced the student to prepare bibliographies, to familiarize himself with the bibliographic aids, or to call upon the services of the Reference Librarian.

A few students volunteered that they were embarrassed over how little they knew about the library. One openly stated, "Swarthmore students hate to appear ignorant about anything as basic as library facilities, especially upperclassmen," while another wrote, "I am often too embarrassed to admit my ignorance and thus never learn where things are." These comments point up one of the obstacles to sophisticated use of libraries. Regrettably, information about libraries is generally regarded as no more intellectually challenging than such "tool" skills as typewriting, and it is often assumed that the student is either already accustomed to using libraries effectively or can easily acquire this ability as if through osmosis. Students tend, consequently, to neglect acquiring the necessary information for extensive use of library resources.

What sort of instruction should be provided to meet this need? Experience has shown that the student derives much greater benefit from instruction in library use when it is given in the normal instructional situation and when it is repeated with increasing sophistication at several levels of the student's career. The student requires the example of scholarship and the motivation provided by the faculty. There is strong evidence in all studies on this matter, including local investigations, that his incentive to acquire the skills necessary for independent study depends primarily on the instructor's willingness to devote time and attention to the development of these skills. For it is only when the student becomes aware of the teacher's emphasis on sources of information and the proper method of using them that he begins to become sufficiently familiar with them himself to develop the capacity for truly independent work.

At Swarthmore, if the ideal of self-education is still paramount, it is clear that the student should have the instruction necessary to equip him to investigate topics and problems independently and the opportunity to put the skills so acquired to use. The fact is that the faculty now teaches much that is indispensable to intelligent use of the library: e.g., foreign languages, careful reading, and critical evaluation of scholarship. Clearly, one reason more emphasis has not been put on use of the library is the faculty's understandable reluctance to devote time to it at the expense of course material to be discussed. What is now suggested would not necessarily take much time away from subject matter and, in fact, should save instructional time in the long run by enabling the student to learn more independently. The suggestion is simply for a conscious effort to train the student in the proper use of the resources of the library as an organized body of information. This training has three aspects: 1) familiarity with library organization and reference sources; 2) experience in quickly and efficiently locating and evaluating materials on a given topic, so that he can inform himself independently on that topic through reading; and 3) research techniques.

Familiarity with Library Organization and Reference Sources

The student's past experience, the library handbook, the library staff, and the occasion to find specific information can normally be relied on to equip him to use profitably such standard library tools as the card catalogue and general reference sources like encyclopedias. However, as the survey of student opinion revealed, he needs more experience in using the less general reference sources, pertinent bibliographies, and periodical indexes. If instructors would make assignments which explicitly required familiarity with the standard reference titles of the discipline, the student would acquire a broad knowledge of basic reference books. Thus, a course in literature might compel him to use the etymological dictionaries; a course in history could require him to examine pertinent biographical dictionaries or subject bibliographies; a sociology assignment might require him to use the periodical indexes in the social sciences. For its part, the library staff could provide annotated bibliographies of local holdings to guide the student to the appropriate source. The need for this kind of information, appropriate to the low-level courses of the curriculum, has been clearly indicated not only by the statements cited above but also by the faculty's concern that students working independently in the library have seldom used time effectively or secured the appropriate materials in the past.

Fact-finding information and knowledge of books about books are obviously necessary for a student before he can proceed to more sophisticated investigations within a specific discipline. Beyond reference sources, the student should begin to develop his capacity to evaluate and analyze the library materials he uses. Assignments can be devised which profitably advance the student's bibliographic techniques and sophistication along with his knowledge of the subject. Examples of projects used elsewhere include compilations of annotated lists of collateral reading which then provide his reading in the course; the comparison of contemporary sources with historical accounts; documented challenges to statements in textbooks; and the examination of the textual evolutions through various editions. It is to be hoped that the faculty will accept the challenge to fashion assignments which will meet this need, and it should be one of the major responsibilities of the Advisory Committee on the Library to foster this kind of instruction.

Recommendation: That experience and proficiency in the use of library materials be made an integral part of courses of instruction.

Independent Reading

By the time the student selects a major department, he should be able to locate and evaluate the written material on a given topic and to instruct himself in it through reading with a fair degree of competence. Incorporation of this kind of instruction into the curriculum should not be difficult. Indeed, its versatility, in addition to its other advantages, strongly recommends it. Independent reading can be used in conjunction with all ranges of instructional situations from the tutorial, where it is traditional, to the large lecture, where it can provide the basic information examined in the course, freeing the instructor from all such responsibility. It is indispensable to self-preparation for the fulfillment of degrees requirements through examination, and it can lend the necessary modicum of structure to such free periods as interim semesters, semesters with reduced loads, and reading periods. It, in effect, provides an opportunity for the College to offer courses not listed in the catalogue and to cover gaps in the curriculum for specific groups of qualified students. Properly administered, it can afford the instructor a greater opportunity to bring his research experiences to bear more directly on his teaching and, through such devices as reading courses, to present his scholarly specialty as a legitimate area for study by his students in the "specialized offerings" described by the Commission on Educational Policy in Chapter III of its Report. It is, therefore, clearly appropriate to the suggestions made by the Commission for changes in the role of the classroom in instruction. While the manner of teaching would depend upon the faculty, the role of the instructor would seem to be appropriately that of guide and critic, of judging performance, as described in the letter by a present faculty member included in Chapter III of the Commission's Report.

From the student viewpoint, the introduction of more independent reading into the curriculum can constitute an effective response to many of the concerns examined by the Commission. It could go a long way to answer the student's desire for more independence and flexibility in his course of study and greatly add to his experience in self-instruction, while furnishing a basis for periodic assessment of his work. Within an appropriate framework, it can provide, for example, an increased opportunity for each student to make his academic experience more relevant by permitting him to investigate in depth specific areas of interest to him. It clearly exposes him to the methods of inquiry and directly meets the need to equip him to continue his education after the completion of his formal instruction. It introduces, as mentioned above, an element of freedom and choice into the undergraduate program which is in fundamental harmony with the widespread desire among undergraduates to abandon highly structured courses and rigidly compartmentalized disciplines.

The very flexibility and freedom afforded by this kind of teaching makes precise description of its mechanics difficult. Within each field, various plateaus of competence will be reached in successive stages as the student progresses through the curriculum. There can scarcely be, in other words, a neat sequence for all students, a set way of determining for large groups of students when or whether they have achieved the desired level of excellence in one field, or virtuosity in several. Only the student and his teachers will know how far he has progressed, and no single examination or thesis will offer sufficient indications of his real competence. Nevertheless, at various times throughout his college career, every student should have the opportunity to exercise his bibliographic ability, by way of testing it for himself, in independent study.

At these times, he should be relieved of whatever regular courseload requirements as may seem justified in light of the scope of his proposed study. For it is generally recognized that the pressure of time is one of the major obstacles to a student's unprescribed use of the library and experience of independent inquiry.

Recommendation: That the curriculum assure experience in self-instruction through independent reading.

In what has been said, there has been no mention of coverage of a given discipline or area of study. To a degree, this concern can be met by a reiteration of the conviction that the purpose of liberal arts education is to develop intellectual maturity and self-reliance, not to accumulate information. (The reader is referred to the discussion of this issue in Chapter III of the Report of the Commission on Educational Policy.) In addition, it should be pointed out that where

coverage is sacrificed to depth, the student equipped with a reading list on a given subject and a capacity for independent study should be able to provide himself with a broad familiarity with that subject.

It is clear that the instructional format described here is not applicable to all educational circumstances or to all subject matter. Indeed, it is not the only form of independent study; "non-bookish" projects such as laboratory experiments and off-campus investigations of social problems are manifestly as appropriate to certain disciplines. There is, nevertheless, a clear opportunity for wider application of independent reading in the curriculum at Swarthmore, and therefore its adoption is urged wherever it presents a feasible alternative to more conventional forms of instruction.

Student Research

None of the situations described thus far necessarily involves research. However, every student should undertake an independent investigation in depth and present a paper based on his research at some point in his undergraduate career. This experience could come at any time at which it might be most profitable to him, beginning with the freshman year, and could be repeated, if such action is deemed advisable by the appropriate faculty authority. The project should be conducted under faculty supervision, and for its duration, the student should be allowed a reduction in course load appropriate to the scope of the project.

Recommendation: That each student should be required to demonstrate some skill at independent inquiry as he progresses through the curriculum and as a major prerequisite for graduation; and that he spend at least one semester with a reduced course load, appropriate to the scope and difficulty of his project, in order to be free for independent study.

The burden of this Chapter has been to argue that undergraduate instruction should aim at teaching the student to teach himself, to point out possible opportunities to do so, and to stress the essential part the faculty must play in this experience. The acquisition of the capacity and inclination for self-instruction seems all the more important in light of the "information explosion." Perhaps recognition of this fact is in part the explanation of the growing emphasis on courses in methods of inquiry in undergraduate curricula. Indeed, nothing proposed here is a marked departure from programs already established and accepted in other institutions. Thus, this segment of this Report simply presents a natural strategy for change and for experimentation for Swarthmore College.

The first two Chapters of this Report have attempted to reveal a distinct viewpoint on the proper role of a library in a college community. The subsequent Chapters will describe in some detail the facilities and staff required to enable a library to fill this role. The material which follows, therefore, is necessarily less concerned with educational policy and more devoted to issues of library administration.

ABOUT THE COMMITTEE

—**The Special Committee on Library Policy** was appointed by Swarthmore College President Courtney Smith to study the function and operation of the library in a liberal arts college. The Committee consisted of four College faculty members representative of the academic program; two members from other institutions, William S. Dix, Librarian of Princeton University, and Carroll G. Bowen, Director of the M. I. T. Press; and the Chairman, James F. Govan, Librarian, Swarthmore College. Ph.d., 1960, Johns Hopkins University.

III
ADMINISTERING THE LIBRARY

For the academic librarian the most difficult task is his constant attempt to establish the significant parameters of his responsibility in terms acceptable to himself and to his environment. The dynamics of this process can be constructive or dysfunctional. Whereas the authority of a concerned high placed academic officer or a strong formula may reduce the degree of tension, the librarian must, nevertheless, operate in the unstable educational marketplace. In his position he is vulnerable to pressure, opinions, circumstance, and the actions of others over whom he has no control. Instead of finding refuge in authority, letting the system become primary, or being easily susceptible to external influence, the academic librarian must learn to manage consent and to appreciate the consequences of executive action.

Government, Organization, and Administration

by E. W. Erickson

By the very nature of the academic environment it is improbable that a library administrator can be satisfied with the relationship between his input and his effect on the decision-making processes which affect the library. This summary of the surveys of academic libraries illustrates the character of the unresolved, and perhaps unresolvable role and organizational difficulties facing the academic librarian. As manifested in the follow-up phase of the study, so long as academic librarians look to solutions solely in terms of structural finites and administrative definition and do not comprehend social processes, their frustration will continue.

Of the approximately 775 recommendations made in the survey reports, 146, or 18.8 percent, dealth with matters concerning the government, organization, and administration of the libraries. Most of these recommendations are found specifically under these categories in the reports, but where surveys have varied in format and terminology the writer has used his best judgment to bring together the recommendations dealing with this general area. This chapter will be devoted to a discussion of the results of these 146 recommendations.

CENTRALIZATION OF LIBRARY RESOURCES AND ADMINISTRATION

At least the basis of the number of recommendations made, the problems caused by decentralization were major ones for all the libraries surveyed. Sixty-four, or 43.8 percent, of the 146 recommendations having to do with government, organization, and administration of libraries were concerned with correcting the ills of decentralization. Each survey report included at least two recommendations of this nature, and two (Indiana and Stanford) had more than ten.

In no case did the surveyors recommend complete physical consolidation of all resources, but they sought means for achieving centralization of administration and a controlled minimum of decentralization of resources. Tauber and Jesse generally expressed the attitude of all the surveyors in this regard when they stated:

The surveyors realize that there are certain advantages to be had through the placement of materials near the students, faculty, and research workers. Hence, they are not in favor of total consolidation of all resources in one central building, even if such an essential building soon becomes a reality at Blacksburg. They wish to make a clear distinction between working laboratory collections, which should be permitted, and departmental libraries, which should be highly restricted. The former, consisting of essential handbooks, dictionaries, specialized periodicals, and other specialized materials which do not overlap into other fields to any great degree, are as necessary as other laboratory materials for effective work. The latter, however, unless carefully controlled, are likely to develop into libraries with overlapping interests to such an extent that the majority of users are hampered in their efforts.[1]

The problem of decentralization existed in varying degrees at all the institutions surveyed, but on some campuses the problem had become more acute than on others. At Stanford University the surveyors found twenty-four departmental libraries, four staffed from the library budget, six staffed from departmental budgets, and fourteen either completely unattended or serviced by departmental secretaries or student assistants.

At Cornell University the surveyors found fourteen departmental libraries connected with the endowed colleges, ranging from units somewhat larger than office collections to large, well-organized libraries. Some were staffed by professional librarians, others by departmental

SOURCE: Reprinted from E. W. Erickson, *College and University Library Surveys, 1938-1952* (Chicago: American Library Association, 1961), Chapter 3, "Government, Organization, and Administration," pp. 20-34, by permission of the publisher and the author.

secretaries. Some were financed by the departments, while others were supported wholly or
in part by University Library funds. Administrative control was in the hands of the deans or
instructional department heads. To complicate
the administrative structure further, the state
colleges on the Cornell campus had nineteen
departmental libraries with even fewer connections with the University Library.

But extremes of decentralization were not
found only in the large libraries. Even at the
Virginia Polytechnic Institute, with an enrollment of 5301 and a book collection of 123,009
volumes, two branch libraries, six departmental
libraries, and fifteen laboratory collections
existed, with only the Main Library and its two
branches under the control of the librarian.

In varying degrees and with the substitution
of names of libraries, the following restrained
comment by Wilson and Tauber regarding the
University of South Carolina situation could be
applied to all of the surveyed libraries in this
study:

> . . . There is clear evidence of tenuous adminis-
> trative relationships between McKissick Library and
> the Education, Law, and South Carolinian libraries.
> In addition, the Extension Library is entirely inde-
> pendent of the McKissick Library, and the various
> office collections are in no way under the control
> of the Librarian.[2]

Of the sixty-four recommendations made concerning the centralization of library resources and
administration, thirty, or 46.9 percent, were
carried out completely; nine, or 14.1 percent,
were achieved to a large degree; three, or 4.7
percent, were achieved to a small degree; and
twenty, or 31.2 percent, were not carried out.
Two (3.1 percent) were in operation at the time
of the survey. Thus it can be said that thirty-nine,
or 61.0 percent, of the sixty-four recommendations
in this category were carried out completely or to
a large degree.

It is interesting to note that of the forty-two
recommendations carried out, either completely
or in part, thirty-eight, or 90.5 percent, were
achieved within five years, twenty three (54.8
percent being carried out during the first two
years following the survey.

It was difficult in many cases for the librarians
of the surveyed institutions to say categorically
that the carrying out of a recommendation was
accomplished as a direct or indirect result of the
survey. However, in the best judgment of these

librarians, nineteen, or 45.2 percent, were
achieved as a direct result of the surveys; twelve,
or 28.6 percent, were indirectly the result of the
surveys; and one, or 2.4 percent, was not the
result of the survey at all. In ten cases the influence of the survey was not ascertainable. It
can be said then that at least thirty-one, or 73.8
percent, of the forty-two recommendations
carried out were achieved as a result of the
survey, either directly or indirectly.

In fifty-nine, 92.2 percent, instances the libraries agreed with the recommendations, and
in five, or 7.8 percent, cases the librarians disagreed. As one might guess, the five recommendations with which there was disagreement
on the part of the librarian were not carried out.

Although the *Revised By-Laws of Cornell
University,* effective June 13, 1955, limit the
director of the University Library to a general
supervision of that library only, exclusive of the
state college libraries, McCarthy believes that
complete centralization of administration as
recommended in the survey might have been
accomplished in 1948 if the college librarians
and deans had been willing. Under the circumstances McCarthy doubts now that centralization as recommended is possible.[3]

Failure to achieve this major recommendation
for centralization of administration does not
mean, however, that conditions were not improved. McCarthy states that, beginning immediately after the survey and increasing during
the ensuing years, great strides were made
toward centralizing the direction of the Cornell
library organization. Although the director's
relationship to the state college librarians is
only advisory, it is an improved relationship.
This relationship also exists with the Aeronautical, Law, and Medical libraries as a result
of the survey. The Regional History Collection
was fully integrated with the University Library,
as recommended, within one year after the
survey and as a direct result of the survey.

At the University of Georgia steps were
taken toward centralization within two years
after the survey, and as a direct result of the
survey. The librarian was acknowledged the
general administrator of all libraries in the
University, including all departmental libraries; all books purchased from University
funds for library purposes were made a part
of the University Library; the Forestry Library was made a part of the College of Agriculture Library; and transfers were made a

part of the Agricultural Engineering Library and the Physical Education Library to the College of Agriculture Library. The survey was a strong factor in the abolition of some departmental libraries, but W. P. Kellam, director of libraries, says that the construction of a new library building in 1953 did more than anything else to eliminate departmental libraries.

Within one year after the survey of the Indiana University Library, and as a direct result of the survey, all the libraries of the University were integrated into a unified system under the director of libraries. Also as a direct result of the survey, the President kept the director of libraries in touch with the building program and regarded him as the University's planning expert when buildings containing a library function were contemplated. Within two years, and as a direct result of the survey, the Medical Library, Dental Library, and Nurses Training Library were merged, technical processes for all three being centralized in the Medical Library.

The following improvements were indirectly the result of the survey and were accomplished in whole or in part within five years following the survey: (1) a statement of policy governing the establishment and maintenance of branch libraries was formulated, (2) a social science reading room was established in the Main Library, and (3) the use of all books purchased with library funds for library purposes was administered through the Main Library or branch units under the administration of the director of libraries.

Five recommendations were not carried out because the director of libraries did not agree with the surveyors. Three of these recommendations were for the integration into the Main Library of three small collections which were later discarded. The other two concerned the supervision of the Law and Business libraries.

Efforts toward centralization at the University of South Carolina Library were singularly unsuccessful. The surveyors made six recommendations, all aimed at integrating the school and departmental libraries (Education, Law, Extension, and South Caroliniana libraries) with the Main Library under a unified control and under the administration of the librarian. The librarian acknowledged defeat in his efforts toward this integration following the Library Committee's negative vote on his proposal to integrate the Education Library with the Main Library. The administrative support necessary for the accomplishment of these recommendations was apparently lacking, Alfred Rawlinson, the librarian, reporting that John Van Male and W. P. Kellam before him had made vigorous efforts to effect the recommended integration.

Of the four recommendations carried out completely at Stanford University, two were concerned with insuring consultation among the administration, the director of libraries, and the party concerned in the case of proposals affecting the administration of the library. Another concerned the development and extension of previously established relationships between the Biological Science, Anatomy, and Marine Station libraries. According to Raynard C. Swank, director of libraries, these were achieved satisfactorily.

The fourth completed recommendation was a major one calling for the administrative consolidation of various related departmental libraries through the establishment of three subject divisional librarianships: one for the social sciences, one for the biological sciences, and the other for the physical sciences and engineering. According to Swank's report for 1947-49 this was achieved within two years following the survey, and in a letter to Maurice Tauber he states that, in addition to the administrative consolidation, some physical consolidation had been effected with more in the planning stage.

Two of the four recommendations which were carried out to a large degree were general in nature, calling for adherence to the principle of centralization and the consolidation of semi-autonomous units in the library system. In 1949, two years after the survey, only the Hoover Library, the Food Research Library, the Business Library, and the Law Library remained as autonomous units. Throughout Swank's report for 1947-49 and in Grieder's account of the reorganization of the Stanford University Libraries[4] great progress is reported. In reference to the consolidation of autonomous units, six years after the survey, Swank reports that it had not yet been accomplished but that relationships with the autonomous units had been greatly improved. The other two recommendations carried out to a large degree involved particular libraries in relation to the total library system.

The two recommendations achieved to a small degree concerned individual libraries, and the extent to which they were achieved represents an improved situation. The recommendation that the Anatomy, Bacteriology, Herbarium, and Natural History libraries be consolidated was frequently considered, but as late as seven years after the survey no progress could be reported.

Because of the unusual circumstances of the surveyor's having been apppointed director of the library within a year after the survey, it is exceedingly difficult to say that an improvement was a direct or indirect result of the survey. Thus throughout this study it will be indicated in the tables that the influence of the Stanford survey is "not ascertainable."

As a direct result of the survey of the Texas A. & M. College Library centralized direction of libraries was achieved within four years after the survey, and a policy was established prohibiting the establishment of new departmental libraries except after study and approval by the President, the librarian, the Library Committee, and the head of the unit concerned. At the other institutions the hand of the librarian was strengthened, but no significant progress was made in the direction of centralization of libraries as a result of the surveys.

STATUTES AND BYLAWS DEFINING LIBRARY RESOURCES AND RESPONSIBILITIES OF THE LIBRARIAN

Relatively little success was achieved by the libraries in the accomplishment of the recommendations made concerning statutes or bylaws that would define library resources and the responsibilities of the librarian. Fourteen specific recommendations were made regarding this matter, including all the libraries except those at the University of Florida and Indiana University, and in the latter two instances the problem was treated incidentally in connection with other recommendations. Four recommendations, or 28.6 percent, including only three libraries, were carried out, two of them completely and the other two to a large degree. Ten, or 71.4 percent, were not achieved. Those accomplished were carried out within two years and were direct results of the surveys, in the opinion of the librarians of the institutions. Despite this significant lack of success the librarians involved agreed with all the recommendations.

At the University of New Hampshire and the University of Georgia statutes were adopted defining the responsibilities of the librarian

and stating what constitutes the libraries of the University, in each case as a direct result of the survey, according to the directors of those libraries. Similar recommendations were carried out at the University of Notre Dame as a direct result of the survey, through the resulting statements were not so specific as Victor A. Schaefer, director of libraries, had requested. Recommendations regarding statutes and bylaws were not achieved at the other institutions.

ESTABLISHMENT AND FUNCTIONS OF LIBRARY COMMITTEES

Fifteen recommendations were made regarding the establishment and functions of library committees, each survey report containing at least one recommendation. Eight, or 53.3 percent, were achieved either completely or to a large degree; two, or 13.3 percent, were achieved to a small degree; four, or 26.7 percent, were not carried out; and in one case (6.7 percent) it could not be ascertained definitely that the recommendation had or had not been carried out.

Of the ten recommendations accomplished eight, or 80.0 percent, were achieved within one year after the survey. Of the remaining two, one was carried out four years after the survey, and the date of achievement for the other could not be ascertained. The achievement of three, or 30.0 percent, of these recommendations was considered the direct result of the surveys, according to the librarians, and in four cases, or 40.0 percent, was considered the indirect result. In one case the achievement was not considered the result of the survey, and in two the influence of the survey could not be ascertained. The librarians agreed with twelve, or 80.0 percent, of the recommendations; disagreed with two, or 13.3 percent; and indicated indifference in one case.

At the time of the surveys all but one (Virginia Polytechnic Institute) of the libraries had library committees of varying quality, composition, and purpose. General criticisms of the surveyors were irregularity of meetings, uncertainty of duties, a tendency toward administrative functions, carlessness in recording minutes, and inadequate faculty representation.

Typical of the recommendations made regarding the establishment and functions of library committees are those made by the surveyors of the University of Georgia Library. They recommended that the committee be advisory, that it concern itself with the usual matters of general policy and apportionment of book funds, that membership be for a definite period of years, that a chairman be elected annually, and that it consist of six members in addition to the librarian. These recommendations were achieved at the University of Georgia indirectly as a result of the survey, but at Notre Dame, Montana, New Hampshire, and Stanford successful results were attributed directly to the survey.

At Indiana University the President offered to revamp the committee along the lines recommended, but Robert A. Miller, director of libraries, declined, disagreeing with the recommendation that a committee consisting largely of faculty members be appointed. He felt that the Library Committee usually dealt with administrative matters which required action by the Dean's Office rather than by the faculty. The librarian at Virginia Polytechnic Institute also disagreed with the recommendation made at that institution, believing that more could be accomplished by direct contacts with individual faculty members than through a formal committee.

The recommendation made at Texas A. & M. College was carried out in large part, indirectly as a result of the survey, but at Alabama Polytechnic Institute, Cornell, the University of Florida, and the University of South Carolina recommendations were achieved either in small degree or not at all.

SUPERVISION OF THE LARGER UNITS IN THE ORGANIZATION OF THE LIBRARIES

The recommendations within this category had to do with the appointment of associate or assistant directors and the heads of larger departments, in order to limit the span of control and to relieve the director of numerous details of supervision. Twelve recommendations were made, including all the libraries except those of the universities of Florida, New Hampshire, and Notre Dame and Alabama Polytechnic Institute.

Eight, or 66.7 percent, of the twelve recommendations were carried out either completely or to a large degree. These included, for example, the appointment of an assistant director at Cornell, an associate librarian at the University of Georgia, an assistant librarian and science librarian at Indiana University, an associate

director at Stanford, an assistant librarian at Texas A. & M., and a head of the order and processing division at Virginia Polytechnic Institute. Four recommendations, or 33.3 percent, were not carried out. Of those achieved five, or 62.5 percent, were accomplished within three years, one (12.5 percent) during the fifth year, and two, or 25.0 percent, after five years.

Six, or 75.0 percent, of the accomplished recommendations were achieved as the direct result of the surveys and one, or 12.5 percent, as an indirect result. In one case the influence of the survey could not be ascertained. It is interesting to note that even the recommendations carried out more than five years after the surveys, were considered by the librarians to have been accomplished directly as a result of the surveys.

In eight, or 66.7 percent, of the cases the librarians agreed with the recommendations; in three, or 25.0 percent, there was disagreement; while in one case (8.3 percent) the librarian agreed only with part of the recommendation.

APPOINTMENT OF THE LIBRARIAN AND OTHER PROFESSIONAL STAFF MEMBERS TO ACADEMIC AND ADMINISTRATIVE COMMITTEES

Recommendations that the library be represented on faculty and administrative committees for the purpose of keeping informed concerning campus developments which affect libraries on the whole, were not very well carried out. Fourteen recommendations were made, including all but the Stanford survey. Seven of the recommendations included all professional personnel, while the rest were concerned only with the director's appointment to committees.

Only two, or 14.3 percent, recommendations were achieved completely, while one, or 7.1 percent, was accomplished to a large degree. Thus, three (21.4 percent) were carried out completely or to a large degree, as compared with eleven, or 78.6 percent, which were carried out to a small degree or not at all. Six, or 42.9 percent, were not carried out at all.

Of the eight recommendations achieved to any degree at all, seven, or 87.5 percent, were carried out within two years of the survey. One, or 12.5 percent, was achieved more than five years after the survey.

Five, or 62.5 percent, of the achieved recommendations were considered direct results of the survey by the librarians of the surveyed institutions, and the achievement of two, or 25.0 percent, was indirectly the result of the survey. In one case the influence of the survey could not be ascertained. In all cases but one the librarians agreed with the recommendations, and, interesting to note, in the case where there was disagreement, the recommendation was nevertheless achieved completely within two years after the survey and as a direct result of the survey.

Some of the committees and councils to which the surveyors recommended that the librarians be appointed were the University Council, the Graduate Council, President's Advisory Council, Administrative Council, and Curriculum Committee. Most of the recommendations concerned the appointment of heads of the libraries to committees, but in several instances it was recommended that *all* professional staff members be considered for faculty committee appointments. In the latter cases the libraries were completely unsuccessful in implementing the recommendations.

USE OF THE ANNUAL REPORT

The practice of writing an annual report was carried out in some form or other in all the surveyed libraries, and only five recommendations were made concerning this matter, dealing with the effective use of reports. These were made for Cornell, Montana State, Notre Dame, Stanford, and Virginia Polytechnic Institute. All of the recommendations were carried out completely or to a large degree within one year after the survey. In three cases the recommendations were achieved indirectly as a result of the surveys; in one, achievement was not the result of the survey; and in the other, influence of the survey was not ascertainable. In all cases the librarians agreed with the recommendations. It is probably safe to say that although the recommendations of the surveyors reinforced the views of the librarians regarding the use of annual reports, they had relatively little influence on the action of the librarians.

ORGANIZATION OF ADVISORY COUNCILS

In five of the surveys (Alabama Polytechnic Institute, Montana, Notre Dame, Stanford, and Texas A. & M.) six recommendations were made concerning the organization of advisory groups,

called variously a Librarian's Council, Director's Council, Advisory Council of Library Department Heads, and Library Council. It was suggested that these groups be organized to consult with and advise the director on matters of policy and operating procedures.

All six recommendations were carried out: five, or 83.3 percent, completely or to a large degree, and one (16.7 percent) to a small degree. Four, or 66.6 percent, were achieved within one year; one, or 16.7 percent, during the second year; and one during the third year.

Two, or 33.3 percent, were considered to be the direct result of the survey, while three, or 50.0 percent, were said to be indirectly the result of the survey. The influence of the survey in one case was not ascertainable. The librarians agreed with all the recommendations, though in one case there were some reservations. At Alabama Polytechnic Institute and Texas A. & M., where a Director's Council and a Librarian's Council, respectively, were organized within one year after the survey, results were excellent, according to the heads of these libraries.

Two recommendations designed to bring about the organization of a Library Council were made by the surveyors of the Notre Dame Library. The first recommendation was for the organization of a Committee of Science Librarians to co-ordinate the work of these branch libraries. The second recommendation was for the organization of the heads of the five departments in the Main Library into a similar group with mutual interests, and this group plus the law librarian and the chairman of the Committee of Science Librarians to meet regularly with the director as a Library Council.

These recommendations were not carried out completely as the surveyors intended, but, at least in spirit, they were achieved to a large degree. According to Victor A. Schaefer, director of libraries, within three years after the survey all the branch librarians were organized into a committee, including the Science, Architecture, Engineering and Law libraries, and weekly meetings were held. The department heads in the Main Library had been organized during the previous years. These groups met separately with the director rather than as one Library Council until September, 1957, when combined weekly meetings were held. In speaking of the organization of the branch libraries particularly, Schaefer says that good results have come from it, including the standardization of practices and hours of opening.

At Montana State University there was an increase in the number of meetings with department heads, but a formal Advisory Council was not established. Raynard C. Swank, swiftly implementing his own recommendation at Stanford, organized an Administrative Council, encouraged the organization of a Library Staff Association, and began publication of a staff bulletin.

STATUS OF THE LIBRARIAN IN REFERENCE TO LINES OF AUTHORITY

Although in most of the surveys recommendations were made that the librarian's position be clearly defined by statute or in some other formal way, in four surveys (Georgia, Indiana, New Hampshire, and Texas A. & M.) additional recommendations were made regarding the status of the librarian in reference to lines of authority. These recommendations were to the effect that the librarian be directly responsible to the President.

A total of five recommendations was made for the four libraries involved. Three, or 60.0 percent, were achieved completely; two within one year and one during the second year after the survey, while two, or 40.0 percent were not achieved. Considering only the number of libraries involved, the recommendations were achieved in three, or 75.0 percent, of the cases, for both of the unaccomplished recommendations were for one library. All three of the achieved recommendations were considered direct results of the survey by the librarians, and in all cases the librarians agreed with the recommendations. At Texas A. & M. College, where two recommendations were made—one that the librarian be responsible to the President, and the other that he be given the status of a dean and be made director of libraries—the recommendations were not carried out, but the librarian's title was changed to library director.

OTHER GENERAL RECOMMENDATIONS

Eleven recommendations made in seven of the surveys (Alabama Polytechnic Institute, Indiana, Montana, Notre Dame, South Carolina, Stanford, and Texas A. & M.) do not fit any of the above categories very well and thus are being considered separately.

Of these eleven recommendations six, or 54.5 percent, were achieved completely; one, or 9.1 percent, was accomplished to a large degree; two (18.2 percent) were carried out only to a small degree; and two were not achieved. Five, or 55.6 percent, of the accomplished recommendations were achieved within one year after the survey, while three, or 33.3 percent, were achieved during the fifth year. The date of achievement in the other case was not ascertainable.

The librarians stated that three, or 33.3 percent, of the achieved recommendations were direct results of the surveys, and four, or 45.5 percent, were indirect results. The influence of the survey could not be ascertained in two instances. In ten, or 90.9 percent, instances the librarians agreed with the recommendations, and in one case the librarian disagreed.

As direct results of the surveys library departments and services at Alabama Polytechnic Institute and Montana State University were organized into four major departments, and at the University of South Carolina the Department of Library Science was transferred to the School of Education. Other recommendations were of a varied nature, including such items as the holding of staff meetings, the compilation of a staff manual, realignment of certain library operations, and transfer of bookkeeping, order work, interlibrary loans, and instruction in the use of the library from the director's office to appropriate departments.

SUMMARY

It has been shown in this chapter that librarians have been fairly successful in carrying out recommendations concerning the government, administration, and organization of the surveyed libraries. Of 146 recommendations, ninety-five, or 65.0 percent, were carried out in varying degrees. Fifty-nine, or 40.4 percent, were achieved completely; twenty-three, or 15.7 percent, were accomplished to a large degree; and thirteen, or 8.9 percent, were carried out only in a small degree. Thus it can be said that while progress was made in 65.0 percent of the cases, considerable achievement can be cited in 56.1 percent instances.

In forty-eight cases, or 32.9 percent, of the recommendations in this broad category the recommendations were not carried out. In one instance it was not possible to ascertain whether the recommendation had been achieved, and in two others the librarians reported that the recommended practice had been in operation at the time of the survey.

As one might expect, greatest progress was made during the first two years following the survey, during which period 67.4 percent of the achieved recommendations were carried out. Thereafter progress was slower, 6.3 percent being achieved during the third year after the survey, 4.2 percent during the fourth, 12.6 percent during the fifth, and 7.4 percent after five years. The date of achievement could not be ascertained for two, or 2.1 percent, of the recommendations.

In the opinion of the librarians of the surveyed institutions, the survey was influential in the achievement of seventy-four, or 77.9 percent, of the recommendations that were carried out. In forty-five, or 47.4 percent of the cases, the achievement was considered the direct result of the survey. Only in three, or 3.2 percent, of the cases did the librarians consider the achievement in no way the result of the survey. The influence of the survey was not ascertainable in eighteen instances, or 18.9 percent of all the recommendations achieved. Sixteen of the latter eighteen recommendations were made for the Stanford University Libraries.

In 131, or 89.7 percent, of the cases the librarians agreed completely with the recommendations, and in three, or 2.1 percent, instances there was agreement with reservations. Only with twelve, or 8.2 percent of the 146 recommendations, was there complete disagreement on the part of the librarians. Librarians generally attempted to carry out recommendations only to the extent that they agreed with them.

The most serious problem found by the surveyors in the area of government, administration, and organization—if the number of recommendations involved can be a measure—was the degree to which decentralization of library administration and resources had taken place. Sixty-four, or 43.8 percent, of the recommendations dealt with this problem, and the librarians had considerable success in the accomplishment, forty-two, or 65.7 percent, being carried out wholly or in part. The achievement of these recommendations was considered the direct or indirect result of the survey in thirty-one, or 73.8 percent, of the cases.

The libraries were least successful in their attempts to carry out the recommendations concerning the definition in statutes and by-laws of what constituted the library and what were the responsibilities of the librarian, and those that concerned the appointment of professional staff members to academic and administrative committees. In regard to the former, only four, or 28.6 percent, were achieved either completely or to a large degree, while ten, or 71.4 percent, were not accomplished. Three, or 21.4 percent, of the latter category were achieved completely or to a large degree, while eleven, or 78.6 percent, were carried out either to a small degree or not at all.

Fair success was achieved in regard to those recommendations having to do with the establishment and function of the Library Committee and the supervision of larger units within the library's organization. In the former case eight, or 53.3 percent, of the fifteen recommendations were carried out completely or to a large degree—all but three as a direct or indirect result of the surveys, according to the librarians. In regard to the latter category eight, or 66.7 percent, of the twelve recommendations were carried out completely or to a large degree, again indirectly or directly the result of the survey.

Fewer recommendations were made regarding the organization of advisory councils and concerning the status of the librarian in reference to lines of authority. The former were achieved completely or to a large degree in five of the six cases, while in one case, or 16.7 percent, the accomplishment was only to a small degree. In all but one instance achievement was considered directly or indirectly the result of the surveys. In regard to the latter category three (60.0 percent) of the five recommendations were achieved, all of them completely and the direct result of the survey in each case.

The other general recommendations which did not fit any of these categories were achieved with fair success. Seven of the eleven, or 63.6 percent, were carried out completely or to a large degree, while two, or 18.2 percent, were accomplished to a small degree. Except for two cases, in which the influence of the survey could not be ascertained, the achievement was considered the direct or indirect result of the surveys.

FOOTNOTES

[1]Maurice F. Tauber and William H. Jesse, *Report of a Survey of the Libraries of the Virginia Polytechnic Institute for the Virginia Polytechnic Institute, January - May, 1949* (Blacksburg: Virginia Polytechnic Institute, 1949), p. 38.

[2]Louis R. Wilson and Maurice F. Tauber, *Report of a Survey of the University of South Carolina Library for the University of South Carolina, February - May, 1946* (Columbia: University of South Carolina, 1946), p. 30.

[3]Centralization was finally achieved on July 1, 1960, when President Dean W. Malott named Stephen A. McCarthy director of libraries for the entire University, including those on the state campus (Library Journal, 85: 2558 [July, 1960]).

[4]Elmer M. Grieder, "The Reorganization of the Stanford University Libraries," *College and Research Libraries,* 13: 246-52 (July, 1952).

ABOUT THE AUTHOR

—**E. W. Erickson,** Librarian, Eastern Michigan University; Ph.D., 1958, University of Illinois. He is now engaged in a study of Swedish language periodicals in America.

Codifying College Library Policy

by Martha Biggs

The findings of this survey illustrate the environment of informality and uncertainty in which academic library administrators tend to function. Codification of those areas outlined should not be seen as a means to establish the library as a quasi-legal organism within the academic structure or to remove the librarian from criticism; rather as an attempt to provide a position, generally acceptable to the institution, from which effective discussion can take place. If the academic library administrator is to operate on a level other than that of expediency and response to random pressures, the protagonists may well require guidelines.

The college library, by being part of the collegiate institution and under its management, is bound by any general or specific statements in its college charter and by-laws to follow the policy there laid down. Within this structure the policies by which the library is governed must be framed. The library of an institution for higher education is no longer a mere storehouse for scholarly works, preserved without regard to the everyday needs of the students and faculty in the institution. As Raymond Hughes has pointed out:

> The library must at all times be the center of the intellectual life of a college or university, from which the accumulated knowledge of the ages flows freely to each department. If the library is inadequately financed or if its administration is ineffective in making all its resources easily available, the flow of knowledge, past and present, is impeded or wholly cut off from some or from many departments. Unless each department can draw easily and surely, according to its needs, on such knowledge as an adequate library can supply, the institution cannot be maintained at a high level of service[1].

The college librarian must know the relation of his library to the rest of the institution: what provision was made for it in the original documents establishing the institution, what developments have followed, what the position of the librarian is in the hierarchy of the college, and what methods can be used to provide the best service to patrons to further the aims of the institution. While attempting to draw up a policy for the government of a college library it became apparent that very few college libraries have such rules in addition to their charter and by-laws. The present study[2] was made in 1948 to obtain information on this phase of administration for the small college; the questionnaire method was employed, its purpose being to learn the present practice in regard to codes of library government, and to find what a given code should contain.

In choosing the colleges to which to send the questionnaire the major aim was to have as large a group of colleges as possible, representing reasonably similar backgrounds in organization, objectives, and financial control. To accomplish this purpose the following criteria were used: (a) that the college be a four-year degree conferring institution, (b) that it be coeducational, (c) that it be privately controlled, (d) that it be accredited by a recognized regional or state accrediting agency, and (e) that it be in the United States.

No attempt was made to limit the study to schools of a similar size except to eliminate very large universities whose organizational plan and financial background could not be compared with the majority of colleges circularized. The institutions varied in size from 130 to 5000 enrollment, the majority coming within the range from 600 to 1500. By checking two standard guides to colleges, a list of 214 institutions meeting all the above requirements was compiled[3]. Sixty percent of the questionnaires sent to the librarians of those colleges were returned. Only 111 were filled out completely enough to be usable for this study, and from them the following information was obtained.

SOURCE: Reprinted from Martha Biggs, "Codifying College Library Policy," (University of Illinois Library School *Occasional Papers,* no. 14, 1951), by permission of the author.

The design for the questionnaire was drawn with the idea of a logical progression from the beginning of a library to the goals sought for it. The questions asked were divided roughly into the following six groups: (a) the college government and the library, (b) the physical library, its contents and divisions, (c) personnel, (d) administration, including financing and the library's objectives, (e) the library committee, and (f) codes for library government. The interrelation of the questions asked is acknowledged and of course would affect an interpretation of the results. All the factors affecting one institution, however, cannot apply to all those in another institution, so the figures in the tabulation can be regarded only as a means of indicating the frequency of one practice or another in a large number of colleges, and of showing by weight of numbers that one or another practice has been generally accepted.

COLLEGE GOVERNMENT AND THE LIBRARY

All colleges and universities receive their authorization by specific action of the individual states rather than under the authority of one uniform act of the Federal Government. The law varies slightly from state to state and so the form and name of the authorizing act may vary, but the fundamental points with which they are concerned are similar. This accounts for some institutions having charters, others having articles of incorporation, and still others being authorized by special legislative acts. The distinction between such terms as charter, articles of incorporation, by-laws, and statutes is important to a discussion of the organization of the college, and therefore to the government of the library. "The by-laws of a college may be likened to the statute laws of a commonwealth, the charter or articles of incorporation corresponding to the constitution of the state"[4]. The charter of the college is concerned mostly with the general statement of authorization. On the other hand, the by-laws of the governing body are the rules by which the institution operates, and if they fail to contain a reference to the library some other method of directing its policies should be provided.

The first section of the questionnaire was devoted to historical material in order to learn whether the age of the governing regulations had any connection with the fullness with which provision for the library was made. In all cases the mention of the library in these rules could hardly be called informative or helpful to the director of the library. Undoubtedly many of the libraries in those institutions are operating on a policy based largely on tradition and expediency.

No statement can be made to the effect that the date of the charter has a bearing on the fullness of mention of the library. Two colleges with charters granted in 1885 and 1887 mention the librarian as a member of the faculty and authorize library purchases, respectively. Three librarians note the following mention of the library in the charters of their institutions: (a) a 1929 charter, listing the librarian's duties and responsibilities; (b) a 1930 charter revision, including the librarian with the faculty; and (c) a charter revised in 1936, giving among the purposes of the college "to provide libraries". All other librarians reporting, whether their college was chartered as early as 1732 or has a charter revision as late as 1944, state that no mention of the library occurs. Tables 1 and 2 show the

TABLE 1
Types of Legal Instruments Authorizing the Institutions

TYPE OF AUTHORIZATION	NUMBER OF INSTITUTIONS
Charter	46
Articles of incorporation	22
Charter and articles of incorporation	39
Other	1
No answer given	3
TOTAL	111

kind of authorizing acts and governing rules under which the 111 colleges operate. The dates of their founding cover the years from 1732 to 1929, the majority being within the nineteenth century. Several librarians noted that frequent charter revisions had been made.

TABLE 2
Rules of the Governing Body of the Institutions

TYPE OF RULES	NUMBER OF INSTITUTIONS
By-laws	84
Statutes	3
By-laws and statutes	8
Other	4
No answer	12
TOTAL	111

Sixteen institutions in by-laws, statutes, or other rules of the governing body mention the library and librarian, but none covers the topic completely. The fullest mention is contained in the by-laws of a college which lists duties and qualifications of the librarian and requires an annual report to the board of trustees. The other fifteen give one or more of these, or mention the librarian as a faculty member, speak of the formation of a library committee of the board of trustees, or of the faculty. On the assumption that additional codes for library government are a comparatively recent development, the librarians were asked whether any principles of library policy had been codified for their libraries, and if so, in what form this codification was presented. Sixteen answered affirmatively and eight submitted rules or policies for examination, which will be discussed later.

THE PHYSICAL LIBRARY

The term "physical library" was used here to mean the library building or its housing, and the materials owned by the college for library purposes. The library building is not of concern here except as it is the house in which the library is maintained, and thus comes under the managerial jurisdiction of the librarian. On the other hand, the contents of the library produce a picture from which much can be gained in interpreting the problems which will arise in its administration. A definition of the contents of the library does not seem to be generally considered necessary by the librarians reporting. Thirty-six gave no answer to the question, and 51 indicated that there is no official statement of what constitutes library materials. Twenty-four named several places where such statements might be found. College catalogs frequently offer some accounting of such a nature, especially the mention of gifts,

special collections, and numerical accountings of library holdings. Other statements appear in the various codes or working policies mentioned, while still other librarians say that staff handbooks include the information.

Departmental libraries vary in definition from college to college and are administered according to their size, location, and the funds available for personnel. The tabulation in Table 3 shows that in 14 of the 54 institutions which have departmental libraries, academic personnel administer or participate in administering them. Some librarians reported that a collection made on departmental loan and circulated from the office of the head of the department is called a departmental library.

PERSONNEL

Faculty status and rank are important to the librarian who for many years was considered merely a custodian for building and books. The formal distinction between status and rank, as indicated from the answers received, may affect the librarian in a number of ways. Status usually includes attendance at faculty meetings, marching in the academic procession, and allows insurance and pension benefits, as well as giving a certain social standing in the college community; while rank may be the deciding factor in regard to voting in faculty meetings, membership on faculty committees, and participation in certain academic activities. As Table 4 shows, only nine report no faculty status for the chief librarian. The variation in rank can be attributed to many factors involving the pay and education of the incumbent,

TABLE 3

Administration of Departmental Libraries

ADMINISTERING AGENT	NUMBER OF INSTITUTIONS
Chief librarian	19
Assistant librarian	6
Chief librarian and assistants	10
Head of academic department	12
Chief librarian and head of academic department	2
Clerical and student help	2
No answer to question	3
TOTAL	54

TABLE 4

Faculty Status and Rank of Librarians

	CHIEF LIBRARIAN	PROFESSIONAL STAFF
Faculty status	101	62
No faculty status	9	30
No answer to question	1	19
Rank:		
Professor	23	
Associate professor	20	
Assistant professor	20	8
Instructor	6	21
Administrative officer	4	
Librarian	2	
"Varies"	4	12
No rank	3	5
Question not answered	19	16
TOTAL	212	173

TABLE 5

Appointment of Librarians

APPOINTING AGENT	FOR CHIEF LIBRARIAN	FOR PROFESSIONAL STAFF
President	52	25
President and board of trustees	24	9
President and dean	4	2
Board of trustees	19	12
President and librarian		22
Librarian		7
Librarian with approval of board of trustees and president		5
Other (committee of faculty, dean, or committee of board of trustees)	9	4
No answer	3	25
TOTAL	111	111

whether or not the librarian is also a teacher, and the presence or absence of a clear statement of policy by the college concerning the librarian's rank and tenure.

It should be pointed out that the large number of non-answers to the question on the status of the professional staff is due in some measure to the fact that several of the librarians indicated elsewhere that there was no professional staff, assistance being by students or clerical workers. A general tendency in the past two decades to give faculty status and some sort of rank to librarians, even though they do not teach, has grown until now it is recognized by most administrators as the accepted practice. The designation of rank varies from place to place depending on the classification plan used in the institution. It is the practice in the majority of cases for the president of the college to appoint the librarian, with or without consultation with the board of trustees (see Table 5). The professional staff also is appointed by the president in his position as an agent of the board of trustees. In many cases, however, the librarian recommends appointments to the president or appoints with the president's approval. In a few cases the librarian seems to be a free agent in the appointment of the staff.

ADMINISTRATION

Ideally library administration connotes the complete direction of the library and its personnel, including staff selection and direction, acquisition of materials for increasing the resources of the library, rules for the use of library materials by the readers, and the public relations involving liaison between administration, faculty, and students in all matters pertaining to the library. The relation

of the librarian and library staff to the college administration indicates the place of the librarian in the hierarchy of the college. Table 6 shows that 70 percent of the librarians reporting have a definite understanding of their relationship to the college administration, yet only 14 percent show that this information could be gained from the college by-laws or other regulations, since only 16 of the 111 colleges mention the library in their charters or by-laws. Some of the answers in Table 6 are ambiguous. Those who answer "same as faculty member" and "departmental" are probably stating that their responsibility is to the president or dean. "Other" here refers to the board of trustees or to some combination of the first four groups. The table does show, however, that in most of these libraries the lines of authority are clearly established.

TABLE 6

Relation of Librarian and Staff to College Administration

RESPONSIBILITY	NO. OF LIBRARIES
To president	32
To president through dean	9
To dean	4
Member of administrative staff	20
Same as faculty member	8
Departmental	2
Other	8
No official statement	2
No answer	26
TOTAL	111

Table 7 shows the practice in regard to the specific duties allocated to the librarian, and that additional activities not necessarily concerned with library management are relatively few in number. Some librarians suggested that fuller cooperation and understanding could be gained between the faculty and library staff if there were more official contacts of the librarian with the faculty and administration by participation in committee work and curricular planning. It is obvious that the delegation of library duties to others is dependent upon size of staff and the particular training of personnel in special fields, although the need for some continuity in planning is a foregone conclusion. Such planning will vary considerably as staff personnel changes and cannot be specifically stated except for the purpose of indicating lines of authority.

The dependence of library administration upon stated objectives is evident. Indeed, objectives are a prerequisite to planning of any kind, and hence are the substance on which the administrative planning is founded, and so form the basis for the evaluation of library services. Library objectives are primarily the same as those of the college,

TABLE 7

Specific Duties Allocated to the Librarian

DUTIES	LIBRARIANS REPORTING
Administrative only	75
Administrative and library committee chairman	2
Administrative and conferences with president on policy	1
Administrative and instructor	2
Administrative and secretary of educational policies committee	1
No official statement	7
TOTAL	88

and are completely dependent upon them. The library's statement will be expressed in terms somewhat different from those for the college as a whole, since it is the instrument through which those objectives are gained.

Table 8 shows that the statement of library objectives occurs most frequently in the college catalog in the section describing the library and its functions in the college program. It is understandable that the statement given in the catalog would be general in nature. To provide a more useable pattern for the management of the library the general statement should be enlarged and made more specific. If a code of practice is being prepared this statement deserves a prominent place. Statements of objectives appearing in faculty handbooks, working policies and committee re-

ports are also effective, but reach only limited groups. In fact, repetition of the statement of purposes in more than one of these places is worthwhile, so that all interested persons may have access to it. Only 31 colleges reported an actual statement of library objectives in existence for their institutions.

TABLE 8

Location of Statement of Library Objectives

LOCATION OF STATEMENT	NUMBER OF INSTITUTIONS
College catalog	14
Annual report of librarian	1
Faculty handbook	1
Working policy	3
Library committee report	2
Statement given but location not mentioned	10
No statement given	63
TOTAL	94

The library objectives which were examined were those which could be found in college catalogs, or were in the handbooks or codes submitted for examination. They all included general ideas given in greater or less detail as the desires of the writer demanded. Certain ideas common to most of them were that the purpose of the library is (a) to teach the students the use of library materials and materials for research, (b) to encourage good habits of reading and study, (c) to broaden students' interests, (d) to provide the necessary materials to meet curricular and research requirements, and (e) to meet community research needs. The statement often contained some definition of library materials as such, and mentioned the method by which the library expected to attain the objectives outlined.

One of the things that the charter or by-laws seldom fails to contain is a statement on disbursement of moneys for the educational purposes of the institution. In the case of many of these documents the statement is general only, although in a few cases it involves the only mention of the library. In most cases the general statement will indicate the officer of the college who is designated as the college purchasing agent, and it is assumed that all financial matters pertaining to the library will pass through this officer's hands at some point. The question of allocating funds for library materials, however, refers to the segment of financial dealings which is within the librarian's scope.

TABLE 9

Agencies Having Power to
Allocate Funds for Book Purchases

ALLOCATION BY	NUMBER OF INSTITUTIONS
Librarian	36
Library committee	19
Librarian and library committee	34
Librarian with approval of president	6
Librarian, library committee and finance committee	2
Consultation with departments	1
President	2
Business office	2
Treasurer of institution	1
Board of trustees	1
President and comptroller	1
TOTAL	105

Table 9 indicates that in 93 percent of the reporting libraries the librarian is included as a budgetary planner. Participation in budgetary matters generally means, in the case of the library budget, allocation of funds for the purchase of library books and periodicals. Regardless of the source of the funds (whether from gifts, endowment, or fees), that portion set aside for the library will have to be apportioned under certain categories covering replacements, continuations and serials, periodicals, and departmental purchases of books. Assuming that the librarian is a member of the library committee, Table 9 shows that in only 7 of the 105 cases reported does the librarian *not* have any voice in the allocation of funds for book purchases. The practice varies somewhat as to who assumes the advisory capacity in the cases in which the librarian does not have the full budgetary responsibility, or even an advisory vote.

LIBRARY COMMITTEE

The faculty committee on the library is common in the majority of American colleges and has been so from the beginning of their history. Whether it is appointed or elected will be decided by the college governing body in its rule on standing committees, or by the faculty body. Of 98 colleges reporting a library committee, 80 have an appointed committee; 11, elected; 1, a combination of appointment and election; and 6 failed to designate the method of selection. Two of the committees no longer function, although they still exist according to the reporting librarians. The usual functions of such a committee are advisory (86 out of the 98 cases), including liaison

duties between the faculty and librarian. The powers of this committee, however, can be of such a nature as to interfere with the work of the librarian and impair the full effectiveness of the library program. In 43 of these 98 colleges, the library committees are concerned mainly with budgetary matters, and in six of these cases the librarians indicated that the committee recommendations in regard to the allocation of funds for book purchases are mandatory.

CODES FOR LIBRARY GOVERNMENT

The query "Do you feel a need for a fuller definition of library administrative policy?" ended the questionnaire. Of 76 answers to the question, 42 either have such a codification of policy or expressed a need for it. Many librarians added remarks to the questionnaire which contradicted their statement that no additional code was desirable. They undoubtedly felt that the status quo was satisfactory for the present, but visualized certain points on which a clarification of policy might eventually be necessary. Three who answered "no" also said that a clarification on salary and tenure would be helpful.

Not all librarians may have the same type of policy statement in mind, as is evident from the eight submitted for examination. They represent seven different ways of presenting such rules for library government, and vary greatly in the detail and manner of their presentation. The oldest policy reported was prepared in 1929, while several are very recent, having been in use only since 1947 or 1948. Sixteen report codes already in use, and 26 feel the need of such a codification in addition to charter and by-laws provisions. The samples submitted run the gamut from rules and regulations for the library, to operating manuals for a college. The various titles for these codes are indicative of the type of rules used, and in a few cases of the method of presentation to the college administration.

One college has what is called "Working Policy" which is a definite statement of 27 specific duties delegated to the librarian. The listing of these points produces a creed by which the librarian can be guided, and mentions all the points that might be expected to arise. It begins, for example, with "To execute such policies and regulations of the faculty as may be delegated by the president"; includes reference to technical and readers' services, and by whom these services shall be performed; and ends with "To represent the college at professional library association meetings".

A faculty handbook, in mimeographed form, includes along with other regulations of the college the rules and regulations of the library, and instructions to the faculty in regard to reserve collections, interlibrary loans, and routines for book selection and purchase. It is an informative manual, prepared for faculty use, but does not attempt to state policies or objectives except by implication. A similar book, mimeographed also, is entitled "Operating Manual" and is intended as a rule book for the use of the college faculty and staff. It outlines in detail the functions and duties of the various members of the college faculty and administration, as well as giving college aims, by-laws, and policies concerning salary, rank and tenure. The librarian is included in the outline as one of the officers of administration, and his functions are given in some detail with regard to the management of the library, personnel, and reporting to the governing body of the institution.

A small university submitted a copy of recently adopted statutes which refer to the library. Statements are made on the title of the librarian and his duties and responsibilities, the definition of what constitutes the library, the status of the librarian, what group rules on individual cases of tenure and promotion, and a very complete statement as to the composition, powers, and duties of the library committee. A small midwestern college has attacked the problem of codification in a less common though no less effective manner. A faculty committee, working with a committee of the trustees, formulated a constitution for the faculty, to define the duties of faculty members and to put in writing some policies governing the faculty. One short paragraph gives the librarian's duties in regard to the administration of the library, the line of his authority to the governing body of the college, and the authority for purchase of library materials. This general statement is amplified in the by-laws of the constitution, which place the librarian as an administrative officer with faculty status, define library resources, account for the composition and appointment of a library committee, and give its chief duties which are advisory, advisory-budgetary, and liaison.

The "Functions of the Library Committee" submitted by one college as a codification of policy lacks the inclusiveness found in the policies mentioned above, but has done for the committee

what a code might do for the library—laid down aims and objectives to follow. Similarly, the library committee minutes of a small university set down the aims and purposes of the university and lists points for their furtherance. It enumerates the type of material to be provided for student use, e.g., reference, visual aids, and cultural materials for the research pursuits of the college and local communities. It should be noted that these aims are drawn up in addition to the college by-laws which mention administrative duties, personnel, and budgeting powers of the librarian, and together round out an adequate statement of library policy. Several answers to the questionnaire state that with fine library-faculty-administration relations no statement of policy was needed. Another group, small but articulate, said that the fewer the rules for the library the better.

SUMMARY

The foregoing material has been assembled to show whether a written code is desirable. The reader must draw his own conclusions as to whether it is clear that some regulatory statements, though not written down nor codified in any one place by 95 of the reporting librarians, are understood by them as the policy of the library. Since the trend toward a written code is reasonably new, conclusions cannot be drawn as to a preference for one form of policy rather than another. The planning of such a policy must be the result of much investigation, a careful study of the aims and policies of the institution as well as of the charter and by-laws under which it operates. It should be undertaken as a guide to the librarian, with the approval and cooperation of the president, and should be flexible enough to meet the changing needs of the college, but should not be considered as a final and irrevocable rule.

Louis R. Wilson pioneered in this field when he drew up the formal statement of rules for the University of North Carolina Library in 1928, representing the statement of "The policy as inaugurated in 1906-7"[5]. These rules have been followed by many large institutions in drawing up codes or revising statutes and can be os use to smaller ones. In the expectation that some college librarians are interested in planning a policy for library government, the following points are suggested for consideration:

I. A clear definition of the physical aspects of the library

A. What college-purchased materials belong to the library.

B. Whether or not there are departmental libraries, and if so where located and whether under department or library control.

II. An unequivocal statement in regard to personnel.

A. Status and tenure of the director and the library staff, both professional and clerical.

B. The relation of the librarian to the controlling body of the college and the officer to whom he is directly responsible.

C. The librarian's major duties in library administration, and where his authority begins and ends.

D. Any additional duties commonly assigned to him.

E. Right of participation of the whole library personnel in group benefit plan.

III. Objectives of the library in relation to those of the college.

A. As an instructional unit.

B. As an aid to research.

C. Additional services to students, faculty and the community.

IV. A statement concerning library finances.

A. Who makes decisions on budget requirements for purchases of materials for library purposes, and for purchase of library equipment.

B. What role the library committee plays in budget planning.

V. A statement on the library committee.

A. How it is chosen.

B. Its composition.

C. Term of office of its members.

D. Its principle functions, and what absolute powers it may exercise, if any.

It should be emphasized that individual circumstances will preclude the inclusion of certain points, and will govern the physical form of the document. To make such a statement effective an effort should be made to have it accepted officially by the administration, and to have it circulated to all who will be affected by its provisions.

FOOTNOTES

[1] Raymond M. Hughes, *A Manual for Trustees of Colleges and Universities* (Ames, Iowa: The Collegiate Press, Inc., 1943), p. 101.

[2] The full report (32 p.) of this study, in typewritten form, is in the University of Illinois Library School Library.

[3] A list of schools was compiled from Carter V. Good, ed., *A Guide to Colleges, Universities, and Professional Schools in the United States* (Wash., D.C.: American Council on Education, 1945) and this list checked against the listing of A. J. Brumbaugh, *American Universities and Colleges* (Wash., D.C.: American Council on Education, 1948) for accreditation in 1946-1947.

[4] Floyd W. Reeves, *et al.*, *The Liberal Arts College* (Chic.: Univ. of Chic. Press, 1932), p. 64.

[5] *Policy of the University Library* (Chapel Hill, N.C.: Univ. of N.C.) 2 p. (mimeo.).

ABOUT THE AUTHOR

—**Martha Biggs**, Director of Libraries, Lake Forest College; M.S., 1950, University of Illinois. Her major research interests are library administration and library buildings.

Advisory Committee or Administrative Board?

by Stephen A. McCarthy

If the library committee of the faculty was originally instituted as a check on a librarian appointed from the faculty, who might be partial to his own department, its continuance is questionable. More to the point, as the author explains, is the need to establish a board/executive relationship which will provide the basis for translating the policy of the institution directly into an effective library response. This explication of the quality of the various relationships between a board, an executive with a professional commitment, and the larger community centers on the need of the academic librarian for an accepted role definition and a reliable power base.

Writers on the administration of the college or university library commonly give some attention to the library committee, council, or board, as it is variously designated in different institutions. The functions usually assigned to the committee or board include liaison between the faculty and the library administration, formulation of policies for the development of the book collection, advice in the allocation of book funds, and long-range planning for library development. The typical point of view is that the committee or board should have advisory power only.

The fear is expressed or at least suggested that, if the board has more than advisory power, it will concern itself in an undesirable way with the internal and detailed administration of the library. Coupled with the fear of meddling by board members is the stated or implied assumption that wherever you find a library board with more than advisory power you will, of necessity, find a weak, ineffective, and inefficient librarian. The implication seems to be that no librarian worthy of the name would or should consider working in an institution in which the organizational plan provides for a library board with administrative and legislative authority.[1]

This view of the faculty library committee may have its origin in observations of institutions in which the situation was clearly an undesirable one and in which the evils noted were to be found. The same view, in effect, has been expressed by some librarians, who, although their institutions have library committees, prefer not to hold meetings of the committees or, when those meetings must be held, arrange to read extensive reports which completely fill the allotted meeting time. Under such circumstances the committee is an empty formality which has no significance for either the librarian or the members of the committee.

Miss Elizabeth Kientzle has recently surveyed certain administrative aspects of a selected group of college libraries in the Midwest. She reaches the following conclusions, among others:

> Library committees serve primarily in an advisory capacity; few of them have responsibility for administrative functions.
> Library committees are least useful when they intrude in library administration and are most useful when they limit themselves to consideration of general policies and to specific means by which the library might better serve the entire institution.[2]

Miss Kientzle's conclusions thus corroborate the principles which have been laid down in the past. They lead her to this final sentence: "If the library committee is no more than the vestigal remains of a forgotten era in librarianship, whose duties can be better performed by others, then there is no reason for its continued existence."

It is the position of this paper (1) that, if library committees or boards in colleges and universities have become vestigal, the library has suffered a serious loss; (2) that the loss of

SOURCE: Reprinted from Stephen A. McCarthy, "Advisory Committee or Administrative Board?" *Library Quarterly* 22: 223-231 (1952), by permission of the University of Chicago Press and the author.

this governmental instrumentality is to be ascribed to the inability of librarians to appreciate its value and to use it effectively; and (3) that one of the chief contributory factors to the decline of the library committee has been the general insistence that it be advisory rather than administrative.

The distinction between these two terms should be made clear: advisory committees or boards do not have final authority or responsibility, but they do have the power to study, investigate, plan, and make recommendations; administrative boards have full authority and responsibility, and, in addition to the functions of the advisory group, they have the further responsibility of determining policy and of seeing that it is put into effect. There are several further points to be noted about the administrative board: the first is that its authority and responsibility are those of the unit, not of individual members; the second is that since obviously a board cannot function in the daily operation of the library, the executive, or, in a sense, the administrative function of carrying out established policies is delegated to the librarian. If these points are clearly understood and observed both by board members and by the librarian, the difficulties suggested by writers on college and university library administration may be minimized, if not eliminated.

A sampling of the textbooks on public administration shows a rather general adherence to the view that boards with administrative authority are undesirable agencies of government. The experts see in the board a slow and cumbersome administrative device: authority divided or fragmented and unable or unwilling to function effectively; individual responsibility shirked or lost in the group; and board action inconsistent with a body in which responsibility is clearly lodged with a single responsible individual. Many examples of the failures attributable to board organization in government are cited by these writers on administration. There is no disposition here to attempt to controvert this view.

Some students of administration see in the administrative board a useful device for the administration of an agency dealing with various groups representing different interests. In such cases it is allowed that a board having more than advisory power may be desirable. Such a board is, first of all, the policy-forming body of the agency, and, secondly, it is responsible for seeing that the interests of all groups are served to the fullest possible extent. Naturally, at times it will be necessary to reconcile conflicting interests. There is reason to believe that this can be done more equitably by a representative group of those directly concerned than by a single individual. Clearly, the actual operation, the day-to-day executive or administrative functions, can be performed only by an administrative officer who represents the board and acts for it.

In the administration of private business, as opposed to that of public agencies, the board has an important place. The board of directors of a corporation certainly has more than advisory power; yet, at the same time, it is not engaged in the daily management of the business. The board of a corporation functions in the manner indicated above: it determines policy; it represents various interests; it authorizes, validates, and reviews many of the decisions of management; but it does not try to operate the enterprise.

It seems possible that, in studying the governing structure of the college or university library, an analysis of the authority and functions of the board of directors of a corporation may furnish a useful guide. It appears that this approach has not been used in the past but, rather, that attention has been focused on what was considered good theory and practice in public administration. The functions of boards of directors of corporations, as described by Baker in his *Directors and Their Functions,* are as follows:

a) The board selects the chief executive and senior officers and makes certain that able, young executives are being developed. Also the board controls executive compensation, pension, and retirement policies.

b) The board delegates to the chief executive and his subordinate executives authority for administrative action.

c) The board discusses and approves objectives and policies of broad corporate significance, such as pricing, labor relations, expansion, and new products, as well as payment of dividends, changes in capital structure, loans, lines of credit, and public relations.

d) The board checks on the progress of the company not only to immediate profits but also as to the discharge of its trusteeship responsibilities. Budgets, reports, inspections, and other controls aid directors in carrying out this function. They serve as the basis for the directors' most effective approach, which is to ask discerning questions from an independent outside point of view. Also, directors arrange for, control, and follow up outside audits and in general maintain vigilance for the welfare of the whole enterprise.[3]

Many of these specific duties do not apply to a library in a college or university; if, however, for the objectives of a corporation the objectives of a university library are substituted and if these objectives are then translated into terms of book collections, services, facilities, and personnel, they would seem to have considerable applicability to college and university libraries. Through this arrangement, centralization of executive authority and responsibility in management is achieved, yet the over-all guidance of the enterprise in the public (i.e., the university community's) interest is assured through the active control exercised by a group of lay members drawn from the community. These board members come from different divisions of the institution, but as a board they act for the benefit of the entire institution, not for the particular division to which they are attached.

Baker, in his study, states that "there are at least four major variations in the way effective boards function on different questions . . . The four types of procedure are indicated by the key concept of what the boards of directors do: *decide, confirm, counsel, review.*"[4]

It would seem that these key words, as well as the more formal statement given above, disclose a broader area of activity than has normally been considered possible or appropriate for a library board. The alternatives have been advisory or managerial, and little effort has apparently been made to examine the possibilities of the situation more closely in an effort to distinguish other useful activities, which, if not developed, may leave important gaps in the organizational structure of a university library. Such gaps, in turn, may permit the development of weaknesses which might otherwise be avoided.

Before it can be shown how the functions ascribed to directors of corporations can be applied to a university library administrative organization, two points deserve comment. The first is concerned with the effectiveness of advisory groups. There are instances in which advisory power has been used skillfully and effectively; in fact, situations exist in which advisory power may become tantamount to legislative or executive power, in

that the organs of authority are guided and controlled by an advisory group. But such situations arise rather infrequently. Much more commonly, advisory groups can express their views and hope to affect the action of legislative and executive authority; they do not command the prestige and influence which assure that their views will prevail. It would appear that this is the status of most library committees having advisory power only. If this comes to be the accepted status of the committee, as understood by committee members, the library administration, and the university administration, then indeed "the library committee is no more than vestigal remains of a forgotten era in librarianship," to quote Miss Kientzle.

It may also be questioned whether there is any analogy between the board of directors of a corporation and the library board of a university. The view may be advanced that, since the objective of a corporation is profit and the objective of a university library is library service of high quality, there is no point in trying to apply to one what is appropriate only to the other. Furthermore, although there are many small corporations, it is true that the rather clear-cut pattern of functions of directors will more commonly be found in the larger corporations. Such enterprises are so large and complex that they dwarf not only a university library but the university as well. The conclusion then might be that is is unreasonable to carry over an administrative device from a large and complex organization to a much smaller one and expect it to work satisfactorily. Such a device might be more elaborate and more detailed than the smaller enterprise would warrant.

This may be a sound objection, but I am disposed to question it. I think that many of the same purposes are to be served in the smaller organization and that, though the need for frequent meetings and long agenda will not exist, the variety of problems to be dealt with may be sufficiently broad in scope to warrant the use of a similar administrative device.

The reasons why boards of directors of corporations have, and must have, more than advisory power are clear. Perhaps some of the reasons why library boards should also have broader powers may be noted and discussed briefly.

The faculty should be deeply concerned about the quality of the book collection, of the services, and of the facilities of the university library, because these materials, facilities, and services are intimately connected with the success of their teaching and research. If faculty members are so concerned, they will accept a share in the responsibility for providing them. They will accept this participation the more readily if appointment to the board carries a full measure of responsibility. Directors of corporations in many instances recognize not only a profit responsibility but a fiduciary responsibility as well. Presumably, one might expect a similar twofold responsibility on the part of a university library-board member, with "profit" translated to mean materials, services, and facilities required by the individual faculty member.

Directors, it must be recognized, frequently do not bring the point of view of an expert to the problems with which they deal. They, or some of them at least, are expected to represent the layman's point of view, to ask penetrating questions, and to bring to the board some specialized knowledge, such as finance, which is deemed useful to the corporation. This would appear to be a prescription for an ideal library-board member in a university.

Although it is by no means new, there is perhaps more general recognition now than there was some years ago of the necessity of securing support for administrative action from those affected by it. Administration by consent is frequently found in government and in business, as well as in universities. Its importance has been learned through bitter experience. In this respect, an administrative board can perform a highly important function for a university library. It can help to test and modify proposed administrative action, if necessary, and it provides a forum in which the full background of administrative action may be presented and discussed. When the decision to act is taken, the university community's acceptance of the decision is more readily secured because the decision is that of its own representatives.

The competition for available funds in most universities is strenuous. There is good reason to expect that the competition will become increasingly severe as demands for personnel, facilities, and services grow and as income fails to keep pace. The library must expect to compete for its funds; it can hardly do otherwise. Yet the library is a service agency; its purpose is ancillary; it does not seek its ends (even such noble ends as a stronger book collection, a

more competent staff, or more adequate facilities) *for itself.* It seeks these things in order to strengthen the teaching and research work of the university of which it is a part. Because in this respect the library is unique, it is important that the presentation of its budget recommendations be the responsibility not of a single individual (the librarian) but, rather, of an administrative board, conscious of its responsibility and determined to press its claims to the utmost. Such a board, working as the group charged by the university with the chief responsibility for the library's welfare, can have a very effective voice in determining the kind of support which the library will receive. As such, the board speaks for the users—the consumers—and does not labor under the handicap of apparent self-seeking.

Although the foregoing arguments in support of an administrative board do not exhaust the case, they are the chief reasons for it, and most other arguments are comprehended under one or another of them.

Turning to a consideration of Baker's key concepts or key words with reference to what boards of directors do, we may now try to determine their applicability to the library board in a university.

Decide

The area of decision for a library board clothed with administrative authority is as wide as that of the board of directors of a corporation, i.e., the board may concern itself with any aspect of the library's operation. A library board which understands the nature of its functions will not, however, interfere with the details of internal management any more than a board of directors will, unless there is trouble. If a bad situation arises, the board not only can but should step in. A library board led by an able chairman can concern itself usefully with matters appropriate to its sphere and its mode of operation and, functioning in this manner, may perform a service which is not provided by any other means.

Among the subjects on this plane on which a library board might well reserve the power of decision are the following:

1. Determination of broad, general policies of operation, particularly as they affect faculty and students.

2. Questions relating to new or additional library space or buildings.

3. Relationships among department and college libraries and between these branch libraries and the central library.

4. Determination of policies to be followed in the preparation of the budget and in the allocation of book funds.

5. Final authority regarding major purchases or major purchasing policies.

Confirmation

The second function noted by Baker may be exercised less frequently in a university library than in a corporation. Under certain circumstances, however, it might tend to include some of the matters noted above as areas of decision. For present purposes, the following items may be considered suitable for confirming action by the board:

1. Proposed budget requests.
2. Proposed book-fund allotments.
3. Solutions for various service problems as developed by the administration of the library and tentatively adopted or proposed for adoption.

Counseling

The third function of directors is one which library-board members can and do fulfill regularly. Advice on all sorts of library problems can be provided by individual board members between meetings, and the reactions of board members may be sought as a sampling or testing device. The special knowledge of individual board members may frequently be drawn on in this way and their assistance secured in dealing with a variety of problems, some of which may never be formally presented to the board.

While it is true that this kind of informal advising can be secured from individual faculty members of a university without the device of a library board, there is some reason to believe that advice is more carefully given when a sense of responsibility is associated with it, such as board membership entails. This is not to imply that sound advice comes only from board members but, rather, to emphasize the importance of the trusteeship principle. Furthermore, after some experience on a library board, a faculty member comes to have a better knowledge of the library and its problems than does the average professor. This combination of experience plus the lay, or public, point of view makes the counseling of library-board members especially valuable.

Review

The function of review occurs normally through the study and criticism of annual and special reports. It is entirely appropriate to a university library board and will take place naturally, if any opportunity for it is given. It can be assured if reports are distributed in advance of meetings and if appropriate items from the reports are included in the agenda.

Lest the conclusion be drawn from the foregoing that the librarian in such a situation has abdicated, it may be useful to recall that this is precisely the way in which many corporations function, although no one concludes that the management of these corporations has retired from the scene. On the contrary, it is very much in evidence and takes a very important part in the deliberations and decisions of the board. The same may be true in a university library situation. The librarian controls the selection and timing of matters submitted for board consideration and the manner in which these subjects are presented. Although any board member may propose topics for the agenda, the librarian is normally in a position to determine the major items for consideration. The manner of presentation, the care with which problems are analyzed, and the soundness of proposed solutions are almost entirely the librarian's responsibility. Both these matters are of the greatest importance in the satisfactory conduct of business with an administrative board. Mistakes in judgment in placing items on the agenda may invite unwarranted interference in internal management; faulty analysis of problems and proposed lines of action that have not been carefully thought out may lead to a lack of confidence in the administrator. Probably much of the dissatisfaction with library boards and committees in universities and colleges has been caused by the librarian's failure to handle the business of board meetings skillfully.

The composition of the library board presents some of the same problems as does the composition of a board of directors. Management must be represented in each case, and it is perhaps not of great importance, so far as a library board is concerned, whether or not this is a voting membership. There is a difference of opinion regarding the number of internal directors that a corporation should have, but in most cases the chief administrative officers are board members. Applied to a university library board, this practice would mean the inclusion of the librarian's principal assistants, and there would seem to be good precedent for extending board membership to these library officers. Perhaps of greater importance, however, is representation from the central university administration. Such representation in the person of the president, the academic vice-president, or the provost is highly desirable; indeed, if it is provided, the library can be assured of a type and quality of understanding in the top echelon of the university administration which can seldom be achieved in any other way. Such representation gives the library board an insight into general administrative policies and problems which enables it to perform its functions in a manner consistent with the general policies; such representation also furnishes an opportunity to present and discuss in some detail, with general board participation, the chief problems confronting the library. It may be objected that the same result can be achieved much more quickly and economically by personal conferences between the librarian and the president or his representative. Actually, this is not the case. The skilful and thorough presentation of problems before the board, the expression of opinions by faculty members as well as by the librarian, and the resolution of different points of view all add up to something more than a personal conference. This "something more" is worth the time and effort it takes to achieve.

There are of course, problems and difficulties connected with this type of administrative organization, as with all administrative arrangements. Obviously, the kind of procedure outlined here is slower and more cumbersome than direct administrative action by the librarian or by the librarian and president. This is seldom as serious an objection as it might seem. For one thing, although by this procedure more time may be required to reach a decision and a policy, the decision, when reached, and the policy, when adopted, tend to be sound and their initiation and maintainance to present less difficulty than do actions and policies adopted after less careful scrutiny. Furthermore, if the president or provost is chairman of the board, decisions can be made quickly in emergencies and the entire matter submitted to the board for confirmation at the first opportunity.

Critics of administrative boards have maintained that authority and responsibility tend to be divided in such a way that no one exercises authority or discharges responsibility. Such a situation may arise but need not, as we can see from the analogy of the corporation. Both management and the board of directors have their respective roles of authority and their areas of responsibility; neither necessarily invalidates or vitiates the other; there is more than enough for both to do, each operating in its own appropriate area. The same may be true in a university library organization. The librarian is held fully responsible for getting results within adopted policies; he is expected to initiate policy; he is required to analyze problems and propose solutions; and he bears, in relation to the board, much the same relationship as does the president or manager of a corporation to the board of directors. If he is not reasonably successful in meeting the tests of developing and maintaining this relationship at a satisfactory level, a change is in order.

The administrative-board form of organization places on the librarian the same kind of task which corporation management assumes. Complex problems must be analyzed, and proposed solutions must be presented with clarity and brevity. These presentations must withstand, at times, rather severe questioning, and the required answers must be produced, or action cannot be taken. Because the inquiries come from several board members rather than from one person and because various approaches may be employed, this kind of scrutiny is frequently more searching than the questioning which a single administrative officer might undertake. There is no disposition to make light of this procedure. The view may be advanced, however, that this course of action can result in more thorough analysis of problems and more careful formulation of proposed policies. If it does so, the procedure is justified.

In the relationship between library board and librarian, as envisaged here, there is always the possibility of disagreement on questions of major policy. Perhaps, on certain occasions, such an outcome is unavoidable. However, the librarian can often deal tactfully with issues on which there is a serious difference of opinion, by taking the time and trouble to insure a full understanding of the problem and by timing its appearance on the agenda. Relatively little experience is required to demonstrate the importance of timing in human affairs. Proposals that were once unthinkable may gain common acceptance at a later date. Members of administrative boards have the same ability to change their minds as do other people, and it is, of course, part of the librarian's job to assist and promote some changes.

Administrative boards, like other human agencies, may sometimes include members who are inclined to be meddlesome. Again, it is part of the librarian's job to deal with the situation. If a suggestion is good, it should be adopted with thanks. If it is dubious, it should be presented to the full board. The manner of presentation and the recommendation of the librarian should help to convey to the meddler the inappropriateness of his interference.

These are by no means all the problems or difficulties of this type of administrative organization, but they are the ones most commonly ascribed to it. While they do not admit all of easy and sure solutions, they are not insurmountable.

The question may well be asked: Does any such library board exist? So far as I am aware, the answer is "No," although there are perhaps some library committees and library boards which may function in a manner similar to the one delineated.

In most universities, as in other institutions, there is an understandable tendency to concentrate administrative authority in the hands of individuals. As applied to the library, such a development may have advantages, but it has also the possible disadvantage of isolating the library from the faculty, thus cutting it off from that group which should have the greatest interest in it, which has the ability to give it valuable assistance, and which can furnish its strongest supporters.

There is little likelihood of reversing the general trend, whatever one's opinion of it. It is more useful to consider how some of the advantages of the board-management relationship may be secured or retained. The most obvious way is to try to develop between the librarian and the existing library committee or board the kind of relationship and method of operation described above. In most institutions this can be done if the librarian is interested and skilful in planning and guiding the operation. In this way, even without legal status, a library board or committee can be developed into the valuable and useful instrument that it was intended to be. A second way in which desirable administrative procedures and devices might be introduced is for librarians and writers on library administration to broaden their horizons and explore the techniques of other fields. Business and government are constantly developing new administrative methods and adapting old ones to new uses. Many of them may have significance for university library administration.

FOOTNOTES

[1]Cf. Guy R. Lyle, *The Administration of the College Library* (2d ed.; New York: H. W. Wilson Co., 1949), pp. 47-52; William M. Randall and Francis L. D. Goodrich, *Principles of College Library Administration* (Chicago: American Library Association, 1936), pp. 28-29, 83-85; Louis Round Wilson and Maurice F. Tauber, *The University Library* (Chicago: University of Chicago Press, 1945), pp. 31-32.

[2]Elizabeth Kientzle, "The College Librarian and the College Library Committee," *Library Quarterly*, XXI (1951), 120-26.

[3]John C. Baker, *Directors and Their Functions* (Boston: Harvard University, Graduate School of Business Administration, 1945), pp. 131-32.

[4]*Ibid.*, pp. 16-17.

ABOUT THE AUTHOR

—**Stephen A. McCarthy**, Executive Director, Association of Research Libraries; Ph.D., 1941, University of Chicago. The author served as Director of Libraries, Cornell University, 1946-1967. His primary interests are in library administration, library building, cataloging and classification.

IV
FINANCING THE LIBRARY

As a significant and regular competitor for resources within the academic community, the library has historically depended upon the mystique of its function, the good will of the resource allocators, and the intuition of the librarian. However successful this was, library expenditures do not necessarily vary in direct relation to increased enrollment, expanded academic programs, or other factors which might suggest the need for considerably greater funds. Yet if the percentage of the increase to the library has remained relatively fixed, the dollar total has reached a magnitude that suggests to the academic administrator the need for analysis. The request for the librarian to justify library expenditures is valid. In spite of the obvious difficulties in determining the cost effectiveness of the library in terms of the variety of the services and materials it supplies, the appraisal of relative needs, and the problem of interpreting data, the library should at a minimum be able to characterize and measure library functions in explicit formulations. Unless this is accomplished, the library will not establish itself as an intelligent ingredient in the determination of academic priorities, but will instead find it increasingly difficult to justify its mandate economically.

Libraries
A Memorandum by the Author of
"Financing Higher Education in The United States"

by John D. Millett

The following two items provide considerable insight into the attitude of academic administrators toward libraries as consumers. Considerably more attention must be given by the academic library administrator to equating and articulating library functions in terms of academic programs if these library responses to teaching and research are to be considered as of other than specious necessity.

Although the total cost of library activities for 1950, as shown in Table 24, was only about 53 million dollars, and although this amount represented only 4 percent of the "educational budget," or 3 percent of the group of expenditures labeled "educational and general," nonetheless library costs have been under great pressure in recent years. Again and again at the institutions we have visited we have found dissatisfaction with and confusion about the library services of higher education.

The library expenditures of institutions of higher education did expand between 1940 and 1950. The expenditures per student increased in this period as well. Yet with mounting costs of library materials and with rising operating costs, higher education was probably spending no more per student on library service in 1950 than in 1940; at private universities and private liberal arts colleges the rate of expenditure per student undoubtedly did not keep pace with rising prices.

At the outset it should be clear that library expenditure is an integral part of the cost of the educational programs of colleges and universities. Higher education requires books and other materials and reading facilities in order to achieve its purposes. Certainly there can be no higher education worthy of its name without adequate library service.

TABLE 24
Library Expenditures, 1930, 1940, 1950

	1930	1940	1950
All institutions	$9,391,367	$18,314,122	$52,706,978
Public	3,268,733	9,202,151	26,416,957
Private	6,122,634	9,111,971	26,290,021
Universities	6,302,531	10,872,012	33,131,896
Public	2,766,593	6,111,112	17,907,153
Private	3,535,938	4,760,900	15,224,743
Liberal arts colleges	2,318,873	4,211,307	10,829,179
Public	197,289	780,062	2,280,053
Private	2,121,584	3,431,245	8,549,126
Professional schools	495,419	2,498,202	6,617,203
Public	121,669	1,841,596	5,027,404
Private	373,750	656,606	1,589,799
Junior colleges	274,544	732,601	2,128,700
Public	183,182	469,381	1,202,347
Private	91,362	263,220	926,353

SOURCE: Reprinted from John D. Millett, *Financing Higher Education in the United States* (New York: Columbia University Press, 1952), pp. 122-126, by permission of the publisher and the author.

Library administrators and others are beginning to realize that the library service for higher education involves two different needs. Undergraduate liberal and professional education requires a general reading collection where the most recent books and other literature, relevant general reference materials, and standard (or land mark) works can be readily available to the student. The other need is for a research collection which will provide extensive resources in government documents, foreign literature, and all kinds of historical materials needed by the graduate student and the scholar. Needless to say, the costs of providing these two different services are very great indeed.

We have found that many colleges and universities do not carefully distinguish between their general reading collection and their research collection. Every college and university must have a general reading collection for each of its various educational programs. But such a collection needs constant review and weeding out. There is little purpose in preserving outdated textbooks and monographic literature of forty and fifty years ago; there is a place, of course, for the small number of works in any field of study which deserve the appellation "land mark." Some colleges and universities are spending so much money taking care of their old volumes that they have too little funds with which to purchase new books. Yet it is the current literature the general student needs most to read: the new volumes which bring together past research into some kind of systematic whole and the new monographs which present the results of present-day research at the frontiers of knowledge.

One study of a liberal arts college library of 180,000 volumes found an estimated 60,000 volumes which had not been used by a single student in the past five years and 20,000 volumes which had not been used in the past 25 years. Yet this library was complaining of a lack of space and was letting book stacks encroach upon student reading space. Librarians constitutionally hate to throw anything away. They always fear that the book they discard will be the one someone wants next month, and they are always chagrined when they cannot at once produce what is wanted. Moreover, the accrediting associations have tended to "rate" colleges by the number of volumes in the library, regardless of whether anyone uses them or not. Librarians rate the importance of their jobs and examine their salary scale in the light of the size of their book collections, the number of their employees, and their total expenditures. The librarian profession as such puts little emphasis on economy; the pressure comes from college presidents and deans when they make up the annual budget.

We have found general agreement as a rule of thumb that a "good" liberal arts college ought to operate with a book collection of under 100,000 volumes, many of which would be duplicates. Moreover, this figure should be an outside limit; the number might be kept considerably lower by a judicious policy of weeding out and discarding. Altogether, there are some 140 college and university libraries in the United States with more than 100,000 volumes.[1] Many of these collections are probably too large for their purposes.

The report of the public library inquiry sponsored by the Social Science Researcch Council from 1948 to 1950 pointed to a number of phases of library operations which require constant analysis by library administrators: (1) wasteful use of professional and other personnel in circulating activities, (2) book selection policy, (3) the cataloguing process, (4) practice of discarding and storing obsolescent materials, (5) handling of periodical literature, and (6) better statistical data on operations[2]. All these needs exist in college and university libraries.

Of recent experiments in college library operations which we have observed, we have been especially impressed by the new Lamont Library for undergraduate students at Harvard University. Here the emphasis has been placed upon comfortable reading accommodations for the student, ready access to books, and minimum operating costs. The volumes have not been catalogued, but classified by broad subject-matter groups and arranged in alphabetical order by the authors' names. The students find their own books; they receive little reference or circulating assistance. The only check is maintained at the door. Incidentally, we may note here that pilferage has been a very great library problem since the end of the Second World War and has added to operating costs because of guard and book replacement charges.

There is a growing tendency at large universities for individual schools and colleges and even some departments to operate their own library facilities. Thirty years ago library centralization was one of the great economy programs at universities; centralization was expected to prevent unnecessary duplication in materials and wasteful utilization of facilities and personnel. Today, the pressures of space and costs have tended to encourage more decentralization. Moreover, as parts of a university build up their own teaching facilities in separate clusters, they tend to want their own libraries as well. Law schools have always insisted upon separate law libraries because of the peculiar nature of their reference needs. Medical schools have done the same. Some degree of decentralization in library operations seems satisfactory as long as central oversight and central cataloguing of reference and research materials are maintained.

This brings us, then, to the peculiar purpose of the university library: to serve as a center for research materials. There are at present eight university libraries in the United States with more than 1,000,000 volumes each. Other university libraries are beginning to approach these proportions. The book collection at Harvard doubled from 1923 to 1943; indeed, it has been estimated that many library collections are growing at that rate, being doubled every twenty years. If this were to continue unchecked, and if much more income is not provided universities, they will soon be in the position of having to drop one or two professors each year in order to keep up the library. This is an obvious absurdity.

The larger universities in the country have been alert to the problem; but ways to limit cost increases have not been easy to devise. Apart from some minor experiments in microfilming newspapers and typescripts (which is also costly), the principal proposal put forth by library administrators has been cooperation among a number of institutions in creating centralized deposit centers. The first experiment of this kind was the New England Deposit Library, which began to function in 1942.[3] Although mostly utilized by Harvard University,

four other colleges and universities in the Boston area have used its facilities for storing books and other materials. The most elaborate effort at cooperative storage of little-used library volumes is the Midwest Inter-Library Center, located on the campus of the University of Chicago and opened in 1951. Thirteen different universities have joined together in this project, which was made possible by grants from the Rockefeller Foundation and the Carnegie Corporation. A Northeast Regional Library has been proposed by librarians of seven universities and the New York Public Library, but has failed of realization because of financial and other difficulties. We should also mention the "Farmington Plan," started in 1948, whereby fifty-two cooperating research libraries set up a program for purchasing library materials in foreign countries. It is expected in this way to buy at least one copy of all foreign books and publications useful for research purposes, which will then be available on loan to all participants.

The future costs of the research library are a very real concern for higher education. In practice, the idea of a central deposit center has encountered several practical obstacles, such as location, type of service to reader, allocation of financial support, agreement upon what to store, the identification of duplicate materials to be discarded, and arrangements for rapid transmission of materials to a requesting library. To some the library center seems likely to become a dead-storage warehouse rather than a library. Nonetheless, some increased degree of cooperation among universities in operating research library centers is the only practicable program thus far suggested to reduce future library costs. Until some better ideas are developed, this one deserves more active prosecution and support than it has thus far received.

It is safe to predict that library operating costs will grow as one of the important expense problems of both colleges and universities.

FOOTNOTES

[1] Robert D. Leigh, *The Public Library in the United States* (New York: Columbia University Press, 1950), p. 71.
[2] *Ibid.*, pp. 182-84.
[3] Thanks to the courtesy of Herman Fussler, librarian of the University of Chicago, we have consulted a master's essay giving the history of this library prepared by Francis Xavier Doherty in 1948.

ABOUT THE AUTHOR

—**John D. Millett**, Chancellor, Ohio Board of Regents; President, Miami University, 1953-1964; Ph.D., 1938, Columbia University. His academic training is in political science and in public administration and he has taught in these areas. His major research interests are in governmental planning, the management of public agencies, and the administration of institutions of higher education.

A Memorandum by the Author of "Financing Higher Education in the United States"

by John D. Millett

I am very much interested in the report that consideration is now being given to the possibility of making a study of the role of the research library in our larger universities. I believe such a study would be quite useful.

I have been disturbed to learn that some of the comments made in my report to the Commission on Financing Higher Education should have been misinterpreted. I should like to call attention to a statement made at the very outset of this discussion, where I declared, "At the outset it should be clear that library expenditure is an integral part of the cost of the educational programs of colleges and universities. Higher education requires books and other materials and reading facilities in order to achieve its purposes. Certainly there can be no higher education worthy of its name without adequate library service." In addition, I called attention to the obvious fact that library service for higher education involves two different needs. One of these is for the general reading collection necessary to the instructional program, and the other is for a research collection to meet the needs of the graduate student and the university scholar. I further pointed out that the costs entailed in these two different services were quite substantial. I also suggested that in many institutions there had been a failure to distinguish between a general reading collection and a research collection.

I should have made clear in a subsequent paragraph on page 123 that my statements about the library profession were statements which were made to me by a sizable number of college administrators. I certainly did not intend to suggest that this was my own personal evaluation of librarians. Indeed, in the course of my investigation, I was astounded to discover the wide gulf which had apparently developed between college administrators on the one hand and librarians on the other. I have a feeling that librarians themselves might give more attention to this situation. It may well be that I talked with the wrong administrators and visited the wrong institutions. I wish to point out, however, that I personally visited all but two of the universities belonging to the Association of American Universities, as well as fifty or sixty liberal arts colleges.

I suspect that a part of this gulf has occurred because of the excellent service librarians have rendered their colleagues university circles. I gather that librarians have exercised substantial initiative in purchasing monographic literature and in acquiring various collections as they have been made available. Oftentimes, the instructional staff and the research scholar appear to be unaware of materials which have been acquired by the library of their own institution. Furthermore, the academic staff appears to be little informed about library costs or about ways and means of rationalizing the handling of research materials.

I should like to suggest that any systematic attack upon the problem of the cost of the research library should be made a joint enterprise of librarians, administrators, and scholars. I concluded from my own brief investigation in this field that a greater degree of cooperation among outstanding universities in operating research centers was the only practical program thus far suggested for meeting the problem of library costs. If a new group could devise some better method of attacking this problem, I am sure its suggestions would be most welcome. If there is no other satisfactory solution, then more attention will have to be given to the

SOURCE: Reprinted from John D. Millett, "A Memorandum by the Author of 'Financing Higher Education in the United States,'" in Association of Research Libraries, *Problems and Prospects of the Research Library* (New Brunswick, N.J.: Scarecrow Press, 1955), pp. 23-25, by permission of the publisher and the author.

ways and means of making inter-university library cooperation more effective.

I think the evidence which has accumulated in the last two years still bear me out in my conclusion that library operating costs remain one of the important cost problems confronting our colleges and universities. Any additional consideration which may result in some improved handling of this situation would be most welcome throughout higher education.

Effect of "The Millett Report" on UCLA's Plans

by Andrew H. Horn

As described in this article, "The Millett Report" had considerable impact on the decision-making processes of appropriating agencies. The budget action is an example of how public policy can be expected to react to the examination of discrete agency practices when these are not defined in terms of an understood and accepted role.

Publication of the "Millett Report" (John D. Millett. *Financing Higher Education in the United States.* The Staff Report of the Commission on Financing Higher Education. Columbia: 1952. Esp. pp. 122-126) late in 1952 seems to have been the principal reason for the failure of the California Legislature to approve funds in 1953/54 to build UCLA's badly needed stack annex. Unless we are able to answer Millett's charges which challenge the competence of librarians as administrators and planners, we can expect further difficulties in defending both our operational and our capital improvements budgets. Our conviction is that university librarians everywhere had better fortify their chancellors and presidents (who evidently require more specific data) to meet the arguments of trustees, regents, and legislators fresh from a reading of Millett:

1. Without a clear-cut distinction between the functions of college, university, research and public libraries;
2. With the impression that: "Librarians rate the importance of their jobs and examine their salary scale in the light of the size of their book collections, the number of their employees, and their total expenditures. The librarian (sic) profession as such puts little emphasis on economy; the pressure comes from college presidents and deans when they make up the annual budget." (Millett, p. 123);
3. Convinced that, since librarians have failed to do so, more competent administrators should put an optimum size on library buildings, collections and budgets, AND;
4. Of the opinion that the problems of growth, finance and cooperation have not as yet been investigated by librarians.

Although we, in California, had ample opportunity to justify our requests, explain the reasons for our needs, and even to offer rebuttal to Millett—still the Millett report was in print (as such it reached persons we could not, and could be quoted or quoted out of context) and it had the authoritative weight of coming from the Commission on Financing Higher Education. Unless the Commission is willing to allow ARL to write an additional volume for its series of reports, on Libraries and Higher Education in the United States, it seems doubtful that the damage will ever be undone. Scattered articles will not have the impact of a comprehensive study; neither will a separate volume be as effective as one connected with the Commission's work.

THIS IS WHAT HAPPENED IN CALIFORNIA

December, 1952

President Sproul suggested to Librarians Coney and Powell that they study the Millett report carefully, since it would probably be considered in connection with library budgets and planning.

January, 1953

Librarian Coney furnished President Sproul comments on the library section of the Millett report, at the President's request. Later in the month, the librarians and assistant librarians of the Berkeley and Los Angeles campuses met in Berkeley for a general coordination discussion. At this meeting the Millett report was discussed, but there seemed to be nothing further we could do at the time. We had given the President the information he needed to appear before the Regents' Finance Committee; and we had been

SOURCE: Reprinted from Andrew H. Horn, "Effect of 'The Millett Report' on UCLA's Plans," in Association of Research Libraries *Minutes* 41 (1953), Appendix 5, pp. 38-42, by permission of the publisher and the author.

able to refer to (and answer) the Millett report in our internal budget requests. Events proved that we had done a fairly effective job in convincing our university administrators and Regents who proposed no cuts of significant amounts in our operating budgets and did not reduce the UCLA library stack from the building budget. The job of selling the University's budget to the Legislature is, of course, out of our hands.

Late in January the Regents met and decided to have a survey made of the financial problems of higher education in California. It was evident that the Regents wanted to know how we measure up to the standards and suggestions coming out of the reports of the Commission on Financing Higher Education in the United States. By this time, evidently the Regents had, or knew about, the *Analysis of the Budget Bill of the State of California for the Fiscal Year July 1, 1953, to June 30, 1954,* a report prepared each year by the Legislative Auditor to the Joint Legislative Budget Committee.

March, 1953

Librarian Powell had been studying the *Analysis of the Budget Bill* with growing concern because the Legislative Auditor had linked the building program of the state college libraries with that of the University, which for 1953/54 was the UCLA stack annex. Powell wrote to the Chancellor at UCLA pointing out again that the Millett report was not adequate or even correct insofar as it dealt with university libraries, and emphasized: "My real concern, however, is over a rather invidious linking of the UCLA campus library with those of the state colleges campus libraries. The two types of institutions are not comparable . . ." By now we were getting concerned, not only about our operating budget but also about our badly needed and long overdue stack annex.

April and May, 1953

In April the Chief Administrative Analyst of the Division of Budgets and Accounts of the Department of Finance of the State of California wrote to Arthur Hamlin, asking if the Association of College and Research Libraries would supply information on the optimum size of college libraries. The Department of Finance was concerned about size, staffing,

and operating standards in the libraries of the various state colleges. Specific reference was made to the Millett report. Hamlin furnished an excellent reply, pointing out what was wrong with Millett's conclusions—indicating also the different levels of responsibilities of different kinds of college and university libraries. Later on (in May), Hamlin sent an advance copy to the Administrative Analyst of the review of the Millett report which has since appeared in *College and Research Libraries* (July 1953, pp. 342-344).

The Administrative Analyst (not the same man as the Legislative Auditor) also consulted Librarian Coney. He was obviously going about things in a very intelligent manner, and he was studying the state college libraries, not those of the University.

It should be understood that the several state colleges in California have no direct connection with the University of California. The state colleges (there are 10 of them) fall under the State Department of Education; the University of California (there are eight campuses) are quite distinct and are under the jurisdiction of a Board of Regents which board has no responsibility to the Department of Education. The Administrative Analyst was not linking the state college libraries with those of the various campuses of the University; but the Legislative Auditor had already done so by implication, and the link was the Millett report. We feared that the legislators would also link them, and they did.

Late May and Early June, 1953

In the closing days of the legislative session, the UCLA library stack annex was eliminated from the 1953/54 budget, as were all provisions for stacks in the state colleges library buildings. The Millett report arguments about limiting library size by weeding and discarding had stuck in the minds of the men who made the decisions. The University's representatives who were called upon to defend the building program or to furnish additional information did a good job, and for a few days the UCLA stacks were "in again, out again". It was a very close decision; but it went against us.

June 8, 1953

At the Chancellor's request, the UCLA Library furnished a statement on the long-range planning for housing books and other instructional materials. Here again, we attempted to show that the Millett report was in no way adequate. We reviewed the work of the University of California Library Council (consisting of the chief librarians of the eight campuses and the dean of the library school) in coordinated planning and in considering storage-library facilities. We also indicated that we would bring the matter of the Millett report to the attention of ARL at its June 21st meeting. Most of the report, however, dealt with a review of UCLA's 25-year plan of library building.

June 12, 1953

Librarian Powell being out of town, Associate Librarian Horn was asked to appear before the President's Administrative Advisory Council to discuss the problem of housing books and other instructional material. Briefly, Horn's report was:

THE PROBLEM

The growth of university and research libraries presents the prospect of planning for "open end" collections because we cannot predict the exact pattern of future teaching or the nature of future research—these are factors of *infinite* potential. Against this must be balanced the problem of planning for the housing and servicing of library collections; and here rather definite factors come into play: the amount of ground space which can be allocated to library buildings—the maximum size and cost of the buildings themselves—and the library operating budget to develop, augment, organize and service the materials of teaching and research.

The above dilemma has been an object of main concern to research librarians for twenty years and more. It is an increasing concern to all university administrations, including that of the University of California—viz., the Millett report, the study recently proposed by the Regents, the questions raised in connection with the State Colleges and the University in the last Report of the Legislative Auditor, and the various discussions in the Library Council of the University.

THE SOLUTION

References

Horn discussed the following briefly, these being the materials which came to his mind at the spur of the moment. The July issue of the *Library Quarterly* had not yet reached us.

Fremont Rider. *The Scholar and the Future of the Research Library.* 1944.
Keyes D. Metcalf. "The Denver Expanding Demand for Materials and the Threatened Decline of Support. How Shall the Gap be Filled?" in *Changing Patterns of Scholarship and the Future of Research Libraries.* 1951.
Ralph R. Shaw. *From Fright to Frankenstein.* 1953.
Ralph D. Esterquest. "The Midwest Inter-Library Center," in *Journal of Higher Education* (January, 1953). "Book Storage and the Microcard," in *Library Journal* (November 1, 1952).
Lawrence S. Thompson. "Research Libraries on the Bargain Counter," in *Midwest Journal* (Summer, 1952).

General

The Library profession has attacked the problem, bit by bit, over the past several years. All of the "solutions" so far proposed are partial, each with its merits and each with its limitation; and the suggestions all rest upon a broad basis of cooperation among libraries and universities which is as yet not fully realized. The several proposals, and others which we can expect to be made in the future, are probably the factors which will combine to cause a flattening of the "exponential curve of research library growth" (from Ralph Shaw's article). Geographical concentration of resources is one of the overall planning factors of prime importance, which must be kept constantly in mind while the several elements of the solution are being considered in connection with any specific institution.

The Elements of the Solution

1. Devices for bibliographical control
2. Cooperative cataloging and indexing
3. Operational economics at the expense of traditional services
4. "Weeding" and selective acquisitions
5. Cooperative acquisitions policies and joint purchases
6. Interlibrary lending
7. Micro-reproduction, micro-publication, and electronic devices

8. Segregation of research collections from teaching collections

9. The attitude of the common pool of scholarship and scholarly resources

10. Storage libraries and inter-library centers

June 16, 1953

It was evident that the University of California administrators wanted to study the problem of storage libraries, and especially wanted to know how we could segregate active from storage collections. Horn and Gordon Williams reported to Chancellor Allen on the studies made to date at the GLS (Williams, Meier, Quinn, Fussler)

which could guide us in plannning for storage operations.

June 21, 1953

At the ARL meeting held at the Clark Library, Horn reported on the problems we had been having as a result of the Millett report. Other universities may already have had parallel experience, some may be facing them next year. These questions might well be included in the agenda of the special conference on research library problems which Mr. Metcalf is proposing.

ABOUT THE AUTHOR

—**Andrew H. Horn,** Dean and Professor, School of Library Service, University of California at Los Angeles; Ph.D., 1948, University of California. At the time this article was written he was Associate University Librarian, University of California at Los Angeles. His major interests are in the history of books and libraries, rare books, college and university library administration, and bibliography.

The Cost of Keeping Books

by Raynard Coe Swank

The statement made here as to why an academic library costs money is simple and comprehensible. It directs itself to the characteristics of research and the book, as well as to factors affecting the operational response of the library. Notwithstanding the savings in costs which might be effected internally, fundamentally the significant expense of the academic library can be attributed to the idea the institution has of itself and of the role the library plays in fulfilling that idea.

My job at this session is to say what university libraries do and why they cost so much. I am supposed also to point out some of the major financial problems of the library. To keep within thirty minutes, I shall have to generalize a good deal, and I shall have to omit all mention of library cooperation and specialization, which are the topics of the next session.

I take it also that I should help to bridge the gap of misunderstanding that often separates the library from the faculty and administration. There never was a great library that was not built by both scholars and librarians, working together—or let us say by people with both interests at heart; indeed, they are a single interest. Yet it seems to grow increasingly difficult for the faculty to diagnose the ailments of the library and for librarians to interpret the needs of the faculty. More than ever before, the closest possible rapport is needed. Librarians cannot attain goals that they do not comprehend or about which the university has failed to advise them. I hope that my remarks, although directed toward costs, will evince the great dependence of librarians upon their faculties and administrations.

The library supplies books to the faculty and students. That sounds embarassingly simple, considering how complicated the service has become. The service has become so complicated, however, and therefore so costly, because university programs and books are complicated. Those are the elements of the library problem, and before talking about library operations as such I should like to say something about each of these elements.

It needs to be said first that the library derives its very nature from the university. It has, and should have, no purpose of its own, no life apart from the institution it serves. It is what it is, does what it does, and costs what it costs primarily because the university has needed and wanted it so.

The library has, indeed, grown up with the university. It did not exist, as we know it, in the old New England college, but arose when the college became a university by assuming the functions of research, graduate study, and professional education—especially research—in addition to liberal education. Some of our problems today, like a number of other university problems, can be traced, perhaps, to the mixture of these functions in a single organization. What kind of library, for example, is appropriate for college freshmen? Certainly not a million-volume research library. And what have we done to the research library in the effort to make it comprehensible to freshmen?

It has been estimated that only a hundred thousand or so volumes should satisfy the limited and relatively stable needs of college teaching, aside from the research needs of the college faculty. Recognizing that possibility, librarians have been experimenting for a number of years with the separation of these books from the research collections, not only to provide the college with a more appropriate service but also to save the research li-

SOURCE: Reprinted from Raynard Coe Swank, "The Cost of Keeping Books," in Association of Research Libraries, *Problems and Prospects of the Research Library* (New Brunswick, N.J.: The Scarecrow Press, 1955), pp. 41-55, by permission of the publisher and the author.

brary for the scholar. Such experimentation has seemed reasonable and good, except that, so far, the withdrawal of the college library has not led to appreciable economies, or modifications of service, in the research library. A new service has merely been added to the old.

It seems to me that any basic consideration of the library problem must begin with the functions of the university and the kinds of library service that each requires. It should include the compatibility of these functions in the library, and the economics of their fusion or separation. This is the first broad problem I would suggest for investigation.

The notable growth of the library during the last half century, however, must certainly be attributed primarily to research. Indeed, the library expresses with remarkable fidelity the ideals of scholarship that have prevailed in the university since the turn of the century. Let me mention several characteristics of that scholarship that have profoundly affected the library.

First, we have assumed that knowledge is elastic, dynamic, and ever expanding. What better monument than the library could there be to this assumption? Does anyone suppose that the library will stop growing as long as man lives and learns? Knowledge, like the human spirit, we suppose to be infinite.

Second, there is always an inconclusive quality about research. It never seems to arrive at any final state. I once heard a historian define a fact somewhat as follows: A fact is a proposition based on the best evidence critically examined and interpreted. If no fact is final, then no evidence has been finally examined and no interpretation finally rendered. That is why the scholar wants at his command the whole amorphous mass of evidence and interpretation to which he aspires to contribute. With good conscience he can and does admit no limit to the library resources that might help him.

Third, not all faculty members are natural scholars, but they make their contributions anyway. They have to, if they hope to climb the academic ladder. By requiring that teachers contribute not only to the intellectual growth of students but also to knowledge itself, we have reared a race of paper writers, whose works the world over bulk large in the research library. Literally hundreds of thousands of scientific papers are published every year. Even librarians write papers. So, when we worry about the vastness of the library, we need to remember who writes the books in the first place. Any forced selectivity of scholarly works for the library may be a richly deserved form of self-judgment.

And fourth, creative activity is unpredictable; it cannot be restricted to arbitrary or even logical definitions of scope. Knowledge simply will not stay classified, nor scholars pigeonholed. For this reason, perhaps, the university's research program, and therefore the library program, tends to remain a vague, elusive sort of thing. The librarian is vulnerable to every imaginable kind of demand from the faculty and has no defense except lack of funds.

These are some of the aspects of the university that make the library what it is today. The mixture of undergraduate teaching and research and, in particular, the characteristics of research have confronted the library with mountainous problems which only the faculty can help to solve. These problems, like those of the scholar himself, are part of the essential pattern of higher education that has evolved since the origin of the modern university.

Books are the other element of the library problem. The quantity of written material produced in recent years is, of course, beyond all belief. Yet mere quantity, contrary to all popular notions, is not the main problem. The real problems derive from the individuality, the diversity, and the multiple uses of written material.

If books were bricks, libraries could handle billions. They could stock them and stack them and dole them out, each like every other. But books are not bricks. Every book, every article, every scribbled note is an individual, different from every other—different in authorship, title, subject, form, or purpose. The library therefore deals not merely in masses of books but in masses of individualized distinctions among books.

Diversity of form—I mean physical form—is another great complication. If only there were just books, how much simpler things would be! But library materials come in a wide variety of packages, and packages within packages, each presenting different problems and requiring special handling. Besides books, there are special publications—journals and monographic series of all kinds and frequencies, tens of thousands of them. There are pamphlets, broadsides, newspapers, and manuscripts; archives, the care of which is another specialty; maps, charts, and pictures. There are microfilms and microprints, motion picture films, lantern slides, film strips, and phonograph records. As though that were not enough, some would also have us collect old furniture, swords, uniforms, and statues. This diversity of physical form, coupled with individuality of content and purpose, explains much of the complexity of the modern library.

The third point about books is the multiplicity of their uses. The library touches upon the work of nearly every faculty member and student in the university—from poets to conchologists, mediaevalists to physicists, freshmen to Nobel prize winners. Books, often the same books, are used in many ways for different purposes. They may be read as literature or as social documents, for information, entertainment, or inspiration. They may be associated by subjects, literary forms, languages, regions, or historical periods. They may be valued for their typography, their illustrations, or their rarity. They may report investigations, or become subjects of investigation. The only thing that exceeds the ingenuity of man in the writing of books is his ingenuity in their use.

The university library, then, must be explained in terms of these two elements: scholarship and books—the ever expanding, inconclusive, unpredictable, paper-writing character of scholarship, and the individuality, diversity, and multiple uses of books. The complex nature of both elements is reflected throughout the library organization. Let us examine now the library as an operation—what it does to provide books for the university program.

I cannot hope to suggest the variety of activities that occur in the library—all, we suppose, of value to somebody. Few faculty members and, indeed, few librarians ever achieve familiarity with the entire operation. There are, however, four library functions that pretty well cover what libraries do. These functions correspond roughly to the four traditional library departments: acquisition, cataloguing, circulation, and reference. Acquisition is the selection and procurement of library resources, the building of the collections.

Cataloguing, or more broadly, bibliographic organization, is the incorporation of these resources, once acquired, into the bibliographic system of the library. Circulation is the physical control of the collections, once acquired and incorporated into the bibliographic system—their care, location, lending, and the like. And reference is personal assistance to individual readers by the library staff.

From the point of view of costs, acquisition is the most blameworthy of all library functions, because all other costs are subsequent to it. If books were not acquired in the first place, they would not have to be catalogued, housed, loaned, and eventually mended. Every time a book is added to the library the university is committed to a series of expenditures that last the lifetime of the book—a series of which the least part is the original price of the ordinary book. Any effort to control library costs in general might well start, therefore, with an attempt to control acquisition.

How many books are enough? It may be possible to limit the number of books for undergraduate teaching, but the only apparent way to limit books for research is to run out of money. As already indicated, the faculty appetite is insatiable, because of the very nature of scholarship. We may add twenty to eighty thousand volumes a year, and never get more than a fraction of the books available. Moreover, if any librarian wilfully sought to limit acquisitions for the mere sake of economy, he would be regarded as a traitor by the faculty—a traitor to both librarianship and research.

Who selects the books? The faculty mostly, and that is as it should be. The faculty know what they need; the library is for them and their students. Yet few faculties can boast of a clear-cut acquisitional program, because of the elusive nature of their own scholarly activities. As a result, the acquisitional program is largely a composite of the individual, sometimes casual, choices of many people. It is a profile of immediate faculty interest, and that interest is frequently inconsistent and spotty. As faculty members come and go, rich collections accumulated through years of devoted effort are often suddenly forgotten. Appalling gaps are sometimes discovered in other fields. Occasionally hobbies are ridden wildly. Perhaps in the long run we could do no better, but this general lack of planning and continuity is expensive.

The library helps to provide continuity; it fills gaps, feeds suggestions to the faculty, and the like. But by and large the acquisitional program is no better than the faculty make it. It succeeds in direct proportion to purposeful, planned faculty participation. Our great collections are almost always built by devoted scholars working hand in hand with equally devoted librarians.

Do we keep all these books forever? We do, for the most part, though some of us would rather not immortalize them all. There is no doubt whatever that our libraries contain much dead wood. Some of it, such as duplicates of old textbooks is thrown away in many cases, but it is more difficult to discard books from a research library than one might think.

There is, of course, the cost of the withdrawal procedure—the cancellation of catalogue records and the like. This is far from negligible. Also, to add a book to the collections the librarian needs the suggestion of only one faculty member—any faculty member; but to withdraw it he needs the concurrence of all faculty members who might claim any conceivable interest in it. Try as he will he is bound to overlook someone; then the fat is in the fire. There is probably no way in which a librarian can arouse faculty suspicion and mistrust more surely than by throwing away the library's books—indeed, the faculty's books—without full faculty approval, individual and title by title. How to do it? I do not know, except by letting the faculty do most of the choosing, so they can blame the inevitable oversights on one another.

The librarian's share of guilt in the accumulation of dead wood is greatest in acquisition by gift and exchange. About half of all books added to some of our libraries are not selected for purchase at all. Some are solicited, some just appear. A great many should be added, but along with the good and relevant material there always arrive tons of stuff that should not. It has often been easier for the library to add almost everything than to select the best and throw the rest out. I think it can be said, however, that librarians, with faculty help, have recently tightened up considerably their selection of "free" materials. No book is ever free by the time it rests on a library shelf.

So libraries acquire books, and more and more books, and the surest way to control library costs in the long run would be to acquire fewer books. The acquisition of books is the second problem we need to study. The third is how to weed the collections of books once acquired but no longer useful.

The second function of the library is the incorporation of books, once they have been acquired, into the bibliographic system of the library. This function is far less well understood by university faculties, and even by librarians, than acquisition, and is harder to explain. But it is absolutely fundamental to the operation of a library.

Whereas the problems of acquisition derive primarily from the nature of scholarship, those of bibliographic organization derive primarily from the nature of books—their individuality, the wide variety of their physical forms, and the multiplicity of their uses. Our catalogues and classifications, together with bibliographies, indexes, and abstract journals try to cope with the entire spectrum of recorded knowledge as approached by a multitude of faculty and students, each pursuing his own special purposes. The bibliographic process is extraordinarily complicated. Even so, faculty members often ask why it costs so much to catalogue books, and librarians ask too. About all that can be honestly said is that nobody yet, either scholar or librarian, has invented a cheaper way to organize the collections.

Librarians have worked hard during the last thirty years to economize in cataloguing—to rid the process of extravagant, though understandable, tendencies toward legalism, perfectionism, and bibliophilic snobbery. Substantial simplifications have been achieved, and rigorous efforts have been made to avoid the duplication in library catalogues of information available in published indexes and bibliographies. Yet there is a limit beyond which such economies are detrimental to the university. There is no point to acquiring books if they cannot be readily found again and used, and there is no point to the omission on important data that students will thereafter have to find for themselves, over and over again.

The problem suggested here is how much the library should do for the reader through its formal systems of organization, and how much the reader should do for himself. How much cataloguing and classification is really necessary? There is also a problem, as our libraries are now organized, of doing nearly everything with all books for all readers, instead of certain things with some books for some readers. For example, we do not distinguish for the most part between cataloguing for research and cataloguing for general education. What specifically are the cataloguing needs of the scholar; can money be saved here to buy more books? Librarians often wonder, but they have not yet been able to obtain clear enough data on the use of the catalogue to risk changes that might wreck the entire service for years. The nature and extent of cataloguing is therefore the fourth problem I would suggest for study.

Once a book has been acquired and incorporated into the library's bibliographic system it is ready for use. The physical handling of the book from there on is circulation, which is the third library function. Included here, in addition to the operation of the various loan desks, are the maintainence of the collections; the management of reserved book rooms, storage areas, and interlibrary loan departments; and in general the control throughout the library system of the locations of books, particularly their continual movement from one place to another. Most of this work is housekeeping. It is the most apparent, the most routine part of librarianship.

There are many problems in circulation: the security of the collections, for example, their preservation, and their decentralization among many temporary service points. There is one particular problem, however, that I should like to stress: the relationship between cost and accessibility. Great numbers of infrequently used books are now commonly intershelved with frequently used books, and the percentage of infrequently used books is increasing. Storage seems to be indicated in order to clear the stack for more convenient and economical access to the active collections, or else the removal of the active collections to other, more accessible areas, such as open-shelf reading rooms. Both approaches are being tried. But certainly the insistence upon treating all books alike, intershelving them in the same high-cost stack and keeping the same hair-trigger machinery cocked to produce any one on a moment's notice, is expensive. Do we really need to produce in five minutes a book that has not been opened in the last twenty years or may never be opened again in our lifetime? A discriminating analysis of what might be called the acceptable stages of accessibility, ranging from open-shelf reading rooms to cold, dark storage at distant places, could be a great help to library economy. This is the fifth problem I would suggest for study.

The fourth function, reference, is personal assistance to individual readers. The larger and more complicated the library becomes, the more help readers need. Most reference work consists simply of helping students or faculty who cannot find what they are looking for—a book, a fact, a bibliography, a reference in the card catalogue. A lot of the work consists, however, of doing the reader's job for him. Here the range of possibilities is tremendous, all the way from answering a simple question by telephone to searching twenty-year files of several hundred journals for every reference to the topic of a new research project.

At Stanford, for example, the Biological Science Librarian knows intimately the teaching and research interests of about fifty faculty members. He and his staff examine currently every issue of more than two hundred journals, type a card for each article of interest to each person, and give it to him. For any research project, they will upon request survey the entire literature of the subject and submit a critical bibliography. The faculty in this case appear to feel that the library can do this job better, faster, and more cheaply than they could do it for themselves.

Such instances are not commonplace in university libraries, certainly not at Stanford, but they do raise an important question about library costs and values. Opinions about such services differ. Many faculty members and some librarians believe that librarians should not participate in the research process, that anybody who is dignified by the good name of scholar cannot afford to leave his bibliographic work to others. On the other hand, more and more research workers in these days have to leave some of this work to others, whether they like it or not, if they want to get anything else done. And more and more librarians are becoming scholars, or perhaps more scholars are becoming librarians. The real issue, therefore, may not be whether, but how much. And that is the sixth problem I would suggest for study. Expenditures for reference service could be greatly expanded or contracted as the university desires.

Those are the library functions—acquisition, cataloguing, circulation, and reference—by means of which books are supplied to the university. All are essential, all expensive in the present context of books and scholarship. To perform these functions the library has evolved an elaborate organization that may employ hundreds of people and divide their work into scores of departments. We may now consider the nature of that organization.

Traditionally the library organization consisted of four major departments for the centralized performance of the four library functions—acquisition, cataloguing, circulation, and reference. As the organization grew, other departments were added to handle especially troublesome forms of materials: government documents, serials, maps, and rare books, for example. Some or all of the functions relating to these materials were transferred to the form departments from the functional departments. Then, because neither the functional nor the form departments were focused on particular parts of the educational program, a multitude of subject departments were added, both inside and outside the main library—chemistry libraries, art collections, and the like. Some or all of the functions relating to some or all forms of materials on particular subjects were thus transferred to subject departments from the functional and form departments. None of the old departments, however, seemed to die; they all lingered on. By now the library is in a state of extraordinary confusion of functional form, and subject departments, overlapping every which way.

Actually, it appears that the university library is lumbering towards the subject basis of organization, as it grows large enough to justify decentralization of functions and forms of materials. At the initial stage this trend has involved the establishment of larger subject units of organization than the departmental library—such broad divisions as humanities and social science libraries. These divisions when staffed by competent subject specialists, have been gradually taking over acquisitional, cataloguing, and other responsibilities from the traditional departments. By now there may be

enough straws in the wind to justify a review of this type of organization, and its relationship to organization by functions and forms. This is the seventh problem I would suggest for study.

One other aspect of the library organization should be mentioned briefly: the possibility of improving operational efficiency by better management and the further application of technological methods. Librarians, like many faculty members, are not always at their best as efficiency experts. Yet more than half of the entire library staff may consist of clerks, typists, and other non-professional assistants, who are engaged in procurement, accounting, paging and shelving, filing, charging out books, and the like, all jobs that are amenable to management techniques. Some librarians, at the risk of being typed by the faculty as administrators instead of scholars, have turned their attention from books to management, and significant progress in this area has been made. Certainly librarians have tried every useful gadget—from IBM to teletype—that has come to their attention. Nevertheless, the odds are pretty good that a great deal has not yet come to their attention. This is the last problem that I would suggest for study.

That is the broad picture, then, of what the library does, why it costs so much, and what problems of cost need study. Again, most of these problems arise from the nature of books and scholarship. If libraries could regiment authors, standardize forms of publication, and prescribe the uses of books, they could save a lot of money. They could save still more if universities would renounce the further advancement of knowledge, forbid the writing of more scholarly papers, and thereby end their existence. But lacking such notable reforms, we must go about our jobs the hard way.

I have suggested eight areas for possible study: (1) the functions of the university and the library needs specific to each function, (2) the acquisition of books, (3) the weeding of the collections, (4) the nature and extent of cataloguing, (5) stages of accessibility of the collections, (6) kinds and amounts of reference service, (7) types of library organization, and (8) management and the application of technological methods. All have broad financial implications, and all involve the faculty, except possibly the last.

They cannot be solved by librarians alone, because they depend upon what the university wants of the library and upon how the responsibilities of the library are defined. While the library can, on its own initiative, pursue minor economies internally, the problem of costs derives fundamentally from the conception of the library in the university and therefore the conception of the university itself. No basic change in the library service can be wisely undertaken without full consideration of its effect on the university and without full faculty understanding and support.

The understanding and support not only of the faculty but also of the university administration are necessary. At present the librarian sometimes rides uncomfortably between the horns of a dilemma—the administration on the one hand urging major economy, according to the financial stringency of the times, and the faculty on the other hand demanding more and more—more books, more cataloguing, more service of all kinds— according to the expanding pattern of university scholarship. When the librarian talks to the president he feels like a faculty member, and when he talks to the faculty he feels like a president.

In the long run, the real problem is to obtain agreement about library values. I doubt that any university librarian is likely to be criticized by his faculty for acquiring too many books or providing too many services, yet even the faculty would admit, under pressure, that library costs cannot be permitted to get out of line with other university costs, or take an undue share of the funds available to the university. The presidents have a point. It is therefore essential, I believe, that, where judgments differ, the librarian get together with his faculty and administration to reconsider jointly the library program—to agree if possible on what is wanted that is really worth the cost. The library, in all its ramifications of service, is in fact capable of great expansion—or contraction. Let us not fool ourselves on that point. The nature of that expansion or contraction, however, should be defined in terms of the educational and research values that the university as a whole expects from the library.

FOOTNOTES

[1] Sincere thanks are due to Elmer M. Grieder and William B. Ready, whose ideas and phrases, elicited during many discussions, have been freely incorporated into this paper.

ABOUT THE AUTHOR

—**Raynard Coe Swank**, Dean and Professor, School of Librarianship, University of California, Berkeley; Ph.D., 1944, University of Chicago. His major interests are in technical processing, academic libraries, and international librarianship.

The Costs of Providing Library Service to Groups in the Purdue University Community -- 1961

by Gerald L. Quatman

Academic libraries have traditionally adhered to the thesis that since the primary purpose of the library is service—an unquantifiable activity—the administration of the academic library is less a science than an art. This study attempts to isolate and measure the components that make up an academic library in order to determine service costs. No less interesting than this example of library cost accounting and statistical techniques is the possibility that it provides as a means of determining educational priorities in resource allocation. In this the educational policy-making role of the academic librarian—and to a considerable extent its financial implementation—is legitimately placed with those ultimately responsible.

The Purdue University Libraries offer their services to many different groups of users. They provide facilities and services for students, both graduate and undergraduate, for faculty members, and for other members of the university community. They provide a wide variety of library materials for those engaged in study, instruction, research and administration.

Most of the expenses for facilities and services are considered the responsibility of this educational institution and the costs are borne as part of the general educational expenses. But the costs incurred for the use of the library facilities and services by persons involved in research sponsored by outside organizations, such as the federal government, are the responsibility of the outside organizations.

The federal government recognizes that library costs are legitimate indirect expenses to be allocated to sponsored research agreements. The U.S. Bureau of Budget Circular No. A-21, revised states that:

> Library expenses should normally be allocated to research agreements on the basis of population, including students and other users. Where appropriate, consideration may be given to weighting segments of the population figures as necessary to produce equitable results[1].

The purpose of this study is to determine the average costs of providing library services and facilities to members of the university community engaged in research supported by organizations outside the university. Such research will be called "sponsored" or "organized" in the present paper.

More specifically the study is designed to determine whether a system of weighting should be applied to population figures to provide "equitable results", and to determine what system of weighting is most appropriate.

For reasons explained in Appendix I, sponsored research personnel's use of the library cannot be accurately measured. But gross relative use by undergraduate students, graduate students, faculty members and others can be measured with reasonable accuracy. Since sponsored research personnel are graduate students and faculty members, a weighting system based on relative average actual use of library facilities and services by undergraduate students, graduate students, and faculty members is developed in this study.

Two approaches to the allocation of library costs are possible. An "intended use" approach has been used by most colleges and universities in the past. In this approach, library personnel estimated the amount of library material (books, periodicals, etc.) and services intended for undergraduate and for graduate and faculty use, and from this they estimated the ratio of costs for sponsored research personnel to the costs for undergraduate students.

SOURCE: Reprinted front Gerald L. Quatman, *The Costs of Providing Library Service to Groups in the Purdue University Community—1961* (Lafayette, Ind.: Purdue University Libraries, 1962), by permission of the publisher and the author.

A second approach—the "actual use" approach—is used in this study. A survey of actual usage is used to distribute library costs to undergraduate students, graduate students, faculty members and others. The "actual use" approach was selected because it was considered a more logical and a more objectively quantifiable method for distributing library costs than the "intended use" approach.

This study was conducted in five steps:

1. A survey of actual use of twenty library services by undergraduate students, graduate students, faculty members and others was conducted and the relative use of the services by the members of these groups was measured.

2. The costs of the twenty library services were computed.

3. The costs of the services were allocated to the using groups on the basis of percentage of use.

4. The total costs chargeable to these four groups were divided by the number of persons composing each group.

5. The ratios of graduate student to undergraduate student library costs, and faculty member to undergraduate student library costs were computed.

Therefore, these ratios reflect the relative use of library services by the using groups as well as the costs of the services. A ratio found to be greater than 1:1 (2:1, 3:1, etc.) would show the extent to which the group with the higher number (2, 3, etc.) used the library services more frequently as well as the extent to which the group used more costly services than the group with the lower number. Experience had led the library staff to expect that the higher numbers in the ratios would apply to graduate students and faculty members. The resulting ratios will be used to weight population figures in the determination of library costs applicable to sponsored research, as allowed in Circular No. A-21, revised.

PROCEDURE AND RESULTS

The description of the procedure and results will follow the five steps previously mentioned.

The Survey of Use

Twenty-three of the libraries in the Purdue University Libraries complex were selected for study. These were the libraries that had full-time employees paid from the budget of the Libraries. One general library, seventeen libraries located in various departments on the University campus, and five off-campus libraries in the University

Extension Centers throughout the State of Indiana were included in the study. Table 1 lists the libraries studied.

TABLE 1

The Libraries Where Usage was Sampled

LIBRARIES

General Library

Department Libraries
  Aeronautical and Engineering Sciences
  Agricultural Economics
  Biochemistry
  Chemical and Metallurgical Engineering
  Chemistry
  Civil Engineering
  Electrical Engineering
  Forestry-Horticulture
  Home Economics
  Industrial Engineering
  Industrial Management
  Life Sciences
  Mathematics
  Mechanical Engineering
  Pharmacy
  Physics
  Veterinary Sciences and Medicine

Extension Libraries
  Aviation Technology (Hangar #1, Purdue Airport)
  Barker Center (Michigan City, Indiana)
  Fort Wayne Center (Fort Wayne, Indiana)
  Hammond Center (Hammond, Indiana)
  Marott Center (Indianapolis, Indiana)

Twenty library services were defined. These are all of the services for which usage was amenable to measurement. The services, the units of measurement, and the methods of measurement are listed in Table 2.

Twenty days were selected to be representative of the days the libraries were open during the calendar year 1961. A description of the selection and characteristics of these "Library Survey Days" is provided in Appendix II.

All of the users who entered the Libraries on the "Library Survey Days" were asked to report their amount of usage of certain services on *survey cards*. The librarians and library assistants recorded the usage of other services on *data sheets*. A detailed description of the methods used to collect and tabulate the data is provided in Appendix III.

Table 3 shows the total amount of usage of the twenty library services by undergraduate students, graduate students, faculty members, and others.

The adequacy of the sampling procedures is reported in Appendix IV. In general the results were:

TABLE 2

A List of the Services Studied, the Units of Measurement Used,
and the Instruments Used in the Sampling of Usage

SERVICES	UNITS	INSTRUMENTS*
Reader facilities	Time in library	Survey card
Card catalog	Number of trips	Survey card

Reserve
  Books
  Pamphlets
  Phonograph records
	Number used	Survey card

Used in library
  Books
  Technical reports
  Other
  Bound periodicals
  Unbound periodicals
	Number used	Survey card

Home circulation
  Books
  Periodicals
  Technical reports
  Other
	Number used	Survey card and
		home circulation
		data sheets

Reference
  Bibliography
  Search
  Ready
  Information
  Catalog information
	Number of
	questions asked
		Reference
		data sheet

Interlibrary loan	Number of items ordered	Interlibrary loan report

*Examples of the instruments used are given in Appendix III.

TABLE 3

Total Recorded Use of 20 Library Services by Undergraduate Students,
Graduate Students, Faculty Members, and Others on the 20 Library Survey Days

SERVICES	UNDERGRADUATE	GRADUATE	FACULTY	OTHER	TOTAL
Facilities for study	47417	15961	1508	1109	65995
Card catalog	8874	5123	1252	780	15329
Reserve					
Books	5351	3763	496	217	9827
Pamphlets	862	506	103	56	1527
Phonograph records	562	115	34	23	734
In library use					
Books	10881	6326	1399	862	19468
Technical reports	1672	1140	401	181	3394
Other	1138	835	212	155	2340
Bound periodicals	5531	6890	1177	562	14160
Unbound periodicals	4227	3593	1689	505	10014
Home Circulation					
Books	4037	2810	1009	543	8399
Periodicals	668	770	324	364	2126
Technical reports	338	230	119	27	714
Other	312	123	117	47	599
Reference					
Bibliography	5	10	4	2	21
Search	384	223	103	61	771
Ready	1541	660	306	170	2677
Information	4151	1690	641	660	7142
Catalog Information	1186	426	194	252	2058
Interlibrary loan	0	45	69	0	114

1. Only 60.7 percent of the users returned usable survey cards.

2. 79 percent of the home circulation usage on the survey days was reported on the survey cards.

3. The sample of survey days was representative of all the days the libraries were open.

4. The amount of usage of home circulation material reported on the library survey cards did not adequately represent the proportions with which the four groups actually checked out material on survey days.

Table 4 shows the computation of a conversion factor for the latter situation. From the first two columns it can be seen that none of the group reported as much usage on the library survey cards as they actually used. The conversion factor was used to equate the amount of home circulation usage reported on the survey cards with the actual usage, which was taken from home circulation check-out cards. Undergraduate students checked out 14 percent more than the reported; graduate students, 37 percent; faculty members, 50 percent; and other users, 14 percent. These variances were due to library personnel being reticent about asking faculty members and graduate students to return survey cards and to these two groups being less cooperative than undergraduate students and others.

The conversion factors were applied to all of the amounts of usage in those sections of Table 3 which were taken from the library survey cards, i.e., the first fourteen services. It was assumed that the conversion developed using home circulation information reported on the library survey cards should be extended to all other information obtained from the survey cards. The converted numbers of uses for the first 14 services are shown on Table 5. These numbers of uses and the information from the data sheets were used to compute the percentages by which undergraduate students, graduate students, faculty members, and others used each of the twenty library services. The percentages will be used later as a basis of the allocation of the costs of each library service to the four groups.

The Allocation of Expenditures to Library Services

Library expenditures were allocated to the twenty library services. The cost accounts used were:

a. Salaries and wages
b. Equipment
c. Space (utilities and building use)
d. Supplies and expenses
e. Materials (books, periodicals, etc.)

It was intended that these accounts reflect the actual expenditures of the Purdue University Libraries during the fiscal year 1960-1961. Actually, only a, d, and e contained expenditures in budgeted library accounts. The method used to compute these costs are described in the sections that follow.

Amounts for general and administrative university expenditures, for fringe benefits, and for tuition and fees remission were not considered because these would have had little differential effects on the allocated expenditures to the library services.

The methods used to allocate the expenditures in the five cost accounts are described in the five sections that follow. Procedures specific to each account were used. In addition, the total amount of library materials (books, periodicals, etc.) used on the library survey days to provide the twenty services was used as the primary basis for the allocation of costs to these services.

Columns (1) and (2) of Table 6 show the total number of pieces of library material used to provide the services, and columns (3) through (15) show the percentages of material used to provide various subcategories of service. These percentages will be used to allocate cost to the library services.

The total amounts of usage in column (1) of Table 6 were taken from Table 3, with the following exceptions:

TABLE 4

The Development of a Conversion Factor so that Survey Card Home Circulation Data are Equivalent to Check-out Data

	DATA FROM:		
	SURVEY CARDS	CHECK-OUT RECORDS	CARD-TO-RECORD CONVERSION FACTOR
Undergraduate	5355	6116	1.1421
Graduate	3933	5404	1.3740
Faculty	1569	2359	1.5035
Other	981	1115	1.1366
Total	11838	14994	

a. The amounts of usage of material by the interlibrary loan section was the amount of material from the Purdue Libraries that was sent to other institutions on survey days, and not the amount of material from other institutions used by members of the Purdue community on survey days. The latter was shown on Table 3.

b. In order to determine the amount of library material used to answer reference questions, all of the reference, departmental, and extension personnel were asked to estimate the average number of books and periodicals used to answer each type of reference question. These estimates were averaged across personnel responding and multiplied by the number of reference questions answered, as shown in Table 3. These products are shown in the reference rows of column (1).

The number of uses was corrected in column (2) of Table 6 because only 4.25 percent of the pamphlets, technical reports and other material were purchased by the libraries. The amount of usage in column (2) was used to compute the percentages in column (3) only.

Columns (4) through (12), except column (7), were computed directly from the number of uses in column (1). The computations for column (7) are described in the library material expenditures section of this paper.

Columns (13), (14), and (15) were computed according to the same percentages used to allocate salaries and wages expenditures. Therefore these percentages reflect time to provide services as well as the amount of material used to provide the services.

TABLE 5

The Corrected Amount and Percentage of Usage of the
20 Library Services by the Four Groups in the University Community

	UNDERGRADUATE		GRADUATE		FACULTY		OTHER		TOTAL
SERVICES	Number	Percent	Number	Percent	Number	Percent	Number	Percent	
Facilities for study*	54,154	68.02	21,930	27.55	2,267	2.85	1,260	1.58	79,611
Card catalog	10,135	50.82	7,039	35.29	1,882	9.44	887	4.45	19,943
Reserve									
Books	6,111	49.79	5,170	42.12	746	6.08	247	2.01	12,274
Pamphlets	984	51.84	695	36.62	155	8.17	64	3.37	1,898
Phonograph records	642	73.20	158	18.02	51	5.82	26	2.96	877
In Library use									
Books	12,427	51.35	8,692	35.91	2,103	8.69	980	4.05	24,204
Technical reports	1,910	44.57	1,566	36.55	603	14.07	206	4.81	4,285
Other	1,300	44.19	1,147	38.99	319	10.84	176	5.98	2,942
Bound periodicals	6,317	34.72	9,467	52.04	1,770	9.73	619	3.51	18,193
Unbound periodicals	4,828	37.49	4,937	38.34	2,539	19.71	574	4.46	12,878
Home circulation									
Books	4,611	43.48	3,861	36.40	1,517	14.30	617	5.82	10,626
Periodicals	763	28.03	1,058	38.87	487	17.89	414	15.21	2,722
Technical reports	386	42.32	316	34.65	179	19.63	31	3.40	912
Other	356	47.22	169	22.41	176	23.34	53	7.03	754
Reference									
Bibliography	5	23.81	10	47.62	4	19.05	2	9.52	21
Search	384	49.81	223	28.92	103	13.36	61	7.91	771
Ready	1,541	57.56	660	24.66	306	11.43	170	6.35	2,677
Information	4,151	58.12	1,690	23.66	641	8.98	660	9.24	7,142
Catalog information	1,186	57.63	426	20.70	194	9.43	252	12.24	2,058
Interlibrary loan	0	0	45	39.47	69	60.53	0	0	114

*Measured by time in library

TABLE 6

The Total Number of Pieces of Library Material Used to Provide the Library Services on Survey Days, and the
Development of Percentages of Usage which will be Used in Determining the Relative Cost of Providing Library Services

LIBRARY SERVICES	(1)	(2)	(3)	(4)	(5)	(6)	(7)	(8)	(9)	(10)	(11)	(12)	(13)	(14)	(15)
Reserve	12,088			Res.											
Books	9,827	9,827	12.97	81.30		11.70		22.52						2.85	8.96
Pamphlets	1,527	65	0.09	12.63		1.82				29.30	16.38			0.44	
Records	734	734	0.97	6.07		0.87				14.08	7.88			0.21	
In library use	49,376			I.L.U.											
Books	19,468	19,468	25.69	39.43	31.80	23.18		44.61						2.68	7.57
Technical reports	3,394	144	0.19	6.87	5.54	4.04					36.42	82.62		0.47	1.32
Other	2,340	99	0.13	4.74	3.82	2.79				44.90	25.11			0.32	0.91
Bound periodicals	14,160	14,160	18.68	28.68	23.13	16.86	62.81		45.62					1.95	5.51
Unbound periodicals	10,014	10,014	13.21	20.28	16.36	11.92	3.14		32.26					1.38	3.90
Home circulation	11,838			H.C.											
Books	8,399	8,399	11.08	70.95	13.72	10.00		19.25						60.17	31.06
Periodicals	2,126	2,126	2.81	17.96	3.47	2.53	9.43		6.85					15.23	7.86
Technical reports	714	30	0.04	6.03	1.18	0.85					7.66	17.38		5.11	2.64
Other	599	25	0.03	5.06	0.98	0.71				11.49	6.43			4.29	2.22
Interlibrary loan	78														
Books	33	78	0.10					0.08							
Periodicals	33	78					0.14		0.11						
Other	12					0.09				0.23	0.13				
Reference															
Bibliography	252	252	0.33										1.29		0.39
Books	181					0.30		0.42							
Periodicals	71						0.80		0.23						
Search	3,484	3,484	4.60										10.87		3.32
Books	1,763					4.15		4.04							
Periodicals	1,721						11.15		5.54						
Ready	4,738	4,738	6.25										10.81		3.30
Books	2,837					5.64		6.50							
Periodicals	1,901						8.04		6.12						
Information	2,143	2,143	2.83										23.93		7.31
Books	1,131					2.55		2.59							
Periodicals	1,012						4.48		3.26						
TOTAL	83,997	75,786													
Card catalog	15,329	88.16											13.00	4.90	10.86
Catalog information	2,058	11.84											9.40	time in library	2.87
TOTAL	17,387														

(1) The total number of pieces of library materials used.
(2) The total number of pieces of library materials used, corrected because only 4.25 percent of the pamphlets, technical reports, and other material are purchased by the libraries.

Percentages of materials used to provide services for the following service categories:
(3) Corrected number of uses.
(4) Reserve material (Res.), material used in the library (I.L.U.), home circulation material (H.C.).
(5) In library use and home circulation.
(6) Total number of uses.

(7) Weighted use of periodicals (Bound periodical usage is weighted eight times unbound periodical usage because each bound periodical contains a median of eight unbound periodicals).
(8) Books.
(9) Periodicals.
(10) Other.
(11) Other and technical reports.
(12) Technical reports.
(13) Reference*
(14) Circulation*
(15) Department and extension*

*See salaries and wages expenditure section of this paper for explanation of methods used to determine these percentages.

TABLE 7

Wages and Salary Expenditures for Sections of the
Libraries During the Fiscal Year 1960-1961

Books Order and Serials Order	$ 105,948.04
Reserve Book Room (General Library)	14,585.08
Circulation (General Library)	70,956.37
Reference (General Library)	74,924.67
Departmental Libraries	122,853.63
Extension Libraries	21,451.28
Card Catalog and Card Preparation	65,207.02
Interlibrary Loan	7,898.09
Shelving (General Library)	13,788.98
Book Marking (General Library)	1,377.84
TOTAL	$ 498,991.00

Salaries and Wages Expenditures

The total expenditures for salaries and wages during the fiscal year 1960-1961 was $498,991.00. The fiscal office of the Purdue Libraries reported the expenditures for those people in the sections of the library listed in Table 7. The above total expenditures include those for administration ($59,120.00) and shipping ($5,320.00). The latter expenditures were considered to be in support of the other sections and were added to the expenditures for the sections in direct proportion to the amount of expenditures involved. Therefore, Table 7 reflects the wages and expenditures for the listed sections during the fiscal year 1960-1961.

The following are descriptions of the methods used to divide wages and salary expenditures of the section personnel into the services used in the study:

1. The Book Order and Serials Order sections purchase all library materials. But the reference librarians estimated that only 4.25 percent of the pamphlets, technical reports, and other materials were purchased by the libraries. Therefore, the number of uses of pamphlets, technical reports and other material were adjusted to reflect this percentage factor. The salaries and wages of these sections were then allocated to the services according to the adjusted number of pieces of material used to provide the services. (See Table 6, column (3).

2. Salaries and wages expenditures for the reserve book room section were allocated to the reserve services according to the amount of material used. (See Reserve Section of column (4), Table 6).

3. A study of the amount of time that the circulation desk personnel spent on various activities was conducted by an Industrial Engineering class in the Fall of 1958. 84.8 percent of the personnel's time was spent on home circulation tasks, 4.9 percent was related to users time in the library (Reader Facilities), 3.5 percent and 6.8 percent were related to reserve and in library use activities, respectively. This information was used in the allocation of the circulation section salaries and wages. The expenditures for home circulation, reserve, and in library use were divided into their subsections (books, periodicals, etc.) according to the percentages in the appropriate categories given in Table 6, column (4).

After the salaries and wages of the circulation section were allocated to the services, the percentages of allocation to each service was computed and transferred to column (14) of Table 6.

4. The reference librarians and the library assistants in both the departmental and extension libraries were asked to estimate the amount of time they spent on the various library services. The average percentages of time are presented in Table 8.

The information in Table 8 was used to allocate the salaries and wages of the reference, departmental, and extension sections to the library services listed in this table. The expenses for these services, except the reference services, were then further allocated according to the amount of

TABLE 8

Average Percentage of Time Spent on Various Library Services

	REFERENCE	DEPARTMENTAL	EXTENSION
Card catalog	13.0	10.9	10.6
Reserve	— —	9.6	5.3
In library use	— —	2.5	0.8
Home circulation	— —	17.0	10.6
In library use and home circulation	21.4	44.8	44.1
Reference	56.3	15.2	28.6
Other material and technical reports	9.3	— —	— —
TOTAL	100.0	100.0	100.0

material usage in the appropriate column of Table 6.

Since different types of reference questions require different amounts of time to answer, the reference, departmental, and extension personnel were asked to estimate the percentage of reference time spent on each type of question. These percentages were averaged to give the results shown in Table 9. The allocation of the reference services expenses was subdivided into the component services according to the percentages shown in Table 9.

TABLE 9

Percentage of Reference Time Spent on Each
Type of Question – All Reference Questions

Bibliography	2.3
Search	19.3
Ready	19.2
Information	42.5
Card catalog	16.7
TOTAL	100.0

Therefore, the salaries and wages for the three sections (reference, departmental, and extension) were allocated to the services using both amount of personnel time and amount of material used as bases. The percentages of allocation for the reference section were computed and transferred to column (13) of Table 6. The costs used in the allocation of departmental and extension sections salaries and wages to the services were combined. The percentages of allocation for these two sections were computed and transferred to column (15) of Table 6.

5. The salaries and wages for the Card Preparation and Card Catalog sections were apportioned between card catalog and catalog information according to the percentages of use given on the bottom of column (2) of Table 6.

6. The salaries and wages for interlibrary loan were charged to that service.

7. In library use and home circulation material are handled by the shelvers. Therefore, the costs of shelving were allocated to the services in these areas according to the use of material. (Column (5), Table 6).   9

8. The cost of book marking was attributed to books according to use. (Column (8) of Table 6).

After the salaries and wages of each section of the libraries were allocated to the twenty library services, total salaries and wages were computed for each library service and transferred to the first column of Table 11.

Equipment Expenditures

The following steps were used to determine the amortized value of the equipment used by the Purdue Libraries and to allocate costs of equipment to the twenty library services used in the study:

1. An inventory of the equipment in all of the twenty-three libraries considered in the study was conducted during the summer of 1961. Each piece of equipment was classified according to its use into one of the following service categories:

    a. For reader use

    b. For the preparation, purchase, or storage of books

    c. For the preparation, purchase or storage of periodicals

    d. For the preparation, acquisition, or storage of technical reports

    e. For the preparation, acquisition, or storage of other library material

    f. For the preparation, acquisition, or storage of material in two or more of the previously listed four categories

    g. For providing reference services

    h. For providing home circulation services

    i. For providing departmental and extension library services, not otherwise categorized

    j. For providing interlibrary loan services

    k. For providing reserve services

    l. For preparation and storage of catalog cards

    m. For in library use only

    n. For library administration use

2. A list of the initial purchase costs of library equipment was obtained from the Office of Property Accounting. From this the average purchase cost of each piece of library equipment was computed. The average cost of each piece of equipment was multiplied by the number of pieces in each of the above categories. Then the total cost of the equipment in each of the above categories was computed. The cost of equipment for library administrative use was allocated to the other categories according to the value of the equipment in the other categories.

3. The value of the equipment in each category was amortized at 6 2/3 percent of original value.

4. The amortized value of the equipment in each category was attributed to the twenty library services according to the following methods (see 1 above for categories):

    a. Reader use entirely to time in the library

    b. Books according to use of books (Table 6, column (8))

c. Periodicals according to use of periodicals (Table 6, column (9))
d. Technical reports according to use of technical reports (Table 6 column (12))
e. Other according to use of other material (Table 6, column (10))
f. Material in two or more categories according use of all material (Table 6, column (6))
g. Reference equipment was allocated first on the basis of time reference librarians spent on the card catalog, reference, etc. and then on the basis of material use within these (Table 6, column (13))
h. Home circulation equipment was allocated first on the basis of home circulation library assistants time and then on the basis of material use within these allocations (Table 6, column (14))
i. Departmental and extension equipment allocated according to time spent on various activities and according to the amount of usage within the activities (Table 6, column (15))
j. Interlibrary loan entirely to interlibrary loan service
k. Reserve according to reserve use (Table 6, column (4), reserve)
l. Card catalog equipment charged entirely to the card catalog and the catalog information services (Table 6, column (2), bottom)
m. In library use equipment allocated according to use (Table 6, column 5, In library use)

5. The total cost for each of the twenty services was computed. The totals are shown in the second column of Table 11.

Space Expenditures

Both the amortized value of the portions of buildings housing libraries and the utility charges for the library areas were included in the total expenditures for space, because both of these cost categories were allocated to the twenty library services according to the space used for the services.

Table 10 shows the computation of space expenditures. The following steps were followed:

1. The value of the buildings on June 31, 1960 (initial acquisition costs plus additions and deletions) was obtained from the Chief Accountant's Office.

2. The value was amortized at two percent.

3. The net space of each library was computed.

4. The total net space in each building in June 1961 was obtained from the Schedules and Space Office of Purdue University.

5. The percentage of total net space occupied by the libraries was computed for each building.

6. The latter percentages were multiplied by the amortized value on each building to obtain the amortized building space costs of the libraries.

7. The library space costs for building use were computed.

8. The total space for libraries was multiplied by $1.60 per square foot to obtain the total costs for physical plant maintenance and operation during the fiscal year 1959-1960. This total was added to building use total to find the total library space costs. Note: The data used in these computations were the most current obtainable at the time of analysis. Although the dates of the information varied, computations were performed because the space and value of the buildings did not change much during this period of time.

The following steps were used in the allocation of space expenditures:

1. The floor space of each piece of equipment in each library was allocated to the same categories as the equipment (see 1, a through n of the previous section on equipment expenditures). For each library the following formula was used to compute the amount of space used for each category of service:

In this way, the total net space for each library was computed for the a through n categories. The total space for each category was computed. The space for library administration was again divided into the other categories according to the percentage of space occupied by the categories.

2. The total for each category was allocated to the twenty services on the same bases as used in the allocation of equipment expenditures (see 4, a through m of the previous section on equipment

$$\frac{\text{Total net space of each library}}{\text{Total space for equipment of each library}} \text{ X Space for equipment in any one category}$$

TABLE 10

Computation of the Total Costs of Providing Library Space

LIBRARY	(1) INITIAL COST OF BUILDING (a)	(2) AMORTIZED AT 2%	(3) NET FLOOR AREA OF LIBRARY (b)	(4) NET FLOOR AREA OF BUILDING (b)	(5) % OF BUILDING HOUSING LIBRARY	(6) COST OF LIBRARY SPACE (2) x (5)
General	$8,544,783.13	$170,895.66	103,443	319,394	32.387	$55,347.98
Aeronautical and Engineering Sciences	275,283.06	5,505.66	2,348	11,130	21.096	1,161.47
Agricultural Economics	75,252.72	1,505.44	884	16,132	5.480	82.50
Biochemistry	974,450.30	19,489.01	628	51,010	1.231	239.91
Chemical and Metallurgical Engineering	467,067.27	9,341.35	878	47,019	1.867	174.40
Chemistry	4,427,952.64	88,559.05	5,024	131,891	3.809	3,373.21
Civil Engineering	202,812.76	4,056.26	2,471	40,764	6.062	245.89
Electrical Engineering	384,041.02	7,680.82	1,420	96,965	1.464	112.45
Forestry-Horticulture	307,964.50	6,159.29	1,324	49,315	2.685	165.38
Home Economics	2,505,443.73	50,108.87	2,568	65,058	3.947	1,977.80
Industrial Engineering	105,581.95	2,111.64	920	31,049	2.963	62.57
Industrial Management	762,050.55	15,241.01	2,537	38,403	6.606	1,006.82
Life Sciences	11,063,957.82	221,279.16	12,636	235,748	5.360	11,860.56
Mathematics	233,140.66	4,662.81	1,924	22,898	8.402	391.77
Mechanical Engineering	788,154.32	15,763.09	1,537	77,574	1.981	312.27
Pharmacy	197,744.69	3,954.89	870	17,250	5.043	199.45
Physics	654,278.41	13,085.57	1,823	66,370	2.747	359.46
Veterinary Science and Medicine	133,456.55	2,669.13	2,894	59,827	4.837	129.11
Aviation Technology	106,031.39	2,120.63	711	31,551	2.253	47.78
Indianapolis (c)	110,000.00	2,200.00	925	28,420	3.255	71.61
Hammond	1,234,100.00	24,682.00	1,584	57,284	2.765	682.46
Fort Wayne	1,400,000.00	28,000.00	2,738	82,858	3.304	925.12
Michigan City (d)	.00	.00	660	9,700	6.804	.00
			152,747		Phys. Plt. Costs —	$ 78,929.97
			X $1.60 (e)			244,395.20
			$244,395.20		Total Costs of Library Area	$323,325.17

(a) Plus the cost of any additions or alterations.
(b) Does not include halls, closets, rest rooms, etc.
(c) The Marott Center was a gift, but alterations were performed.
(d) The Barker Center was a gift.
(e) The cost of physical plant services was computed to be $1.60 per square foot in the fiscal year 1959-1960.

expenditures). The total space for each of the twenty services was then computed.

3. The expenditure per square foot of library space was computed by dividing the total expenditures for library space by the total space for the libraries ($323,325.17/152,747 = $2.1167). This cost per square foot was then multiplied by the space involved in providing each service to obtain the total space cost for each service. The latter is shown in the third column of Table 11.

Supplies and Expenses Expenditures

The total expenditure for supplies and expenses for the fiscal year 1960-1961 was $35,080.00. The following means were used to attribute supplies and expenses to the twenty library services:

1. A detailed record of the supplies acquired by the department and extension libraries and the sections of the general library was maintained from December, 1959 through March, 1960. No more recent records were maintained. Librarians and library assistants were asked what these supplied were used for. Each item for which use could be isolated was placed in one of the following categories:

    a. For reader use
    b. For card catalog
    c. For reserve material
    d. For reserve books
    e. For home circulation
    f. For home circulation books
    g. For home circulation periodicals
    h. For two or more types of material
    i. For books
    j. For periodicals
    k. For other material
    l. For reference
    m. For interlibrary loan
    n. For circulation
    o. For departmental and extension

Only $4,280.49 of the $35,080.00 was assigned to the above categories, therefore the total cost allocated to each category was multiplied by $35,080.00/$4,280.49 or 8.19532. In this way the entire $35,080.00 was allocated to the *a* through *o* categories.

2. The expenditures in each of the above categories were assigned to the twenty library services on the following bases:

    a. Reader use to time in the library
    b. Card catalog to card catalog and catalog information (Table 6, bottom column (2))

    c. Reserve material to reserve according to use (Table 6, column (4), reserve)
    d. Reserve books to reserve books
    e. Home circulation to home circulation according to use (Table 6, column (4), home circulation)
    f. Home circulation books to home circulation books
    g. Home circulation periodicals to home circulation periodicals
    h. Two or more types of material to all material according to use (Table 6, column (6))
    i. Books to books according to use (Table 6, column (8))
    j. Periodicals to periodicals according to use (Table 6, column (9))
    k. Other material to other material according to use (Table 6, column (10))
    l. Reference according to time and use (Table 6, column (13))
    m. Interlibrary loan to interlibrary loan
    n. Circulation according to time and use (Table 6, column (14))
    o. Departmental and extension according to time and use (Table 6, column (15))

3. The total expenditures for the twenty services were computed. They are shown in column 4 of Table 11.

Library Material Expenditures

The expenditures for library materials for the fiscal year 1960-1961:

Books	$128,634.03
Phonograph Records	41.16
Periodicals	139,306.34
Binding	37,000.00
TOTAL	$304,981.53

The expenditures for materials were allocated to the twenty library services on the following bases:

1. The expenditures for books included expenditures for technical reports and other material. But only 4.25 percent of the technical reports and other material were purchased by the library. Therefore, number of uses of these two items was multiplied by 4.25 percent. The total expenditure for books was allocated to the library services using books, technical reports, and other material according to the adjusted amount of usage (Table 6, column (3)).

2. The expenditures for phonograph records were attributed to that service entirely.

3. It was estimated that five percent of the binding costs were for the rebinding of books. This expenditure for rebinding books was allocated according to the use of books. (Table 6, column (8)).

4. Bound periodicals cost more than unbound periodicals for two reasons:

   a. The cost of binding (95 percent of the total binding cost) is included in bound periodicals.
   b. The average bound volume contains a median of eight issues (based on a random sample of 200 volumes).

Expenditures for periodicals were allocated to the services according to use. For the services which used bound periodicals, the usage was weighted by a factor of eight, and the cost of binding periodicals was included in the amount to be allocated. The resulting percentages are shown in column (7) of Table 6.

The total costs of providing material for the twenty library services is shown in the fifth column of Table 11. Table 11 also shows the total costs of providing the twenty library services.

The Computation of the Ratios of University Community Groups' Costs for Library Services

Allocation of Library Services Expenses to Community Groups.

The total costs of the twenty library services were computed in Table 11. Then, the cost of each service was allocated to the four population groups according to the percentages with which the population groups used each service (see Table 5). These computations are shown in Table 12. The total costs of providing library services to undergraduate students, graduate students, faculty members, and others are shown on the bottom of Table 12.

Number of People in the University Community Groups

In order to compute the costs for library services per member of the university population groups, it was necessary to compute the number of people in each of these groups. Table 13 shows this computation.

Table 13 shows total numbers of people in the university population groups (both the Lafayette and Extension Campuses) for the semesters during which the survey of use was conducted. The numbers of undergraduate students and graduate students were taken from the registration report published by Office of the Registrar each semester. These numbers of people were weighted by five months for the academic year semesters and by two months for the summer sessions. The total number of months was then divided by twelve to compute the number of people per year.

The number of full-time equivalent ten month and twelve month faculty appointments was taken from the salary analysis published by the Payroll Department. "4" – "7" personnel are assistant professors, associate professors, professors, and head professors excluding administrative personnel. The number of "4" – "7" ten month personnel who signed separate summer session contracts are not reflected in the salary analysis. These were counted, using personnel records. Most "3" personnel (instructors) are graduate students. Those "3" employees who were enrolled in graduate courses are reflected in the graduate student registration data. The "3" employees not enrolled were considered faculty members. They were counted, using Central Business Data Processing information. The number of "3" personnel not enrolled in graduate courses during the fall semester 1961-1962 was not available. Therefore, the number for the fall semester of 1960-1961 was used.

The total number of faculty members per semester was computed. Again, the semesters were weighted for months and the total number of months was divided by twelve to compute the number of people per year.

It was not possible to compute the number of people in the other group.

The Ratios of Library Costs Per Member of University Community Groups

Table 14 shows the computation of the ratios of library costs per member of the university population groups. The cost per group was taken from Table 12 and the number of people in each group was taken from Table 13. The library costs per person in each group was computed by dividing costs by number of people. The ratio of library costs per person in each group was computed by dividing costs by number of people. The ratio of library costs per graduate student to the costs per undergraduate student was found to be 2.800 : 1. The ratio of library costs per faculty member to the costs per undergraduate student was 2.267 : 1. A hypothetical example showing how the ratios will be used is provided in Appendix V.

TABLE 11
Total Costs of Library Services

	SALARIES & WAGES	EQUIPMENT	SPACE	SUPPLIES & EXPENSES	MATERIAL	TOTAL
Reader use	$ 3,476.86	$ 8,205.28	$117,459.80	$ 41.32	$ .00	$ 129,183.26
Card catalog	82,891.61	3,638.76	13,482.16	9,954.21	.00	109,966.74
Reserve						
Books	40,128.17	1,395.78	4,726.33	2,402.06	27,169.74	75,822.08
Pamphlets	2,240.57	538.08	661.11	1,429.14	180.09	5,048.99
Records	2,010.85	258.50	317.25	686.58	41.16	3,314.34
In library use						
Books	48,738.43	2,359.20	32,717.74	1,761.75	53,817.53	139,394.65
Technical reports	7,434.38	335.94	5,325.57	2,751.04	398.77	16,245.70
Other	5,121.96	813.72	10,290.38	1,896.83	270.13	18,393.02
Bound periodicals	35,025.77	3,060.52	42,152.38	2,587.11	109,567.67	192,393.45
Unbound periodicals	24,776.23	2,164.30	29,808.49	1,829.53	5,474.74	64,053.29
Home circulation						
Books	103,012.22	1,522.57	18,608.48	3,284.25	23,215.69	149,673.21
Periodicals	26,004.99	594.53	7,460.41	1,022.90	16,458.81	51,541.64
Technical reports	8,544.10	116.07	1,501.59	770.12	77.18	11,009.06
Other	7,158.35	246.39	2,954.83	646.46	64.32	11,070.35
Interlibrary loan	8,005.14	52.16	487.11	462.33	344.99	9,351.73
Reference						
Bibliography	1,968.60	64.01	811.46	54.87	1,780.95	4,679.89
Search	19,829.55	906.62	12,052.66	760.98	26,705.43	60,255.24
Ready	20,996.03	938.59	12,553.16	771.00	25,678.99	60,937.77
Information direction	32,719.12	660.49	7,735.11	570.45	13,735.33	55,420.50
Catalog information	18,908.08	549.32	2,219.15	1,397.06	.00	23,073.61
TOTAL	$498,991.00	$28,450.84	$323,325.17	$35,080.00	$304,981.53	$1,190,828.54

TABLE 12

Distribution of the Costs of Library Services to the Four University Community Groups

SERVICES	PERCENT UNDERGRADUATE	UNDERGRADUATE COSTS	PERCENT GRADUATE	GRADUATE COSTS	PERCENT FACULTY	FACULTY COSTS	PERCENT OTHER	OTHER COSTS	TOTAL COST OF SERVICES
Reader facilities	68.02	$ 87,870.45	27.55	$ 35,589.99	2.85	$ 3,681.72	1.58	$ 2,041.10	$ 129,183.26
Card catalog	50.82	55,885.10	35.29	38,807.26	9.44	10,380.86	4.45	4,893.52	109,966.74
Reserve									
Books	49.79	37,751.81	42.12	31,936.26	6.08	4,609.98	2.01	1,524.02	75,822.08
Pamphlets	51.84	2,617.40	36.62	1,848.94	8.17	412.50	3.37	170.15	5,048.99
Phonograph records	73.20	2,426.10	18.02	597.24	5.82	192.89	2.96	98.10	3,314.34
In library use									
Books	51.35	71,579.15	35.91	50,056.62	8.69	12,113.40	4.05	5,645.48	139,394.65
Technical reports	44.57	7,240.71	36.55	5,937.80	14.07	2,285.77	4.81	781.42	16,245.70
Other	44.19	8,127.88	38.99	7,171.44	10.84	1,993.80	5.98	1,099.90	18,393.02
Bound periodicals	34.72	66,799.01	52.04	100,121.55	9.73	18,719.88	3.51	6,753.01	192,393.45
Unbound periodicals	37.49	24,013.58	38.34	24,558.03	19.71	12,624.90	4.46	2,856.78	64,053.29
Home circulation									
Books	43.48	65,077.91	36.40	54,481.05	14.30	21,403.27	5.82	8,710.98	149,673.21
Periodicals	28.03	14,447.12	38.87	20,034.24	17.89	9,220.80	15.21	7,839.48	51,541.64
Technical reports	42.32	4,659.03	34.65	3,814.64	19.63	2,161.07	3.40	374.31	11,009.06
Other	47.22	5,227.42	22.41	2,480.87	23.34	2,583.82	7.03	778.25	11,070.35
Reference									
Bibliography	23.81	1,114.28	47.62	2,228.56	19.05	891.52	9.52	445.53	4,679.89
Search	49.81	30,013.14	28.92	17,425.82	13.36	8,050.10	7.91	4,766.19	60,255.24
Ready	57.56	35,075.78	24.66	15,027.25	11.43	6,965.19	6.35	3,869.55	60,937.77
Information	58.12	32,210.39	23.66	13,112.49	8.98	4,976.76	9.24	5,120.85	55,420.50
Catalog information	57.63	13,297.32	20.70	4,776.24	9.43	2,175.84	12.24	2,824.21	23,073.61
Interlibrary loan	00.00		39.47	3,691.13	60.53	5,660.60	00.00		9,351.73
TOTAL COST PER GROUP		$565,433.58		$433,697.42		$131,104.67		$60,592.83	$1,190,828.54

TABLE 13
The Number of People in Three Population Groups – 1961

POPULATION GROUPS	SPRING SEMESTER 1960-1961	SUMMER SESSION 1961	FALL SEMESTER 1961-1962	TOTAL
Undergraduate	14,616	4,284	17,425	
Weighting for months	x 5	x 2	x 5	
	73,080	8,568	87,125	168,773/12
				14,064.42
Graduate	3,287	3,130	3,857	
Weighting for months	x 5	x 2	x 5	
	16,435	6,260	19,285	41,980/12
				3,503.00
Faculty members				
"4"-"7" 10 month appointments	500		512	
"4"-"7" 12 month appointments	602	652	652	
"4"-"7" extended into summer		126		
"3" appointments	237	181	252	
TOTAL	1,339	959	1,416	
Weighting for months	x 5	x 2	x 5	
	6,695	1,918	7,080	15,693/12
				1,307.75

TABLE 14
The Computation of the Ratios of Library Costs
Per Member of Three University Community Groups

	COST PER GROUP	NUMBER OF PEOPLE IN EACH GROUP	COST PER AVERAGE PERSON IN GROUP 1 / 2	RATIO OF COST PER PERSON
Undergraduate	$565,433.58	14,064.42	$ 44.22	1.000
Graduate	433,697.42	3,503.00	123.80	2.800
Faculty	131,104.67	1,307.75	100.25	2.267

DISCUSSION OF RESULTS

The computation of the ratios of the library costs per faculty member and per graduate student to the cost per undergraduate student was the object of this study. These ratios show how much more faculty members and graduate students used the library facilities at Purdue University than the undergraduate students. These ratios also reflect the fact that faculty members and graduate students use more costly library services than undergraduate students.

These ratios can be used to weight library expenses for faculty members and graduate students in relation to undergraduate students in any allocation of library expenses to these groups during the fiscal years 1960-1961 and 1961-1962.

The ratios were computed on a cost per member of the university community basis. If the library facilities and material holdings increase proportional to the increase in the number of members of the university community in future years, and if the members of the groups continue to use the facilities to the same extent as this year, the same ratios can be used after 1961-1962.

These ratios will be used to weight library expenses for faculty members and graduate students in relation to undergraduate students in the determination of indirect library costs applicable to organized research contracts. But these ratios should be considered underestimates of the actual relationships between library expenses for organized research personnel and the library expenses for undergraduates for the following reasons:

1. The libraries provide more services for faculty members and graduate students than were covered in the study of use.

These two groups:

a. Use library facilities after closing hours
b. Suggest what library materials should be ordered
c. Often see new material first
d. Are allowed to use home circulation material longer
e. Have families who use library facilities. Some of the families' uses of the library was undoubtedly directly beneficial to the graduate students and faculty members.
f. It is very probable that the materials used by graduate students and faculty members cost more than materials for students.

2. The libraries provide more services for organized research personnel than for other graduate students and faculty members. The organized research personnel:

a. Work primarily in science fields. Science and technology materials cost more and the costs have increased more than material in other fields.[2] Science materials also depreciate in value more rapidly than other materials.
b. Use more current materials and need the library materials more quickly.

APPENDIX I

Methodological Problems

It would have been extremely difficult to measure "actual use" of library facilities by organized research personnel. The graduate students and faculty members at Purdue University often have teaching and non-sponsored research duties, in addition to sponsored research duties. They are also responsible for their own professional development. The graduate students and faculty members generally perform all of their duties in the same area of study. Therefore, they could not report accurately which library materials and services they used for sponsored research and which were used in connection with other university duties. Furthermore, they could not report the library services that would enable them to perform more efficiently on sponsored research projects in the future.

Because sponsored research personnel could not report their library use directly with dependable accuracy, no attempt was made to determine the library costs for organized research personnel on this basis. Instead, library use was surveyed and the average costs of providing library services to groups in the university community and the ratios of costs between groups were determined. These ratios of average costs will be used to allocate library cost to organized research personnel on the basis of the number of full time equivalent organized research personnel in the population groups. That is, if a graduate student was employed one-half time on a sponsored research project, one-half of the library costs for the average graduate student was apportioned to organized research.

The implicit assumption here, and throughout the study, was that the average graduate student or faculty member engaging in sponsored research used the same amount of library services as the average graduate student or faculty member employed in other university duties.

APPENDIX II

The Design of the Sample

Entire days were used in the sample of usage. The "Library Survey Days" were selected to be representative of the total number of days the libraries were open from January 30, 1961 (the beginning of the spring semester, 1961) to January 28, 1962 (the day before the beginning of the spring semester, 1962). The days were selected to represent as equally as possible other days with similar characteristics.

The "Library Survey Days" occurred during the last half of the spring semester, 1960-61 and the first half of the fall semester, 1961-62. The fourteen survey days during the semesters occurred in fourteen separate weeks. The first, seventh, fifteenth, and eighteenth weeks were not represented. The one survey day representing the school year vacation period was taken in the spring vacation, 1960-61.

APPENDIX III

The Collection and Usage Data

The usage of the twenty library services was measured by the library *survey cards* completed by the users and by *data sheets* maintained by the library assistants and librarians.

Displays and Instruments Used

A sign and a box were provided to implement the sampling of usage as measured by the survey cards. On the twenty "Library Survey Days", a 14" x 22" yellow and black sign was placed in a conspicuous position near each entrance to each library. The sign announced that this was a "Library Survey Day" and asked all who enter to:

"Please pick up a card
Fill it out while here
Return the card as you leave"

Blank 4" x 6" survey cards (see example) were made available in one side of a 7" x 9½" wooden box which was placed on a table near each of the signs. The boxes were partitioned to provide two slots for cards. The slot facing the entrance had a 2½" x 6" sign stating:
"Take a card"

A sign on the other side of the box faced users as they departed from the library. It requested the users to:
"Return cards here"

Encouragement of User Response

The signs and boxes were placed near the library assistants' desks. As people entered the library they were encouraged to take survey cards by the library assistants. As the users departed they were asked to return the cards. These encouragements were provided only when the assistants were not engaged in other duties.

Three articles explaining the nature of the study and urging cooperation were published in the student newspaper, "The Exponent." Copies of the first article were made available to library users as they entered the library. Other copies were placed in faculty mail boxes.

Other articles were published in Extension Center newspapers.

Requests for cooperation were read to the students in their dormitories by dormitory presidents and by announcers on campus radio stations.

Source of Information

The survey cards measured user time in the library, the number of trips to the card catalog, the use of reserve material, the use of material in the library (excluding reserve material), and the use of home circulation material.

The use of reference material by undergraduate students, graduate students, faculty members, and others was measured by the reference data sheets, which were completed by the reference librarians on "Library Survey Days." The reference librarians recorded the bibliographies compiled, and the number of search reference, ready reference, information and direction, and catalog information questions asked by the four groups.

Home circulation library assistants reported the amount of library materials distributed to the four groups on the home circulation data sheets. The information for these sheets was taken from the check-out cards. This information was collected for each day from the first survey day until the last. Home circulation information was obtained from both the check-out cards and the survey cards in order to provide a basis for checking the adequacy of the sample obtained from the survey cards. The adequacy of the sample is discussed in Appendix IV.

On "Library Survey Days" the interlibrary loan section records were reviewed to determine the amount of materials provided for groups within Purdue University which it serves (graduate students and faculty members).

Tabulation of Results

The survey cards, data sheets, and interlibrary loan reports were sent after each survey day to one central office for tabulation. Some of the survey cards were returned blank. Others contained highly exaggerated reports of usage. These were not counted in the tabulation.

When a library was closed on "Library Survey Days" no information was obtained from that library. No other days were substituted.

The amount of usage of library materials by undergraduate students, graduate students, faculty members, and others was tabulated for each survey day. Then the totals were accumulated for all survey days. The total amount and percentage of usage of the twenty services by the four population groups were computed (Table 3).

LIBRARY SURVEY CARD*

The information from this questionnaire will be used by the Libraries to improve service to you. Please answer as accurately as possible all questions applicable to this visit to the Library.

CLASSIFICATION: Undergraduate _____ , Graduate _____ , Faculty _____ , Other University Staff_____ , University Family_____ , Non-University _____ .

ABOUT HOW LONG WERE YOU IN THE LIBRARY? _____HOURS _____MINUTES

HOW MANY TRIPS DID YOU MAKE TO USE ANY OF THE CARD CATALOGS?_____

HOW MUCH RESERVE BOOK ROOM MATERIAL DID YOU CHECK OUT FOR HOME OR LIBRARY USE?
HOW MANY: Books _____ , Pamphlets _____ , Phonograph records _____

HOW MUCH OTHER LIBRARY MATERIAL DID YOU USE IN THE LIBRARY?
HOW MANY:
Books _____   Periodicals:
Technical reports_____   Bound volumes _____
Other (theses, college catalogs, etc.)_____   Unbound issues _____
HOW MUCH ARE YOU GOING TO <u>CHECK OUT</u> OF THE LIBRARY?
HOW MANY:
Books _____ , Periodicals_____ , Technical reports _____ , Other_____ .

Please turn in this card to any check-out desk as you leave the Library.

THANK YOU

*This was printed on a 4" x 6" card.

APPENDIX IV

Adequacy of the Sample

On the first fifteen "Library Survey Days" a count of the number of users leaving the General Library was made by the library assistants nearest the five exits. The count showed that 34,717 people used the library. 21,069 users, or 60.7 percent returned usable survey cards. The count of people is only approximate because:

1. People who were in the library only a couple of minutes were counted. These people were not asked to fill out survey cards.
2. The library assistants had other duties. The count was probably an underestimate at some times and an overestimate at other times because of overcompensation.

Nevertheless, it is evident from the statistics that a sizeable proportion of the people using the library on "Library Survey Days" failed to return usable survey cards.

The purpose of the sample was to determine the percentages of under-graduate students, graduate students, faculty members, and other users who availed themselves of the various library services. The question of adequacy, therefore, relates to the extent to which these percentages were represented accurately by the usable survey cards returned.

The home circulation check-out cards are accurate measures of home circulation library material usage by undergraduate students, graduate students, faculty members and others because:

1. The library assistants require that the check-out cards be filled out correctly in order to prevent the loss of library materials.
2. The status of the lender is indicated on the check-out card and is verified by the users' identification cards.

Home circulation usage measured by the survey cards was compared with the home circulation usage of the four groups measured by the check-out cards and reported on the data sheets in order to determine the accuracy of the survey card information. Table 4 was computed from this information.

It was reassuring to note that as much as 79 percent (11838 of 14994) of the home circulation usage was reported on the survey cards.

Table 15 compares the amount and percentage of home circulation material that was used by the four groups on survey days with the amount and percentage used on days when there was no survey. Both sets of information were obtained from home circulation check-out data. The percentages of group usage were very similar, indicating that the sample was representative of all the days the libraries were open.

APPENDIX V

A Hypothetical Example

Below is a hypothetical example of the use of the ratios to compute the costs of providing library services for organized research personnel:

Undergraduate students	5000 x 1.000 = 5,000 = 50%	
Graduates	1071 x 2.800 = 3,000 = 30%	
Faculty members	882 x 2.267 = 2,000 = 20%	

$$50\% \times \$100,000 = \$50,000$$
$$30\% \times \$100,000 = \$30,000 \times 1/6 = \$5,000$$
$$20\% \times \$100,000 = \$20,000 \times 1/5 = \$4,000$$
$$\overline{\qquad \$9,000}$$

1. Suppose there are 5000 undergraduate students, 1071 graduate students, and 882 faculty members.

2. The number of people in the groups is multiplied by the corresponding ratios to weight the population figures.

3. The weighted population figures are then divided by the total weighted population figure (10,000) to find the percentages of library cost that should be allocated to each group.

4. Suppose further that the total library expenditures are $100,000.

5. Then the percentages are multiplied by the expenditures to find the total cost per group.

6. Again suppose that 375 graduate students are employed one-half time on organized research projects, so that 187.5 full-time equivalent or 1/6 of the total graduate students are employed on organized research. And suppose that 176.4 full-time equivalent of the 882 faculty members (1/5) are employed on organized research.

7. The library costs for graduate students and faculty members are multiplied by 1/6 and 1/5, respectively.

8. Therefore, in this example, the costs of providing library services for organized research personnel would be $9,000.

SUMMARY

The purpose of the study was to determine the cost of providing library facilities and services for those members of the university community doing sponsored research during 1961. To accomplish this the average costs of providing the facilities and services for undergraduate students, graduate students, and faculty members were computed.

The following procedures were used to compute these costs:

1. The amount of usage of twenty library services by undergraduate students, graduate students, faculty members, and other users on a sample of twenty days was used to project the amount and percentages of usage of each services for the year.

2. The cost of each library service was determined using various cost accounting methods. The elements of cost considered were salaries and wages of employees, amortized costs of equipment, amortized costs of library buildings, physical plant services, (utilities, custodial, etc.), supplies and expenses, and library materials (books, periodicals, etc.).

3. The cost of each service was allocated to the four user groups according to the percentages with which they used the services. In this way the total cost of providing library services to the four user groups was computed.

4. The costs for undergraduate students, graduate students, and faculty members were divided by the number of people composing these groups to find the average cost of providing library services for each group.

5. These average costs showed that the costs of providing library services to graduate students were 2.800 times as much as the costs for undergraduate students and that the costs for the average faculty member were 2.267 times those for undergraduate students.

TABLE 15

Home Circulation Usage by the Four University Community Groups on Survey Days

	SURVEY DAYS		NON-SURVEY DAYS	
	Number	Percent	Number	Percent
Books				
Undergraduate	5,246	42.92	41,019	40.47
Graduate	4,286	35.06	34,778	34.31
Faculty	1,674	13.70	14,138	13.95
Other	1,017	8.32	11,434	11.27
TOTAL	12,223	100.00	101,358	100.00
Periodicals				
Undergraduate	561	26.08	5,947	33.55
Graduate	909	42.26	7,121	40.17
Faculty	602	27.99	3,963	22.36
Other	79	3.67	695	3.92
TOTAL	2,151	100.00	17,726	100.00
Technical Reports				
Undergraduate	192	51.89	1,687	50.77
Graduate	121	32.70	1,188	35.75
Faculty	48	12.97	400	12.04
Other	9	2.43	154	6.09
TOTAL	370	100.00	3,323	100.00
Other				
Undergraduate	117	46.80	1,489	58.90
Graduate	88	35.20	811	32.08
Faculty	35	14.00	154	6.09
Other	10	4.00	74	2.93
TOTAL	250	100.00	2,528	100.00

FOOTNOTES

[1] U.S. Bureau of the Budget. Principles for determining costs applicable to research and development under grants and contracts with educational institutions. Circular No. A-21 revised (January 8, 1961).

[2] Kurth, W. H. U. S. book and periodical prices—a preliminary report. *Library Journal,* 1960, *85,* pp. 54-56.

ABOUT THE AUTHOR

—**Gerald L. Quatman,** Associate Professor of Psychology, Xavier University, Cincinnati; Ph.D., 1963, Purdue University. He has taught courses in psychological statistics, psychology, occupational information, and job analysis. His major research interests are in the areas of advertising effectiveness and motivational factors in work with the disadvantaged.

V
THE STRUCTURE OF THE LIBRARY

For the academic library administrator a prerequisite to organizational effectiveness is an arrangement which can best provide unity and responsiveness. In this way stability and uniformity can be maintained within the total organization, responsibility can be assigned, accountability achieved, and the librarian has a definite idea of his authority. This, however, presupposes that such an arrangement occurs within the larger institution itself. In reality, while the function of each is constant, neither the school nor the library is static, instead they take on the shapes which can best accomodate constant changes in program and pressures. Too often the academic librarian is limited by the library machinery created to respond to institutional change. Stability and uniformity in the library can best be achieved by responding from the substantive nature of the library function. In this way finding more effective modes would become a regular and deliberative process.

The Future Policy of the University Libraries

The Chicago University Commission on the

Future Policy of the University Libraries

This faculty committee report illustrates the self-interests which the various components of the academic community have in the structural arrangement of the academic library. The arguments of the principals are less a result of differences in interpretation of the function of the library than they are a conflict between the administrative impulse to attempt to bring together what is apparently similar and the user impulse for convenience. Unless the library administrator can suggest and satisfactorily implement alternatives he should be aware that the outcome will probably not be a plan for maximizing the impact of the library on the educational environment, but rather a condition of expediency.

PLAN I:
CENTRALIZATION

55. The first plan calls for a great central library building including (1) all non-departmental books; (2) the general library stock of the Departments of Philosophy, Political Economy, Political Science, History, Sociology, Household Administration, Romance, German, English, General Literature, the Biology Departments, and the Medical School; (3) the general library stock of all or nearly all of the following Departments, for which new library construction is already, or will soon be, necessary: Psychology, Geography, Mathematics, Astronomy, Physics, Chemistry; and (4) the general library stock of all other Departments or Schools disposed to enter the central library (the other Departments are Comparative Philogy, Greek, Latin, History of Art, and Geology; and the other Schools are the Divinity School, the School of Education, the Law School, the School of Commerce and Administration, and the School of Social Service Administration). Such a central library building would presumably be located in the broad space which now separates the northern group and the southern group of buildings on the campus. The main axis of the building is conceived as vertical rather than horizontal, in part on the principal that the administration of a great library is though to be more economical on a vertical plane, in part on the expectation that more rapid and satisfactory service would result, and in part in view of the architectural promise involved in the treatment of such a structure. The architectural aspects of this problem will be treated below.

56. This plan varies in range from complete to incomplete centralization. Complete centralization would involve the transfer to such a building of the general library stock of all Departments and Schools in the University. Incomplete centralization would involve the housing elsewhere than in the central library of the books of one or more of the Departments and Schools referred to under (3) and (4) in the preceding paragraph.

57. The central building proposed by this plan, as has been said, would presumably be located in the broad space that now intervenes between the northern group and the southern group of buildings on the campus. Its plan would presumably be somewhat like a thick H, the cross bar running from north to south, thus:

SOURCE: Reprinted from Chicago University Commission on the Future Policy of the University Libraries, *Tentative Report, January, 1924* (Chicago: University of Chicago Press, 1924), Section 8-Section 11, pp. 28-44, by permission of the publisher.

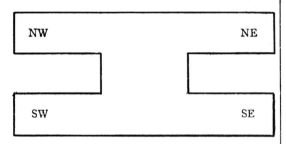

58. The extremities of the two western wings might be connected by one or more bridges and a subway; so also the extremities of the two eastern wings. The central portion would contain the rooms of a central and general character, including the catalogue room and the delivery room, preferably on the first floor, reading-rooms on the middle floors, and administration rooms on the upper floors. The four wings would contain stacks and seminar rooms planned, in each case, in accordance with the principles set forth above. The southeast wing would serve the Social Science Departments (including Philosophy, Psychology, Household Administration, and Geography), the Department of Geology, the Law School, and the Schools of Commerce and Administration and Social Service Administration. The southwest wing would serve the Language Departments, Classic and Modern, the Department of the History of Art, and the Divinity School. The northeast wing would contain the nondepartmental books and would serve the Departments of Mathematics, Astronomy, and Physics, and the School of Education. The northwest wing would serve the Department of Chemistry, the Biology Departments, and the Medical School. Other plans would, of course, be possible—the foregoing is merely a reasonable suggestion. From east to west the building would probably extend about 300 feet, from a line about 250 feet west of University Avenue to a line about 250 feet east of Ellis Avenue. From north to south the building would probably extend about 200 feet, from a line about 75 feet south of Kent and Ryerson to a line about 75 feet north of Rosenwald and the proposed Divinity School. In height the building, as a whole, would probably rise to some ten stories. Should it be thought wise, the name "Harper Memorial Library" might be transferred to this new building.

PLAN II.

COMPLETION AND DEVELOPMENT OF THE HARPER GROUP, WITH SEPARATE LIBRARIES FOR THE SCHOOL OF EDUCATION, MEDICINE, AND THE PHYSICAL SCIENCES

59. The essential features of the second plan are (1) the continued use of Harper as a part and presumably for a long time the headquarters of the whole library system of the University; (2) the erection of a building between Harper and Classics; (3) the erection of a building east of Harper, extending to Foster, the latter also being probably eventually converted to library purposes with such reconstruction as may be necessary; (4) the erection of the Theological Building north of Haskell and the installation in it of the Divinity School Library; (5) the erection of a Science Library (perhaps subdivided as suggested below) at such point as may seem best on the north half of the main quadrangle; (6) the eventual erection on the site of Haskell a much larger building devoted wholly to library purposes, the memorial interest in the present building being conserved by the erection elsewhere of a more adequate Oriental Museum, bearing a name fulfilling the trust; (7) the erection, if and when necessary, of a building joining the north end of the building replacing Haskell and the north end of the Law Building, thus yielding a Harper court 150 x 210 feet and a fore court between Rosenwald and the Theological Building; (8) if and when necessary, the conversion of the Law School Building to library purposes and the erection of a Law School Building at some other point. The proposed science library should be connected with Harper by a tunnel to carry pneumatic tubes and book conveyors and to enable the passage of persons and book trucks from one library to another. The basement of the new Divinity Building might be connected with this tunnel and give pneumatic tube connection between the library desk of that building and the main desk in Harper.

60. It is of the essence of this plan that it will proceed by stages, providing in the near future the buildings west and east of Harper, the Theological Building, and the Science Library Building; then some years later, replacing Haskell, which is recognized to be inadequate for even the immediately future

development of the Oriental Museum, and to be incapable of enlargement on its present site, by a much larger building, and when another expansion is called for, erecting the building across the north end of Harper Court. It is thus adjustable to needs of the University, as these develop, in ways and to an extent that is it not now possible to foresee with exactness. If carried out in all the respects indicated above, the four buildings surrounding Harper court would constitute a hollow square, and the buildings east and west of Harper would constitute immediately connected wings. The total capacity of these buildings devoted to Library purposes would exceed that of the central building suggested in Plan I. It would be contemplated that all the buildings would be so connected in the basement and on one or more of the upper floors that the books of the several classes would occupy the space proportioned to their number and bulk and that the same would be measurably true of the studies and offices.

61. In general, and subject to the foregoing principle, library facilities would be provided for the several departments as follows:

(1) The Classical Group in Classics Building.

(2) The Modern Language Group in the building to be erected west of Harper.

(3) The History and Social Science Group in Harper and the building to be erected east of Harper. Commerce and Administration might be included in this group, or preferably be located in its own building when one of adequate size is provided.

(4) Geology in Rosenwald.

(5) Geography, for the present in Rosenwald, eventually probably in connection with the Social Science Group if its development continues to be in that direction.

(6) The Divinity School in the Theological Building.

(7) The School of Education in a new building to be erected on its own quadrangle.

(8) The Law School in the Law Building, for years to come the present one, eventually perhaps a new one.

(9) Medicine, Biology, and Chemistry in a Science Library; Physics, Mathematics, and Astronomy, in this building or in an extension of Ryerson.

ARGUMENTS FOR PLAN I AND AGAINST PLAN II

62. In the consideration of the educational and administrative advantages and disadvantages of either plan, the fundamental criterion should be the degree to which each promises to facilitate and encourage research. This is more important than any other consideration, administrative or aesthetic. And in the long run, financial economy will coincide with the provision of facilities which will in reality facilitate and encourage research. Any attempt to economize by failing to provide such facilities will surely defeat its own ends.

63. The several departments and schools of the University are interrelated to a large degree in the use of books, and the closeness of such interrelations is clearly on the increase. This increasing interrelationship is, of course, due fundamentally to the increasing sense of the essential unity of knowledge, and in particular to the sense that research cannot be limited by departmental barriers. The results of a study of the degrees of closeness of the present interrelationships of the several departments and schools are presented herewith in tabular form in Appendix A: we commend that table to the particular attention of the readers of this Report. As the research conducted by the University extends in scope, interrelations between Departments and groups of Departments will largely increase. The stock of books used most frequently by a given Department will be used more and more by members of the Faculty and graduate students of other Departments. No Department has a prescriptive right to the exclusive possession of any book; every book is potentially needed by students in many Departments. It follows that all books should be so located as most fairly and readily to satisfy such interdepartmental needs. A great central library provides just such a location.

64. A central library makes the non-departmental books—general periodicals, publications of learned societies, general reference works, etc.—equally accessible to all Departments and Schools.

65. A central library makes a great central catalogue equally accessible to all Departments and Schools. From the point of view of the facilitation and encouragement of research, the

use of such a catalogue is preferable to the use of a smaller departmental catalogue; in the first place, because a great central catalogue can be maintained on a level of expert excellence, both as regards inclusiveness and as regards analysis, which cannot reasonably be expected in a series of minor catalogues; and in the second place, because the habit of consultation of a general catalogue is in itself a broadening educational habit.

66. In a central library there is a tendency for members of different Departments to meet and compare notes as to the progress of research much more frequently and naturally than would be the case otherwise. Such informal conferences are of great value in the stimulation of research.

67. A central library permits excellent supervision by properly trained librarians over the various branches of the library. This applies to all phases of the library service, as, for instance, reading-room management, shelving, and stack service. Excellence in these respects contributes directly to the facilitation and encouragement of research.

68. A great central library permits access to the whole stock of books by members of the library staff. This, in turn, particularly as it applies to the Reference Department and to searchers for "difficult" books, reacts directly upon the convenience of those consulting the library.

69. A central library eliminates the great delay caused by the mechanical transfer of books from one building to another. In the case of dispersed libraries, such transfer is necessary not only in the case of books specially called for by or from a departmental library, or wanted for a temporary reserve, but in the case of all books added to the permanent library stock, since all books are necessarily purchased and catalogued in a central building. This applies with particular force to periodicals, which come first to the main library, are then sent unbound to the dispersed libraries, are later sent back to the main library for binding, and eventually returned to the dispersed libraries.

70. On the administrative side, a central library is, in the view of those who favor this plan, greatly to be preferred. The expert in any branch of the service has greater range than in the case of dispersed libraries, both in respect to his individual duties and in respect to the supervision of his subordinates. He is, there-

fore, employed with greater efficiency and greater economy.

71. The concentration of effort on a single central catalogue, already referred to as desirable from the point of view of research, is exceedingly desirable from the administrative point of view. Such duplication in the preparation and filing of cards is required by the maintenance of dispersed libraries is a matter of very heavy expense. This applies not only to the original making and filing of the cards, but to the necessity of entering the frequent changes of location of a given book upon all the cards concerned—the cost of which runs to 35 or 40 cents per card.

72. In a central library the charging system may be kept simple. In the case of dispersed libraries, duplication in charging frequently occurs, as, for instance, when a book indefinitely loaned to a special library is in turn loaned for reserve to another special library. This not only makes unnecessary charging, but is certain to cause the reader considerable annoyance and loss of time in being sent from library to library. Efforts are being made to reduce the cost of duplication, by charging all books which are sent to departmental libraries instead of marking location symbols on the catalogue cards. This expedient, however, results in a huge accumulation of charging cards and means that every call slip must be compared with this file before being sent to the stacks. Results of recent investigations made at the University of Illinois for a number of departmental libraries indicate that between 25 percent and 30 percent of the entire expenditure is for cataloguing. In the case of dispersed libraries, unnecessary and undesirable duplication occurs also in the sending out of notices at the end of a quarter for books charged to Faculty and students.

73. Those who favor Plan I believe that the administration of the library upon this plan would be much less expensive than upon Plan II. This opinion appears to be shared unanimously by a number of librarians to whom the matter has been informally presented in general terms.

74. The building of a central library would obviate the necessity of erecting new buildings for the Social Science Departments and for the Modern Language Departments. The classrooms, laboratories, and other non-library facilities of the Modern Language Departments

could be located in Cobb Hall and (if the Classics books should be transferred to the central library) in the Classics Building.

75. Similarly, the building of a great central library would release for other purposes—as, for instance, offices, classrooms, and conference rooms—spaces in many departmental buildings now given to stacks and reading-rooms; and would thus add appreciably to the resources of these buildings for work other than library work. The separation of library collections from the departmental facilities (as classrooms and laboratories) will become inevitable in the near future in some cases under any circumstances; in other departments this disadvantage would be to a considerable degree offset (a) by the presence in each departmental group, or school building of a limited reserve; and (b) by the development of a system of subways connecting the central library building with other buildings.

76. Such a building as that proposed in Plan I would, of course, afford a great architectural problem. It is the belief of the advocates of this plan that it would afford a magnificent architectural opportunity. In its proportions it is greater than any building now on the campus. It would occupy the center of the campus and might well be treated as the dominant and unifying architectural member of the whole University design—as the towering center toward which the other buildings lead up, around which they cluster like supporting buttresses. Furthermore, the fact that several portions of the building differ somewhat in character and the fact that the wings might well differ from each other, to some extent, in size and in shape would afford the architect an excellent opportunity for the avoidance of monotony and for the development of that principle of variation which is a vital principle of Gothic architecture. In its vertical emphasis, also, the building would be absolutely within the Gothic tradition. The architectural difficulty and opportunity are both increased by the fact that the building should be so planned as to be capable of enlargement in the centuries to come. The designing of a structure thus prepared for extension is by no means impossible. Some of the notable buildings of Europe have grown to be what they are through a series of additions.

It is within architectural power to design a building conceived not as a thing definitive and limited, but as a living, growing organism. It is the belief of the advocates of this plan that architects would be eager to meet the challenge of such an opportunity in the conviction that such a building might well be made one of the greatest buildings of the New World.

77. It is true that such a building would necessarily destroy the present character of the open campus and would diminish the independent architectural effectiveness of the buildings which are built upon that space. In this respect, however, it may be noted that though the cross-campus view of Ryerson, for instance, would be lost, it is equally true that a beautiful building remains beautiful even if higher buildings are erected near it, that it may indeed gain in poignancy and may even more intimately reveal its fineness.

78. A great central library has further the very real value of symbolizing the unity of knowledge and of educational endeavor. The conception of such a building certainly stimulates the imagination. If it should receive a loyal architectural expression, it might well kindle to good purpose the imagination of thousands of students.

79. The presence on the campus of a great central library would serve notice on the city and the country that the University considers its library as the heart of its educational equipment, and that it proposes to house its books properly and to provide proper access to them. Under such conditions gifts of collections of books or gifts for collections of books would be far more likely to be forthcoming than in the case of dispersed and less impressive libraries. Indeed the obvious stimulation to the imagination provided by such a structure might well result in general gifts to the University as well as in specific gifts of or for books.

80. A great central library, properly designed, would make possible the indefinite extension of resources in a much more economical manner than would otherwise be practicable. The present Report envisages immediately the situation which will presumably exist in 1950-51; but no one believes that the growth of the University libraries will cease at that time. If a great central library, properly designed, is built in the location above referred to a large addition could be made, say once in

twenty-five years, as a single homogeneous piece of construction under a single contract; and the space available is such that by the proper utilization both of horizontal and vertical opportunities, the needs of the library could presumably be supplied for several centuries. If, on the other hand, growing libraries are maintained in a number of different buildings, frequent piecemeal additions of new wings to existing buildings will be necessary; and since the ground available for such wings is limited, and the height of the wings could hardly exceed that of the original buildings, a point will eventually be reached beyond which such piecemeal construction cannot go.

81. In the opinion of those who favor Plan I, there are certain disadvantages inherent in Plan II. One fundamental difficulty is that it tends to disjoin the sciences from the other departments. Omitting to speak of the specific cases which now bridge the gap between them (Psychology, Philosophy, Geography, etc.), those who favor Plan I desire to call attention to the strong prevailing tendency toward the introduction of scientific methods in the social sciences and the recognition of the social sciences as belonging to the science group. Already the American Association for the Advancement of Science has a section (K) devoted to the social sciences; the newly organized Social Science Research Council is already co-operating with the National Research Council, and steps are under way to affiliate it with the National Research Council and thereby with the National Academy of Sciences. A number of professors of Political Science are now preparing a series of studies for the National Research Council. The mutual interest of the natural sciences and the social sciences in such fields as public health and sanitation, the study of the causes of mental disease, delinquency, and crime, applied engineering, and many others is sufficient indication that each group of departments is now and will in greater degree be vitally interested in the books and program of the other. It is obvious, therefore, that Faculty members and students working primarily in the sciences will need in increasing measure to work among the Humanistic books and vice versa. Plan II recognizes the need for contact between the two collections by proposing a tunnel connection between the buildings. The advocates of Plan I cannot help feeling that the degree of interrelation desirable is more effectively obtained by a single library building.

82. In the opinion of those who favor Plan I, a second fundamental fault of Plan II is that it contemplates the indefinite expansion of the library on a horizontal plane. It is thought that true library economy demands the construction and operation of a great library on a vertical plane rather than a horizontal plane. Greater efficiency in service, greater rapidity in delivery of books, greater access to books, higher efficiency in library administration, and more intensive use of ground space are all inherent in vertical construction. The difficulties of administration on a horizontal plane, already apparent in the operation of Harper Library, will be rapidly increased as the elements of Plan II are realized.

83. Those who favor Plan I find a third important weakness of Plan II in the fact that the plan appears to make inadequate provision for the growth of the Social Science and the Modern Language Departments. Examination of Appendix B will show that the space requirements of the Social Science Departments for facilities other than library facilities are such that they could at once use the whole of Harper to advantage for non-library purposes. And if one or more of the four closely allied departments—Philosophy, Psychology, Household Administration, and Geography—should join the group, the space requirements would be so much the larger.

84. The proposed building for the Modern Language Departments, if large enough to accommodate the libraries and other facilities of the Departments concerned, would already be too large for the space west of Harper, and would have no room for expansion. Calculations show that the total stack space for books now required by the Modern Language Departments (Romance, German, English, and General Literature) is 30,780 cubic feet; that the space which would now be needed for professorial studies is 41,760 cubic feet; that the space which would now be needed for individual working spaces in the stacks is 22,000 cubic feet; that the space which would now be needed for reading rooms is 111,200; and that for 1950-51 the corresponding figures would be 150,789; 74,880; 48,000; and 198,000. Nor do the foregoing figures provide for classrooms and other non-library facilities.

85. Plan II involves also a large-scale duplication. In the Harper center there would be of necessity a single inclusive catalogue with proper analyticals and shelf lists. In the Science Library it would be necessary to duplicate this equipment for the 80,000 books now in stock and the thousands of yearly additions. In addition each card in the Harper catalogue belonging to a book in the Science Library would need to bear a special symbol showing the permanent location of the book. The maintenance of two large separate libraries would mean a considerable duplication of administrative and supervisory staff. In short, from a purely business standpoint the duplication in building, staff, and operation does not recommend itself to those who favor Plan I.

86. Library administration while somewhat improved over the present system by Plan II would still be open to difficulties easily remediable by a single library. The processes of ordering, cataloguing, recording, and binding would presumably continue to be centralized in Harper, thus necessitating the constant transfer of books from one library to the other and the constant requirement that the library staff go from one building to another.

87. It should also be noted that Plan II continues to hold a very large stock of books underground in the Harper stacks, where they are not readily accessible to research students. Provision of studies on the ground floor of Harper would only partially remedy this difficulty.

ARGUMENTS FOR PLAN II AND AGAINST PLAN I

88. The reasons which favor the plan now under consideration may be presented under four heads:
1. Educational Considerations
2. Architectural Considerations
3. Financial Considerations
4. General Considerations

Educational Considerations

89. It is the opinion of those who favor Plan II that there are substantial advantages in the location of books used by the Humanistic Departments and Schools where they may be most conveniently accessible to instructors and students; and correspondingly, serious disadvantages in their concentration in a common central library building. The value of reference to a collateral reading and the consultation of authorities is in many cases directly in proportion to the facility with which such reference may be made *at the moment.* It is important, therefore, to avoid in every practicable way whatever would tend to render such immediate reference physically inconvenient. Moreover, the location of books conveniently adjacent to classrooms lends additional interest, emphasis, and significance to the work of the related courses. The plan now under consideration seeks to secure these advantages by the arrangement described in paragraph 61.

90. The plan now under consideration contemplates the reconstruction of the first floor of Harper in accordance with the original plan of the building whereby a considerable number of studies for instructors and graduate students may be provided having adequate natural light; and when the other buildings of the group east, west, and north of Harper are constructed as contemplated in this plan, provision for this kind of study in immediate contiguity to the stacks will be very generally increased. Space for the expanding catalogue may be provided and other similar needs met in the building proposed to be built on the west of Harper.

91. The problem presented by the libraries of the Departments of the Physical Sciences has its peculiarities and special difficulties. In a sense laboratories are to the Physical Sciences what libraries are to the Humanities. But the Physical Sciences also have their libraries which for practical purposes need to be in as close connection as possible with the laboratories. If the literature of each science were sharply differentiated from that of all the other sciences, the best arrangement for the specialist investigator would be a library of his own science immediately adjoining his own laboratory. But account must, of course, be taken of the fact that the literature is not thus sharply subdivided, and that the student in one field is obliged to consult the literature of other fields. It remains, however, that in the interest of the laboratory investigator, the books of his subject should be within as easy reach of his laboratory as possible. If, having had our past

experience and reached our present development, we were beginning to erect buildings on a new site, it is not impossible that we should find the best solution of our library problem, so far as respects the Physical Sciences, in one huge building, at the center of which should be the library of sciences, and in the various outlying portions, the laboratories, classrooms, etc., of chemistry, biology, and physics.

92. This condition, however, does not exist. The buildings already erected for the several sciences, not to mention also the easily foreseen necessity for additional buildings, especially for biology and medicine, exclude any such solution of the problem, and compel us to seek instead an arrangement which, though not furnishing ideal conditions, shall contribute most highly to the future development of this group of subjects.

93. It is the conviction of those who favor the second plan that this cannot be done by removing all the libraries of the sciences to a central building, with the result that none of the scientific groups would have immediate and easy access to the books of its subject. On the other hand, it is desirable to group the libraries of related sciences as far as practicable. Perhaps there is no better solution than the establishment of a library of chemistry, the biological sciences, and medicine in a building in as close connection with the buildings of these subjects as practicable, and in Ryerson, or an extension of it, to develop a library for physics, mathematics, and astronomy. The former library might well be built on the main Quadrangle on some portion of the unoccupied land, south of Snell and west of, and connected with Kent. Such a location will eventually be near the center of the biological group and adjacent to the buildings of the Medical School. This does not probably provide ideal conditions for Biology and Medicine, but such conditions are in any case rendered impossible by the detached character of the buildings already erected and of the fact that the buildings still to be erected for the hospitals and laboratories of the Medical School must be separated from the existing buildings by intervening streets.

94. Adequate library space is thus provided by the second plan for the period which the present report includes, both for the Science Departments and for the Humanities. The plan makes provision also for Faculty studies and graduate-student working spaces in the stacks and for seminar rooms adjacent to the books. The plan recognizes substantially the existing interrelationships of Departments, and groups the library facilities in accordance therewith. It raises no difficult architectural problem, but provides for new construction of exactly the type which has prevailed. The plan lends itself readily to partial completion, one new building after another being built as the necessities of the situation require. These are all substantial advantages necessitating full and careful consideration of this plan as an alternative to Plan I.

95. Centralization, it may be conceded, has many advantages from the point of view of the library administration which it would be desirable to secure if this could be done without sacrificing the advantages of readers and investigators. If it could be carried out in full it would likewise serve excellently the convenience of the occasional visitor from outside of the University and the scholar whose interests range over many departments. But it cannot be too strongly stated that the library administration exists to facilitate research and instruction by placing the resources of the library where they can be used with greatest facility by those who are engaged in research and in giving or receiving instruction. The interests of the occasional visitor and of the widely ranging scholar are not to be forgotten, but, affecting, as they do, a relatively small group, should not be allowed to control to the detriment of the much larger number of the other class.

96. For example, housing the chemistry library in the same building with the Humanities removes the library of chemistry from contiguity with its laboratory. The former relationship is desirable, but the latter, contiguity of the chemistry library and laboratories, would probably serve the interests of research to ten times the extent that the location of the Chemistry library in the general library building would.

97. There are advantages in a building of ten stories over one of four for library purposes, but these may easily be overestimated. It must not be forgotten that a building which is to provide reading space for 5,000 readers, assigning many of these individual studies, or reserved desks, working space for a staff of 200, storage for 2,000,000 volumes, and cor-

ridors and elevators for communication and transportation, cannot be other than a large building, with many rooms and with considerable distances between the more remote portions. To go from one part to another of this building will inevitably consume time, and the advantages in the greater height over a group of connecting buildings of lesser height may be easily overestimated. If one is to walk he can do so more easily on a level than up and down stairs, and often waiting for an elevator is more time-consuming than walking.

Architectural Considerations

98. The advocates of Plan I concede that their proposal has great architectural difficulties. To those who favor Plan II, these difficulties seem fatal to the plan. The University has led the way in planning its buildings on a consistent plan and giving due consideration to the educational value of architectural symmetry and beauty. The erection of a ten-story building in the center of the main quadrangle, approaching within 75 feet of the much lower buildings north and south of it, would, in the judgment of those who favor the second plan, go far toward undoing what has been done in thirty years to create a group of buildings characterized not only by the architectural beauty of each building, but by a unity and symmetry of plan. To them it would be an architectural disaster not to the University of Chicago only, but to the city and to the country. Such a sacrifice might be made if it were required by educational efficiency. But when educationally also it sacrifices the interests of many departments to the convenience of the administrative staff and the occasional student of exceptionally wide interests, it is in the opinion of those whom this paragraph represents, quite indefensible.

Financial Considerations

99. The financial problem proposed by the first plan is very difficult. It calls for perhaps four million dollars for one building which will far exceed immediate needs. This sum will be exceedingly difficult to obtain unless from one giver, as in the case of the Widener Library. The University must soon ask its friends for several millions to enable it to make new educational advances. In this sum it may be possible to include a million or a million and a half divided into two or three sums, each for a building. It is to be feared that it might wait a long time, much longer than it can afford to wait, for the single gift of four millions for a single building.

General Considerations

100. In reference to the problem as a whole, it is the opinion of those who favor the second plan that it is wiser to make necessary modifications in the plan which was approved in 1902 and has since been partly carried out than to abandon this and adopt a new one which twenty years hence may, in its turn, prove to have somewhat missed the mark. Perfect foresight of the future is not given to us and is, perhaps, no more likely to be achieved now than twenty-one years ago. Evolution and modification seem wiser than discarding a half-completed plan and beginning all over again.

101. To those who favor this second plan, moreover it appears wiser to proceed by gradual development than to attempt to arrive at the goal by one great effort. The assumption on which the first plan is based, that we must expect the University to increase the number of its students at the rate and to the extent which a statistical study of our history would suggest, seems to the advocates of the second plan to rest upon very precarious grounds. Not only is it doubtful whether the extraordinary increase in the number of young people seeking a college education within the last twenty-five years will continue indefinitely, but even if it should so continue, it is quite among the possibilities that the University may, a few years hence, decide that its duty lies rather in the improvement of the quality of its work than in the increase in the numbers of its students, and that the conservation of quality demands the setting of a limit to the number of students far below which a mere statistical inquiry would suggest. It is already clear that to meet the needs of the libraries well as to provide necessary space for other educational work will demand the early erection of additional buildings—certainly the buildings east and west of Harper, the Theological Building, and the building which shall eventually replace Haskell. Manifestly, also some provision must be made

at a very early date for the libraries of medicine and the physical sciences. But in view of the uncertainty as to the precise character of our future development and the extent of the future increase in our student body, it seems to the advocates of the second plan wiser to proceed from our present status by a process of gradual development than to attempt now to formulate a plan based on a statistical prediction of our future growth.

102. Further, it seems to those who favor the second plan, a serious objection to Plan I that it converts the Harper Memorial Library to a use for which it was not originally erected and to which it is not easily adaptable. Its capacious basement stacks would not be easily convertible to the purposes of a departmental building, nor is it a satisfactory disposition of the most beautiful reading-room in the world to employ it as an exhibition room for a museum of the historical and social sciences. Similarly, the plan proposes no use for the Classics Building, and none for the spaces east and west of Harper which are needed to complete the Quadrangle; and instead it proposes to occupy the space in the center of the main Quadrangle, which from every point of view should be left vacant as long as possible, if not permanently, with a building wholly out of scale with the existing buildings.

103. Plan II, on the other hand, retaining the use of the William Rainey Harper Memorial Library for the purposes for which it was originally built, conserves the sentimental interest attaching to this building, given to the University by more than two thousand donors, who made their gifts not only as a memorial to the first President of the University, but in the expectation that it would be the central unit of the University system of library buildings.

General Organization and Administration

by Louis R. Wilson, Robert B. Downs, and Maurice F. Tauber

In this chapter the authors examine the library response of a diverse institution, organized to provide service to particular groups of users. When measured against the prescriptive concepts of administrative efficiency this response is not satisfactory. These would hold that if the library administrator is to be responsible for the library function he must have systematic control over the variables which affect performance. Yet even given the opportunity to create an organization, the academic librarian must organize the library to provide for the advantages inherent in such factors as functionalism, form, the special requirements of particular clients, geographic decentralization. All this conditioned by his ability to define the end use and quality of service to be provided and capable of support by his resources.

PRESENT ORGANIZATION

To show the present administrative organization of the libraries of the University requires three charts, because of the complexity of the situation. In Figure 1 is represented all divisions, in Ithaca and elsewhere, and for the principal units the administrative authority or responsibility is indicated. Included, in addition to the University Library, with its several special collections and seminar rooms, are the four major state-supported libraries, the Law and Medical libraries, and 33 autonomous or semi-autonomous departmental libraries and laboratory collections.

Figure 2 represents the organization that went into effect on July 1, 1947, for the University Library, replacing a plan under which virtually every member of the staff reported directly to the Librarian. Though the span of control has now been narrowed, especially for the readers' service departments, some further changes affecting the technical divisions are advisable.

Finally, Figure 3 shows the form of organization, following a traditional pattern of the Agriculture Library, largest of the independent college libraries.

Following are comments on the present types of library organization in the University.

University Library

The Assistant Director in charge of Readers' Services has direct responsibility for the Circulation, Reference, and Periodical Departments, for special collections, and for seminar and departmental libraries under main library control. He also shares in the general administrative work of the Library, including such specific functions as employment of part-time staff members, care and supervision of the library building, preparation and submission of hourly wages payroll, preparation of vacation schedules, and investigation and reports on requests for new equipment.

Nearly all public contacts, faculty and student, with the University Library are through the several readers' service divisions mentioned above. A brief outline of their functions is therefore given here. The Circulation Department employs 12 full-time staff members, plus part-time desk assistants and pages. Here lies full responsibility for the circulation of books for use in the library building or for home use.

SOURCE: Reprinted from Louis R. Wilson, Robert B. Downs, and Maurice F. Tauber, *Report of a Survey of the Libraries of Cornell University for the Library Board of Cornell University, October 1947-February 1948* (Ithaca, N.Y.: Cornell University, 1948), Chapter 5, "General Organization and Administration," pp. 53-63, by permission of the publisher and the authors.

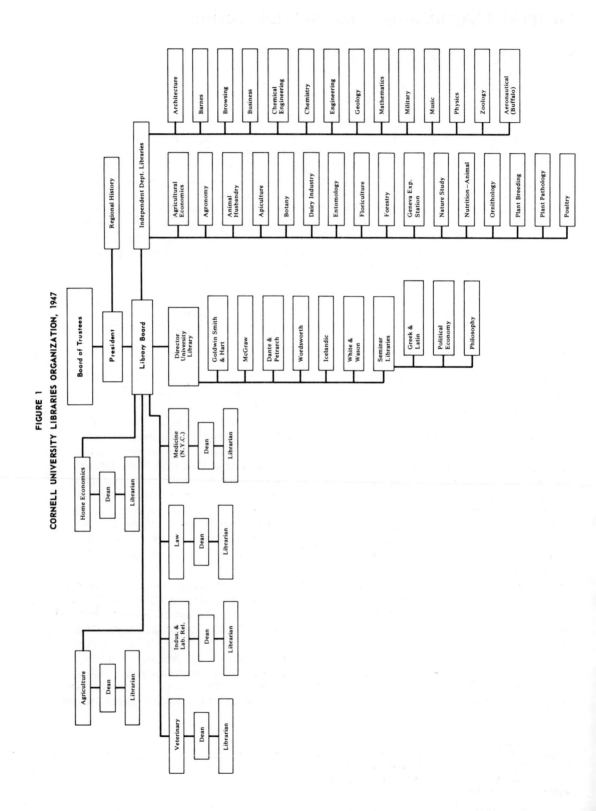

FIGURE 1
CORNELL UNIVERSITY LIBRARIES ORGANIZATION, 1947

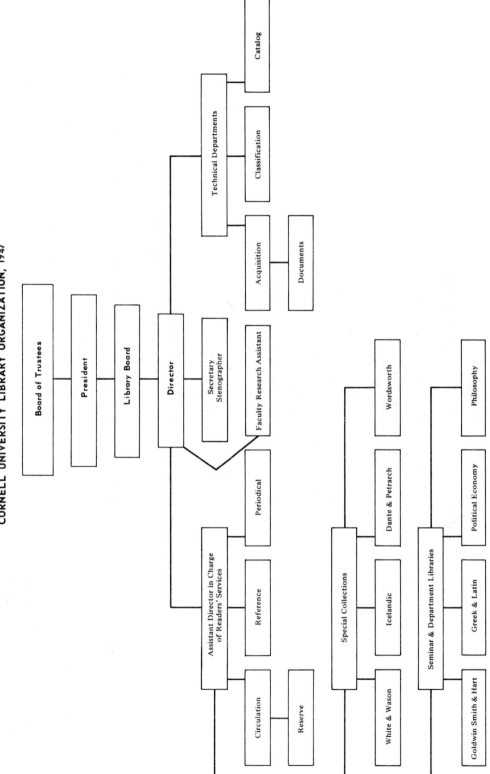

FIGURE 2
CORNELL UNIVERSITY LIBRARY ORGANIZATION, 1947

FIGURE 3

COLLEGE OF AGRICULTURE LIBRARY ORGANIZATION, 1947

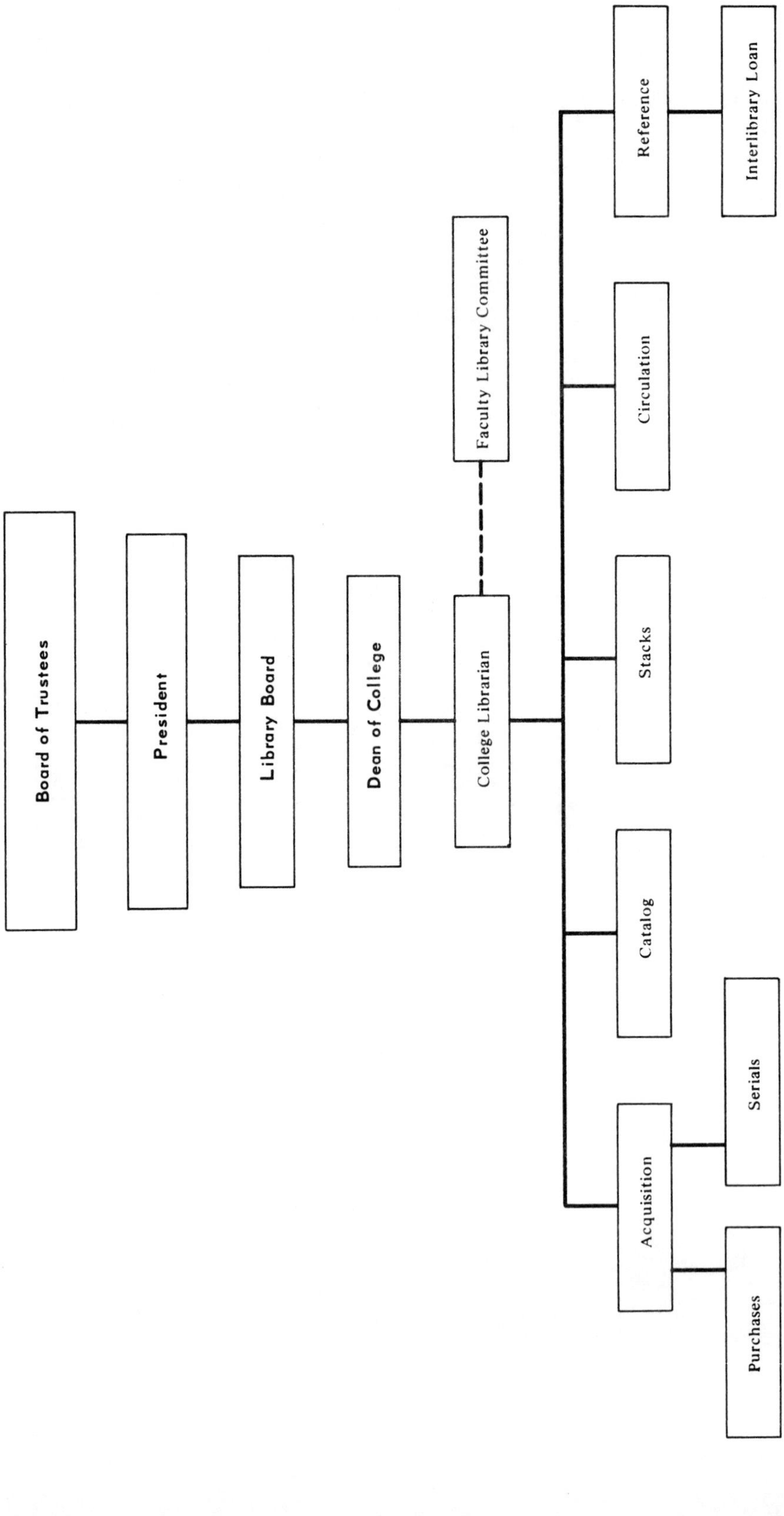

The Department has charge of reserve desks or rooms and of the library stacks and storage areas. The Reference Department has three professional librarians and two half-time graduate assistants. Until 1947 the Cornell Library did not posess a separately organized reference division with its own staff, and there is still under way selection of an up-to-date reference book collection and other materials needed to carry on its functions. The Reference Department is responsible for the provision of reference service to the users of the Library, for interlibrary loans, for reference service on government documents, and for instruction and training in the use of the Library. In the Periodical Department are the Periodical Librarian, three clerical assistants, and part-time desk attendants. For current periodicals, the Department is responsible for maintaining files, keeping records, and giving reference service. Sets of the most used general periodicals are housed in the Periodical Room. Another responsibility of the Department is the preparation of materials for the bindery, and the receipt and checking of shipments from the bindery. The special collections—White and Wason, Icelandic, Dante and Petrarch, and Wordsworth—have curators to provide expert research assistance and to select items for acquisition. Goldwin Smith Library, in Goldwin Smith Hall, composed of reserve books, is in charge of a librarian, with part-time desk assistants. The three seminar libraries—Greek and Latin, Political Economy, and Philosophy—are unstaffed.

The Technical Services are primarily concerned with the acquisition of library materials and their preparation for use. Each of the three divisions, Acquisition, Classification, and Catalog, has a head who reports to the Director. The Acquisition Department has the responsibility for acquiring all materials added to the Library by purchase, gift, or exchange. This includes government documents as well as books and periodicals. The Department is also in charge of the Library's duplicate collection and is responsible for its disposition through sale, gift, or exchange. The Catalog Department has responsibility for cataloging all materials added to the Library, except for the Icelandic Collection. The Classification Department has similar duties, classifying all material added to the main Library and a

number of departmental libraries on the campus. In view of the closely-related nature of their activities and the many points at which they touch, appointment of an Assistant Director for Technical Services, corresponding to the Assistant Director for Readers' Services, would be a logical next step. As a matter of fact, the Acquisition Librarian has recently been assigned the additional responsibility of coordinating the activities of all the technical service departments, in line with the above recommendation. The Catalog and Classification Librarians, however, are continuing to report directly to the Director concerning the activities of their departments.

Departmental Libraries in the Endowed Colleges at Ithaca

Some indication of the organizational complexities of departmental libraries at Cornell was given in the chapter on Financial Administration. Finances, however, are only one aspect of the problem, which is characterized by a bewildering variety of practices resulting from the lack of central direction. Libraries connected with endowed colleges on the campus include Architecture, Barnes (religion), Browsing (Willard Straight), Business, Chemistry, Chemical Engineering, Engineering, Geology, Law, Mathematics, Military, Music, Physics, and Zoology. These range from units which are little larger than office collections, e.g., Military, to large, highly-organized libraries such as Law. In some instances professional librarians are in charge, in others part-time secretaries. All technical processes may be carried on, as in Law, or acquisition and cataloging may be handled by the University Library. The supporting college may provide all funds for salaries, books, and other costs, as previously mentioned, or books may be purchased in whole or in part from the University Library appropriation. Despite recent efforts to achieve some uniformity in hours open for use, schedules still vary widely. Administrative control of the major departmental libraries is usually in the hands of the college deans, to whom the librarians report directly, while the smaller libraries are ordinarily supervised by department heads or departmental library committees. In the case of the Regional History Collection, the curator is directly responsible to the President of the University.

Departmental Libraries in the State Colleges

No less diverse are the libraries connected with the State Colleges, which include the Agriculture, Agricultural Economics, Agronomy, Animal Husbandry, Apiculture, Botany, Dairy Industry, Entomology, Floriculture, Forestry, Home Economics, Industrial and Labor Relations, Nature Study, Nutrition (Animal), Ornithology, Plant Breeding, Plant Pathology, Poultry, and Veterinary libraries. Their connections with the University Library are fewer than those of departmental libraries in the endowed colleges, though a number of endowment funds for the purchase of materials in fields covered by the State College libraries are held by the University Library, and two University endowment funds are administered by the Agriculture Library. A majority of libraries in the state group are essentially laboratory or office collections directly under the administration of department heads or committees, and not exceeding 3,500 volumes in size. Conspicious exceptions are the Agriculture, Agricultural Economics, Entomology, Home Economics, Industrial and Labor Relations, Plant Breeding, and Veterinary libraries, which range from 10,000 to 160,000 volumes. Eventually it is planned to merge the Agriculture, Agricultural Economics, and Home Economics libraries in a new library building projected for the campus of the State Colleges, but at present each is largely autonomous. Exceptions which might be noted are the handling of technical processes for the Home Economics Library in the Agriculture Library, and the chairmanship of the Agricultural Economics Library faculty committee, held by the Agriculture Librarian. These two connections permit a limited degree of coordination.

GENERAL CRITICISM

At numerous points the existing library situation at Cornell violates sound principles of administration and organization. It is obvious also that the longer the extreme *laissez-faire* methods of the past are allowed to continue, the more difficult it will become to achieve any effective administrative organization. Accordingly, decisive measures

should be taken as promptly as possible to reorganize the libraries from the point of view of administrative control and over-all planning. Certain steps to effect these changes are proposed in this chapter.

Long experience, some costly and bitter, in universities throughout the country has demonstrated beyond reasonable doubt that unity of management and control of all library staff, materials, and facilities is essential to economical and efficient service to the whole university. The tables on expenditures in Chapter 4 reveal that Cornell is spending substantial sums of money for library support, but it is certain the returns from these expenditures, from a University-wide point of view, are far less than the benefits which would come from the same funds spent with the needs of the entire institution in mind.

It should be made clear at this point that the surveyors do not favor too extensive consolidation of book collections. They recognize that some degree of decentralization is necessary and desirable to facilitate instruction and research and in order to provide the most useful library service. On the other hand, the multiplication of departmental collections too small to be staffed or serviced economically or which require an extensive duplication of books is unnecessary and undesirable. As new building plans mature around the campus, it should be quite feasible to merge departmental libraries in closely related fields into larger units, perhaps along broad divisional lines, such as biological sciences or physical sciences, especially if the teaching departments they serve are contiguous. These larger units would then be in a position to employ better trained staffs, maintain longer hours of opening, eliminate duplication of purchases and records, and serve more students and faculty members.

Under existing arrangements, the Director of the University Library has little campus-wide library authority. By direction of the Library Board, he collects data for annual reports from all libraries and he may be called upon to act as advisor to departmental libraries whenever questions of mutual interest and concern arise. When problems related to the libraries in general are under consideration, the Director may present his own point of view and reasons why a given course of action appears desirable. Whether or not suggestions made by the Director are followed, however, is a voluntary matter. Such casual relationships, with the Director possessing only advisory functions, could never result in a really effective organization. A specific illustration is the matter of library buildings, with no less than seven University decisions now preparing library plans independently, without consideration with the Director of the Library Board.

PROPOSED ORGANIZATION

The reorganization represented in Figure 4 is submitted to show the general character of the changes which the surveyors recommend. It will be noted that this chart accepts all library divisions as they now stand. There are definite plans, however, to transfer Business, Goldwin Smith, and Regional History to a new University Library building, and to merge Agriculture, Agricultural Economics, and Home Economics in the new Agriculture library building. Other consolidations, revisions, or changes are matters for further study.

The first recommendation is for the appointment of three principal administrative officers for the Library, to work with the Director: (1) Associate Director for agriculture and related libraries; (2) Associate Director for departmental libraries in other fields and for readers' service departments in the main library building; (3) Assistant Director for technical services. Fortunately, this proposal could be carried into effect without employment of additional staff. It would merely require an expansion of the duties and responsibilities of three existing officers, namely the College of Agriculture Librarian, the Assistant Director of the University Library, and the Acquisition Librarian, all of whom are fully competent to assume the broader functions.

Under the Associate Director for Agriculture and related libraries would be placed jurisdiction over the following group: Agriculture, Agricultural Economics, Agronomy, Animal Husbandry, Botany, Dairy Industry, Entomology (including Apiculture), Floriculture, Forestry, Geneva Experiment Station, Home Economics, Nature Study, Nutrition (Animal), Ornithology, Plant Breeding, Plant Pathology, Poultry, and Veterinary libraries. The second Associate Director would take responsibility for the Circulation, Reference, and Periodical Departments and the several special collec-

tions in the main library and the following college and departmental libraries: Architecture, Barnes, Browsing, Business, Chemistry, Chemical Engineering, Engineering, Geology, Industrial and Labor Relations, Mathematics, Military, Music, Physics, Regional History, and Zoology.

The Assistant Director for Technical Services would supervise not only the technical processes carried on in the main library, as at present, but would coordinate and direct acquisition, cataloguing and classification everywhere in the library system. Given existing space conditions, any complete centralization of such work for the entire campus must probably await a new general library building. Less revision in future will be called for, however, and a smoother operating organization achieved immediately if some one capable person is given oversight of all activities involved in the preparation of material for use. Among the Assistant Director's responsibilities would be the completion of a union catalog in the main library, recording of all books on the campus belonging to the University; promotion of a uniform classification scheme throughout the library organization; setting up of standards of binding and arranging contracts with one or more qualified firms to bind material for all the libraries; obtaining maximum value from book appropriations in various library divisions by thorough familiarity with the book market, by getting bids on periodical subscription lists, by quantity purchasing, and by standardized order routines; and the development of photographic reproduction facilities, especially microfilm, to serve library needs.

It will be noted that in the chart of the proposed organization three divisions would maintain their independent status—Aeronautical, Law, and Medicine. Because of the nature of legal materials, the slight amount of overlapping in collections, and the excellent organization now found in the Law Library, the advantages of central control would be relatively slight, and a loss of its present autonomy might be injurious from the point of view of College of Law support and interest. On the other hand, certain collections in Law, such as League of Nations and United Nations documents, are of interest to students in other departments of the University, and library resources elsewhere on the campus may be use-

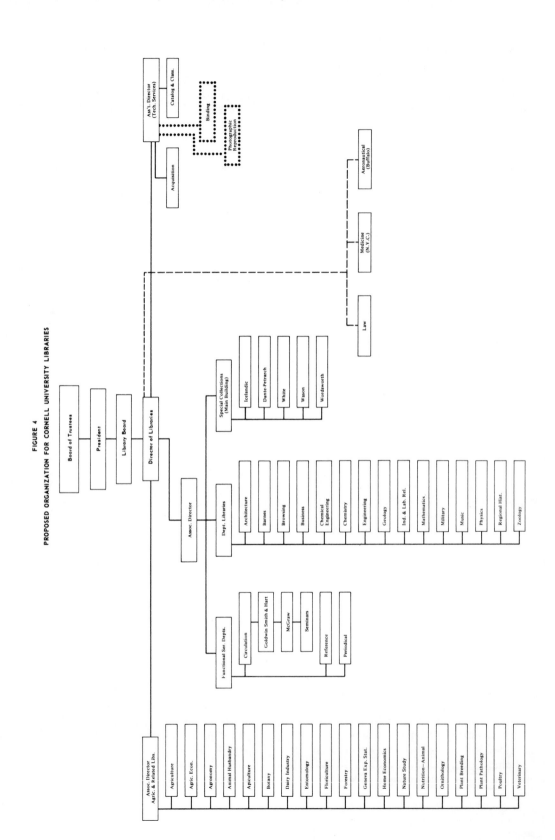

FIGURE 4
PROPOSED ORGANIZATION FOR CORNELL UNIVERSITY LIBRARIES

ful to law students. Consequently close relationships and a high degree of cooperation
should exist between the Law Library and
the general University Library system. The
Director ought to be consulted on the new
Law Library programs and act in an advisory
capacity to the Law Librarian as occassions
arise.

As for the Medical Library in New York
City, and the Aeronautical Library in Buffalo,
their specialized character and remoteness
from the Ithaca campus would make control
by the Director of somewhat questionable
value. Again, however, cooperative efforts
of mutual advantage should be encouraged,
and all divisions should submit annual reports, or any special reports which may be
desired, to the Director of Libraries.

The status of the Regional History Collection calls for special comment. During its
relatively brief career, this division has brought
together an extensive and valuable collection
of manuscript and printed materials. Conditions under which these documents are
stored leave much to be desired, and eventually
it is planned to transfer them to the new Agriculture Library building, when erected, or
to the University Library building when space
can be provided there. Meanwhile the growth
of the collection without close consultation
with the Library administration, which probably must ultimately assume responsibility
for its care and use, is creating problems for
the future. The experience at Duke University, the University of Virginia, University of
North Carolina, and other institutions which
have developed large manuscript sections of
similar character demonstrates that a close
tie-up with the university library has numerous advantages. Effective use of manuscript records, it has been found, cannot be
made without ready access to printed works,
such as government publications, biographical dictionaries, reference tools, historical
treatises, and, in fact, the entire resources
of a large research library. Because of this
indispensable relationship, it is proposed that
the Regional History Collection be made an
integral part of the University Library system,
and its future program be planned jointly by
the principal interests concerned.

The Director's Office

The recommended form of organization
for the library system would delegate considerable authority and responsibility by the
Director to strong associate and assistant directors. It would be an impossible assignment
for the Director to undertake the whole administrative task alone, even if he devoted his full
time to general administrative problems.
More effective service in the University Library has already come from delegation
of certain duties to an assistant director, and,
of course, the proposed organization would be
far more complex and ramified than the present
comparatively limited general library functions.
In any case, the Director should be relieved of
routine technical matters in connection with
library operations, in order to be able to devote his time and energy to faculty contacts,
to planning for the library in all its phases,
working toward improved coordination of library activities, developing the program of
the Library Associates, and promoting the
interests of the libraries generally.

Several additional activities in connection
with internal administration of the libraries
might well concern the Director's office. Continuation of the excellent "Library Staff
Memorandum" series, started in 1947, would
be useful in informing the staff of administrative decisions and policies and for reporting on
matters of general interest. An informal mimeographed news sheet for distribution to the widely
scattered libraries of the University could serve
a like purpose. A general staff manual relating to procedures, organization, personnel,
etc., has been found valuable in numerous
large libraries, and compilation of such a
manual for the whole library system might
be sponsored by the Director's office. Staff
meetings at frequent intervals, including the
general administrative officers, division chiefs,
and principal departmental librarians, should
be held to discuss library problems and to
keep the staff informed of matters of interdepartmental concern. Organization of a
general staff association which would interest
itself in professional and social affairs and arrange for gatherings of the entire staff would
contribute much to a strong *esprit de corps.*

CONCLUSION

The recommendations contained in this chapter involve something of a revolution in the Cornell library picture, and differences of opinion are likely to be expressed about their desirability and feasibility. Nevertheless, there seems no sound alternative . The results of extreme decentralization of control when applied to libraries is all to clear at Cornell. Until the principle is thoroughly established and maintained that all library materials which are the property of the University (regardless of how acquired or where located), and all library personnel employed by the University are integral parts of the University library system, library service of first-rate quality will be lacking on the Cornell campus. The library's sole object should be, and undoubedly is, to supply the best possible service to all instructional and research departments. Accordingly, the proposal for centralized direction should not be interpreted as a move to deprive any division of anything it may now possess, but as a measure to insure that every department of the University will get the largest possible returns from the University's investment in library service.

RECOMMENDATIONS

It is recommended:

1. That the Cornell Library organization be revised to bring about centalized direction.

2. That to assist the Director, three general library administrative officers be appointed: (a) Associate Director for agriculture and related fields, (b) Associate Director for departmental libraries in other fields and for readers' service departments in the main library building, and (c) Assistant Director for technical services.

3. That the Aeronautical, Law, and Medical Libraries remain largely autonomous, but that they cooperate closely with the remainder of the library system, furnish such reports as may be required, and that the Director advise in their further development.

4. That the Regional History Collection be fully integrated with the University Library.

5. That, freed from some of his routine administrative responsibilities, the Director devote attention to such matters as general planning for the libraries, building up an able staff, developing the book collection, working with the faculty, promoting the Library Associates, and otherwise strengthening the librarie's place in the University.

ABOUT THE AUTHORS

—**Louis R. Wilson**, Dean Emeritus, Graduate Library School, University of Chicago; Ph.D., 1905, University of North Carolina. At present his research deals with the men and movements of the University of North Carolina.

—**Robert B. Downs**, Dean of Library Administration, University of Illinois; M.S., 1929, Columbia University. His current research interests lie in the study of influential books, American library resources, and intellectual freedom.

—**Maurice F. Tauber**, Melvil Dewey Professor of Library Service, Columbia University; Ph.D., 1941, University of Chicago. His teaching and research interests include technical services, documentation, library education, and library administration.

The Place of the Law School Library in Library Administration

by Miles O. Price

This article provides the academic library administrator with the essential arguments for alternative structural arrangements to achieve the satisfaction of specialized needs. While the author sees in the quality of personalities—rather than in particular organizational and operational schemes—the ingredients which will determine accommodation among the library components, he does suggest that the specialized library response offers an advantage to its clientele and its particular library staff.

The administration of the law school library—whether as an autonomous unit under the dean or integrated as a unit of the university library system under the director of libraries—has long been a sore point with both deans and directors.[1] The matter was brought to a head on March 10, 1958, by a letter from John G. Hervey, Advisor to the Section of Legal Education and Admissions to the Bar, of the American Bar Association, addressed to the deans of all "approved" schools, in which he set forth the rule, adopted by the council of the association, that

> . . . it [the law school library] should be administered by the law school as an autonomous unit, free of outside control. Exceptions are permissible only where this is preponderance of affirmative evidence in a particular school, satisfactory to the Council, that the advantages of autonomy can be preserved and economy in administration attained through centralizing the responsibility for acquisition, circulating, cataloging, ordering, processing, or payment for books ordered. . . .

This Council action was reaffirmed at the 1959 Annual Meeting of the American Bar Association.

It is my earnest belief that, with respect to the place of the law school library in the administrative scheme, whether autonomous under the dean or integrated under the director, personalities are much more important than formal organization. With all concerned—law school and central library—working for the benefit of Dear Old Siwash, any set-up will work admirably within budget limitations. On the other hand, a group of prima donnas bent more on maintaining their personal perogatives than on achieving their function of service to their university will wreck any scheme. Granting this, there are still measurable theoretical advantages and disadvantages under either arrangement.

It should be borne in mind to begin with that very few law school libraries are either entirely integrated or autonomous. Most "autonomous" libraries are subject to one or more of the following: book binding fund allocations by the central library, technical processing controls, university-wide salary regulations, division of librarians' duties between library administration (paid for by the director) and teaching (paid for by the dean). The principal stigmata of the so-called "autonomous" law school library are closer budget control by the law school, hiring and discharge of library personnel, and book-selection autonomy. It is in the discussion of the exercise of these functions, as between director and dean, that the most significant analytical fallacies occur.

SOURCE: Reprinted from Miles O. Price, "The Place of the Law School Library in Library Administration," *Journal of Legal Education* 13: 230-238 (1960), by permission of the publisher. Originally published in *College and Research Libraries* 21: 13-19 (1960).

To advert to personalities: The dean is the most important single factor in developing the collection and rendering reasonably satisfactory service—and this whether the library is autonomous (as most law school libraries are to some extent) or integrated (as some of the largest and best are). With a library-minded dean, conscious of the place of the law library in his scheme of things and willing to fight for it, success within budget limitations is almost assured under either system. On the other hand, if the dean is indifferent to the library needs, or weak, the autonomous library is a mess (and for every unsatisfactory law library in a centralized system, I can show you an autonomous library just as bad). Contrariwise, in a centalized system, the law library may or may not be a stepchild, depending upon how enlightened the director is and how willing he is to cooperate in solving the peculiar problems of the law library.

The next important factor in a successful law school library is the law librarian. The dean's interest in his library is only one of his many interests; the director's is spread throughout the whole campus system; but the law library is its librarian's career. Properly chosen by reason of education, experience, and personality, he can, if given his head to a reasonable extent, develop his collection and render good service to his clientele, regardless of the formal organization.

ASSERTED ADVANTAGES OF THE AUTONOMOUS LAW LIBRARY

The principal argument advanced in favor of law school control of the library is that the library serving the law school occupies a unique position among professional libraries and so should not be governed by general administrative rules. It is the laboratory of the law school, the repository of source as well as of secondary material. Its material is not only highly specialized (a quality it shares with the libraries of other disciplines, such as medicine and engineering), but the books are of a most complicated character, requiring for their effective selection and service training in their subject matter and make-up. Library training and experience in general libraries alone are not sufficient. Since the law faculty is so much more familiar with the problems involved than the central library administration, it should control the library; the control should be close, not remote from an ivory tower.

The only point in the above that is not common to all professional school libraries is the uniqueness of the law library as a laboratory, with such highly specialized types of books as to require special knowledge and techniques for their effective utilization in serving the clientele. As a librarian with nineteen year's experience in general university and technical and scientific libraries before coming into law, I can vouch for the validity of this point; until directors come to understand this and act accordingly, there will be lack of *rapport* between the law school and the general library.

Another point stressed by the law school is that the faculty, all law-trained and requiring for the key library positions law-trained personnel believes that it, not the central library, is uniquely equipped by understanding of the subject matter and curriculum to select the library books and to appraise the qualification of the librarian and professional staff. It concedes the value of professional library training—which it more and more requires of its staff—but asserts the paramount necessity of law training in addition; and, since librarians trained in both disciplines are now available, it sees little reason for the intermediation of the central library.

As a law librarian who learned his law and law books on the job, I believe wholeheartedly in the need of the law-trained librarian. In addition, however, he needs broad library training and experience, a fact that law schools concede, as is shown by the fact that, particularly since World War II, practically all the better jobs have gone to both law and library school degrees. A fallacy in the reasoning of the law schools, however, is that the director does not realize the professional needs of the law school library. In fact, as will be pointed out later, it is common practice for the head and assistant librarians of law schools to be chosen only after consultation with the law school.

Most of the other advantages claimed for the autonomous law school library fail to withstand factual analysis—always granted that prima donnas and empire builders do not interfere with library operation.

Budget Control

It is commonly asserted that in the integrated library, the dean has nothing to say about library funds. That is up to the dean and is not inherent in the organizational set-up. Budgets are not made, and certainly not adopted, in a vacuum in the director's office. In the integrated library, the law librarian with any sense has his ear to the ground to learn of the dean's desires. So at budget time, he consults the dean as to all his financial needs for the coming year, for books and continuations, for staff, and for major equipment.

Furthermore, the dean is a very important member of the university administrative community. He is usually a member of the council or senate considering budget demands of all university departments and has his day in court on library as well as law school matters. Paradoxically, the dean is in the position of being able to fight more wholeheartedly for integrated library budget items than if the library were under his complete law school control. It is no skin off his nose if they are granted; whereas if on the law school budget, they might make his total too large and result in cuts for other law school items. In two recent instances known to me, autonomous libraries actually encountered this situation and suffered.

As for fund control after the appropriation is made, there is considerable of this, by moral suasion if not directly. For example, the director follows budget lines or departs from them only in unusual circumstances and by permission. Law library items in the central budget commonly have their own lines and are not merely a part of a lump sum, juggled more or less at will between departments by the director. Neither is the law library budget necessarily a fixed percentage of that of the entire library system, as is true of book funds for some outstanding autonomous law school libraries.

Acquisitions and Technical Processes

Book Selection

Frustration in this in the integrated library is a universal argument brought up against integration, also without much basis in fact. It all depends upon the cooperation between director and dean. A vigorous dean, through his library committee, makes his policies and immediate wants known: a wise director goes along, with a liberal exercise of his directionary powers. I know book-selection policies among law school libraries very well, and I am quite certain that where the law library is on the general library campus, the nonduplication policy general among the libraries is observed by autonomous libraries to just about the same extent as by the integrated ones; to do otherwise would be indefensible. It is elementary that money spent for duplicating book A, which is in Business, cannot purchase book B, which is not in Law but needed there; and that if the needs of Law can be served by borrowing book A from Business, Law may then buy book B. Within broad guidelines, established in consultation between general library and law school, the law librarian's discretion should seldom be interfered with; it is by no means inherent in the integrated scheme that it should be.

Gifts and Exchanges

These are important. In the integrated setup, those received by the central library are sent to Law if of appropriate subject matter. In the absence of difficult personnel, this policy can just as well be followed for the autonomous library.

Cataloging

This is a most important aspect of law library service, but no problem of organization should be involved. In many autonomous libraries, the cataloging is farmed out to the general library. It is important, however, that the work be done in Law (for expedition and opportunity of consultation with law-trained personnel) and that Law, within the confines of decent cataloging policies, be permitted to set the policies.

Book Classification

It is charged that sometimes the general library forces the integrated library to classify its books according to some general classification scheme. If this has been done anywhere, it is very silly, indeed. There is at present no satisfactory classification scheme for Anglo-American law books, though the Library of Congress is about to embark seriously upon the study of its Schedule K for law.

Binding

In my own experience, the allocation by the general library in integrated schemes works better than that in autonomous. At least binding money is spent for binding and not diverted to some other law school purpose. It is not, however, inherent in either scheme and is not an argument for either setup.

Order Routine

Delay and misunderstanding caused by channeling orders and books received through the central library acquisitions department are common and often justified. There is inherent some delay, and law librarians feel that they lose many antiquarian books through delay, lack of knowledge of sources, and the like. If shipments are made in gross from abroad to the central library, Law frequently does not receive its continuations as promptly as it would in an autonomous setup. On the other hand, the expertise of the central library saves the law library many a headache in routine matters. The difficulty is that in both cataloging and order work, processing outside of Law causes delay.

A point not always considered by the critics of the integrated library is that of staff quarters. The law school building and its library quarters must be substantially enlarged if the technical processes are to be done in Law. Furthermore, at least at Columbia, many supplies are provided by the central library free to Law, which, in the autonomous setup, would have to be provided by the law school.

Staff

Frequent objection is voiced to any degree of staff control by the director, whether appointment, payment, or supervision, and there is often validity, particularly when the director equates all central library salaries to those of supposedly similar law jobs.

The degree of control varies widely. In some universities, the law school has complete control; in others, the director. A not uncommon arrangement is the splitting of the head librarian's salary payment between the dean and the director, with the dean paying the librarian a stipend for whatever teaching he does, and the director paying him for his services as librarian. This device also helps solve the problem of faculty rank and status, which are important to the librarian.

In the fully autonomous library, appointment and salary are Law matters; but even here, in all schools with which I am acquainted, the central library salary scale is substantially followed for most jobs, certainly for clericals and professionals other than librarian, first assistant librarian, and perhaps the reference librarian. In the autonomous library, the three positions mentioned, calling for professional subject-matter competence, properly tend to be compensated as law jobs. As for the rest, there is no good reason why a routine professional or clerical job performed in a law library should be treated differently than in any other learned library; and as far as I know, the campus-wide library scale is carefully adhered to, even in autonomous schools.

Real trouble comes for the integrated library when, as too often happens, the director equates the law positions with all others in his system. The really pernicious practice is to limit the law librarian's salary to the amount of the assistant director's. This is an indefensible practice that has resulted in the actual and potential loss of many a good head law librarian in integrated schools.

A major point in the American Bar Association directive is that appointments should be made by the dean, and that those carrying faculty rank should be approved by the faculty. This is flogging a dead horse. Integrated library appointments of librarian or assistant librarian (particularly when the latter also is limited to those with law degrees) are "by and with the consent" of the law faculty. It would be a most unusual case in which the director would arbitrarily appoint either without the full knowledge and consent of the law faculty, which body normally would have met and carefully considered candidates for the position. Lesser positions can just as well be filled from the larger reservoir of central library personnel files.

The size of the staff causes some difficulty between the integrated library and the dean. The dean may feel that additional personnel are needed, but he has only persuasive powers to enforce his will and may dislike interfering in another officer's jurisdiction. By the same token, it is my own experience that the small integrated library has a better staff than a similar autonomous library. Librarianship is the central librarie's business, and they are equipped and anxious to give and appreciate expert operation. The same is too often not true of the autonomous library.

Staff control by the director may result in continual frustration if the director is a prima donna or empire builder, jealous of his perogatives and unwilling to delegate sufficient of them to the law librarian.

ASSERTED ADVANTAGES OF THE INTEGRATED LAW LIBRARY

Such advantages as there are inhere chiefly in the library really too small to stand on its own feet as an efficient, separate administrative unit. Running a library is library business, a matter for experts in this profession. Any university having a law school has a fairly large and well organized library system, staffed by experts who make library administration a career and are especially trained for it. Librarianship is not static, and its developments must be followed, as is true of any learned profession. Librarians, through their associations, do this; the dean lacks time or interest for it.

In a small autonomous law library, the librarian tends to be a lawyer plucked from a graduating class, with little or no training or interest in the science of librarianship, though this is by no means always true. On the other hand, increasingly, the law school librarian of medium and large-sized libraries is both a law and library school graduate, with a staff and collection comparable with those of many college libraries. Such a librarian should be able to stand on his own feet, fully professional as to both the law and the library sides of his job. I believe there may be definite advantages in autonomy for the large, self-contained library, though by no means to the extent claimed for it.

University-wide, the integration of all units of the library system under the director is said to make for added efficiency and economy. This the dean is likely to deny.

An objection earnestly made to autonomy is the consequent difficulty of intralibrary loans, between Law and any other central library department. It is asserted seriously that, following such autonomy, the central library would refuse or be reluctant to lend its books to Law, and that as a consequence, Law would have to purchase material it would otherwise borrow. I cannot conceive of any university president who would permit such an absurdity.

HEAD LAW LIBRARIAN'S ATTITUDE

One factor of great importance remains to be mentioned, the head librarian's attitude. Massey[2] has recorded the almost unanimous preference of law school librarians answering her questionnaire for the autonomous library. This accords with the knowledge of other school librarians and with my own long and extensive experience in placement work. This preference is very important to the school seeking a qualified law librarian. There is now a bull market in qualified law librarians; and to a great extent, such a person can pick and choose among law school jobs. Therefore, the library seeking an outstanding person must have something to offer.

Salary

This is probably the first attraction. The minimum now paid in large or fairly large law school libraries is about $12,000, with ranges up to above $16,000. Head librarians' salaries in autonomous libraries definitely average higher than in integrated ones because deans tend to think in terms of law faculty status and salaries generally, directors in terms of the usually lower library ranges. Librarians have the feeling, also, that they benefit more by across-the-board faculty salary increases, but this is by no means always true. In any event, the law librarian's heart follows his pocket book, other things being equal.

Academic Status and Rank

These are dear to the law librarian's heart and perhaps of even greater importance than salary alone (partly because salary and status are so often tied together). The librarian accorded academic rank and status in his institution is thereby made a member of the lodge in good standing, which is significant in his relations with both faculty and students. To be sure, in most schools, professional library staff members have a sort of academic status, varying greatly with the institution, but it is an *ersatz* arrangement, generally regarded as inferior to that of a seat on the faculty served.

The difference is both a matter of prestige among his faculty and students and of direct communication between faculty and librarian. Given anything like equal opportunity as between jobs, the law school librarian will almost invariably accept the autonomous library position. All this has one important by-product, tending to raise the quality of head law school librarians: The schools say, with perfect logic, "If you're to be made a member of our faculty, you've jolly well got to measure up to the same selection standards as the rest of us." This separates the men from the boys. It may be noted that integrated librarians also have been accorded full professorial rank and status by the law schools served, and that autonomous libraries have rejected it. Here, again, it is a matter of personality rather than of organization.

SUMMARY

Nearly all of the advantages urged in favor of the autonomous law school library and against the integrated one fall before careful analysis. Given a strong and interested dean and a capable and reasonable director, either will work. Either will just as assuredly fail if the dean will not fight for his library and the director is an empire builder. Just as many, proportionately, fail of realizing their potential under one scheme as the other, but the results from the autonomous library are more likely to be unsatisfactory with the small library than with one large enough to be self-sufficient under the leadership of a well-trained and otherwise competent librarian.

Budget control, book selection, and processing need cause little difficulty under either system. The quality of service to users need not be dependent at all upon formal organization. We have a saying at Columbia that every time the dean sneezes the library says "God bless you." The dean of any school can always get the sort of service he wants from the integrated library, within budgetary limitations, and is likely to be relieved thereby from many arduous routine detail and space troubles.

The principal dangers and disadvantages of the autonomous library are the too frequent lack of interest or aggressiveness on the part of the dean, resulting in a poor technical staff and administration, as opposed to the expertise of the central library and its constant contact with agencies aiming to improve library methods, and its insistence upon high technical standards.

The disadvantages said to be inherent in the integrated library (though in practice they are less than in theory, except as to faculty rank and status) have chiefly to do with control: an empire-building director, unwilling to delegate sufficient power of operation to his law librarian, tying his salary to that of his assistant director, and paying too little deference to the desires and needs of the dean can play hob with library development and service if the dean lets him. It has been done. The law librarians, with practical unanimity, prefer the autonomous library; the large integrated library, at least unless it can persuade the law school to grant full professorial rank and status to its librarian, stands in danger of securing only second-rate head librarians. A fairly common solution of this dilemma is the joint appointment of the law librarian (especially of an integrated library) by both dean and director, in which case, the major share of his combined salary is paid by the director. Academic rank and status are thus granted, and the librarian is satisfied on this point.

To repeat my first observation: Personalities are more important than formal organization; it is like marriage, which succeeds or fails on the basis of the parties participating. There is much to be said for either the autonomous or the integrated library, but both the dean and the director should realize that cooperation is vital.

Mr. Hervey's dream of a law school library without "outside control" is, of course, just that. Any agency of a university is subject to control. There is no Santa Claus, and placing the law library under the dean is not going automatically, to solve all problems in which money is involved, which is about all of them.

FOOTNOTES

[1] Since, with one exception, the statements of law librarians on the subject of this paper have been the product of those from autonomous libraries and without general library or integrated law library experience, perhaps I should state whatever qualifications I may possess for intruding my views on a controversial subject. Prior to becoming librarian of the Columbia Law Library (an "integrated" library) thirty years ago, I had been in library work in other fields for nineteen years, in two large universities and (for seven years) as librarian of one of the largest technical libraries, with a staff then of thirty-eight. My university library work included such diverse positions as that of circulation assistant in a divinity school library, supervision of a 50,000 volume modern languages library, general reference work, and heading gifts and exchanges. As law librarian and teacher of a course in law librarianship, I, for many years, was active in personnel placement work in the field, during which time I had extended and constant contact with the deans and directors of many schools employing law librarians, and with whom, by correspondence and personal interviews, I discussed at length their library problems.

[2] Massey, *Law School Administration and the Law Librarian,* 10 J. LEGAL ED. 215 (1957).

ABOUT THE AUTHOR

—**Miles O. Price** (d. 1968), Law Librarian and Professor of Law, Columbia University, 1929-1961; B.L.S., 1922, University of Illinois; L.L.B., 1938, Columbia University Law School. His major interests were law and administration.

How Much is a Physicist's Inertia Worth?

by Jesse H. Shera

The classic arguments of the academic library administrator for centralization are presented cogently in this article. However many times they are stated as administrative orthodoxy they apparently do not give centralization immutability. That these arguments are not wholly acceptable does not diminish their validity. This should suggest to the librarian that this ideal library arrangement is at variance with the reality in which faculty live. What is indicated is a fuller comprehension by the academic librarian of this reality and, consequently, clearer substantive definitions of the functions of the library in the academic community before an organizational response is fixed.

In an article entitled "Individual Departmental Libraries vs. Consolidated Science Libraries" *(Physics Today,* May 1961, pp. 40-41), Professor D. A. Wells of the University of Cincinnati reported on a poll of 126 chairmen of physics departments with respect to their opinions of consolidated science libraries. His results indicated that 84 "were strongly in favor of departmental libraries", 17 "made no positive committment", 3 favored consolidation, and 22 did not reply. Professor Wells follows these statistics, which he does not refine to show which of his respondents were and which were not served by a centralized library, with a series of quotations setting forth the arguments favoring individual departmental libraries. But, he fails to present the reasoning for the other side. Without providing the reader with the opportunity to judge for himself, and by carefully suppressing any point of view that differs from his own, he concludes: "The few arguments which may be advanced in favor of the consolidated library can easily be given their proper perspective." This is scarcely scientific objectivity. In the interest, then, of permitting the reviewer to establish his own perspective, it would seem only proper and fair to enumerate arguments in support of consolidation.

Convenience

None of the statements quoted by Professor Wells sets forth any argument for individual libraries other than the convenience of the user. No one will disagree that a book in the hand is more convenient than twenty down the hall, but according to Dr. Wells intensity of scholarship in physics is much like that of light—it varies with the square of the distance. Moreover, Dr. Wells concerns himself only with the convenience of the faculty, he does not appear to be concerned with the convenience of the student who may be compelled to go to the physics library for his physics books, the mathematics library for his mathematics books, the chemistry library for his chemistry books and God-knows-where for the books that fall between. Only one who, like the present writer, has struggled, both as a student and a faculty member, with the more than twenty departmental collections of the University of Chicago can appreciate the headaches such a system imposes. An academic library is not a private estate from which the great unwashed are to be barred. No one would deny that there are certain basic titles, perhaps even the files of *Physics Today,* which every faculty member must have constantly within reach; but these materials should be the personal property of the scholar. They represent expenditures that are tax deductible, and in the income bracket at which most physicists find themselves scientific books probably cost only ten cents on the dollar. Certainly the Federal Government is doing all it can to

SOURCE: Reprinted from Jesse H. Shera, "How Much is a Physicist's Inertia Worth?" *Physics Today* 14: 42-43 (1961), by permission of the publisher and the author.

revive the tradition of the book-lined office of the nineteenth century German scholar.

Interdisciplinary Relationships

The steady erosion of the old disciplinary boundaries is an important characteristic of mid-twentieth century science, and the emergence of such interdisciplinary studies as biochemistry, biophysics, physical chemistry, and solid state will increasingly demand that the scientist in one field will need access to the materials in other departments. This is as true for libraries as it is for reactors and computers. During our career as a practicing librarian we have been called upon more than once to arbitrate an angry interdepartmental tussle for the possession of an unusually expensive volume or a long file of a scientific journal. Thus, we suggest that the modern science center might present an architectural configuration of a great wheel, or pentagon, in which the science library would be the hub, the radiating spokes the major disciplines—physics, mathematics, chemistry, the biological sciences—and the rim the laboratories. In such a way cross-pollinization could take place both in the laboratory and in the library, and the inner courts could provide an hospitable retreat for the dove of peace. The scientist can no more afford bibliographic isolation than can a nation endure political isolation. The cross-fertilization of disciplines, therefore compels either library consolidation or extensive duplication. With the costs of scientific publications rising almost at an exponential rate, one can seriously doubt whether university administrators, confronted by budgets that are themselves finite entities, will place a very high premium on the inertia of the physicists.

Economic Advantage

A centralized library service is a more efficient economic unit than one that is dispersed. This holds true for personnel, book stock, supplies, and overhead. Money saved on library budgets may be available for the physics department.

Improved Service

Fragmentation of library service into small departmental units results in poor library service. Small departmental libraries are not attractive to trained library personnel and most university libraries cannot afford to supply it to such small, uneconomical units. The larger unit can offer far greater service to its patrons than can a small departmental library presided over by a secretary or a part-time graduate student. There is no reason why a well-organized central science library could not arrange to deliver materials on request to the office of the footweary physicist. That Professor Wells and his respondents cling so tenaciously to the horse-and-buggy service of the departmental library may well be due to the fact that they have never experienced a truly modernized library service.

Improved Book Collections

Dissipation of the library's book collection among a number of small departmental libraries militates against the formulation of a sound book selection program. Not only does it encourage the excessive duplication of expensive materials, but also it conceals lacunae in the collection and generally diffuses responsibility for the purchase of books in those areas which cross departmental lines. By contrast, a well-organized science library coordinates book purchase and generally maintains professional supervision over the growth, development, and balance of the book stock.

The Revolution in Librarianship:

Dr. Wells is apparently unaware that, through the introduction of automation into library service, a very important revolution is taking place in the profession of librarianship. (See *Fortune,* June 1961, p. 186.) This automation, which in many aspects revolves about mechanization through large computer-like devices, will compel centralization, and a university that does not establish a centralized library service that provides for this new equipment will very soon find that its instruction and research in all areas of science will be seriously handicapped if not actually outmoded.

A Snare and a Delusion:

Finally, even Professor Wells' argument from convenience is illusory, for a strong, centralized science library is capable of saving the scientist many hours of tedium and repetitive searching. When we were a graduate student at Yale, Karl Young was wont to remind us that "Scholarship depends as much on your legs as it does on your head." One of the tasks of modern librarianship is to ease the physical burden that has handicapped intellectual toil.

Many decades have passed since we studied college physics, and we understand that the old Newtonian theories have received considerable buffeting in the intervening years. Nevertheless, we believe that density is still mass per unit volume and that static masses have within themselves a latent force that resists change and moving objects a force that opposes alteration of course. Since this force varies directly with the magnitude of the mass there would seem to be some relationship between density and inertia. Department-chairman Wells would do well to contemplate the characteristics of bodies at rest.

ABOUT THE AUTHOR

—**Jesse H. Shera**, Dean, School of Library Science, Case Western Reserve University; Ph.D., 1944, University of Chicago. Dean Shera is currently studying the sociological foundations of library education. His major research interests are in library history and the theory of communication in relation to librarianship.

Professional School and Departmental Libraries

by Walter Hausdorfer

This paper provides both a survey and an analysis of the reality of library organization and operation. And while, in the years since it was prepared, there may have been considerable change within the groups included in the survey, it is problematical that the substantive issues posed by the findings have, in fact, changed. In order to affect reality the library administrator must identify it, must understand it, and must provide acceptable and possible alternatives.

When the University and College Group was formed a few years ago, some of the members felt a need for more detailed and accurate information than existed at the time on special libraries within universities. Outside the A.L.A. "Survey," which was then ten years old, there was little in print that was not merely a description of some special collection, or a discussion in which a few facts were concealed by the fog of controversy.[1]

The lack of information is not due to the recent origin of libraries for professional use, because some of the earliest libraries in America, namely, those established by the "Bray Foundation," 1697, were for the use of ministers. By 1800 there were at least four professional school libraries in universities, but the greatest impetus to their development was given by the increasing professionalization of various occupations during the nineteenth and twentieth centuries. Departmental libraries experienced a sudden, forced growth in the last quarter of the nineteenth century, with the introduction of seminar or reserved book collections, and an equally violent reaction since. Concern over their increase was apparent even in the last decade of that century. In the confusion of argument, meanwhile, their usefulness was overlooked.

At the outset it may be well to differentiate the professional college or school library from the departmental library: the former is generally recognized as covering a much wider field, as having a larger and more varied group of materials, and as providing information with a view to its value later in the practice of a profession. The latter is a "collection of books pertaining to the work of a single academic department,"[2] such as chemistry, history, or mathematics, physically separate but inherently a part of the general collection covering the broader phases of science and the humanities. The latter may exist in an arts college, but the former usually is present only in a university, or in an independent school devoted to training for a profession. There is still a third type, often not under control of the university library at all, though intended for graduate or faculty use: the research library. Examples are the Scripps Foundation for Research in Population Problems, Miami University, and numerous industrial relations, and governmental research libraries throughout the country. These are of even more recent origin than the departmental library, but they have a strong resemblance to the old seminar libraries, at least, in being a laboratory for particular departments of instruction.

What is the place of each of these types in the educational work of the library? Whatever may be said against the departmental library as a factor in scattering the collections of the main library, its function in maintaining a live collection of materials in a special field, in serving intimately a group of faculty and students that might otherwise have only the impersonal and often hurried service of the general loan desk or the too limited service of a

SOURCE: Reprinted from Walter Hausdorfer, "Professional School and Departmental Libraries," *Special Libraries* 30: 75-81, 116-120, 150-156, 191-195 (1939), by permission of the publisher and the author.

reference department, and in affording ready access to materials for both research and study, has been important. The future of this type of library depends on its ability to justify its existence by performing better than the loan and reference departments of the general library the functions mentioned above, and by preserving a liberal policy of interchange with the general library and with other departmental libraries—in short, by complete cooperation. Some of the suggested substitutes for departmental organization are staff specialization,[3] segregated collections housed in the central building but consisting of merely a group of books on indefinite loan from the main collection, and duplicate rental collections. Whatever adjustments may be made in the structure of the library, its function in providing service in special fields, and in keeping collections in these fields active through close faculty cooperation, will be preserved.

The professional school library performs to an even greater degree the previously mentioned functions but, more than that, it serves as a laboratory. The very success of training depends on the immediate availability of accumulated facts and recorded experience that the student needs in order to develop professional knowledge. Part of this is transmitted in the classroom of the laboratory, by the faculty, but much more, to attain desired confidence and skill, must be acquired through individual study in the library. All the activities of the library must serve to assist the student in that aim: material must be acquired for their utility, not for their contribution to a well-rounded collection, or for their inherent value as records of civilization; cataloging must be based on professional use and terminology, not on the academic or standard; loan and reference service must depend on far more specialized subject knowledge than is present or possible in a general library. The school library differs from the departmental also in the completeness of its collection: it can in no sense be a fragment of a larger body of material, such as the departmental of the general collection, and still be adequate. Because of the nature of its materials and purpose, the professional school library can never become any more than affiliated with the general library.

The research library, like the professional, is limited in its clientele: it may serve a separate research staff, the faculty of a special department, graduate students, or all three. In some instances it is supported by a foundation or special fund. Like the professional also, its policy in purchasing, cataloging and servicing is colored by limited and specialized use. Unlike the professional library, its subject field is usually very restricted. Often its quarters contain desks or tables of research workers. Its materials, usually for reference use only, are likely to have a large percentage of original data, and to be of the ephemeral sort that creates problems of handling quite different from those of books.

The above are the principal types of libraries included in the survey.[4] Although there are variations and combinations of these three, the main features of one or the other are sufficiently prominent in each of the fifty-one libraries to classify them under these main heads. Still another grouping is possible: by subject or field covered, as art, architecture, music, economics and business, and the like. Because the purpose of the analysis is to make comparisons of special libraries in institutions of higher education, to see if there are common factors, rather than to show differences between the types mentioned, the subject grouping is used throughout. Such is the composition of the libraries surveyed.

METHOD

The device employed for obtaining first-hand data was the questionnaire. Of the numbered questions, totalling 193, there were under the divisions given below the following:

DIVISIONS	NO. OF QUESTIONS
Management	50
Personnel	14
Quarters, equipment, etc.	20
Organization	53
Discovery and selection of material	11
Lending	13
Information, reference, and research service	28
Publicity	4
TOTAL	193

Counting the sub-heads under each numbered question, however, the total would be between six and seven hundred.[5] After the preliminary draft of the questionnaire was submitted for criticism and revision at the 1935 Convention, it was mimeographed and distributed through local chairmen of the Group, and to individuals during the years 1936 and 1937. Selected replies were tabulated in 1936 and 1937, and these were presented for discussion at the Convention in 1936 and at Group meetings of the New York Chapter in 1937. Although the final total of usable returns reached only 51, the coverage for each library was sufficiently intensive to warrant analysis. A conservative estimate of answers tabulated would be 30,000. To show the source of returns, the following table gives the number of libraries

FIELD	NO. OF LIBRARIES COOPERATING
Art, architecture, music	6
Economics and business	10
Journalism	2
Law	4
Medical and dental	4
Sociology and education	6
Scientific and technical	17
TOTAL	51

in each field: In order to preserve consistency in interpretation, and to afford one person a sufficiently broad view of the whole range of answers, the final tabulation was made by one person, the Chairman. For the present results of the comparison and interpretation of replies, therefore, he alone is responsible.

Apart from defects which may have arisen from the use of this method, the questions as to representativeness of the sample and the efficiency of the device used to secure data, the questionnaire, must be faced. Geographically the 25 institutions from which returns were received are fairly well distributed in different sections of the country.[6] The nature and size of these institutions also are varied; and the fields covered, and organizational set-ups as well, seem to present a reasonably good picture of the whole. Whether, of course, the proportions of the different elements are quite true is not verifiable from our present knowledge. For the purpose of analyzing and comparing special libraries in institutions of higher education, to discover what the situation is, and not what it should be, the present group seems adequate.

Limitations of the questionnaire as a device for securing information are never so apparent as after the returns are examined. Among the principal weaknesses that are apt to appear

are: whether there were too many or too few questions, whether the emphasis was placed where it should have been, and whether the questions were really as clear as one thought them to be. Regarding the first, the failure of some librarians to return answers, and of others to complete each section, showed too great wealth rather than paucity of questions. Less information on Quarters and Equipment, and more on Personnel would have been desirable. Lack of clarity was apparent where obviously incorrect answers were the rule rather than the exception. In spite of the above weaknesses, present to only a minor degree, the questionnaire produced a wealth of information, and received a fair amount of praise. Had it been possible to carry on extensive correspondence to supplement the data obtained, most of the above defects might have been remedied.

PLACE OF THE COLLEGIATE AND DEPARTMENTAL LIBRARY IN THE ADMINISTRATIVE ORGANIZATION

Collegiate[7] libraries on the whole seem to have a closer administrative relationship with the school than with the university library. Although only 19 are reported as being operated as a department of the school, of the 28 libraries that are under the direction of the university librarian, 12 are departmental. That the university, however, has a hand in the administration of such units is apparent from the fact that 19 of the librarians are subordinate to him; and 12, both to him and to a faculty committee; while 14 are responsible only to a library committee. Thus in 31 of the 45 cases he has a degree of direction. Because the size of the unit might have some relation to the degree of dependence on one or the other administrative group, it should be pointed out that over 90 percent of the libraries included in this survey rank as to volumes, attendance, and size of staff in the upper half of all the libraries of their respective institutions. In several other respects the position of the departmental or collegiate library is made clear. In 21 instances purchasing is carried on through the university library; in 14, by the departmental. For that reason the evil of duplication, or, at least, of the unwarranted sort, is minimized: 4 libraries report none and

26 report that there is very little. The degree to which the departmental library handles its own cataloging also is an indication: 28 libraries report central cataloging, while only 14 report departmental. A further fact is that in the majority of cases the university librarian shares in the appointment of assistants: in 9 instances he appoints directly; in 6, in consultation with the dean or director, or library committee, and in the 13 libraries where the departmental librarian appoints, the university librarian about half the time approves selections. Although 19 libraries are operated as a department of the school, the dean or director appoints assistants in only 8. Finally, further evidence of control appears in the extent to which income is derived from the general library budget: 33 report income from that source, and of the 33 only 3 show as low as one-third or one-half of their income obtained therefrom. Of the 21 that receive appropriations from departmental funds, 13 are dependent also on the general library budget, thus leaving only 8 independent of the latter.

While it is true that the university librarian or director of libraries enjoys a large degree of administrative control, he shares it in 12 libraries with a faculty committee, and in 14 is subordinate to such committee. Such a situation exists particularly in collegiate libraries. The problems involved in the administrative relationships of departmental and collegiate libraries are by no means solved in existing circumstances. Some advance has been made since the appearance of the A.L.A. survey and the Works study,[8] but the condition of the libraries themselves is evidence of the need for closer cooperation between the director of libraries, representing with the departmental librarian, professional interests, and the department or school, representing the subject and teaching interests.

Another factor that complicates the situation is the poorly defined or greatly limited powers of the university librarian. It has been pointed out that:

> As a matter of fact, the implication or tenor of many statutes is that the office of librarian is more to carry out orders than to formulate plans or to determine policies. Too often such phrases as "duties that the president may assign," or "to carry out such policies as the committee may decide upon," or to "have oversight of the library under the direction of the committee (or president)," appear. Vagueness of this sort exists even when the more important functions are mentioned.[9]

Between the struggle of the librarian to secure definite control through statutory powers of all library facilities, against the administrative encroachments of the faculty and officers, and the controversy in library circles over the place of the departmental unit in the organization, the position of the departmental library has been made difficult. Some of the evils ascribed to the system are due to the above circumstances, for insufficient book funds, cramped quarters, and inadequate staff are traceable to shortsighted (or enforced) economy on the part of the university librarian, or to a failure on the part of the faculty or officers to understand the function of a library.

QUARTERS AND EQUIPMENT

The physical condition of the libraries is in many instances highly unsatisfactory: space and equipment are insufficient, lighting and ventilation poor, and the general arrangement unsuitable for greatest efficiency. In the first place, the median square footage of space occupied is 2,500, representing not much more than one large room to house stacks, tables and chairs, and work space for the staff. Seven libraries, in fact, report between 1,001 and 2,000 square feet. One point that seems to be overlooked by administrators in planning quarters is that because subject fields overlap and interest in a given subject is wider than a particular school or department, the possible use of a given library is much greater than that estimated on the basis of school or subject registration. The following table illustrates the number of libraries serving different groups. Although the number served within the group, and the intensity of service would vary with the different types of libraries, the directions from which demands must be met is fairly well indicated:

Because much of the equipment must be concentrated within a very limited space, there are insufficient seats to take care of peak periods of demand. Of the 43 libraries reporting, 52 percent have 80 seats or less, while only 37 percent have over 101 seats or more. The median number of seats for all libraries is 66. In connection with this fact it must be noted that the library is used as a

LIBRARY SERVES	NO. OF LIBRARIES
Officers and employees	36
In connection with work	23
On all subjects	17
Entire student body (for the subject covered)	42
Faculty of school or department	46
Graduate students	42
Alumni	39
Selective student group	31
Research workers	41
Persons by correspondence	30
Persons unaffiliated with univ.	28
General public	21

[Total libraries reporting: 46]

reading room on an average of 275 man hours per day, that 60 percent of the staff's day is devoted to reference and circulation, and that in many cases the routine work as well must be performed within the same room. Under such conditions tables seating 10 or 12 readers, such as are used in many of the libraries, are impracticable, both for the comfort of the reader and for the maintenance of quiet.

Other factors that give rise to serious problems are the housing of the library and physical arrangement. One of the difficulties lies in the location of quarters within the departmental building. Although some of the librarians report such a condition satisfactory, possibly on the grounds of convenience of access for faculty and students, most of them feel the need of greater provision for expansion, and of quarters that were designed functionally for a library. Of the 38 that report location in the departmental building, only 8 consider the conditions satisfactory; of the 7 in the university library building, one reports conditions unsatisfactory. Two libraries are in separate buildings. With space thus limited, open shelves are the rule: 38 of the 43 libraries have them. Book losses range from 3 to 150, the average for all groups being 13 a year:

LIBRARIES	AVERAGE BOOK LOSSES PER YEAR
Art, architecture, music	15
Economics and business	43
Journalism	15
Law	23
Sociology and education	39
Scientific and technical	27

Other problems connected with quarters are the use of library rooms for seminar classes, unsatisfactory lighting, difficulty of supervision, need for staff room, workroom separate from reading room, and conference and typewriter room for students, presence of faculty offices with access through the library, and the general inconvenience of arrangement necessitated by the size and shape of the room.

Equipment shows a great variety which cannot be wholly explained by the varying requirements of the libraries. Wood shelving alone is used by only 14 of the 46 libraries; metal, by 21; and both, by 15. What is most surprising is that 13 libraries have non-adjustable shelving, and 6 have sectional bookcases. Outside of 7 instances in which the shelves were made by Library Bureau, and 5 by Snead and 3 by Art Metal, the equipment was manufactured by smaller or local concerns, or by the carpenter shop (8 instances). For current periodicals 29 of the 46 libraries use the same type of shelves as for books. Ten of the others use some form of the magazine display rack; others use a special table, cubby holes with doors, and a separate case with flat shelves.

Card cabinets on the whole seem to be more uniform: all 47 of the libraries use the standard for 3" x 5" cards, but in addition 10 use other sizes ranging from 3" x 6" to 5" x 8" for special purposes. Only 3 of the 8 using metal cabinets employ them exclusively, and of those 3 one reports the type unsatisfactory. Library Bureau seems to be the preferred manufacturer in about 55 percent of the cases, others being Yawman & Erbe, Shaw Walker, Gaylord, and Globe Wernicke.

For the preservation and organization of miscellaneous printed materials, all 49 of the reporting libraries use vertical files: 28 use metal; 21 wood; 7 use both; 22 have legal size; 22, correspondence size; 9, both. The manufacturers found most satisfactory were Library Bureau (7), Yawman & Erbe (3), Art Metal (3), Shaw Walker (2), Berger, Globe Wernicke, Macey and Wagemaker (1 each). Files are not, however, the only type of equipment used for occasional material. It may be interesting to show the use of other sorts: See table on page 198.

The principal advantages of the pamphlet binder as reported are that it protects the pamphlet, that it can be shelved better with

EQUIPMENT	NO. OF REPORTING LIBRARIES	USING	NOT USING	SATISFACTORY	NOT SATISFACTORY
Pamphlet binders	42	32	10	22	1
Makes:					
Gaylord	28				
Local	3				
Library Bureau	1				
Strapflex	1				
C & C Grip	1				
Pamphlet boxes	43	35	8	26	3
Makes:					
Library Bureau	10				
Gaylord	3				
Schultz-Ill. Str.	2				
Wm. A. Church	2				
F. H. Ulick	2				
7 others	1 each				
Loose-leaf binders	42	18	24		
Types:					
Ring	10				
Spring	8				
Bar	3				
String	3				
Post	2				

books, and that it is easy to use; the disadvantages are that the binding disintegrates, the pamphlets are not held securely, the backs are too narrow to mark, and they are too expensive. The advantages of pamphlet boxes as set forth are mainly that they are convenient and that they keep periodical issues and other like materials together; the disadvantages are that the contents get dusty, the boxes are awkward, expensive, and easily broken, the material sags and is apt to be lost or stolen. Another method of keeping loose materials in order, the loose-leaf binder, is employed for accession records (1), mimeographed sheets (4), services (9), periodicals (6), and dissertations (1).

Although 7 of the 11 users of visible filing equipment consider it an economy, 31 do not have it at all. Where it is used it serves for pictures, lantern slides, records of persons who owe fines, records of periodicals and services, and borrowers' cards. Its advantages lie in permitting quick checking and ready consultation. Of the various makes, Kardex ranks first, with 7 users, Van Dorn, G.S. Maler, and Acme tubes have 1 each.

There seems to be little use of photographic equipment: only 15 of the 42 report the presence of either photostat or films, and of those 15, 13 have photostat; 3, films; and 1, lantern slides. Seven report equipment in the central library, and 2 have the work done outside the university. Here again, there is a lack of equipment, projection especially, that would open up possibilities of a much wider field of specialized literature for the departments that could most benefit by it.

Rubber stamps—time-savers if they can be readily found—exist in great number and variety. To classify the types for various divisions of work: accessioning, cataloging, circulation, and correspondence, there are 11 sorts in the first division, the main ones being the name of the library, date, special collections or funds, and special location. In cataloging 7 are used: location, special collection, type of material, "see reference," "in process" or "in progress" or "in bindery," L. C. stamp, and serial records. In loan work also 7 are used: date, type of material (reserved, etc.), length of loan, and overdue warnings being the main ones. For correspondence there are personal names, of the librarian and of the faculty, and a special stamp with the name and address of the library. It is very easy, of course, to multiply the number of stamps beyond the point at which their value as time-savers declines. In any event, it would be worth while to go over those in use from time to time to see whether any can be eliminated, or whether there is some way by which their ugliness can be lessened, for the reaction of patrons even to such minute details should be considered.

Among the problems arising from quarters and equipment those most frequently mentioned relate to provision for expansion, adequacy of equipment, and housing and equipment planned primarily for library use. The treatment of special types of material also offers persistent difficulties: clippings, unbound newspapers, maps, atlases, and oversized books of plates. As most of the major problems have already been discussed above or in great detail in other library literature, it is unnecessary to review them here.

PERSONNEL

Since the staff ranks next in importance to the book collection it deserves special consideration in the organization of a library. Until recently little has been written about qualifications of collegiate or departmental librarians, but with the increasing emphasis on the role of the librarian in the teaching program of the university, more attention has been given to academic qualifications. What applied to the college librarian, as presented in most of the recent books and periodical articles on administration, applies as well to the staff of a departmental or school library. Such movements are as illustrated by the Library Project of the Association of American Colleges are of vital concern to the profession, for the indictment set forth by Dr. Harvie Branscomb in his circular describing the project and in his paper presented at the Regional Conference of the Association on October 23, 1937,[10] must be satisfactorily answered for the faculty and presidents of universities. As Professor Lucy E. Fay stated in a paper presented at the November 30, 1937, Group meeting in New York:

> If we show no more awareness than that [expressed by the attitude of "sticking to our last"] of what is going on and of why the Association of American Colleges and the American Association of University Professors are going ahead with their present investigations of college libraries, then I think we shall deserve every criticism of our work that may come out of these studies. We may also wake up to the fact that college presidents will insist on appointing professors with the Ph.D. degree as librarians and departmental librarians without any professional training or experience whatsoever. Such a procedure would not only hurt the profession of librarianship but it would be a retrogression calculated to set the college library back fifty years.[11]

Thus the requirements set forth are professional training and experience, and subject specialization. How far these are met may be seen in conditions revealed by the survey.

Referring to the previous section on the place of the collegiate and departmental library in the organization, one may see how the variation in set-up would affect the character of the staff. Under central library administration the director of libraries appoints the librarian, as he controls also the hiring and firing of assistants; hence the professional requirements (if he is not short-sighted) are apt to be met. Where the dean or faculty committee, or both, make the decision, emphasis is likely to be placed on acquaintance with the special subject. In either case the danger lies in a situation where salaries are low and inferior people must be accepted. According to the published statistics of the American Library Association for 1935, 1936, and 1937 the medians of the highest salaries of department heads were $2,295, $2,296 and $2,328 respectively, while for school or collegiate librarians the medians were $2,000, $1,870 and $2,130, and for departmental, $1,800, $1,632 and $1,700—$400 less than for department heads, or $200 less than for collegiate librarians. If both requirements are to be met, professional training and experience and knowledge of special field, fair salaries must be paid. To compare teaching salaries with those of librarians, in 1935 the median for associate professors in land grant colleges was about $2,900;[12] for assistant professors, $2,500; and for instructors, $1,960. If, as is the situation in leading institutions, the director of libraries, or chief librarian has the rank of full professor, the librarian of the school or department should have at the lowest the position corresponding to assistant professor. Unfortunately the salary scale indicates a rank, even for the median highest paid group, of instructor, while for departmental librarians the grade is even lower. The income class (considered regionally, of course) into which these library salaries fall, according to the "Urban Study of Consumer Purchases" of the U.S. Bureau of Labor Statistics, is somewhere between the clerical and wage earner, a situation inconsistent with the requirements of the position.

In the matter of authority also, the varying degrees of control over the professional or departmental library by the central library and the school or department have affected the administrative control of the librarian. The qualifications, appointment and pay of staff members, the size and distribution of the budget, and interpretation of functions performed by the librarian and staff are all influenced by the above condition.

Under central library administration the director of libraries appoints assistants, after consultation with departmental librarians, and sometimes with a faculty committee. In a few instances the school or departmental librarian appoints, with the approval of the dean or director of libraries. In one instance the office manager approves on recommendation of the librarian and of the dean; in another, the state civil service officials have the power. It is hard to see how some of these individuals could have much notion of the needs of the special libraries. Even with a most detailed and forceful presentation of requirements, which the librarian should prepare when he does not make the selection himself, he will have greater difficulties in securing and retaining a strong staff than if he had the direct authority to appoint.

Before qualifications for various positions in the library can be discussed, some form of work analysis should be made. On the basis of time distribution revealed by the survey, the percentages for different activities were:

ACTIVITY	PER CENT	HOURS PER WEEK
Administration	10.8	9
Book selection and ordering	9.7	8
Cataloging and processing	16.9	14
Circulation	22.9	19
Service to readers (Ref., etc.)	16.9	14
Miscellaneous	22.8	19
TOTAL	100.0	83

Obviously some of these activities involve more clerical than professional work. Even where there is an element of the professional, as Brewitt and Carter have shown in their study, [13] the amount of clerical labor in Administration, Book ordering, Cataloging, Circulation, and miscellaneous activities runs well over 50 percent, so that of the average 83 work hours per week about 39½ are spent in clerical tasks.

It is therefore apparent that a great deal of clerical assistance is necessary in order to free the professional members for book selection, bibliography, reference, and such other duties requiring library training and experience. Thus, typing of letters and lists, checking of bills, keeping of statistics, and so in the other categories of book ordering, cataloging, circulation, and miscellaneous, clerical help is less expensive and in many respects more satisfactory.

In any analysis it is likewise important to know what services are demanded by the users of the library. Since only two organizations of the whole group report that they function primarily as reading rooms rather than as libraries, the rest must fulfill demands made upon a library. That the facts support this assumption is borne out by the types of service mentioned: of the 47 libraries 42 report circulation; 43, assigned reading; 47, reference; and 43, research. The type of service activity that is considered most important and most appreciated by patrons is that of reference, while circulation, reserved book work and cataloging are rated much lower. Other types are related to the first, such as compiling bibliographies and indexes, listing periodical articles, maintaining a clipping file, and digging out new material. Some libraries, however, carry the whole burden of cataloging and order work as well, both of which are heavy time consumers. In the extensive list of 22 new activities initiated between 1933 and 1935, apparently on expressed or implied need, most of them were aimed to increase the effectiveness of the reference service, while the rest were scattered over a wide range of library work.

Since the librarian and his staff are responsible for the success or failure of the departmental or collegiate library, they must be able to undertake the charge creditably. They must not only be able but they must be allowed the time to perform the functions of administration, reference, book selection, contact with faculty and students, and research, well; otherwise the whole library system will suffer. One weak unit in the university libraries will damage the reputation of the whole quicker than various forms of good publicity can repair it. Thus there are two aspects of staff adequacy: qualifications of the members, and the number of persons who are assigned the given units of work.

Much has been written about the first aspect, characteristics of good professional assistants, but the two qualities that have been most emphasized are knowledge of the special field of subject and competence in library technique. Such writers as Dr. Bishop and Mr. Noé would have scholars or genuine scientists in charge. There is some question, of course, as to whether competent persons in special fields could be lured away from the delights of scholarship to concern themselves with bibliography, reference, and book selection. Those trained in special subjects who have not been successful in their fields, unless they have a greater aptitude for library work, are not likely to be any more fortunate in their second as in their first choice. Even the best scholars, moreover, are not always the most competent in bibliography, for they may be quite familiar with lists and sources in their field of particular interest, but not with those in general or tangental ones. The alternative suggested, therefore, by Professor Lucy E. Fay,[11] and others[14] is that of subject literature specialization based on a fair understanding of the subject. It is more useful to have a knowledge of the literature of a wide field than acquaintance with a narrower portion of the same field.

Qualifications revealed by the survey indicate that most of the members of small staffs are college graduates, that, except in three instances, one member at least has library training, and that but for eight libraries some member has special knowledge of or a formal degree in the subject. In cases where no training or experience were reported, reference was made to clerical or student assistants. General library experience seemed less common than the first three qualifications mentioned. Apparently a working knowledge of the subject sufficient for the purposes of the library was less frequent than general education or training. That is borne out also by educational lacks most often mentioned as found in assistants, for eight libraries report such a situation. More frequent, however, was inability to read or to understand foreign languages, particularly French and German. Other deficiencies lay in general background of information, knowledge of library techniques, especially of reference, and ability to organize ideas. Qualities most difficult to obtain in assistants were, first of all, accuracy, ability

to follow things through, imagination and good judgment.

Considering the other aspect of staff adequacy, the number of persons required to take care of given units of work, one must conclude, after observation of the data available in this survey, and in other published sources, that norms have not yet been established. So much depends on factors varying in each institution that no definite figures can be set down. This does not mean, however, that individual libraries, after an analysis has been made of the work involved in maintaining the collection and service at high levels, may not determine their own staff requirements.

Although one cannot set up general standards, he may observe certain dangerous conditions existing in the libraries. One of the most striking facts is the general absence of regular clerical assistance, as only 9 libraries report having any. On the other hand, there are an average of 3 student assistants and 4 N.Y.A. assistants to each library, as against the average number of regular staff members of between 1 and 2. In some instances there are as high as 16 such temporary assistants to 4 regular members. Such practice must in the end prove costly in terms of quality of service, and tend to lower the morale of the whole organization.

There have been, from time to time, discussions of certain quantitative factors that affect the size of a staff:

> Hours library is open.
> Size of student body. One survey recommends 5 members for each 500 students to 1,000; 10 for 1,000 students, and 4 additional for every 500 students.
> Size of faculty. A suggestion was made of 1 library staff member for every 10 teaching staff members.
> Number of volumes in the library.
> Rate of growth of the library.
> Character of building or quarters.

Qualitative factors suggested were:

> Sufficiency for technical operations and service functions of high grade.
> Method of instruction. Subjects offered in curriculum.
> Nature and extent of work the library undertakes.

Once the work of the library is thus analyzed and classified, job analyses may be prepared, and qualifications be established. [15] With respective duties well defined the administrative organization can be clarified, yet kept flexible for emergencies. Not the least advantage is a sound basis for requesting an adequate staff.

Another helpful result of analysis will be a staff manual, or book of procedures, a very useful instrument.[16] It will eliminate much repetition of instructions to new staff members, and avoid possible misunderstandings. Unfortunately its use does not seem to be general among departmental or collegiate libraries, as only 11 of 45 reporting have such a book, while 9 other report partially written procedures. Student assistants (since they must still be considered) will find aids of that sort quite valuable in orienting themselves in the library.

Working conditions of the staff follow as a rule those of the university library. Where the librarian is on full time, he works on an average of 39 hours a week, though the time varies from 37 to 44. In a number of instances the summer schedule is lighter, from 30 to 33 hours. A fairly liberal vacation policy on the whole is observed: the range is from two to five weeks with regular assistants often enjoying the same privileges as the head librarian, though in a few instances their vacations are shorter by one or two weeks. For part-time employees the practice varies from no vacation to 15 days. As for sick leave, where a definite statement has been made, the allowable absence with pay is two weeks, though in about one-third of the libraries the rule is flexible. Leave other than that for sickness is usually taken without pay.

In spite of the small staffs in most of the libraries, meetings or conferences are reported as held in 13. In only 3 instances do they occur jointly with the university library meetings. Doubtless the advantages of such occasions for discussing problems that arise in the course of work, new books, new bibliographies, or other reference equipment, are fully appreciated, but the time for such activities, however desirable, is not usually available during library hours. To demand part of the leisure hours of the staff for that purpose is not conducive to good will. It would doubtless be much better to encourage members in continuing professional education either through formal courses or by individual courses of study. In other words, the initiative should be theirs, though stimulated by suggestion and example. That, at least, is the tenor of suggestions made by those who offered definite recommendations.

Among the personnel problems the most frequently mentioned relate to the use of student assistants. Whatever may be said to condone the evil of that sort of part time help, the fact remains that some of the students are not dependable, the turnover from year to year is almost 100 percent, hence such members cannot be trained as part of the staff, they are unable to handle difficult reference questions, thus to maintain a uniform quality of service—in brief, they can never, however numerous, be an adequate substitute for regular members. No student assistant can feel that the work he does in the library is of major importance, so long as his primary purpose is success in his studies. He cannot, therefore, have the same degree of job satisfaction that the full-time member enjoys, a very important element in the most efficient organization of the staff.

The whole question seems to turn, in the final analysis, upon the requirements of highly specialized knowledge and professional training, the cost of which cannot be met by the meagre budgets usually allowed the departmental or collegiate library.

FINANCIAL ADMINISTRATION

Since the position of the library in the administrative organization affects the financial set-up, it may be well to recall what was previously mentioned in passing. Of the 48 reporting libraries, 19 are administratively subordinate to the university librarian; 14 to a faculty committee; and 12, to the librarian and faculty committee. Of the same libraries, 28 are operated as departments of the university library, and 19 as departments of the school. The sources of income present a rather interesting though somewhat confusing picture: See table on page 203.

Seven libraries in addition received money from fines, and 1 from the sale of duplicates. The totals are on the whole rather small, though they cannot be taken as absolute, because some items of expense may be and often are assumed by the general library. Without further information, therefore, it would be impossible to work out standards that have any significance.

SOURCES OF FUNDS	NO. OF LIBRARIES
University library budget only	16
Departmental fund only	4
Endowment only	3
University library budget and departmental fund	5
Departmental fund and endowment	2
University library budget, departmental fund and endowment	4
Endowment and gifts	1
Departmental fund and gifts	1
University library budget, departmental fund, gifts and endowment	2
Departmental fund, endowment and gifts	1

ANNUAL BUDGET (1,000's of dollars)	NO. OF LIBRARIES
1- 3	13
4- 6	10
7- 9	8
10-12	3
13-15	2
16-18	3
19-21	0
22-24	0
25-27	1
28-30	1
31-33	1

Although there is a wide range in the relative amounts of the budget spent on various items, the means or averages for all and for individual groups are:

CLASS	ALL GROUPS %	A %	B %	L %	M %	S %	ST %
Salaries	57	63	69	45	62	60	56
Books and pamphlets	19	30	15	17	11	21	20
Periodicals and services	18	5	14	32	17	5	16
Binding	4	2	2	6	9	9	8
Miscellaneous	2	0	0	0	1	5	0
TOTAL	100	100	100	100	100	100	100

In individual cases these percentages also are affected by the nature and amount of expenses borne by the general library or some other department. Where salaries absorb 80 to 90 percent of the total budget, it seems likely that books, pamphlets, periodicals and binding are paid for principally out of other funds.

In lieu of an average based on figures which would include amounts derived from the university library or other budget, one must take into account all of the main factors presented by Miss McCrum [17] and Randall and Goodrich [2] and adjust them to the actual situation in a given library. By that means one may arrive at some standard.

Difficulty arises from the same source in attempting to establish costs, for allocation of expense would be so complicated and time consuming that it would not pay. This does not mean, however, that the resulting data would not be valuable, especially in presenting arguments for an increased budget, but that the instrument of costing, devised for a production organization, needs a far more careful adaption to non-profit enterprises than has been apparent in recent studies. [18]

Although one need not install such an elaborate system of accounting as costing implies, he can use a simple method, and thus have a degree of control over the funds that are in his care. Such method should, of course, be built on the one in use in the university, so that there may be a basis for checking the results of one against the other. It is certainly desirable to have some records that will furnish information on the state of the funds, and on the proportions of expenditures for different purposes.

ACQUISITION

However advantageous it may be to have members of the faculty show their interest in the collection by recommending the acquisition of new materials, such arrangement cannot be depended upon to keep the library abreast of the times. As previously mentioned, the process of watching for and acquiring new materials takes about one-tenth of the staff time per week, a fact that shows how much

CATEGORIES	ART	BUS.	LAW	MED.	SOC.	SCI. AND TECH.
Readable	55	30	1	13	25	30
Reference	45	70	99	87	75	70
Current	20	75	—	66	63	38
Historical	80	25	—	34	37	62
Facts and figures	13	60	—	15	57	70
Theory	87	40	—	85	43	30
Elementary	18	25	—	6	2	10
Technical	82	75	—	94	98	90

of the task devolves on the library. The faculty, moreover, usually have too many additional calls on their time to take on what they consider rightly the function of librarians. Before going into the problem of methods it may be well to examine the nature of the collections and the rate of accretion. Some notion of the character of the stock in different groups may be seen in the rough percentage distributions within the pairs of categories: See table above.

In spite of the fact that there is a great variety in the interpretation of terms, hence of percentages assigned by different librarians, the ratios appear to represent the general opinion. The extent of the stock and the rate of increase per month may be seen in the table below.

Keeping in mind the character of the collections one may turn to methods and policies in discovery and acquisition. For literature in these special fields the value of the trade bibliography is secondary. The source found to be most fruitful is professional and trade periodicals. As these, however, do not always cover documents as fully as books and pamphlets, they need to be supplemented by the *Monthly Catalogue of United States Public Documents* and the *Monthly Check-list of State Publications,* which rank second in frequency of use. Third in the list is the "Publications of special interest" in SPECIAL

LIBRARIES; fourth, the *New York Times Book Review;* fifth, *Publishers' Weekly,* and sixth, publishers' catalogs.

In art and music libraries the principal sources are respectively periodicals, publishers' catalogs , and the *New York Times Book Review.* Business librarians find that they use periodicals, SPECIAL LIBRARIES, *Monthly catalogue,* and *Monthly check-list about equally,* though they find the *New York Times* and *Industrial Arts Index* helpful. Besides periodicals the source found valuable for law literature are the two documentary catalogs and *Publishers' Weekly.* For medical and dental literature the journals, are, again, first, with publishers' catalogs and special bibliographies next. In the sociology and education group, in addition to periodicals, the field is evenly divided among the document catalogs, *Public Affairs Information Service* and the *New York Times.* Finally, among scientific and technical librarians, the use of periodicals far exceeds that of any other medium, the document catalogs and SPECIAL LIBRARIES being mentioned only by a third as many as the first.

Some implications of the above facts are that such publications as the *Cumulative Book Index, A.L.A. Booklist, Book Review Digest,* and *Saturday Review of Literature* are of little or no value in discovering new material for these libraries; that checking

	ART	BUS.	JLSM.	LAW	MED.	SOC.	SCI. AND TECH.
Stock:							
Books	7,000	12,000	—	101,000	15,000	12,000	15,000
Pamphlets	—	50,000	—	—	9,500	3,500	8,500
Additions per month:							
Purchases:							
Books	30	91	12	480	17	38	87
Pamphlets	5	30	46	150	2	10	7
Gifts	22	408	90	59	109	345	151
Exchanges	4	8	2	20	4	100	101
TOTALS	61	497	150	709	132	493	346

the type of sources indicated usually requires more time than going through the usual book listing services; and that the selection of important items demands a good working knowledge of the subject literature field. The latter point especially is significant in that it shows how little more than a central purchasing office the general library acquisition department can be for these special libraries.

Concerning the details of acquisition there are some interesting points revealed by the survey. While purchasing is carried on by the university library in 60 percent of the cases, duplication between the central and departmental libraries exists in 75 percent.

Having accumulated great quantities of material of both temporary and permanent value, do the librarians follow any definite plan or schedule in discarding? Most of them do not. Rather, about once a year, during the comparatively quiet intersessional period, the librarian goes about the task of weeding out shelves and files. The principal bases of selection appear to be whether or not the particular item has been superseded, and how live or currently useful it may be. To a certain extent the disposal of clippings and pamphlets is automatic; the age of clippings is checked by the date or by the different colors of the mounting paper (changed

	ART		BUS.		LAW		MED.		SOC.		SCI. AND TECH.	
					[Books: B, Pamphlets: P]							
Percent received	B	P	B	P	B	P	B	P	B	P	B	P
by Gift	9	5	42	45	–	8	40	41	37	30	8	14
Purchase	82	92	57	54	–	92	48	44	52	60	83	69
Exchange	9	3	1	1	–	–	12	15	11	10	8	17
TOTAL	100	100	100	100	–	100	100	100	100	100	100	100

Gifts come in largely without asking from users of the library, or as a result of a previous mailing list request, though a fair number of desirable items require an individual letter. Another effective method is that of typed or printed post cards. Least used are printed or mimeographed letters, and the telephone.

For material on exchange there are several kinds of publications used: theses or dissertations; duplicates, publications of staff members, or the university, or of affiliated organizations.

The extent to which records are kept of requested material depends apparently on who makes the request; the departmental or the university library. Since over 60 percent of the ordering is done centrally, records kept in the order departments are considered in many cases sufficient. About a third of the libraries, nevertheless, keep a duplicate order card or a slip as a check against the main library; others keep the carbon copies of letters, and still others make lists. For serials, however, the department usually keeps a check card, as the information supplied thereon is useful in reference as well as in order work. The departments, at any rate, usually follow up their own continuations regularly, except where in the smaller one-man libraries that task is taken over by the central library.

each year); later editions of pamphlets, when they arrive, replace those in the files. Even here, however, a degree of caution needs to be used, because in the university library the historical value of an item must be weighed carefully, for historical study and research are often as much a part of the educational program as the examination of contemporary matters. Duplicate textbooks, no longer used on reserved book shelves, or replaced by later editions, are as a rule discarded. Whatever ingenious systems may be devised for weeding out materials, the final determinant is the judgment of the person responsible for the task. At best the estimate of future value is a guess which time will pronounce either good or bad. Such a guess may, nevertheless, have a basis in the knowledge of previous use made, or of demands created by what and how certain courses are taught.

A major problem in this activity of book selection and ordering is the background and judgment of the librarian. Much of the criticism aimed at librarians by college presidents and professors is that they are not qualified by subject knowledge to choose what is important; hence these investigations, mentioned above, of libraries by associations of colleges and university professors.

As Professor Fay has said:

> Until professional assistants on college and university staffs . . . are interested enough to become subject literature specialists, we shall continue to be regarded as incompetent to give the service essential to faculty and students in the mutual process of education.[11]

PREPARATORY PROCESSES ORGANIZATION

Fundamental to the organization of any group of aids, such as catalogs and indexes, is the realization that their functions is to make not only the existence of certain books and periodicals in different fields known but also to make the information they contain more accessible. To regard the catalog as a printed or manuscript bibliography rather than as a living and changing guide to new facts and ideas is to give it a false value and to deny it its true place in the library. All the processes and details, therefore, should be governed by that purpose.

Such questions, for example, as the degree to which material in a library is cataloged have no meaning unless one considers what other methods are possible or better for certain groups. Thus the variations in percentages of material cataloged must be related to types of material that are self-indexing, and to possibilities of geographical, corporation, or numerical arrangement. Deviations from the general average for material cataloged of 82 percent are considerable: percentage cataloged in Art libraries, 83; in Business, 80; in Journalism, 70; in Law, 92; in Medical and Dental, 91; in Sociology and Education, 76; in Scientific and Technical, 88. Of the 43 libraries reporting uncataloged material, 30 have it arranged so as to be self-indexing; 4, not; and 2, partially. Material arranged by units is as follows in table above.

Methods of arrangement principally used are the corporation, geographical, and numerical. Libraries having groups of material filed by company or organization name and those that have not are about evenly divided. Of the above types, No. 4, Corporation material, accounts for the largest group, with a total of 6, and No. 11, Society publications, with 4. Also represented are No. 1, 3, 7, 10 and 17. Geographical order, used in 19 and not used in 17 libraries, likewise includes No. 1, Government documents (7 libraries), and No. 10, Maps, together with numerous other mis-

TYPES	NO. OF LIBRARIES HAVING SUCH UNITS
1. Documents	19
2. Periodicals	6
3. Clippings and pamphlets	14
4. Corporation material	6
5. Theses and dissertations	5
6. College catalogs	5
7. Trade catalogs	4
8. Directories	1
9. House organs	4
10. Maps	2
11. Society publications and transactions	6
12. University publications	1
13. Press releases	3
14. Syllabi; courses of study	3
15. League of Nations publications	1
16. International Labor Office publications	1
17. Trade union material	1
18. Business services	2

cellaneous types, such as folk songs, guide books, directories (No. 8), biographical dictionaires, market surveys, foreign law, statistical data, and slides and plates. Publication number is used by 20 (of a total of 36); in 6, for arranging No. 11, Society publications; in 6, for No. 1, Government documents, as well as for Nos. 12, 13, and 15. The above examples show the possible methods of treating certain types of material without cataloging, and with the object of increasing their accessibility by some other means.

The time thus freed by eliminating cataloging can be used for the creation of special indexes that serve to analyze contents more completely. That such practice is fairly common may be seen from responses to the question of card records other than the catalog, for of 43 libraries, 31 have indexes to special materials, 13 have special indexes; 6, a quick reference file; 1, a contact file for companies; and 3, sources for borrowing. Other records include a continuations file (15), order file (6), accession (23), books recommended file (1), shelf list (16), and subject and name authority lists (7).

Since the catalog is, however, the tool most widely known by the public, its importance in making materials available ranks high. Some appreciation of this point has been shown by catalogers themselves. [19] All of the libraries report having a catalog separate from that of the main library. In spite of the fact that in 28 cases the cataloging is done by the general library, as against 18 by departmental, the difference between the two records is considerable. In the first place, in 7 libraries the departmental collection is not listed in the general catalog; in 11, only in part, the degree ranging from a few entries to all except special material. For the most part, fullest information is given in the departmental unit, as additional subject and author entries, and cards for special collections are present only in the departmental. Because the catalog is used more by the clientele than by the staff, the type, classed or dictionary, must be chosen that is most comprehensible to the first group; hence the prevalence of the dictionary arrangement. Estimates of the number of times it is used by different groups for every ten times consulted support that contention:

USED BY	FOR EVERY 10 TIMES USED	
Library staff	3.8	
Clientele	6.2	
Faculty		.9
Research workers		1.5
Students		2.8
Others		1.0

Considering the process of cataloging, as mentioned above, except for books, and to a certain extent for pamphlets, about as much cataloging is done by the departmental or collegiate as by the general library. Where formal codes are used, the A.L.A. is most generally employed, namely in 16 libraries, though the Library of Congress is almost as common, in 14. Less frequent are those individually compiled, 5; library school rules, 4; Fellows, 2; Cutter, 2. Variations to codes, covering points not treated therein, are made by 10 libraries, and not made by 12. Such differences are apparently not extensive enough to justify the compilation of a special code for this group, as 22 are against, and only 8 in favor.

Of the principal schemes of classification, the Dewey is most often used (31 libraries), the Library of Congress next (11), and Brussells, least (2). Other libraries used special systems, or the Dewey so modified as to change the grouping radically. Considerable dissatisfaction, expressed and implied, with existing schemes, is shown by the fact that 22 libraries (against 12 that have not) have modified or expanded classes pertinent to their collections; 14 have found it desirable to develop special classifications, though 24 have not; and many of the problems mentioned relate to revision and expansion, as well as to the inelasticity and lack of provison for new developments. Besides books, in 15 libraries vertical file material is classified, and in 8 others, pictures, sheet music, lantern slides, colored reproductions and photographs are so treated. For most groups the same scheme is used throughout, though in 12 libraries it is not. In classification, as in the field of subject headings, the principal difficulty seems to be the inadequacy of existing standard schemes and lists for the specialized material of departmental and collegiate libraries.

Since in the dictionary catalog subject heading play an important role in acquainting readers with types of material available on specific subjects, they must be very carefully worked out. Here again, as noted above, the standard lists and entries are not satisfactory. While it is true that 15 libraries use Library of Congress headings, and 8 others use a list based on L. C., 20 have found it necessary to compile their own, a rather expensive and troublesome process. Varying degrees of completeness are apparent in such lists as 22 use "see"; 21, "see also" references; 9, "refer from"; and 10 include definitions. On the whole, for material in special fields of the library narrow headings are used, narrower than those of the Library of Congress, and in a few cases, even narrower than those of "Public Affairs Information Service." For the compilation of special lists some 31 different indexes and bibliographies are mentioned, most of them limited in scope to the particular field of interest. Use of the same group of headings throughout the library is common to 24 libraries, whereas in 12, the exceptions are for pictures, music, and vertical file material. Since the maintenance of individual lists is rather costly, the suggestions made in connection with cooperative cataloging regarding cooperatively compiled and maintained lists is worth considering.

In spite of the fact that much of the material is uncommon to general university and public libraries, Library of Congress cards are obtainable and can be used (with modifications) for about 85 percent of it. These are as a rule ordered through the central cataloging department. For books, for which L. C. cards are not printed, besides the usual typed, the mimeographed, carbon copy, and photostated cards are made. The number of cards per book averages between 5 and 6, and for pamphlets, between 3 and 4. Deviations from the usual practices include omission of author card, in a few libraries, the inclusion of more and fuller notes on both author and subject cards, the disuse of the title card, inclusion of analytics for bibliographies in magazines or in the vertical file, the use of the serial check card with author card, and brief cataloging and the omission of collation for such material as press releases.

If, with all the carefully worked out catalog, books cannot be found on the shelves, the system breaks down. The inventory, therefore, has a place in giving service through the catalog, for missing books can be discovered and replaced, errors in classification can be corrected, the physical condition of the collection can be checked, old material can be weeded out, and mis-shelving can be straightened out. The average frequency of inventory is once a year, though variations run from the continuous to five year periods. Correspondingly the length of time it takes varies from 8 to 300 hours, the mean time being about 50 hours.

The two points that are repeatedly stressed by librarians in the survey are the simplification of processes for time saving by both the staff and the public, and the provision, in whatever schemes that may be devised, for future growth.

SERVICE TO THE CLIENTELE: CIRCULATION AND REFERENCE

Apart from the preparatory processes the two activities that require most time of the staff are circulation and reference: circulation taking 19 of the average 83 hours a week, and reference, 14. These, with the work of book selection, are most closely related to the teaching methods and curriculum of the department or school. Of the two, reference is considered the most important both by the librarians and by the clientele. Why, then, does circulation rank lower in the estimation of both? One

reason may be found in the system of reserved readings, which, though absorbing much of the time of students and the staff, involves much mechanical loan desk work and causes the most difficulty to all the circulation service. To a certain extent the practice of open shelf reserves, adopted by about 10 of the libraries, lessens the burden of rush hours at the desk, but does not solve disciplinary problems, or decrease the expense of duplication. Special rules set up for this type of material cover time of withdrawal for overnight use, usually limited to an hour before closing, the time for return, varying from 15 minutes to 2 hours after opening the next morning, the minutes' grace allowed (about 15), and the penalties imposed for late return, usual amount being 25 cents for the first hour and 5 cents for each additional hour. In general, two policies in duplicating books are observed: one is to use the size of the class, with or without a fixed ratio of the number of copies to the number of students. The other policy calls for a fixed maximum number, from one to six. In some cases the department itself supplies duplicates and, in others, fees are charged to the classes. It is felt by most administrators that such fees are not conducive to the best relations of students and faculty with the library. Much less objectionable is the duplicate rental collection.

Another problem in connection with the two services has been that of an adequate measure of use. Although 36 of 44 libraries keep records of circulation, and 8, of reference, only 16 feel that the former is very indicative of the value of the library, and 12, that the latter is significant. Alternative suggestions are: data on the class of material used, on the class of user, while a third considers a composite, short-time study best. After an examination and analysis of reported circulation one must conclude that the lack of a standard method for counting is indicative of uncertainty as to the value of this measure of use. It seems hardly credible that if circulation work takes on an average of 19 hours of staff time a week that the mean circulation per *month* would be no more than 1,375, or that the upper quartile could be no more than 4,125. Apparently in some cases, as suggested by others who did not give statistics, data were not kept for items used in the reading rooms, or for reserved book circulation. In other cases the libraries were reported as strictly reference.

Another factor affecting service is the total hours the library is open per week. The range for all types is from 24 to 91 hours, the average for each being: for Art, 47 hours; for Business, 73½; for Journalism, 61½; for Law, 75; for Medical and Dental, 60; for Sociology and Education, 59; and for Scientific and Technical, 59. When libraries are not open sufficiently long, faculty often demand access after hours, and are, in 29 instances, given keys or some other means of entering, but in 18 are denied the privilege. Such access gives rise to problems of having charges properly made for items taken from the library. Although faculty members are required to leave signed book cards, or call slips, they are sometimes forgetful; hence in two cases the use has been restricted to reference, and in 8 there is great dissatisfaction with the arrangement. Other librarians feel, however, that the faculty should be encouraged to use the library intensively.

Loan records on the whole are comparatively simple: only 11 libraries use borrowers' cards, against 27 which do not; and in 35 cases the library staff make the charges, though in 10 the borrower does it.

For the problem of getting books returned the most effective solution found is that of making a special appeal to the individual. Devices used are telephone calls, follow-up forms, faculty reminders and lists.

Since, however, the loan desk is one place where contact with the clients is possible, the atmosphere should be inviting. There should be a certain liberality in lending different sorts of material, so that readers will be encouraged, but this should never degenerate into favoritism. That is, of course, one of the objections to student assistants, that their interests are more closely associated with their classmates than with the library. Stronger, not weaker

members of the staff should be given some duty at least at the desk, for they should have this opportunity to become acquainted with the borrower, to study his attitude toward the library, and to discover what difficulties he may have in getting what he wants. [20]

In the specialized fields represented by libraries included in this survey reference work plays a very important part, as the very nature of the materials calls for that sort of intensive use. A few of the factors influencing the kind and extent of such demand are: the methods of instruction in the school, the composition of the clientele, and the activities of faculty or other members of the university staff in research. If the faculty requires students to carry on independent investigations, to write papers or essays, or to work out problems or projects, students will need all the special assistance the library staff can give. In a school where the registration is largely graduate, and masters' essays and doctoral disserations are the usual requirement, much of the students' work will have to be done in the library, and the staff will have to give each student a greater amount of time than is necessary in an undergraduate college. Again, where the faculty are active in research, or where special projects are set up and worked on by a group of research assistants, the library will have to supply not only a quantity of technical and factual material not ordinarily used by the students, but also a great deal of bibliographic and reference assistance.

Evidences of such demand appear in the amount of time the staff spends in reference activity, an average of 14 hours per week, in the number of requests per month for information, ranging from 50 to 1,875, and in the high rating of reference among the service activities by both the librarian and clientele. As the average percentages of requests coming from different groups are interesting in their implications, they may well be presented in detail:

GROUP	ART %	BUS. %	JLSM. %	LAW %	MED. %	SOC. %	SCI. AND TECH. %
Faculty	16	10	4	9	35	33	35
Graduate students	15	24	5	12	6	17	24
Students (undergrad.)	61	50	85	69	56	29	35
Officers, etc.	2	6	2	1	1	3	2
General public	5	3	4	9	1	8	3
Others	1	7	—	—	1	10	1
TOTAL	100	100	100	100	100	100	100

Concerning the manner in which requests are presented, the most common, and one preferred by librarians, is that made in person, for 40 of the librarians feel that it provides a channel for the best service by increasing personal contact, by giving the clients a better understanding of the library, and by affording a fuller and more accurate statement of the problem. The average percentages of requests received are: by telephone, 7.6; by memo, 3.7; by letter, 4.7; in person, 84. Some of the reasons given for preferring other channels are that with a memo or letter more time is allowed for answer, and that through the telephone, on the other hand, one can give quick service to faculty in their offices. Encouragement of one method of request or another is given through suggestion or polite insistence.

Perhaps because relationships in a university are more informal than in a business office, and because there is so much other paper work, request forms for information are not generally used. In two instances, nevertheless, they are employed: in one, for extensive bibliographies, and in another, to advertise the services of the library.

Although for the most part requests are made by readers of any member of the staff who is on duty at the time, they are referred to the librarian alone in 8 instances, and in 11 they are made directly to him. When other members of the staff supply information, there are various ways by which the librarian maintains contacts. The principal means are by having the staff report continuously, either in person or by written memorandum, by having difficult questions referred to him, by consulting with the staff during a discussion of new bibliographies and sources of information, by having reports of projects sent to him by the faculty or research workers, by serving at the loan desk from time to time,

and by personal contact, either in talks with the clientele, or in faculty committee meetings.

Since all members of the staff, as noted above, in the section on Personnel are not equally qualified to supply information, and since there are occasions when even the well-trained assistant may be unable to locate desired data, there must be some procedure, in order to assure uniformly good service, for handling such situations. In 30 libraries the request is referred to the librarian, either verbally or by note or memorandum; in 9, to other members of the staff; and in 3, to other libraries. If the information still is not obtained, the faculty, as a last resort, are consulted. For future guidance, and in order to save time, 9 libraries keep a permanent record on cards or in notebooks of requests for which information cannot be found, while 33 either do not keep such a record or else do not consider it necessary. Similarly, only one library uses a form for recording searches, while 38 do not. As a method of increasing ability to answer reference questions, buiding up one's knowledge of the special subject field is effective. Besides the most obvious means, that of taking courses in department or school (provided one has not already graduated from the school), one frequently employed is that of reading or skimming through new books. A variety of other ways are available, namely, attending occasional or special lectures, auditing classes, travelling, discussing questions with faculty and students, reading professional journals, and carrying on research.

What is the nature of requests and what are the techniques employed? As there is a significant variety in the percentages for different types of requests, it is better to present the data in tabular form:

REQUEST FOR	ART %	BUS. %	JLSM. %	LAW %	SOC. %	SCI. AND TECH. %
Specific book or article	27	27	50	58	30	46
Specific fact or facts	10	21	10	15	18	10
Material on broad subject	27	12	15	5	14	8
Material on useful methods	3	1	0	0	3	8
Theories, opinions	12	8	3	13	10	8
Short, selected bibliographies	8	7	10	4	7	5
Extensive, selective bibliographies	1	3	2	2	4	6
Material for speech or paper	12	21	10	3	14	9
TOTAL	100	100	100	100	100	100

Run of the mill requests are met principally by giving the inquirer a few books or pamphlets, or by showing him how he can use the catalog or indexes more effectively. Where ephemeral, current material is important, in business and journalism, the pamphlet and clipping file is found very helpful. In very few cases do librarians have either the time or the call to make extracts, abstracts, or reports. Perhaps in research libraries such practice may be common, but in departmental and professional school libraries, it is most uncommon. Other devices to obtain desired information or material such as borrowing from the central library, are usual, just as telephoning, writing, or visiting outside libraries is exceptional.

In the course of developing an efficient reference organization certain procedures and devices have been evolved. One is that of keeping a collection of quick reference aids at the loan or reference desk, varying in number and from 5 to 300, the average or mean being 15. These are arranged for convenient use by class or subject or, if few, alphabetically. Another is that of making lists of where material most often requested may be found. A third is that of supplying students with a handbook or guide. A fourth, worked out in a chemical library, is that of using a chart of procedure in searching chemical literature. Several other procedures have been developed for searching in fine arts, in music, in law, in business, and in technical literature, but are too detailed to describe here.

Special reference tools also have been collected and indexes compiled. For work with government documents, besides the usual *Monthly Catalogue, Monthly Check-list,* periodical indexes, Boyd, Schmeckebier, and Wilcox, there are special sources, far too numerous to list, whose usefulness is limited to particular fields. It should be noted, however, that federal departmental lists and the Government Printing Office price lists receive frequent mention. Similarly, long and specialized lists of guides, bibliographies and indexes are presented under the head of books useful in statistical reference questions, and in the particular fields covered by invididual libraries. Among the indexes compiled to supply information not elsewhere available are those to periodicals not included in any of the current indexes, to special files and collections, to statistical sources in news-papers and magazines, to research in progress, and to pictures in unusual collections. There are also lists of societies, of California municipal documents, and union lists of medical books, and of trials. While a union catalog of all these might be very desirable, undertaking the projects suggested, on a national scale, by the Special Libraries Association is considered neither advisable nor practicable. Projects recommended for commercial enterprise, however, include the following:

> Art index before 1929
> List of geographic names, each name in the principal languages
> Cumulation of the American Society of Landscape Architects' *Bi-monthly Index*
> Index to music periodicals, past and present
> Library manual for students of business
> Sources of foreign statistical series
> Inclusion of foreign and dental periodicals in *Index Medicus*
> Complete list of school surveys for the past thirty years
> Index to pharmaceutical literature.
> International catalog of scientific literature brought up to date
> Lists of serials by state departments of agriculture.

Many other guides and indexes are suggested as possible ways of improving present equipment for information service, but they are too numerous to itemize.

One of the ways by which the reference service of the university libraries might be generally bettered is by an agreed or implied allocation of fields to be covered by each department. Often the general reference department spends a great deal of time in answering questions which should be referred to a library where pertinent material can be found. A special index or list compiled in the departmental or school library may save the reader and the staff a great deal of time. On the other hand, the departmental library should cooperate by referring to the general reference room such questions are definitely general and out of its field. In this way a much wider use of the whole library will be encouraged, and more efficient service given than if each tried to do the work of the other.

If some statistical measure of performance could be devised, such a condition described above might be discovered and eliminated. If standards of performance were set up, a different organization of work might result. Without such measure, furthermore, the personnel requirements of this service as against circulation or cataloging are hard to justify. Economically it would be put in the luxury class of services. But since it is to the public the clearest expression of professional competency, it should not be hampered by an inadequate staff.

PROMOTION-PUBLICITY

In spite of the fact that many of the methods for advertising public libraries are not available or appropriate to departmental or professional school libraries, there are many ways in which the latter can build up good will for the organization. The first problem, that of acquainting a changing student body with the existence of the library, and suggesting ways in which the library could be of use, has been solved in part by the use of display. Such devices as bulletin boards, for example, used by 25 libraries, exhibits in the halls and reading rooms, employed by 14 libraries, and notices or articles on new books or special collections in the library in the campus or school paper are all effective. They must, however, be placed strategically. If, for instance, the library is not housed in the same building in which classes are held, bulletin boards, and displays if possible, should be utilized within the classroom buildings. Enough news interest should characterize contributions or notices sent to campus papers so that they will be given prominence. Another type of printed publicity is a statement about the library in the school or department catalog of courses. Too often such description is limited to a few lines, and not even prepared by the librarian.

One of the most effective means, of course, is personal contact with both faculty and students. Within the small community represented by the department or school it is easier to learn more about the individuals comprising it than in the larger community served by a public library, hence to discover new ways of serving them. Formal talks to students on how to use the library to the best advantage, or personal conferences in connection with papers or essays may be arranged. Discussions with the faculty on building up certain types of material, leading to an exposition of their method

of presenting certain subjects, or questions about researches in which they are engaged are all very effective in increasing their interest in the library.

For bringing to the attention of the clientele the resources and services of the library two principal methods have been employed. The first is that of publishing or sending around memos or notes of new acquisitions or magazine articles of special interest. Sometimes lists of new books or articles are posted on bulletin boards; in other cases weekly or monthly bulletins are issued and sent mainly to the faculty. In a few instances periodicals themselves are routed to the faculty.

The second method is that of advertising service through service. Once a reader has discovered the library's interest in helping him find what he wants, or in serving him promptly, he will not only return but will also send others. It is particularly important that the faculty be made to understand the library's attitude in giving good service, for under the teacher-pupil set-up in universities, the faculty influence considerably the student's attitude toward the library. If, however, the quality of service is uneven, due perhaps to lack of sufficient professional help, adverse reports of the students on the library will tend to break down the faculty good will that the librarian has struggled to create. As shown elsewhere in the survey, indirect means, such as organizing materials so that the student can help himself, as well as the direct method of personal assistance, will increase the effectiveness of the service. A handbook or library guide also is useful for this purpose.

Although one may not conduct an elaborate advertising campaign, he should realize, as one librarian points out, that persistent rather than intermittent efforts bring the best results. After one has made a study of the clientele, of the curiculum and methods of teaching, he will have a sound basis for such methods, however simple, that he may use.

It is hoped, in conclusion, that the survey will provoke other more detailed studies to strengthen our knowledge of collegiate and departmental libraries, and thus to furnish a broad factual basis for determining their proper position in the library structure.

FOOTNOTES

[1] Mention should be made, however, of a survey limited to school of business libraries by the Lippincott Library, *University of Pennsylvania: Questionnaire submitted to libraries of schools of business . . . Report, May 10, 1933.* (Philadelphia, 1933.) 16 1., mim.

[2] William M. Randall and Frances L. D. Goodrich, "Principles of College Library Administration." (Chicago, American Library Association, 1936), p. 199.

[3] Peyton Hurt, "Staff Specialization: A Possible Substitute for Departmentalization." *(Bulletin of the American Library Association,* July, 1935), vol. 26, pp. 417-421.

[4] For a discussion and definition of types see the American Library Association's "Survey of Libraries in the U.S.," vol. 1, p. 170 ff.

[5] Questions were derived by a committee from the New York Clinic Questionnaire, with the advice of Miss Linda H. Morley, the compiler.

[6] See list of cooperating libraries.

[7] "Collegiate" is used throughout in the sense of professional school.

[8] American Library Association, "A Survey of Libraries in the United States." (Chicago, 1926-27), 4 vol. Works, George A. "College and University Library Problems." (Chicago, Amecan Library Association, 1927).

[9] "Statutory Powers of The Head of a College or University Library." (An unpublished paper).

[10] See B. H. Branscomb. "Library Project." *(Bulletin of the Association of American Colleges,* November, 1937), vol. 23, pp. 368-369.

[11] "New Tendencies in College Libraries." (An unpublished paper.)

[12] U.S. Office of Education. "Salaries in Land Grant Colleges, 1935." (Washington, February, 1936), 18 p. (Circular no. 157).

[13] Theodora R. Brewitt and Mary Duncan Carter, "Professional and Non-Professional Work." *(Library Journal,* October 15, 1938), vol. 63, p. 773-775.

[14] Gladys Burrows and Rita McDonald, "Specialization of Staff in Library Work." *(Pacific Northwest Library Association. Proceedings,* 1936), pp. 67-73.

[15] Two bibliographies may be suggested: Industrial Relations Counselors, Inc. "Job Analysis and Its Allied Activities" *(Suppl. to Lib. Bull., 1932);* R. M. Berg, "Suppl. to Management Bibliography, 1931-1935." *American Soc. of Mech. Eng.,* 1937, p. 21. For Libraries: "A.L.A. Budgets, Classification and Compensation Plans for University and College Libraries." Chicago, 1929: Bur. of Public Personnel Admin. "Proposed Classification and Compensation Plans for Library Positions." Washington, D.C. 1927.

[16] Lucy E. Fay, "The Staff Manual for The College Library." *(Bulletin of the American Library Association,* August, 1937), vol. 31, pp. 464-468.

[17] Blanche Prichard McCrum, "An Estimate of Standards for A College Library." Rev. ed. Lexington, Va., Washington and Lee University, Journalism Laboratory Press, 1937.

[18] See the articles of F. Rider, "Library Cost Accounting" *(Library Quarterly,* October, 1936, vol. 6, p. 331-381), and Robert A. Miller, "Cost Accounting for Libraries; Acquisition and Cataloging." *(Library Quarterly,* October, 1937), vol. 7, p. 511-536.

[19] See the article of Grace O. Kelley, "Subject Approach to Books: An Adventure in Curriculum." *(Catalogers' and Classifiers' Yearbook,* no. 2, 1930), pp. 9-23.

[20] For a detailed discussion of circulation work SEE: Charles H. Brown and H. G. Bousfield's "Circulation Work in College and University Libraries," Chicago, *A.L.A.,* 1933.

ABOUT THE AUTHOR

—**Walter Hausdorfer,** Librarian of Temple University, 1946-1962; M.S.L.S., 1930, Columbia University. His major research interest is in the area of economic history. The author wrote this article when he was Librarian, Columbia University School of Business Library.

VI

THE MANAGEMENT OF THE LIBRARY

The academic librarian must give a shape to the library function. This shape—in terms of people, library materials, facilities, relationships with similar organizations, and operation—must be, however, predicated on a sound conceptual base. At present, the base for librarianship is not comprehensive or adequately developed in any one area to provide other than perfunctory conclusions. The readings in this section define the significant issues and offer sufficient analytical interpretation to demonstrate the character of academic librarianship and to provide a basis for generalizations on the relationship between academic administrative events.

PERSONNEL

If academic librarianship is to gain the initiative and to participate in the dialogue relevant to its function, the academic librarian must not be a functionary, accommodating the library to the institution. Instead he must perceive the richness of higher education, be dedicated to the possibilities of its enhancement through the discipline of librarianship, and be uncomfortable within the structure of the discipline.

What Type Research Librarian?

by Louis R. Wilson

If the "message" of the library is the image the academic community has of the librarian—certainly in the person of the library administrator—Louis R. Wilson's suggestion of a discipline in the practice of librarianship offers recommendations for professional preparation. As Wilson suggests, participation in the academic process requires considerably more than vocational training and attitude.

What Type Research Librarian? Against the background of the papers and discussions of this Symposium that have thrown into high relief the importance, complexity, and problems of research libraries, I am assigned the task of answering the question, "What type research librarian?" Specifically, I am asked to answer the questions whether research librarians should be scholars whose minds have been conditioned by long experience in research; and should they be encouraged to participate actively in research? Or should they be administrators, highly competent in the organization of large and expensive enterprises (men who "can get things done")? Or should they be technicians, expert in the minutiae of technical processes? Or, finally, should they be primarily promotors? Or, as an afterthought, should they perhaps be educators?

Not an "Or" But an "And" Proposal

In answering these questions, which have already been considered in part in the foregoing discussion, I can do little more than express an individual opinion, a procedure that librarians have followed all too frequently and that unfortunately holds out little probability of illuminating the subject and providing a solution of the problem. Nevertheless, I shall answer them in the light of my experience as a librarian, as a director for ten years of a library school that emphasized the importance of training librarians for research libraries, and as a surveyor of and prescriber for such libraries when they have encountered administrative or other difficulties.

The terms scholar, administrator, technician, promotor, and educator, used by the organizer of the Symposium were not intended, I assume, to be mutually exclusive, though there have been and there are those who think of them as such. Individuals from each of these categories, and from other categories, with different types and amounts of general education, graduate and professional training, and experience, have administered research libraries in the past and will be needed to direct the highly complex and intricate service required of them tomorrow. My first answer, then, is that the research librarian need not be a scholar *or* an administrator, but rather a scholar *and* an administrator, as well as a technician, a promotor, and an educator. After all, it is the qualities and abilities of the individual that count rather than the label he wears. In my opinion, all of these qualities and abilities may be embraced in the comprehensive term "librarianship," to which librarians may devote themselves unreservedly in the conviction that by so doing they can make their greatest contribution to society.

My second answer is that the categories mentioned do not comprise all the types of individuals and qualities and abilities desired in the research librarian. At an early period, the specifications submitted by the employers of research librarians may have called for only the technician with personality. Later they called for the technician and administrator; then for the administrator, technician, and scholar. Then the educator and the promotor were added. Today the formula runs somewhat like this: an individual is wanted with high intelligence, fine personality, wide educational interests, and an understanding of how the library can contribute to the advancement of educational and research programs; he must

SOURCE: Reprinted from Louis R. Wilson, "What Type Research Librarian?" in *Changing Patterns of Scholarship and the Future of Research Libraries; A Symposium* (Philadelphia: University of Pennsylvania Press, 1951), by permission of the publisher and the author.

have imagination, sound common sense, and intellectual drive. These are basic even if they are all too rare. He should also be an experienced, capable administrator and a dynamic leader. Scholarship, knowledge of languages, understanding of the spirit of research, and ability to engage in fruitful research or to direct members of his staff in it, are likewise set down sometimes as fundamental requirements. Frequently, it is also insisted that the librarian shall have a broad, humanistic outlook on books and all that enriches life, or that he shall have had training in research in the social and natural sciences, in order that he may be able to attack experimentally the problems confronting him with greater prospect of solving them.

TYPE OF LIBRARIAN DETERMINED BY THE NATURE OF POSITION

These are general or idealistic qualifications. Such librarians as they describe are, like the ideal university president, rarely to be found. Now, to be more specific, I shall point out qualities and abilities that should be possessed by the director and other members of the research library staff who fill the more important positions of associate and assistant directors and division and department heads. The abilities of all members of the staff combined are required if maximum efficiency is to be attained.

As the papers presented at this Symposium have demonstrated, the matters with which the director of a major research library must deal are extremely varied and complex. If they are to be handled effectively, it seems to me that the librarian should be first of all an experienced administrator of vision and leadership who has had considerable academic, professional, and educational training. His total academic and professional training should be as extensive and as exacting as that provided through curricula leading to the doctorage, including knowledge of research methods and an understanding of the spirit of research. A fundamental weakness of librarianship in the past has stemmed from the lack of librarians who have undergone training in librarianship of this range and exacting nature.

For a director of a research library devoted to a more limited field, such as the Clements or Folger libraries, with a corresponding limitation of administrative responsibility, emphasis may well be shifted from administrative ability and extensive knowledge of librarianship to exacting scholarly attainment in the subject field, proficiency in research, and experience in teaching and publication.

For associate or assistant librarians and other staff members in charge of major divisions and departments, qualities similar to those demanded of the head librarian may be required. I shall illustrate with three positions:

1. The assistant librarian in charge of technical services will find it advantageous to be more of the technician than of the scholar or the administrator. Knowledge of the technical processes involved, training in research, and ability in experimentation in solving technical problems will be essential to the efficient performance of his duties. Even so, he should be an administrator as well, since he must direct the activities of others working under him.

2. The assistant librarian in charge of building up collections may require still other qualifications. Materials are fundamental to teaching and research. It is not enough for the acquisition librarian to know the book trade and the technical processes involved in securing materials. Knowledge of their content assumes major importance. The scholar or subject specialist or bibliographer is indicated for this position. His knowledge of bibliographical sources may well exceed his knowledge of technical processes and his administrative skill. Nevertheless, he must know the interrelationships of all parts of the library and be able to coordinate the work of the faculty and members of the library staff in a purposeful, well-integrated program of acquisition. This is essential because faculty members work intermittently at building up resources or select materials that are related to their own interests rather than to those that are important in a well-conceived long-range plan. Due to their teaching and research, they lack time for continuous application which successful selection requires.

3. The assistant librarian in charge of readers services should have still other abilities. His knowledge of the contents of materials must be extensive and he should also know how to assist students and scholars in securing the greatest educational benefit possible from their study and investigation. The roles of the bibliographer, the subject specialist, and the educator may, therefore, be the most important for him to play, whether as assistant director in charge of readers service, or as head of a divisional reading

room, or of a major reference service. He cannot, however, neglect his role as administrator, since he is the library's representative in meeting its clientele and he must be able to provide it with a well-directed, smoothly functioning service. In doing this, his knowledge as a technician may also have to be brought into play, since much of the service he directs is dependent upon technical operations.

THE ROLE OF THE PROMOTER

Whether the research librarian should be primarily a promoter or public relations expert is a matter about which there may be question. Certainly there is need for such abilities as a promoter possesses. Possibly it is a matter of definition or of personality. Is the promoter to be a planner who is to project a long-range building program; or is he to develop an extensive cooperative enterprise like the Midwest Inter-Library Center or the Farmington Plan; or is he to organize a campaign for securing endowment for library purposes; or is he to aid councils of learned and scientific societies, educational foundations, federal agencies, and possibly international organizations, in carrying out some bibliographical or other important library programs? Opportunities for the exercise of such abilities occur daily in the life of the research librarian and the success of his library in many aspects of its work depends largely upon his wise utilization of them.

WHAT IS THE ROLE OF THE SCHOLAR-RESEARCH WORKER?

I have reserved for final consideration the question, "Should research librarians be scholars whose minds have been conditioned by long experience in research and should they be encouraged to participate in research?" This has long been a controversial question and doubtless will continue to be. What I have said earlier indicates that I believe the librarian can acquire a scholarly outlook and ability to engage in research and to understand its spirit as readily in librarianship as he can in other disciplines, and that in addition he has the opportunity through librarianship to become acquainted with techniques and administrative theories and principles that are essential to effective library administration but are lacking in scholarly training in other disciplines. Certainly the research librarian should be a person of scholarly attainment and should know how

to formulate research problems and set himself or others to work on their solution. Otherwise, progress in meeting changes in library service will be slow indeed. He should likewise thoroughly understand the spirit of research, and know how to assist scholars in securing maximum benefits from the use of materials. Without such understanding, intelligent cooperation and maximum efficiency are impossible. The shortage of librarians having such ability and understanding has, more than anything else, caused university presidents and boards of trustees of scholarly libraries to turn to holders of academic positions for directors of libraries under their control. But that a scholar-director whose mind has been conditioned by long experience in research will be able to carry on a sustained program of research in the field in which he has worked previously, or that he should do so, is a different matter. In comparable European libraries, such programs of investigation and publication have frequently been carried on. Their organization and methods of procedure have made this feasible. But the administrative process in American libraries makes such constant and pressing demands upon the librarian's time and energy that he has but little left for such activities, unless he largely turns over the administration of the library to an associate librarian. In that case the library is apt to suffer because the librarian cannot represent it properly before the governing body because he lacks first-hand information and experience, and the associate librarian cannot represent it because he is usually not charged with this responsibility.

In the first twenty-five years of my service as a practicing librarian, when I was studying library periodicals and reports for guidance in developing a research library program in a region in which large, well-functioning libraries were totally lacking, two of the major academic libraries of the nation were administered by professors who continued their research and publication in their special fields. One was a professor of New Testament Greek; the other, a professor of history. They contributed little by way of guidance in library matters because they continued their previous activities and did not have sufficient time or library experience to prepare extensive reports on the administration of their libraries or to read stimulating papers before library conferences. During the past twenty-five years, the libraries which I have been called on to survey have most frequently been those where administrative ability has been lacking or an effort has been made by a scholar-librarian to play a double role with the result that usually follows the attempt to serve two masters.

THE TRAINING OF THE
RESEARCH LIBRARIAN

The lack of knowledge of research and of an understanding of its spirit which the scholar-librarian appointment attempts to supply has been and is being met in a number of ways. In France, through the École de Chartes, the prospective librarian pursues a curriculum of university studies with heavy emphasis on archives, manuscripts, diplomatics, palaeography, language, literature, history, and the theory of archival administration. In England, university studies have been considered basic for librarians holding university library posts. Training through apprenticeship in university libraries and passing the British Library Association examinations have likewise been required, and have generally been preferred until recently to library school training. In Germany, until the late 1930's, the prescribed program of training for scholarly librarians called for university training leading to the doctorate and two years of training in the theory and practice of librarianship in the Prussian State Library, the Library of the University of Berlin, or a few other major state libraries. In the United States a number of library schools have developed faculties and curricula that have made possible training leading to the doctorate in librarianship. As a result, students who possess imagination, sound judgment, and the quality of dynamic leadership may master the theory and practice of librarianship and become proficient in carrying on research in that and related fields. They may likewise gain knowledge of subjects that closely support librarianship as well as of the ways in which scholars work and of the spirit which motivates them. Finally, through their study and investigation, such library school students may acquire a clearer understanding of the role of the library at various levels of education and research and may deepen their devotion to the library as an effective instrument for the achievement of high educational ends. Such mastery, such attainment, such knowledge, and such understanding, coupled with experience gained in service, should be sought by prospective research librarians if the libraries which they will direct are to make their full contribution to the civilization of tomorrow.

In their discussion of the preceding papers, two of the discussants have sharply challenged this point of view of librarianship. They insist that the librarian, whose training has been acquired in this way, may acquire skill in analyzing library problems and in applying established principles to library situations; but they deny him the possibility of acquiring a scholarly outlook and of joining in the quest of truth. In this they reflect the scholar's pre-occupation with his subject field and his lack of understanding of librarianship in its broadest aspects. If they looked more closely at history and English, for example, they would find that scholars even in those mines rich in the ore of truth frequently spend much time in date checking, word counting, and the like, and that librarianship, while concerned with problems such as have been considered in this Symposium, in which librarian and scholar have participated on a common basis, is also concerned with other matters to the study of which the librarian may devote himself with the assurance that he too will discover richly rewarding ore. They would find that librarianship is concerned with classification, fundamental to all science; with bibliography, the key that unlocks accumulated resources for the scholar's use; with the history of writing and libraries, that parallels the long course of man's cultural development; with the accumulated records of civilization in all fields that are of supreme importance to librarian and scholar alike; and with the communication of ideas that have affected man's long upward climb and will continue to shape his future destiny. In all these areas, the librarian may find abundant opportunity not only to make easier the quest of truth for others, but to participate significantly in the quest himself.

ABOUT THE AUTHOR

—**Louis R. Wilson**, Dean Emeritus, Graduate Library School, University of Chicago; Ph.D., 1905, University of North Carolina. Currently his research deals with the men and movements of the University of North Carolina.

The Status of Academic Librarians

by Robert Ward McEwen

Within any society or organization a process of differentiation can be expected to take place. In the typically artificial caste system that has evolved in higher education, the librarian is not included as a member of the primary group, the faculty. Academic librarians should be aware that differences in disciplines, in themselves, do not provide the basis for this informal structure. This article rehearses the value structure of an environment jealous of traditional roles and suggests means by which academic librarians might achieve legitimate recognition and equity.

There has been considerable discussion during the past few years of the status of the librarian and of members of library staffs in colleges and universities. It has been discussed in courses in library schools, in books on college library administration, in journal articles. Dr. Branscomb[1] notes that we do not have objective data necessary to a critical analysis of the problem. We need dependable statistical studies of the problem, studies involving classification of types of institutions. We need to know in how many and in what kinds of institutions the librarian is technically a member of the faculty, an administrative officer, or both. We need to know his rank as a member of the faculty and whether that rank follows automatically with the position of librarian or is the result of special circumstances. We need to know whether department heads, the assistant librarian, and the professional library staff members who are not department heads are classified as members of the faculty, administrative officers, or as part of the clerical staff of the institution. The data, to be significant, must indicate the exact meaning of the technical rank assigned to college librarians. If they are classified as members of the faculty, does that mean full voice and vote in faculty meetings, participation in academic functions, freedom to use facilities reserved for members of the faculty, inclusion in special privileges granted to members of the faculty?

But the interest of this paper does not require statistical studies as its basis. It may suggest, rather, an interpretation of that data when it is available. It deals, as well, with certain problems on which it would not be practicable to secure statistical data. We are concerned here with two main questions: (1) What status do college librarians want? (2) What can college librarians do to achieve it? As is evident from every discussion of the problem, this is an area of joint responsibility on the part of the college president, the head librarian, and other members of the library staff. As a paper at a meeting of college librarians, we address ourselves solely to our own responsibilities in the matter. The problem is considerably different for the large university and for the college librarian for reasons that will be apparent. We are here concerned primarily with the problem of the college librarian. The term college librarian is used to refer to all professional members of the staff.

Status is commonly defined as relative rank or position. Satisfactory status would then mean for the college librarian a relative position in the situation and community in which he lives and works which would express satisfactorily his sense of his relation to that situation and community.

We are assuming from the current concern for status an existing situation which is felt to be less than satisfactory and turn our attention first to an attempt to understand this dissatisfaction.

WHAT STATUS DO COLLEGE LIBRARIANS WANT?

Certain outstanding characteristics of satisfactory status will be clearly recognized, involving the natural wish for security and for recognition from the most important groups with whom the

SOURCE: Reprinted from Robert W. McEwen, "The Status of College Librarians," in Robert B. Downs, ed., *The Status of American College and University Librarians* (Chicago: American Library Association, 1958), pp. 169-176, by permission of the publisher. Originally published in *College and Research Libraries* 3: 256-261 (1942).

individual is concerned. Any individual wants his position to be a fair expression of his significance and value in the situation concerned. Here the college librarian is handicapped.

The mysteries of his craft, the intricacies of cataloging, even according to the old rules, the adventure of bibliographical search, these are dear to his heart and important to his function. But they are largely lost on the great majority of those among whom and with whom he works—members of the faculty, administrative officers in other aspects of the college's program. For these others do not commonly have opportunity to see his mysteries in operation, let alone understand them. Their contact with the college librarian is primarily expressed in one form—getting a book they want. Nor can we expect the professor, as he waits at the circulation desk, to meditate often or long on the wonderful organization, the meticulous scholarship, the professional skill that must be expressed in the process of making that book available to him. In the normal experience of getting a book he thinks no more about cataloging than he would about the generating plant and the linesmen while he was snapping on a light. He expects smooth functioning in both instances. And the librarian can humbly say to himself, "They also serve who only stand and wait." But it will not make him feel that his significance and value in the academic scene are properly recognized.

Desire for Acceptance

Secondly, any individual wants a feeling of group-belongingness, an assurance of acceptance as one with his fellows. This feeling of group-belongingness may appear to be the outgrowth of a common professional interest but its expression goes beyond the professional activities to the whole social life of the group. Invitations to dinner parties, bridge clubs, teas, are as important as service on committees as marks of this acceptance. Here again the college librarian is handicapped. The university library staff may be large enough to provide within itself for this aspect of status. A member of a large staff has status as a librarian in a group of librarians. But the college librarian belongs to a small minority group on campus and may even be the only representative of his craft.

Status in the whole college scene is set by the majority group—the faculty. By this we mean that the sense of group-belongingness

most characteristic of the college campus is organized around the life of the faculty group, which group professionally share common interest in teaching and research. The college librarian naturally seeks social acceptance from this majority group. But the librarian is commonly excluded by the nature of his task from any complete acceptance in this fellowship.

Status as we have discussed it thus far may seem to be primarily identified with the individual's desire for recognition, with social status. It is obvious that this is an important part of the status college librarians want.

There is another approach to the problem, however. In order for any individual to feel secure and therefore to achieve satisfactory status, there must exist for him some clear understanding of the nature of the areas in which he functions. Knowledge of the character of his problems, definition of the limits of those problems, and the goals which their solution concerns, brings confidence in attacking them and a sense of security follows in the process. The more sharply defined the area and meaning of his task, the greater will be his sense of security and status in it.

Area of Activities

The public librarian defines the area of his activities for himself. He studies his community, defines the objectives of library service to his community, builds his professional activities, his routines, his functions as a skilled craftsman in the direction of these objectives.

But the college librarian's problem at this point is much more complicated. Many of his professional activities, many of his routines are like those of the public librarian. And he has been taught to regard himself as a professional librarian. But the college library functions as a service agency to the educational process. The dominant area of activity in the library as in the college is academic. The validity of any routine must be determined not with reference to its place in librarianship but rather on the basis of its meaning and effectiveness in and for the academic community and primarily in its relationship to the teaching and learning process as defined by the college.

The definition of his problem and the sense of security achieved through such definition is therefore much more difficult for the college librarian. His area of activity as librarian overlaps the area of teaching but only in part. Some of his functions are obviously in both areas but not all of them. And frequently neither he nor his profession nor the college has any clear definition of these relationships.

Emphasis on Professional Training

Recent emphasis on professional training for librarianship has largely assumed that the area of the librarian's activities could be defined, and that a professional course of study would give the librarian the knowledge and understanding of the field requisite for effectiveness in almost any job in any library. But that assumption clearly breaks down when, as in the college library, the area of librarianship overlaps the academic area and the academic area is obviously the major determinant. In such a situation is the college librarian to regard himself as primarily a professional librarian, and hence as primarily an administrative officer in the college? Or is he to feel, seeing that the teaching process is the heart of the college and that the library exists on campus to collect, preserve and make readily available the facilities of print for use in teaching—is he to feel that his function as a librarian is essentially a branch of the teaching process and hence think of himself as primarily a member of the faculty? The sensible college librarian will do both and therefore be uncertain at many points in his definition of his function, resulting in a sense of insecurity and lack of status.

This particular uncertainty is aptly illustrated in Randall and Goodrich's discussion of the status of the college librarian. In the first edition of their book there appears this statement:

> As a matter of fact, the proper status of the librarian seems to be rather administrative, in the class of the deans, the secretary, etc., than pedagogical, in the class of the actual teaching faculty.[2]

In the revised edition, which has just appeared, the sentence quoted is preserved but is qualified, to say the least, by concluding sentences added to the paragraph:

> Even though the librarian conducts no classes, his teaching function is important. If a distinction in rank is to be made, is professional responsibilities should place him with the faculty group rather than the administrative.[3]

What status do college librarians want? Primarily they want status, any satisfactory status.

They are concerned about it because their situation makes difficult any wide recognition of their specialized function, marks them off as a minority group separated from the satisfactions of group-belongingness, places them in over-lapping areas of function which are not clearly defined. In this situation it is possible, of course, for the college librarians to partially satisfy their desire for status by turning their backs on their problems. They can say:

> We are librarians. It is only natural that these faculty folk, benighted individuals who have not had the advantage of special studies in bibliography, should be unaware of our real function in their midst. We don't care. We will go to the librarians' conferences and associate with other librarians. There we will be recognized. We will solve the problem created by the overlapping of library and teaching processes by turning our attention directly and solely to the proper professional problems of all good librarians, and let the faculty take care of the teaching process, and forget the overlapping.

The speaker would suggest that this attitude, increasingly rare but not yet extinct, affords only partial and temporary solace and no solution.

Why has there been a concerted effort in recent years on the part of college librarians to acquire faculty status? Because faculty members have status. Because faculty status, once achieved, brings the desired sense of inclusion and acceptance, which involves a recognition of the significance of their specialized tasks and which assists somewhat in clarifying the extent to which library processes and the teaching process do overlap.

WHAT CAN COLLEGE LIBRARIANS DO TO ACHIEVE IT?

The interest of the speaker in this subject arose from the observation that librarians are, for the most part, concentrating on one technique in achieving this desirable end. That technique is the attempt to secure formal recognition and appropriate rank as members of their faculties through action on the part of college administrators. The extent of progress in this attempt is the subject of the statistical studies suggested at the outset. We ought to know what the situation really is. And the speaker heartily approves that attempt. Formal status and appropriate rank are really important—often absurdly important—to members of faculties, and formal granting of that status to college librarians will in itself assist in solving the problems we are discussing. But one is reminded of the story, which every librarian will recognize as Abraham Lincoln's. You will remember that Lincoln asked how many legs a dog has if we count the tail a leg. The response was "Five." But Lincoln replied, "No, four, for calling a tail a leg doesn't make it one."

Formal Classification

Formal classification of college librarians in the college catalog as members of the faculty will solve the problem only if with it there comes actual status in the minds of those who alone can give it—the teaching faculty themselves. We have said that the sense of group-belongingness most characteristic of the college campus is the shared interest of the faculty in teaching and in creative and productive research. Any complete acceptance of college librarians as full colleagues must therefore await proof that the librarians are genuine participants in these shared interests. Librarians may therefore teach a course, or courses, in subject fields in which they are equally qualified with other members of the faculty. And librarians may undertake independent research in fields of special interest. Some activity in these directions seems to the speaker highly desirable for most college librarians. It will not be practicable or desirable to staff college libraries exclusively with people equipped to offer courses in the curriculum. But there would seem to be every reason to expect individuals who wish to make a career of college librarianship to be deeply interested in some subject field, perhaps but not necessarily in bibliographical problems within that subject field, and to expect that interest to issue eventually in research of a level that will gain the approbation of their colleagues outside the library. But again, such activity, whether in teaching or research, must be the result of genuine interest and ability and not a device to secure status.

Individual college librarians can therefore, it is believed, be recognized as colleagues through the results of their own participation in the basic interests of the faculty in teaching and research. But it will be as individuals, as individuals who are doing research or teaching courses, that that acceptance will be won. And it is obvious that acceptance need not carry over to the recognition of the professional and educational character of the work of those individuals as librarians.

Directly Attack Confusion

A third aspect of the solution seems equally clearly indicated, if more difficult of achievement than those we have discussed. College librarians can directly attack the existing confusion in the relationship of their work to the teaching process. The primary responsibility here may fall on the head librarian but it need not be his alone. If almost all contacts between members of the faculty and the librarians *are* at the circulation desk and *are* limited to getting a book, we can hardly expect our teaching colleagues to see the importance of our tasks in their work. But the situation can be changed. We know that our tasks are important in their work. But we have not clarified that function in our own minds. And we have not educated them in what we have clarified. Is it not time that we listed and defined some of the functions performed by college librarians which are definitely adjunct activities in the teaching process? A faculty member sends a student to the library to find information on a specific subject. The librarians, as teachers, commonly require the student to think through the problem of finding the specific material, suggest the necessity of reading material on all sides of a controversial question, call attention to the effect of the lapse of time on the treatment of the problem. The good librarian will seldom be satisfied with finding the book, turning to the page, and saying to the student, "Here it is." The librarian may feel with some justification that he gets no credit for his pains. But that credit waits on the clarification of his function and an understanding concerning it with the faculty. Students come to the library to work on term papers. What is the librarian's teaching task here? To what extent is he responsible for the education of the student in the methods of study involved in such an undertaking? He commonly advises the student to define his problem first, turn to the dictionary for definitions of terms involved, to the proper encyclopedia for a preliminary but organized statement of the nature of the problem. He then may assist the student in forming a reading list. He does not do that for the student. All this is teaching, is it not? And these are only samples.

Objective Measurement of Functions

Is it not time that we devised some relatively objective measurement of those functions and substituted such measurement for the type of statistics commonly kept in college libraries? What does it mean to say that the reference librarian answered so many "search questions" and so many "general questions" last year? Granted that we have no substitute for them at present, what do our circulation records actually mean, even if they are broken down in terms of the Dewey Decimal Classification?

Is it not time that we thought through the areas of responsibility of college librarians with reference to faculty research? To what extent can a small staff provide expert bibliographical knowledge at a level that can be useful to our teaching colleagues? Should we be informed of special research interests of every member of the faculty? If so, what can we do when we have that information? It may be the special responsibility of the head librarian, with the cooperation of the college administrator, to undertake the task of re-education of the faculty in this area. But the actual definition and the new activities that would grow out of it, require concerted and cooperative effort.

The final result of such a program might be that we would still be unsure occasionally whether we were tail or leg. But with formal recognition of some faculty status, with some individual participation in teaching and/or research, and with a clearer understanding of the extent and meaning of the overlapping between our work and that of our teaching colleagues, the speaker believes it would not matter very much.

FOOTNOTES

[1] Branscomb, Harvie. *Teaching with Books.* (Chicago, A.L.A., 1940) pp. 95-96.
[2] Randall, William M., and Goodrich, Francis L. D. *Principles of College Library Administration.* (Chicago, American Library Association and University of Chicago Press, 1936), p. 31.
[3] *Ibid.,* revised edition, Chicago, 1941, p. 31.

ABOUT THE AUTHOR

—**Robert Ward McEwen** (d. 1967), President, Hamilton College, 1949-1966; Ph.D., 1933, University of Chicago. At the time this article was originally published, the author was Librarian of Carleton College. His academic interests were in the history of religion and in philosophy.

What Librarians Do and What They Think

by Anita R. Schiller

The following chapter examines the characteristics of academic librarians. The data and the comments suggest significant areas where understanding and subsequent change can affect the quality of academic librarianship. Preparation as a professional, a professional commitment, involvement, academic and professional equity are all requisite to a high order of academic librarianship, no less than to better manpower utilization and the recruitment of talent.

CHARACTERISTICS OF PRESENT POSITIONS

Position Level

Nearly one out of seven academic librarians is a chief librarian (Table 16). The high proportion of chiefs to other librarians results from the small size of many of the nation's 2,000 academic libraries. While a handful of the largest libraries have professional staffs numbering 150 or more, roughly half of all academic libraries have professional staffs of less than three (FTE) and in some libraries professional staffing falls far below minimum standards.

One-fourth of the chief librarians in the sample supervise two employees or less. At the other extreme, about one-third supervise ten or more people. While most libraries are small, many librarians are concentrated in just a few institutions. Nearly one-third of all librarians work in the 50 largest libraries alone.

Relatively more of the men (21.6 percent) than of the women (11.8 percent) are chief librarians. A trend toward hiring males to fill top administrative positions has become particularly apparent over the last few decades. In 1930, for example, of the 74 institutions with enrollments of 2,000 or more, accredited by the Association of American Universities, there were 55 men and 19 women chief librarians.[1] As women chiefs retired, men were hired to take their place. The 1967 *ALA Directory* shows that 70 of these libraries are now headed by men and only four by women. Furthermore, not one of the 50 largest academic libraries listed in the 1967 *Bowker*

Annual is directed by a woman.[2] The recent appointment of a male chief librarian at Barnard College was considered newsworthy enough to make headlines here, and was even reported in the British press; but the appointment of a woman librarian as head of a major library would be far more unusual.

Number of Years in Present Position

Over three-fifths of all academic librarians have held the same position for less than five years. Nearly one-fifth of the women (but only one-tenth of the men) have held the same position for eleven years or more (Table 17). These figures may reflect the fact that the women tend to have had more professional experience than the men.

Job Mobility

Over one-fourth of the women but only one-sixth of the men have had eleven or more years of professional experience in their present institution (Table 18). This greater mobility on the part of the men is not unexpected since "virtually all of the studies [of job mobility] agree that the more mobile are to be found among male rather than female workers."[3] John F. Harvey has studied advancement level mobility of librarians and a significant factor associated with mobility is being a man.[4] The mobility of male librarians is taken as a matter of course, yet women who, because they may withdraw from their employment for marriage or family reasons, are sometimes considered to inhibit the "development of

---

SOURCE: Reprinted from Anita R. Schiller, *Characteristics of Professional Personnel in College and University Libraries* (Washington, D. C.: U. S. Office of Education, Bureau of Research, 1968), Chapter 4, "What Librarians Do and What They Think—An Overview," pp. 45-60, by permission of the author.

TABLE 16

Position Level, by Sex
(Percent Distribution)

POSITION LEVEL	TOTAL	MEN	WOMEN
Chief Librarian	15.3%	21.6%	11.8%
Assoc./Asst. Librarian	10.4	11.4	9.7
Dept. or Division Head*	36.0	36.9	35.5
Other Professional Asst.	38.3	30.1	43.0
TOTAL	100.0%	100.0%	100.0%
Base	2279	831	1448

*Includes Head of College, School or Department Library.

TABLE 17

Number of Years in Present Position, by Sex
(Percent Distribution)

NUMBER OF YEARS IN PRESENT POSITION	TOTAL	MEN	WOMEN
Less than 5	64.0%	69.7%	60.5%
5-10	20.3	20.2	20.4
11-20	12.3	8.4	14.6
21 and over	3.4	1.7	4.5
TOTAL	100.0%	100.0%	100.0%
Base	2263	828	1435

TABLE 18

Number of Years of Professional Experience in Present Institution, by Sex
(Percent Distribution)

YEARS	TOTAL	MEN	WOMEN
Less than 5	54.1%	60.2%	50.5%
5-10	22.3	23.3	21.8
11-20	16.2	12.3	18.4
21 and over	7.4	4.1	9.2
TOTAL	100.0%	99.9%	99.9%
Base	2270	828	1442

solid, long-range library programs."[5]   Whether this situation is actually as paradoxical as it seems cannot be determined by the present survey which was limited to those who are now working.

High turnover rates may indeed have serious effects upon the stability of library operations, but how high they are, and whether it is the women who are most culpable, has not been demonstrated (although the findings of the present study show that many of those women who are now employed had left their library positions at some earlier point).   Where men leave one position for another, for example, the disruptions may be particularly strongly felt, for men are more likely to hold administrative positions and thereby to be responsible for library policy and planning.   Turnover in these positions may have more harmful effects in the long run than changes in personnel at the lower levels.

Just as the drop-out problem affects both the profession as a whole and the status of its women workers, mobility or lack of mobility brings with it similar consequences.   Recent studies of special librarians[6] and of current library school graduates[7] have shown, for example, that those who are able to move can and do earn considerably more than those who are not.   The general lack of mobility among women librarians operates as a restraint upon their own career advancement.   At the same time, worthwhile employment opportunities may remain unfilled, and trained manpower, although available generally, cannot be channeled where it is needed.

Attrition, turnover, and job mobility rates are important concerns, both for the profession as a whole, and for the future advancement

possibilities of its individual members.   It is quite evident, for example, that men who vacate a position for a better one will maintain their professional commitment, thereby enhancing their value to the profession as well as improving their own future career opportunities.   On the other hand, when women drop out of librarianship for marriage or family reasons (even though they may return later), they may find themselves at a disadvantage.   When women leave their employment for other than professional reasons, for example, they are likely to do so at exactly that point when their library careers are just becoming established.   When they return, they are likely to find that they have been overtaken by others who have maintained their professional involvement.   While continuing education and increased part-time employment opportunities for women have been recommended as important steps toward overcoming one aspect of this problem (i.e., the "social wastage of women, particularly [of] those who hold a professional qualification")[8] even these solutions may be only partial.   It has been suggested, for example, that increased part-time employment may serve only to perpetuate and reinforce existing disparities in status between the sexes.[9]

Number of Employees Supervised

Few librarians supervise large numbers of people, but most librarians have some supervisory responsibilities (Table 19).   Just over one-quarter of the respondents supervise more than five people and an equal proportion of respondents supervise no one; nearly half supervise from one

TABLE 19

Number of Employees* Supervised, by Sex
(Percent Distribution)

NUMBER OF EMPLOYEES SUPERVISED	TOTAL	MEN	WOMEN
None	26.6%	18.7%	31.1%
1-2	28.5	26.1	29.9
3-5	19.0	17.5	19.8
6-9	9.8	11.8	8.7
10-19	8.4	11.4	6.7
20-49	4.6	8.2	2.5
50 and over	3.1	6.3	1.3
TOTAL	100.0%	100.0%	100.0%
Base	2238	815	1423

*Excludes student assistants.

to five people. Here again, just as men are more likely than women to be administrators, they are also more likely to supervise larger staffs. One-quarter of the men as opposed to one-tenth of the women supervise more than ten people. At the same time, 31 percent of the women (compared to 18.7 percent of the men) supervise no one.

Job Activities and Specialization

Selection and acquisition, cataloging and classification, reference service, and circulation of materials are the traditional library functions. Librarians are also administrators, and a few of them direct large organizations with annual operating expenditures of a million dollars or more. Respondents to the present library survey hold all types of library positions, and perform an enormous variety of library activities. College and university librarians all contribute to the educational programs of the institutions where they work, regardless of whether or not they have any direct teaching duties, although some of them do teach formal courses or provide informal instruction in the use of the library. Librarians deal with all kinds of printed and other materials, developing and carrying out ways to make these materials, along with the knowledge, ideas, and facts that they contain, accessible to students, faculty, and research workers. Librarians draw on their total educational backgrounds to perform their work. All kinds of non-library as well as library specializations are represented in the present survey. Foreign language competencies, subject field and area specializations, knowledge of specialized forms of materials, and other professional specializations requiring non-library skills each have applications in certain types of library positions. The sampled librarians were asked the following question: "Is your *major* activity associated *primarily* with any of the following? A particular foreign language or group of languages? A particular subject field or geographical area? Another professional specialization?" Table 20 summarizes these data.

TABLE 20

Academic Librarians Whose Major Library Activity is Associated with a Non-Library Specialization, by Type of Specialization
(Percent Distribution)

ACTIVITY	TOTAL	MEN	WOMEN
Foreign Language			
Yes	8.0%	9.7%	7.0%
No	85.6	86.8	85.0
No Report	6.4	3.5	8.0
TOTAL	100.0%	100.0%	100.0%
Base	2282	831	1451
Subject Field or Area			
Yes, Subject Field	26.2%	26.2%	26.2%
Yes, Geographical Area	4.2	6.5	2.8
No	63.4	63.5	63.3
No Report	6.2	3.8	7.7
TOTAL	100.0%	100.0%	100.0%
Base	2282	831	1451
Materials or Other Specialization			
Yes, Special Collections	4.3%	6.0%	3.4%
Yes, Other Materials[1]	6.3	5.9	6.5
Yes, Other Prof. Specializations[2]	4.1	6.6	2.6
No	75.9	75.0	76.4
No Report	9.4	6.5	11.1
TOTAL	100.0%	100.0%	100.0%
Base	2282	831	1451

[1]Includes A-V, documents, maps, music scores, etc.
[2]Includes administrative specialization (i.e., personnel, public relations), automation, systems analysis, etc.

The desirability of foreign language skill is stressed by library administrators and is generally required of entering students in the library schools. Academic librarians as a whole seem to be fairly well-equipped in this respect. The Romance languages (including Portuguese, Italian, Romanian, French, Spanish and Catalan), the Germanic languages (including Danish, Dutch, Flemish, German, Icelandic, Norwegian, Swedish and Yiddish), and the Slavic languages (Polish, Russian, Serbian, Ukranian, Bulgarian, Slovak, Czech, etc.) were fairly common among the respondents. Other languages mentioned were: Latin and Greek, Hungarian, Finnish, Estonian, Turkish, Celtic, Hebrew, Chinese, Japanese, Korean, Arabic, Persian, Hindi, Indonesian, Tibetan, Manchu, Mongol, and Islamic.

Although library schools place particular emphasis on language study, specialization on the job in a subject field is much more common among academic librarians than is specialization in a language. Only 8 percent of the respondents stated that their major activity is associated with a language while 26.2 percent noted that their major activity is associated with a subject field or fields. Of 598 people who specialized in a subject field, the subject specialization reported most often (185 people) was science. This included the health sciences, biological and agricultural sciences, physical sciences, engineering and mathematics. Following the sciences were the humanities and arts (177), social sciences and law (161), education and psychology (62), and "other" (17).

Area specializations were less common but included regions of the United States as well as foreign regions. Altogether 4.2 percent of the respondents (6.5 percent of the men and 2.8 percent of the women) specialized in a geographic area.

Of all respondents, 6.3 percent dealt primarily with a form of material such as U.S. government publications, or other documents, newspapers, maps, music scores, A-V materials, microforms, slides, or microprint.

Men more than women tend to have their major activity associated with special forms of material or with "other professional specializations." Six percent of the men work primarily with archives, manuscripts, rare books, and other types of special collections while only 3.4 percent of the women are active in these areas of specialization. Other professional specializations mentioned include: adminis-

tration, personnel, buildings and equipment, business management, automation, systems analysis, information science, documentation, public relations, exhibits, publications, graphic design, photography. Altogether 4.1 percent of all the respondents (6.6 percent of the men, as compared with 2.6 percent of the women) stated that their major work was associated with one of these specializations.

There is some overlapping of responses between various portions of Table 20. An individual who uses a foreign language, for example, may also specialize in a geographic area, or someone whose major activity deals with a subject field (such as history), may also deal with archival or other special materials. The proportion of all librarians who are associated with at least one of these specializations, however, is certainly no less than 40 percent, and the figure is probably even higher. While administrators have repeatedly emphasized the need for specialized personnel, the library schools have not yet come to grips with this need in preparing library school students for their future employment.

Returning again to the differences in the library activities pursued by men and women, it can be noted that relatively equal proportions of men and of women are engaged in "subject" and in "other materials" specializations, while in the "other professional specializations" category, the men tend to be represented more than women.

Table 21 is further evidence that more men than women tend to be identified with special "non-library" endeavors. Three percent of the respondents employed in professional positions on college and university library staffs regard themselves as something other than librarians. (It is important to note here, however, that others employed in similar types of positions, think of themselves as librarians.) Relatively more of the men (5.4 percent) than the women (1.7 percent) consider themselves as other than librarians. It is clear from the table, of course, that the vast majority (95.2 percent) of all respondents regard themselves professionally as librarians, although one respondent facetiously supplied the self-description "high-paid clerk."

Nearly 11 percent of the 2,282 respondents are involved in the application of electronic data processing at an administrative or supervisory level; 18.1 percent of the men are so involved while only 6.4 percent of the women are.

TABLE 21

Regards Self as Librarian or Other, by Sex
(Percent Distribution)

REGARDS SELF AS	TOTAL	MEN	WOMEN
Librarian	95.2%	92.4%	96.9%
Librarian and "Other"[1]	1.8	2.2	1.5
Other Professional[2]	3.0	5.4	1.7
TOTAL	100.0%	100.0%	100.0%
Base	2262	828	1434

[1]Generally "Librarian and Teacher."
[2]"AV Specialist," "Graphic Designer," "Historian," etc.

Comments from some respondents working in this area help explain the extent of their involvement:

> I am acting as co-ordinator between the [circulation] department and the systems analysis staff [during] the implementation of an interim based processing program.
> . . . . .
> We have data processing equipment here or on order and will probably go to at least automated circulation. Two of the central staff and I are trained in this area.
> . . . . .
> We [conducted] a partially successful experiment with a machine-produced serials list.
> . . . . .
> [I wrote a] detailed proposal for a new acquisition routine combining the rule of punched cards with machine-produced multiple copy orders . . . From this proposal, our new acquisitions control program was developed . . .

Nearly 15 percent of the respondents teach courses for credit. Almost one-fifth of the men teach such courses, in comparison with just over one-tenth of the women. Most teach at the same institution although a few teach at other institutions.

> I teach as a visiting lecturer at . . . . This is not within the scope of my position [here] but rather done outside of library hours. I usually teach during the Fall and Spring quarters.

Of the 322 who recorded the names or areas of the courses they teach, 76.4 percent teach library courses only, 20.2 percent teach non-library courses and only 3.4 percent teach both. More men (27.7 percent) than women (12.9 percent) teach non-library courses. Examples of non-library courses taught include: Oriental thought, legal research and writing, American legal history, seminar on legislation, directed reading, medical history, Spanish, chief English writers, and Old Norse. Bibliography courses in subject areas such as: music, horticulture, medicinal chemistry, law, Japanese literature, Chinese literature, social sciences, social work, science and technology, and religious literature were some of the others mentioned.

Apparently, library policies differ in encouraging or discouraging staff to teach. One librarian wrote,

> I received an offer to teach a foreign language at . . . University three hours per week, but the library did not grant permission to accept in spite of the fact that I offered, of course, to make up time (3 hours per week.)

Association Memberships

Two-thirds of the academic librarians reported that they belong to a national, state, or regional library association; half belong to only one association and one-sixth belong to two or more. Men and women are represented in very similar proportions. The state or regional library associations are the most popular (with nearly three-fifths of the respondents as members). Half of the respondents belong to the American Library Association. Special Libraries Association memberships are held by one-tenth of the sampled academic librarians.

Comments from the respondents who do not belong to ALA are of interest because one reason predominates—high dues.

> Dues for ALA too high
> . . . . .
> I read the publications regularly of ALA, ADI, SLA, but do not belong because of the cost of dues with so little return.
> . . . . .
> The high cost of membership in the ALA prohibits a recent graduate from joining until his financial situation is more stable.

Younger librarians are the least likely to be ALA members. Although half of all the respondents belong to ALA, the percentage who are members varies among the different age groupings. Only two-fifths of those under 30 are ALA members, while half of those between 30 and 49 years of age and three-fifths of those who are 50 and over are ALA members. Various committees in the ALA "are making a determined effort to include new, young, or relatively untried members in the activities of the association." The Reference Services Division Board and the Board of Directors of the Association of College and Research Libraries both have established a program of intern committee membership on an experimental basis. Both will seek out and add junior members to committees for a one-year term.[10] Perhaps such recognition will inspire the interest and participation of other younger librarians.

In contrast to the fairly extensive membership in library associations is the more limited affiliation of librarians with national non-library associations. More than half of the 2,282 respondents do not belong to any national non-library organization, while 27.8 percent belong to one only and 12.2 percent belong to more than one such organization. Non-response to the question on association membership (6.3 percent) was relatively high. The American Association of University Women, Modern Language Association, National Education Association, and American Political Science Association are some of the more frequently noted associations to which librarians belong. Examples of some other non-library associations mentioned by respondents are: Mediaeval Academy of America, Estonian Learned Society in America, Guild of Carillonneurs of North America, American Guild of Organists, Society of History of Technology, Society of Architectural Historians, American Association for Engineering Education, National Association of Social Workers, and the Association for Asian Studies.

One-fifth of the 2,282 respondents belong to the American Association of University Professors, over one-sixth of the women (16.5 percent) and over one-fourth of the men (26.2 percent) are members. This membership rate is evidence of the interest librarians show in this organization and in this means of identification with the faculty. When one considers librarians on many campuses are not even elibible for mem-

bership in the AAUP because they do not have faculty status, this membership rate seems fairly high overall.

OPINIONS OF LIBRARY CAREER

The respondents were asked, "To what extent has your library career fulfilled your expectations?" The most common reply was, "About as expected," with over one-third of the respondents giving that answer. Table 22 shows, however, that half were more satisfied with their library careers than they had expected.

Only 11 percent felt disappointed with their library careers. Morrison found that only 13 percent of the academic librarians in his sample were uncertain about or dissatisfied with their library careers, and that "fewer academic librarians than other professional people are dissatisfied with their occupational choice."[11]

Although only about one out of ten of the respondents to the present survey considered that their careers did not measure up to their expectations, the question did serve to bring forth many added comments on present library practice which pointed to specific inadequacies in individual library careers. While the reasons for their opinions were not requested, those who stated that they were dissatisfied were much more likely than others to add comments to explain why. Many such criticisms were in close accord with one another on specific issues. Together, they reveal a basic concern for better manpower utilization and for improvement in the status of the profession ("The profession is just not what it could be."). Time-consuming clerical duties were one of the major sources of dissatisfaction. The following remarks are typical.

> I seem to have been hired only as a typist and file clerk in spite of my qualifications. Though I am a professional person, I am not doing what I consider professional work.
> . . . . .
> The reason I find library work disappointing is that I have not been given work of a professional nature to do. Far too much of my time has been tied up with clerical duties.
> . . . . .
> My negative reaction to librarianship is based on the 15 to 20 hours a week that I check out restricted materials from our section of the library. Although I certainly expected to perform certain clerical duties, I did not realize I would spend 40 to 50 percent of my working time engaged in such tasks.
> . . . . .

TABLE 22

Extent to Which Library Career Has Fulfilled Respondents' Expectations, by Sex
(Percent Distribution)

OPINION OF LIBRARY CAREER	TOTAL	MEN	WOMEN
Very disappointing	1.3%	1.5%	1.3%
Somewhat disappointing	9.6	10.3	9.1
About as expected	37.2	38.2	36.7
More satisfying than expected	25.4	26.4	24.8
Much more satisfying than expected	26.5	23.6	28.1
TOTAL	100.0%	100.0%	100.0%
Base	2246	825	1421

Poor distinctions between professional work
and clerical work account for [my disappointment].
. . . . .
. . . may I plead for better utilization of personnel? For better administrative practices? Reap-
praisal and tightening of clerical routines? Private
industry would go bankrupt supporting some of
the library habits I have witnessed!

Many respondents criticized what they considered inflexible policies and administrative
rigidity. The need for shared decision-making
responsibility at all levels also was emphasized:

Ingenuity and innovation are repressed due to
over-supervision and demands made for minor
jobs, errands, and "busy work" and no opportunity to renovate, use other than long-standing procedures whether they fit the times or not.
. . . . .
We are organized so that entire responsibility
rests with the Head Librarian. The Head Librarian will not delegate any authority to anyone else.
. . . . .
The chief reason for the many years of dis-
appointing experience are: a) working under
authoritarian supervision and b) working under
people who have little love for or interest in the
content of books.
. . . . .
Often younger librarians are held in check
professionally by stodgy administrative personnel too timid to venture into the mid-twentieth
century technological age.
. . . . .
While librarianship strives to be professional,
the professionals are not serving in a professional
capacity. Their recommendations or opinions
are not sought and not welcomed if proferred.
There is still a strong "authoritarian" concept of
librarianship. Those who just "follow orders"
are likely to be "time servers."
. . . . .
Where is this "new librarian" that library
schools present to us? I guess the "new breed"
somehow clashes with the "old breed!"
. . . . .

Librarians in administrative positions are the
greatest barriers to academic recognition of the
profession. Most resist new ideas or suggestions
of change in existing routine.
. . . . .
As a new librarian I am surprised . . . at the
predominance of "little old ladies" of both
sexes in library administration who are totally
lacking in enlightened concepts of management.
. . . . .
Having recently graduated from library school
I was filled with a great deal of enthusiasm and
developed in my mind's eye an image of the "new
librarian": full of zip, interested in new ideas, up
on what's new in the field, having rapport with
the patron whether adult or youth. Once I began
work many of the so-called "stereotyped" images
seemed to present themselves—and particularly
resistance to change!

The lack of challenging work seems to be
cause for some librarians to think about leaving the profession.

My disappointment in my job centers around
what I do all day. To me it is . . . redundant,
short-sighted, and continues to make something
out of nothing. I would be more satisfied at the
same salary with more responsibility and meaningful work. I hope to find a way out of the library
field.
. . . . .
University libraries seem to have a common
fault—an appalling waste of talent. People with
broad backgrounds and lively interests are placed
in jobs which are, at best, dull and repetitive. No
new challenges nor incentives appear and there is
a singular lack of chance for advancement. The
person is expected to remain in the same rut. The
only way out is simply to leave the system. The
system thus loses the time and money it has invested in the person. Sadly enough, this situation
is perpetuated by librarians entrenched in their
position and unwilling to accept new ideas or re-
linquish power.

I am presently planning on leaving librarianship. I feel there is always an administrative

ceiling on creativity, and conventionalized routine can induce boredom.

How many others who seek intellectually challenging careers never consider librarianship to begin with is unknown. Its public image, however, does not portray librarianship as a stimulating and exciting career. Agnes Reagan has reported that college students "seem more likely to dismiss the profession as a possible career because of their impressions of the work, which they term uninteresting, than because of any other one consideration."[12] Wilson and Tauber have stated further that

> In order to attract individuals who, by native ability, background, and training, are able to develop into effective chief librarians, assistant librarians, and professional assistants, it must be shown that university librarianship is many sided and affords an opportunity for challenging, creative work; that it presents many opportunities for administrative and scholarly activity; and that ability is rewarded with promotion, extension of responsibility, and ample financial compensation.[13]

Current demands on librarianship are immensely challenging. There are certainly many librarians who are indeed presented with the opportunity, both in their day to day work, and in their other professional activities, to deal with the urgent problems which face the profession. It is also clear, however, that not all library positions offer these opportunities. ("How can one who is motivated to do something really creative in library work find an administrator who is not complacent?") Some 40 years ago, Williamson noted that

> the development of library work as a profession has been hampered by the tendency on the part of the public to look upon it as wholly clerical in nature. The library schools and the actual organization of libraries have not only done little to remove this handicap but have even done much unconsciously to perpetuate it.[14]

Judging from the spontaneous comments of the respondents quoted above, these points still merit special attention in the academic library field.[15]

Other sources of dissatisfaction ranged from nepotism rules which "stand in the way of granting faculty status to librarian-wives of professors" and the "strong tendency when there is a vacancy to replace women by men," to the lack of faculty status and inadequate salaries. Status and salaries are dealt with elsewhere but each of these matters were major areas of concern, and in some cases dissatisfaction with salary was great enough to cause librarians to decide to leave the field.

> By preference, I would like to stay with academic librarianship, but I am even now looking for a position with more remuneration.

Additionally, the desire for time off to take courses and to attend professional meetings regularly was often voiced.

> [I am] somewhat saddened by the lack of interest in the professional development of librarians by library and university administrators.
> . . . . .
> How can we be asked to "publish," "do research," while holding down an 8-5 job? How about a quarter or semester off to do research?

Nearly all of these comments were offered in sincere concern for improving the library profession. All point to legitimate problems librarians live with, but we must not lose sight of the vast majority who commented on the fulfillment of their library career expectations with comments such as these:

> I *expected* satisfaction and get it from my work.
> . . . . .
> Every moment has been fascinating—even the troublesome ones and that's what I expected.
> . . . . .
> I expected to like it, and I do.
> . . . . .
> It's Great!!!!!

FOOTNOTES

[1] Zimmerman, Lee F., "The Academic and Professional Education of College and University Librarians," Unpublished Master's Thesis, University of Illinois, 1932.

[2] Jordan, Robert T., in a letter to the editor of *Library Journal*, 90 (December 1, 1965), 5126, states that "only seven of the 46 largest public libraries are directed by women and there are no women among the directors of the 74 libraries in . . . the Association of Research Libraries."

[3] Marshall, Howard D., *The Mobility of College Faculties* (New York: Pageant Press, 1964), p. 19.

[4] Harvey, John F., "Advancement in the Library Profession," *Wilson Library Bulletin,* 36 (October, 1961), 144-47.

[5] Gaines, Ervin J., "Library Education and the Talent Shortage," *Library Journal,* 91 (April 1, 1966), 1771.

[6] Special Libraries Association, "A Study of 1967 Annual Salaries of Members of the Special Libraries Association," Special Libraries 58:217-254 (1967).

[7] Frarey, Carlyle J., "The Placement Picture - 1966," *Library Journal,* 92:2134 (1967).

[8] Ward, Patricia L., *Women and Librarianship,* Library Association Pamphlet, no. 82 (London: The Library Association, 1966), p. 7.

[9] Rossi, Alice S., "Barriers to the Career Choice of Engineering, Medicine, or Science Among American Women," Jacquelyn A. Matfield and Carol G. Van Aken, eds., *Women and the Scientific Profession* (Cambridge, Mass.: M.I.T. Press, 1965), p. 73.

[10] "A Look at ALA Activities," *ALA Bulletin,* 62 (April, 1968), 419.

[11] Morrison, Perry D., "The Career of the Academic Librarian," Unpublished Ph.D. Dissertation, University of California, 1961, p. 243.

[12] Reagan, Agnes L., *A Study of Factors Influencing College Students to Become Librarians,* ACRL Monograph, No. 21 (Chicago: Association of College and Research Libraries, 1958), p. 22.

[13] Wilson, Louis R. and Maurice Tauber, *The University Library,* 2d ed. (New York: Columbia University Press, 1956), p. 297.

[14] Williamson, Charles C., *Training for Library Service* (New York: Merrymount Press, 1923) p. 26 and 32.

[15] This tendency is sometimes reinforced by the very materials which are used to describe the profession to possible recruits. The 1966-67 *Occupational Outlook Handbook,* for example, contains a photograph showing a librarian at work. The caption reads: "Librarian checks out book."

ABOUT THE AUTHOR

—**Anita R. Schiller,** Research Associate, Library Research Center, University of Illinois; M.L.S., 1959, Pratt Institute. Mrs. Schiller's major research interest is in library manpower.

THE COLLECTION

The academic librarian is charged with providing a significant portion of the information from which knowledge is produced. While the assumptions that he and the academic community have as to how this can best be done may differ as to priorities and techniques, it is further assumed that there must be a rationale to collection development. For the academic librarian, the latter is an expected response to professional conditioning, the desire to provide intelligence in the budgetary process, and an attempt to establish the means to regulate the competition for resources.

Research in a College Library

by Eileen Thornton

This speech on the expectations and behavior of various components in the academic community provides insights into the function of the academic librarian as the deliberate developer of a library materials collection. The speaker suggests the need for a determination on the nature of the collection and the acceptance of this definition by the institution as a whole as basic to reducing tension. So long as a policy vacuum exists, because of his relationship with a significant resource, the book budget, the librarian will not be able to avoid the unenviable position of being a major ingredient in the success of programs and research. In much the same way he should not be left with the long range responsibility of determining for the institution its future program or research development,

Librarians speak to librarians, they write for librarians, they gripe to librarians and about them. It is heady wine to have a chance to speak also to presidents, to deans, to faculty members, and to the others here assembled. I might as well confess that the temptation is almost irresistible to rupture rather than enrapture the captured.

Lancelot Gobbo and I have a lot in common. Caution dictates: "Be nice. Don't get carried away. Don't try to cover everything. Sugar catches more flies than vinegar. Don't sound petulant: the throat you cut may be your own. Coin a few new clichés. Remember you have a whole little book in your possesion by Matthew Arnold and it is entitled *Sweetness and Light.*"But my other thumb tells me I may never get another chance like this even if I speak a soothing piece, so I might as well speak what I laughingly call my mind. If worse comes to worst I can live on a janitor's pay. Goodness knows I have had enough experience in that line of work.

First, I think there are two things that ought to be said at this juncture: I know who should be up here and so do you, and that's Newton McKeon. His "The Nature of the College Library Book Collection"[1] is a landmark piece, timeless and valuable. I shall crib from it and occasionally differ from it, but I shall take it as read by most of this audience.

If you have not read it, do so. Another thing I ought to say: I wish the program had started with Verner Clapp instead of ending with him. He will take a shot at the future, and, if he is right in his predictions, it might have made unnecessary Fred Wagman's agonizing and mine to try to tell you what we are up against now. If the cure is in Mr. Clapp's saltshaker we need not worry.

My assigned segment of this topic has changed its title a number of times, and I am not dead sure just what it is I am supposed to be speaking about. From the last letter of instructions, I gathered that I was to give a capsulated case history of how one specific library, probably Oberlin, came to have research and resource materials. This brought me back to the matter of the word "research" as I culled up from the G.L.S. shades, "Course No. 301: Methods of Research. Tenet 1: Define your terms." It struck me then that it would never be possible for me to come closer to it than to say that "research" and "research materials" are relative rather than absolute terms.

For about twenty-five years now I have personally and unsystematically collected college novels. After about ten years of this effort I found out that I knew quite a bit about college novels, so I started to toy with the idea of writing a book. Now here is where I am a

SOURCE: Reprinted from Eileen Thornton, "Research in a College Library," in *The Place of a Research Library in a Liberal Arts College; Proceedings of a Symposium Held at Bowdoin College, February 21-22, 1963* (Brunswick, Maine: Bowdoin College, 1963), by permission of the publisher and the author.

failure. Had I been a faculty member I would have dignified this whole lazy and pleasant enterprise with the title of "research," and out of the discipline that the very word imposes (I am quite serious about this) I think I might have got on with the job and might have done a book. Furthermore (this is only incidental but perhaps worth mentioning) I might have wangled a leave or two for this project, as it would have been research, and the institutional investment would have produced a better librarian if not a better book.

But back to our dictionaries and definitions. Webster's, both edition two and edition three are fortunately for once in agreement and say: "Research (with the accent there): (1) careful or diligent search, a close searching; (2) studious inquiry or examination; specifically and usually, critical and exhaustive investigation or experimentation having for its aim the discovery of new facts and their correct interpretation [some of this sounds almost like my struggles with my checkbook], the revision of accepted conclusions, theories, or laws, in the light of newly-discovered facts, or the principal applications of such new or revised conclusions, and so on. The word comes from the French, so I went one step further: "Recherche: noun: search, quest, pursuit, inquiry, investigation, examination, scrutiny . . .: addresses, suit, courtship [we have lots of "recherche" at Oberlin among the student body, and much of it goes on in the library]: figuratively, studied elegance or refinement, affectation [I am sorry to say we have some of that too]."

Bergan Evans adds a bit: "Research has become very popular in the United States since the outbreak of World War II. As Henry D. Smyth has observed, the idea that the object of research is new knowledge does not seem to be widely understood, and a schoolboy looking up the meaning of a word in a dictionary is now said to be doing research. Indeed, it has become debased even further. Research is frequently used to describe reading by those to whom reading, apparently, is a recherché activity, and for many a graduate student it is a euphemism for wholesale plagiarism." I am glad to say we are talking about undergraduates here.

I am concerned with both student research and faculty research, as I think most college librarians are and most college faculties are. Is it always a matter of new knowledge? And where students are concerned, even in the best programs, is part of the research activity aimed at teaching the discipline of research or is it always purely the search for new knowledge? This seems to me rather vital for us to know in small academic institutions, for in college libraries we can do a good deal to develop materials of research quality in selected fields, but only in selected fields. In using these, our ablest students can both acquaint themselves with research methodology and find areas for original contributions. But if, on the other hand, the selection of a research topic may be a matter of immensely wide latitude for the good undergraduate, in order to be sure that the chances of turning up new knowledge are enhanced, then it becomes close to impossible for even the best and very richest college libraries to predict needs and to develop the enormous universe of resources they should have. Most college librarians have had the experience of advanced students lighting on a topic in which resources are slim, while closely adjacent topics, in which the library does have rich resources, gather dust.

The complex university library system, in part because of sheer mass and in part because of the structure of the institution and the numbers of persons to be served, can perhaps make sharper distinctions among categories of users and categories of materials. In the college, both research materials and research activity are less sharply defined. Both shade down from the most rarefied to the near mundane. There is a wide grayish band, not a sharp black line. Basically the problem of meeting research need is easier, at least in theory, in the college, which can restrict its universe, stabilize its programs, control changes, control quantity and quality of student body, experiment with methods and keep tab on their results, and plan to provide both breadth and depth in a closely watched education program. Most colleges use strong faculty members rather than graduate assistants in elementary courses. This helps to identify the kinds of ability in students and permits the relatively early improvement of some students in independent and advanced programs.

While I am sure there is a lot of self-deception and outright falsity in statements to the effect that "Our students, our advanced juniors and seniors in colleges, engage in work that would be on the graduate level at a large state institution," there must be cases where this is true. If it is, it puts a special burden on college libraries to respond to this capacity.

College faculties are more like university faculties than may be apparent at first glance. Many college faculty members increasingly engage in research, some of it pointing upward and outward to enhance the world's stockpile of information. Some of the best faculty members publish upward and outward because it is just in them to engage in this kind of activity and it emerges in the form of publication. But many of them do more than this, as I am sure university teachers also do: they carry on research that is inward and downward too. I doubt that they consciously separate these kinds of research very much. The good ones extend themselves as teachers through this latter process, for this kind of research affects their teaching and in turn affects their students. This constant research-backed teaching is obvious to discriminating students, and it can be contagious.

But we all know that to get and hold a faculty, especially a faculty that continues to develop as a community of live scholars while still dedicated basically to the teaching function, is a difficult affair. Facilities for research are as important to many candidates as are salaries and course assignments. When colleges lose faculty members to universities, library inadequacy is often an important reason.

The discriminating faculty member and the thoughtful administrator are the great allies of librarians. Their vision should be our vision. One of our great failures as librarians is that we have often failed to make clear to administrators and faculties what it takes to build a library collection and library services. Communications flow well in one direction and not very well in the other. For instance, painful as it may be, let's go back to Millett's ten-year-old book of the financing of higher institutions and to his statements about libraries and librarians.[2] This is very dangerous territory, because Millet's brutality always brings

out the brute in me.

According to him, more than a hundred college presidents and deans told him three things:

> 1. That librarians constitutionally hate to throw anything away. They always fear that the book they discard will be the one someone wants next month, and they are always chagrined when they cannot produce what is wanted.
> 2. The librarian profession (sic) as such puts little emphasis on economy.
> 3. We have found general agreement as a rule of thumb that a "good" liberal arts college ought to operate with a book collection of under a hundred thousand volumes, many of which would be duplicates.

Jesse Shera recently wrote in the *Wilson Library Bulletin*[3] that this is all so absurd that it has become a toothless lion. I am sorry to say I think it is still doing great damage, and I regret to state that I have rarely heard or seen anything by presidents or deans which would help in its refutation.

To me the Millett statements are schizophrenia academia at its worst. But within the past year I have heard a college president (not my own, thank heaven) say what boils down to this: "We want the library that can help us hold good faculty, enable distinguished scholarship, support independent and advanced student work and fully satisfy all the needs of the college. We also want a tight little budget, a permanent little building, a snug little collection and no nonsense about salaries and staff shortages out of those damned librarians."

I am typical of the librarians who simply chatter ineffectually with rage over this sort of thing, so let me quote one of many librarians whose reactions are reasoned and clear. Gordon R. Williams wrote in the *Proceedings* of the Western Conference Association for 1956:

> To the librarian, most of the criticism cited by President Millet seems unjustified because it is isolated from a consideration of the basic purpose of the library. To make this clearer, and perhaps to help correct this situation which is so serious for the library, let us look at some of the comments in detail.
> The first of these says the "Librarians constitutionally hate to throw anything away. They always fear that the book they discard will be the one someone wants next month," etc.
> It is not the fact that this is true that upsets the librarians, but the fact it is said in criticism;

we had been assuming all along that this was our job. How long would any librarian last on your campus who started discarding books that someone did want next month? Or, assuming that he had not already given the book to the Goodwill, how long would he last if he could not at once produce it, or at least tell you where it was? I think it is safe to assume that within a very short time indeed after either of these events the faculty would be marching to the president in a closely packed body, dragging a much disheveled librarian in their midst.

The point I am trying to make is that if it is indeed a crime to keep the library's books instead of discarding them, it is the faculty who are guilty, not librarians. To accuse the librarians of this, as a crime, is to say that the purpose of the library is not to provide the books and services which the faculty require in order to do their teaching and research.

On the economy matter:

Not only are we looking, and in the true academic tradition holding conferences on this subject, but we can actually point to practical accomplishments in this direction. But it is also true, as one of my colleagues puts it, that he did not believe he had been hired to save money for the university, nor to spend it either. It seems to us that our responsibility is to try and provide the library services which the university requires. We would be as false to our obligation and as guilty of a disservice to the university were we to hide the library's needs from the administration in order to point with pride to fewer dollars spent as we would be if we did not economize when this was clearly feasible.

If we accept the concept of the function of the library and the librarian as that of providing what the institution needs, then the faculty must share with us in the responsibility of making this clear to the administration, for in the last analysis it is the faculty who must in practice accomplish the educational goals; goals which they themselves have helped to shape, and in so doing have determined the role of the librarian. If they, who need the library's books and services, do not speak up directly in support of the library programs that they wish, this program is in danger of being modified so it can no longer serve adequately either them or their institution.

I have only a few words to add to this, but it is a constant bugaboo that the library itself is expected to be contained while the rest of the program grows more complex, more costly, and more rich. I can only do it in this form:

Dear Clementine Paddleford: I need your advice. Recently I made an angelfood cake from your recipe but it wasn't very good. What shall I do now?

P.S. Your recipe called for twelve eggs and I only had two.

If the growth of libraries is a bother, we have several options about them. If the main criticism is that college libraries have little business to develop research resources, there is one handy cure, among several, that I could recommend for your consideration: Cut some of this off at the source. Prohibit college faculties from doing research, from publishing research, and from feeling responsible for keeping up to date in their fields by reading research reports of their peers. When we separate the problem of backlog research resources from the current output of research reporting, the problem is at least halved. That half that comes from the current scholarly record shows up most sharply in the proliferation of journals and serials, most of them destined to see very little use in terms of quantity. Perhaps they are accorded a too prestigious position today anyway, what with the glamor of science. (This is, of course, THE route to achieving high status in scholarly scientific circles; the glamor of science is now established.) Why not just wait for a few years and let a single book synthesize and abbreviate all this independent source material? Isn't a secondary and simplified version enough for our undergraduate students, even if it is five years out of date and watered down by the biases or limitations of the synthesist? If the faculty man is determined to base his teaching on either his own explorations or on the work of the most advanced persons in his field, let him subside and go back to the textbook. This would have an added advantage to the money powers of any institution; salaries would be lower, and there would be very little competition for the services of these faculty members. If carried on long enough, there would not be any students to bother with and the endowment could be used as scholarship money to send students elsewhere, where there *are* library resources and good faculties.

How do you get a strong library? The best preliminary advice that I can give you is this: From a librarian's point of view, the best way to have a library capable of supporting at least some research is to select most carefully your predecessors. If the Oberlin experience counts for anything, the qualities to look for in these predecessors are:

1. Absolute, unshakable conviction that a "great" library is what is wanted.

2. A clear intention to build a great collegiate library without waiting for the college to catch up to it.

3. Scholarly, bookish interests and knowledgeability and great independence of mind. Azariah Root was at Oberlin for forty years and was in large measure responsible for the nature of its collection. (Root must have been a highly independent one-man selection committee, and I suspect that he was the first person to have said that a camel is a horse designed by a committee.)

4. A sharp eye for a bargain, a good gift, a lucky find and something of the dragnet approach.

5. To some extent, a blithe assumption that all else in what we have come to call "Library Administration" will somehow take care of itself. Concentrate on the collection.

6. Especially in the early days, enough intelligence, vigor, and incisiveness to cut a pretty broad swath in the institution's total affairs and hence have it taken for granted that you know what you are doing and should be left alone to do it.

7. Finally, with these qualities established, the status of the library has been confirmed and what little money there is in the institution tends to be paralleled out so that the library gets a healthy cut. But you have to persist.

Most of us in this room have libraries that really are extraordinarily rich in resources and in research materials. These resources and materials are not widely spread but they extend in some depth and with a considerable amount of system. I wish I could tell you easy and sure ways of systematic development and enrichment of them. All I can do is to point out some of the problems that I think are most urgent for us to solve.

For instance, in trying to ready myself for today I wanted to bring up to date my information regarding the sources of American scholars and other notables. Publication 582 of the National Research Council is titled:

Doctorate Production in U.S. Universities 1936-1956. It appeared as though it might be more up-to-date than anything I had had in hand before. I was interested in seeing where American scholars come from. The book is probably a very good book. I will never be sure and never will know where American scholars come from because we don't have the book. It wasn't worthy trying to rush as a purchase or a loan, and in fact there wasn't time. But it brought to me this: What ought to be our policy with regard to major and minor series of somewhat marginal importance and of a mixed content? Don't we increasingly need these as bed-rock in our collections, research or otherwise? How do we balance off this ever-increasing bite on the budget against our periodical commitment, the necessary purchase of monuments, the flurry of new fields and courses, the problem of new teachers, the problem of the great abstracting services and bibliographies, the great tools? How do we know when we have reached a reasonable saturation in any given and precise field, no matter how small?

One of our advanced students did a paper last year on Baudelaire. Our catalog showed almost a hundred titles about him and about his works, to say nothing of our holdings of his works, many of which contain important and critical and biographic commentary. Yet for this one honors student we had to borrow ten or twelve books and several journals from friendly libraries. It would look to me as if we had had enough material there in a very precise area. But how do we know? How can we gauge this? It does not seem as if we can ever win.

We do not have at Oberlin Gmelin, the major resource, probably, in inorganic chemistry. As a matter of fact, our program in inorganic has not been tremendously extensive, nothing to compare with what we do in other areas of chemistry. But somewhere I discovered via the grapevine route that National Science Foundation funds had been received by the college to implement the teaching of inorganic chemistry. A member of the library committee, a very fine person who is a close friend and a good library committee member, sat on the committee for the appeal to the National Science Foundation and helped to devise that budget. He told me: "I simply never thought of the library implication."

Because of an intelligent provost, a Way Will Be Found to deflect some of this money into the purchase of Gmelin. But how do we catch up with this sort of thing? Even smaller colleges now are receiving grants and engaging in programs that commit them to the development of scholarly resources. All too frequently this is not thought of at the time the plan is drawn up, the appeal made, or extra funds sought. It seems almost fundamental dishonesty to undertake programs of this sort or to fill our catalogs with purple prose about the content of courses or programs unless we have what it takes to back them up.

What do we do about the chopping and changing of a curriculum that is somewhat related to the coming and going of faculty members?

Take the case of our Mr. C. He replaced a professor of some thirty years whose specialty had been intellectual history, especially of Europe. The new man had a specialty of French medevial history. By the time he got to the campus he had been promised the moon by someone upstairs. We had, he told us after two days on the place, nothing in his field. We were particularly void in the areas of his own research. (This one already had his doctorate, so we couldn't suggest that the institution from which that degree would come might reasonably help him out a little bit and help us.) Not only did we have nothing for his own research (it was perfectly respectable research), but we had nothing for his reserves and for general book needs of his students. We did not have many of the major works in his specialty, that is true— and they were good works, so we set about getting them at the cost of some squeeze to other history and general interests. After a month or two, he rather shamefacedly told us he had discovered that we may have lacked some of the basics, but he was pleased to find that we had much of the marginal and the exotic that he did not expect us to have. His reserve duplicates, which were many, have been used very heavily.

Before he came, he had a grant from the college for the purchase of microfilm. I did not tumble to this until fairly late. I am not sure whose the microfilm is. Some of it,

incidentally, was of material we do have, which was a bit of a shocker. Now in February we are catching our breath, and we feel that although the cost was high we have acquired much good material in this specialty; and it is not an unreasonable specialty for us to have. We have acquired a great deal of lower level material that probably will continue to be worth the investment for as long as the courses continue, and quite a stock of rather personally related material not likely to be used by faculty members with other specializations.

And what is the news? Mr. C is leaving us in June. His successor will probably have his own private little stake-out in the scholarly world, so we will begin again to develop a little peak of excellence, limited in scope and time, costly to get and hard to get quickly. The enrichment of the collection, even though this will do us no harm, is pretty expensive in these terms. The erratic quality of the collection is situations like this (of which there are always many for any lively college), makes it hard for me to describe to those ever-loving library school students ever-writing: "What is your acquisitions policy? Please answer in three easy paragraphs."

It has often been suggested, especially by the universities, where the problem must be multiplied by the hundreds, that we should ship the special collection that surrounds a movable man along with him to the next institution.

What can we do, living in a real world, about money? The constant problem is to be sure we are using our money properly.

Madame X, one of our professors of Russian, came to see me not long after the rather sudden creation of a major in this field. She asked if we couldn't put in a special plea for about $1500 to break the back of our most urgent needs in Russian. One candidate, she said, had already turned us down because of the poverty of library holdings. I agreed that we needed extra money for this and for a few other new developments, and we did ask for additional funds. No money has yet been turned up for this purpose.

I must admit that I found it hard to be cordial and enthusiastic in congratulating Madame X on an an award, then just announced, of a $1500 travel grant permitting her to go to Russia and be scholarly there. I do not see any way in which Oberlin could have deflected this travel money to the development of a collection which would have permitted her to be scholarly at home, but I must say that I wonder, when it all comes out of one pocket, how the choice is made. Perhaps one pocket knoweth not what another pocket doeth.

There is another area in which I wonder about money. I searched some old and new college catalogs and found half a dozen in which figures were given for about ten years ago and for today on tuition, board and room, and the probable outlay the student would have to make for personally-owned books. The suggested figure for books was static in three cases, had risen about 10 percent in the fourth, about 15 percent in the fifth, and was actually lower for today than yesterday in the sixth. Other costs, of course, has risen astronomically.

All of us are concerned that students shall not depend solely on textbooks, and all of us want students to start building personal libraries. We expect them to meet the cost of purchasing some materials. The rise of the paperback book should relieve libraries and help students, and it does more of this than is apparent. There are, however, many book problems the paperback does not solve and some fields in which the paperback is not yet serving well. For instance, a few years ago when our library was pressed to buy a host of fairly costly duplicates in philosophy, I was told by a teacher of that subject that paperbacks didn't help at all, as all that got into paperback versions were the dead philosophies. I hadn't realized that philosophy, of all things, had a short life.

The cost of some kinds of books is higher today than ever before, and the cost of other kinds if relatively lower than it has been in the memory of most of us. There is no formula that I can suggest which tells a student how much to expect to spend for personal books. The fact that he must spend $13 for a chemistry text instead of the $6 of ten years ago is a blow, but it does not mean that he should not buy some basic materials of lasting worth as constant support to history and literature courses. He needs to own books in many fields, and he can own them at a modest cost

if guided by faculty members and librarians in his selection. The library is not inevitably the only source of heavily used materials. There are times when I wonder if libraries are not trying to be too much of everything to every student and, perhaps, to every faculty member.

This inevitably brings me around to the reserve book situation, and here I differ somewhat from McKeon. Ten years ago, he thought librarians were not generous enough in supplying multiple copies. Today I am convinced that we supply too many multiple copies, or, more precisely, that we and the faculty should be far more discriminating than we are in this matter.

At Oberlin, I asked for some information on reserve book use this past fall. Out of about six thousand volumes on closed reserve, one-fifth had an astonishing record of non-use between the opening of college and the start of the Christmas vacation. Some five hundred books had not been used *at all* and the other seven hundred had an average of two and one-half uses in twelve weeks. None was used more than twelve times, or the equivalent of once a week.

Now these are allegedly our most heavily used books. I wish they could have been left in their regular places on the shelves, where they might have fed into the kind of library use that appeals so strongly to librarians. Had they not been tied up with reserve's red tape, they might have been leafed through, borrowed, or even read.

I do not quibble about the cost of single copies, whether on reserve or not; I am cavilling at what seems to me great waste in the purchase of unnecessary extra copies. We estimate that the unused extra copies spotted in our modest study cost approximately $2400. I wish we might have used that money for the purchase of valuable and enduring titles which we lack.

Perhaps I am too much concerned with coverage, but I think not. The more we turn away from the text and the lecture and the more we teach by methods approximating those characteristic of research, the greater will be our need for depth and diversity in our college library collections. There simply is no money, and there is not liekly to be money, to squander. Every dollar counts. I find it hard to keep facts which suggest extravagance swept under the rug while I'm busily showing the holes in said rug to our administrators in the hope that they can find us money for vital patching.

What does it take to increase and develop the research holdings, the scholarly materials, and the intermediate books of lasting value in our libraries? We have some assets in this struggle, and some liabilities. Our librarians and faculty members work well together. We have our feuds, we have our difficulties. Doubtless we have fools and prima donnas on both sides. But on the whole the college community cooperates effectively when the common aim is clear to all. We never have enough money, and we never have too many book and dollar angels. We have, however, an intellectual geography in which the library is, or can be, truly central. By and large, our communities are compact enough that instructor, librarian, student, and book can be effectively related to each other as individuals rather than as one mass to another mass. Though our collections may be limited in size and in richness, we can know them well enough to see that they are used to the limit. New library buildings, designed to promote the learning and research needs of modern colleges, are the order of the day.

But the crucial problem for a great many college libraries is personnel. I react like a Pavlov dog to the T-V jingle, "Support the college of your choice." This electrifying iambic tetrameter is followed by the information that every college needs a good faculty and good laboratories. Now and then, for a slightly more expensive plug, mention is made of the need for good libraries. I have never heard, however, that colleges need good librarians, or any librarians, for that matter.

No matter how small a faculty body, it contains specialists. A small library staff normally cannot contain matching specialists, hence we need librarians of high quality. They are scarce. We need versatility, intellectual curiosity, strong backgrounds, resourcefulness and scholarly bent. To keep the show on the road for ninety hours a week, we need some management skills, health, and a genuine desire to be of service to all comers. A love of books is a fine start, but it isn't the only essential for a career in college librarianship.

One of my favorite faculty members at Oberlin came in one day, carefully closed the door of my office, and said: "I must talk to you about a student. He is a very good student. He does unusually good work. He is not good enough to make a college teacher, but he will make a wonderful librarian." It is not too early for faculty members to start helping us rather than hindering us in the matter of recruitment. The student of today will shortly be out in the employable world, and if the student isn't good enough to be a teacher but can be trained into being a good librarian, I will have to settle for that at this point, although I would hope that we might get the student who is going to be an excellent librarian but who could be a good teacher.

We are very short of all kinds of librarians, particularly of librarians for academic purposes. All of our libraries are trying to make do with staffs too small, with staffs that are too burdened, and, in many cases, with staffs that are not appropriate. In the matter of the book collection, we need more time from more skilled staff to work with faculties and other librarians on the development of our collections. The lack of time for planning is inevitably a costly factor. Because of it we will make injudicious purchases and we will make unsystematic approaches to the examination, evaluation, and enrichment of our holdings.

This summer at Oberlin we face the prospect of having a number of new projects in a college which normally gathers moss and not much else from Commencement to Convocation. We will have one hundred high school brighties as special students. This is wonderful. It is a fine program. I wish I had heard about it earlier; I read about it in the paper. They will undertake independent work in six fields: biology, English, French, history, mathematics, and religion. These students will be taught, in part, by Master of Arts in Teaching candidates, whom we also have in the summer. The MAT students—a brand new brood each summer—are college graduates who have seen the light and wish to become secondary school teachers. They themselves know relatively little about libraries. They come from all sorts of backgrounds. We in the library have worked on a program to help them know more about books and libraries for secondary school use, and from that experience we are aware of how little beginning MAT students really know about materials for their own use, to say nothing of materials for the use of high school students. It is distressing to us to face the consequences of their instructing a hundred high school students in the use of the Oberlin College Library.

For the first time in our history, we will have a summer Honors College in Oberlin, made up of twenty to forty of our own students. The work will be highly individualized. We have, of course, no clues as to the areas students will select for exploration in depth. It's an exciting prospect but in this case, as in the case of the high school students, I am afraid we may not have on hand enough staff or the right sort of staff to serve our public.

It has been our practice to put aside during the academic year all of those things which could possibly wait till July and August. These are large internal projects that must be done but are best done when we have uninterrupted blocks of time for them. Staff vacations are already jelled; we always have to arrange them early in order to be sure we have the right teams on hand to carry through on the summer projects. Some departmental libraries are closed, and any staff time thus salvaged is put into special summer work. With more educational programs developing for the summer, and with all of them highly desirable as services Oberlin College can render to society, we must, of course, find some way of staffing the library as best we can. There is an economy, too, in operating a good college plant around the year. But this sudden bulge into a considerable academic program for the summer, combined with increasing efforts to turn our regular students loose to do independent work (largely through library use) is putting new pressures on us. While we may be able to conserve faculty time by increasing independent work in the academic year, and while these summer programs offer additional compensation for those of our faculty members who wish to participate in them, we have not made clear that there are additional costs in the library. A large part of that cost will be for personnel.

If Bowdoin can bear with it for a moment, I would like to speak about its situation.

There is nothing like an old statistic to give comfort in current times, if it works the right way around. In 1960-61, according to the figures reported by the Office of Education Bowdoin's library budget was divided roughly as follows: 44 percent went into personnel and about 48 percent went into material and binding. This seems to me just fantastic. The actual amount spent for material was not out of proportion at all to the institution's needs for books and periodicals, and was fairly typical of the amount that was spent by roughly comparable colleges; but the amount spent for personnel was astonishingly low. How that amount of material could be acquired and incorporated into the collection with a staff that cost so little, I do not know. I would like to know if it was a trick, but I suspect it was simply the hard task of finding people, or perhaps not enough awareness of the need for them. Such lack of awareness is not peculiar to Bowdoin; it can occur anywhere. But the amount spent for personnel at Bowdoin was so low in relation to the amount for books and binding that I wonder if the library does not have a problem of backlog, especially with a program on to bring its house into better order. I do congratulate the College; I hope there is no secret about Bowdoin's success in gaining administrative support for its venture to overhaul its whole cataloging operation.

We know that we can greatly enrich college and university library collections via microforms of all sorts and that many things we used to think were completely out of our reach are going to be available. Tonight we may hear from Verner Clapp about the possible containment of the world's literature in a saltshaker, and we have already heard of the great potentialities of Verac from Fred Wagman. "Utopia is just around the corner" should be my message of cheer. In the meantime, I think we should not be timid in our efforts to add more and more of the necessary research and resource materials to our libraries. It is slow work and it is difficult work, but it is important. Let us not give up, as the man did who read so much about the harmful effects of smoking that he decided to give up reading.

FOOTNOTES

[1] *The Library Quarterly,* XXIV (1954), 322-335.
[2] John David Millett, *Financing Higher Education in the United States* (New York: Columbia University Press, 1952), p. 123.
[3] Jesse H. Shera, "Libraries Are for Growing," *Wilson Library Bulletin,* XXXVII (1963), 498-99.

ABOUT THE AUTHOR

—**Eileen Thornton**, Librarian, Oberlin College; M.A., 1945, University of Chicago. Currently Miss Thornton is doing research on the college and university novel. Her major research interests lie in higher education and in academic libraries.

The Research Library in Transition

by Herman H. Fussler

As a primary participant in the process of communicating information, the academic library tends to respond to the changes in scholarly methodology and interests. For the research library of today and tomorrow this involves significant expenditures in acquiring and making available increasingly greater quantities of materials. It also involves considerable risks if it is to support areas of research not as yet defined–nor, perhaps, defineable. This essay offers to the academic librarian the possibility that intelligent decisions on alternatives to incremental growth exist through studying the use by and needs of scholars for library materials. The author explores significant changes occurring in information handling which reflect the attempt to respond to the problems of volume, bibliographic control, and storage.

This paper is directed toward some of the problems relating to the communication of knowledge and information at the graduate and research level in the American university. It is a generally accepted axiom that university libraries have the obligation of selecting, acquiring, organizing, preserving, and making available the full record of man's achievements in all of their important and many of their minor aspects. It is clear that the survival and advancement of our civilization are critically dependent upon our ability to communicate with one another successfully and to understand quickly and fully what our fellow men are doing and thinking as well as what they have accomplished and thought in the past. These tasks are reflected in the modern world-wide production and use of print in an increasing diversity of forms. Furthermore, rising literacy, the spread of technology and commerce, growing nationalism among heretofore colonial peoples, and many other factors have changed and are continuing to change the magnitude and uses of print in ways that have already created formidable problems for both research libraries and those who use them.

There are other forces, some new, some traditional, that seem to be pointing toward an increase in these problems and the strong probability of changes in the research library in response. Among these forces one of the most conspicious is the extent to which research has become a dominant force in shaping the character and functions of the modern university. Until late in the nineteenth century and the beginning of the twentieth, the function of the university was primarily to preserve, interpret, and transmit what was thought to be a fairly stable cultural heritage. Anyone at all familiar with the modern American university will be aware of the extent to which these traditional functions, while probably not neglected, have had to make room for a new one–the advancement of the frontiers of knowledge and our understanding of the universe in which we live.

The concept of an ever-advancing frontier of new knowledge is most conspicious, of course, in the physical and biological sciences, but it is also strong in the social sciences, many professional disciplines, and is not foreign to the humanities. While the frontier may not always be advancing, scholars, almost universally, behave as though it were.

This preoccupation with research and the resulting continuous change in the state of knowledge in many subject fields are important aspects of even more general and basic intellectual changes. The late Pierce Butler, in a thoughful essay a number of years ago, laid the general philosophical groundwork for part of the situation that

SOURCE: Reprinted from Herman H. Fussler, "The Research Library in Transition," in *The Library in the University; The University of Tennessee Lectures, 1949-1966* (Hamden, Conn.: Shoe String Press, 1967), pp. 121-148, by permission of the publisher. Originally published as University of Tennessee Library Lecture, No. 8, April 17, 1956.

the modern research library faces in these words:

> It would seem self-evident that modern thought is essentially different from the various intellectual habits which were current in other periods. Not merely has the content of our knowledge changed; its very texture is something new; where the medieval mind appealed to authority and the renaissance mind to a sense of values; the modern mind demands an objective realism. Older types persist; there are still men whose thought is essentially medieval or humanistic. Perhaps no mind is wholly free in every phase of its activity from survivals of incongruous mental habit, yet modern man, in so far as he is modern minded, does think in modes that are new to the intellectual history of humanity.[1]

It seems reasonably clear that print—in the broadest meaning of that term—is serving as one of the major instruments by means of which scholars try to attain "objective realism." But we also, consciously and unconsciously, have an attitude toward the book that seems in part to be a survival of the medieval appeal to authority as well. Furthermore, no matter how common or inconsequential, redundant, trivial, or ephemeral were the purposes for which a book was prepared, both librarians and scholars tend to treat it as unique and of at least potential permanent significance. This attitude surely reflects to some extent what we now regard as careless errors of the past, and our own experience that much of the day-to-day "trivia" of the past has often become some of the most important—and scarcest—historical source material of today.

In addition to the technological, economic, and social and cultural changes that are spreading with great rapidity throughout most of the world and resulting in increasing use and production of print, we must note that Western scholarship has traditionally tended to ignore much of the literature and culture of the Orient and other civilizations where major language barriers have seemed to intervene. It is abundantly clear that this pattern of scholarship is also changing, and the growing production of print from many other parts of the world must, in consequence, become increasingly accessible in the United States.

These kinds of changes are closely related to another basic characteristic of modern research. As Dan Lacy has recently put it:

> The higher learning is no longer disengaged, as during most of its history, from the daily life of the people. On the contrary, agriculture, industry, communications, government, and every other activity utilize and are indeed shaped by the university-fostered sciences and professions, so that every step in the progress of learning has its impact on everyday affairs.[2]

This intimate relationship between the concerns of the university and many aspects of daily life, has made it imperative for the university to have access to a vast quantity of information and data, that, not long ago, would have been regarded as largely irrelevant to the proper concerns of the university. All of these various changes, along with others that have not been mentioned, have greatly increased the diversity and scope of university studies, the complexity of the corpus of knowledge, the number of people engaged in serious investigation, and have resulted in a huge increase in the bulk of the universe of recorded knowledge and very large increases in the size of research libraries.

While it has been a basic characteristic of the university library to accumulate books and retain most of them permanently, the growth of the research library—in the sense of demanding very substantial quantities of space and very large funds both for capital expenditures and current operations—is a modern phenomenon, really one of the twentieth century. Harvard had about 560,000 books and pamphlets in 1900, two and a half million in 1925, and has about six million today. While Harvard's collection is well in excess of that of any other American university, the *rate* of growth for a large number of other institutions appears to be closely comparable. If these growth rates continue at the past levels, it will be only a matter of time—and perhaps not as long as some of you may think—until The University of Tennessee may have to find space for six million books too.

This matter of research library growth is not yet well understood; in consequence there is no shortage of strong opinions concerning it. Growth, per se, is not in itself alarming; it becomes alarming only as it may create intellectual difficulties in relation to use, and space or financial demands that are beyond the reasonable capacities of the library's parent institution. The evidence is not clear by which one may, with any confidence at least, determine whether there are genuinely serious, long-range intellectual and financial problems at the moment or not. Characteristically, for example, university costs for space are hidden and unrecognized in functional or operational budgets. While it seems to be a fundamental characteristic in the research library for the unit costs of acquisition, cataloging, circulation, etc., to increase as the size of the collection increases, there is no evidence that the economies resulting from improved efficiency and other offsetting technical changes have not, in the better-managed libraries at least, kept ahead of the so-called inevitable cost increases. Although librarians have recently been accused of putting little emphasis on economy,[3] the librarians are convinced that this criticism would not be supported by an impartial examination of the facts.[4] Certainly the evidence seems reasonably clear that, while all the costs of university libraries have increased sharply along with almost all other costs, the actual percentage of university expenditures allocated to library purposes has shown no general increase. To the contrary, there is evidence that at least some research libraries have received in recent years a gradually declining percentage of the university dollar.

However, it is argued by some that if university libraries are not difficult to house now, they show a good many indications of becoming difficult—not sometime in the distant future, but quite soon. This is because an ever-larger number of university libraries are becoming intrinsically large in the amount of university space occupied—there are now nineteen universities with more than one million volumes. American university libraries in the past seem to have grown exponentially rather than arithmetically. That is to say, there is a good deal of evidence that the annual additions to any university library—within limits—tend to be proportional to the size of its holdings rather than to some external constant. A careful study of growth in the largest university libraries reveals that this percentage has been declining for the past twenty-five years. One might in consequence conclude that, after a library reaches a certain size, it will begin to "mature" and will no longer grow as rapidly as it does

in its adolescence. The average rate for the annual increase in size of seven large endowed university libraries has declined from about 4.3 percent in 1930 to about 2.6 percent in 1955. Even so, during this period they grew from an average size of 1,270,000 volumes to 2,600,000 volumes. Four large state-supported libraries, that now average 2,260,000 volumes, showed a decline in annual growth rate from about 6 percent in 1930 to about 3½ percent in 1955.

There is nothing too alarming about any of this until even these reduced figures are extrapolated into the future. The projection of almost any ascending exponential curve, if carried far enough, is likely to produce totals that can scare the daylights out of most prudent people. Assuming that the 6 percent annual rate of growth that the University of Tennessee enjoyed in 1954/55 continues—and it is a very reasonable rate of growth—it is easy to calculate that Tennessee will have more than three-quarters of a million books by 1967, one and a half million by 1979, and about six and one-quarter million by the year 2000. The current evidence, of course, suggests the possibility that by the time Tennessee's library reaches a total of somewhere between one and two million books, the annual *rate* of increase may have dropped by about one half; thus instead of doubling every twelve years, it will be doubling about once every twenty-five years. By extending prior growth rates, without such diminution, Fremont Rider showed several years ago that Yale sould have about 200,000,000 volumes in 2040, occupying 6,000 miles of shelving, with a card catalog of three-quarters of a million trays, and new books coming in at the rate of 12,000,000 volumes a year.[5] Rider's calculations showed an average annual growth rate for a group of university libraries of about 4¼ percent between 1831 and 1938, producing a doubling of the library every sixteen years. Using his same institutions, but measuring the growth from 1938 to 1955, reveals an average annual rate during this period of 3.3 percent, which would produce a doubling about every twenty-one years. The time between 1938 and 1955 is short, of course, and acquisition patterns during it were certainly influenced by six years of war, but it does suggest at least the possibility of some decline in the velocity of growth.

If these projections of statistical trends do not give you pause, let me quote some figures from a recent report of the Librarian of Congress. In the fiscal year 1955 the Library received some 5,340,000 pieces, including unbound newspaper issues, as compared with 4,588,000 in 1954. By the exercise of "careful selectivity," the Library whittled this 5 1/3 million down to a mere 1,206,000 items for addition to the collections, with the 1.2 million including a mere 357,700 volumes and pamphlets. This one year intake for the Library of Congress almost equals the total size of the University of Tennessee's Library, and brought total holdings to 10½ million volumes and pamphlets, and a total of 34,359,174 pieces altogether, including manuscripts, microprint cards, music, etc.

There tend to be at least three typical answers to projections of growth of this kind. One answer usually takes one form or another of the following: "Obviously these rates will slow down—there won't be that many books to collect; or some better solution is bound to turn up—microfilm, Rapid Selectors, or some other mitigating (but unspecified) steps will take care of it." A more common answer takes one form or another of the vernacular: "So what? Books are the lifeblood of scholarship; you can't have too many of them, and until there is evidence that the university library is growing far more rapidly than knowledge and its parent institution, why worry?" A third position deplores the quality of much current scholarly and other writing, points to tons of seemingly useless books—usually in someone else's subject—in the typical library, and concludes that rigorous selection and heroic weeding are really all that is necessary. As a final note in this context we should recognize that universities as well as libraries grow and change.

While I see no need to be panic-stricken by this matter of growth, I am convinced it deserves serious attention. And growth is not just the problem of the few very large university libraries; it concerns us all, for there is no university that does not aspire to do good research, graduate and undergraduate instruction, and these activities require books—lots of books. There seem to be four principal reasons for concern: 1) While current library growth rates may

prove manageable with traditional approaches, the velocity of growth strongly suggests that the traditional techniques of selection, organization of materials, and service may prove inadequate. 2) There is some reason to believe that, despite the growth of research libraries, our library resources are often found wanting and too inflexible to accommodate rapidly changing, widely searching research and teaching programs. 3) Many university presidents seem to be disturbed by the apparently insatiable demands of the research library, and the presidents' understanding and support are clearly essential to the proper management of the library. 4) Finally, there appears to be some reason to believe, in view of the broad intellectual and social changes that are occurring, that the nature, quantity, and uses of print will follow patterns that may demand fundamentally new attitudes and solutions from the research library. These four aspects of library growth may not convince you that the research library is already in transition to some new form, but perhaps they will suggest the possibility that it might be or that it ought to be.

However, the services and resources of the research library are not simply the consequences of the number and shape of books published each year. The dominant characteristics of the university library are largely the result of scholarly customs and needs as they relate to recorded information. The library must adapt itself to the needs of both print and scholarship as well as it can. Thus in order to assess the current operations of libraries and the prospects of change, it is important that everyone concerned recognize, perhaps more clearly than we may have in the past, the nature of some of these other external forces and their effects upon the library, for the academic library is anything but a free agent when it comes to changing the character of its resources or its methods of making its resources accessible. Furthermore, growth is not just a library administrative and financial problem—this may indeed be its least important aspect. It is evident that growth may already have reached levels where the fundamental communication of scholarly information in some fields is being impeded by the sheer mass of the data. This impediment may take several forms: the library may have the material, but the traditional methods of organization may not make the data sufficiently accessible to the scholar who needs it; the mass of data may be so great so as to be beyond the financial capacity of the library to acquire it in the first place and house it in the second; or, perhaps most significantly, the library may possess, and be able to produce on demand, more *relevant* data than the scholar can digest and use. Yet an investigator who is not fully in touch with the relevant data and the progress of others on a common problem, simply cannot be as thorough or as scholarly as he ought to be. Alternatively, if he faces am "impossible" mass of data, he may—consciously or unconsciously—turn from an important topic of investigation to one that is more "manageable" but possibly of far less significance. Faculty members, when they go on public record about the library, very often seem to say, "What we really need are bigger and better libraries." According to Millett[6] the presidents appear to be saying, "The library is too big and expensive already, let's see that the librarians handle this thing more efficiently." The issue is clearly more complex and more important than either of these two over-simplified opinions would suggest.

The library exists only to supply the resources and services that are necessary for the fulfillment of a university's major functions. This sounds easy enough except that many of the major concerns of a university are elusive and uncertain matters—thus making a vast quantity of recorded information subject to at least potential, if not probable, demand. Nor is the pursuit of knowledge unfailingly orderly, systematic, and without its own peculiar wastes and diversions. Universities, while generally recognizing this situation, have been willing thus far to circumscribe the scope of their formal teaching and research programs only in very general terms. Furthermore, university research and teaching interests shift with the findings of new research, with changes in the composition of the faculty, and with changes in the interests of individual faculty members. Out of this freedom comes much of the strength of American universities. But the impact upon large research collections often seems less attractive; new research undertakings seldom

are planned with consideration for the added library resources that they will entail, and substantial strength built up over a long period may stand idle and neglected when a departing specialist is not replaced, or even more likely, replaced by a man whose interests are in a field where the resources are, in his judgment, meager and insufficient.

This enormous diversity and unpredictable character of university research have forced libraries into something of a dual function: first, the library builds and maintains a "working" library, oriented around the reasonably clear needs of students and faculty members and the materials most likely to be used in support of current research and teaching; and secondly, the library acquires, keeps, and services a collection of "permanent record" in which many future needs are anticipated as far as good judgment and available resources permit, and in which the relatively inactive acquisitions of the past are retained for possible future uses. These future uses, it is recognized, are often entirely different from the original purposes of the publications. Clearly, the more complete or larger the library's holdings, the more likely it will be able to meet the occasional esoteric and unanticipated demand. The distinction I am trying to make here between what I loosely call a "working research library" and a "library of permanent record" requires many important qualifications, for in many fields of research it is not a very obvious distinction. In some disciplines or types of literature the distinction probably does not exist at all, while in other fields it would be subject to sharp dispute by scholars working in the same subjects; but, finally, in many fields the distinction almost certainly does exist, and there would be general agreement about the books in the working library and those falling essentially in the "permanent record" category.

This distinction between research books for which there is a probable demand as distinguished from those with a possible demand, is, I think, extremely important, for it is likely to be a major factor in future research library development. I hasten to point out that while the distinction has a close relationship to the amount of use it is not synonymous with a quantitative measure of use. A good research library is not likely to emerge from a census of the most-used books, for little-used books are a prime necessity in much research—

conspicuously so in the humanities, nearly as much so in the social sciences, and to a considerably lesser degree in many of the natural sciences, where the concentration of most current research literature in journal form produces quite distinctive patterns of use. Thus not only must little-used books be available, but the number and quality of such books may be a real index of research potential. Despite this general need in research for seldom-used materials we are beginning to have some evidence that suggests that there may be, in many fields, real and predictable differences among the little-used books. These differences, if they do indeed exist, have yet to be incorporated into the practices and philosophy of research libraries.

In summary, it would appear that the growth of research libraries can be largely attributed to the following elements: 1) There has been a vast increase in the amount of print. 2) There is a real growth of knowledge and a need for more information about the world. 3) Up to the present, both individual scholars and university administrators have been willing to set few or no boundaries on access to recorded knowledge—indeed it can and has been argued that any scrap of paper may at some point in time be used or needed for serious purposes. 4) Traditionally the best means of gaining practical access to recorded knowledge has been to see that the local research library acquired as many books as its funds and space would permit. 5) No book ever seems to become entirely obsolete. Books that were once useful may fall into desuetude, but they are by this fact not dead. The most obvious case, of course, is where the state of knowledge has changed and made the book substantively obsolete—and even misleading—to the man working at the research frontier as well as to the student or anyone else who is trying to ascertain the current state of knowledge. But such a book may be regarded as indispensable by the historian of a discipline, of educational methods, or of something else. There are many such variations in use, and they cannot easily be dismissed or ignored. It is this pattern, of course, that has tended to force the research library to retain everything it has once acquired.

These are also the factors that have led large research libraries to treat all books alike in their bibliographical organization and to keep them equally accessible, though the logic for such action seems open to much greater doubt than does simple acquisition and retention. In the well-managed university library, equally accessible has meant that any book not actually charged out to another borrower should be delivered to a reader within a few minutes even though it has quietly been gathering dust quite undisturbed for thirty years. All books have been cataloged in approximately identical fashion. And even more characteristically the American scholar has expected to be able to walk into the stacks and find any book, no matter how infrequently used, beside all other books on the same subject. Librarians seem to have concluded that if these kinds of access were desirable for some books, then they were equally desirable for all books. All are costly services, and convincing evidence of their efficacy in relation to their cost is yet to be fully established.

It is clear that we are dealing here with various aspects of three major concerns:

1) What are the characteristics of "print" itself? In answering this question we must also answer others: How much print is being produced? Where? For what purposes? What is the present distribution pattern of print? How long will it last without showing serious physical deterioration? How repetitious is it? What forms does it take, etc.?

2) What are the actual needs of current and future investigators? The subordinate questions here must include: Of the total production of print, current as well as retrospective, how much is relevant to the predictable needs of society in such a way as to require a deliberate effort to collect, organize, and preserve it within libraries? How do investigators get at their materials? How do they use them once they have them? How quickly do they need them? For how long? How often? In what form can various kinds of materials be used? How well are users able to locate and secure access to what is now available, etc.?

3) The third concern would revolve around an evaluation of current library services and techniques in relation to these two major areas and a consideration of all alternative schemes that might produce better results or equally good results with greater efficiency.

What have been the approaches thus far to these problems? They are really very few. We have already made reference to those who say that publishing should be curtailed. Clearly, these are whispers tossed into winds of hurricane force and will be of no effect. Secondly, there are arguments that research libraries should collect much more carefully and selectively. The proponents of this view should, and some do, adhere to the position that libraries should quite ruthlessly toss out the trivial and inconsequential, the secondary, the once-useful-but-now-neglected items. After all it is evident that the production and use of print in the twentieth century is based upon a completely different intellectual, technological, and economic structure from that prevailing during medieval and renaissance periods when many of our current attitudes toward books were shaped. I, myself, think there is some merit in this position, but I think it runs counter to many current scholarly trends, and general agreement on what is trivial seems never to occur. More selective acquisition and retention are most applicable where the state of knowledge for a subject has changed or is changing rapidly, e.g., physics, or where there is an immense secondary literature, or where there is a large literature really intended for the general public and of a somewhat transitional character, e.g., "How to make money in the stock market." It is hardly applicable at all to creative literature, where an author's work is, of course, never superseded except as new editions may follow older ones year after year and libraries must try to decide whether they need all editions, the first, the last, or what appears to be the most definitive. The only effective way under these conditions to acquire more selectively is to limit the library's collecting to particular authors, periods, or languages. The difficulties are obvious.

There have also been suggestions that libraries should store their books more compactly or place them in microfilm or microcard form, but no library seems to have found ways of using these devices as yet that offer evidence of substantial permanent space relief or other economies.

The fourth and by far the most commonly suggested remedy is inter-library cooperation. The argument for cooperation is simple. It is agreed that the total task facing the research library is immense and well beyond the capacity of any library acting alone, but by sharing the burden in some way, it is argued, that we can accomplish together what we cannot alone. We should note that the current widespread conviction that the individual library is unlikely to be able to meet with its own collections *all* the literature needs and aspirations of its faculty and graduate student body is a very fundamental change it itself from the attitude that seems certainly to have been prevalent as recently as twenty-five to thirty years ago.

Cooperation can be helpful only as it 1) extends the range of material usefully available beyond limits that would otherwise obtain, or 2) maintains approximately the same levels of access that would otherwise obtain, at less over-all cost in space or money to the participating institutions. The form of cooperation must be such as not to impair scholarship except as there are offsetting gains to scholarship or economies that justify the impairment in the eyes of those competent to weigh the alternatives.

While there are many important cooperative ventures among libraries, there are only two nationally discussed cooperative plans that I will comment upon here to illustrate a point to be made shortly.

The first of these is the Midwest Inter-Library Center, which, along with other functions, receives little-used materials from its sixteen member libraries, eliminates the duplicates, and makes the materials received from each library available to all other members by means of loans. It can thus have the effect of transferring at least a part of library growth from a large number of member libraries and concentrating it in one where less space will be required because of the elimination of duplicates.

Such an enterprise assumes that a scholar will be able to identify as useful certain kinds of material by means of reference citations, bibliographies, card catalogs, or other devices, and that a delay in access of overnight to forty-eight hours will not be harmful. The plan gives the librarian an opportunity to make local space available for more important or more frequently used material without irrevocably discarding or surrendering future rights of access to an item for which the probable demand is slight. Since the Center distributes catalog cards or other descriptions of all its holdings to its members, participating libraries should be able to discard directly titles that are no longer needed locally if a copy has already gone to the Center; and, even more significantly, a member may, if it wishes, decline to acquire a title that it finds already available from the Center.

The Center has gone one step further by setting up its own acquisition program. While the acquisition program has moved slowly and is still being viewed with fear and apprehension by some member university presidents and librarians, it seems altogether likely that joint acquisitions will continue to expand slowly because of the important savings they can create for all member libraries. The Center is, for example, acquiring the current documents of the forty-eight states (and has consolidated the retrospective state documents holdings of many member libraries to the enrichment of the region), thus relieving the member institutions of acquiring all but the most needed state documents. The savings in space acquisition and and cataloging effort, binding, etc., can obviously be very substantial. The Center has several other acquisition programs that are quite similar.

In summary, there can be little doubt that the Center has saved space and money for most of its members. It has extended the joint resources of the region. How much further it can go in expanding its program is difficult to determine. We do not yet know too much about the effects on scholars of the brief delay in access, nor do we know well users are able to identify relevant resources—largely unknown in the usual library also. The major difficulties thus far have grown, not out of these problems nor those of a technical or procedural nature, as one might have expected, but instead out of the different concepts of the member institutions as to the services and resources that must be provided locally and those that can successfully be provided through the Center by joint action. For several years there has been a substantial interest in the Northeast in creating a regional library, but these different views as to its scope, services, location, method of support, etc., have not yet been resolved. Other regions of the country have watched the Midwest Inter-Library Center with interest, and more such

libraries may come into being.

The other cooperative venture is theFarmington Plan, in which a large number of libraries tried to insure a more thorough coverage of current foreign monographic publications by agreeing to accept on a blanket basis all publications from a certain country or all publications in a certain subject from a series of countries. The Plan has undoubtedly achieved its goal of more inclusive coverage. We doubt, however, that it has had any very material effect upon the growth and coverage problems of individual research libraries. The reasons seem to be that access to Farmington Plan publications seems too uncertain and difficult, scattered as the books are through many different libraries, and with, at the moment, only very limited bibliographical information about them readily available in the average research library. Under such circumstances, there is likely to be a disposition to go ahead and order a book in question. With more direct knowledge of holdings and more direct patterns of accessibility—if, for example, the Farmington books for the Midwest had gone to the Midwest Inter-Library Center—the acquisition patterns of the local libraries might be reduced perceptibly for many publications that are marginal to the institutions' current interests.

It has been argued by several distinguished librarians that a national plan of subject specialization among libraries for retrospective as well as current publications is the best— and some say the only—solution to both growth and coverage problems.[7] Such a scheme would seem to offer major economies in effort and cost, but it has inherent in it difficulties that may be extraordinarily difficult to overcome. In such a plan, University A accepts the responsibility for collecting comprehensively or exhaustively in, let us say, physics; University B accepts the same responsibility in chemistry, etc., through the entire range of books and knowledge. The plan does not prohibit University B from acquiring books it wants in physics, but it assumes that B will limit its acquisitions and holdings to the most essential materials and borrow the rest from A and other universities or research libraries. Such cooperation is achieved automatically where a university already has a major, sustained interest in a field, and where other institutions have only a limited interest. Cornell's Icelandic collection is the most frequently cited example. Few universities today seem likely to embark upon a comprehensive program of collecting Icelandic literature. But this very illustration seems to point up some of the inherent difficulties in the plan. A university faculty that has a major interest in a subject field is unlikely to be satisfied with a plan that puts the major collection in the subject in a distant library with physical access to the material a matter of inter-institutional courtesy and considerable delay while the location is determined and the materials are borrowed. A direct access to complete locational bibliography and even high-speed, low-cost facsimile transmission of texts from one institution to another would not overcome some of these admittedly traditional objections.

Even more fundamental is the impact upon the institution collecting in the special field. If knowledge and books continue to increase in the field of specialization, and if comprehensive coverage is deemed an imperative concomitant of the plan, more and more space and money will have to be put into the special field. If the library's total resources in space and money are growing equally rapidly no great difficulty may appear, but if these resources level out, or even worse, are curtailed, then an increasing proportion of the specializing library's resources will have to be put into materials in the special subject for which the library has accepted responsibility. Even this might not prove too awkward if the specializing institution retained its major interest in the speciality. But any history of universities suggests that sustained high-level interest and academic strength in a particular subject are relatively rare. Academic departments wax and wane in strength, and the high inter-institutional mobility of faculty members in American academic institutions is a tradition of long standing. Even where the faculty members remain the same, they are free to change their subject interests, and it is a freedom they are not likely to surrender. Inter-institutional subject agreements to be helpful must be reasonably permanent; some of their difficulties in this connection will become apparent if you will try to determine what your library would probably have chosen to specialize in fifteen,

twenty, or twenty-five years ago and compare it with the subjects you would like to specialize in today. They will seldom be the same.

The response to this generally acknowledged situation is that it is extravagant and wasteful with respect to research library resources, and that every university cannot expect to conduct high-level research and graduate instruction in every field of knowledge. This is perfectly true, and in practice universities do not, of course, conduct high-level research in all fields of knowledge simultaneously, but they have traditionally been free to do so. While universities have long recognized that it is not fruitful for all of them to engage in every discipline, the practical effects of this have been noticeable primarily at the level of the professional school and in subject areas where the equipment—other than libraries—is notoriously expensive or the teaching and research personnel scarce, or the number of interested students has characteristically been small. In the major, traditional, basic academic disciplines it seems to me very unlikely that many universities will take a position in which they assert that they will not support or permit extensive research and advanced teaching. To be the most effective, library specialization based upon a division of subject fields demands such institutional limitations, and they must be long-term limitations.

There is a final difficulty; the division of books into neat subject compartments is by no means easy, and some will declare it to be impossible. Thus the books which University A is specializing in may be equally relevant to the studies and subject speciality of University B. While books and scholars may both be forced into nice systematic compartments, both groups have a tendency to keep popping out and moving into adjacent fields and into what often seems to be singularly remote subject areas. Despite increasing specialization of knowledge and scholars, the constant vigor of research in inter-disciplinary fields suggests, in addition to the reasons already cited, that efforts to attain a sustained, comprehensive, and systematic national plan of library specialization by the division of subject fields among universities may possibly be doomed to failure because of inadequate recognition of these basic intellectual forces. In this vein Mortimer Taube has taken the position that literature cannot really be divided in this way and still be useful in historical studies, where the problems are most acute.[8] A recent study of the material used in the preparation of doctoral dissertations also suggests basic intellectual problems to this cooperative approach.[9] Clearly where universities can limit their fields of endeavor—and abide by the decision— the available resources—library and otherwise— will go further and dilution will be avoided, but this does not mean that the major research library obligations can be materially modified by inter-institutional subject specialization agreements.

It will be seen that both of the cooperative schemes described result in two major changes from traditional library-scholarly relationships: 1) the scholar must be able by means of citations, bibliography, checklists, or similar devices to establish the probable relevancy of a particular item to the work in hand (in other words he can no longer count on finding his material by walking through the bookstack of a library or by thumbing through volume after volume of a large unanalyzed set), and 2) there will be a delay in getting the material to him after he has determined what he needs. The kinds of books that can be used under these conditions with the least impairment of good scholarship are, to say the least, not well known. The working scholar's initial response to any proposal that seems to make any considerable number of books less accessible is likely to be something less than wild enthusiasm, for traditionally, a book not in the local library, even if available on inter-library loan, has not been regarded by the man who wants to check something in it, as very accessible. Many faculty members are likely to welcome new schemes of library operation involving deferred access to certain kinds of material only as they become convinced 1) that a continuation of the present methods of collecting and making materials available may lead to quite unreasonable capital or operating costs in relation to any probable gains, or 2) that the traditional methods are already too cumbersome and expensive for current needs, or 3) that some alternative scheme might greatly extend access to needed resources at relatively little cost and not too much inconvenience.

As soon as one begins such an analysis, it quickly becomes evident that the problem is not simply what materials can be

used with some form of deferred access, but what materials are really needed for current and future scholarly operations and how these materials are used and thus most usefully made available. A recent report on problems of library growth by a special committee of the trustees of Harvard, Yale, Columbia, and the New York Public Library said that answers were needed to such questions as the following to assess the merits of a joint integrated storage library:

What is the bulk of such material which would be removed from present collections?

What use of the joint library would be expected; how frequently, by whom, how, and for what purposes?

Is there a practical basis for eliminating entirely from the libraries of the Northeast, materials with little inherent value to society in the future? [10]

The trustees hastily point out that "These questions are so vast and complex that the main challenge presented to your Committee is not merely to ascertain what facts are needed to arrive at a sound course of action, but rather *how* to gather these facts accurately and expeditiously."

To gather these facts the committee must begin to ascertain more than any of us now know about the characteristics of large numbers of books, the habits and needs of scholars in relation to print, and the relationship in all of this between value and costs. The latter is an extremely important part of these considerations. What is research worth? How much should a university spend in the pursuit of knowledge? What is an education worth? What is the value of an idea? The elusive and highly intangible quality of these matters requires no elaboration before an academic audience. Yet these are the intangible reasons for which the research library exists, and, if the library is weak in its resources and inadequately supported, these weaknesses will inevitably be reflected in the educational and research programs that are dependent upon library resources.

But simply because many of the ultimate qualities of a library and of scholarship are intangible does not mean that the processes of both, particularly in relation to one another, should be exempted from objective observation and analysis. And indeed these matters have not been entirely neglected; we are beginning to learn a little more about the kinds of material that appear to be essential in the support of serious research and how these materials are used. For the most part, these studies so far have revealed nothing startlingly new nor unexpected, but they have confirmed and extended some ideas about research literature that, with further study, may help us to plan a more sensible and efficient research library structure than the one we now have. A number of these studies have been based upon a careful examination of the characteristics of the literature cited by scholars in their own work. Citation analyses are subject to all kinds of flaws—one of the most common being stated in the maxim "what was cited wasn't read, and what was read wasn't cited"; nonetheless, the data may be helpful until more precise research techniques can be developed to give us a clearer picture of the scholarly uses of print.

A number of these earlier studies investigated literature characteristics in the sciences, simply because the more compact literature of science, in terms of age and the heavy dependence upon serial and periodical publications, made it easier to approach. Almost any physicist will tell you that physics publications more than a few years old will be of very limited usefulness to the scholar or student of modern physics. To what extent can this be confirmed? By way of illustration, an ananlysis of certain carefully selected scholarly journals in physics published in 1939 revealed that some 88 percent of all references to serial articles were to articles that had appeared within the previous ten years—surely evidence that there is a fairly high rate of obsolescence in physics serial literature at least as measured by frequency of citations.

In chemistry the rate is not as high, but even so some 71 percent of the serial references were only ten years old or less at the time they were cited in 1939. References in chemistry that were eleven to fifty years old at the time they were cited amounted to 26 percent of all serial references, which may be compared to the 11 percent of serial references in physics that were this old.

Other relevant characteristics of the ma-

terials used by scholars emerge from careful analysis of such factors as subject and title dispersions, the countries in which cited literature is published, the form in which the used literature appears, etc. Studies in history, literature, political science, sociology, economics, etc., reveal literature citation patterns that present, as one would expect both similarities and sharp contrasts from one discipline to another. In some disciplines the current literature seems to be more or less quickly superseded almost in its entirety. In others, such as history, there appears to be only a limited pattern of obsolescence, while in still other disciplines, distinct parts of the literature are apparently superseded in terms of frequency of use. Modern books on philosophy are a fairly obvious example; many of them seem to fall into disuse fairly quickly, while the classical works remain as popular as ever.

Some of the results of citation analyses have proved interesting when compared with the actual frequency with which books of different kinds seem to be used in a research library. Analysis of the use of books in a library is a complicated business. It is subject to hazards quite similar to those governing citation analyses: much library use is quite unrecorded and, as any user of a library is well aware, a record of circulation does not mean that the book borrowed was ever read. There are statistical problems too: of any one thousand books, some are likely to have arrived in the library yesterday and have not yet had a chance to be used, while others may have been sitting on the shelf hopefully for fifty years. In most libraries, changes in circulation systems will also raise questions about the adequacy and reliability of the data on the earlier use of particular books. Recognizing all these, and many other unlisted but equally dangerous traps, what is the evidence? Again, it bears out common knowledge: most of the recorded use of a large research library is produced by a relatively small percentage of the books used in the library. In one study [11] of this problem at the University of Chicago, the following results were obtained: In physics only 3.4 percent of the collection appears to produce some 42½ percent of the total use, 8.7 percent of the collection supplies 61 percent of the use, and all apparent recorded use is met by 52½ percent of the collection on a volume-by-volume basis. The results were similar in many respects in chemistry, botany, and zoology— in all three instances less than 50 percent of the collections supplied 100 percent of the use.

A similar study [12] in the social sciences and humanities revealed that use is more widely scattered, but even so, that some 30 to 40 percent of the books in the collections will produce about 85 to 95 percent of the use and the quantity of material showing no recorded use at all will also be high (30 to 45 percent). Some of these percentages are probably quite different for libraries of different size, and they will certainly be affected by local curricular and research patterns.

It is evident however that the supplying of the last few percentage points of use in a research library requires geometrically increasing numbers of books and that most of these books will be used very seldom and many of them not at all. These circulation studies also suggest that the use of a book in the first five years after it is acquired may be a crude index of its probable use thereafter. There was a surprising agreement in this respect among all the subjects studied. Of the books that were not used at all during the first five years they were held by the library, some 60 to 70 percent showed no subsequent use. And when these books *were* used subsequently, the use appears to be very infrequent and widely scattered. While this may sound wasteful, the problem of the research library is made clearer if the figures are presented the other way. Of all the books in a research library that showed no recorded use at all during their first five years in the collections, some 30 to 40 percent of them will be used at least once later.

The present data *tend*—and the highly tentative nature of this must be emphasized—to suggest the following points: 1) A very high percentage of the literature needs of distinguished research in many subject disciplines can probably be met with a very carefully selected collection, the size of which, while still unknown, may be considerably smaller than has commonly been supposed to have been necessary. 2) If this collection is kept closely matched to the demands of many disciplines, its contents will change as the state of knowledge or fashions of study change. 3) To supply the last few percentage points of total research use,

i.e., the last 90 to 95, or 95 to 99 percent, will require extremely large book collections in many disciplines. Indeed, the last percent or fraction of a percent will require collections so large as to be well beyond the means of any single institution except in very narrow or modern specialities, for the collection that is to supply all possible use would clearly have to contain all the books in the world. The great bulk of this mass of material that is to satisfy the last few percentage points will, of course, be used very infrequently if at all. 4) Certain kinds of research studies, most typically those of an historical or literary nature, will not follow these patterns. The required literature in these instances will be dependent solely upon the topic chosen for investigation and is likely to be of the infrequently used type. These topics are not likely to be very predictable. 5) Only in literature, bibliography, and a few similar areas does it seem likely that a basically accumulative pattern of local library growth may be indispensable to good research *if there are other means of gaining quick and easy access to the infrequently used materials when they are required.* 6) Different treatments and patterns of access to parts of very large research collections may be both feasible and desirable.

It would be highly premature at this point to try to make more specific judgments as to the long-range significance of studies of these kinds for the research library. The research methodologies are still tentative and unsatisfactory in many important respects, and the data are much too meager and scattered. Nonetheless we believe that data of this kind are helpful in describing more precisely the complex phenomena that occur in the use of books by serious scholars. Furthermore we are convinced that no rational solutions of the major problems of the larger research libraries are likely to emerge except as we improve our understanding of what scholars use; what they could have used, but didn't; how they identify what they need; and the extent to which serious studies are impaired, postponed, or otherwise affected by the availability of research library resources.

Although studies of the type described do not yet justify any firm conclusions about the future research library, it is interesting to speculate upon the kinds of changes that could occur or that seem already to be occurring.

In the first place it seems evident that bibliography of all kinds and for a great variety of purposes will be increasingly conspicuous in the future research library. Bibliography will be in the form of monographic books, cards, serial publications, and, more likely than not, parts of it will be on punched cards, magnetic tapes or drums, film, and other media, with high unit capacities and capable of very fast manipulation for purposes of selection and analysis. It will be produced by scholarly organizations, national libraries, governments, inter-library cooperation, individuals, corporations, and many other agencies. Its proper application to local problems will make constantly increasing demands upon the professional skills of librarians.

The necessity for bibliography is, I think, fairly obvious. Although libraries are growing rapidly, they are almost certainly not growing as rapidly as print itself. In consequence, the percentage of the universe of print contained in the individual library seems likely to be a gradually declining one. Since the boundaries between what is relevant to serious investigation and what is irrelevant have yet to be drawn—and may never be—bibliography, and greatly improved bibliography at that, will be a prime essential to the scholarly constituency of any research library. Furthermore some of the more space-consuming elements of the present library, e.g., the effort to arrange the books on the shelves in accordance with elaborate subject classifications, are devices that seem designed to make up, in part at least, for bibliographical deficiencies. Possibly in the library of the future, bibliography will become good enough to make it so superior an approach to information and print that the effort to arrange large numbers of physical books by subject can be abandoned, since such arrangement inevitably results in many arbitrary decisions. In fact the total effort given to local cataloging is likely to be minimized as the national, subject, and other forms of bibliography improve. Incidentally, it is evident that, if satisfactory bibliographical apparatus is to be constructed, scholarship itself needs a greatly improved understanding of its own needs and methods.

A second change in the future research library is the probability that the books to be acquired and retained in original form in the local library will need to be subjected to much more rigorous appraisals than have been common in the past in order to try to judge the probable current and future usefulness of the material. It may no longer be possible to say of a book simply that someone someday may wish to look at it. Such a judgment is almost infallible, but it may not be sufficient for the future building of a strong research library. Present canons of selection are often singularly broad and inclusive—and often for the very good reasons that I have tried to make clear—but the space and the overhead costs in relation to the scholarly benefits may simply become too high to continue what often seem to be collecting policies that go beyond probable needs. As a library grows and its collections become more inclusive, acquisition policies tend to become increasingly inclusive also.

If scholars and librarians are going to cast a more critical eye on what goes into research collections—as I think they will—then they are also logically forced to take a more critical look at what is already there. In both contexts we encounter the plight that I have already referred to: the librarian has heretofore had no real choice between indefinite retention and outright discard. One of the most logical and economical solutions to the preservation of many such books seems to be the regional or even a national cooperative deposit library. Such libraries can also play a very significant role by acquiring much marginal material either directly or by transfer from the current acquisitions of member institutions. This concept of a major, continuous withdrawal of less useful or largely superseded materials will require intensive study and great care in its implementation.

A fourth category of change would be related to technological developments. One author [13] has already suggested that the local research library may be entirely superseded by high-speed, low-cost facsimile transmission from one or a few comprehensive collecting centers. One would simply dial for the texts desired, and they would start feeding out of a box either in what survives of the local library or in the scholar's office. Alternatively, an image of the desired text would appear on an electronic screen, while the pages would be flipped by pressing a button. Mr. Ridenour did not suggest it, but when pressing the button grows tiresome, it may be only a matter of time to go to the next step: merely to fasten two electrodes from the central transmitter to a suitable part of one's scalp and have the desired information fed electronically directly to the brain—preferably while sleeping. With the possible exception of the last step, none of this is impossible, for most of the basic technology is already in being. An affection for books and a mild fear of technological unemployment induce me to pass hastily on to other technological alternatives—equally repellent to some librarians and scholars I am sure, but perhaps less distant than the vista just described.

It may be possible by means of high-reduction microfacsimile techniques to store an immense amount of information in a very small space. Let us suppose that this great corpus of books or knowledge could be reproduced inexpensively and thus widely distributed. Let us also suppose that either built-in or auxiliary bibliographical techniques can be developed to assure good access to the contents of the corpus. This mass of material could obviously be added to routinely by massive selection from both the current output and deteriorating wood-pulp materials on which copyright has expired; these copies could be distributed automatically by blanket subscription or something of the sort. I would conceive of this material as a supplement to the regional library and the local, more dynamic book collection, but it could obviously supersede large parts of the regional library and perhaps much of the local research collection as well.

The microtext suggested here will differ in important particulars from what is now in common use. The reductions will be moderately high, making it possible to handle large quantities of text on a relatively small surface and in a small space. The costs of the original reproduction must be much lower than anything we are now accustomed to. Preferably the costs should be less than the current annual cost of storing a book in original format in the average research library. The microtext will be in a form that is reproducible quickly and very inexpensively in the local library. In consequence it will be quicker and less expensive to make a copy of such a microtext "book" on demand than to charge a conventional book out of the library and return it to the shelves. The recipient will therefore keep the microtext permanently—in the meantime the library's microtext "master" will remain instantly accessible for the production of another copy for another borrower or for consultation in the library.

Each scholar would normally have his own microtext reader just as he now owns his own typewriter. The projectors will, of course, be easy to use, free of eyestrain, inexpensive, and capable of producing paper enlargement prints quickly and inexpensively when the scholar needs a full-size copy for purposes of comparison, detailed consultation, editing, etc. Under the conditions described, one can visualize a research library of great scope, occupying a moderate amount of space, and providing a high level of access to both frequently and seldom used materials. One can also see the possibility of the individual scholar having at his fingertips as extensive a collection as he needs of the works relevant to his own studies or investigation. This microtext, it should be emphasized, would serve as a supplement to a conventional—and still large—book collection; I do not believe that it is likely to take its place.

In gazing into the future, experience suggests that our visions of what can be accomplished are more likely than not to fall far short of reality, and the illustrative ideas outlined here for changes in the research library are neither very revolutionary nor very new. Almost every technical or organizational element suggested has either been realized or appears sufficiently well developed in the general state of technology as to present few obstacles to its full technical development if we want it and *can pay for it*. In consequence one can probably anticipate that the changes outlined for the research library are not nearly radical enough, yet we must also recognize that neither the research library nor scholarly methods are changed easily. Experimental alterations in the procedures for arranging or making accessible hundreds of thousands or even millions of books, each of which must be uniquely identified, are not made lightly or inexpensively. It is for reasons of this kind that the university library may sometimes seem more inflexible and more rigid than it really wants to be.

Yet the advancement of human knowledge

and understanding are goals that civilized men must hold high. Full and easy access to the record of what man has thought and achieved in the past and what our fellow men are now thinking and achieving are indispensable to any real advancement of knowledge. The university library is the principal instrument of society by which this record of the past and present is maintained and communicated. The techniques employed by the research library for accomplishing these goals must be kept on a par in imagination, resourcefulness, and efficiency with the importance of the goals themselves.

FOOTNOTES

[1] Pierce Butler, *An Introduction to Library Science* (Chicago: The University of Chicago Press, 1933), pp. 2-3.

[2] "Tradition and Change: The Role of the College Library Today," *Essential Books* (October, 1955), p. 30.

[3] John D. Millett, *Financing Higher Education in the United States* (New York: Columbia University Press, 1955), pp. 122-123.

[4] Paul Buck, "Looking Ahead," in *Problems and Prospects of the Research Library,* ed. Edwin E. Williams (New Brunswick, N.J.: The Scarecrow Press, 1955), pp. 147-148.

[5] Fremont Rider, *The Scholar and the Future of the Research Library* (New York: Hadham Press, 1944), p. 12.

[6] John D. Millett, "A Memorandum by the Author of *Financing Higher Education in the United States,"* in *Problems and Prospects of the Research Library* (New Brunswick, N.J.: The Scarecrow Press, 1955), pp. 23-25.

[7] R. B. Downs, ec., *Library Specialization: Proceedings of an Informal Conference Called by the ALA Board on Resources of American Libraries, May 13-14, 1941* (Chicago: American Library Association, 1941).

[8] Mortimer Taube, "The Realities of Library Specialization," *The Library Quarterly,* XII (1942), 246-256.

[9] Rolland Stevens, "The Use of Library Materials in Doctoral Research. A Study of the Effect of Differences in Research Method," *The Library Quarterly,* XXIII (1953), 33-41.

[10] *Progress Report to the Trustees of Harvard, Yale, Columbia, and the New York Public Library From Its Special Committee to Consider the Problems of Library Growth* (New York: Cresap, McCormick and Paget, 1952).

[11] Hal Smith, "The Recorded Use of a University Library's Books in Two Areas: Biological and Physical Sciences," Unpublished Master's Thesis, University of Chicago, 1951.

[12] Lilian E. Middleswart, "A Study of Book Use in the University of Chicago Library," Unpublished Master's Thesis, University of Chicago, 1951.

[13] Louis N. Ridenour, *Bibliography in an Age of Science* (Urbana: University of Illinois Press, 1951).

ABOUT THE AUTHOR

—**Herman H. Fussler,** Director, The University of Chicago Library; Ph.D., 1948, University of Chicago. His major research interests are in research library resources and their use, and in library buildings.

The University Library

by Wilhelm Munthe

This view on collection development, maintenance, and use in academic libraries provides, through contrast, an incisive commentary on the fundamental premises of academic library practice. Valuable for its analysis of particular procedures, it also examines the question as to who, in fact, is or should be responsible for the collection.

THE LIBRARIAN AND THE PRESIDENT

In approaching this problem the university librarian starts out with an advantage that his European colleague does not as yet have: he is a member of the faculty and as such takes part in many important conferences where he can present the library's case directly and in time. But, on the other hand, he is accountable in a greater degree to the president of the university, and the permanence and power of this latter office has no counterpart in the European democracies. The president is not elected by the professors and does not always have to be a scholar, yet he is the one who determines the university's library policy, fixes the budget for purchase of books, and apportions it between the general library and the departmental libraries. Even though he may usually accept the librarian's budget proposal, duly indorsed by a faculty committee, and recommended it to the board of trustees, he is still the most decisive factor in financial and administrative matters. Hence, the librarian comes to be dependent, even more than we Europeans imagine, on the president's personal feelings and goodwill, and the library's funds are subject to much greater fluctuation than in Europe, where the library director knows that his budget proposal goes all the way to the appropriating body and becomes, as a rule, the basis for a permanent legislative grant.

LIBRARY COMMITTEES

Between the president and the librarian we usually find a committee composed of faculty members. Whether appointed by the president or elected by the faculty, its powers are largely of an advisory character, and seldom does it take a hand in the actual administration of the library. It is, however, the champion and the preserver of the outmoded system, which is still found in some universities, of parceling out the funds by departments of instruction, or between the general library and the departmental libraries—the latter usually coming out ahead. In certain instances the approval of this committee is an intermediate step in book buying, and this may be carried so far that the director who is responsible for the use of the funds actually has control over but an insignificant fraction of them.

In the larger European libraries this is a discarded set-up, although the rudiments of it may still be seen—on paper—in the written regulations of certain libraries. In Germany, Denmark, and Norway the entire responsibility for the purchase of books rests with the university librarian, instead of being dispersed among the shifting and compromising membership of a library committee. There may exist such a committee, but usually only as a regulatory body, and with the tacit understanding that it will interfere only if the librarian's buying policy gives occasion for just complaints.

I think that both American and European librarians consider the interpolation of a purchasing committee a drag on efficiency. Why should a professor have to go round by way of a committee that often includes no representative from his own field, rather than directly to the librarian, who by the very next

---

SOURCE: Reprinted from Wilhelm Munthe, *American Librarianship from a European Angle; An Attempt at an Evaluation of Policies and Activities* (Chicago: American Library Association, 1939), excerpts from Chapter 13, "The University Library," pp. 114-129, by permission of the publisher.

day will have to come to a decision and have placed the order? It has been our experience in Europe that the elimination of the purchasing committee has speeded up the acquisition of books, made the funds more elastic, and contributed to the development of a long-range buying policy, while the method of quota division leads to an improvident frittering away of the funds.

BOOK BUYING

In practice, of course, the director of a European library will not be able to attend to the entire business of book buying himself. Instead, this part of the work has been developed into a separate branch (pre-accession) in which the aim is to call on the services of both the teaching and the library staff. As an illustration, I shall take a northern European university library: In the circulation department, and at numerous other places on the campus, blank suggestion-cards are provided and each year lists are sent out to the teaching staff on which they are asked to put down new books of importance in their respective fields. In addition, all requests from borrowers for books not in the library are collected and gone over by the pre-accession department. Each member of the professional library staff is expected to keep up on certain subjects, or certain critical journals, and to make suggestions on the basis of his reading. Then, every week the librarian holds a conference in his office at which decisions are made on all the suggestions that have come in from these various sources: some are approved for immediate purchase and go right to the order department, some are referred to other libraries or are kept for closer examination, while those that are rejected are sent back to the individual suggesting them, with a brief explanatory statement.

It is not to be expected that an ordinary library will have on its staff specialists in all subjects, but this fact does not prevent its carrying out the plan as far as it can. And, in my opinion, too high a value cannot be placed on the responsibility that the entire professional library personnel must thus assume as co-workers, with their special subjects to keep up on. Here is a veritable fountain of youth in the midst of the deadening routine.

In the libraries of Austria this system of staff responsibility for the various subject fields is well established; in Germany, too, it operates successfully in the larger libraries. The United States should find the plan even easier to introduce, since there the university libraries seldom include medicine or jurisprudence, and these are the fields for which it is most difficult to get competent staff representatives.

The School of Medicine is frequently located in another town or at a considerable distance from the main campus, and hence generally has its own library. The Law School, too, as a rule, has its own library in a separate building, but in many instances this collection has been brought under the direction of the university librarian, although usually only in such a manner as to leave it a large measure of self-government. The authority of the university librarian may be limited to nominal supervision, or may be extended to involve central purchasing and cataloging and, finally, even joint book funds and staff personnel. The active emergence of the related social sciences that come under the domain of the general library has brought the law library out of its former isolation, but there is probably no instance of its forming an integral part of the university library.

The segregation of medical and legal literature also has its practical advantages. The architectural problems of the university library are complicated enough as it is, without the necessity of providing space for a mammoth reading room to house the legislative and judicial literature of the forty-eight states, and research accommodations for the professors besides. With such requirements as the alternative, separation is to be preferred even though it means considerable duplication of material.

In this respect the continental university library is, as we have seen, in a more fortunate position: it is really an organic part of the university as a whole and an integrating factor among all of its various divisions. True enough, in Germany and Austria, individual voices have been raised for a bipartition of the university library, into a humanistic and a medical and natural service branch. But, aside from a few localities where lack of space and similar factors have made themselves felt, the idea has not gained acceptance. Neither is the time favorable for proposals that involve increased running expenses and artificial lines of cleavage, with the attendant overlapping.

DEPARTMENTAL LIBRARIES

If Europe is ahead in the respect just mentioned, it cannot be denied that she is behind on another point; namely, coordination of and cooperation between the university library and the departmental libraries in the European sense; that is, the special collection attached to the university's museums, institutes, laboratories, observatories, hospitals, and seminars. For the last hundred years these special collections have been allowed to grow wild and remain mutually independent, so that now, when they have become large in size and strong in historical tradition, it is increasingly difficult to bring them into effective cooperation with one another or with the general library.

The directors of institutes ordinarily have complete power and freedom in the selection and purchase of books, no outside approval being required. The general library is given no list of their acquisitions, and access to the collections if often quite difficult. And if the director shelves his own books and pamphlets together with those that belong to the institute, then the collection takes on the appearance and also the exclusiveness of a private library.

We can see easily enough that this is wrong—but to correct it is not so easy, for here we come up against sacred traditions and the rights of a group of professors whom the Germans, not without reason, call *Institut Barone.* These gentlemen look upon every proposal for coordination as an encroachment upon their baronial rights and a veiled attempt to make them subordinate to the university librarian. Such reform proposals are then usually quietly buried by the university administration or amended to the point of complete ineffectiveness.

Actually this "systematic lack of system" is not so troublesome at the universities in the smaller countries, because there it is difficult for the institutes to get very large grants for books, but in Germany the dissipation of energy and resources that it causes has become an economic problem. The holdings of the German university libraries total thirteen and one half million books, against

which we have the institutes with around five million. In an effort to do something about this splitting up of the book funds, they have tried the plan of setting an arbitrary limit to the number of books in each institute, say 5,000 or 10,000 volumes (*numerus classus*). When new accessions bring the total in excess of this figure, a corresponding number of books must be turned over to the university library. This is not exactly to the advantage of the latter, nor is it a step toward coordination, but it should, at any rate, prevent these special collections from assuming such proportions as will eventually lead either to chaos or to demands for larger staffs and larger appropriations. It is safe to say, however, that results have not come up to expectations—whatever these might have been. At present Prussia has a government committee at work trying to bring all institute libraries under centralized control—in accordance with the *Fuehrer* principle.

SECRET BOOK FUNDS

This all looks very nice on paper, of course, but it does not take care of all the difficulties. The departments gradually demand more and more duplicate sets of handbooks and periodicals, as long as they are not paying for them out of their own funds. One way of preventing some of this is to assign definite portions of the total budget to the main library and to each department. This is, as a matter of fact, the usual practice and incidentally it has complicated the bookkeeping so as almost to frighten European visitors. In practice other complications also come up. Certain departments buy books on their ordinary maintenance budget, or receive gifts of periodicals, for instance, which they wish to continue. So, alongside of the book fund administered by the university librarian, there develops a non-library book fund for books and periodicals that seldom get into the public catalogs. Of course, the greater part of these "hidden" periodicals would be duplicates of others already in the main library or in another department. Private exchange arrangements, in addition to the official ones of the main university library, are particularly widespread.

There is no panacea for these disorders, but

they are relatively small when compared with the complications that arise when the departmental libraries become more powerful than the main library. The origin and cause of decentralization can often be traced back to the time when the university either had no university librarian, or else one without professional rank, and hence incapable of interfering with the department heads in their parceling out of the book funds. The University of Chicago's library situation has become unusually involved, because from the very beginning they built on a decentalized system, in which the department libraries were entirely independent, and the lack of coordination resulted in uneven growth and conflicting policies. Unfortunately, it is probably already too late to wipe out the traces of this confusion and in its place set up one great central library with the departmental libraries reduced to minor subordinate divisions. Incidentally, Johns Hopkins University has had something of the same trouble.

The most effective way of changing the course of development and of counteracting these centrifugal forces is for the main library to embark on a program of expansion that will attract and care for the overflow from the departmental libraries. At Chicago, for example, a new central stack tower with enlarged study facilities would be a better centripetal force than any amount of discussion and resolutions.

On the other hand, it might seem as though Yale had hit upon the ideal solution of this controversial problem: the main library automatically buys copies of all books in the departmental libraries. But who can, in the long run, afford this solution in these days when the rate of book production plays havoc with all library budget estimates? Unwarranted duplication can never be defended.

SEPARATE BOOK FUNDS AND UNION SERVICE

In practice, the best solution is probably for the general and the departmental libraries to have separate book funds, but combined service arrangements. The department heads are then to do their own book selecting, but are not to buy books or subscribe to periodicals that fall outside their field, without consulting with the university librarian. All ordering, bookkeeping, cataloging, binding, etc., is done through the main library, which thus maintains contact with the departmental libraries and can keep a union catalog of the entire resources of the university. The university librarian must then make it his business to call the attention of the department heads to recommendations that he considers superfluous, either because he knows that the work in question has already been bought for another collection or because of other circumstances. But if the department still insists, the university library must comply—provided the departmental budget can stand it.

It is also of great importance that the assistants in the departmental libraries be appointed in the same manner and on the same terms as the staff of the main library, in order to facilitate transfer or advancement from one library to another. The objection to the positions in the smaller libraries is that there is no future in them, and consequently they are often taken by persons of mediocre ability who do not mind the prospect of ending in a blind alley. Here the interests of both libraries should be one: the better the chances for advancement, the better the qualifications of the staff.

DEPOSIT SETS

An unfortunate practice that has also found its way into American universities is that of buying books and periodicals on the general book fund and then turning them over to a departmental library as deposits. It happens, for instance, that the general library subscribes to a periodical and has the numbers sent to a department as they come in, later gets back the completed volume for binding at its own expense and then returns it to the department for shelving. This sort of thing gradually eats into the book budget. I found cases of it in my own library but managed to get the set back, either outright or in exchange for something else. In general, the main library need not worry too much about turning over a current periodical to a special library, if the condition is made that it will be lent to anyone who would be entitled to borrow it from the main library. But no administrator should stand by and see his budget undermined.

SEMINAR LIBRARIES

In our comparison of American and European university libraries we must also note the different roles played by seminar libraries. In America, these are mostly rather small reading rooms for graduate study, located in the upper stories of the university library building, with a more or less permanent collection of books taken from the main stack. In Europe the situation varies greatly, but we can best take a single university as an illustration.

The largest university in Sweden, Uppsala, has a library of 700,000 volumes, 17,000 bound manuscripts, 70,000 maps, etc. But its reading rooms are used chiefly by research workers and special students preparing for a doctor's or other higher degree. The ordinary graduate students work in the reading rooms of the various "faculties" (divisions), which are independent of the main library and are under the control of the respective faculty committee. This committee usually appoints one of the officers of the university library as inspector—as a rule one who has taken his degree in that particular school or "faculty"—and thus is brought about at least an unofficial connection. The humanistic seminar library, for instance, contains about 20,000 volumes and seats 100 persons in its two reading rooms. In addition there are some minor special seminar reading rooms. The actual situation is, then, that the students get their recreational reading from their student union libraries, their ordinary study material in the "faculty" or seminar libraries, and use the university library only when borrowing books for home use or when carrying on special investigations.

THE BOOK COLLECTION

As we walk past the rows of shelves in an American university library we realize at once how it differs from its European counterpart. The former seems primarily adapted to serve a teaching institution, while the latter looks more like a general research library. One might put it this way—that the American university library starts at the bottom, on the undergraduate level, and progresses up-ward, through graduate studies and faculty research, to the heights of pure science and knowledge—while the European starts at the top, and works itself down from the highest scholarly and scientific literature to the level of the students. Books for the European student's daily use occupy a very modest place, both in number of volumes (there being no duplicates) and in number of titles. All in all, the development in America has followed a more natural course.

On the other hand, the basis on which the German and Scandinavian university libraries are built is much broader. They are really great universal libraries whose task is to serve not only the university community but the entire scholarly and scientific life of their country or province. They have long since transcended university lines, and hence cannot be compared with institutions that are so restricted.

Most of them are copyright deposit libraries, to which all printers and publishers in the country or region send a copy of everything they issue. This, of course, fills them with an enormous mass of printed material that has nothing to do with ordinary university work. From an exclusively university point of view, this may seem a burden, yet it cannot be denied that such a complete collection of national or regional literature is of great value for all historical and social study. All domestic newspapers and periodicals come in free, and there is no trouble in getting the fugitive material that certain American university libraries (Princeton, Stanford, Baker Business Library at Harvard, etc.) are trying to get through special acquisition organs.

This situation also has its effect on the use of the library. It is obvious that the deposit copies of fiction and popular books cannot be lent to students for recreational reading. They are archive copies, and as such must be reserved for special use. The students have to take care of the problem of entertainment literature through their student unions. It is even too dangerous to put all this "deposit literature" in the general stacks. Scandinavian libraries have gone so far as to shelve all their national literature in a separate stack where it is cared for by a staff specially trained for this work.[1]

FOOTNOTES

[1] See my article, "National Departments in Scandinavian Libraries." *Library Quarterly,* 4: 296. 1934.

ABOUT THE AUTHOR

—**Wilhelm Munthe** (d. 1965), University Librarian, University of Oslo, 1922-1953; Ph.D., 1911, University of Oslo. His major research interests were in mediaeval history, palaeography, library administration, and international librarianship.

HOUSING THE LIBRARY

The educational function of the academic library is not a building. Yet the facility, representing as it does an approximation of the concept of the library, has a significant effect on the nature of its function and the priorities of its educational roles. An analysis of the library's physical requirements provides the academic librarian with the opportunity to affirm the principles of his discipline and their implementation.

The Concept of a Library

by Ralph E. Ellsworth

This study of the multiplicity of factors which are involved in library architecture illustrates the need for extensive analysis of the different responses the library makes to the educational process, as well as the effectiveness of the possible alternatives in fulfilling its role. If the planning of library buildings is to be solely an exercise in interpolating present assumptions, the consequences are merely suggested by this reading.

When within the lifetime of one individual one sees new libraries constructed to replace relatively new buildings that were supposed to be adequate for a century or so, structures that are still new looking and in sound physical condition (as at Washington University in St. Louis and Temple University) one is forced to admit that either there was something wrong with the old planning methods, or that the colleges and universities have changed their natures, or that the function of the library has changed so radically that a basically new type of structure is needed.

Actually, all three of these forces have been in operation in colleges and universities during the last twenty-five years.

There were three reasons why the old fixed-function types of library have frequently failed to serve the purposes for which they were designed. (1) Inadequate attention was given to proper programming with the result that architects did too much of the planning on their own responsibility. (2) These buildings were inflexible and not easily adaptable to changing conditions at a time when all conditions were changing. And (3) they were too small to house book collections and student enrollments that during the last twenty-five years began to grow far more rapidly than anyone in the pre World War II days realized could happen.

Each of these errors can be illustrated from the University of Colorado library building (with which I was associated from the beginning): (1) C. Z. Klauder planned the building from the outside in, to fit in with a Master Campus Plan. Exterior sketches and outlines came first. Some modifications to meet the needs of a working plan were permitted, but not if they forced changes in the exterior design. There was no formal written program setting forth the University's wishes and needs. Thus, both the architect and the University were to blame.

(2) The second error can be illustrated by the fact that the building contained a book stack well surrounded by a series of reading rooms. There is no way of merging the two functions and yet the need for merging began to show itself soon after the building was put into operation. Two sets of stairwells located at the two ends of the stack well, dividing the building into three parts, effectively blocked any attempt to establish the kinds of rooms that were needed to meet new demands.

These demands have immersed us in problems and prospects we have not and do not, today fully understand. There is a mountain of literature on the subject of what should be taught, how we should teach and what tools we should use.

The Ford Foundation has set up a subsidiary organization called the *Educational Facilities Laboratories, Inc.* whose task it is to peer into the future and find new answers to the questions of how we are to teach the coming hordes of students with staffs that cannot be increased with equal rapidity in buildings we are unable to afford.

It is argued that we are wedded to methods that are characterized by "too much teaching and too little learning". Some of us think that

SOURCE: Reprinted from Ralph E. Ellsworth, *Planning the College and University Library Building: A Book for Campus Planners and Architects* (Boulder, Col.: Pruett Press, Inc., 1960), "Introduction" and Chapter 1, "Concept of a Library," pp. 1-21, by permission of the author.

existing methods are still based on pre-Gutenberg times, when books were scarce and knowledge had to be transmitted orally from the teacher to the class.[1] The technology of the communication process has evolved rapidly but the teaching methodologies have not. And so it is that the Eurichs, Rumls, Gores, McGraths, etc. propose reforms that professors consider pie-in-the-sky but that Legislators welcome as possible ways of meeting the future at a cost level they think the public can afford.

Stephens College, which has traditionally been interested in new methods, in planning its new library, questions the validity of all the accepted assumptions, and tries to conceive a library that could house all the learning media and the new techniques and methods.[2] Some of the questions they ask are: Is a library a place where only the printed book is used? Or a place where the student has access to all communication media? Why think of the book, as we know it, as the ultimate vehicle for containing the record of knowledge? And why assume that the lecture method is the only suitable one for undergraduate instruction? Why assume that existing assumptions of space utilizations will continue to dominate?

(3) In terms of conception of size and rate of growth, the University of Colorado building reached the saturation point sooner than was expected. In 1937, when the building was planned, there was no evidence that the birth rate would soon begin to change, or that we could soon have an expanding economy that would provide the money that would enable the University to increase its book funds five fold and to double the size of its faculty. The process of globalization as we know it today was simply not a factor to be reckoned with at that time. Thus, it seemed perfectly normal for the University to conceive its future growth in terms of past history. Colorado's experience is duplicated in practically every university in the country and in many of the colleges.

Normal schools and teachers colleges have become universities overnight and immediately demand library collections of university scope. State colleges of agriculture and engineering, too, have expanded their scope to coincide with university programs. For example, the very new library building at Central Michigan State College was hardly open before the college became a state university and its nature

and size began to increase rapidly. In a period of five years the library became too small. Fortunately, it can be enlarged.

At this very moment, in most states, legislative study committees and university planners are trying to develop patterns of growth for the various state institutions to take care of the future. Should the state university be allowed to increase its enrollment from 10,000 to 20,000? Or would it be better to convert the existing teachers colleges into strong liberal arts colleges, or universities, and thus permit the university to hold down its size? Or should new state colleges be created? Orderly and logical solutions to these and other related problems are not always possible, because of political and emotional considerations that seem to dominate thinking about higher education everywhere in the country.

Nor have we come to an answer about the role of Federal Aid to higher education, or the financing of private colleges and universities.

In short, a library building that was, or is, planned to match assumptions about size and growth has soon outgrown its usefulness unless it was planned for changing assumptions— which few fixed function buildings were!

Nor do we have any assurance that we have better control of our destiny in 1960 than we did in 1937. Yet in the midst of all this uncertainty we must proceed to build libraries as best we can, anticipating future developments as best we can, and profiting as much as possible from cumulated experience.

The central problem in planning is in programming, or attempting to decide exactly what the library system for each college or university is to be. In a small college the problem may be narrowed down to the internal arrangements of one building, whereas at the other end of the scale, the large university problem is always one of developing a cluster of libraries with the central library in the center. The complexity of the problem in each case will depend on size, traditions, the geography of the campus, the nature of other facilities available, and other purely local matters.

Programming is a relatively new idea in library planning because the need for planning was not acute in the 19th Century, when college and university libraries were small and when library use by students at the undergraduate level, was slight and uncomplicated. Almost any castle or palace or home of an American magnate could be adapted to serve the needs of the community.

In the period from the turn of the Century to World War II, there were buildings that were planned carefully in terms of function (the University of Illinois and Cincinnati for example) but for every one planned in this spirit there were many that were planned by architects without the benefit of careful analysis and presentation of function. In fact, I have been unable to find for any college or university library in the United States built prior to World War II a carefully compiled and written program such as is taken for granted today.

And even when the planning was obviously based on a well thought out program, even though it was not written down, all buildings prior to World War II (with the possible exception of the Colorado State College of Education and Skidmore College) were fixed function buildings and, as such, have seldom been sufficiently flexible to meet changing conditions, or properly planned so that economical additions could be made without causing clashes in tone and feeling with new materials, concepts and spaces. For example, it is impossible to subdivide large reading rooms with ceiling heights from fifteen to thirty feet into small study rooms, or individual studies, without running into unpleasant room proportions.

At this point it is necessary to define what is meant by a fixed-function building in contrast to what is now called a modular building.

Before World War II it was assumed that in each building the architect designed each space to meet the needs of each function or operation to a maximum degree of efficiency and appearance. Thus, a self supporting separate book stack was planned for the number of books the institution would own, the ceiling heights of which were usually 7'2", or just high enough to take seven shelves of books. Since the weight of the books was carried on the columns spaced 3' x 4'6" centers, the floors could be very thin (4"). A book stack could be used for no other function. It was highly specialized and efficient. Likewise, the main reading room was to be a beautiful room in which to read, and because of the necessity of reliance on natural lighting and natural circulation of air, the ceiling height was high—sometimes 30'–40'. The stairways were thought of as opportunities for the architect to create elegance. Each space, in fact, was thought of as an architectural gem as well as a place in which to perform a specific function. If each space were large enough and if all the spaces were properly related to one another so that the readers and staff could do their work without too much walking, and if the spaces were thought of as beautiful, the building was said to be successful. The monumentality of a library was accepted as a symbolic measure of respect for knowledge in the minds of the university community.

But the more successful each of these buildings was; that is, the more precisely each fulfilled its functions, the more unsuccessful each building became when the old order began to break up in the late 30's. By this I mean two specific things: first, the rapid and unanticipated growth of the book collections and secondly, the expression of desire for new patterns of service and for access to books by students—expressed well in two books published in the late thirties.[3]

Faculty members began to wish to work with their students among the books; students began to want to go directly to the stacks instead of working exclusively through the card catalogs and bibliographies; and students began to want to study in groups among the books. None of these was possible in the fixed function buildings, nor were these buildings easily remodelled for these and other needs.[4]

Angus Snead Macdonald, an imaginative pioneer in the field of library construction, began in the early thirties to sense the need for a type of library in which spaces might be used for either the storage of books or work space for people. Spreading the spacings of the columns in the Library of Congress Annex was an early expression of his ideas, which were spelled out in a precedent setting article in 1933.[5] The Colorado State College of Education used his system in its library addition in the middle thirties, but until the University of Iowa urged him in 1943 to continue the development of this idea, nothing more was done till be built a mock-up of a modular library in 1944. Princeton and Iowa began modular buildings soon after, though neither used the hollow column system proposed by Macdonald. Hardin Simmons was the first to use his system of construction and the North Dakota State College of Agriculture, in Fargo, was the second.

This concept has come to be called modular planning—a special use of the term modular. Although there has been some disagreement as to the exact meaning of the term, everyone knows that a modular library is one in which most of the floor space, except the core service areas, can be used to support free standing book stacks, or to subdivide into rooms.

Lighting and air supply are mechanically available to all areas. Around this central idea, the concept of modular planning varies considerably. It has been confused with methods of construction, organization of space, ceiling heights and various other irrelevancies.[6]

The concept originated out of the need for internal flexibility and adaptability and its essence continues to be its ability to provide these qualities, though the way in which the concept is interpreted continues to develop.

The relationship of program planning to fixed-function *vs* modular planning now becomes fairly obvious. In theory, a fixed function building would have to be programmed and planned with great care and precision, whereas a modular building should need no programming except for the proper location of fixed core elements and areas and for the provision of the proper amount of floor space.

But in practice the latter part of the theory breaks down. Although it is true that if the service core elements are properly located a modular building can sometimes be reorganized so as to work properly, it seems to work out that colleges and universities that use modular planning spend as much time on programming as do planners of fixed function buildings, for the obvious reason that experience shows that unless you get the fixed core elements in the right places and relationships nothing else works out right and also that it is wise to give up some of the complete flexibility in order to achieve more variety in architectural treatment in the introductory parts of the building.

He who is satisfied that the concept of modular planning is the ultimate and final

basis for library planning is lacking in both hindsight and foresight indeed because it should be obvious to all that the technology of building construction is still in its infancy in some respects. Buildings still cost too much, use materials that are too heavy, can't be moved readily, haven't mastered proper ventilation and lighting, or sound proofing, havn't provided interior remodeling procedures that are sufficiently inexpensive and haven't made sensible use of new materials.

THE CONCEPT OF A LIBRARY

Until the year 1940, practically all college library buildings were minor variations of each other, e.g., Augustana in Moline, Illinois was a small version of the Oberlin College Library; and all university libraries copied one another, e.g., California at Berkeley, Illinois, Michigan, Stanford, Minnesota and Harvard. Then there was the tower group as represented by Yale, Texas and Rochester. Libraries were for books. Undergraduate teaching was pretty much confined to the textbook method. Research called for seminars in the German manner and stack carrels.

Today no one can say for certain what a library should contain, how teaching methods will change in the next twenty years, what physical carrier will be used for the recording and preservation and transmission of knowledge, or even whether the alphabet as we use it will continue to be used as the basis for our symbols of communication. Certainly, no one knows the ultimate limits of our ability to design machines for the bibliographic control of the literature of our knowledge.

Thus far only Yale and Harvard in their multi-house libraries have departed from the philosophy of scarcity in providing books for use on a campus. When the microcard was introduced we envisioned the time when we would give each entering freshman, to keep in his dormitory room, a complete college library in the form of a few shoe boxes of microcards and we expected to turn our central library buildings into purely research centers, but we have failed to do this, not because the idea was unsound but because we failed to develop good reading machines, and because of the economics of the problem. We still haven't developed the machines but we know that the economics of the problem are no barrier. The introduction of widespread use of the paperbacks has permitted us to move into building planning on a philosophy of plenty, but we have done so slowly.

Since the library needs of a strictly liberal arts college like Knox, Colorado College or Swarthmore differ radically from those of a vast and complex university like Illinois or UCLA they cannot be discussed at the same time. Still, a university system begins with a college of liberal arts and on top of this adds layers and circles of service for research and professional training. Thus, it is proper to start with the concept of a college library.

What Should A College of Liberal Arts Library Building Be Like When It Is Not Part of a University Library System?

Surely we have come far enough along in our thinking to know that it should be a "center for learning" in the sense that it should be capable of housing and permitting the use of all the kinds of carriers of knowledge, not just books, but all the things we class as audio-visual, and that it should be capable of housing (unless these can be more appropriately housed in other buildings) all the kinds of teaching and learning where it is essential that the student, the teacher and the material be present in one place at the same time.

The trouble is that we don't know enough about the nature of all the carriers or the teaching and learning methods to know how to plan for them. All we really know is that we should provide a good deal of uncommitted floor space that can accommodate rooms of varying size, each well lighted, properly ventilated, with access to wiring ducts from which electrically powered machines can draw their power, and with good sound proofing qualities. Such a building can be set up to meet the needs of the college at the present time and for the known future. This is about as far as our existing knowledge will permit us to go.

Our assumptions about the amount of space needed are based on our past experience, which may or may not be valid for the future. Therefore, our buildings should be capable of major expansion or of conversion to other uses. The days of a college library building all four walls of which are monumental and indispensable to the aesthetic tone of the campus are gone, whether we know it or not.

This is the theory we should follow, and are following in many of our new college library buildings. Thus far, no architect has been able to come up with the proper expression of a suitable skin for such a building, probably because our public isn't ready for this and still expects a library to look like a library.

In the independent college, the library will be expected to house some functions that in the university-connected college would not need to be in the college library—faculty research studies and provisions for storing newspapers and other research materials, for example.

The College Library Building Within a University.

Until recent years few universities recognized that there was any need for separate facilities for the college function in the university. Columbia University provided a small college library, consisting mostly of required readings, in Butler. The University of Chicago established a separate college library in Cobb Hall when it embarked on its experimentation with a separate college library,[7] but later moved this into Harper.

The University of Colorado in 1940 established a Lower Divisional Library as a center for freshman and sophomore reading but later abandoned the idea for purely local reasons.

But until Harvard sanctioned the idea with the establishment of Lamont—the concept of an undergraduate library had few supporters, now it is being generally accepted—Michigan, Illinois, Indiana, California, Southern Methodist University, etc.

There is still a basic disagreement as to whether it is better to limit the college library to a relatively small number of titles suitable to the introductory level—as Yale does—or to a collection of some one hundred thousand volumes—as Harvard does—for all undergraduates to use.[8] The agrument pivots on the question of whether or not advanced undergraduate majors do or do not use the same materials young graduate students use and if so why try to isolate or duplicate these materials.

It is not easy to determine how large a book collection should be to meet the needs of an undergraduate student body (disregarding the question of the number of duplicates needed). At Earlham College—a strong, high quality liberal arts college in a separate city a good collection of 115,000 volumes is not large enough to satisfy the needs of their best students. I would guess that they should have about 250,000-300,000 volumes, the goal Colorado College has set for itself. If this is proper then it should be true that the needs of the college students in a university will be less than half met in an undergraduate library of 100,000 volumes.

Yale solves the problem by providing some thirteen sets of libraries (one in the main building and twelve in the houses) containing duplicate copies of the heavily used books in the larger, more or less introductory courses. Their assumption is that the undergraduate, once he has passed the level of need, can best be taken care of by the book stack collection. This concept has been defended by William Dix, librarian of Princeton, who believes that the conditions of library service that are right for graduate students are also the right ones for young undergraduates in a university like Princeton.[9]

There are many factors to be considered in arriving at a decision on what the scope of the college library should be, among which is the money available for duplication of titles. Harvard and Michigan can afford to duplicate the materials used in common by the advanced undergraduates and the graduate students; Colorado thinks it must use this money to buy badly needed new titles.

The question of the role of dormitory or house libraries in the total picture is debatable. If the university can afford to provide enough books in the dormitory libraries, and can staff them adequately, so that students can find there most of the books they need for their course work—with the nucleus of a reference collection—then these libraries do affect the nature of the college library in the university library system.

But the trouble is that few universities can afford this. When they cannot, the dormitory libraries constitute an uncertain element, usually a sort of browsing library, a nice luxury but offering no relief on the main job for the library system. There is also a question of whether or not it is cheaper to provide this study space in the dormitories

or in the library. For the serious student it is a nuisance to work in a collection that can't satisfy more than elementary needs. And then there is the matter of fairness. What about the students who don't live in the dormitories? Where are their needs taken care of?

There is also a body of opinion that holds that it is a silly luxury to provide separate facilities for the undergraduates, that they should learn how to use the main collections just like everybody else. The answer to this argument is that the youngsters in most universities aren't ready to work in a research library and that either they get crowded out and thus fall back on the text book or else they create so much noise and confusion in the stacks they spoil these areas for the researchers. One can see this most clearly in departmental libraries in the university, which exist in reality to satisfy the needs or desires of the faculty.

The evidence of experience points to the desirability of separate facilities for the young students, the nature of which will depend on many local elements.

The Nature of the Rest of a University Library System

Once the question of the nature of the liberal arts college library within the university has been decided—and in the American university, as contrasted with the European system, the college is basic—the rest of the problem is one of providing space for the technical processes, for reference and research and for the professional schools.

For Technical Processes

The space needs for these operations are pretty well known and are always different for each university. They will be dealt with later.

For Reference and Research

The concept for these services is not standardized and will vary from campus to campus depending on purely local conditions. The traditional pattern was for the main library to contain a reference service based on type of material, that is: an inclusive reference and bibliography room, current periodical room, a government documents room (unless government documents were treated the same as other books); a special collections room and a book stack for everything not in departmental libraries. Separate departmental libraries for the professional schools and science departments usually exist.

The question of how a university library should organize its reference and reading room services (both within the main building and throughout the campus) is, strictly speaking, not a building problem at all and is thus outside the scope of this book, particularly when modular buildings are under consideration. But not all buildings are modular, and even when they are the question of organization of service should be thought out in advance.

The first real break with the traditional university library building organizational pattern came in 1940 when Colorado and Brown opened subject divisional libraries.

There had been, prior to that time, examples of subject divisional libraries within university library systems—the social science reading room at Chicago and the Life Science Library at the University of California, Berkeley, for example, and several large public libraries had been set up on that basis, but Colorado was the first university library to be conceived on a complete subject divisional basis. Brown used the idea on a more limited basis.

Since that time many universities have used the plan with all kinds of local adaptations. Typical examples can be found at Nebraska, Oregon, Wayne, Michigan State, Georgia, Florida State and Louisiana State, etc. The literature on the subject is extensive. Lundy has written on all phases of the concept. McNeal's paper "The Divisional Organization in the University Library" (read before the Southeastern Library Association, Spring, 1960) is the most recent critical examination of the plan.

The concept originated as a sensible way of reaching a compromise between the old closed stack concept and a departmental system, between general, inclusive reference and departmental reference service, and as an attempt to arrange reference and reading room service on a subject basis rather than on a type-of-material basis.

Nebraska is the only university that has tried to make a consistent and inclusive application of the plan (see articles by Lundy). By this I mean the subordination and merging of acquisitions, processing and reference operations to the subject division. But Nebraska has had to do this in a fixed-function type building (as did Colorado) with the result that their freedom to marshall staff, rooms and equipment is limited. At Colorado the physical rigidity of the building prevented us in the very early life of the building from evolving the plan and solving the problems that experience presented us. When the plan was started there was no experience to draw upon and consequently we did not anticipate the dilemmas that would confront us.

It is not my intent in this book to evaluate the subject divisional plan, but rather to say that it is dangerous to contemplate the inauguration of this, or any other, type of organization the full implications of which are not known in advance, in a fixed-function type of building in which one cannot make major rearrangements of space at will.

This point is important enough to be illustrated in a specific manner. Soon after the plan was put into operation at Colorado it became clear that the terms "Social Science" and "Humanities" caused jurisdictional disputes over specific groups of books and faculty attitudes. Much of this trouble could have been eliminated had we been able to rearrange the second floor of the library and merge the two sets of divisional staffs, and book collections. But this was impossible because two sets of stairwells and a row of seminars separated the rooms. The problem remains.

By way of contrast, in the University of Iowa building we experimented with a method of setting up a Lower Divisional Library by arranging the books according to chronological periods. The idea was a failure. It was a simple matter (and was accomplished during a summer session) to rearrange the entire first and second floors of the building without any construction alterations.

The concept of service in the main building of a university library system will always be dependent on the nature of the amount and kind of decentralization necessary on each campus. Although the pattern will always differ widely from campus to campus, there are certain problems and generalizations that are common to all.

Problems and Generalizations

1. When faculties want departmental libraries they are usually thinking of their own convenience and seldom are willing to think of the needs of their students. They shrug off responsibility for providing adequate reading space for students and seldom realize that students need good reference service even though the faculty think they, the students, do not.

2. Scientists claim special privileges because of the laboratory and are seldom willing to see that the researchers in history or literature have library needs that are very much like those of the scientists.

3. Each man knows which books and journals he needs but finds it difficult to understand that other scholars may need the materials he thinks of as his.

4. The older the discipline, the easier it is for scholars to see the interdependence among departmental literatures and the reason for centralized or at least divisional groupings of collections, and *vice versa*.

5. Although scholars in professional schools like pharmacy, business, nursing, or journalism publish the results of their research in their own professional journals, in doing their research they do not draw upon the professional journals nearly as much as they do the journals of the parent disciplines out of which the schools evolved. Thus, for example, pharmacists use the basic journals in chemistry, biology, and botany and medicine (both human and animal). As long as such schools can be housed close to the parent disciplines no problem exists, but when they move into separate buildings away from their home base, the cost of providing duplicate collections of the basic journals is formidable.

What this means is that in campus planning, buildings should be located consistent with the intellectual relationships of disciplines, other things being equal. These relationships are easily traced through the use of the literature of scholarship.

6. Although demands for departmental libraries by accrediting agencies of professional associations are numerous and annoying they can mostly be disregarded if a university is able to offer a good service to the school concerned even though its pattern doesn't match that of the accrediting agency.

7. Sometimes first class photocopying and delivery-upon-demand service to departments will be an acceptable substitute for a departmental library.

8. On the other hand, librarians who fail to make it possible for scientists to get at their literature late at night and on weekends are asking for trouble.

9. The constant desire for some kind of subject grouping of library materials is not just a sign of perversity or laziness in the faculty, but rather a natural response to a need. The research scholar's time is limited and the older he becomes the less he is interested in spending it on irrelevancies that stand between him and his immediate concerns. As libraries become large, the more obstacles they present to the research scholar unless they are arranged in such a way that his subject literature is segregated. But, at the same time, minute segregation itself becomes a problem to the scholar because it causes him to waste his time hunting materials in marginal and other areas. Thus, geographical conditions permitting, some kind of decentralized divisional grouping may turn out to be the best solution.

For example, Colorado is moving from a completely centralized plan into a central library for the "college" and the social sciences and humanities; a life science library for botany, biology, zoology and psychology; an earth science library for geology and geography; a physical science library for chemistry, mathematics, physics, pharmacy, home economics and nursing—the latter three being included because the departments are now located in those buildings, a separate engineering library and a High Altitude Observatory Library because those two departments are located a good half mile from the rest. Law, of course, is separate.

10. It should be realized, particularly by librarians that new developments in methods of scholarship may create problems that can't be met by the old patterns of librarianship. For example, when anthropologists began to apply the cross cultural method of analysis to world cultures, they found that the mechanics of assembling relevant data was practically impossible as long as their data were locked up in books, journals, et cetera, classified in all areas of knowledge. To solve their problem they developed the Human Relations Area Files, an expensive solution to be sure— but a solution that enables them to do their

research. In other areas, too—petroleum geology, physical education, journalism, for example—scholars are using microfacsimile reproduction techniques to get around the problem of the rigidity of the traditional containers for knowledge we librarians tend to accept as inevitable.

In fact, in developing patterns for a library system in a university, we would do well to realize that the old order is breaking up. No one can see what the future will be like but we should be watching for the developments.

Anyone who watched the two political conventions in the summer of 1960 must know that historians of the future will need access to the visual and auditory tapes of these proceedings as much as to the printed record of what happened. Will they find these tapes in our libraries? Is the bound journal the right container for new research, now that we have microfilms, cards, prints, and fiche? Aren't all of our accepted containers and storage methods that are tied to a philosophy of scarcity of print likely to be outmoded now that it is possible to adopt a philosophy of abundance of print?

Yes, but how do these ideas change the planning of library buildings? No one knows. The best we can do is to make certain that the space we provide is capable of adaptation. The Bell Telephone Laboratories in New Jersey are still the best place to study library planning.

People and Plans

Too often planning is done without consideration for the capacities and limitations of the librarians who will offer the interpreting services in the libraries. Machines for storing and retrieving information are with us and they will undoubtedly increase the power of librarians to help users of literature but they will not replace the need for librarians. [10]

The essential question is how wide a span of scholarship can a librarian manage effectively? This is a matter of levels of use. For the "general education" or "liberal education" levels of higher education a librarian like Mrs. Roberta Keniston is, and will continue to be, the right kind of librarian. The generalist, well educated in the mainstream of our basic ideas, well trained in the general reference and bibliographic tools and approaches to scholarship, is exactly the right kind of librarian to manage that kind of library. Fortunate indeed is the university that can find a person also with the knowledge of young people, the respect of the faculty and the personal charm of a Mrs. Keniston!

For the higher and more specialized levels of scholarship, however, the days of the generalist reference librarians are past. A division of two or three departmental literatures is as wide a span of mastery as one can expect. A librarian who has specialized up to the Ph.D. level in one subject can master the reference and bibliographic tools and the basic literature of a division well enough to serve the needs of researchers.

Thus, it would follow that in developing building plans for a university library pattern at the research level, the subject division is as broad a grouping as one dares use. Of course, it is possible to assemble a pool of reference specialists who will work from a more inclusive collection. The danger is that financial limitations will force the scheduling of these specialists in such a manner that each will be forced to act as a generalist. An academic community soon learns the capabilities of the Reference staff and places demands on them accordingly.

FOOTNOTES

[1] R. E. Ellsworth, "College Students and Reading," *The American Scholar,* Fall, 1958, pp. 473-481.

[2] L. B. Mayhew, *New Frontiers in Learning.* (Columbia, Mo., 1959), 38 pp.

[3] Harvie Branscomb, *Teaching with Books;* and Wilhelm Munthe, *American Librarianship from a European Angle.*

[4] R. E. Ellsworth, "Library Architecture and Buildings," *Library Quarterly,* 25: 66-75, Jan., 1955.

[5] A. S. Macdonald, "Library of the Future," *Library Journal,* 58: 971-5, Dec. 1; 1023-5, Dec. 15, 1933.

[6] R. E. Ellsworth, "Determining Factors in the Evaluation of the Modular Plan for Libraries," *College and Research Libraries,* April, 1953, pp. 125-129.

[7] Chauncey Boucher, *The Chicago College Plan.* Chicago University Press, 1935.

[8] R. E. Ellsworth, "To What Extent Can We Integrate?" *College and Research Libraries,* 8: 401-4, October, 1947.

[9] William Dix, "Undergraduate Libraries," *College and Research Libraries,* 14: 271-2, July, 1953.

[10] J. Myron Jacobstein, *Law Library Journal* (forthcoming issue, probably November, 1960). "Law Librarianship, Documentation, and Semantics."

ABOUT THE AUTHOR

—**Ralph E. Ellsworth,** Director of Libraries and Professor of Bibliography, University of Colorado; Ph.D., 1937, University of Chicago. Currently he is preparing a volume on book storage. His major interest is library building planning.

Libraries

by Alvin Toffler

In this presentation the author traces the evolution of the modern academic library and suggests directions for the future. In the past, the physical and ascribed characteristics of information media resulted in a library building, however this building might be influenced by engineering capability or architectural style. That this certainty may now be questioned by changes in educational concepts and an advanced technology does not diminish the need for information functions and professional competence in its management.

Fifteen years ago a revolution swept the planning of college and university libraries. A new type of library sprang up on the grounds of many campuses—a clean-lined contemporary library that emphasized efficiency and economy, occasionally at the cost of beauty or comfort. Today the initial force of that revolution has spent itself. Campus planners, architects, and librarians are, modifying its principles, softening the lines of the revolutionary model, adding grace to its form, and shaping the library to accommodate man in all his individual variety. The result is a more human library than any we have ever known. But already a new revolution is brewing, one that promises to be more profound and far-reaching than any to date. For while the changes of the recent past adapted the library to man, the coming revolution must adapt the library to the machine. And there are those who insist that this is impossible, that, in fact, the library will be completely swallowed up by the machine.

Some argue forcefully that the library and the book itself are mere relics of an inefficient past, that the job of storing, retrieving, and transmitting information will, in the future, be accomplished without either. They point out that there is nothing inviolable about the book or its storehouse, that cuneiform tablets gave way to papyrus rolls, that medieval manuscripts gave way to books, and that books are already sharing the job of communicating information with other carriers. Already most libraries store records, tapes, films, slides, and other non-book materials. The rise of the computer and the development of a whole new technology of information, these prophets charge, will inevitably transform the role of the book in modern society.

It is ironic that the death or downgrading of the book should be debated seriously today. The American higher education community is in the midst of a library-building boom of unprecedented scope and thrust. According to the U. S. Office of Education, between 1958 and 1959, 52 new campus library structures rose at a cost estimated at $29,500,000. Between 1960 and 1961 another 69 new campus libraries sprang up at a cost of $38,650,000. And in the five-year period 1961-1965, fully 504 more libraries will come into being on college or university campuses at a cost of approximately $466,600,000. This means we are spending an annual average of over $93,000,000 on these new buildings designed to bring book and scholar together. These impressive figures do not include the cost of the books themselves, of salaries, or other operating expenses.

Why, at a time when the book is for the first time in history being challenged, are we pouring so much time, energy, and money into new libraries for our institutions of higher education? Campus libraries are overcrowded. Educators believe that college and university libraries should be able to seat anywhere from 25 to 50 percent of the total enrollment of the institution at any given time. Yet the latest figures of the U. S. Department of Health, Education and Welfare paint a stark picture of

SOURCE: Reprinted from Alvin Toffler, "Libraries," in Educational Facilities Laboratories, *Bricks and Mortarboards; A Report on College Planning and Building* (New York: 1964), pp. 71-87, 97-98, by permission of the publishers.

shortages in capacity: "For the aggregate United States, as of December 31, 1957, the number of students who could be seated at one time in higher education library reading rooms represented 16.2 percent of the fall of 1957 enrollment." Construction since then has done little to narrow the gap. In fact, it may have widened since this report.

Behind the shortage of teaching capacity lies the powerful surge in student enrollment. And of the swelling wave of students descending on the colleges and universities, an increasing proportion go on to graduate study. According to Francis H. Horn, president of the University of Rhode Island, "They require much more service than do undergraduates. More space is needed. ... This means that libraries cannot be expected to provide for twice as many students in the future just by doubling present facilities, staffs, and appropriations." Furthermore, students at all levels are using libraries more than in the past. According to an announcement from Cornell University, "Students have been reading more books, too; during 1959-1960 a total of 873,903 books are recorded as having been used by Cornell students," not counting reference books. "This means that students at Cornell on the average are consulting annually—in addition to their regular texts—more than 80 library books each—a stack of books from 12 to 15 feet high." By 1960-1961 the average had climbed further to 89 books per student.

An increase in library usage is reported almost everywhere. Says Stephen A. McCarthy, director of Cornell University Libraries: "This phenomenal rise in library use—steady over the last few years—apparently results from changes in teaching methods and from a greater sense of urgency and purpose on the part of the students." Henry James, assistant librarian at the Lamont Undergraduate Library at Harvard adds: "Today education is more sophisticated. Assignments are made not from a single book, but from many books, from government documents, pamphlets, journals, and magazine articles."

Meanwhile, another explosive force is at work. This is the accelerating growth in the number of books, journals, and other materials that libraries must house. The world has never known such a rapid proliferation of knowledge. In the words of the *Wall Street Journal:* "Every 24 hours enough technical papers are turned out around the globe to fill seven sets of the 24-volume *Encyclopedia Brittanica.* The output is rising every year. This year's crop: some 60,000,000 pages or the equivalent of about 465 man-years of steady around-the-clock reading." A more recent estimate by Charles P. Bourne of the Stanford Research Institute put the number of significant journals being published around the world at 15,000, with perhaps 1,000,000 significant papers in them each year. These figures do not include books and other forms of publication. Information specialists say that the sheer quantity of information is doubling every 10 years.

The library that expects to serve its readers, and especially faculty researchers, must somehow attempt to keep up with this tidal wave of data. No library can store everything. But as intellectual disciplines subdivide into specialties and the relationships between disciplines multiply, collections must grow. The fantastic information explosion not only means that storage space must be expanded rapidly or some other means of storage developed, but that the costs of cataloging, clerical processing, and retrieving material are skyrocketing. Scholars, faculty researchers, and graduate students are drowning in a sea of data, and locating and obtaining any specific item of information is becoming harder and more time consuming.

Under such pressures the campus library is being transformed. The library of the University of Illinois Chicago Undergraduate Division, for example, will have to grow 1,000 percent in less than 10 years, and is making preparations to do so. Cornell's new seven-story library, completed in 1960 at a cost of $5,700,000, houses 2,000,000 volumes, is cataloging new titles at the rate of 80,000 a year, and will be hard pressed for space again within 15 years.

At the same time, colleges and universities themselves are undergoing changes that must affect libraries. Colleges are becoming universities, meaning that their libraries must increase their collections to permit graduate research and more faculty use. Universities are broadening their scope to encompass new specialties. Moreover, educational philosophy itself is changing. As a result, according to Ralph Ellsworth, director of libraries for the

University of Colorado, and a leading consultant on library construction: "Most libraries built before 1950 are either totally unusuable or need to be remodeled or enlarged." The challenge confronting planners has never been so massive or so complex.

How may this challenge be met? How may the urgent demands of the present be confronted without compromising the future? How real is the threat to both book and library as we know them? To answer these and similar questions, it is necessary to cast a glance backward at the traditional library, at the upheaval that so recently replaced it, at the mood of library planners as they consolidate the gains of the past, and only then at the multiple possibilities of the future.

MONSIEUR LABROUSTE'S SKYSCRAPER

Libraries have been in existence at least since Assurbanipal, the Assyrian emperor of 2,500 years ago, kept a crew of copyists busy collecting and copying samples of the literature of his time. And builders have been worried about library design since the Roman Vitruvius urged that library rooms face east so that scholars might have the benefit of the morning sun as they bent over their scrolls. But the classic design of the library in modern times was established by a French architect, Henri Labrouste. M. Labrouste built a great library in Paris, the Bibliothèque Nationale, begun in 1858 and finished 10 years later. In doing so, he created a tradition that endured almost a century. The Bibliothèque Nationale was a monumental structure with vast, high-ceilinged reading rooms, elaborately decorated and covered with a huge dome. Inside it, M. Labrouste constructed what was, in effect, a small skyscraper within a building— a five-story framework of cast iron columns and wrought iron beams—a gigantic rack to house the shelving for 900,000 volumes. Since this part, the stack, was closed to the public and not visible to outsiders, M. Labrouste felt free to do away with the ornamentation that covered the public spaces, and therefore to create a truly functional building within one that was not.

This same basic concept embracing two sharply differentiated parts, one grandly elaborate, the other Spartan in its simplicity, became the model for hundreds of libraries subsequently built elsewhere, and today monumental libraries, descendants of M. Labrouste's Bibliothèque, still dominate scores of American college and university campuses.

In these, as a rule, the section open to the public is an aggregate of reading or working rooms clustered around a central reading hall whose ceiling towers as much as 30 or 40 feet above the long tables and straight-backed chairs ranged below. Natural light filters in from windows set high above the floor. Huge marble stairways wind leisurely from floor to floor, and upstairs, somewhere near the top level, there may be small book-lined seminar rooms in which groups of students can meet with their professors. Each room is set off from the others by thick, immovable, load-bearing walls. The stack area, either housed within the main building or in a separate annex connected with the main building, consists of tier after tier of shelves, narrow staircases, and cramped aisles. Often floors are constructed of translucent glass tile so that light from a skylight in the roof may seep downward into the warehouse-like gloom.

While some of the monumental libraries that dot American campuses are, in their way, beautiful buildings, most were neither beautiful nor efficient from the beginning, and most are cripplingly inefficient today. Yet monumentalism reigned over the American campus right down through the 1930's. One after another, major new library buildings cropped up on university grounds, each a variation of the same basic theme. At Harvard, at Stanford, at Minnesota, Michigan, Illinois, and elsewhere the same lofty ceilings, impressive stairways, and ornamented walls turned up. Architects vied to make the buildings look imposing. To quote Ralph Ellsworth again, "The monumentality of a library was accepted as a symbolic measure of respect for knowledge in the minds of the university community."

The monumental library turned out to be hard to wire and light artificially, and almost impossible to heat and air condition efficiently. It was wasteful of space too. As much as 25 percent of its gross space was assigned to wide stairways, impressive lobbies, thick walls, and service facilities, leaving only 75 percent for actual library functions. But its chief drawback was its rigidity. Each room or working space was designed to serve a single function and, set off by load-bearing walls, could be altered only with extreme difficulty. As functions changed with the passage of years, the rooms became increasingly inefficient.

This is illustrated by the change in the function of the stack. Throughout history, until fairly recently, the book (or the tablet or manuscript) was expensive and frequently rare. The library was primarily a repository, and the librarian's first impulse was to protect the collection from the reader. In the Middle Ages, books were chained to iron bars on library desks. In church libraries, monks wrote "book curses" into them to deter thieves. In our own country in 1667 the overseers of Harvard University ruled that "No scholar in the College, under a Senior Sophister shall borrow a book out of the library." This air of possessiveness was reflected during M. Labrouste's time in the exclusion of readers from the stack.

By the 1920's, however, the whole philosophy of librarianship had begun to shift. Service to the reader became far more important than it had been. Books were cheaper, more easily available. On campuses, libraries came to be regarded less as passive repositories and more as an active part of the teaching machinery. This new emphasis was reflected in a movement to throw the stack open to the student. Educators came to believe that there is positive intellectual value in encouraging the student to browse among thousands of books. By the 1920's the open, or at least partially open, stack had become commonplace among small- and medium-size libraries. The stack had thus become something more than just a place for storage.

This shift in the function of the stack dramatized the rigidity of the old monumental library. The tightly packed stack, created for maximum storage, lacked adequate aisle space for browsing. There was no handy place to set a table for readers to use near the shelves. Lighting and ventilation were inadequate for the increased traffic in the stack. Nor could the old-fashioned stack, designed to exclude rather than welcome people, be easily converted. The change in the philosophy of service created a conflict between function and form.

Similarly, as other concepts of librarianship changed with changing times, the frozen forms of the old monumental buildings stood

more and more in the way of simple, efficient, and modern operation. Constricted by the walls around them, librarians took up the cry for more functional surroundings. During the 1930's the Depression slowed down the construction of new facilities. But by the early forties the attack on the monumental library had gained great force.

ENTER MR. MODULE

Ever since the mid-thirties Angus Snead Macdonald, a manufacturer of library shelving, had urged a radical change in library design. By 1943 he had built a mock-up of a completely new kind of library building. The contemporary library, Mr. Macdonald argued, should throw out the cliches of monumentalism. It should be built of light steel columns, beams, and panels. The columns should be hollow, providing vertical ducts for air conditioning. The cool air should flow into hollow chambers in the floors and be distributed into the rooms through registers in the ceilings. The ceilings, themselves, should be built to permit installation of flush lighting fixtures. And most important, each room should be set off, not by load-bearing walls, but by easily movable steel partitions.

Mr. Macdonald campaigned vigorously in articles and speeches for his idea of simple, wide-open spaces in libraries, broken only by impermanent walls that could be moved as functions in the library changed. Instead of thick walls to bear the weight of the upper stories, carefully distributed columns would do the job. The spaces bounded by these columns, i.e., the structural bays, were termed "modules," and Mr. Macdonald soon became known in the library profession as "Mr. Module," a tribute to his persistence and vigor.

Mr. Macdonald's ideas struck a responsive chord in Ralph Ellsworth, then librarian at the State University of Iowa. Dr. Ellsworth, a tall, husky, outspoken man, energetically proselytized for experimentation with Mr. Macdonald's ideas, and promptly began, with the backing of his institution, to build a so-called modular library at Iowa. The dominance of monumentalism came to an abrupt end.

The swiftness of the modular revolution was amazing. From the time Dr. Ellsworth built his new library at Iowa down to the present, hardly a single major campus library has been built in this country that has not, in one way or another, followed his lead. Few accepted every jot and tittle of Mr. Macdonald's mock-up. Even Dr. Ellsworth was unable to make use of the hollow columns. But free-flowing space became an article of faith in what can now be called the modular era. The modular library made possible an easy intermixture of reading spaces and stack spaces. The stack, instead of being structurally independent, was part of the building. Readers could move freely and comfortably through those stack areas open to them. The elimination of space-wasting stairways, thick walls, and elaborate decoration proved economical. Up to 85 percent of gross space could actually be turned to true library use.   Electrical outlets and ventilating ducts were easier to install and to alter. But most important of all, the modular plan made possible libraries that, in the words of one librarian, "you don't have to blow apart with dynamite to change."

The modular revolution affected almost every physical element of the building. The stack, the most rigid element of the traditional campus library, was transformed. In the traditional multi-tier stack, a series of vertical columns thrust up from the base to the top of the stack building. Floors were built around them, usually at intervals of about 7-1/2 feet. The vertical columns were set in rows 3 feet apart, and the shelving actually hung on them so that all the weight was borne by these columns rather than the floors. The floors, in consequence, were relatively thin.

In the modular library the stacks are not structural elements at all. Instead, they consist of free-standing bookcases easily shifted from place to place. For standardization purposes they are still usually made in sections 3 feet long, but while the traditional stacks were made in rows set apart 4-1/2 feet center to center, the aisle can now be made any desired width. Ordinarily, the 4-1/2-foot width is still used, except where tables and other furniture are interspersed with bookcases. These dimensions, 3 by 4-1/2, are often used to help determine the horizontal dimensions of the module or

bay. Today architects strive to make the bay as large as possible in an effort to minimize the number of columns necessary and thereby enhance the easy convertibility of the space. Architect Gyo Obata, whose firm, Hellmuth, Obata and Kassabaum, is helping to create a new $25,000,000 campus for Southern Illinois University at Edwardsville, Illinois, has designed a library that uses a 30 by 30 foot module, and at the University of Illinois at Chicago, architect Walter A. Netsch, Jr., of Skidmore, Owings and Merrill, has planned what is probably the largest module of any in the academic library field—30 by 45 feet.

One factor that limits the size of the module is floor strength. The farther apart the columns are spaced, the stronger the floors have to be. This adds to cost. According to Mr. Obata, after a certain point, as the span widens, "You have to begin to do extra things like tensioning the reinforcing steel or using higher strength concrete to get the bigger span. The depth of your structural floor system gets much deeper, and you take on more height in the building." Just where the convenience of a larger bay warrants extra expenditure and where it does not is a point in hot dispute among architects and librarians, with most building planners leaning toward dimensions of 22-1/2 feet or 27 feet.

As the bay or module expands, the floors tend to grow fatter. In modular buildings the books may be stored anywhere, and the floors must be able to carry a load of about 200 pounds per square foot. In addition, false ceilings are often hung beneath the structural floor leaving space above to accommodate ducts, wiring, and lighting fixtures. This, too, adds thickness. Some modern libraries have floors as thick as five feet. At Washington University, whose new $3,000,000 library opened this fall, the architects, Murphy and Mackey, used flat slab concrete floors 9 inches thick, with drop ceilings hung from them only in certain parts of the buidling and not over the stacks.

The modular library concept also radically altered classical notions about the vertical space between floors—that is, room height. An adult can comfortably use a bookshelf that is about 7 feet tall. In traditional buildings, with the stark structure divided into stories roughly 7-1/2 feet high, the surrounding reading rooms were frequently built so that their floors tied into certain stack floors. This meant that room heights were almost always multiples of the basic 7-1/2-foot height of a single story in the stack. The lowest ceiling in a reading room was likely to be two stack levels high, or about 15 feet. The great reading hall, of course, was likely to be much taller. The consensus was that human beings are uncomfortable in rooms with low ceilings.

The modular library directly challenged this notion. According to Keyes D. Metcalf, Librarian Emeritus of Harvard and the dean of library construction consultants, the death knell of the high ceiling came when Princeton performed an unusual experiment. In preparing to build its own modular library, he says, "Princeton built a two-bay mock-up with a fake ceiling and cranked it up and down. They brought in librarians, students, architects, college presidents, faculty members, and others and asked them to holler when it got uncomfortable. They found the users could take it as low as 8'4" in a room as large as 25 by 36 feet." At Iowa, the library Dr. Ellsworth built has 8-foot ceilings. Today, most modular libraries incorporate heights of about 8'6" for their reading areas.

The modular library brought with it air conditioning. The musty odor of the old-fashioned stack and the suffocating closeness of the cavernous reading room have been replaced by scientific comfort control. Libraries now being built are using air-conditioning equipment to accomplish a whole number of ends. First, temperature and humidity control make readers and staff comfortable all year around. Second, in many libraries, the air is electronically filtered to remove odors, smoke particles, and dust, thus reducing the time and money that must be spent cleaning the rooms and the collection. Many new libraries are "pressurized"—i.e., the air-conditioning level is such that when a door or window is opened air is forced out, thus keeping dirty or dusty air from rushing in. Third, the noise level of the system is so adjusted that it masks distracting sounds like the click of heels on tile, the clatter of a typewriter, or the opening and closing of doors. The air-conditioning system, in ef-

fect, maintains a comfortable backdrop noise. (Where the air-conditioning system has been set to operate too quietly, library users complain the building is noisy.)

The most important distinguishing characteristic of the modular library is the so-called loft space that is created by this type of design. Librarians are given great, wide-open spaces, whole floors broken only by a minimal number of fixed vertical elements. Architects, aware that any immovable vertical element constricts the librarian's freedom, have attempted to cluster the service areas in places where they get in the way of library functions as little as possible. In many libraries they are pushed outward toward the walls to leave the internal space clear. At Southern Illinois University this idea is to be carried one step further. Mr. Obata's plans call for pushing the service cores part way outside the walls. Thus, around the squarish three-story building rise six four-story towers. Each juts out from the walls of the building, rather than consuming space inside the walls. These house the elevator shafts, stairways, toilets, mechanical equipment, etc.

The modular revolution gave the librarian economy, efficiency, and a new sense of openness never before experienced. It also gave him the freedom to adapt his buildings to change.

THE HUMANIZATION OF THE MODULAR

Today the modular revolution, having triumphed, is in a new phase. The period of revolutionary zeal is over. A period of revision has begun—a period in which architects, librarians, consultants, and planners are rethinking their principles and applying them in new ways. Modularism is undergoing humanization.

When the modular revolution began, shortly after World War II, its critics charged that it would create large numbers of standardized, factory-like libraries across the country. Similar design principles had been used in the hasty construction of aircraft plants and similar structures during the war. Characteristically, they were long, low, unrelievedly bleak, and unimaginative. The loft spaces in them were too big, emphasizing the closeness of the ceilings and giving the interiors a claustrophobic appearance. The ruthless elimination of ornament heightened their look of grim, uninviting efficiency.

It is true that the modular revolution, like most revolutions, brought with it some excesses. A number of early modular libraries shared these unpleasant characteristics. But since the mid-fifties increasing attention has been paid to making college and university libraries livable.

What might be called the new humanism of the library can be seen in the way space is cut up and put together, as well as in the way it is subsequently furnished.

Inside the library, space must be set aside for a number of basic functions. Apart from the stack and the reading rooms, there must be space for a lobby, a centrally located card catalog, a reserve book room where students can come for assigned reading of books which are stocked in multiple copies by the library, a periodicals room, a reference room, a circulation counter and work space for the staff, receiving and shipping rooms, and work space for cataloging, mending, binding, ordering, or otherwise processing books.

Most new libraries now add to the basic areas listed above, special rooms for typing, for record listening, for seminars, small offices for faculty members engaged in research, conference rooms, lounges for student and staff, rare book rooms, exhibition spaces, and special lounges and study rooms for smokers. (Some libraries now permit smoking throughout and provide a few no-smoking rooms.) The Temple University library now being built in Philadelphia will even provide special study areas for blind students. Increasing attention to the needs of the individual rather than the mass is leading to increasing variety in space assignments.

This accent on the individuals is reflected also in the growing importance now placed on providing private and semi-private study space for students . The large reading room of the past, with its long wooden tables and its institutional climate, is now being replaced by smaller rooms and alcoves, some formed by imaginative stack arrangements. According to Ralph Ellsworth: "It has been proven over and over again in college libraries that students don't like to read in large open reading rooms. They like the privacy and the intimacy of small groups. They do not want

to sit at flat tables in the middle of a large reading room."

This finding is strongly supported by the results of a survey conducted by four institutions, Amherst, Smith, Mt. Holyoke, and the University of Massachusetts. Nearly 400 students were polled on their preferences for certain types of study space. The results, in the words of the subsequent report, are a "challenge to the typical large library reading room. It may be economical in terms of the cost per student user, but it is expensive in terms of the quality of work done."

Just as the size of the reading room is growing smaller, more space is being devoted to individual seating, and especially to the use of carrels. (The study carrel is a small table with a raised partition on one, two, or three sides to screen off from the seated student visual distractions that interfere with concentration.) Says Keyes Metcalf, who planned the Lamont Undergraduate Library at Harvard and who has served as consultant to hundreds of other libraries around the world, "Since 1915 many libraries have provided large numbers of carrels for graduate students. Since 1949 we've had a great many individual seats in all parts of libraries, and I dared to put in up to 50 percent individual seating when we were designing Lamont just after World War II. That was as far as I could go then. Today if it were done, I'd go to 75 or 80 percent individual seating—and this for undergraduates." In university libraries, where many graduate students make use of the library, the proportion might even be higher. Carrels are often interspersed in or near the stack areas. At the just-opened Van Pelt Library of the University of Pennsylvania, individual work desks are built directly into the stack bookcases.

In many large libraries where long tables are still used, fewer students are placed at them. Thus at Washington University in St. Louis the large reading rooms are furnished with tables intended to seat eight, but only six chairs are ranged around them. At the beautiful new library of Colorado College, in Colorado Springs, the main reading room is furnished with small round tables for four.

This scaling down of space in the campus library for use by individuals or small groups rather than masses—this humanization of the modular library—has been accompanied by attempts to make the spaces themselves more inherently interesting and varied. Walter Netsch bluntly calls it "demodularization." and thinks it is a good thing. As he sees it, architects are now seeking to combine the beauties of the classical library with the efficiencies of the modular. "The classical idea of the dome is gone. But the new idea of the box is gone also," he says.

Behind this impulse toward modification of the box, Mr. Netsch says, is the need of mankind for a variety of space, rather than a uniformity of space. "You can have a world that's nine feet tall. It's technically feasible. . . . But there is no universal space. Mankind needs different kinds of spaces for different kinds of activities."

Architect Obata expresses the need for variety and beauty in other terms: "Within the essentially horizontal spaces of the pure modular library we have very little chance to create any spaces that would add a new dimension for a person going through the building."

Ralph Ellsworth sees what is happening as less of a retreat from the modular than an advance in our ability to handle it. "We went through a period," he says, "when the architects took the modular idea and wrapped it up and put a cover around it. It's ugly. But now they are viewing the structure. They're learning how to use the medium, and some of the new modular libraries are extraordinarily beautiful."

One way in which architects are striving to regain the human element, the variety they find lacking in the unrelieved horizontality of the modular libraries, is through the creation of contrasting high-ceilinged spaces. At Washington University, designed by Murphy and Mackey, this takes the form of a small court that cuts through the building like an off-center hole in a donut and reaches up to open to the sky. This small square patio is moved off toward one corner of the large building so that it interferes little with the free space within. At Colorado College, a much smaller library achieves relief from the horizontal quality by creating a reading area that is two stories high with a mezzanine running around all four sides above it and a skylight roofing it over. This atrium, is indeed, a throwback to the high-ceilinged reading room of the past. But because it is in a small building, and is carefully furnished with small tables and groupings of lounge furniture, it avoids the institutional look. Its scale is human and intimate, its appearance warm and inviting.

This same concern for warmth and individuality is evident in the way in which new libraries are being outfitted. The old library, says Ellsworth Mason, librarian of Colorado College, speaking of his campus, "kept a lot of students out simply because it was totally unaesthetic and in a style that was dead as far as these kids were concerned. So we've paid very careful attention to appearnce. The looks of a building influence very greatly whether or not the student wants to come in."

Today libraries are taking on some of the comfort of the home or of a well-furnished dormitory. The accent is on the provision of a variety of furniture forms so that each individual temperament can find some comfortable working space. As the four-college report on study habits declared: "Most institutional furniture is bought in standard sizes, but students don't come that way."

In consequence, libraries are getting away from the so-called standard items and sizes. Here is what one architect, Theodore Wofford, of Murphy and Mackey, had to say about his firm's findings after building the new Washington University library and working on several others: "In a modular building the furniture becomes very important. We found that the traditional library suppliers had standard sizes, mostly geared to high-volume high school libraries, and much of it badly designed. So we gambled and went to high-quality furniture houses. Working with the library staff, we programmed each piece of furniture for them, giving them the size, its purposes, etc., and asked them if they would be interested in a no-strings-attached arrangement to develop designs to meet our requirements. Many did. And so did some of the regular library suppliers.

"This took two years. We worked with Knoll, Herman Miller, Jens Risom, Dunbar, Steelcase, General Fireproofing and others, including Art Metal and Remington Rand. Some of the houses came up with a full line of designs. The fine furniture houses are increasingly aware of the volume of library building and are eyeing this market.

This whole process paid off. We took the best furniture we could afford, and we feel we have a more attractive and comfortable library than we might have gotten by doing things the standard way."

Fabric or leather-covered armchairs, coffee tables, couches, and table lamps turn up with increasing frequency in alcoves, lounges, or lobbies of the humanized library. In the study rooms a variety of carrels are being tried out, offering different kinds of partitions, some with shelves for storing books, others with extra large surfaces, some made of wood panels, others of various kinds of peg board composition. Says Walter Netsch: "We need to do more research on the efficiency of different kinds of study room furniture. Aside from the standard carrel, consideration should also be given to the old-fashioned stand-up carrel. Maybe some people like to work that way. Remember Thomas Wolfe wrote standing up. And how about the big over-sized tablet arm that Ben Franklin had on his chair. We need maximum variety."

The concern for comfort is also more and more evident to anyone who looks downward in a library. Carpets, once unknown in the library, and bitterly opposed by maintenance people, are now turning up as a pleasant, efficient, economical addition to modern campus libraries. "A reference librarian walks eight miles a day," says Colorado's Mr. Mason, "and our beautiful carpeting is wonderful for the staff. But the kids love it, too. They will sit down in front of a stack right on the floor to browse through a low shelf. I find myself doing it!"

Says architect Eugene Mackey, "There's been a terrific breakthrough in carpeting, on price as well as in the kinds there are—acrilan, nylon, dacron—and others. And you can use them to provide color."

A cost analysis drawn up for the John Crerar Library at Illinois Institute of Technology shows the comparitive costs of carpeting, cork tile, vinyl asbestos tile, homogenous vinyl tile, and asphalt tile. Initial costs for carpeting are still higher than for any of the other kinds of floor covering included. But maintenance costs are significantly lower, and the most expensive grade of carpeting analyzed in the study turned out to be cheaper to own and maintain than all other types of covering in less than 8 years. The carpeting was given a life expectancy of 15 years.

Carpeted, colorful, and quiet, tastefully designed and decorated, offering a variety of spaces and furnishings for its users, the humanized modular library of today is a far cry from the rather formal, artificially hushed, poorly ventilated, and dimly lighted library of the not-too-distant past.

THE STUPIDEST MONK PROBLEM

Hundreds of years ago Leibnitz predicted that, "If the world goes on this way for a thousand years and as many books are written as today, I am afraid that whole cities will be made up of libraries." Today more books are being written than ever and although no city has yet been drowned under a sea of paper, thoughtful librarians have long been pondering whether libraries must—or can—continue to increase the size of their collections *ad infinitum.* The increase is swelling both the size and the cost of campus libraries.

A growing body of opinion holds that librarians must get over the traditional idea that the bigger the collection, the better the library. Perhaps the most vociferous critic of the size of libraries today is Mortimer Taube, a former librarian, now chairman of the board of a company called Documentation, Inc. "Libraries are too big today," Mr. Taube charges. "The question is how much of the total past are you going to embalm? The stupidest book written by the stupidest monk in the Middle Ages is a rarity today. We want to own it, not because it contains useful information but because it's a historical artifact. This attempt to embalm the living past is silly. Why, we're worse than the ancient Egyptians. We're trying to mummify the past. An enormous number of the books collected today are not collected as books at all. Nobody wants to read them. They are collected because their very existence is presumed to tell us something about the society that produced them. Is this the job of the library? And how many copies of each one do we need?"

To date no way has been found to stem the ever swelling tide of material that is finding its way into campus collections. But a number of positive steps have been taken. Libraries have begun serious programs aimed at weeding out insignificant items from their collections, and determining use patterns for the books and other materials they own.

Libraries are also banding together to carry out two other programs to help alleviate the problem of mushrooming collections. First, groups of libraries are linking up to create regional storage warehouses for their least-used materials. Thus there are today three interlibrary storage centers. The Mid-West Interlibrary Center in Chicago serves about 20 libraries from Kansas to Minnesota and Ohio; the Hampshire Interlibrary Center services Amherst, Smith, the University of Massachusetts, and Mt. Holyoke; and the New England center handles overflow from a dozen libraries in the Boston area, including Harvard, Tufts, and the Massachusetts Institute of Technology.

But putting books into storage is clearly not a final solution to the problem. While it is cheaper to store materials in warehouse space than in library space, there is a limit, too, to how much storage is practical. Says Mortimer Taube with a snort: "Dead storage is like making four copies of everything before you throw it away."

The second and more imaginative interlibrary program is designed to restrict the size of collections by birth control rather than *ex post facto* means. Called the Farmington Plan, this program brings together some 60 libraries into a systematic division of labor. Each participant is given responsibility for building its collection in a special field of knowledge. Thus Cornell has the nation's best collection of Icelandic literature: Harvard has the best collections in philosophy and law; Princeton's chief specialty is mathematics; and the University of Minnesota boasts the best Scandinavian collection. Each institution buys the periodicals in its own field, and goes lightly in other fields. In this way the nation's campuses can support first-rate collections without heavily duplicating one another's activity. All collections are recorded in the National Union Catalog so that scholars can locate their materials through a central clearinghouse.

Another step being taken by campus librarians to keep their expanding collections under control is called compact storage. Here, certain materials are stored in big drawers jammed full. They take up less space than they would if ranged on shelves in the normal manner. Though they are cumbersome to handle, some

libraries find this eminently practical for books and other materials that are called for infrequently.

But the most important and most promising steps to control the physical size of collections have to do with microreproduction, that is, the reduction of the materials to diminutive size. The best-known technique for doing this, of course, is microfilm. Here, the pages of periodicals or books may be reduced to fingernail size on strips of film. These, when needed, are fed through reading machines which enlarge the image and convert it to black on white. Microfilm techniques are hardly new, but they are being used more widely than ever before. One reason for this is the availability of more and more material in this form. At St. Louis University, for example, scholars have access to 600,000 manuscripts, including histories, biographies, chronicles, annals, notes, and other documents from the famed Vatican Manuscript Library. Between 1953 and 1955 crews of technicians shot 873,000 feet of film in the Vatican to compress 11,000,000 manuscript pages into manageable proportions, and thereby, with the permission of the Vatican, brought to the United States one of the world's great collections of the history of theology, philosophy, the church, and Renaissance humanism.

Today the librarian can also use similar techniques to compress collections. Microreproductions are available on index cards—microcards—and in other shapes and sizes. These techniques are regarded as especially important today when all libraries face the problem of book embrittlement. Recent studies have shown that much of the book paper produced since the turn of the century is subject to rapid deterioration. A recent test revealed that, of 400 books manufactured between 1900 and 1939, the paper in 89 percent of them had a fold strength less than that of newsprint. What this means is that the sheer passage of time will, before too many decades, literally destroy vast sections of present book collections. Microreproduction is looked to as a way of saving some of these doomed materials.

However, microreproduction techniques are not a panacea for the problem of sprawling collections. First, the need for a machine of some kind to enlarge the images means that users do not have the physical freedom that book users enjoy. The Council on Library

Resources is supporting studies aimed at developing a simple, light-weight, and effective pocket reader—an enlarging lens and bracket of some kind that readers can carry with them anywhere. But there are a number of prickly optical problems to be solved before this can be accomplished. Secondly, many readers, especially researchers, need the convenience of a book. Study through a reading enlarger makes it difficult to flip through pages to scan, or to browse for material. The machines often must be used in subdued light.

It is, of course, now possible to have photographic enlargements made of each frame of the microreproduction but this is still a fairly costly and time-consuming method. However, University Microfilms, Inc., in Ann Arbor, Michigan, has started a service through which Xerox copies, in paperbound form of microfilmed books can be obtained at 3-1/2 cents a page. Copies of doctoral dissertations run slightly higher—4-1/2 cents a page. But the service is limited to the firm's existing microfilm collection: 15,000 books printed in English prior to 1640, 6,000 out-of-print books, and 50,000 doctoral disserations.

From the point of view of the library planner, too, microreproduction is less advantageous than might seem at first blush. While the compression of collection material into diminutive form is, of course, a great space saver, the reading machines require space. As a result, until a library has a fairly large collection in microform, it is not likely to save much in square footage.

According to Verner W. Clapp, president of the Council on Library Resources: "Microfilm will enrich collections, not replace them. It is possible to make microfilm almost as convenient as books. But we haven't done it yet. At present it's downright abominable." Nevertheless, it is predictable that more and more use will be made of microreproduction in years to come. It is a sign of the times that the Mormon Geographical Society in Salt Lake City is building a reading room that will house 750 reading machines. The switchover to microfilm was partially responsible for a decision to abandon plans for a 15-story archives building to house the Society's records.

THE WIRED-IN STUDENT

The day is thus long past when libraries stored books alone. In addition to microform material, all new libraries now must make provision for new forms of material like phonograph records, tapes, films, slides, even, in some cases, kinescopes, and, of course, the machines needed to make use of these information carriers. Apart from special racks and storage facilities, and in some cases, special catalogs, the introduction of audio-visual equipment often brings with it the need for special areas in which it may be used. With instructors assigning spoken word LP records to their classes, so that the student may hear T. S. Eliot reading his own poetry of John Gielgud doing Hamlet, the listening booth or earphones have become commonplace in the campus library. Rooms are also set aside for the projection of movies, filmstrips, and slides.

The tape recorder is cropping up with ever greater frequency in college libraries, and the library stocks taped lectures, foreign language lessons, and similar material. In some libraries tape recorders are installed in booths or carrels. In others the student may pick up a portable unit at the reserve desk and carry it to a place set aside for listening. At Washington University a room has been set aside for mobile tape recorder units into which a number of students simultaneously may plug their earsets. With ever greater emphasis being placed on educational television, libraries are also equipping themselves for closed-circuit reception.

Another form of material that may be expected to become important in campus libraries is the teaching machine program. Librarians are talking about the day when teaching machines will be signed out as books are now.

Perhaps the most ambitious project presently in the development stage is the so-called environmental carrel. Unlike the traditional carrel which is nothing much more than a small table partially enclosed by partitions, the environmental carrel would be equipped to receive information electronically in a number of forms, and to dial out for the data needed.

Sol Cornberg, former director of studio and plant planning for the National Broadcasting Company and now head of his own firm of "designers in the communication arts," has been engaged by Grande Valley State College, a new institution near Grand Rapids, Michigan, to install the most up-to-date audio-visual equipment possible. The library now being built there will contain 256 carrels, each outfitted with a microphone, two loudspeakers, an eight-inch TV picture tube, and a telephone dial. As Mr. Cornberg describes it: "Any information stored in a 'use attitude' will be available to the student. There will be up to 310 audiotapes—that is, 310 talking books. These will be programmed for self-learning. On a typical day the student would go to his class or laboratory. That is, he would participate in a group learning activity. After his lesson he goes to his carrel for individual learning. There, by simply dialing a code number, he will be able to get a repeat of the lecture, excerpts as they apply to his assigned lesson, a list of problems. He will use the microphone to record his answers on tape, erase and correct them, if necessary, then dial his instructor. He then plays the tape for his instructor."

The advantage of this system, Mr. Cornberg says, "is that it presents a controlled environment. The student works at his own pace. There is no problem of being too shy to raise one's hand or too exhibitionistic and, therefore, a disruptive influence in the class. It's a more objective learning situation."

Such carrels could, in theory, be placed anywhere on the campus, not only in the library. But even if they were not housed in the library, the library would have the responsibility for storing the tapes, videotapes, films, and other materials. A similar system is envisioned as being part of the new library now planned at Stephens College in Columbia, Missouri. So far, it must be cautioned, no such fully equipped carrel has been placed in actual operation anywhere, but the technical problems of producing them are not overwhelming. Their usefulness, of course, will depend largely on how much information will be stored "in a use attitude"—that is, how much will be available in the appropriate forms and how much of that will be properly coded for remote dialing.

With the development of such mechanical teaching aids still in its infancy, it is impossible to predict just how deeply they will affect campus libraries. But already the audio-visual invasion has created design problems for academic libraries. The biggest and most important of these is whether, in fact, the entire audio-visual function should be a part of the library. At the Southern

Illinois University, where this question was thoroughly explored, the decision reached was that a separate "communications building" right next door to the library should house TV production studios and all audio-visual materials. "We felt it was developing so fast that it was important to put it in a separate building," says Mr. Obata. At Stephens College, a pioneer in the use of closed-circuit TV for teaching, the decision of the architects and planners again was that a special building was needed. "We started out to put all the audio-visual into the library," says Joseph Murphy of Murphy and Mackey, the architects. "We ended up finding that this was not as practical as it seemed. While the user in the library still has access to a full range of audio-visual resources, it was more sensible and economical to put the TV production and the master control facilities in a separate building. What we had was not a group of flexible spaces, but a group of specialized spaces and equipment that required studios and office space, and eventually needed a whole building."

In contrast, there are strong arguments for including audio-visual centers in library buildings. One is that libraries are equipped to acquire, process, and catalog the materials needed. Another argument is put forward by Keyes Metcalf, who points out that "We tend to build libraries about twice as large as they are needed at the time of construction because libraries double their collections in 16 years. This means that for the first few years you have extra space in the library. We have no idea how far audio-visual can go in the next few years, and it is therefore foolish to put up audio-visual buildings as such. The new library can give it space for the next 5 years, until we know more about how far it will go in higher education."

This fundamental policy question has not been decided by campus planners yet. It is likely to arouse heated controversy in the next few years.

BUILDINGS OF THE FUTURE

Before it committed itself to plans for a library at Edwardsville, Illinois, Southern Illinois University dispatched consultant Donald G. Moore to survey the technological advances that might affect its decision. Mr. Moore interviewed 43 experts employed by companies like

IBM, Lockheed, the Martin Company, Information Handling Services, System Development Corporation, Thompson Ramo Woolridge, Teleprompter Corporation, and R.C.A., as well as the Stanford Research Institute, and the University of California Radiation Laboratory. His preliminary report presents a striking and imaginative picture of the possibilities of the future. But his findings clashed directly with the views of Mr. Cornberg. The report declared: "There was nothing found that would conflict with the conclusion that the Edwardsville campus should have a book-containing library."

This conclusion is shared by hundreds of other librarians, architects, scientists, and technical experts. The present large-scale assault on the problems of information retrieval and storage, Mr. Moore reported, "is certain to have an impact on modern library facilities," within 10 years. But not so deep an impact as to make the library of books obsolete.

Today the library profession is watching the technological revolution with hawk-like concentration. "We know," says Ralph Ellsworth, "that the era of the 'handcraft' library is at and end." But this does not wash away the pressing need for new libraries *now,* the miracles of technology notwithstanding.

Today hundreds of colleges and universities go ahead with plans for new and better libraries than ever before. At the same time, they are keeping an eye cocked on the future, preparing for it as best they can. Hollow floors and ceilings going into new buildings are concealing miles of electrical conduit and ventilation ducting so that computers, punch card machines, TV screens, or other devices can be plugged in at any point. At UCLA, alert to the possibilities, a pneumatic tube planned for a new building was increased in diameter so that it might carry IBM cards without the need for them to be folded.

At the National Library of Medicine, which has had more experience with the machine age than any other library in the country, preparations are being made for bringing in a computer so that it may improve and speed up the work now done by punch card equipment in the compilation of *Index Medicus.* The changeover

has meant the installation of a false floor in the computer area to contain the wiring required and to serve as a plenum to dissipate the heat generated by the machine. Such floors now come in standard modular sections so that any section can be pulled out at will. A special 50-ton air conditioner is being readied, and another set aside for emergency service. Space is being allotted for the computer, for related machines, for parts and test equipment. A special fireproof vault is being built to store the precious magnetic tapes—the computer memory—when they are not in use.

The lack of extensive experience to date makes it impossible to predict accurately all the adjustments that must be made in the design of modern library buildings if they are to take full advantage of the coming age of automation. But the uncertainty that accompanies an age of rapid social and technological change proves the essential rightness of the modular revolution. For today, more than ever before, library buildings must avoid becoming frozen forms. They must be easily and swiftly convertible from one use to another. In the words of Ralph Ellsworth: "All we really know is that we should provide a good deal of uncommitted floor space that can accommodate rooms of varying size, each well-lighted, properly ventilated, with access to wiring ducts from which electrically powered machines can draw their power, with good soundproofing qualities. Such a building can be set up to meet the needs of the college at the present time and for the known future. This is about as far as our existing knowledge will permit us to go. . . . Our buildings should be capable of major expansion or of conversion to other uses."

The avalanche of technological discoveries, the accelerating pace of change may, as has been suggested, transform the library, eliminate the book, and provide still-unthought-of methods for collecting, storing, recovering, and communicating information. But for the foreseeable future the campus library, with all its primitive faults, will remain a vital part of our intellectual landscape. We need the know-how, money, and courage to make it just as good as humanly possible.

ABOUT THE AUTHOR

—**Alvin Toffler** is a former associate editor of *Fortune.* He teaches at the New School for Social Research. Mr. Toffler has done extensive research on culture in America and has acted as an advisor to the Rockefeller Brother's Fund Study of the Performing Arts.

Student Reactions to Study Facilities

The Committee for New College

The academic librarian tends to become bewildered when the manifest logic of the need for additional space to meet the library's requirements to house more students, more materials, and greater operational obligations elicits no regular response. In this he reflects, on a smaller scale, the sense of the academic administrator. The following study of the options provided students to support an aspect of educational behavior—an aspect in which the academic library has historically had a major commitment, legitimately or otherwise—illustrates how the definition of the library's role has direct implications for the total academic building program.

THE STUDY IN DETAIL

Subjects

For an explanation of the purpose and the origin of this study, the reader is referred to the Foreword. It is sufficient to state here that the purpose was to discover what kinds of study space were used by students, why they used it, and what they would prefer. It was hoped that the answers might be helpful to the planners of college buildings which were to be used as places in which study would take place.

The study was based upon samples of student behavior and opinions from Amherst College, Mount Holyoke College, Smith College, and The University of Massachusetts. Sophomores, juniors, and seniors were selected from a variety of dormitories, fraternities, and sororities. The following tables will indicate their distribution.

TABLE I.

College, Sex, and Residence of the Subjects

COLLEGE	MALES	FEMALES	DORMITORY RESIDENTS	FRATERNITY OR SORORITY RESIDENTS	TOTALS
Amherst	96		56	40	96
Mt. Holyoke		92	92		92
Smith		93	93		93
University of Massachusetts	35	40	56	19	75
Totals	131	225	297	59	356
Percentages	36.8	63.2	83.4	16.6	

TABLE II.

Distribution by Major Divisions of Study

MAJOR STILL UNSELECTED	HUMANITIES	SOCIAL SCIENCES	NATURAL SCIENCES	OTHERS
N 80	91	91	55	39
% 22.5	25.6	25.6	15.4	10.9

SOURCE: Reprinted from The Committee for New College, *Student Reaction to Study Facilities, with Implications for Architects and College Administrators. A Report to the Presidents of Amherst College, Mount Holyoke College, Smith College, and The University of Massachusetts* (Amherst: 1960), pp. 18-42, by permission of the publisher.

TABLE III.

Distribution by Classes

SOPHOMORES	JUNIORS	SENIORS
N 151	93	112
% 42.4	26.1	31.5

TABLE IV.

Distribution by Preparatory School Attended

PUBLIC HIGH SCHOOL	PRIVATE SCHOOL	PAROCHIAL
N 240	110	6
% 67.4	30.8	1.7

TABLE V.

Distribution by Number of Roommates

NONE	ONE	TWO	THREE-OR-MORE
N 77	198	45	36
% 21.6	55.6	12.6	10.1

There were 12 dormitories and 8 fraternities and sororities represented in the study. In some dormitories a better degree of cooperation was found than in others, but the total response, 49 percent, was good in view of the amount of work asked of the students. Only one group, the fraternities at one institution, failed to respond adequately. There was an attempt to select dormitories and other residences which would reflect such variables as old and new buildings, those near to and remote from the libraries, those with reputations of studiousness and those with less enviable records, representative of both large and small houses. The students showed a wide range of distribution throughout the curriculum, high school backgrounds, and residence conditions. In terms of academic ability there was less range, for the students in these institutions are highly selected. In terms of socio-economic scale there was a considerable range although the great majority were in the upper half as indicated by paternal occupation and education. There was a slight preponderance among the 356 respondents of students from the upper halves of their academic classes, 56.3%, in contrast to 43.7% from the lower halves. There is a predominance of women but no sex differences of significance appear in the findings.

The heterogeneity of four different institutions, residences, and diversity of libraries, rules, regulations, etc., was deliberately sought in the hope that either contrasts would show up, or that generalizations would appear which would have high validity and wide application because they existed in such diverse conditions.

Differences in the amounts of time devoted to study in the four colleges were slight. In the study diaries kept on each campus for four consecutive days, the range of the mean number of half-hours of study recorded by institutions was from 45.3 to 48.6. Dormitory residents studied a bit more than fraternity and sorority students at the same institutions, but not significantly. In one institution there was a difference between such groups of 1.9 hours per student in four days, while in the other it was one hour. As a consequence in some comparisons dormitory, fraternity, and sorority members were put into the same category, viz., dormitory residents.

Major Sources of Data

Each student participating in the study kept a study diary of where he studied, when he studied, and for how long. These diaries were kept on record sheets furnished to the students with the request that they be filled out each day. The time used consisted of four days, Dec. 1 to Dec. 4, 1959, Tuesday, Wednesday, Thursday, and Friday. These days were chosen in order to have an equal amount of time on each of the class schedule cycles in each institution and most students reported these days as "quite typical" or "fairly typical." The period chosen seemed a fairly representative time of study, with habits established and no unusual distractions or pressures. This could not, of course, be equally true of all subjects, but the time sample proved reasonably good. A few students, less than ten percent, used a different four days. The total number of hours of reported study was 8,375. It should be noted, however, that other periods might be weighted heavily with reviewing or paper writing which could conceivably shift the loci of studying somewhat. For an illustration of the diary form, see Appendix A.

A second source of information consisted of comments made by the students on a special sheet at the end of the study diary, on which they were asked: "1. What comments can you make about each of the study spaces used which will show in what respects it was satisfactory or otherwise? 2. Do you have any suggestions for the *improvement* of the study spaces in the dormitories, fraternities, library, etc?" The replies were informal and consequently difficult to organize or quantify. Yet they did yield good insights into student reactions to their own study space or what they conceived of as more ideal; and the fact that certain kinds of comments were repeated frequently did show a consensus.

A third source of data was an opinionnaire. This was divided into two sections. The first stated 72 specified study conditions and asked the students to indicate their opinion as to how desirable each of the conditions would be in an ideal college or university. A seven point scale was used. The second section consisted of 22 specified study conditions and asked the student to declare *how often* he would study under each condition. Responses were also to be recorded on a seven point scale running from "always" to "never". Since these duplicated a sample of the items in the first section, they served as a check upon consistency in student replies. For a sample opinionnaire, and the results obtained, see Appendix B.

Both the study diary and the opinionnaire were refined by try-outs with samples of students.

Supplementary Sources of Information

Interviews were conducted with the librarians at the different schools, with heads of houses, and other officials who might be able to throw some illumination upon student habits of study. These were not standardized interviews and consequently proved more useful in providing leads for further study and for interpretation of data than for tabulation.

Discussions with students were held both individually and in small groups before the study diary and opinionnaire were fully developed. These provided helpful suggestions about items for inclusion, the choice of dormitories to be studied, etc. They also shed interesting insights into local conditions and practices which might affect student reactions to study spaces. Their discussions helped to crystallize the belief that they, the customers had a great deal of valuable information about how study space worked out in fact as well as theory.

Visits to dormitories, fraternities, and libraries added another angle of observation. One could readily see why one dormitory proved a poorer place to study in than another. Mistakes in construction, lighting, heating, organization and operation were pointed out by student guides in the dormitories. Some of these errors were remediable and others avoidable in new construction. Similarly it was possible to see difficulties in the libraries—many of which were not so easily remediable. Some interesting attempts to adapt existing space to improve it for study purposes were seen. Again, these observations did not lead to tables and statistics, but they were helpful in confirming things indicated elsewhere.

The validity of such data as these depends upon the seriousness and competence of the students who contributed them. Partial checks for these lie in the consistency of behavior and opinions. If students had chosen study places which contradicted their opinionnaire or informal data, no confidence could have been placed in them. Instead the three major sources of data corroborated each other with a very high level of consistency on significant factors. On items which showed a wide range of opinion and behavior, and consequently much variability, no conclusions have been drawn. Having several sources of opinions and information also helped to make much more valid interpretations of behavior than if only once source had been tapped with a single method. For example, having an expression of attitudes on a seven point scale concerning specified conditions of study, plus informal written comments without specific questions, and free discussions with different groups of students or individuals, enabled us to test opinions and information for their consistency and meaning. There have been few attempts to make comparisons between small groups, living under specialized conditions; for such samples are too small to be reliable. Occasional speculations have been attempted, but these are so identified.

Methods of Handling Data

As much data as could be handled by machine tabulation was so treated. The opinionnaire readily lent itself to this, and the study diaries did also with some supplementary coding. Students used the code for different types of study successfully, and wrote out activities which they were not sure fitted into the codes. The latter were coded or discarded by the committee. Place names for studying had to be identified as to type by the representative or a deputy, on each campus, before being turned over to clerks for tabulation. Time reported by students showed a marked tendency to round numbers. In order to find some quick but accurate method of counting time for our purposes, several methods were tried and one of them proved accurate to an average of 7.5 minutes difference on 32 days of actual reported study time. Since we were interested in relative amounts of time spent in different places in varied activities, this was accurate enough for our purposes. The method consisted of counting anything less than 40 minutes reported in a given hour as a half hour, and anything over that as an hour. In an occasional record of three activities in a one hour period, one of the activities was almost invariably related to the work of a previous or subsequent hour and consequently could be attached to that hour. Rules for preparing the diaries for clerical workers were made and used so that uniformity of treatment at the four institutions could be obtained. Later clerical work was done for the most part by skilled clerks and an IBM sorting machine operator. Tables were compiled by the committee.

FINDINGS

Size of Space

The most conspicuous physical characteristic affecting student choices of places to study in is size. There is an inverse relation between the size of study places and their desirability. Even the compulsion of having to study in some large places in order to secure books or other materials is not enough to disguise the relation. Study space was divided into four categories of size. In the small size were dormitory rooms, library carrels, and studies for honor students. In the second category went such places as dormitory lounges, smokers, study halls, and library seminar rooms. Into a category of "moderately large" places were put empty classrooms, laboratories, studios, departmental libraries, dining rooms, and public social rooms like restaurants. The category of "large" contained only one type of space, large library reading rooms. The following tables show the differences in the use of such rooms and preferences expressed for them.

The verbal opinions of students agree very well with their behavior. There is not unanimity of opinion, but the tendency to prefer smaller places is clear and strong. Students are not completely free, of course, to study where they wish, and the compulsions to study are apt to be strongest in the large library reading rooms, since so many books are obtainable there only. There is compulsion of a similar sort about studio and departmental library work. For most students there is relatively little pressure to study in their rooms, although most college libraries could not meet the demand for chairs if all students suddenly decided not to study in their rooms any more. There is a very clear desire on the part of the majority of students to escape from large study places and use small ones. The dislike of the large places is not merely because of their size, but the fact that large study places normally have large populations of students. Students will use such large places as empty classrooms for study, but only if they are not required to share them with many others.

TABLE VI.

Student Use of Study Space of Different Sizes
(The figures represent half-hours)

TYPE OF SPACE	TOTAL HALF-HOURS USED	NO. STUDENTS USING SPACE	MEAN HALF-HOURS USED	PERCENT OF TOTAL STUDY TIME USED
Small	9434	424*	22.0	56
Intermediate	2794	196	14.2	17
Mod. Large	2291	340	6.7	14
Large	1935	173	11.1	12

*The number is larger than the total number of students in the study because three different kinds of study space were included and since some students used more than one of them, they would be counted more than once.

Thus size and population are interwoven influences in determining student reactions, as can be seen by comparing Tables VII and VIII. In one table there are responses to size; in the other, responses to the number of other students present and studying. The correspondence of the answers not only serves as a check of consistency, but also as a key to interpretation.

TABLE VII.

Expressed Preferences for Study Places of Different Sizes

SIZE OF SPACE	OPINIONNAIRE REPLIES % PRO	% CONTRA	NO. OF FAVORABLE COMMENTS FROM STUDY DIARIES
Small	80.2	11.2*	126
Intermediate	68.1	16.0	87
Mod. Larger	not included		21
Large	24.7	63.0	10

*The percentages do not total 100 because neutral opinions are not included in the table. See items 07, 08, 09 in Appendix B.

TABLE VIII.

Attitudes Toward the Number of Persons Using a Given Study Space

NUMBER OF FELLOW STUDENTS IN SPACE	OPINIONNAIRE REPLIES % PRO*	% CONTRA	NO. OF INFORMAL FAVORABLE COMMENTS
No one else	85.5	7.6	92
2 or 3 others	64.5	24.1	40
About 7	37.0	41.5	22
About 20	27.5	54.0	11
100 or more	15.3	71.1	7

*i.e., the percent on the positive side of the neutral point in a seven point scale.

The dislike for fellow students in the same study area increases directly with their number. This is not an evidence of misanthropy, but a desire to escape the distractions which increasingly large numbers of students inevitably produce. How important this is can be seen from the fact that students in their informal comments about study space mentioned the annoyance and distractions of people-produced noise and movements 295 times; while the second most frequent complaint, poor lighting, was made only 167 times. The opinionnaire also supports this attitude by high percentages of dislike for the same types of noises. The movements are not annoying solely because of the accompanying noise, but also because of the strong tendency to look up and identify the persons and movements seen dimly in the periphery of vision. This was mentioned by a number of students, but it can also be easily verified by walking down the aisles of a large reading room and watching the heads turn. It is almost inevitable that more noise will be made by a large number of people than a small group in a study area. There will be more movement, more coughing, more chair scraping, more whispering, more page turning, etc., etc. So the student who wishes to escape such distractions tries to avoid the larger and more highly populated study spaces.

There is a small minority, however, which does not want to study alone. Some of these seek out noisy places to study, e.g., coffee shops and some of them prefer the large study halls. Discussions of their choices with such individuals shows that they usually have a reason to offer. Those who like to study in the atmosphere of coffee, cigarettes, sandwiches, juke boxes, buzzing conversations, and streams of student traffic, protest that these conditions are fairly continuous and consequently tend to lose their power of attracting attention; while the distractions of the large library reading room are intermittent and consequently maintain their ability to distract. The public sees this student more than the great majority who study in their rooms or in the library, and assumes that he is typical. But this is not true. Most students do not want to study in a tavern atmosphere. An occasional student reports inability to study alone and finds the large study hall keeps him awake and busy. So this individual may have a private room in a dormitory, own all the books he reads, and yet carry them back and forth to the library to read because he needs pacemakers and a formal atmosphere to keep him working. Others report that they like to study with a congenial roommate or other friend; or an occasional small group finds discussion of studies a stimulating intellectual exercise. But most students are anxious to diminish people-produced distractions and consequently choose small places in which to study.

Distinctions Between Good and Poor Students

Is there any disagreement between good and poor students in their preference for large *versus* small, or well *versus* sparsely populated study places? Two attempts were made to answer this question in relation to study in dormitory rooms and large library reading rooms. In one of these a contrast was made between students in the top three deciles of their classes and those in the bottom three in the amount of studying done in their rooms. The high group reported 23.9 half-hours of study in their rooms in four days; while the low group reported 22.4 half-hours. A few persons in each group, 5.6% in the high group and 7.1% in the low group, did not study in their rooms at all. The little difference that exists might be due to the fact that a slightly greater proportion of students in the lowest three dociles had more than one roommate; and such students study less in their rooms than those with one roomate or none. (See p. 27ff.)[1]

A second contrast was made between students labeled "under-achievers" or "over-achievers." The former were arbitrarily defined as those whose academic decile rank in class was two or more deciles below that of their Scholastic Aptitude (Verbal). The latter were defined as those who had an academic decile rank two or more deciles above that of their Scholastic Aptitude. There were 51 under-achievers and 115 over-achievers. The large library reading rooms were not used at all by 56.9 percent of the under-achievers or by 44.3 percent of the over-achievers. The mean number of half-hours studied in these rooms by under-achievers was 3.96; and 7.49 by over-achievers. Since approximately half of each group did not use them at all, and since the difference between the means of use amounted to less than a half-hour per day per student, it is hard to believe that the large library room is an important factor in determining under or over achievement, except for the occasional student who, as has been said before, needs pacemakers and a formal atmosphere of study. The means for studying in the dormitory rooms were 24.1 for under-achievers and 21.7 for over-achievers. This amounts to approximately one half-hour per day—not a material difference. A few did not study in their rooms at all—3.96 percent of the under-achievers and 6.1 percent of the over-achievers.

It might be noted for use in interpreting the above facts that the under-achievers reported a mean total of 44.7 half-hours of study in the four days, while over-achievers reported 48.6. Those in the lowest three deciles of their classes studied 47.5 half-hours; and those in the highest three deciles, a mean of 48.5.

In the light of all the evidence, there seems to be little distinction between good and poor students in their choices of dormitory rooms and large reading rooms as places in which to study. A high percentage of both groups use the large library reading rooms very little or none at all. A few from each group use them more heavily; and over-achievers slightly more than under-achievers. But, in general, it is evident that what is recognized by one group as desirable study space is so identified by the other.

The Dormitories as Study Places

The students were all in residence at their various institutions. Since there were no sororities at the women's colleges, and since few replies were returned from the fraternities in one institution, the large majority, 83 percent, lived in dormitories. The fraternity and sorority dwellers were not treated separately since they comprised a small group scattered through eight houses, and their amounts of study were not significantly different from those of students living in dormitories. So the results are those essentially of dormitory dwellers, living largely in single or double rooms—78 of the former and 199 of the latter. Forty-five students had two roommates and 36 had more. The houses operated under different rules with respect to closing hours, smoking, quiet hours, etc. They also differed in their provision for special study rooms, social rooms, smoking rooms, typing places, etc. Some were near the library; some were distant. Some were new; some were old. None was arranged in suites with a study room for the six or eight students who might live in them. Students were chosen for dormitories by lot in some places and were allocated in others. With these facts as background, the following data will be presented.

TABLE IX.

Studying Done in the Dormitories in a Four Day Period
(Reported in Half-hours)

COLLEGE	TOTAL TIME STUDIED	TOTAL STUDIED IN DORMITORIES	PERCENT OF ALL STUDY	TOTAL STUDY IN STUDENT ROOMS	PERCENT OF ALL STUDY	PERCENT OF ALL DORMITORY STUDY
Amherst	4623	2751	59	2252	49	82
Mt. Holyoke	4300	2365	55	2194	51	93
Smith	4521	2593	57	1537	34**	59
U. of Mass.	3306	2565	78*	2091	63	82
Total	16750	10274	61	8074	48	79

*This high percentage is due in large part to the inadequacy of the old library. This may drop when the new addition is in service.

**The smaller proportion of studying done in student rooms here is due largely to the greater provision and use of special study rooms in which smoking is permitted.

Well over half of all the studying done in each of these institutions was done in the dormitories; and with one exception, more than four-fifths of the studying done in the dormitories was done in student rooms. This makes the dormitories the most important study space in these four institutions, and of all types of places, the dormitory student room carries the greatest burden of study. In the light of the desire of the students to escape from studying with others, this is not surprising, even though students do complain about lack of observance of quiet hours, and the casualness with which students wander into the rooms of others.

The effect of the number of roommates upon the amount of study in student rooms is of interest. One might expect from what has been written previously that the amount of study in student rooms would decrease as the number of roommates increased. Table X shows us, however, that this is not the case until the number of roommates becomes greater than one. Indeed students in single rooms study slightly less in their rooms than those in doubles. Some of those who live in single rooms, but did practically all of their studying in the library, offered such explanations as: "I just go to sleep if I try to study alone"; or "I need others around who are studying to keep me busy." Those who do not have habits of self-discipline at study apparently do better when they study in a situation where studious behavior is expected. Students who have only one roommate come close to approximating the study conditions desired by most students (see p. 36f) unless they have some specially awarded, private space as is frequently given to honor students. If roommates have different schedules, then the room becomes in effect a single room part of the time. Also one student may study in the library while the other uses the room. Two students, with good habits of study, may work together quite congenially. If one wishes to study late and the other to sleep, a special study hall in the dormitory may resolve the problem. But these solutions become increasingly difficult with added roommates, and consequently study in the rooms tends to decline as is shown in the bottom line of Table X. If a dormitory is to be constructed so as to encourage study in the rooms, then singles and doubles are almost equally desirable. But if more students are housed in a room, or suite, then special study space must be provided.

TABLE X.

Amounts of Study in their Rooms by Students with Different Numbers of Roommates
(Recorded in Half-Hour Units)

COLLEGE	NO ROOMMATES			ONE ROOMMATE			TWO ROOMMATES			THREE OR MORE		
	N	TOTAL STUDY	ROOM STUDY	N	TOTAL STUDY	ROOM STUDY	N	TOTAL STUDY	ROOM STUDY	N	TOTAL STUDY	ROOM STUDY
Amherst	12	607	441	23	1082	735	37	1836	727	24	1140	304
Mt. Holyoke	25	1183	625	64	2978	1490	3	165	79			
Smith	34	1669	574	59	2864	963						
U. of Mass.	6	272	147	52	2232	1698	5	173	79	12	594	200
Totals	77	3731	1787	198	9156	4886	45	2174	885	36	1734	504
Percent of Total Study Time Spent in Study in Their Rooms			48			53			41			29

One reason which no doubt makes a student's room a desirable place to study in is that a student can frequently deal with some matters of distraction, personal comfort, and efficiency more easily there than in a study hall which must serve many. That these have importance can be seen from the frequency of their mention in the informal comments in the study diaries shown in Table XI. Some of these are supported by the opinionnaire, see items 27-35, 46-49, 15-16, 50-55, 56-59, Appendix B; but others cannot be tabulated in the same way.

Most of the complaints made about the above were in relation to large reading rooms, although some were made about lack of respect for quiet hours in dormitories. Almost all of the complaints about temperature and light were of too much heat, and inadequate lighting. But the lighting and temperature problems were almost completely those of large places. In these, students could not open windows or turn on another light, for they had no control over these things such as usually exist in one's own dormitory room. The opinionnaire responses placed a strong emphasis upon

TABLE XI.

Problems More Easily Remedied in a Dormitory Student Room than in One Shared with a Number of Students

	PEOPLE-PRODUCED NOISES	LIGHTING	TEMP. VENT.	EASY AVAILABILITY OF MATERIALS	FURNITURE	RELAXATION NEEDS
Frequency of Mention in Study Diaries	295	167	156	152	124	68

the desirability of easy access to materials needed for study, and for most of these students,
with the exception of senior honor students,
their rooms were the best places to collect and
have available such materials as they needed,
even though their collections were limited.
Chairs grow uncomfortable after awhile, and
a dormitory room is more apt to provide a
change than a large reading room. Dormitory
desks were complained of where two students
had to share one in common, but otherwise
there were few comments. On the opinionnaire, most students expressed a preference
for a larger desk size than most dormitories
furnish, but the comments did not indicate
any serious unhappiness with what they had,
although an occasional student did report a
need to spread things out when writing a
paper. In many rooms the desk surfaces
were made still smaller by using the back eight
inches as a book shelf. This space might be
salvaged for work by putting a book shelf above
the desk within easy reach. The need for a
seventh inning stretch is as urgent in study as
in a baseball game; and one's own room provides an opportunity to relax with vigorous
and undignified stretches which are not per-
missable in a large reading room. A snack, a
turn around the room often provide the needed shift which refreshes. Students recognize
these as dangerous diversions if they are in-
dulged in too much, and some find them so
tempting that they cannot study in their
rooms. "The bed is inviting for a ten minute
nap; but when I wake up, it is time for dinner."
Some students deliberately seek the restraints
of the large reading room as a way of handling
their own inability at self-discipline. But on
the whole most students can find it more possible to mold their own rooms closer to the
heart's desire than to do anything about the
large study places.

There are no doubt some intangible values
for many individuals obtained by studying in
their rooms. These rooms offer the little privacy obtainable in a college, the substitute
for home, a sense of belonging. Here are collected many stimuli which are dear to the
students but may compete with needs for
study—a pin-up gallery, trophies of success,
school pennants, attempts at college humor,
collections which are an extension of one's
personality, etc. Indeed many student rooms
are as revealing of their inhabitants as a pro-

jective technique session in a psychiatric
clinic.

The question is often raised as to whether
the distracting stimuli in a student's room,
and the multiplicity of its uses do not nullify
its value as a place to study. (But, paren-
thetically, it should be noted that the student
will not necessarily escape from them simply
by going to some other place, for he can carry them within his memory). Some propose
as a solution, that rooms should be arranged
in suites, with one special room for study.
For example, two sleeping rooms might house
three students each, and an adjoining study
room have six desks. Our dormitories did
not provide such facilities or we would have
evaluated this proposal carefully. As it is,
our data indicate that students would prefer to study in their single or double rooms
rather than in a room with five others. The
latter situation leads to more people-produced
noises and distractions than the former. Yet
we did visit fraternities in which special
study rooms had been fitted with booths
which cut down visual distraction, and the
students were so determined to enforce quiet
rules that even a visitor was not allowed to
speak. The students were quite pleased with
these study conditions.

Students need to talk. They also need to
study. Reconciling these two needs is a difficult problem. One group of students was
asked to jot down, without further reflection, the things which the found satisfying
about dormitory life, and also the things which
they found most unsatisfying. One of the
most conspicuously satisfying things was
"the bull sessions"; while one of the most
annoying was the inability to escape from
the "chatter." There should be space designated for social activities, but even then
dormitory traditions need to be built up
which respect symbols of request for quiet
or periods of study. A single individual with
a homemade sign on the door requesting
quiet is not apt to secure much respect for it,
but a dormitorywide symbol adopted by all,
and with respect for it taught to each incoming group, will produce results. It has long
been known that an honor system in a college
will work only if the students want it and
work seriously at maintaining it. The same
thing is true about respect for privacy and
study quiet. These things can be obtained by

building up in the students a code to which they give their allegiance.

Informal discussions with upperclass students reveal that they regard the freshmen as one of the most serious sources of noise in a dormitory. Their exuberance and uninhibited freshness in a new and highly stimulating world are frequently expressed in noisy vitality. Freshmen retort that the upperclassmen "make more noise than we do trying to shush us." Upperclassmen recommend that the problem be diluted by not allowing more than a limited percentage of freshmen in any one dormitory and by not putting too many on one floor. They declare that a dormitory may not deteriorate substantially in its observance of good study decorum simply by having too large or too concentrated a group of freshmen in one year. This sounds like the voice of experience which should be heeded, although we have no objective data on the subject.

Some construction problems in dormitories deserve comment. These were observed or called to our attention by students living in dormitories with the problems. Partitions which do not screen sound well enough are all too frequent. Lack of noise dampening construction at strategic points permits noise to disturb those living near, and to render some rooms particularly undesirable, e.g., rooms near elevators, noisy toilets, bathrooms, and stairways. Long, unbroken halls permit reverberations. Hall noises may be reduced by attention to flooring, ceilings, and placing room closets against hall walls. Dormitories built in L, T, or hollow court patterns are considerably noisier than straight line dormitories when windows are open. The location of study rooms in dormitories should be in quiet places—something which is not always done. Telephones constitute an annoying problem unless properly handled. Often they are placed at points on each dormitory floor where they will be heard by the largest number of students. Usually they ring until the person with the least patience, or the greatest hope, answers. Most of the time the call is for someone else, and the answerer then noisily calls "Bill," or "Jane," as the case may be. By this time everyone has been distracted from study. The best system observed was a central desk downstairs which took all incoming calls and then buzzed the desired student's room. If the student was

in, he pressed his buzzer to let it be known that he was taking the call, and then went to the telephone which was enclosed. Thus little disturbance was produced. In view of the amount of telephoning which goes on, and the heavy use of dormitories as study halls, such an investment is worth while.

There is need for other study places in a dormitory than just student rooms. Such needs arise for students who wish to smoke in dormitories which forbid smoking in rooms. The occasional student who wishes to study late while his roommate wants to sleep, must have some other place to work. A need to spread out papers, or type late may also create too heavy or improper demands upon a student room. Dormitories in these institutions which have rules against smoking in student rooms, provide special smoking rooms. An occasional student uses such a room almost consistently as a place for study; but less than half of the users of smoking rooms as places for study used them for more than an hour a day. Some smoking rooms are social rooms also, others may be restricted for study. One large dormitory had a commodious study room for non-smokers, but it was rarely used by more than three students and often by fewer. If smoking is not permitted in student rooms, then non-smokers usually study there. It is evident that if students are allowed to smoke in their rooms, or do not wish to smoke, then much less demand will exist for study space outside the rooms.

At first thought dining halls might seem attractive places to study in when empty; but our data show that in four days of recorded study for 356 students, in no instance did more than three students use a dining hall at the same time. This fits perfectly into the dislike expressed by our students for large, well populated study places; but additional reasons exist in inadequate lighting and furniture. These are designed for dining, not studying. But even if these faults were remedied, it seems reasonable from what we have learned that students would still use them in small numbers at most. Converting a dining hall into a study hall physically is not likely to make it a popular place to study, although a couple of tables of desirable height and adequate lighting might be useful.

Lounges, date parlors, lobbies, and visiting parlors, are unused for substantial amounts of time each week, but they do not seem to be attractive places in which to study. An occasional student who is reading without taking notes will use them; but for serious work, they are avoided. The chairs are too comfortable for many students, often there is no place to write, and the lighting is frequently inappropriate. In addition these places are subject to people-produced distractions.

But these dual purpose rooms are not really satisfactory places for study, for they are not subject to the control of individuals who wish to use them solely for study. It is desirable in a dormitory to provide special rooms for students who for one reason or another cannot study in their rooms. There is probably no exact formula which can be used to determine how many students will want to study in the dormitory, but outside their rooms, at any one time. Numerous variables have to be considered, e.g., the more distant the dormitory is from the library, the fewer will be studying in the dormitory while the library is open; the smoking rules and the addiction of the students to smoking; the number of other small and desirable study spaces on the campus; the hours at which most students tend to go to bed; the hours the library is open; how long reserve books may be kept out; rules about typing in the dormitory; and possibly others. Our sample indicated that from ten to twenty percent might want to study in the dormitory building but outside of the dormitory rooms at any one time. If the dormitory is large enough, then it is better to make several small study rooms than a single large one. They should be located in quiet parts of the dormitory, and furnished with good sized tables and a variety of chairs rather than a single type and size. The lighting should be excellent. If smoking is permitted, especial care must be taken of the ventilation, for even the most devoted smokers dislike stale smoke. Possibly typing should be restricted to one of these rooms, at least at late hours, although our data about typing are not clear on the subject.

It seems probable that most colleges will continue to plan for the use of dormitories as places in which to study. Consequently they should take this function of a dormitory seriously and plan it accordingly; and in old buildings they should correct errors as far as can be reasonably managed. At this point it seems desirable to attempt a description of the hypothetical kind of study space which most students appear to want.

Ideal Study Space

No study space is ideal for everyone. That fact clearly emerges, even though students may like a given pattern by an overwhelming majority. Consequently there must be variety. Some like plush comfort, most like their study furniture and surroundings rather plain and reasonably comfortable. Discomfort distracts; so does too much comfort. The tall and the short are both apt to be uncomfortable in chairs designed for average persons. Some like it hot; some like it cold. Some want to smoke; some don't. Some like company and pacemakers; most do not. But like most compilations of human behavior and preferences, there are distint trends which characterize most subjects, with variability on both sides of the normal trend. Below is an attempt to state the characteristics of the study space which would be at the mode of student choice and use. The items are roughly in order of importance as derived from the various data available to the writers.

Characteristics of Good Study Space for the Typical Student

1. A small room where one may study alone or with possibly one or two other students.
2. A place being used exclusively for study—at least at the time.
3. Freedom from distractions of movement and noise caused by other people.
4. Freedom from distractions of noise from physical sources, e.g., telephones, plumbing, clanking radiators, typewriters, etc.
5. Good lighting.
6. Temperature and ventilation under personal control.
7. Easy access to books and other study materials.
8. Comfortable chairs, adequate desk space, and book shelves.
9. Some chance to relax, wear "easy" clothes, etc.; and for smokers, freedom to smoke.
10. Decor and furnishing which are plain but not ugly, definitely not plushy or arty.

It should be noted that the order of importance given above, and even the presence of items, may be affected by the conditions which students found existing in their institutions. If, e.g., students had had all the light they wanted, the subject would probably not have been mentioned, and light would not have appeared in the list at all. But architects can feel assured that the items listed above are matters of significance to students even though their rank order is not unassailable.

It should also be noted that some of the preferences for lighting and temperature are matters of previous conditioning. The amounts of lighting in some of our older libraries were considered adequate by the parents of contemporary students for they had like amounts at home and elsewhere. But we are now accustomed to many more foot candles than was true when Abraham Lincoln considered his firelight or candle sufficient, and consequently the contemporary student wants more light than he often gets. Temperatures desired are much affected by custom, experience and clothing—cf. the American preference for warmer buildings than the English like. No doubt compromises will have to be made on the control of temperature and ventilation, because people differ in the amounts of heat they need, both from habituation and also from bodily structure. One student's comfort in such matters may be another's discomfort—a factor which may make studying in one's dormitory room, where such matters can be controlled, particularly desirable to those who deviate from the norm. Perhaps libraries might be designed with thermostats which allow variability in different study rooms or in parts of the library.

The Library

That the library is central to a college education is a fact which needs no proof or defense. But how much students use it, and how they use it do need investigation. Numerous factors determine the answers to these questions.

1. Educational policies and practices are of prime importance. What dependence upon textbooks exists? How varied are the sources which students must consult? How are reserves managed? How much research on the

part of students is required or encouraged? How much independence do the students have? Is there an honors program?

2. There are alternate physical facilities for study to be considered. Among these are the dormitories, student unions, coffee shops, empty classrooms, laboratories, and possible special study halls. How do these compare in functional attractiveness with the facilities of the library? What is the capacity of these alternate facilities?

3. Then there are extra-curricular activities which may invite some students and repel others, e.g., making the library a place of rendevous and courtship.

4. But important also are the building and its management. Are the stacks open? Do they have tables and carrels scattered through them? Are there small rooms in which students may study? Must most of the students study in large study halls? Are there enough study stations to supply the demand? Is there much traffic through study places? Are books easily obtained? Is the lighting good? Are the temperature and ventilation soporific or stimulating? Are the desks and chairs comfortable enough to permit study for considerable periods of time? Are there suitable places in which to collect materials for writing? Are there rooms for typing?

No doubt there are other variables which determine how much and how students will use a library, but these will serve to show that no simple answer will do.

With this *caveat* in mind a study of Table XII will provide some interesting insights into the wide differences in how students used the libraries in these four institutions. The reader should keep in mind that differences in the average amounts of study done by the students in these institutions is trivial.

No doubt the reader will be struck by the differences in the total amounts of use of the libraries as shown in the last column. In the case of Amherst, competing study facilities, arranged especially for honor students at Churchill House, siphoned off 343 half-hours of recorded study from the library. Here the honor students in the humanities or social sciences were provided with attractive studies, where they might collect books and other materials to use. Another reason for less use of the Amherst Library lies in the fact that the library provided plenty of copies of books

TABLE XII.

Where Time Was Spent in the Libraries
(Stated in half-hours)

INSTITUTION	LARGE READING ROOMS		CARRELS		SEMINAR ROOMS		DEPARTMENT LIBRARIES		SMOKING ROOMS		TOTALS
	N	%	N	%	N	%	N	%	N	%	
Amherst	470	48.3	119	12.2	82	8.4	36	3.7	265	27.3	972
Mt. Holyoke	734	50.0	446	30.4	92	6.3	163	11.1	33	2.2	1468
Smith	502	34.6	397	27.4	192	13.3	264	18.2	94	6.5	1449
U. of Mass.	229	63.4	55	15.2	15	4.2	62	17.2			361

on reserve and permitted them to be withdrawn after dinner and kept until the next day. This is probably one reason why Amherst students studied more in their dormitories than did the students at Mt. Holyoke or Smith. Another possible factor is that they studied later at night than did students in the women's colleges, and not enough library space was left open late enough to satisfy them. In the case of the University's low total use of the library, one need seek no further than the inadequate size of the library at the time of the study. At this time it could seat only about ten percent of the student body so most students had to study elsewhere. The "elsewhere" usually proved to be the dormitories, where they studied 78 percent of their time in contrast to the nearest competitor, Amherst, which studied 59 percent of the time in dormitories. The University is now opening a substantial addition to their library and it seems most reasonable to expect a large gain in the amount that the library will be used.

Carrels proved attractive at Mt. Holyoke and Smith, but less so at Amherst, and hardly used at the University. None of the institutions had closed carrels, but those at Holyoke cut off the most visibility and communication. They were assigned to honor students first but other students might use them when they were not occupied. They, like the carrels at Smith, were around the stacks, and books and materials might be accumulated in them. Use and comment agree in attesting their popularity at both Mt. Holyoke and Smith. At Amherst honor students and most seniors were provided with better assigned study places than the carrels. The carrels were unhappily located next to radiators and were dimly lit, so that they were not much

sought after. At the University there were no real carrels—only a few tables and chairs at the back of the stacks. This situation is obviously attributable to the fact that the library addition was long over-due.

Seminar rooms were used more generously by Smith students than by the others. This is due to a greater abundance of them and the fact that smoking was permitted in them, as was not the case at the other libraries. Again the low total at the University was a building deficiency. One thing which holds down the use of seminar rooms as study rooms is the tendency for students to regard them as more or less private offices on a first come, first served basis, a practice which is in conformity with their desire to study with few others around.

Department libraries are unevenly represented in our figures and probably in large measure because our sample of students using special libraries is low and uneven. E.g., department libraries of art may be quite adequate and desirable, but if our sample has only one or two art majors from the colleges that have them, their use is apt to look very small indeed. All of the colleges have department libraries, but any generalizations about them from our data are dangerous. Some research on the student use of such facilities is definitely in order.

Smoking rooms were provided in all the libraries except at the University—again probably a function of the limited space there. At Amherst one large room had been reserved for smokers. It was fitted so as to make individual study booths on the tables by partial partitions which cut down visibility and communication, and provided facilities for assembling study materials. It was also kept open after the main library closed. How much these additional reasons added to its attractiveness as a smoker is hard to say, but probably a considerable amount. Amherst students are permitted to smoke in their dormitory rooms, which may be a factor in siphoning off some smokers from the library to the dormitories. Since smoking was permitted in the seminar rooms at Smith, there were numerous places where students could smoke. At Mt. Holyoke, only one small room was reserved for smoking and it was more fitted for social conversation than study. Quite possibly a combination of study facilities and smoking privileges would see more use than our study shows at Mt. Holyoke.

The use of the large reading rooms at the four libraries was affected by several variables. First, is the existence of competing study space within the library, department libraries, and other supplementary space designed particularly for study. A second was the regulation of the use of reserve books and the extent of the supply of these. A third exists in terms of temperature, ventilation, and lighting. A fourth involves smoking regulations. A fifth is concerned with hours at which facilities are available. It is not possible to evaluate all of these, and since this study is particularly concerned with the relation of physical space to study, only the first variable will be pursued. The following table represents an attempt to balance the use of competing smaller study spaces within the library complex against the large reading rooms.

TABLE XIII.

Distribution of Time Between Large Library Reading Rooms and
Competing Study Places Within the Library Complex

INSTITUTION	TIME SPENT IN LARGE READING ROOMS	TIME SPENT IN COMPETING SPACE	TOTALS	PERCENT OF TIME SPENT IN LARGE READING ROOMS
U. of Mass.	229	132	361	63
Mt. Holyoke	734	734	1468	50
Amherst	470	845	1315	38
Smith	502	947	1449	35

Within the total library complex, the University of Massachusetts had the least amount of alternate types of study space competing with the large reading rooms; Mount Holyoke came next, and then Amherst and Smith with different but probably somewhat comparable amounts of competing study space. If one examines the last column of Table XIII it can be seen that the percent of time spent in large reading rooms varied inversely with the provisions of smaller competing study places. Between Amherst and Smith the difference is negligible. It should be remembered that these choices on the part of the students were not completely based upon size. Some of the other variables mentioned in the previous paragraph may accentuate the preference for the smaller places. But along with this reservation, it must also be remembered that there was an undersupply of these smaller places in the opinion of the students, and consequently some people used the large reading rooms who would have used smaller places had they been available. It seems clear that the students have weighed the large reading room in the balance and found it wanting.

How large should reading rooms be in the library of the future? What percent of the students should they be expected to house? There is no precise answer to such questions, for other variables than student preference are influential. Among them are such matters as educational policy, problems of supervision of the library, architectural planning, and building costs. Educational trends, as will be pointed out later, seem to indicate an increasing need for smaller study places. Costs cannot be assessed until plans for different kinds of space are available. Solutions to supervision problems are matters for librarians to evolve out of their experience. The only contribution to be made from this study is an examination of student preferences and use. These obviously have been on the side of small study space in contrast to large, but not unanimously so. This minority opinion may help to answer the questions cited at the beginning of the paragraph.

TABLE XIV.

Percent of Students Checking Attitudes Favorable or Against Studying with Specified Numbers of Others

NUMBER OF OTHER STUDENTS	TOP FOUR POINTS ON THE SCALE	NEGATIVE THREE POINTS ON THE SCALE
0	75.9	22.4
2 or 3	63.8	34.4
About 7	37.5	61.2
About 20	24.9	70.6
Over 100	17.6	81.3

Opinionnaire data on the frequency with which students would study under certain conditions, items 82-86 inclusive, show roughly what might be expected. The following table is constructed from these items by adding together the percentage of students checking the three positive points and the neutral point of the scale—the top four points of the seven—to obtain the percentage disposed to use rooms with varying numbers of other students also studying. It is assumed that these students would use a given study space enough to make it functional space; and that the lowest three points on the scale, "occasionally," "rarely," and "never," indicate too low a use of space to justify construction of it for students using these three points.

Without considering factors of cost, supervision, etc., it would appear that rooms holding 20 students will be sufficiently used to warrant their construction, even in a library which has an ample supply of small or individual study places. Roughly 25 percent of the students would use these rooms with a fair amount of frequency, but very few would use them "always" or "almost always." Some of the users of such rooms would use smaller places also. So it is hardly necessary to plan for seating a full 25 percent of the student body in such rooms. Study of peak loads by librarians might give better guides to what proportion of the potential users of such rooms would need to be seated at one time. If a library does not provide an ample supply of individual or other small study places, then the number of larger rooms must be increased.

Is a room for 20 students the maximum size a library should build? The data presented here do not provide a continuous opinion on different sizes. Rooms for 100 or more do not seem to have enough favorable reactions from students to warrant constructing them—if student preference is

to be the only guide. But there may be sizes between 20 and 100 which will satisfy those who voted for either of these in preference to the other. Without further evidence it looks as though there is no sharp and clearly defined best number between 20 and 100; and it may be quite possible that different sizes between them are satisfactory, although the percentage of satisfied students is bound to decrease slowly as the number increases.

Student attitudes might be shifted toward greater tolerance of larger rooms than 20 if imaginative designing could cut down traffic and break up the study area with other library facilities and functions which would not interfere with study, but which would not require expensive partitions.

Any attempt to revise library architecture should certainly be concerned with educational trends and the development of mechanical devices for presenting information. A vigorous drive toward more independence and research on the part of undergraduates would certainly call for a reduced emphasis upon large reading rooms and an increase in the number of small study stations where students may collect and utilize materials in the fashion of mature scholars. One can expect that there will be an increasing use of microfilms. Perhaps these will be paralleled by auditory devices which will enable individuals as well as groups to listen to famous speeches or unusual music. The use of television is now thought of as a means for mass instruction, but it may possibly be adapted for small groups or individuals. Instructional machines for use with individuals are receiving much encouragement at the present time. If they fulfill their promise, they will provide a new medium of study—at least for routine learning. Language laboratories have come into their own. These devices will, for the most part, require small spaces rather than large, and consequently fit into the direction of library development previously indicated, viz., away from large study rooms and toward smaller, individualized work rooms or spaces.

Since some individuals desire to study at late hours, and librarians must have both rest and sleep, conflict occurs as to how late libraries should remain open. A compromise has been achieved in some libraries by construction which will close up all but some designated study space, but leave this open around the clock, or as late as seems desirable.

A Defense of Student Desire for Small Rooms

Critics of these proposals for smaller study places believe that they will coddle the students instead of helping them to learn to work in the presence of distractions as so many adults do in offices or elsewhere. But it should be noted that these adults are, for the most part, working at things with which they are reasonably familiar while students are not; the adult has his motivations well established, whereas students are often beginning a new area of study which they have not yet learned to like or to work with; adults are apt to find reprisals fairly quick for wasting time in social chatter on the job, while students do not; and adults often forget their early inadequacies and difficulties at working on a job with distracting activities around them, and think of only their established habits. Intellectual work of an abstract nature is not easy, particularly for the novice, and colleges should give him every chance to succeed instead of throwing obstacles of distraction in his way.

Empty Classrooms

Empty classrooms are sometimes suggested as excellent places to study in; or that they would be if the furniture were modified. Such rooms were used extensively at one of the colleges and slightly at the others. Yet the total number of half-hours reported for four days of use in the college where the greatest use was made was only 249. A walk around to these classrooms in the evening usually disclosed one student in each room. The room might be large enough for forty students, but custom declared that squatter's rights gave possession to the first to begin studying. In effect the students were making private offices out of classrooms, frequently at considerable expense for

lighting the whole room. In view of the attitude found among the students toward studying in large groups, it seems improbable that empty classrooms will become much used places for study unless there is a drastic shortage of other places. Somewhat the same problem exists with reference to seminar rooms in the library. If study materials can be used there *only,* then the room gets used by several students at a time; but otherwise the first student to take possession regards it as his property and tends to drive others out with cool courtesy or obvious irritation. Whether such customs can be broken has not been adequately tested; but since the custom is grounded in the students' desire for a study place answering the description on page 37, it will be difficult to conquer.

Study Activities in Relation to Places

During the period of four days covered in the study dairies approximately 45 percent of the study time was spent in reading, either with or without note taking. Reviewing took up 15 to 20 percent of the time; and preparation of papers about 14 percent. This distribution is probably fairly typical, although it might shift considerably at some special time. If reading and reviewing are added together, then the typical student was spending approximately two-thirds of his time in activity which could readily be carried on in many different places, as it actually was. The great preponderance of these activities did occur in the dormitories and libraries as previously indciated, but they were carried on in emough different places to make it clear that no particular kind of space was needed, although some kinds were much preferred to others. The preparation of papers also took place predominantly in the dormitories or libraries, with a marked preference for working in isolation where materials could be accumulated, e.g., in a student's room or a library carrel. The remainder of the study activities were scattered through the list given in the study diary. Some of these, e.g., creative art work calculating with machines, projects of various sorts, had to be carried out in special places where proper conditions and equipment existed. But it appears that except for studies which require special tools or conditions, no architectural stipulations beyond those already discussed as characteristic of good study space are needed. No doubt the distribution of study activities would differ in a specialized institution, e.g., art, engineering, or music schools, and consequently less time would be spent studying in libraries and dormitories.

A SUMMARY OF FINDINGS FOR THE USE OF PLANNERS OF STUDY SPACE

1. Students are good sources of information about study space, but they should be consulted in numbers, because a single individual may not be typical.

2. There is a strong preference for studying in small places where one may study alone or with one or two others. (P. 22f).[1]

3. The large library reading room is disliked by most students even though it may be used. Its faults are that it inevitably produces more distractions from other people than a small study place. (P. 33ff).

4. Reading rooms large enough for 20 to 40 students need not be provided for more than 15 to 20 percent of the students provided there are plenty of smaller and individual study stations. (P. 36f).

5. The larger the study hall, the more it should be broken up with other functions and facilities which may reduce traffic and noise without interfering with study.

6. Fifty-six percent of the studying was done in dormitory room and carrel size places, and probably the percentage would have been considerably larger if more such space had been available. (P. 22f).

7. The visibility of traffic in a study hall is almost as bad as the noise it produces. Can it be reduced, rerouted, noise dampened?

8. Freedom from the distraction of equipment noises is desired; and is most apt to be infringed upon in dormitories by telephones, plumbing, kitchen noises, etc. (P. 29f).

9. Good lighting is much wanted. Don't spare the wattage, and arrange it so that visibility is at a maximum, and eye strain at a minimum.

10. Heating complaints are mostly of too high temperatures in study halls, particularly in libraries. Students adjust their own dormitory rooms to suit themselves for temperature and ventilation. Perhaps libraries can manage more flexibility and user controls in these matters. (P. 28).

11. Casual observation gives the impression that libraries should provide more space for typing than they frequently do, but the planning of typing facilities for libraries needs more attention than it has received in this study. Dormitories frequently permit typing in student rooms except at late hours—a practice which seems to arouse little complaint.

12. Each dormitory needs some special rooms in which some students may study outside their rooms. For dormitories with single and double rooms, probably space to house ten to twenty percent of the residents will be adequate. Variability of need will be related to smoking regulations, hours the library remains open, hours at which sizeable numbers want to go to sleep. Dormitories with many rooms having more than two students to the room will need more special study space. A large dormitory should have several small study rooms rather than a single large one. (P. 30f).

13. For a list of common structural faults in dormitories, see page 29f.

14. Some social space should be provided in a dormitory so that those who wish to talk may do so without disturbing those who wish to study.

15. Smoking regulations need careful consideration. Students who are heavy smokers want to study and smoke simultaneously much of the time. Moderate smokers are satisfied with an occasional period of smoking and studying in some special room. Non-smokers prefer to study in rooms which are not smoke filled. Populations of students differ in the percentage belonging to these groups, and consequently regulations and allocation of study space to these groups will vary. (P. 30, 35).

16. Most students want to study in a place where nothing but studying is going on at the time. This requires respect on the part of students for such regulations as may be agreed upon. Building up traditions on these matters is educationally like the problem of building up an honor system which is a matter of pride among the students. P. 29f).

17. The few students who like to study in the clatter of public social places to the accompaniment of chatter, juke boxes, and food, can be trusted to find their own heart's desire without help from the college.

18. The dream of using empty classrooms and dining halls as study halls is probably a

vain hope. Our data indicate that they will be used by only a few students. (P. 30, 38f).

19. Places to collect and use study materials are highly prized, and no doubt account in part for the popularity of carrels and dormitory rooms as study places.

20. Open carrels, arranged to reduce visibility, assigned to individuals but permissible to others when not in use, proved popular, especially when well lighted and under conditions of good temperature and ventilation.

21. Institutions tend to provide only one size and type of chair in study halls; but students come on no such scale of uniformity. Diversity which would conform to student measurements is a goal to be sought. Variety is easier to provide in a dormitory, but more can be done in a library. (P. 15f).

22. Variety is needed in types of study space as well as in chairs. There is no place which will be equally liked by all, although the description given on page 32 would probably please three-fourths of the students.

23. A high concentration of freshmen in a dormitory or in one part of a dormitory tends to increase the decibels of sound, and reduce the quality of the dormitory as a place for study. (P. 29).

24. The development of new devices such as the use of microfilms, individualized instructional machines, language laboratories, and other future possibilities, require more use of small study and work spaces and less of the large reading rooms. (P. 38).

25. The more colleges tend to develop independence on the part of students and require greater amounts of individual research, the more need there will be for carrels or other small places for study.

26. There seems to be little distinction between good and poor students in their choice of dormitory rooms and large library reading rooms as places in which to study. A high percentage of both groups uses the large library reading rooms little or not at all. A few from each group use them more heavily; and over-achievers slightly more than under-achievers. But in general both groups are very similar in their ideas about the nature of desirable study space. (P. 24f).

27. There are many unanswered questions about the construction of desirable study space, and many of the generalizations cited in this study must be translated into specifics. It is hoped that the present study will stimulate further inquiry, and generate numerous proposals for solutions to the problems raised.

FOOTNOTES

[1] Pages cited in text refer to pages as numbered in original publication.

ABOUT THE COMMITTEE

—After the publication of *The New College Plan,* the Committee, representing the four institutions, received a grant from the Fund for the Advancement of Education which provided it with the opportunity for this investigation. The Chairman, **Stuart M. Stoke,** is Professor Emeritus of Psychology and Education, Mount Holyoke College; Ed.D., 1926, Harvard Graduate School of Education. He taught education and psychology and served as Coordinator of Cooperative Activities for the four schools; his major research interest was in higher education.

LIBRARY COOPERATION

In spite of the impediments to library cooperation—such as the voluntary character of academic cooperation, social and academic attitudes toward institutional exclusiveness, and legal and budgetary strictures—economic requirements and technological possibilities can be expected to contribute greater impetus in this direction. Academic librarians, while responsive to the advantages of multilibrary arrangements, as well as to the uncertainties of future support, nonetheless must continue to be primarily receptive to the requirements of their immediate environments. The kinds and the degree of library cooperation can be expected to be a function of the ability of academic librarianship to demonstrate alternatives capable of obtaining sufficient approbation for implementation.

Cooperation in the Development of Library Resources for Research

by George Alan Works

The character of interinstitutional arrangements which tend to affect the functioning of the academic library is essentially not influenced by the librarian. For the librarian to demonstrate duplication of materials and replication in acquiring, providing file control, and warehousing, may be only a form of professional irrelevance. Certainly the magnitude of library cooperation now taking place—much, if not all, directly attributable to the librarian—has not made a significant impact on the behavior of the academic library. As illustrated in this chapter, libraries will function in conjunction when institutions do so. Yet while resource considerations do now and will continue to force change, the nature of involvement by institutions in their arrangements will continue to influence the future of library cooperation.

In this study no special objective measures were devised for determining the adequacy of the printed resources of the library for purposes of research. On the part of the faculty members, the statement was very frequently made that these resources were inadequate, both for their own needs and for those of their graduate students. In a few institutions the faculty members were inclined to place the responsibility for this situation on the librarian. It was stated: "He has no adequate conception of the place of scholarship"; "It takes vision and scholarship to be a librarian. His purchases in biology were rubbish." He was also sometimes accused of spending too large a proportion of the library funds on duplicates or frittering them away on books that had little or no value in the college or university library.

There can be little doubt but that a keen appreciation of the needs of research is an indispensable characteristic of the person who attempts to serve successfully as librarian in a modern university. That this quality is lacking in some instances cannot be gainsaid. However, as a result of the work on this study, it is the opinion of the writer that to apply the above-mentioned criticisms to all librarians would, in the great majority of cases, be unfair—at least it would be unfair in the group of institutions included in this study. A considerable proportion of the criticism is due to conditions that are beyond the control of librarians.

The data presented on page 14 show that for the group of institutions studied the increase in number of graduate students has been very rapid. This is one objective measurement of the demands made upon the libraries of these institutions to contribute to research. This demand on university libraries has become greater, not only as a result of the increased numbers of graduate students in a given group of institutions but also because of the growth in number of institutions giving graduate work. A further factor is the growth in size of facilities. Data on growth of graduate work and of faculties for institutions reporting to the United States Bureau of Education are given in Figure 8 and Tables N and O (see Appendix). As a result of these developments the demand for certain materials has become so great that it is only with very great difficulty that additions in certain fields can be made to the resources of the library. What the faculty member is sometimes inclined to attribute to the weakness of the librarian is due to causes that lie entirely beyond his control.

An illustration may be a means of helping to make this point clear.

"The University of Washington has made special effort during the past few years to se-

SOURCE: Reprinted from George Alan Works, *College and University Problems; A Study of a Selected Group of Institutions Prepared for the Association of American Universities* (Chicago: American Library Association, 1927), Chapter 3, "Cooperation in the Development of Library Resources for Research," pp. 51-62, by permission of the publisher.

FIGURE 8

Increase in Graduate Work and Size of Faculties in the College and Professional Schools
Reporting to the U.S. Bureau of Education
(See Tables N and O)

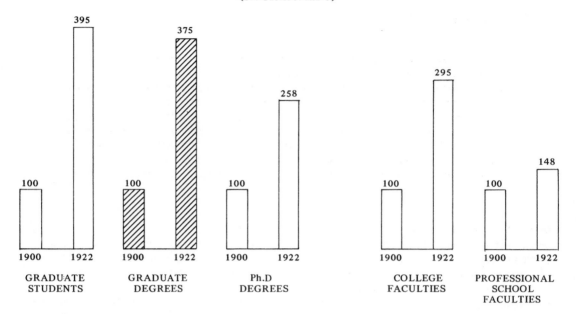

cure books for its young but promising graduate school. On account of the growing scarcity of periodicals and the serial publications of academies and learned societies, purchases have been concentrated upon this type of material. From titles selected from departmental requests, the library committee caused the preparation of a preferred buying list of the most essential items. On this list the sets of supreme importance were double-starred. One copy of the list thus prepared was submitted for quotations to the chief library agent in each of the leading European countries. From the resulting offers it has been impossible during the past six years to spend even the modest amount of money available. Not a single quotation has been received from any source on complete sets of any of the double-starred items.

"As a consequence of this failure to make proper headway towards the acquisition of those necessary books which must form the background for any extended research, I was sent to Europe to establish personal relations with dealers, to place direct orders and to examine existing book stocks. I devoted four months to visiting the principal book establishments in England, Scotland, The Nether-

lands, Germany, Italy and France. Some excellent material has been obtained in this way and the personal relations thus established will doubtless make matters easier so far as future orders are concerned.

"One fact however stands out above all others obtained from this first hand observation of European book stocks, namely, complete sets of fundamental research publications are scarce and in many cases the available supply is already exhausted. Some of the items on the list were easily found, but in a considerable number of cases the sets purchased were the only ones encountered in Europe. Of a number of the most important items desired not a single set was located. On one item requested by many departments in the University, I was informed by a dealer in one of the smaller cities that he had already six standing orders for the set from as many American libraries. Another dealer speaking of a desired set said, 'If this should come into the open market all of the principal dealers in London will bid for it and the library with the longest purse will pay the bill.' Speaking of a group of German periodicals, our Leipzig agent confirmed the statement previously made by letter, 'Germany is already sold out. These magazines are no longer to be had.'

"These experiences of the past summer are offered in evidence of a condition already understood or suspected by a considerable number of librarians in the United States. The gradual exhaustion of the market has been progressing steadily for years. The heavy buying that followed several years of interruption by war, increased no doubt a wish to take advantage of the favorable state of exchange, has suddenly sent prices soaring skyward and made strikingly evident the shortage in international books. Emphasis has been thrown upon a condition already developing and bound to arrive regardless of the war."[1]

Quite obviously these conditions are beyond the power of the librarian to remedy. In view of the limited supply of printed materials available in certain fields of knowledge, it becomes evident that it is no longer possible for each library to be strong in all departments of knowledge. Money with which to buy will not correct this situation.

If there is to be the largest possible development of research in this country, there will need to be fuller definition on the part of higher educational institutions of the types of research they will undertake. These limitations should be established in the interests of scholarship and as a means of effecting financial economies. There are fields of research so specialized that there is need for only a limited number of centers. In some fields of knowledge the printed resources are so limited that there are enough for only a very few centers. These conditions call for a coordination of effort on the part of higher institutions of learning. An arrangement of this type lies beyond the power of librarians. It is a problem for trustees, administrative officers, and faculty members. It means that most institutions will have to make a choice between mediocrity of work in a wide range of subjects and a relatively high type of research in a limited number of fields.

As has been implied, the acceptance of this idea of cooperation in the development of library resources does not stop with the library. It raises at once the whole question of cooperation in the development of graduate instruction and research, at least in certain fields. In discussing this problem before the twenty-first annual conference of the Association of American Universities, James R. Angell, president of Yale University, made the following statement:

"At no point in the present administration of research interests in educational institutions is there perhaps more need for searching analysis of present practices than in the methods, or lack of methods, whereby particular lines of research are undertaken. Almost every great university is put in the position of attempting to foster all the major fields of research and an unlimited number of accessory ones. Local pride has repeatedly led to the effort to develop forms of research which may be intrinsically of minor consequence and altogether anomalous in the regions where they are undertaken. State institutions are constantly subjected to pressure of this character, leading to the formation of new departments, some of which have no substantial justification beyond the gratification of the ambition of some energetic professor or some small group whose interests will be theoretically promoted in this way. There exists at present no adequate device by which an indefinite continuation of these conditions may be avoided. Indeed, it is but quite recently that there has grown up any considerable body of opinion recognizing the wastefulness of the present practices. It is of course a matter of the utmost delicacy, and one calling for great breadth of knowledge and great sanity of judgment, to attempt in any fashion to allocate responsibility for particular kinds of research. At the very outset one is met with the contention that any such artificial distribution of functions would operate seriously to cripple individual initiative. And yet the contrary consideration is quite as urgent. To equip every university in the country to carry on research in agriculture, in forestry, in all the branches of engineering, and, for that matter, in all the physical, chemical, and biological sciences, would obviously be wasteful of equipment and physical resources, and all but impossible of execution in the matter of personnel. Certain rough lines of division are in point of fact at present operative. Some institutions by mere virtue of the fact that they secured an

early occupancy of a field have developed
to a considerable degree of advancement
research work in special directions which
might perhaps have been more advantageously
developed elsewhere. But meantime, being
in possession of the property, it would be
ill-advised to attempt to dispossess them.
In any event while it is futile, and were it not
futile it would be unwise, to attempt any
arbitrary and coercive methods in the solution of this general problem, it is not too
much to hope that by intelligent voluntary
cooperation something may be done to
safeguard the situation against an indefinite
continuation of the present condition."[2]

In the judgment of the writer this is one
of the most important problems treated in
this report. It will also be a very difficult
one with which to deal as it runs counter
to most of the current practice. In spite of
the difficulties it presents, there is much that
can be done if those administratively responsible become convinced of its desirability. It is
hardly to be expected that institutions that
have already well-developed lines of research
with good library facilities will drop them.
On the contrary, the proposal implies that
these would be the very lines with which
they would go forward. There were, however but few libraries among those included
in the study that were not, as a result of
pressure from faculty members, attempting
to secure library resources for research in
the fields in which they are not now strong
and in which the supply of printed matter
is so limited that a strong collection could
not be obtained.

Guy S. Ford, dean of the graduate school
of the University of Minnesota, has made a
forceful statement bearing on the interests
of graduate schools in this problem:

"The interest of the Graduate School is in
the reasonable accessibility of the necessary
books. That may be secured for practical
purposes when a long run of a rare periodical,
a first edition, or a valuable set of source material is in the local city public library or in
the library of a neighboring university. At
present, too many universities are buying
without due reference to the neighboring
collections. Four or five universities within a radius of a hundred to two hundred
miles of each other in both eastern and middle western sections are bidding against each

other, paying higher and higher prices for
rarely used sets to which occasional access
is necessary, but sets of which one or two in
a section would by the courtesy of inter-
library loans supply all needs.

"The matter of competing in single purchases as between libraries that should be
cooperating is significant of a more expensive competition into which we may be led
by imitation or the zeal of departments. I
hesitate to name the universities whose libraries—irrespective of their faculties—
furnish 'unrivaled facilities for studying
western history'; the list of these 'strong in
the pamphlet and other source material of
the Frrench Revolution' is equally extensive.
The next decade will see us bidding and
building against each other for South American and oriental history, politics, and literature—not a selected country or period or
phase—but all South America and the whole
Orient. All the middle western and perhaps
the eastern universities may have to check
influences within and without that would
want to make them the greatest centers for
the study of the history, literature, and institutions of all the countries which have
contributed large numbers of immigrants to
the tax-paying population of their section.
All this means spreading out—horizontal distribution of funds—mediocre results at greatly enhanced expenditure.

"Is it wise or necessary or possible for all
Universities to be all things to all advanced
students? Are not the responsibility and the
necessity upon most of us to be respectable
in our library equipment in all the fields—
where the personnel of the faculty justifies
work for the Master's degree; to be good in
what our location or traditions or special
departmental strength justifies and to be
the best where all these three combine and
make us the logical place where library excellence is to be expected? Should we not
make our special treasures immediately
available by special bibliographies, by gen-
erosity in inter-library loans, accepting
commissions to photograph or copy whenever the demand is made and the expenses
paid? Then in those fields where we are
wisely and respectably mediocre let us
depend upon loans ourselves and send our
students on to the greater opportunities
that offer elsewhere in the fields where

we have determined not to be a claimant for pre-eminence."[3]

Reference has been made to the fact that competition among the libraries is not only greatly increasing the cost of securing material but, much worse, results in the scattering of the material. From the standpoint of a large development of research, it would be better if there were more concentration of the materials treating of highly specialized fields of knowledge and of those in which there are distinct limitations in the supply of printed materials.

Would it not be possible to divide the country into regions and in each secure agreement among the educational institutions with reference to the lines of highly specialized research each will undertake? In some instances there may not be need for more than one center in this country. When the regional divisions have been determined, there should be cooperation among the libraries of each region in securing the needed book resources. To secure the cooperation of the librarians would not be very difficult. Many of them realize the weaknesses of the present practices and are in favor of correcting them. References will be found to the problem in their literature. A portion of a statement dealing with this question follows:

"This leads us very naturally to consider this problem of supplying the full record of science to our men of science. It is not a local problem merely. It is also a national problem. The difficulties in the way are partly those of finance, partly those of time, partly competition, not alone among American libraries, but with those of Japan and China, of South America and South Africa, of New Zealand and Australia. Very much of the material required by this group before me was published in but a small edition, running from a couple of hundred in the case of certain very costly books, to a thousand or more for certain journals. In their beginnings journals and transactions are frequently issued in only sufficient numbers to meet the actual number of subscribers. You all know how the wastebasket yawns for odd numbers, and what chances of destruction stray copies must run between careless or absent-minded owners, house-maids, janitors, the frugal housewife and the rag-man. Wars and disasters intervene to reduce the numbers of copies in existence. I have no hesitation in saying that the possibility of securing sets of certain very much valued books and journals is diminishing even to the vanishing point with each year that goes by. The world war was destructive of reserves, caused restriction in the number of copies printed, and increased enormously the cost of printed matter of all sorts. In some cases known to me no copies were printed beyond the actual home demand, totally ignoring foreign or enemy subscribers. I know of one American journal which actually printed last December one hundred and fifty copies less than its regular subscription list, because paper took a sudden jump in price and only the stock on hand was used. This sort of thing makes the task of securing sets anything but easy. The chief source of supply is the libraries of deceased professors as they come on the market—and professors who own and bind long files of journals and transactions are becoming rarer with the high cost of living and the decreasing amount of shelf space in modern homes and apartments. The necessity of quick action cannot be stressed unduly in view of the present circumstances. It is not a question any longer of waiting for a favorable opportunity. Rather are we faced with the necessity of getting what we need whenever the chance comes up. The competition from the newer countries and the newer libraries is keener every year. Thirty years ago there was no large scientific library west of us—not one. Now we may mention the Universities of Chicago, Illinois, Wisconsin, Minnesota, Iowa, Nebraska, California, Leland, Stanford, Washington, and the John Crerar Library, without even exhausting the list of institutions of the first rank—for special libraries in a small field are equally dangerous competitors for the valuable books and sets in their own line. In those same thirty years South Amercia, South Africa, Japan, Australia, and Canada have come into the field eager to provide their scientists with the record of science. McGill University bought just before me last fall very many sets of journals long on our list of desiderata. I found Japanese buyers had been everywhere with the government purse to draw on. The fact is that we must both hasten our own purchases and combine with our neighbors if American learning is to be kept on an equality with that of Europe.

"The need of cooperation and of a policy looking to the elimination of certain forms of competition is brought home to me more keenly each year. We should be able, it would seem, to agree on certain fields which we can cultivate intensively, securing everything of moment in them, as far as we can raise the funds. Certain general works, general society transactions, journals of a wide appeal we must *all* have. But must we—take a concrete case— *all* try to buy the publications of the smaller and less important societies? May not half a dozen sets spread over the country suffice with the development of the inter-library loan and of photo-duplicating machines? Can we not agree with Chicago, Urbana, Cleveland, Columbus, Pittsburgh, and Ithaca on a limit in purchasing such local society publications? Thus we might *all* save money, keep down prices, gain in the total number of sets available, and lend freely between ourselves. This matter seems to me highly important—even vital to our success. It has been much discussed among librarians. There would be small difficulty in arriving at a policy, if it were a matter to be decided by librarians alone. But it concerns far more deeply the faculties of the various universities and their governing boards. We librarians cannot, for example, get together and agree on a limitation of our several fields of specialization. We must first gain adherents to a policy of limitation, then form an agreement through some joint committee of professors, and finally secure the consent of boards of regents and trustees. The facts are most clear and patent. We simply cannot all have everything. There isn't enough to go 'round, nor money enough to buy everything. What we must do, then, in common sense is to stop trying to get everything in each library, and go for the things we can reasonably expect to secure in cooperation with our neighbors. If any one doubts the success of this plan, I refer him to the results of the agreement between the Chicago libraries made in 1895 and carried out since to the lasting benefit of scholarship. There is every reason why we should enter into a similar pact with neighboring libraries."[4]

Such practical problems as the extreme loyalty of the alumnus who cannot tolerate having a rival institution possess a better Goethe collection than his alma mater would

have to be met; also that of the prospective choice for a faculty position who stipulates as one condition of his acceptance the practically unlimited expansion of the library on the side of his research interests. The result frequently is the collection of materials which remain unused when the faculty member migrates. Several cases were found in which very expensive collections remained unused as a result of this procedure.

A further difficulty that would present itself would be the inability of an institution to give to each graduate student, regardless of his interests, library resources for the conduct of his research. This would make it necessary for him to go to another institution for at least a part of his work. It should be pointed out that this problem is not peculiar to the proposed plan. It is also a characteristic of the present unsystematized procedure. The proposed plan would have the advantage of making it possible for the graduate student to find the specialized materials in which he is interested concentrated at one institution. There is no doubt at all but that it would be cheaper in many instances for institutions to pay all the expense incident to his going to another institution to secure access to the materials he needs for his research than to purchase them, even when this is possible.

It should be relatively easy for the librarians and research workers of a given region to decide upon the fields in which the materials are so limited or so expensive that it is either impossible or too costly to duplicate collections. When this has been done and the specialized interests of each institution are known to the others, the cooperation could be readily carried forward. A more serious difficulty to be met is that of securing some agreement on the part of the universities with reference to the highly specialized fields in which each will undertake research and graduate instruction. If an agreement were reached on the development of library resources that aspect of the problem might eventually be more easily solved.

It would be desirable to have some organization sponsor such a program of cooperation. Without some general attempt the cooperation is almost certain to be confined to such more or less accidental efforts as will be mentioned later. This is not adequate. Would it not be appropriate for the Association of American

Universities to interest itself in such a program? It is a matter of vital concern to graduate schools.

It should be recognized that a measure of cooperation is to be found at present. It exists between Stanford University and the University of California, with reference to the Hoover War Library and the Bancroft Library, respectively. The University of Michigan Library does not buy genealogy because this is a field in which the Detroit Public Library specializes, nor does it endeavor to secure unusual books that are to be found in the White Collection of the Cleveland Public Library. There also is cooperation between the New York Public Library and the Columbia University Library. The library of the University of Minnesota has an agreement with the Minnesota Historical Society covering genealogy and local history. It is also cooperating with the Minneapolis Public Library and James Jerome Hill Library of St. Paul with reference to

the purchase of certain kinds of materials.

It is unnecessary to point out that this proposal does not imply that each university will not have the publications necessary for its undergraduate work. Neither does it mean that among the cooperating institutions there shall not be research in each of the institutions in such major lines as are appropriate to the institution and in which there are book resources as well as competent workers. It means only that it will be applied in the highly specialized fields, or in those lines in which the publications are so limited that it is impossible to secure adequate resources. It means concentration of resources rather than their dispersal, with the result that each institution will recognize the special interests of its neighbors. It is believed that this type of cooperation if continued over a period of fifty years would mean a larger development of research than can possibly result from the present procedure.

FOOTNOTES

[1] Charles W. Smith. The Vanishing Supply of Research Periodicals, *The Library Journal,* XLIX (1924), p. 117.

[2] The Organization of Research, *Journal of Proceedings and Addresses of the Twenty-first Annual Conference of the Association of American Universities* (1919), p. 29.

[3] The Library and the Graduate School, *Journal of Proceedings and Addresses of the Fifteenth Annual Conference of the Association of American Universities* (1913), pp. 43-44.

[4] William W. Bishop. *The Backs of Books* (Baltimore: The Williams & Wilkins Co., 1926), pp. 289-92.

ABOUT THE AUTHOR

—**George Alan Works** (d. 1957), Dean, University of Chicago Graduate Library School, 1927-1929; Ed.D., 1925, Harvard University. His major efforts were in the study of the administration and organization of institutions of higher education.

The Indiana University Regional Campus Libraries: Self-Survey, 1965

by Michael M. Reynolds

The need to provide higher educational possibilities for an ever increasing number of students has modified social and political attitudes about the geographical exclusiveness of higher education. Whether in a single school or as a system of higher education, these new pressures have resulted in the rapid proliferation of educational facilities and the consequent rise of the multiversity, with the subsequent demand for significant library resources at each location. As described in this report, competition for library resources is compounded in a multi-locational institution. This will produce a trend toward conformity in the development of the library at the different places. The academic librarian can, on the other hand, attempt to effect substantive changes in the attitude of the institution toward the role of the library and aim toward an integrated system, capable of supporting diversity within its components.

PRESENT CONDITIONS

Analysis

It would not be meaningful to review the historical development of the libraries on the Regional Campuses in terms of liberal arts colleges serving comparable numbers of students, much less the Indiana University Library at Bloomington. As it spread its too limited resources and energies to meet the various and changing commitments at the various centers, the Extension Division could not have appreciated the type of library which is considered necessary in a liberal arts curriculum. Indeed, this would not even have been pertinent.

Despite the diversity existing among the various Regional Campuses they share the same common problems. With respect to collection, services and space, the libraries at the Regional Campuses up to the past five years could have been called college libraries only out of kindness; and, while considerable improvements have taken place, they are still patently inadequate. Now with graduate work being offered at the Centers, an ever-increasing number of courses in science and technology, and the continuing requirements of the faculty to keep abreast of the professional literature in their fields and, for whatever the nexus of reasons, to publish, the collections can only be viewed as grossly substandard.

Program

The six libraries comprising the Regional Campus Libraries had originated as separate entities and had grown as parts, each one performing the full spectrum of its functions independent of each other or of the General Library at Bloomington. As the President's Committee on Library Problems of the Regional Campuses (1964) indicated, possibly the most effective arrangement for the development of the campus libraries into installations capable of supporting junior and four year college programs would be to centralize technical processing (purchasing, the recording of bibliographic information, and book preparation) at Bloomington. In this way the staff at each Regional Campus would be able to concentrate on the most important functions of a college library, support and intensification of the educational experience and building and maintaining a collection that reflects the school's program.

In essence this is the course being followed at present. The burden of technical processing is being shifted from each library to Bloomington and a Regional Campus staff, separate

SOURCE: Reprinted from Indiana University Regional Campus Libraries, "Regional Campus Libraries: Self-Survey, 1965" (Bloomington, Indiana: 1965), mimeographed, by permission of the author.

from that of the University's General Library, is now evolving techniques whereby the libraries at the Regional Campus will receive library materials ready for use. Within this arrangement each Regional Campus continues to initiate the requests for the material it needs. No attempt is being made by the Bloomington staff to provide common book collections, control the growth of the collections, or reduce the duplication among the libraries or between them and the Bloomington Campus libraries.

However, as the local professional staffs have been freed from a major portion of their previous responsibilities, it is anticipated that they will be instrumental in building a corpus of library materials which the particular school has to have to meet the requirements of a two, three or four year program. In addition, the Library Committee at each campus has been requested to make definite allocations of the book budget to the individual departments and to assign a part of the budget to the library. It is hoped that this procedure will provide a modicum of the supportive library materials needed for current and future academic and research commitments and will make the book budget an instrument for a reasoned growth of the collection.

In providing funds for building the collections, considerable care must be taken that a balance between the library needs of the academic program and the library needs of the faculty as individuals be maintained. It is one thing to support an active member of a faculty; it is another to accede to the theory that the faculty has *carte blanche* spending privileges, thereby losing control of the money to buy the standard high-use monographs and journals.

Fostering this balance between the systematic development of the collection and the book hunger of a faculty which must be aggressive to be successful is one of the most difficult problems now facing the Regional Campus Libraries. And if the present practice of hiring academics with terminal degrees is continued and the reward system is kept within the structure of the departments at the Bloomington campus, the growing faculty will make a proportionately larger demand for books to support individual interests. Yet unless this balance can be effected and maintained, a generation of students will be faced with a lack of basic materials in their own library.

The establishment of a base of library operation at the Bloomington campus has made it possible for the Regional Campus Libraries to extend the volume of library materials and range of services they can offer to the students and faculty on the Regional Campuses. Members of the Regional Campus Libraries Bloomington staff working in conjunction with the local staffs attempt to supply materials and information not available locally. Fortunately, the size and quality of the collections at Bloomington are such that they can act as an effective backstop collection. However, in keeping with the concept underlying this service—that location need not be a limitation—and even to promote its acceptance and stimulate its greater use, items requested from the campuses but not owned by the university are located at other libraries and these libraries too are asked to lend them. In many instances this material could only have been located through the use of a major bibliographic collection, such as exists on the Bloomington campus. In the future as the staffs at the Regional Campuses are able to devote more time to their patrons and as the patrons themselves are conditioned to expect this service as a normal library activity, this network should play a significant part in the growing role of the libraries at the Regional Campuses.

While a major move in the direction of making more efficient use of the University's total library resources and one which can be expected to develop techniques for expediting the movement of library materials, this concept should be analyzed for the ramifications it may have in all parts of the University's library system. For notwithstanding the certainty that there will be an increase in the size and quality of local collections and staff, the need for, and the expectation of materials and services beyond those which can be supplied at the immediate libraries will increase at an even greater rate.

Goals

There is still some lack of understanding of an agreement on the function and duties of the Assistant Director of Libraries charged with the development of Regional Campus Libraries. However, what is lacking in definition is more than offset by the tangible support and the encouragement from the administrative officers of the Extension Division and the University Library. The Assistant Director has assumed that if he is charged with the development of libraries, all library activities and all things pertaining to libraries come under his purview.

Needless to say the sudden introduction of this office and of this idea of comprehensive responsibility into the Extension Division has raised organizational difficulties. On the assumption that the above organizational pattern is intended and that it is desirable, it will require from three to five years to define and to refine the management arrangements to a place where the components of the Regional Campus Libraries can work systematically and logically. Among the areas which must be deliberately improved are the following:

1. The assignment of, and agreement upon, the role of the faculty, faculty library committee and the Regional Campus Librarian in policy making, building of the collection and operation of the library.

2. The reporting relationships of the Assistant Director of Libraries and the Regional Campus Librarians to the Extension Division, the University Library, Regional Campus Directors, Regional Campus Library Committees, etc.

3. The character and quality of the staffs at the Regional Campus Libraries and at Bloomington. On the local level this will mean developing college/university librarians who are capable of administering the rapidly expanding campus libraries and are able to work within the context of the Regional Campus Libraries system. At Bloomington it will mean developing a cadre capable of supervising a line operation and, at the same time, assuming responsibility for administrative and staff functions.

4. The budgeting and accounting procedures under which Regional Campus Libraries operates in order to provide better instruments for planning and control and to take advantage of the new techniques in electronic accountancy and bibliographic recording.

5. The standards of performance, management tools, and work routines at the local libraries.

The present organizational arrangement of the Regional Campus Libraries offers many obvious and covert advantages. The sum of these is the improvement in the quality of the library function at the Regional Campuses and the increased effectiveness and economic efficiency of the human and material resources available for this function.

Direction for the Future

If the University wants the libraries at the Regional Campuses to develop into college or university type installations, the present Regional Campus Libraries organization is basically sound, though it may be, at best, medical care for a type of library organism which may already be dead. The hard fact is that even given optimum conditions for growth, the Regional Campus Libraries will continue to suffer a relative diminution of ability to provide resources and services. In turn, if the General Library at Bloomington is not given an opportunity to bring its administrative expertise to bear on the piecemeal development of Regional Campus Libraries, the resources for total University Library growth can well be dissipated. The object should not be to repeat the past piecemeal, but to stress the proposition that a broadly based approach is vital.

Much of the current effort of the Regional Campus Libraries in organizing the individual libraries for service and in establishing standards of operation is necessary. Yet to expect *a priori* that each Regional Campus library can and should provide total immediate or in-house access to information for every part of its clientele is clearly unsound. It would be equally unsound to accept for the Regional Campus Libraries many of the traditional ideas of the acquisition, storage, bibliographic control, retrieval and use of library material and information.

The forces of modern technology have made these ideas obsolete. With the development of rapid communication and transportation systems and with the existence of a major research collections, the capabilities are present to create a true Indiana University Library serving all parts of the University.

There are more problems involved in developing such a total University Library system than can be enumerated here. Not the least of these is the concept mentioned above that each separate library should provide immediate access to all general and professional publications at the moment they are required. Faced with the informational demands of his environment the academic user demands and is conditioned not to expect otherwise. To satisfy the book needs of the faculty and students at the Regional Campuses, the research library facilities at the Bloomington Campus will have to become a regular and natural extension of their own libraries. As a library for the Regional Campus libraries, Bloomington should also play an important part in resolving the problems of inventory.

At present, and in spite of their limited means, the Regional Campus librarians are alert to the potential directions of the teaching and research activities on their campuses, and in order to avoid being found wanting by newly appointed faculty or faculty whose research interest has shifted, tend to provide minimal collections in a multitude of areas. The direct cost of these capital speculations added to the costs of processing, space, storage and overhead costs might be better used in other areas of the Center's program. By the same token, continuing to house low-frequency use material, whether monographs, serials or the accumulated efforts of departed faculty members, will almost certainly require the continuous expansion of library facilities without a corollary of increased use of the collection. It would be far less expensive to supply low use materials from a central source than to attempt to build major collections—which would still not be adequate—at each Regional Campus.

In addition to establishing a principle, methodology, and procedural basis for the development of the collections, a better relationship must be sought between the physical requirements of the various Regional Campus activities. On an urban campus these requirements are not the same as those of the traditional home-away-from-home institution.

The difference between the function of a library and that of a study area is a very real

and obvious one—though the functions are not always mutually exclusive. It costs too much to construct, maintain and service a library to use it as a study hall. The commuting student must be provided with a place to study other than the library.

While the needs for space, which were so critical to 1965, are being met, and the prospects for the near future are encouraging, there is still the need for better expression of the library's space requirements. This can be determined only on the basis of the number and kind of undergraduate, graduate and faculty library user, the ultimate size of the collection, the functions and quality of these functions the library is to perform, and the activities other than library performed by the library.

Unfortunately, it is far easier to suggest problems and insist they be resolved than to resolve them. Yet it is essential that choices—even difficult choices—be made. In an institution with infinite resources, it would be far easier to suggest, as many public libraries do, that everyone must be served equally and that every library service and piece of information must be provided. Implementing the educational function of Indiana University as expressed at its Regional Campuses, however, requires that even at a mediocre level of operation, considerable judgment must be exercised. The immediate and future goals of the Regional Campus program must be so outlined as to make calculations of what is essential to attain given ends.

A chair is for sitting. It is not for decorative effect, for matching a table, or to be made necessarily of plastic, wood or steel. A Regional Campus Library is for supporting the educational role of the Regional Campus; it is not for decorative effect, for buying and storing books, or for the personal gratification of faculty, students, or librarian. This function may best be realized by withering away preconceived ideas on the development of the Regional Campus Libraries and working within the framework of a University Library system.

ABOUT THE AUTHOR

—**Michael M. Reynolds**, Associate Dean, University of Maryland School of Library and Information Services; Ph.D., 1964, University of Michigan. At the time of this survey he was Assistant Director of Libraries for Regional Campus Libraries at Indiana University. His major research interests are in multi-library cooperation and library administration.

THE LIBRARY PERFORMING

Professions characteristically have a practical orientation, as much because of a lack of an understanding of fundamental ideas as from the need to respond to the immediacy of operational obligations. The academic librarian must be constantly alert to the tendency of a particular activity to develop a separate validity, urgency, and form.

The Dual Assignment: Cataloging and Reference

by Frank Arthur Lundy, Kathryn R. Renfro, and Esther M. Schubert

Of the variety of issues raised by this article, the most significant for the academic library administrator might well be that of manpower utilization. In questioning the traditional functional cleavages, analyzing them in terms of their interrelationships, and integrating them into a total process to provide information to library users in large—but relatively discrete—service areas, the educational and professional preparation and the performance expectations of librarians are given a different perspective.

THE DIVISIONAL CONCEPT

The divisional concept in librarianship is based upon an approach to all organization and service through subject matter. The initial approach is made in the divisional reading room. The divisional reading room, in contrast to the departmental reading room, serves three or more departments of instruction and research in an institution of higher education; hence, the word divisional, implying a group of closely related subjects, such as the humanities, the social sciences, the biological sciences, the physical sciences.

Prior to the introduction of the divisional concept in the organization of a college or university library, the public service departments were based upon other concepts altogether, such as reference work and reference books, periodicals and newspapers, documents in the connotation of that word peculiar to librarianship, and reserved books. The divisional concept of subject matter may have had its first applications to librarianship in the consolidation of two or more closely related departmental reading rooms or branch libraries. It should be noted in passing that the divisional concept has long been applied successfully in a few large public libraries, quite apart from the academic environment of higher education.

The concept of the divisional reading room offered an opportunity to present the undergraduate student with a well-rounded open-shelf collection of books and periodicals suited to his interests. The humanities reading room thus immediately became a reading room full of books and periodicals in the humanities, commonly including such subjects as English and foreign languages and literatures, together with philosophy and religion. The fine arts may be included here, or they may be made the subject matter of a fine arts division. Under this plan the library on the campus now for the first time offered the undergraduate student a reading room full of books selected to serve conveniently his own special interests, instead of those of the librarians in charge. Here, in one place, he could find books and periodicals in the field of his undergraduate major, together with their special indexes and the related encyclopedias, without being routed around from place to place; from the card catalog to the loan desk and book stack; from the reference room to the current periodicals room, or to the reserved book room.

The concept of the divisional reading room also offered the librarian an opportunity to select and employ his staff on the basis of their subject interests and training as well as for their professional interests and training in librarianship. Reference librarians now become humanities librarians, or social science librarians, or physical science librarians. Ideal educational training under this concept is recruit-

SOURCE: Reprinted from Frank A. Lundy, Kathryn R. Renfro and Esther M. Shubert, "The Dual Assignment: Cataloging and Reference: A Four-Year Review of Cataloging in the Divisional Plan," *Library Resources and Technical Services* 3: 167-188 (1959), by permission of the authors.

ing would include two master's degrees or their equivalent, one in an appropriate subject and one in librarianship. Librarians in training, with bachelor's degrees and possibly some graduate work in one of the languages or literatures, in philosophy, or in the fine arts, would become ideal recruits for appointment to the humanities division. In the science division, on the other hand, one would seek librarians in training, who had majored in one of the physical or biological sciences, or in mathematics. The logic of assigning new recruits to librarianship in accordance with their known subject interests and training, since all college graduates commonly present a major field of interest as a *fait accompli,* would seem to be so obvious as to need no defense here.

Extensions of the Divisional Concept

The idea of the divisional reading room, stocked with books and periodicals covering a broad but closely related group of subjects, and staffed with librarians whose special interests qualify them for work in these subjects, is commonly understood and accepted. The extension of the divisional concept beyond the boundaries of the reading room is, however, neither commonly understood nor accepted. It is for this reason, therefore, that this paper summarizing an eight-year experience with the extension of the divisional concept into cataloging may be of more than casual interest to many readers.

A first extension of the divisional concept of staffing already described would logically occur in book selection. Why not apply the formal training and the personal interests of the reference staff in the humanities division to the selection of books and periodicals for the library? On the academic campus this becomes a shared responsibility, and the humanities staff will find that a large part of its work in book selection will find expression in stimulating selection on the part of the faculty and in correlating all book selection within the established budget framework. The staff will inevitably, of course, make a major contribution of its own to book selection. Under this plan of management the acquisition department is no longer the sole or principal agency for book selection within the library walls. The acquisition department must, however, assume its share of responsibility for selection in the fields of general bibliography

and incomplete sets. All subjects, as such, are assignable to the subject-oriented divisions.

Book selection, properly conceived as a function of librarians, must assume some of the technical aspects of precataloging. To be selected as an appropriate addition to the library, the book must first be correctly identified, bibliographically speaking. This initial effort, properly recorded, becomes the first step in the cataloging process. The useful and useable knowledge of the reference librarian in the subject division is immediately extended by this first-hand acquaintance with books and periodicals newly selected for acquisition. The books selected may not be new books altogether, but they will be new to the library. The librarian involved in their selection, identification, and preliminary checking will then be better informed of the resources shortly to be available to him.

Contrary to common practice, it seems illogical at this point to introduce a new staff to catalog and classify these same books. As we have described it, book selection and pre-cataloging have already become a function of the reference staff in the subject division. We now extend this responsibility to include full cataloging and classification of all newly acquired material, limited only by the boundaries of subject matter; that is, the humanities staff catalogs only humanities materials.

Briefly stated, this plan implies that a divisional staff is recruited on the basis of its formal training, both in subject matter and in librarianship, in order effectively to serve the public in a library organized by subject divisions. This same divisional staff is given a broad assignment of responsibility including not only reference work with students and faculty but also a major share in the selection of materials for acquisition. Since book selection involves many of the elements of precataloging, this same reference staff is assigned to the full cataloging and classification of all new materials appropriate to the division involved. So assigned, the same staff divides its time between the public service and the technical service. The same individuals select materials for acquisition, catalog, classify, and use them to serve the public. This we call the dual-assignment: the ultimate extension of the divisional plan.

WHAT IS A CATALOGER?

Guy Lyle[1] has explained that a cataloger must graduate from college and also from library school; that he must have a knowledge of books, of the uses of catalogs, bibliographies, and book lists, and of classification and cataloging procedures; that he must have a reading knowledge of one or more foreign languages; that he must have an understanding of modern library organization, procedure, policy, aims, and service, particularly in relation to cataloging; and that he must have an appreciation of the objectives of higher education. He says further that a cataloger must be resourceful and exhibit good judgment, orderliness, and accuracy; that he must have ability to organize work and to follow instructions; that he must get along well with supervisors, co-workers, and subordinates. These are the qualifications expected of almost any librarian. They are especially pertinent to reference librarians, as well as to catalogers.

Catalogers sometimes tend to work in an ivory tower situation. Cataloging can become a cult, the end of which is cataloging for the sake of cataloging. Such cataloging may produce perfection in the principles of entry, adequacy in cross-references for subject headings, and accuracy in filing. Without direct contact with students and faculty, however, and without continuous communication with colleagues throughout the library, such cataloging will inevitably fail to reflect in the classification of materials the actual use made of them. It will also fail in some degree in the use of subject headings and analytics with appropriate adaptation to actual classroom instruction and research. It should be remembered at all times that the catalog is the basic bibliographical tool in the library. It is the most important tool the reference librarian has at his disposal.

In some libraries the catalog department, being somewhat apart from the public eye, has become the repository of all of the library's unsolvable personnel problems. It has become an escape hatch for inept administrators. The ivory tower complex and the maladjusted personality seem to go well together, but such a combination is not suited to the creation of a card catalog conceived to be in the public interest

and with the specific needs of the reference librarian uppermost in mind.

WHAT IS A REFERENCE LIBRARIAN?

Something should be said on the other side of the question as to what is a cataloger. The reference librarian tends to wear a halo, albeit sometimes the halo is too small for the individual trying to wear it. This has been a tendency all to prevalent in recent years both in reference departments and in library school courses in reference work. The reference librarian is the individual who can and should be the most helpful in interpreting the library's collections to the user, be he student or teacher or public library patron. If it is true that the most important tool in the library is the catalog, then the reference librarian's very work itself must depend upon a high degree of expertness in understanding the card catalog and in exploiting its contents in the public interest.

It is often said that the best way to learn a subject is to teach it. It can also be said that the best way to master the card catalog is to participate in its making. A card catalog of over a million cards is a complicated instrument, even at best and with a reasonable degree of simplification. Effective use of such a card file requires a comprehensive grasp of the rules of entry and an understanding of all the essential elements of bibliographic description. Nowhere is such an understanding better acquired than through actual experience in cataloging. If all administrators had actual experience of some duration in the catalog department of a well run library, some of these same administrators would then be less prone than they now are to make absurd public pronouncements on the costs and procedures of cataloging.

More important still, if reference librarians could have substantial experience in actual cataloging, not only would they be less critical of the work of catalogers who must forever be seeking the perfect compromise between the actual book and the appropriate cataloging rule or classification theory; they would by the very experience itself become more expert in the use of the card catalog. They would then be less inclined to blame the catalogers for what appear to them at first glance to be the intricacies and omissions of the card catalog, an attitude which is too often based upon their own ignorance of current cataloging practice. It follows, too, that if the reference librarians take a hand in actual cataloging, the card catalog will tend to become better adapted to public need. This can be true in many important respects: in the choice of subject headings, for example, or in modifications of the classification scheme, or in the selection of details of descriptive cataloging.

WHAT IS A LIBRARIAN?

Unless the library is so large that a high degree of specialization in its staff is inescapable, the library will benefit in many ways if its professional employees can practice their profession broadly rather than narrowly. On the academic campus the librarian's principal responsibility is the organization of the collections for use and their interpretation to the community of students and scholars. This work implies the continuous use of several common library processes which are based upon sound bibliographic technique. The more obvious of these processes are book selection and pre-cataloging; full cataloging and classification; and interpretation through the use of books and reference tools.

In all of these closely interrelated processes sound bibliographic technique is essential. It implies a fundamental knowledge of book analysis and book description, and a comprehensive grasp of the content and relative usefulness of book lists of all kinds, whether they be subject bibliographies, printed catalogs of libraries, indexes, abstracts, or dealer's lists, or the card catalog itself. Sound bibliographic knowledge and technique are to librarianship what algebra is to all higher mathematics, or human anatomy to the whole field of medicine.

A reference librarian who is intimidated by the card catalog, or one who shies away from the cataloging process, is actually no rererence librarian at all, but an information clerk. We believe it to be equally true that a cataloger who is intimidated by the notion of working with books in relation to people, who wants to hide behind a stack of books in a catalog department and without an actual first hand acquaintance with the use to which the card catalog is actually put in the daily work of the library, is not a cataloger in the best interest of the library, but a recluse of one sort or another.

THE UNIVERSITY OF NEBRASKA: A CASE-STUDY OF THE DUAL-ASSIGNMENT

The Technical Service Division consists of two departments: Acquisition and Catalog. The primary responsibilities of the Acquisition Department may be described as purchases, gifts, and exchanges. This Department also has secondary functions, including centralized serial records and bindery preparations. The primary responsibilities of the Catalog Department are the cataloging and classification of printed materials in all their forms. Its secondary responsibilities include the processing of materials. The Technical Service Division serves the central university library and all the branch, departmental, and laboratory libraries on the two Lincoln campuses of the University.

The present staff of the Catalog Department has three full-time professionals: a Catalog Librarian and two Senior Assistant Catalogers; eight half-time Junior Catalogers assigned from the divisions: two each from Humanities, Social Studies, and Science & Technology, and one each from Agriculture and Law; and nine full-time classified service personnel: two Junior Librarians, two Library Assistants, and five Clerk-Typists.[2]

Administrative responsibility and authority for all cataloging and classification reside in the Catalog Librarian and her two full-time Senior Assistant Librarians. These three break in and direct the work of the eight half-time catalogers. They also undertake their share of the more difficult original cataloging and the direction of the many special projects which inevitably fall to the lot of the Catalog Department. Librarians from the subject divisions catalog and classify the great bulk of the materials flowing into the Catalog Department, but they do so under the supervision and authority of the Catalog Librarian. Centralized authority for supervision assures continuity in the work and at least a reasonable level of uniformity in cataloging practice.

The University of Nebraska's card catalog is a union catalog of all the University's books. All books owned by the University are considered to be a part of the University Library. A reasonable degree of continuity and uniformity in cataloging practice would, therefore, seem to be highly desirable in the maintenance and development of the catalog records of the collections. The card catalog is the primary bibliographic tool of all librarianship in the university library, and a costly one too, be it noted. The University of Nebraska is estimated to have invested three-quarters of a million dollars in direct cataloging costs.

The librarians from the subject divisions are responsible for descriptive and subject cataloging and also for the classification of all materials flowing into their respective subject areas. This includes materials for which Library of Congress cards may be had, serial cataloging, and original cataloging. Each of the divisional librarians brings to this work an interest in special subject areas. For example, one of the librarians from the Division of Science & Technology majored in the biological sciences, and another is now completing a master's degree in physics. In the practice of librarianship these special interests inevitably broaden to include cognate subjects. This special knowledge is also applied to cataloging. Questions of classification practice, for example, are discussed between the Junior and Senior Catalogers in the Department. Policy decisions are referred to the Catalog Librarian and may also involve the Assistant Director for Technical Service and the corresponding officer in the subject division. Such exchanges of ideas and information have developed practical approaches to mutual problems and an *esprit de corps* that would be hard to duplicate in an organization where such easy communication did not prevail. Full and open discussion of such problems does not in any way imply a loose organization. Responsibilities, with commensurate authority, are clearly assigned and this is fully understood.

The nine classified service personnel are assigned to marking and bookplating the physical volumes, typing catalog cards, and filing or withdrawing cards from the dictionary catalog or the shelflist. The Library Assistants and the Junior Librarians, who are sub-professionals, handle added volumes, copies, and editions; card filing and its supervision; the training and supervision of the Clerk-Typists including revision of their card typing; revising and releasing books after processing; and so-called brief cataloging. It is essential that an adequate complement of classified service personnel support the catalog program in the dual-assignment situation. The subject specialists from the divisions are too valuable in catalog-

ing and in reference work to have their time and energies dissipated upon any of the tasks which can as well or better be delegated to supporting personnel. Their bibliographical work is highly professional, and maintaining it on this level helps to sell the program to reference librarians who thought they never wanted to catalog books.

Productivity and Cost

Questions are frequently asked concerning the cost and productivity of Nebraska's cataloging program. The general impression seems to be that it may cost more to catalog books under this plan than in a traditional catalog department and that productivity may be less. Is this true or false? It is true that there are no statistics available with which we can uniformly compare our production and costs. This study, however, attempts to define and describe Nebraska's catalog program and to isolate special factors affecting it during the period 1954/55 through 1957/58. Tables I and II summarize cataloging personnel and personnel costs during this period.

The Catalog Department is the centralized agency for the system of libraries on the two Lincoln campuses. The College of Medicine Library is not included in this operation since it is located over fifty miles away in Omaha. In addition to the union catalog in the Love Memorial Library (the central university library), the Catalog Department supplies the cards and maintains the catalogs in four divisional reading rooms (humanities, social studies, education, and science), in two major branch libraries (agriculture and law), and in five departmental libraries. All processed books and all catalog records emanate from the central agency and, with the exception of a simple play and short story index prepared in the Humanities Division, no special indexes or supplementations to the catalogs are made locally in the public service departments. This means that the total cataloging cost is represented in our tabulations.

The operations performed by the Catalog Department include: descriptive cataloging, classification and subject headings, shelflisting, preparation and filing of cards, and the processing of the physical volumes. It is important to note here that the major portion of time expended in Library of Congress card searching and in bibliographic searching is not charged to cataloging. At Nebraska, the bibliographic work both for card ordering and for establishing correct entry is done by the subject specialists in connection with book selection. This we have already referred to as pre-cataloging. All essential bibliographic information is recorded on the order cards and these will go forward with the books to cataloging. This eliminates duplication of initial searching. Some new materials do, of course, require additional bibliographic work by the catalogers.

Excepting only the collection in the University High School Library, Library of Congress cards are obtained for all materials insofar as they are available. We do not blindly accept these printed cards, but give them critical review for local adaptation. We have not measured the actual extent of this process of local adaptation.

The Cost of Cataloging

Table III presents an itemized record of cataloging costs. The unit cost *per title* catalogued in 1954/55 was $3.58; in 1955/56 $3.86; in 1956/57 $4.54; and in 1957/58 $5.47. During the same period the unit cost *per volume* was as follows: $2.32 in 1954/55; $1.83 in 1955/56; $2.47 in 1956/57; and $2.34 in 1957/58. It is apparent that the unit cost per title has steadily increased, but that the unit cost per volume reveals no similar pattern. Personnel is the largest and most significant item of cataloging cost. The payroll has increased from $41,228 in 1954/55 to $56,480 in 1957/58. Major increases in salaries occur in 1955/56 and 1957/58, the initial years of the biennial appropriations provided by the State. There is no observable consistent ratio between the cost of personnel and the cost of cataloging, since the human factor and many other variables are involved.

The cost of printed catalog cards is next to personnel in importance. Even though expenditures for books, periodicals, and binding increased from $112,769 in 1954/55 to $149,887 in 1957/58, card costs decreased from $4,655 to $4,109. Here again, such factors as one-time purchases of large groups of Library of Congress cards for recataloging projects in Law and Agriculture explain the deviation.

In view of all the factors involved, the eval-uation of the cost of cataloging with particular reference to the dual-assignment is exceedingly difficult. The variables from year to year such as those mentioned do directly affect cost. However, salaries paid to the professional staff are comparable to those we would otherwise have had to pay full-time catalogers, and certainly the clerical salaries are not very much affected by the organization of the Department. The really basic question is are we getting as much production with this organization as we might get otherwise.

Productivity in Cataloging

Table IV details the production record for the years covered. *Title unit output* for the Catalog Department was 905 in 1954/55; 862 in 1955/56; 724 in 1956/57; and 649 in 1957/58 During the same period the *volume unit output* fluctuated as follows: 1,397 in 1954/55; 1,777 in 1955/56; 1,336 in 1956/57; and 1,518 in 1957/58. It is apparent that in overall production the year 1955/56 was the best. This can be explained only by a careful examination of the individual cataloger's statistical records and an evaluation of related employment factors. Production in 1956/57 suffered because of turnover in staff. A Senior Cataloger resigned in September and was not replaced until July of the next fiscal year. In addition, five new people were trained for junior cataloging positions on half-time assignment. The staff increased in 1957/58. Three people were added to the clerical group and all professional positions were filled during most of the year. But the major factor influencing production at this time was the conversion from a 44-hour clerical week and a 41-hour professional week to a 40-hour week for all employees. A corresponding loss of cataloging time is reflected in the statistics for the year.

These figures of title and volume production do not take into account the other jobs and projects which are a part of the operation of the catalog department. The training of new staff members, both professional and clerical, teaching them the policies of this particular library system, and orienting them to the work of the Department, are important phases of management. The Catalog Librarian does the initial training of each Junior Cataloger. During the period for which we are

TABLE I

Catalog Department Personnel: University of Nebraska Libraries[1]

	PROFESSIONAL FULL-TIME BUDGETED POSITIONS[2]	PROFESSIONAL FULL-TIME EQUIVALENT[3]	PROFESSIONAL HALF-TIME BUDGETED POSITIONS[4]	PROFESSIONAL HALF-TIME IN FULL-TIME EQUIVALENT[3]	CLERICAL FULL-TIME BUDGETED POSITIONS[5]	CLERICAL FULL-TIME EQUIVALENT[3]	STUDENT ASSISTANTS IN FULL-TIME EQUIVALENT[6]	TOTAL STAFF IN FULL-TIME EQUIVALENT
1954/55	3	3	8	3.42	6	5.42	2.43	14.27
1955/56	3	3	8	3.83	6	5.91	2.9	15.64
1956/57	3	2.5	8	3.41	8.5	8.5	1.25	15.66
1957/58	3	3	8	3.92	9	8.83	1.46	17.21

[1] The College of Medicine Library is not included.
[2] Full-time catalogers include the Catalog Librarian and two Senior Catalogers (revisors and supervisors).
[3] The "full-time equivalent" is computed on the basis of a full-time position for twelve months employment. To illustrate by example from column four: two Junior Catalogers working respectively 8 and 9 months on half-time assignment during a fiscal year equal .71 in full-time equivalent. This is calculated as 1/2 of 8/12 plus 1/2 of 9/12.
[4] Half-time Junior Catalogers include two people from each subject division i.e. Humanities, Social Studies, and Science and Technology, plus one person from each branch library: Agriculture and Law. This equates to four full-time positions filled by eight half-time people.
[5] As classified by the University Personnel Office, the clerical complement for 1954-1956 consists of one Junior Librarian, one Library Assistant and four Clerk-Typists. In July 1956, two Clerk-Typists were added and in January 1957 one Junior Librarian. On July 1, 1957, a Clerk-Typist was reclassified to Library Assistant.
[6] Student Assistants are employed on an hourly schedule. The total hours per year have been converted to full-time equivalents on the basis of a 44 hour week during 1954-1957 and a 40 hour week since July 1957. Student Assistants are used to supplement the clerical staff and perform related tasks such as filing, typing and processing.

TABLE II

Catalog Department Personnel Costs: University of Nebraska Libraries

	SALARY EXPENDITURES FOR FULL-TIME CATALOGERS	SALARY EXPENDITURES FOR HALF-TIME CATALOGERS	SALARY EXPENDITURES FOR CLERICAL EMPLOYEES	EXPENDITURES FOR STUDENT ASSISTANCE	TOTAL COST OF PERSONNEL
1954/55	$13,010.37	$13,011.88	$11,406.90	$3,799.41	$41,228.56[1]
1955/56	14,500.00	15,375.00	12,791.57	4,676.70	47,343.27[1]
1956/57	12,923.12	14,456.75	17,358.09	2,447.35	47,185.31
1957/58	15,500.00	18,819.50	19,997.58	2,163.62	56,480.70[1]

[1] Major increases in rates of pay occur bienially.

TABLE III

Catalog Department Costs: University of Nebraska Libraries[1]

	COST OF PERSONNEL	COST OF CARDS[2]	COST OF MISCELLANEOUS SUPPLIES[3]	TOTAL CATALOG DEPT. COSTS	NUMBER OF TITLES CATALOGED	NUMBER OF VOLUMES CATALOGED[4]	UNIT COST PER TITLE CATALOGED	UNIT COST PER VOLUME CATALOGED
1954/55	$41,228.56	$4,655.87	$339.55	$46,223.98	12,912	19,936	$3.58	$2.32
1955/56	47,343.27	4,223.73	479.75	52,046.75	13,482	27,798	3.86	1.83
1956/57	47,185.31	4,003.58	412.75	51,601.64	11,345	20,917	4.54	2.47
1957/58	56,480.70	4,109.64	494.90	61,085.24	11,177	26,125	5.47	2.34

[1] These costs include processing, card production and catalog maintenance. The College of Medicine Library statistics are not included.
[2] The card costs include Library of Congress, H.W. Wilson, and Xerography cards, location and check cards, and card stock.
   The cost of Library of Congress cards is the largest part of this item: 1954/55, $3,907.97; 1955/56, $3,651.33; 1956/57, $3,072.69; 1957/58, $3,396.03. These figures include Library of Congress cards purchased for the College of Medicine Library since there is no convenient way to separate this item of cost.
   Library of Congress cards, when available, are purchased for all titles. Photostat reproductions are purchased when L.C. cards are not available and more than four cards are needed, they are reproduced by Xerography. If cards are typed, the main cost is in the personnel figure. H.W. Wilson cards are pur-chased for the University High School Library and were purchased for the first time in 1956/57. The figures for card stock are estimated.
[3] Supplies include book pockets, book cards, book plates, paste, rubber cement, transfer paper, temporary colored cards and miscellanea such as rubber stamps, pencils, ink, desk pens and rubber bands. These figures are estimated.
[4] A volume is a "bound physical volume," not a "bibliographical unit."

TABLE IV

Catalog Department Production: University of Nebraska Libraries

	AMOUNT SPENT THROUGH THE ACQUISITION DEPARTMENT[1]	NUMBER OF TITLES CATALOGED (MONOGRAPHS AND SERIALS)	NUMBER OF TITLES RE-CATALOGED	TOTAL NUMBER OF TITLES CATALOGED	NUMBER OF VOLUMES ADDED[2]	NUMBER OF VOLUMES RE-CATALOGED	TOTAL NUMBER OF VOLUMES CATALOGED	TOTAL STAFF IN FULL-TIME EQUIVA-LENT[3]	TITLE UNIT OUTPUT PER PERSON FOR CATALOG DEPARTMENT[4]	VOLUME UNIT OUTPUT PER PERSON FOR CATALOG DEPARTMENT[5]
1954/55	$112,769.50	10,445	2,467	12,912	16,831	3,105	19,936	14.27	905	1,397
1955/56	117,567.67	11,757	1,725	13,482	25,110	2,688	27,798	15.64	862	1,777
1956/57	118,287.86	10,434	911	11,345	20,002	915	20,917	15.66	724	1,336
1957/58	149,887.64	10,173	1,004	11,177	24,948	1,177	26,125	17.21	649	1,518

[1] Includes Expenditures for Books, Periodicals and Binding on the Lincoln campuses, excluding the College of Medicine in Omaha.
[2] A volume is a "bound physical volume," not a "bibliographical unit."
[3] See Table I for definition.
[4] Title unit output is calculated by dividing the number of titles by the number of cataloging staff in full-time equivalent.
[5] Volume unit output is calculated by dividing the number of volumes by the number of cataloging staff in full-time equivalent.

presenting statistics, three new Junior Catalogers were trained in 1954/55; two in
1955/56, five in 1956/57, and one Senior
Cataloger as well as three Junior Catalogers
in 1957/58.

Is there any special difference in the training of a cataloger at the University of Nebraska? The rules and forms of entry and
the general policies of the Catalog Department are basic for all librarians. Some newcomers will have more knowledge of cataloging method than others, and some will
have more experience. Many of the Library's policies and routines, especially
classification policy, will be learned in the
divisional reading rooms. Each cataloger
must have a knowledge of cataloging method,
of languages, and of basic subject matter. The
cataloging methods of a given library are much
easier to teach a librarian with a broad background in the whole field of library work than
to one who knows and is interested in only one
special department. A knowledge of cataloging
procedure is still important, but we have come
to believe that subject background is indispensable.

It is impossible to tell whether the number
of trainees would have been larger or smaller
with full-time catalogers and with what periods
of vacancy. In recent years it has become almost impossible to recruit and employ full-
time catalogers under any circumstances. The
task of training two people for each full-time
position cannot be discounted, but it can be
counterbalanced by the fact that one resignation means only a half-time replacement and
that meanwhile at least half of the work of this
position will go steadily forward.

The training of new clerical staff members
and student assistants is done by the Senior
Catalogers and the Junior Librarians (sub-professionals). Six new clerical assistants were
trained in 1954/55; three in 1955/56; eight in
1956/57; and ten in 1957/58. A student of
group dynamics could find interesting data for
his studies among our clerical employees. Approximately half are recent graduates of high
schools within our region. These are seeking
husbands and, to fill in the time, are content
with short-term careers in clerical work.
Some find husbands in the local community,
and others come to us for work in order to help
support husbands who are enrolled as graduate
students. In 1956/57 a majority of the instances

of turnover in employment within this group
were due to pregnancy; in 1957/58 a majority
returned to college to finish degrees; in 1958/59
a majority are finding better paid employment
in other offices in downtown Lincoln. Obviously, group dynamics are at work; which is simply
to say that these young women are friends, they
share their experiences, and they influence each
other in many ways.

The Catalog Librarian and her two full-time
Senior Catalogers do the cooperative cataloging
for the Library of Congress, supervise reporting
to the National Union Catalog, and catalog special materials such as microfilm and microcards.
One of their important tasks is supervision and
revision of material catalogued by the Junior
Catalogers. The cataloging is not completely
revised except during the first six weeks or two
months the cataloger is new to the Department.
The main purpose of revision is to sustain reasonable uniformity in the general policies of the
Catalog Department and to maintain consistency
in technical details.

Do we spend more time on revision than is
spent in a traditional department? All material
does flow through the hands of a second person.
The added volumes, copies, editions, and so on
are revised by a Junior Librarian (sub-professional).
All other materials are revised by the Senior Catalogers or by the Catalog Librarian. The reviser
soon learns which type of detail needs to be
checked for a given cataloger. For some a brief
glance at classification is sufficient, or to note
if there is any special problem with the material
in hand; for others all details must be checked
more closely. We try to keep actual revision at
a minimum, but some checking proves to be
worthwhile.

In addition to the regular work of the Department, special projects are invariably in
progress. During 1954/55 we initiated the
reproduction of cards by Xerography at the
University's central Duplicating Service, and
procedures were worked out with that office.
The special Wyer classification scheme for the
College of Agriculture was discontinued, and
books for this Library accordingly were included in the union shelf list. A special classification and procedure were developed for
Agriculture Experiment Station and Agricultural Extension publications in the College of
Agriculture Library. Work was continued on
transferring records for collections previously
moved into the Love Memorial Library from

teaching departments where they had formerly been housed. The Catalog and Acquisition
Departments worked together to establish a
central serial file. An assistant in Acquisitions
worked in the Catalog Department part-time
for a couple of months to demonstrate how
the Catalog Department could use information
forwarded from the Acquisition Department
and why such information had initially to be
ascertained as a part of precataloging. Government agency history cards were purchased and
filed in the public catalog to facilitate the use
of "document" materials. The card catalogs
in the Architecture and Geology Libraries
were refiled to conform with current American
Library Association filing rules.

During 1955/56 the Department cataloged
a large collection of music scores received from
the Department of Music. Russian materials
which had accumulated for several years were
cataloged, and rare book cataloging was re-
sumed. Subject cataloging for University of
Nebraska theses had been eliminated from
1945 to 1952 because of lack of staff, and
during 1955/56 some of these were given
subject cataloging. The routine for all serial
cataloging was revised, and cards for serials
in Law and Medicine were pulled and stamped
for the serial file. A brief but special classification scheme was developed for the Law Library. Further work was done on revising
subject headings and adding necessary cross
references. During the summer the cards were
shifted in the sections of the card catalog that
had become too tight and new labels were
made for all cases.

During 1956/57 new routines were established for periodicals and continuations for
which holding records are in the Postindex.
Work was also done on transferring the holding records from the public catalog and shelf
list to the Postindex. The routines and policies for the University High School Library
were reviewed, and a manual of cataloging
procedures written. This Library was needed, and recataloging with H. W. Wilson cards
was initiated. New binding forms were designed, and new routines established for material sent to the bindery from the Catalog
Department. New forms were devised for
use by public service divisions in indicating
to the Catalog Department that corrections
and additional references are needed in the
public catalog. Analytics were pulled from

the public catalog for a selected list of
United States government publications in
accordance with new policies for handling
all government publications. Work was
continued on adding necessary subject
cross-references in the public catalog.

During 1957/58 the project of typing new
subject cross-references for the public catalog
was completed. Work continued on transferring
holding records for periodicals and continuations from the public catalog and shelf list to
the Postindex. The special classification
scheme in entomology at the College of Agriculture was discontinued, and work was initiated on the reclassification of this collection and its transfer to the Library from the
Department of Entomology. And last but
not least, refiling the public catalog in the
Love Memorial Library to conform with current American Library Association rules was
initiated.

Despite increasing appropriations for materials and an increasing flow of new acquisitions into the Department, the Catalog Department has been busy with an unusual
number of special projects. These special
projects are the inevitable consequence of the
total reorganization of all library services insti-
gated by moving into the new divisional plan
central library in 1945. These special projects
have substantially affected the cost of cataloging per title and per volume. Their chief
effort has been to divert some of the time and
attention of the entire Department away from
direct application to the steady flow of new
materials into the Library. During the trial
period of the dual-assignment, too, from
1951 forward, a general reorganization of
the work procedures and habits of the entire
Technical Service Division was called for.
This, unquestionably, has affected productivity. It may, therefore, be too soon to attempt to measure the actual operation of the
dual-assignment as we have defined and described it in this report. We look forward,
therefore, to a second four-year study to be
undertaken immediately in what we hope
may prove to be a more normal situation for
concentration upon the advantages and disadvantages of the dual-assignment, without
all the distractions described in the immed-
iately-preceeding paragraphs.

We are trying continually to control and
reduce cataloging costs by other means; for

example, by clarifying the distinctions between clerical and professional tasks, by better organizing the flow of work, by simplifying or eliminating procedures wherever possible, by writing down routines so that they are easier to follow with consistency, and by an increasing coordination of all related aspects of the twin departments: Acquisition and Catalog. We recognize that a price must be paid for value received. A study of costs is not meaningful unless the final product is taken into account. Quantity alone is not entirely valid basis for judging the work of a library department—not even such piece work as the cataloging of books. We believe that through the dual-assignment we are producing a catalog better adapted to the needs of a divisional library.

To Be Specific

The evaluation of the quality of the cataloging produced under the dual-assignment system is elusive. There are no commonly-accepted quantitative measures of quality in this field. Evaluation of some kinds we have, of course. Student and faculty response to the card catalog and to the local library is an indirect evaluation to observant and sensitive librarians. Many of the faculty and students have worked or studied on other campuses, and their comments may sometimes be taken as comparative judgments. The library staff, too, represents a wide range of training and experience in other universities, and its composite judgment determines the specific applications of our present program. Exchange librarianships for the purpose of further evaluation might also prove to be significant to the program.

The degree of expertness in the public interest developed by the cataloger who is also and at the same time a reference librarian is observable in many specific and practical ways. These catalogers are personal acquaintances and working colleagues of the graduate students and faculty. Because of this close relationship, Dewey classification numbers, for example, are assigned with greater discrimination since the cataloger knows at first-hand what teaching and research interests are being served in the local academic community. On the other hand, to make sure that the cataloger who is also a reference librarian does not do violence to the basic principles of consistent classification policy, we have centered cataloging authority in the person of the Catalog Librarian. A Humanities Librarian might, for example, prefer to group all the works of a significant literary author together on the open shelf, but it is a basic principle of the Dewey classification to separate literary works into groups distinguished by their literary form. The classification system, under centralized direction, could be adapted to serve either concept, but not both at once. In the interest of administrative efficiency and economy the basic decision on this point, having once been made, must be adhered to despite changes in staff and in personal preference.

The reference librarian brings to cataloging a breadth and depth of subject knowledge and interest that is reflected time and time again, for example, in the choice and application of subject headings. In rapidly developing fields of research this advantage is especially noticeable. The card catalog no longer need be twenty-five years behind contemporary science. The reference librarian's intimate personal knowledge of subject bibliography enables him to suggest the elimination of expensive and time-consuming analyses in the card catalog in instances where this work is being done adequately in published sources. Added entries and analytics suggested by the reference librarian for inclusion in the catalog he helps to make are apt to be selective and discriminating. This may prove to be especially true, for example, with added entries for editors, translators, and illustrators.

By channeling the bibliographic process continuously into the hands of the reference librarians from the subject division, not only have we eliminated nearly all of the duplication of bibliographic research that is so commonly noticeable in libraries where this function is divided among separate groups of staff, but we are also developing a degree of bibliographic expertness in our reference staff that was not possible under a system of divided and widely separated bibliographic responsibilities. In other words, in this system the reference librarian develops a systematic and comprehensive knowledge of all new acquisitions in his area starting at that moment when the new title first appears as a suggestion for purchase or acquisition by other means. This process accumulates a wide variety of useful knowledge within his comprehension and memory, having to do with initial identification of "the book", its acceptance or rejection for acquisition, and the solution of immediate practical problems growing out of editions, multiple copies, necessary duplications, the location of copies, restrictions on their use, their availability, and ultimately with respect to their content and usefulness to student or faculty. Anonymity of authorship, changes in title, items numbered in series, variety and complexity in corporate entry, and especially in government authorship, and the inescapable intricacies of filing a million cards—none of these is any longer a mystery to the reference librarian working under the dual-assignment, and every cataloging decision permanently affecting the library's bibliographic record is tempered to some degree by experience gained in the reference function.

Does this system sacrifice uniformity and essential bibliographic detail in the card catalog? To the extent that such uniformity and detail are desirable and economically reasonable, the answer is "No"! We have assurance on this point because the system affords a maximum application of cataloging theory and practical reference experience to the making of such decisions. All three of the authors of this report have at one time or another been head catalogers for a substantial period of time. Among the three there is also a considerable accumulation of direct reference experience. The ultimate application of the divisional concept in the dual-assignment of librarians to a combination of reference work and cataloging was an outgrowth of much reflection upon the accumulative experiences of long years of service in university libraries where these primary functions were held to be entirely separate and sacred, each from the other. In this new system librarians are urged to concentrate upon and to grow intellectually in subject areas of special interest to them, and they are given every encouragement to apply to their work as librarians a comprehensive knowledge of all the essential elements of librarianship.

Recruiting and Indoctrination

Sometimes newcomers are shocked by the breadth of their responsibilities in the dual-assignment. Newcomers are therefore given a carefully-planned induction consisting first of three to six months full-time work in the reading room of the subject division before the half-time assignment to the work of technical service is initiated. Without taint of prejudice or pious hope, we can say that conversion to full support of the plan comes sooner or later and invariably within the first year of the experience.

The problem of adjustment to the dual-assignment, however logical the plan may appear to be to those who defend and direct it, usually derives from attitudes developed in library school or in previous employment. Cataloging is sometimes unfortunately taught as the advanced calculus of librarianship rather than as its elementary algebra. Catalog departments, too, have in some situations become known as the home of the insecure personalities in librarianship. Reference work is sometimes taught as though it were the only consistently intellectual effort in the curriculum and also, curiously enough, as though it could be mastered and practised in a discipline divorced from the elements of cataloging and classification. This situation thus described is not wholly true, of course, but there is enough truth in these impressions to cause some trouble in a library which wishes to merge cataloging and classification with reference as one unified application of sound bibliographic technique.

It may be, too, that inadequacies in ability and in training are more accurately observed and measured in cataloging, where the work is subject to more or less continuous review, than in reference work where qualitative and quantitative standards of performance are more likely to be nebulous or merely arithmetic. The individual who either can't or doesn't want to catalog books proves to be inadequate at the reference desk.

Scheduling

Scheduling is one of the perennial problems in all library practice. The work-week at Nebraska is now forty hours. The central university library is open seventy-five hours and expects in the near future to extend this schedule. No librarian can reasonably be expected to apply himself to any one task forty hours continuously during the week. A diversity of assignments is highly desirable in the interest of alertness and efficiency on the job. The Assistant Librarians in the dual-assignment find that dividing their time between the technical service and the reference desk provides the diversification that is both necessary and desirable. Nebraska experimented with a variety of schedule patterns and has discarded the divided day and the alternate day in favor of the divided week. In this system none of the work is ever referred to as monotonous. In fact, since a major work assignment must be accomplished within two and a half days, the tendency is for the Assistant Librarian to step up his own pace.

Training for Promotion

The system of dual-assignment described in this report was initiated at the University of Nebraska in 1951. The elements of the plan were explained and discussed in staff meetings. Several members of the staff volunteered their cooperation. Initially and experimentally only two librarians were involved. Gradually the plan was extended to its present full-scale application. During the eight years since 1951, twenty-six Junior Catalogers have been trained into the program. To the Catalog Librarian each of these twenty-six was a half-time cataloger who required a comprehensive training effort. Viewing this effort selfishly from the point of view of the Catalog Department, one might conclude that it is administratively expensive and also unreasonable. However, certain obvious facts can be set in opposition to this conclusion.

Cataloging at the University of Nebraska is viewed not only as a means of organizing new materials for use and accompanying them with adequate records, but also as a continuous training for the public service staff in the essential elements of sound bibliographical technique. In this system, young librarians, including many newly graduated from library school, are soon immersed in the elements of book selection, pre-cataloging, cataloging and classification, and reference in actual practice. The breadth of this experience develops a mature comprehension of librarianship. Promotion in line with special personal interests becomes possible in either direction, that is in either the technical service or the public service.

Out of this group of Assistant Librarians, working in the dual-assignment system, Nebraska has developed three full-time Senior Assistant Catalogers whose reference experience was in the humanities and the social

studies, an Order Librarian whose reference experience was in science, and an Acquisition Librarian whose experience included both reference work in the humanities and full-time supervisory experience in cataloging. From Assistant Librarianships in Law where the work also included cataloging, one individual moved into science, the home of his first "academic love," and another into the position of Public Service Librarian in order to broaden his experience. Previously the position of Public Service Librarian had been filled by promotion from the Education Librarianship which had also included cataloging. It is also worth mentioning that the Librarians in Agriculture and Law now share the dual-assignment with their Assistant Librarians, dividing both their schedules between the technical service and the public service within their subject areas.

Mention should also be made here of another supporting argument. During the past decade "catalogers" have become increasingly hard to find in the employment market. In fact, they have almost reached the vanishing point in some geographic areas. During this same period Nebraska has developed a full staff of "catalogers" and "reference librarians," recruiting and employing them as "librarians" in the humanities, in the social studies, or in science, and encouraging them in the continuous application of all the essential elements of librarianship which they learned in library school.

Staff Comment

Mary Doak, Social Studies Librarian speaking for the Social Studies Division, says: "The librarian who works in both the technical service division and at the reference desk in the divisional reading room is not only able to catalog more efficiently, but is also able to give better service to students and faculty. Having the advantage of observing the actual use of books, the cataloger is able to classify them where they will be of most value. The reference librarian in this system acquires a better working knowledge of the card catalog and a more thorough acquaintance with the collection. The librarian working in a dual-assignment learns to understand the intracies of problems in both areas. He gets a clearer overall view of the organization and works toward an integration of its diverse elements. The dual-assignment broadens the experience of the beginning librarian and gives him better preparation for future responsibilities."

Richard Farley, formerly Assistant Director of Libraries for Science & Technology and now Associate Director of Libraries, and here speaking for the Science & Technology Division, says: "The most significant consequence of the dual-assignment to cataloging and reference, from the science librarian's point of view, centers in its freedom of action. So long as we stay within the general framework of good cataloging practice, we are able to maintain direct control over the assignment of classification numbers, analytics, and subject headings to science materials. To librarians who were formerly bound to accept anything and everything that came out of the catalog department, this is an exciting and revolutionary modification of traditional practice. It has become especially significant in areas of science where we are able to apply our special knowledge of scientific biography, a knowledge which incidentally is best acquired only through direct and continuous contact with research personnel and students."

Mr. Farley says further: "Certain side-effects of the dual-assignment should also be noted. The informal pressures we apply to each other within the division to complete all unfinished cataloging cannot be discounted. We are so enthusiastic about getting our science materials into the hands of our patrons that a backlog of fifteen or twenty titles becomes a matter of serious concern. We gain immeasurable good will through being able to catalog a title for any faculty member during the time it takes him to browse through the current journals. And finally,

we like a system that contains built-in checks and balances that do not permit careless habits in bibliography. We are confident that our skill as catalogers increases our skill as reference librarians."

Bernard Kreissman, Assistant Director of Libraries for the Humanities, says: "There really is no single outstanding characteristic of the integrated reference-and-catalog plan, the dual-assignment. Like an efficiently functioning organism, each characteristic derives benefits from all the other features of the plan, and it in turn provides the other elements with the value of its own processes. They all dovetail and interlock; they all work together. To detail this statement very briefly, the librarian in his reference capacity knows the collection more intimately than one who has never seen 'the book' until it appears on the reference shelf, and in his catalog function he has an intimate knowledge of the use to which he and his patrons will put a particular text. It is thus far the only system I have known in which the reference librarians are one hundred percent satisfied with the classification and description of the collection; and the catalog librarians are wholly satisfied that the reference group are fully capable of interpreting the catalog. In all fairness, I think we may turn the question around and ask: 'Where and how did you get the idea that any organism, a library included, is better served when run in two separate walled-off compartments rather than in one single unit:' "

ADDITIONAL READING ON THE DIVISIONAL PLAN LIBRARY AT THE UNIVERSITY OF NEBRASKA

Lundy, F. A. and Renfro, K. R. "New Frontiers for the College Library." *Library Journal*, 76: 1091-1096. July 1951.

Lundy, F. A. "The Divisional Plan Library." *College and Research Libraries.* 17: 143-148. March 1956. (Part of "A Symposium: Library Service to Undergraduate College Students.").

"The Divisional Library at Nebraska." *Library Journal*, 80: 1301-1303. June 1, 1955. (With administrative Chart.)

Chapman, J. D., Hopp, R. H., and Vennix, A. J. "The Role of the Divisional Librarian." *College and Research Libraries*, 15: 148-154. April 1954.

Marvin, Patricia. "Circulation in the Divisional Library: the New Plan of Service." *College and Research Libraries*, 12: 241-244, 265. July 1951.

Vennix, A. J. "Two-Hour Reserve Desk at University of Nebraska." *Library Journal*, 77: 1040-1041. June 15, 1952.

Kreissman, Bernard. "Browsing-Room—Divisional Style." *College and Research Libraries*, 17: 228-230. May 1956.

Blanchard, J. R. "Departmental Libraries in Divisional Plan University Libraries." *College and Research Libraries,* 14: 243-248. July 1953.

Lundy, F. A. and Johnson, E. M. "Documents in the Divisional Library." *College and Research Libraries,* 19: 463-466. November, 1958.

Renfro, K. R. "Cataloging in the Divisional Library." *College and Research Libraries,* 15: 154-157. April 1954.

Lundy, F. A. "Reference vs. Catalog: a Basic Dilemma." *Library Journal,* 80: 19-22. January 1, 1955.

"The University of Nebraska Plan." *PNLA Quarterly.* 22: 40-41. October 1957.

Nebraska University. *Look to Your Library: Your Handbook of the Libraries.* September 1958 edition. 23 p.

Salmons, R. M. "A Legacy of Gracious Living." *Wilson Library Bulletin,* 26: 54-55. September 1954.

"University of Nebraska Library." *Library Journal,* 79: 569. April 1, 1954. (Library Outline" 262)

Lundy, F. A. and Stuff, M. A. "A Dream Come True." *The Nebraska Alumnus,* 41: 4-5. May 1945.

FOOTNOTES

[1] Lyle, Guy R. *The Administration of the College Library.* Second edition, revised. (New York: H. W. Silson Company, 1949), p. 96.

[2] The professional classes of employment in The University of Nebraska Libraries are as follows: Director; Associate Director; Assistant Directors; Librarians (e.g. the Catalog Librarian); Senior Assistant Librarians (e.g. Senior Assistant Catalogers); Assistant Librarian (e.g. Junior Cataloger). The classified service classes of employment include the following: Junior Librarian; Library Assistant; Clerk-Typist.

ABOUT THE AUTHORS

—**Frank Arthur Lundy,** Director of Libraries, University of Nebraska; M.A., 1948, University of California. His major research interests are in management and administration.

—**Kathryn R. Renfro,** Associate Director of Libraries for General Services, University of Nebraska; A.B. with Diploma in Library Science, 1939, University of Denver. Her major research interests are in technical services, university libraries, and library administration.

—**Esther M. Schubert,** Catalog Librarian, University of Nebraska; M.S.L.S., 1940, University of Illinois.

The Administrator Looks at Classification

by Robert B. Downs

One of the most significant investments made in the academic library is the development, application, and modification of a system of material management intended to meet the requirements of the library user. The author warns that the academic librarian must be critical of the assumptions of this activity and conservative in supporting its tendency to involute. The librarian must constantly analyze the systematics of library operations in terms of relevance, least work, and redundancy.

A strong case can be made out, I am convinced, for the proposition that many librarians are obsessed with classification for the sake of classification. With rare exceptions, investigation has revealed, library users are totally indifferent to classification, so long as it does not actually interfere with their finding the books they want. If they have thought about the matter at all and were given a choice, the readers would vote for the utmost possible simplicity in whatever scheme of classification is adopted. Logical sequences, a fetish worshipped by numerous classifiers, mean little to all except an occasional professor of philosophy.

Though I would not argue for it, there is a good deal to be said for the accession order in arranging the books in a library—simply numbering the first book received 1, the second 2, and so on *ad infinitum,* filling every shelf to capacity, and saving much space. Such a plan appears to have worked satisfactorily in the half-million volume library of the London School of Economics, but that is a closed shelf collection and perhaps belongs to a special category.

Carrying the thesis further, I would maintain that librarians, principally in colleges and universities, have been guilty of wasting millions of dollars in elaborate and unnecessary reclassification programs, using funds that could have been spent to far greater advantage to everyone concerned in building up their book resources. To be specific, consider the cases of two of the most poverty-stricken university libraries in the country: The University of Mississippi and the University of South Carolina, both of which have expended tens of thousands of dollars in recent years, changing from one standard system of classification to another. Meanwhile their book budgets were at about the level of a college library without any university pretensions. Here is almost incontrovertible support for such critics as Lawrence C. Powell, when they charge that librarians are more concerned with housekeeping than with books and reading.

What exactly does the library patron—scholar, research worker, student, or general reader—have a right to expect of library classification? One thing he should *not* expect, because it is a practical impossibility, is to find *all* the materials on any given subject grouped together. This was, of course, convincingly demonstrated by the Kelley studies.[1] A characteristic of the literature of virtually every modern field is that it cuts across subject lines. There are no longer any watertight compartments—if there ever were. The physicist, to illustrate, is interested not only in the strictly physical literature, but in biology, chemistry, engineering, mathematics, and other related areas. The lawyer is concerned not simply with legal treatises, but with psychology, medicine, political sciences, economics, sociology, and nearly everything else under the sun. Every classifier is familiar with innumerable cases of border-line books—books that could just as logically be

SOURCE: Reprinted from Robert B. Downs, "The Administrator Looks at Classification," in Thelma Eaton and Donald E. Strout, eds., *The Role of Classification in the Modern American Library; Papers Presented at an Institute Conducted by the University of Illinois Graduate School of Library Science, November 1-4, 1959* (Champaign, Ill.: 1959), pp. 1-7, by permission of the publisher and the author.

placed in one classification division as another, or perhaps several others, with the final decision usually resting upon the interests of the particular institution.

No less responsible for the scattering of materials on a specific topic is format. Even if it were possible to group together all the separately-printed monographic titles, vast quantities of references on most subjects must remain scattered in periodicals and other serial publications, government documents, newspapers, collections of essays, reference works, and bibliographical compilations.

We can only conclude, therefore, that the most perfect system of classification ever devised by man, or likely to be invented, can be but partially successful in any aim to bring together all related materials on whatever subject. It follows logically, therefore, that the users of libraries must anticipate supplementing the undoubted values of classification with catalogs, periodical indexes, documents indexes, essay indexes, printed bibliographies, and similar tools. The deficiencies of classification can be partially offset by expert cataloging, with which classification must always remain interdependent, but even the combination does not provide a complete answer. Eventually, perhaps, some form of automation, indexing every idea dealt with in the library's collections, may furnish an adequate solution.

When people enter a library to find a book, I suggest that they will ordinarily use one of three approaches. If there is a specific title in mind, it will be located through author or title in the catalog. This approach is characteristic of the scholar who, in most instances, will know or is presumed to know exactly what he wants. The only significance of classification for him is as a finding device. The student and general reader, on the other hand, are often uncertain about their requirements, except that they are interested in a subject. They may attempt to solve their problem by going direct to the shelves (assuming there is an open stack system), or through inspection of subject entries in the card catalog. Of these two approaches, the catalog is almost invariably more reliable and more complete, though that method lacks the psychological satisfaction of seeing and handling the books themselves.

Whether the library collection is to be arranged for the convenience of the specialist or for the generalist, simplicity of classification is to be preferred. Here is another spot where the librarian is frequently tempted by art for art's sake, stringing out the classification symbols, whether letters or numbers, to interminable lengths. It may be mistaken judgement to fix an arbitrary limitation, but it seems to me difficult to justify a subject classification of more than six characters for any book, and if author and title symbols are added, these too should not be allowed to exceed a half-dozen. Anything beyond that number complicates location and shelving problems, and increases the labor and expense of classification.

But, assert perfectionists among the classifiers, scientific and exact classification often requires carrying numbers out to eight, ten, or even more places. This, to me, is comparable to the value of pi in mathematics. No matter how far it is extended, it is still imperfect, and for ordinary purposes I am willing to settle for 3.14 instead of 3.14159265 or pi extended to infinity.

As an old New York Public Library alumnus, I recall how simple, yet generally efficient, is the scheme developed over sixty years ago by Dr. John Shaw Billings for that great research institution. Here, in one of the world's largest libraries, three letters are usually sufficient to classify any book in the collection. The principle of the classification is so clear that a new stack attendant can readily grasp it in a few minute's time. Cutter numbers and minute subdivisions do not clutter up or confuse finding a book on the shelf. This also is a closed-stack system, though that fact I think does not destroy the validity of my argument. Given the class number, any intelligent person can quickly locate a specific title.

When life can thus be so uncomplicated, why should college libraries of less than 100,000 volumes adopt, as dozens of them have done, anything so detailed and complex as the Library of Congress classification? Some are apparently under the delusion that they will eventually reach the size of Harvard or the British Museum, and consequently they must be ready for the future. Meanwhile, as the price of preparing for that unlikely contingency, their students and faculty for generations to come must struggle with a system too involved for them to understand or appreciate, a scheme they have not met in high school and will probably not find in any public library they may use later, and which puts unnecessary obstacles in their way in using the college library.

It is not proposed here to weigh the respective advantages and disadvantages of the Library of Congress and Dewey Decimal classifications. That has been done *ad nauseam* and by experts. According to Eaton's investigations[2], less than two percent of the academic libraries in the United States use anything other than one of these two schemes, and the percentage is at least as high for public libraries. As a practical matter, it would be difficult to justify adoption of any classification other than Dewey or L.C. in an American library, except perhaps for an occasional highly specialized collection. These two are the only schemes for which any provision has been made to keep updated, and both possess the important advantage of having their classification numbers printed on Library of Congress cards. Despite their acknowledged defects, the Dewey and L.C. have proven themselves in the fire of several generations' experience.

From the point of view of an administrator, the chief question in my mind is this one: Having adopted one scheme, either L.C. or Dewey, for a library, is it wise to change? Assuming classification has been in the hands of competent personnel, and has been applied as efficiently and expertly as human frailties permit, can the librarian make a reasonable case for reclassification? My candid opinion is that he cannot.

According to Maurice Tauber, who has studied the matter more exhaustively than anyone else, to my knowledge:

> Most of the reasons for reclassification have been based on either or both of two assumptions: (1) That the use of the new classification achieves a grouping of the books in the collection that is of greater educational significance and shows to the users the currently accepted relationships among the branches of knowledge more effectively than did the system being replaced, and (2) That the adoption of a new classification will reduce the costs of technical processes.[3]

Tauber believes that there has been considerable rationalization among librarians who have attempted to justify reclassification. There is little concrete evidence that the hoped-for benefits actually materialize.

We do know, however, that the cost involved in complete or extensive reclassification runs into large sums of money, that it frequently extends over decades of time, and may seriously interfere with the use of the library while the work is in progress. Another consideration brought out by Tauber in a further study is whether an inferior classification system and catalog appreciably handicap library users. His findings cast substantial doubt on the matter, from which he concludes:

> The burden of proof rests upon the librarian to show that the outmoded classification and the antiquated catalog interfere with the use of library materials or increase the cost of operating them for use. It is not possible to answer definitively the question of whether a particular library should reclassify or recatalog. If its present status is such as to interfere greatly with the proper functioning of the library in its service to scholarship, then a change is indicated; otherwise, changes should be made with considerable caution. Only as greatly improved service can be seen to result from reorganization may the tremendous costs involved be justified.[4]

A case study of the difficulties of reclassification was described by Harriet MacPherson.[5] The project was to transfer about 4,000 volumes from the 650 class in Dewey to a special classification developed for the Columbia University School of Business Library. This would seem a rather small operation. Yet the reclassification involved the removal, frequent remaking, and the refiling of 4,000 shelf cards, and the actual handling of the volumes. The last step meant verification of the books with the cards, frequent recataloging of the books, fitting the books into the new classification scheme, and labeling the volumes with new numbers. The entire process required the services of two people for more than two years. Their work was continually hampered and retarded by delays in locating the books, caused by such factors as many books being charged out to readers, some volumes being on reserve in departmental libraries, professors on sabbatical leave having carried off a few volumes, some books being in the bindery, and others having been lost. Here in microcosm are the problems confronting a large library in even more aggravated form when it decides to reclassify.

The question of whether a library afflicted with an obsolete and wholly inadequate classification should reclassify poses quite a different problem from the decision to change from say, Dewey to L.C. or from L.C. to Dewey. About a dozen years ago, I was a member of a survey team for the Cornell University Library. We were called upon to advise on the retention or abandonment of a homemade plan, the Harris classification, adopted in 1891. Some 800,000 volumes at Cornell had been arranged by this curious scheme, based on the old British Museum system of press numbers, a fixed location device. The surveyors agreed that there was no alternative to discontinuing this outdated, inflexible, and inconsistent arrangement, which had for all practical purposes broken down, and replacing it with the Library of Congress classification. Under such conditions, there was no question that reclassification was essential, even though it involved the Library in estimated expenditures of $600,000, and fifteen to twenty years of disruption.

Undoubtedly, more studies are needed of the way people actually use library catalogs and classification, as a basis for administrative decisions. We then might be able to operate more on fact than on theory. Paul Dunkin, who, as Head Cataloger at the Folger Shakespeare Library for a number of years, had an excellent vantage point from which to view scholars at work, offered some observations on how, specifically, an Elizabethan scholar proceeds with his researches. Such a scholar, reports Dunkin:

> works with Elizabethan handwriting (palaeography), Francis Bacon (philosophy and law), Elizabeth and Essex (history and biography), 'rogues and vagabonds' (sociology and economics), and Thomas Cartwright (religion), as well as with the plays of Shakespeare (literature).[6]

Comparing their basically different approaches to classification, Dunkin pointed out that, "The librarian's classification is, so to speak, vertical; the scholar's, horizontal." Perhaps the twain are destined never to meet.

In the Classics Library at the University of Illinois is a prime example of the scholar's horizontal classification, achieved mainly by ignoring the librarian's classification. Discarding the literature classification in Dewey for the Classics, all Latin authors are arranged in one large alphabetical group under a single class number, and similarly all Greek authors are in a straight alphabetical sequence under another number. There have been assembled here philosophy, church fathers, economics, the languages, the arts, the literatures, antiquities, history and biography, without any effort to subdivide by specific topics. The basic concept is to bring together books according to their use. This scheme, which was devised fifty years ago, for a library of 35,000 volumes, is apparently exactly what the scholar wants, and generations of them have expressed their satisfaction with it. The essential idea has been incorporated into the L.C. classification's treatment of the classical literatures.

As a general rule, however, tinkering with a classification arrangement creates more problems than it solves. If one has adopted the Library of Congress or Dewey scheme, it is best to adhere to it and not attempt to introduce innovations to meet what may be regarded as special situations. As a keen critic of classification, Berwick Sayers, remarked, "Librarians are seldom able to leave their classification alone." Mr. Sayers added that "the moving about of classes to suit the convenience of the furniture arrangements, the adjustments made with biography, fiction, other literature, and in music, occur to one as often causing difficulties . . . changes are often unskillfully made and the advantages they give are not always so great as their authors imagine."[7] It is the adoption of special, homemade schemes of classification and radical modifications of standard classification schedules that have more frequently brought about the need for reclassification than has dissatisfaction with an established plan. The amateur usually fails to realize the complexities of classification, when he starts changing it.

In trying to represent the point of view of the administrator in this paper, my aim has been to consider those aspects of classification that involve administrative problems and relationships. Chief among these are costs, efficiency, the convenience of the reading public, and the relation of classification to the library service as a whole. Those are considerations that concern every professional-minded librarian, and not merely administrators.

Classification means different things to different people. Robert Graves in his book *5 Pens in Hand* relates what he calls his favorite story about nomenclature:

> An old lady was taking a pet tortoise by train in a basket from London to Edinburgh, and wanted to know whether she ought to buy a dog-ticket

for it, as one has to do in England if one takes a cat by train—because cats officially count as dogs. "No," said the ticket inspector, "No mum! Cats

is dogs, and rabbits is dogs, and dogs is dogs, and squirrels in cages is parrots, but this 'ere turkle is a hinsect. We won't charge you nothing, mum!"[8]

FOOTNOTES

[1] Grace O. Kelley, *The Classification of Books, an Inquiry into its Usefulness to the Reader* (New York: H. W. Wilson Co., 1937).

[2] Thelma Eaton, *Classification in Theory and Practice, a Collection of Papers* (Champaign, Ill.: Illini Union Bookstore, 1957), pp. 29-42, 45-58.

[3] Maurice F. Tauber, "Subject Cataloging and Classification Approach the Crossroad," *College and Research Libraries,* III (March, 1942), 153-54.

[4] Maurice F. Tauber, "Reclassification and Recataloging in College and University Libraries, Reasons and Evaluation," *Library Quarterly,* XII (October, 1942), 845.

[5] Harriet D. MacPherson, "Reclassification of College and University Libraries," *College and Research Libraries,* I (March, 1940) 160.

[6] Paul S. Dunkin, "Classification and the Scholar," *College and Research Libraries,* III (September, 1942), 336.

[7] W. C. Berwick Sayers, "Failures of Classification Considered," *Library World,* XLIV (March, 1942), 129.

[8] Robert Graves, *5 Pens in Hand* (New York: Doubleday, 1958), pp. 333-34.

ABOUT THE AUTHOR

—**Robert B. Downs,** Dean of Library Administration, University of Illinois; M.S., 1929, Columbia University. His current research interests lie in the study of influential books, American library resources, and intellectual freedom.

The Use of the Subject Catalog in the University of California Library

by LeRoy Charles Merritt

In response to recurrent crises the contemporary academic librarian is often forced to examine the propositions of the library, only to find that the evidence reveals the need for more complex responses. This study exposes what may be, unfortunately, an example of the character of decision-making in the library. Decision-making can not be based on occupational inclinations but must depend on evidence capable of supporting professional conclusions.

Serious questioning of the value of the subject catalog has been a popular armchair sport of American librarians from their very beginning. In 1944 Swank was able to write a sixteen-page summary of the important critical discussion which had gone before.[1] The course of the battle has ranged wide from an almost universal acceptance of subject bibliography in 1876 through a growing reliance on the card catalog which may be said to have reached its peak during the third decade of the twentieth century. Reliance on the subject catalog is no less today, but a growing critical literature gives evidence of serious doubt in the minds of catalogers and administrators about the physical and economic possibility of long continuing the feeding of more and more cards to an insatiable and many-headed Gargantua.

Such doubts are strengthened by isolated evidence that even existing bibliographies are as good as, or very nearly as good as, if not better than existing subject catalogs. Two students have made independent investigations in the field of English literature. Swank[2] was able to conclude that for candidates for the doctorate in English literature, both the classification and the subject catalog were less adequate than the subject bibliography, the *Cambridge Bibliography of English Literature* and the *Cambridge History of English Literature* being particular cases in point. Simonton[3] compared bibliographies of Shakespeare and Chaucer with subject entries in a large university-library catalog and discovered that the bibliographies revealed more than ninety percent of the titles shown in the card catalog.

In the field of the social sciences Brown[4] observed 33 graduate students' work at the card catalog in the preparation of term papers and concluded that the subject catalog was for them an unsatisfactory and inefficient instrument. At the 1950 midwinter meeting of the American Library Association, Rutherford D. Rogers of the Grosevnor Library reported comparing twenty-five outstanding subject bibliographies with the subject catalogs of Grosvenor and the Library of Congress. He concluded that good subject bibliography could replace the subject catalog.[5]

All of these efforts have been directed at showing that a given subject bibliography or group of bibliographies could be used in place of the subject catalog in a given institution with comparable or even superior results. All of them may be said to be concerned with the use made of these tools by the comparatively advanced student making an extended study. None of them is concerned with the more casual use of bibliographies and catalogs by the average college undergraduate. Bibliographical tools serve different men in different ways, and it is possible that, whatever the theoretical evidence against the subject catalog, it may still be so useful to such large numbers of people that printed bibliographies can never practically supplant it.

The Situation at California

In the postwar period of rapidly rising costs, when the cost of cataloging each volume enter-

SOURCE: Reprinted from LeRoy Charles Merritt, *The Use of the Subject Catalog in the University of California Library* (Berkeley: University of California Press, 1951), by permission of The Regents of the University of California and the author.

ing the University of California Library rose to $3.34,[6] it was inevitable that there should be much discussion of modifying cataloging processes sufficiently to save a considerable amount of time and money without seriously diminishing the value of the general card catalog. Such discussions ran the gamut from establishing the entry in descriptive cataloging, through modifications of subject-cataloging procedure, to the possibilities of making savings in the final manufacture of the cards. It was finally decided to look at subject cataloging first as the point of attack most likely to result in the substantial savings being sought.

That decision involved a number of basic assumptions which are best stated as follows:[7]

> a. Authorship is an essential aspect of library material. The author catalog cannot be eliminated, nor can it be modified so as to produce much saving in time and cost.
> b. Modification of descriptive cataloging will not produce important savings.
> c. Quantity of use is an important determinant of areas of subject cataloging subject to modification.
> d. Identification of groups of books seldom approached through the subject catalog will suggest areas in subject cataloging where modifications can be made.

The subject catalog is used by a variety of people for a variety of purposes, not all of which were included in the intent of its creators. Basically and fundamentally, the subject catalog in a university library is intended to assist patrons of the library to find books on the subjects in which they are interested when they do not know the authors or titles of particular books. It is this need for a subject approach to a library's collections which justifies the time and money expended in the operation and maintenance of the subject catalog. If it could be shown that certain categories of books, be they identified by subject, date, language, or other criterion, are not, in fact, approached through the subject catalogs by the users of the library, then the administrative course of action would be clear: those categories of books should not have the benefit of subject cataloging.

The patron of the library has not yet attained his objective when he comes away from the subject catalog with a number of apparently satisfactory references in hand; he must still obtain the books across the loan desk of the library or directly from the shelves if he has access to the stacks. The use of the subject catalog is not complete until the book noted in the catalog comes into the hands of the user—until that transaction known as "charging" a book is completed. So it is that this study of the use of the subject catalog is based on the record of all such completed transactions created by the charging process. While it was thus not necessary to create any new records or vary any normal procedures to make the study possible, one addition to the record, one additional procedure, and several additional assumptions had to be made; these are described in the following section.

THE SAMPLE
Preexisting Conditions

The subject-catalog inquiry was made possible because of two preexisting conditions; had either one been absent, the study could not have followed the particular course it did. The fact that the University of California Library had divided its dictionary catalog into an author-title catalog and a subject catalog[8] facilitated the separation of author-title-catalog use and subject-catalog use. The whole study is predicated on the assumption that this separation of use was successfully accomplished. The additional fact that the library installed an IBM charging system in August, 1948 placed at hand a body of raw data in the form of IBM call cards representing completed charges of books from the University Library. It was necessary only to induce the users of the library to indicate from which of the two parts of the divided catalog they had obtained the call number of each book.

This was done by imprinting on each card the set of boxes shown in the upper right-hand corner of figure 1.

The two catalogs are placed at either end of the loan desk in the University Library, the author-title catalog at the east end, and the subject catalog at the west end. The catalogs were thus designated "East Catalog" and "West Catalog," respectively, and large, bold, white-on-black, identifying signs were placed on top of each catalog. The users of the library were not informed of the significance of the two signs or of the procedure, but no secret was made of either when curious users or inquiring reporters[9] asked about them.

The "No Catalog" box was provided to record the use of books located without reference

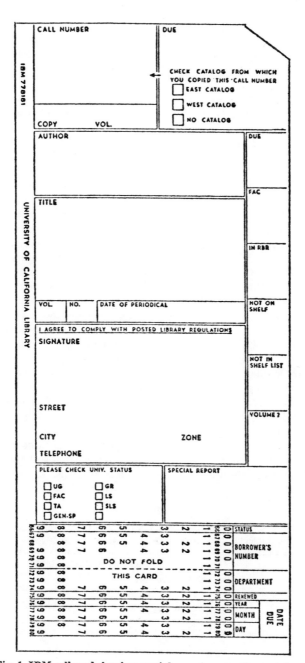

Fig. 1. IBM call card showing special area for recording catalog use.

to either author-title or subject catalogs. Borrowers who have access to the stacks, for example, frequently find books without using a catalog; and some professors provide call numbers in their syllabi, thus making student use of the catalog unnecessary. Attendants at the loan desk and at the stack exit were alerted to the need for making sure that one of the three boxes had been checked, but constant administrative pressure was necessary to hold the unchecked cards down to a maximum of 10 percent. A typical day's "take" of call cards is represented by the 1,094 books returned on March 14, 1949:

SOURCE	BOOKS	PERCENT
Author-title Catalog	435	39.8
Subject Catalog	287	26.2
No Catalog	268	24.5
Not Marked	104	9.5
TOTAL	1,094	100.0

Ten separate samples of approximately 4,000 cards each were drawn from the loan-desk circulation at different times during the academic year, as shown in table 1. All samples included call cards for books returned during the period specified. The books were taken from the library almost any time previously, but not before October 12, 1948 for samples 1, 2, and 3, and not before December 6, 1948 for the other seven samples. The original stock of specially imprinted call cards was placed in use on October 12, 1948, and became exhausted two weeks before December 6, when a new shipment was received and placed in continuous use for the duration of the study.

Cards Excluded

Each sample represents all call cards for books returned within the period specified which had been checked as having had their call numbers derived from either the author-title or subject catalogs. This statement implies certain omissions which should be noted. Excluded from each sample are the call cards (approximately 10 percent of the total) which the user did not check at all. Excluded also from the sample are all those cards which were checked "No Catalog" because the study was concerned with the relative use of the author-title and the subject catalogs, not with direct use without benefit of catalog. Some tentative analyses of the cards checked "No Catalog" were made for samples 1 and 3; these will be found in the appendix but do not comprise a portion of the subject-catalog inquiry.

One other progressively decreasing exclusion consisted of call cards for books which had been withdrawn before the specially imprinted call cards were placed in use. These represent books withdrawn before the beginning of the study and returned during the study; they cannot be considered as forming part of the study, even though they do represent books which were returned during the several sample periods.

The subject-catalog inquiry has been concerned with monographs only, and has considered serials not at all; thus it was necessary to exclude all cards from the sample which represented withdrawals of individual volumes of serials. A count of these exclusions of serial loans was made for samples

TABLE 1

Schedule of Separate Samples of Call Cards Drawn from Total Circulation for Subject-Catalog Inquiry During Academic Year 1948-49

	PERIOD IN WHICH SAMPLE WAS TAKEN	
SAMPLE	INCLUSIVE DATES	WEEK OF TERM
	Fall Term	
1	Oct. 12-26, 1948	4-5
2	Oct. 27-Nov. 3, 1948	6-7
3	Nov. 15-Dec. 5, 1948	9-11
4	Dec. 6-17, 1948	12-13
5	Jan. 3-10, 1949	16
	Spring Term	
6	Mar. 14-20, 1949	5
7	Mar. 28-Apr. 1, 1949	7
8	Apr. 11-14, 1949	9
9	May 9-12, 1949	12
10	June 6-10, 1949	16

1 and 3, and will be found in the appendix, table A. Here it need only be noted that loans of serials amounted to 37 percent of all loans.

Size of Sample

The ten samples shown in table 1 contain a combined total of 25,010 cards. All ten samples were drawn during fiscal year 1948-49, during which the loan desk circulated 361,843 books. When this figure is reduced by 37 percent to exclude loans of serials, the total circulation of monographs is found to be 227,961. When this figure is further reduced by the monographic loans made without benefit of either catalog, estimated at 29,526, the total circulation of monographs through the author or subject catalog is 198,435. When this figure is related to the sample of 25,010, the sample proves to be 12.6 percent of the total circulation of monographs with catalog assistance.

Reliability of Sample

The reliability of the sample was checked by correlating several of the small samples shown in table 1 with the whole sample of 25,010 cards. This was done by applying Spearman's rank-difference correlation formula to the distribution of call cards by library classification (see p. 12), which represents the most detailed distribution of data in the study. The following samples were so correlated with the whole sample with consistently high and positive results: See table below.

Validity of Sample

Since this entire study is based on library users' indication of the catalog from which they obtained the call numbers of the books they borrowed, considerations of validity are largely predicated on the assumption that the checking of the boxes on the call cards was accurately and honestly done. It must also be assumed that those cards which were not checked at all (10 percent of the total) would have been checked in conformity with the re-

sultant pattern if checking had been insisted on by the desk attendants.

The study is based on charges which were actually completed, on books which were in the possession of the borrower for an undetermined period of time ranging from a minimum of one minute to a maximum of 176 days (December 6, 1948 to June 10, 1949). The loan desk reports, however, that about 48 percent of all call cards presented do not result in completed transactions; books are discovered to be already in circulation, are located elsewhere in the library, or are otherwise unobtainable at the moment they are requested. Thus it must be further assumed that these additional call cards, representing incompleted transactions, had also been checked as to catalog source of call number in conformity with the pattern described herein.

Preparation of Sample

From the day the IBM charging system began operation on August 1, 1948, all call cards withdrawn from the files in the process of discharging returned books were delivered to the desk of the writer. This routing was firmly established by the time the first run of specially imprinted cards was placed in use on October 12, 1948. It was necessary only to segregate the call cards relevant to the study from this daily accumulation of cards for discharged books. All cards bearing the specially imprinted boxes were so segregated, and then sorted (each day) into four groups according to the checking on the card. Whenever the percentage of cards which were not checked at all tended to rise above the minimum 10 percent, loan-desk personnel responsible for nonchecked cards were again asked to be more careful.

Samples were drawn from this backlog of call cards for the arbitrarily selected weeks shown in table 1 by taking out all cards which had been checked "East Catalog" (author) or "West Catalog" (subject). Each of these groups was again sorted to separate the charges for monographs from those for serials. The classification number on each card was then

Author Catalog	Correlation	Subject Catalog	Correlation
Sample 3	Positive .9674	Sample 2	Positive .9714
Sample 6	Positive .9668	Sample 5	Positive .9588
Sample 9	Positive .9560	Sample 8	Positive .9842

punched into the card on an IBM 031 Duplicating Punch which is so constructed that the call number can be read from each card while the punching is being done. Following this the cards were arranged in order by classification on an IBM 080 Sorter. This step was necessary in order to facilitate checking each sample with the library shelflist in order to add this information to each card: (1) imprint date of book; (2) language in which book was written; and (3) whether book had been cataloged on an LC (Library of Congress) or CU (University of California Library) card. At this point the language and date were punched into the cards on the 031.

The cards were then hand-sorted according to whether the books they represented had been cataloged on LC or CU cards; each of these groups was hand-sorted again by status of borrower. These two items of information were then gang-punched into the cards on the IBM 513 Reproducer. The cards were than ready for mechanical sorting on the 080 to produce the data forming the next four sections of the study.

THE BORROWERS

Before reporting the library borrowers' respective use of the author and subject catalogs, it is well to record the more general finding that use of the two catalogs by all borrowers for locating call numbers was almost evenly divided. Subject-catalog use was represented by 50.8 percent of all call cards in the sample; author-catalog use by 49.2 percent of all cards.

Detailed analysis of subject-catalog-derived (SCD) and author-catalog-derived (ACD) loans

according to the university status of the borrowers is shown in Table 2. The number of undergraduates shown in column 1 has been reduced by 227, the number of the student library staff, for virtually all of the latter are undergraduates. The number of faculty shown has been reduced by 433, the number of teaching assistants. Special borrowers are individuals, not members of the university community, who pay $6.00 a year for the privilege of borrowing books from the university library.

It is seen at once that the several classes of borrowers use the two catalogs very nearly in direct relation to their numbers (rank-difference correlation between column 2 and each of columns 3, 4, and 5 is a positive 0.8710). Undergraduates, student library staff, and library staff are shown to use the subject catalog more than they use the author catalog, while the converse is true for graduates, faculty, special borrowers and teaching assistants. Of the seven classes of borrowers, only the graduates, faculty, and teaching assistants use the subject catalog less than their numbers warrant, and of these, only the faculty use it significantly less.

PUBLICATION DATE

Because a large university library acquires many books many years after they are published, it was thought important to record and tabulate the publication date of the 25,010 books represented by the sample. If it were found that the subject catalog was used only in the location of comparatively recent books, then it might be possible to make an administrative decision that is uneconomical to give

TABLE 2
Status of Borrowers: Percent of Subject-Catalog-Derived, Author-Catalog Derived, and
Total Loans Related to University Population

| BORROWERS | AVERAGE UNIVERSITY POPULATION | | SCD LOANS (12,705), PERCENT | ACD LOANS (12,305), PERCENT | ALL LOANS (25,010), PERCENT |
	NUMBER	PERCENT			
	(1)	(2)	(3)	(4)	(5)
Undergraduates	17,929	70.8	72.8	63.7	68.3
Graduates	4,620	18.3	16.2	21.0	18.7
Faculty	1,196	4.7	2.1	3.4	2.7
Special borrowers	708	2.8	3.6	4.9	4.3
Teaching assistants	433	1.7	1.5	4.4	2.9
Student library staff	227	0.9	0.9	0.6	0.7
Library staff	206	0.8	1.4	1.0	1.2
Status not shown	—	—	1.5	1.0	1.2
TOTAL	25,319	100.0	100.0	100.0	100.0

subject treatment to all books acquired more than x years after they were published. If books loaned with the help of the subject catalog were found to be less than ten years old, for example, considerable savings might result from eliminating subject cataloging on all books more than ten years old at the time of acquisition.

This distribution of the sample by date, reduced to percentages for ease of reading is shown in table 3. Column 2 shows the percentage of the 12,705 subject-catalog-derived loans whose publication dates fall within the several periods shown in column 1. These percentages are cumulated in column 3, where it is possible to read, for example, that books published within the last 20 years (since 1929) represented 49.6 percent of all subject-catalog-derived loans. Similar analyses for the author-catalog-derived loans are shown in columns 4 and 5, and for both catalogs together in columns 5 and 6. It can be seen at once that there is comparatively little difference in the distribution of publication dates between loans derived from the two catalogs. Books withdrawn with the aid of the author catalog tend to be somewhat older than those deriving from the subject catalog, but the difference is not considered significant.

The University of California Library is a regular contributor to the union catalog in the State Library in Sacramento. One main entry card for each book cataloged is made for this purpose and kept in Berkeley pending more or less regular quarterly shipments to Sacramento. In the summer of 1948 it was possible to tabulate the publication dates of such a three-month accumulation of main entry cards representing very nearly all of the books cataloged between April 21 and July 15, 1948. The results of that tabulation are shown in table 4, where it is seen (column 6) that books less than twenty-one years old represent 71 percent of current cataloging.

If it is assumed that the distribution in table 4 has been approximately the same in the past, and will continue so in the future, it is possible to postulate a policy of applying subject cataloging only to books less than twenty-one years old which would decrease the present coverage of subject display by 15 percent. It was shown in table 3 that 49.6 percent of the books loaned with the aid of the subject catalog had been published with-

TABLE 3

Publication Date: Percent and Cumulative Percent of Subject-Catalog and Author-Catalog Loans
Related to Publication Date of Books Loaned

PUBLICATION DATE	SUBJECT CATALOG		AUTHOR CATALOG		BOTH CATALOGS	
	PERCENT	CUMULATIVE PERCENT	PERCENT	CUMULATIVE PERCENT	PERCENT	CUMULATIVE PERCENT
(1)	(2)	(3)	(4)	(5)	(6)	(7)
1940+	22.8	22.8	20.0	20.0	21.4	21.4
1930-1939	26.8	49.6	23.4	43.4	25.2	46.6
1920-1929	17.6	67.2	19.4	62.8	18.5	65.1
1910-1919	11.5	78.7	11.0	73.8	11.3	76.4
1900-1909	8.0	86.7	9.0	82.8	8.4	84.8
1800-1899	12.2	98.9	15.2	98.0	13.7	98.5
-1799	1.1	100.0	2.0	100.0	1.5	100.0

TABLE 4

Age and Publication Dates of Books Cataloged Between April 21 and July 15, 1948

AGE IN YEARS	PUBLICATION DATES	NUMBER	PERCENT OF TOTAL	CUMULATION	
				NUMBER	PERCENT
(1)	(2)	(3)	(4)	(5)	(6)
1-5	1944-1948	2,537	45	2,537	45
6-10	1939-1943	871	15	3,408	60
11-20	1929-1938	608	11	4,016	71
21-49	1900-1928	818	15	4,834	86
50-149	1800-1899	653	12	5,487	98
150-449	1500-1799	142	2	5,629	100

in the last twenty years. By corollary, 50.4 percent of these loans had been published more than twenty years ago. But 71 percent of these would have had the benefit of subject cataloging, since they would have come into the library within their first twenty years of life, leaving only 15 percent without representation in the subject catalog. These 15 percent, from the beginning of such a postulated policy, would not be found by users of the subject catalog. Such a policy would cause a reduction of 29 percent in the amount of subject cataloging.

SUBJECT DISTRIBUTION

One of the objectives of the subject-catalog inquiry was to discover whether the subject-catalog-derived use of books in the several major subdivisions of the Library of Congress and Rowell classifications corresponded in any way with a similar subject distribution of current cataloging. If it could be shown that much cataloging was being done in certain subject fields which the users of the library did not approach through the subject catalog, it might be possible to decide that subject cataloging in those fields could be curtailed without seriously hampering the usefulness of the catalog.

It was possible to study the subject distribution of current cataloging by analyzing the circulating shelflist for a nine-week period during October and November, 1948. The circulating shelflist is an accumulation of each week's output of shelflist cards which is circulated among key staff members before the cards are filed. Nine such accumulations, a total of 5,403 cards, were tabulated during the test period. Their distribution by subject in percentages, is shown in column 2 of table 5.

Comparison may be made with the subject distribution of subject-catalog-derived loans in column 3. While it is true that the two columns roughly approximate each other (rank-difference correlation is positive .7571), certain major differences are immediately apparent. The only subject, however, which shows a sharp enough difference between books cataloged and books used to raise serious question about the need for subject cataloging is LC class P, Language and Literature, which normally calls for a comparatively small amount of subject cataloging.

Comparison may also be made between subject distributions of subject-catalog-derived books and author-catalog-derived books (shown in column 4). These distributions are remarkably similar, as

TABLE 5

Distribution by Subject: Subject-Catalog-Derived Loans and Author-Catalog-Derived Loans Related to Catalog-Department Output During October and November, 1948, Expressed in Percentages

SUBJECT		BOOKS CATALOGED (5,403)	SCD LOANS (12,705)	ACD LOANS (12,305)
	(1)	(2)	(3)	(4)
A	General	1.2	0.1	0.2
B	Philosophy-Religion	5.2	7.7	7.1
C	Philosophy-History	0.9	0.8	0.6
D	History	18.0	9.8	9.1
E	American history	1.6	2.8	5.0
F	U.S. history	3.3	4.4	3.5
G	Geography-Anthropology	2.1	4.2	2.1
H	Social science	13.5	18.4	11.4
J	Political science	5.1	4.7	3.8
L	Education	1.9	3.9	2.0
M	Music	5.1	2.2	3.2
N	Fine arts	3.6	3.9	1.6
P	Language-Literature	16.8	1.2	2.1
Q	Science	3.5	6.2	3.2
S	Agriculture	3.4	1.7	1.0
T	Technology	2.9	5.4	2.2
U	Military science	0.0	0.5	0.2
V	Naval science	0.0	0.2	0.1
Z	Bibliography	1.4	0.7	0.2
200	California biography-Law	0.0	0.1	0.1
300	California theses	1.4	5.4	2.4
600	Philology	0.0	0.2	0.2
700	Languages	0.0	1.5	5.1
800	Literature	3.2	2.2	6.6
900	English literature	5.9	11.8	27.0

TABLE 6

Language Distribution: Relation Between Subject-Catalog-Derived Loans
and Author-Catalog-Derived Loans, Expressed in Percentages

LANGUAGE	SCD LOANS (12,705)	ACD LOANS (12,305)	ALL LOANS (25,010)
(1)	(2)	(3)	(4)
French	2.0	3.8	2.9
German	1.9	3.5	2.7
Spanish	1.4	2.9	2.1
Russian	0.34	0.64	0.49
Italian	0.32	0.45	0.38
Other	0.24	0.41	0.33
All foreign	6.20	11.70	8.90
English	93.80	88.30	91.10

is revealed by the rank-difference correlation of a positive 0.8163. Subject for subject, approximately the same number of books are located with the help of the author catalog as are located with the help of the subject catalog.

LANGUAGE

The full sample of 25,010 call cards was also distributed by the language in which the books were written. This distribution is shown in table 6, where it can be immediately seen that books in foreign languages are approached by author very nearly twice as often as they are approached by subject. Total foreign-language loans account for less than 10 percent of the circulation, and loans derived from the subject catalog account for only 6.2 percent of all subject-catalog-derived loans. Thus, if one wishes to postulate the elimination of all subject cataloging of foreign materials, one can then conclude that the efficiency of the subject catalog would be impaired by only 6.2 percent. Such curtailment would, however, result in a 50 percent saving in subject cataloging, since one-half of all titles cataloged by the University of California Library are in foreign languages.

SUMMARY AND CONCLUSIONS

It was revealed (table 3) that the use of books progressively diminishes as they become older, and that somewhat more recent books are chosen from the subject catalog than are located in the author catalog. When a convenient age limit of twenty years is set, it is found that 49.6 percent of all loans through the subject catalog are not more than twenty years old. It was shown further (table 4) that 71 percent of books currently being cataloged are not more than twenty years old. When

these two facts are related it is possible to anticipate a reduction of 29 percent in the amount of subject cataloging by postulating a policy of providing subject display only for books less than twenty-one years old. Such a policy would, over a period of years, result in a reduction in subject coverage of only 15 percent based on books loaned through use of the subject catalog. That is, users of the library would borrow 15 percent fewer books through use of the subject catalog than they do now.

The subject distribution of books loaned through the subject catalog (table 5) revealed no major subject areas in which curtailed subject cataloging could be instituted. While it is true that more detailed subject analysis might reveal certain specific subjects to which (1) much current cataloging is being done, and (2) which are seldom or never approached through the subject catalog, the professional task of selecting those books *before* cataloging would more than offset any savings made by eliminating subject display.

The major discrepancy between books cataloged and books loaned was discovered among foreign language material. Although 50 percent of all titles currently being cataloged are in foreign languages, only 6.2 percent of all books loaned through the subject catalog were written in foreign languages (table 6). Thus the subject-cataloging load could be reduced by 50 percent while reducing the efficiency of the subject catalog by only 6.2 percent, on a purely quantitative basis.

To this 50 percent reduction in subject-cataloging load on foreign material it is possible to add a 29 percent reduction of the remaining half of books in English if subject cataloging is eliminated for books more than twenty years old, resulting in a total reduction in subject-cataloging load of 64.5 percent. Concomitant reduction in the amount of subject display affected by use of the subject catalog would be 21.2 percent. Phrased differently, and in rounder numbers, if subject cataloging were to be dropped for all foreign books and for all English books more than twenty years old, subject-cataloging load would be reduced immediately by 65 percent. The efficiency of the subject catalog in terms of books circulated with its help would progressively decline to a level not lower than 80 percent of its present effectiveness.

APPENDIX

No-Catalog-Derived Cards

The following tentative analyses were made of the call cards which were checked "No Catalog" by the borrower. All figures for samples 1 and 3 only, and give a provisional indication of the ways in which direct use of the library stacks differs from use made through the author-title and subject catalogs. Abbreviations SCD (Subject-Catalog-Derived), ACD (Author-Catalog-Derived), and NCD (No-Catalog-Derived) are used throughout the following tables.

TABLE A

Relation of Monographs to Serials Among Loans Derived from the Subject Catalog, Author Catalog and No Catalog

LOANS	SCD	ACD	NCD	TOTAL
Monographs	2,715	737	460	3,912
Serials	617	766	906	2,289
TOTAL	3,332	1,503	1,366	6,201
Percent serials	18.5	50.9	66.4	37.1

TABLE B

Status of Borrowers: Percentage of SCD, ACD, and NCD Loans Related to University Population

BORROWERS	AVERAGE UNIVERSITY POPULATION NUMBER	AVERAGE UNIVERSITY POPULATION PERCENT	SCD LOANS (PERCENT)	ACD LOANS (PERCENT)	NCD LOANS (PERCENT)
Undergraduates	17,929	70.8	79.0	80.1	17.6
Graduates	4,620	18.3	12.8	11.6	46.3
Faculty	1,196	4.7	0.7	1.2	10.1
Special borrowers	708	2.8	3.7	2.8	4.6
Teaching assistants	433	1.7	0.5	2.3	5.2
Student library staff	227	0.9	0.5	0.1	6.7
Library staff	206	0.8	20.8	0.5	6.7
Status not shown	—	—	2.0	1.4	2.8
TOTAL	25,319	100.0	100.0	100.0	100.0

TABLE C

Cumulative Percentages of SCD, ACD, and NCD Loans Related to Publication Date of Books Loaned

PUBLICATION DATE	SCD	ACD	NCD
1940-	21.3	18.5	24.6
1930-1939	46.2	44.9	47.6
1920-1929	64.9	64.4	66.5
1910-1919	77.0	76.7	79.3
1900-1909	85.2	84.9	89.5
1800-1899	99.1	99.1	99.7
-1799	100.0	100.0	100.0

TABLE D

Distribution of SCD, ACD, and NCD Loans by Broad Library of
Congress and Rowell Classification, Expressed in Percentages

CLASSIFICATION		SCD	ACD	NCD
A	General	0.2	0.0	0.2
B	Philosophy-Religion	8.6	6.4	8.0
C	Philosophy-History	1.1	1.3	0.9
D	History	6.8	8.3	8.3
E	American history	3.0	5.4	2.6
F	U.S. history	5.3	2.9	5.2
G	Geography-Anthropology	4.0	1.1	1.1
H	Social science	18.4	13.6	6.7
J	Political science	3.5	4.4	2.0
L	Education	5.1	1.9	2.0
M	Music	3.2	2.2	2.8
N	Fine arts	4.0	1.2	1.7
P	Language-Literature	0.9	1.4	2.4
Q	Science	6.5	4.0	3.0
S	Agriculture	1.7	0.4	0.2
T	Technology	4.7	1.5	1.1
U	Military science	0.7	0.3	0.4
V	Naval science	0.2	0.0	0.0
Z	Bibliography	0.4	0.0	1.1
X-8	Current books*	0.0	0.9	7.5
200	California biography-Law	0.0	0.1	0.0
300	California theses	7.9	4.0	2.4
600	Philology	0.0	0.0	0.2
700	Languages	1.2	4.2	3.3
800	Literature	1.7	5.5	8.0
900	English literature	10.9	30.8	28.9

*New, uncataloged books so segregated for a brief period.

TABLE E

Language Distribution: Relation Between SCD, ACD, and NCD Loans, Expressed in Percentages

LANGUAGE	SCD	ACD	NCD
French	2.3	1.9	4.6
German	2.6	3.9	5.3
Spanish	2.0	2.4	1.4
Russian	0.1	0.4	2.3
Italian	0.6	1.1	0.3
All foreign	7.5	9.7	13.9
English	92.5	90.3	86.1

FOOTNOTES

[1] R. C. Swank, "Subject Catalogs, Classifications, or Bibliographies? A Review of Critical Discussion, 1876-1942," *Library Quarterly,* XIV (1944), 316-332.

[2] R. C. Swank, "The Organization of Library Materials in English Literature," *Library Quarterly,* XV (1945), 49-74.

[3] W. C. Simonton, *Duplication of Entries in the Subject Catalog of a University Library and in Subject Bibliographies in English Literature.* Unpublished Master's dissertation, Columbia University, 1948.

[4] Margaret C. Brown, "The Graduate Student's Use of the Subject Catalog," *College and Research Libraries,* VIII (1947), 203-208, 217.

[5] Rutherford D. Rogers, "Subject Bibliography Versus Subject Catalog and Periodical Index," *College and Research Libraries,* XI (1950), 211-214.

[6] University of California, General Library, *Catalog Inquiry Memo No. 3,* January 20, 1949.

[7] Adapted from *Catalog Inquiry Memo No. 1,* January 3, 1949.

[8] Amy F. Wood, "California Divides Its Catalog," *Library Journal,* LXIII (1938), 723-726.

[9] *Daily Californian,* March 10, 1949, p. 5.

ABOUT THE AUTHOR

—**LeRoy Charles Merritt,** Dean, School of Librarianship, University of Oregon; Ph.D., 1942, University of Chicago. His major interests are book selection, censorship, and intellectual freedom.

VII
THE ACADEMIC LIBRARY TOMORROW

The degree of concern of those involved with the information process is undergoing dramatic change as they continue to be subject to growing societal and technological tensions. There is less certainty in higher education and librarianship that the function traditionally assigned to the library can be best performed by the mode now institutionalized. Academic librarians have begun to sense the need for new attitudes and new potentials; and the need to reject historical accretions and evolve a more appropriate model. If radical change is to take place in the library the total institution must understand and accept the risks in terms of commitment of resources and time. The components of the institution and especially the librarian must also be cognizant of the risks in not affecting change. New models, however, to be capable of viability, must be found in continuous analysis of the information process, in hypothesis and experimentation, rather than in organizational modification. This will require that academic librarianship bring to this process contributions from the pure, applied, and social sciences, and that the research and experience from these areas be focused on the information process.

Computers, Cooperation, and the Library's Work

Harvard University Library

If the computer and rapid technological change are expected to make fundamental changes in the behavior of the academic library, this look into the future by responsible librarians does not indicate it. For the academic librarian, the implications of technology continue to suggest only modifications of the same overall response. As a supportive agency faced with major operating obligations and resource limitations the academic library must, of necessity, live in a meantime condition, modifying rather than innovating, all the while doing what historically has become expected.

In thinking about the future of the Library, we have necessarily had to give careful attention to the effect of computers and other technical innovations on the performance of various library functions. There are some who assert that computers and new techniques of electronic transmission of texts will shortly render existing libraries obsolete or at least enable them to reduce the extent of their holdings. As William S. Dix, the Princeton Librarian, recently wrote in his 1965 annual report, "It is easy to envision the world's store of books reduced to a quite small bulk by micro-reduction, controlled by a computer-stored catalogue which will give instant access to whatever is wanted by a scholar through a much greater depth of subject analysis than is now available, transmitting to him instantly from the central store either an image of the printed text on a screen or a full-sized paper copy." But as Dix and others have pointed out, the problems of constructing and installing such a system have still to be resolved, and the costs at this stage appear prohibitive unless very heavy government subsidies are made available. The best advice that we have been able to obtain makes it appear thoroughly unrealistic to expect that electronic transmission of texts will become so inexpensive during the next decade that we shall be able to draw instantly upon the resources of distant libraries and thus significantly curtail our expenditures for books. In planning the development of the library, the only reasonable assumption at present appears to be that nothing will replace books and journals during the next ten years as the backbone of research collections, though books and journals will undoubtedly be supplemented by an ever-increasing number of tapes, microreproductions, and other materials for research.

When it comes to technological innovation and cooperative projects that may vitally affect cataloguing and other library operations and services, we can be more sanguine, and the problem, in any attempt at ten-year forecasts, is to draw a line between reasonable expectations and those hopes that probably will have to wait more than a decade for their fulfillment. It seems desirable to examine the major divisions of the Library's work and to consider what important changes in each can be anticipated within ten years.

Selection, it is evident, must become more rigorous rather than less so as the output of printed books increases, as the scope of collecting is extended, and as it becomes necessary to consider more and more "non-book" material. Recent meetings with the Faculty have confirmed our belief that a good job is being done in subjects for which the Library has selection specialists on its staff, but that additional specialists are needed. Neither cooperative efforts nor machines can be ex-

SOURCE: Reprinted from Harvard University Library, *The Harvard University Library, 1966-1976; Report of a Planning Study Submitted to the President of the University by the Director of the University Library and the University Librarian* (Cambridge: 1966), Chapter 2, "Computers, Cooperation and the Library's Work," pp. 11-16, by permission of the authors.

pected to take over the work of selecting what is added to our collections or what is removed, but machine products, such as the published Widener shelflists that have already begun to appear, promise to be useful tools for the selector.

The acquisition of ephemera and of publications of under-developed countries is much more difficult than the acquisition of books and journals issued by publishers in countries with a well-organized book trade and good current bibliographies. Cooperation with other libraries will help, and it can be hoped that the federal Public Law 480 program, which now brings us current publications of Israel and the United Arab Republic, will be extended. Still, it must be expected that ten years hence Harvard will still have much to do for itself; a vigorous exchange program will still be needed, as well as occasional buying expeditions by members of the staff and assistance from members of the Faculties who travel abroad.

In the area of order records, serial receipts and claims, payment of bills, and handling of accounts, the computer ought to make substantial contributions before the end of the decade. Services can be improved if mechanization makes these processes quicker and more effective, and some increase in the productivity of clerical personnel can also be anticipated.

Cataloguing accounts for a larger segment of the staff than any other function and here, fortunately, the prospects seem brightest for a major break-through within ten years. With the mechanization and publication of portions of the Widener shelflist, the computer has made its first tangible contributions to cataloguing in Harvard's central collections; these are useful to scholars as well as to members of the staff engaged in selection, classification, weeding, and maintenance of the stacks, and they have provided valuable experience in the mechanical manipulation of bibliographical data. It should be recognized, however, that this has been a means of improving the shelflist and various library services deriving from it, rather than a means of reducing costs of shelflisting.

Better tools will be provided for Harvard cataloguers by mechanization projects here, but it appears that hopes for major reductions in the costs of cataloguing depend upon the use of computers in a cooperative or centralized cataloguing system. The Library of Congress has been printing catalogue cards since the beginning of the century, and there have been a number of cooperative cataloguing projects. For public libraries, chiefly concerned with current American publications, the benefits have been substantial, but much less has been done for foreign publications, and most foreign-language cataloguing that is done by the Library of Congress becomes available too tardily to be useful to Harvard. Now, at last, funds are being provided to enable the Library of Congress to expand and speed up its foreign acquisitions, and it is about to start the experimental distribution, to Harvard and a few other major libraries, of catalogue information in machine-readable form.

We are eager to do all we can to push forward with this, but the pace of development obviously depends on Congressional legislation and appropriations as well as on the Library of Congress and other institutions. Indeed, it would be unwise to develop automated cataloguing procedures here that might prove to be incompatible with those that will be adopted nationally and, ultimately, internationally.

We depend very largely on other organizations for the indexing and abstracting of serial publications; the prospect is that we soon may be able to depend on a national center for cataloguing many of our books, and that mechanization will enable this center to provide subject analysis in greater depth and to analyze parts of books to a considerably greater extent than individual libraries have been able to do. If we contribute cataloguing data to a national pool, we may expect to be cataloguing fewer books ourselves but to be dealing with more specialized materials and providing more information on their content than is now practicable. In the long run, the gains for scholarship resulting from improved bibliographical control may well be more significant than savings in costs of cataloguing.

The first major benefits of bibliographical mechanization seem likely to come in medicine, where the National Library of Medicine is providing strong leadership, and in some of the other sciences. In the social sciences and humanities, scholars working on contemporary problems will probably be the first to benefit; data on new publications will be fed into computers before libraries go back and attempt to deal with vast retrospective collections.

While the next decade cannot be expected to bring mechanical analysis or storage of the texts of books on a practicable scale, it ought to bring great advances in the storage and manipulation of bibliographical data. Mechanization of the National Union Catalog is a major objective. Reference librarians obviously will need to be familiar with the capabilities of available machines and skilled in communicating with them; already members of the Countway staff are going to Washington for training in retrieval of information from the computer tapes that will be supplied by the National Library of Medicine when Countway becomes a regional search center of the Medical Literature Analysis and Retrieval System (MEDLARS).

The coming decade will not produce a bibliographical utopia; it will not transform the Library's services unrecognizably, but it will bring solid improvements. The punched-card circulation system that has operated successfully in Widener since 1963 will be further perfected and similar systems will probably have been installed in several other major units of the Library. Card catalogues will not yet for the most part have been replaced by computer memories and console displays, but they will be supplemented by an increasing number of computer products, including accessions lists and shelflist printouts produced at Harvard as well as national bibli-

ographical services for many subjects. More information will be available and instantly available on holdings throughout the Harvard system as well as on holdings of other research libraries throughout the country. It should be possible to supply "made to order" bibliographies of recent publications at least in some subjects. Instant copying machines will no doubt continue to proliferate, and it should be cheaper and even more convenient than at present to obtain copies of journal articles and parts of books.

Many of these developments will benefit new and relatively weak libraries even more than they benefit Harvard. If ours is still to be a better library than any other for many scholars, it must maintain both the quality and the accessibility of its collections. This will not be easy as more and more books become too rare or fragile to remain in the stacks and as more and more of the total content is made up of films, archival collections, tapes, and other records that cannot be shelved in stacks where the scholar works and browses. Neither will it be easy to maintain a balance between a degree of decentralization that promotes accessibility and a fragmentation of collections that will cripple interdisciplinary research. Technology can help to make the library a finer instrument of scholarship than it has ever been, but it would be disastrous to let bright prospects in this direction blind us to the need for continued building of the collections, recruitment of a strong staff, and provision of adequate space.

ABOUT THE AUTHORS

—**Merle Fainsod,** Carl H. Pforzheimer University Professor and Director of the Harvard University Library; Ph.D., 1932, Harvard University. Currently his research is on the relationship between the United States and Russia. His major research interests lie in the study of Soviet government and politics.

—**Douglas W. Bryant,** University Librarian, Harvard University; A.M.L.S., 1938, University of Michigan. His major research interest is in university library administration.

Document vs. Digital Storage of Textual Materials for Network Operations

EDUCOM

Regardless of current and future technological applications discussed in this report, the continuity of a library function is manifest. The instincts are the same; only the terminology is new. Also new is the growing involvement of non-librarians in the dialogue, reflecting the diversity of higher education's information requirements and the growing number of scientific and technical agencies that are concerned with the development of information sources. These other disciplines are now affecting, and will have considerably more effect on, the conventions of the academic library, operationally and organizationally.

On the morning of October 31, the Council heard a report of an all-day invitational conference which had been held on October 30, financed by RCA and chaired by Professor Allen Kent, Director of the Knowledge Availability Systems Center at the University of Pittsburgh. In addition to Professor Kent, the members of the panel presenting the results of the conference to the Council were Dr. James G. Miller, Vice President for Academic Affairs, Cleveland State University, and Vice President and Principal Scientist of EDUCOM; Mr. William Lonergan, Vice President, Radio Corporation of America; Miss Mary Stevens, National Bureau of Standards, who also reported the contributions of Dr. Gerald Salton, Professor of Computer Science at Cornell University and Mr. John Markus of the McGraw-Hill Publishing Company; Mr. John Simonds of Eastman Kodak Company; Mr. Thomas Paterson, Manager, Corporate Planning Program, Radio Corporation of America; and Mr. Samuel Alexander, Chief, Information Technology, National Bureau of Standards.

Dr. Miller began his presentation with the assertion that digital storage is almost basic to any kind of network operation. He suggested that we should begin to stress the importance of access to *ideas* in documents rather than to the documents themselves. Such a point of view would favor digital storage, permitting manipulation of text, over document storage.

Libraries should have available materials in digital as well as in book form. The ideal mix, however, is yet to be decided. Over the long run, the saving on buildings and books for each institution might be greater than the cost of storing the information in one or more computers accessible to scholars and institutions throughout the country. Copyright problems remain to be solved. And it is unlikely that an operating information network would not have additional costs for securing rights either to input or output copyrighted material. Dr. Miller does not believe those problems are irresolvable, however.

Dr. Miller concluded that we have the technology; cost is the problem, especially for inputs. In summary, he raised three central questions:

1) Is it necessary for all institutions to have access to the same resources?

His conclusion was that it is necessary because the small college could therefore spend a large part of its library budget on the costs of accessing the system instead of on its library and, as a result, could enjoy the advantage of an excellent library service and attract better scholars to its faculty.

2) Why not capture information at its source? Could we not begin with new information that is generated now and have it digitalized for storage while it is being published?

SOURCE: Reprinted from "Document vs Digital Storage of Textual Materials for Network Operations," *EDUCOM* 2: 1-5 (December, 1967), by permission of the publisher.

This might be excellent for a few areas, science for example, because the body of knowledge is primarily current. This approach would not be as useful for such disciplines as law and history, which are heavily dependent on the past.

3) What should be done to solve the problem of digitalizing Greek letters and mathematical symbols, for example, if we hope to take advantage of the speed and accuracy of input afforded by optical character readers?

The problem cannot be solved immediately, but it is still possible to take advantage of the optical character reader (OCR) by using multifont print readers and inserting exceptions by hand.

Mr. Lonergan discussed the concept of a library as a system. He suggested that the index, which would be comparable to the card catalog in the traditional library, should be available on all of the college campuses hooked into the net. The scholar would enter the system through the index. Finding titles of interest to him, he would ask for an abstract to be displayed. The abstract file would probably be digital, and would be directed to him through the computer over some common carrier to a display system at his location. He would then decide from the abstracts which document he wished to examine and would possibly then be shown the table of contents, select the chapter, and have the pages of interest displayed—probably on a television receiver.

The document file can be digital or not; Mr. Lonergan felt that it probably should not be. He commented that although all of the hardware for these systems is on the market or near realization, all of it, both present and soon to come, is very expensive.

He recommended that an ideal EDUNET index would list everything in every library in the system. This would probably mean a listing of indexes to about a billion documents. Ideally, every school should have the total index. At every terminal there should be provision for the production of hard copy if it is desired. Obviously, it is highly unlikely that a scholar would want a hard copy of an entire book, but he might want several pages of hard copy and provision should be made to produce them.

The major area of discussion of the conference had been the state in which documents should be stored—as images or digitally. The arguments for pictorial or image storage are, of course, that more kinds of information can be stored; there are many references, for example to chemical apparatus, that would be difficult to store digitally. On the other hand, the information which can be digitally stored can be manipulated by the computer and is, in some cases, more valuable in that form to the user.

Although the ability to reduce size of documents has greatly improved the possibilities for image storage, it would still involve a rather heavy cost. There are systems on the market which can reduce the material sufficiently so that about 10,000 pictorial documents can be shown on a 6 x 4-inch card at reasonable cost. However, a library with a million books would consist of about 300 million pages. The cost, at the moment, than seems prohibitive. The largest unknowns in the library equation are the needs of the users. Although his presentation had attempted to hypothesize an automated library system, Mr. Lonergan said that the essential first step was to learn the problems of the users. Only after these problems are understood with some precision could specialists attempt to work out a system which would take into consideration such problems as queuing and selecting the proper trade-offs. The ultimate form of all parts of the system should be related to the users' needs, the traffic in the system, the method by which it was to be entered, and the form in which the final product was desired.

It was suggested that the determination of user needs nationwide might be a task which EDUCOM is particularly well suited to undertake. Only after these kinds of information are available could any long distance general transmission system of library information be designed.

Miss Mary Stevens, in her presentation, suggested that one of the significant purposes to be served by digital storage is accessibility. That direct accessibility is to people, to machines, and to communications links. Digitally stored material would permit on-line editing and rewriting of the original manuscript.

The second important purpose to be served

by digital storage is manipulability. Material can be reformatted; it can be reorganized—e.g., material in low demand can be transferred to slow access devices, material much in demand can be moved into rapid access devices. Digital storage allows the production of transcriptions and transliterations and permits convertibility with respect to multiple modes of input, output, and transmission. Included in these characteristics are the advantages for automatic analysis. These include computational linguistic studies, concordance making, and word frequency counts; development of machine-compiled indexes; research on auto-extracting and machine translation; automatic classification and indexing; full text searching; dynamic user-oriented services such as selective dissemination of information (SDI); and the introduction of procognitive systems including problem solving, machine-aided inference, and decision making. Large amounts of machine readable textual materials must be available to permit such research to go forward.

Even if automatic indexing might not be ultimately feasible, there are many valuable by-products including, for example, the ability to reclassify an entire file over a weekend and be ready for human consultation immediately thereafter. The third advantage is recomputability, which makes possible error detection and correction, reconstruction or enhancement of digitized images, and enhancement of information by synomym reduction and homograph resolution. Another advantage in this category is the possibility of encrypting and decoding in transmitting classified information over the system.

The digital storage of information also lends itself to the control of redundancy. It is possible for example, to store only unique words and index to their occurrence; to check duplicates by the use of machine logic to delete the same message appearing more than once in several different forms; to update automatically various materials affected by a revised edition; to achieve minimal redundancy store and minimal paraphrasing.

Miss Stevens then discussed the points of view expressed by Gerald Salton in the previous day's conference. Dr. Salton has designed a storage system with a variety of text processing and search strategy options. He has found that the retrieval effectiveness of even his least sophisticated options seems to be better than that resulting from human analysis.

He has also found that titles alone are not effective for data searches; abstracts are considerably better; but full text provides only slight improvement over abstracts. Dr. Salton does not believe that automatic character recognition is needed because he believes that we are moving toward tape-controlled type setting, which would provide enough machine-readable materials as a by-product.

Reporting for Mr. John Markus, Miss Stevens said that the computer is a valuable tool in proofreading and correction of errors and development of word frequency lists. Computer processing is particularly hopeful for the preparation of some types of directories and dictionaries.

Mr. Markus has concluded that the storage of a book on a shelf in a library costs about 25 cents per year. The storage of a magnetic tape with 18 books on a reel costs about $5.28 per book per year, not including the cost of human handling. On the other hand, there is a space reduction of about 18 to 1, books to magnetic tape. Furthermore, as Miss Stevens pointed out, the cost of 25 cents a year per book in the library must be multiplied by many copies of the same book in many libraries. Therefore, it might seem that even at present costs, magnetic tape would be very little more expensive than traditional library storage.

Mr. John Simonds reported that technology does not have all the answers and that new steps must be taken before the system which Mr. Lonergan had hypothesized could be realized. But, Mr. Simonds continued, many of these technological problems can be solved and will be solved.

Mr. Simonds introduced as one example of the unsolved problems, that of the storage and transmittal of pictorial elements. He noted that an 8 x 10-inch photo would require 10 million bits for transmission if it were in black and white, and 10^9 bits for paper. The average English word can be stored or transmitted with 30 bits. It is possible now to encode graphics in digital fashion, but there is still a large problem in storing and transmitting pictures.

It is estimated that in two to five years devices reading 5,000 characters per second at a cost of .0001 cent per thousand bits will be available. With current technology, however, graphics do not interface well with either computer or transmission technologies.

New techniques—presently only in the research stage—are being studied to allow digital storage and transmission of pictorial images. It is expected that in the next few years special scanners, analog to digital converters, encoders (which will also reduce redundancy), and techniques for storage in photo-digital form will be available, along with computer terminals which reconstitute the picture.

Some devices that should be available in the 70's were described by Mr. Simonds. He expects that the speeds and packing densities of magnetic tape will increase significantly. He also believes that read-only memories with a 10^{11} bit capacity will be available. He sees them as the hope for the future for photo-digital storage. The first ones will probably be slow access. He warned that his predictions may be upset significantly by new technologies, among which would be the development of laser technology in this area.

Mr. Simonds perceives EDUCOM's immediate goal to be one of fostering the development of a network that is evolutionary so it can take advantage of new technology when it comes. He believes that EDUCOM should begin a network of finding keys which, though simple, will be a start; that it should go on from there to define a sub-set of operations that will lead to the day when the complete EDUNET as defined in the summer study will be possible. That day is coming, it has not arrived.

Mr. Thomas Paterson reported that, as a result of the conference, he was convinced that the problem of document vs. digital storage is not the central issue now. He agrees that the existence of a multifont print reader is essential but it is not the basic requirement of a successful communications system. It is his feeling that the goal should be an evolutionary system that does not require reinvestment in either hardware or software due to obsolescence. It should have compatibility, facilitating linkage of computers. The state-of-the-art should be projected at least ten years and expressed in quantitative terms—e.g., cost per page on-line and, perhaps more important, cost per page retrieved. This kind of projection is a task for which industry is eminently suited.

On the other hand, Mr. Paterson feels that the definition of what is desirable is the user's task and that those desirable elements must be defined in terms of specifics. In particular, he mentioned the need to;

1) order priorities,
2) define purposes to be served,
3) clearly delineate objectives.

One of the enormous jobs of an EDUNET is the need, in defining compatibility, to arrive at common standards and preferred practices. This agreement must be reached so that the network can grown in an evolutionary way and bridge the gap between generations of computers and of programs.

Mr. Paterson referred to Mr. Samule Alexander's advice that EDUCOM should begin with a network which would constitute a controlled experiment in a sheltered environment where the alternatives which are possible can be studied. A program, looking ahead at least ten years, that considers both user requirements and supplier capabilities must be designed. The experimental network must be operational and have produced the answers to questions involved in the national net before the larger net should be attempted.

Professor Allen Kent said that it was agreed at the conference that the network was important and needs to be fostered and that library materials or reference to them must be stored in machine readable form. Before a network can be designed, however, a test system must be operated. Before the test system must come the predictive model of the network. Before the predictive model must come a determination of what is practicable to serve present and future library needs in terms of the projected technical state-of-the-art. He said that industry has agreed to prepare a report on what will probably be technically feasible in the next twenty years for libraries or information networks. The EDUCOM universities, or at least a representative group of them, will be asked to determine the size of their libraries, considering not only volumes, but the number of pages, the kinds of material on the pages, the patterns of use, and the nature of the library operation. This latter should include a study not only of the kinds of people from what disciplines use the library, but also their opinions as to what is wrong with the current library function and how it could be improved. Obviously, the study of each library will be based on a reliable sample.

Mr. Kent suggested that the EDUCOM staff should prepare, in about a month, the instrument which can be used by the EDUCOM universities in conducting their part of the study which is needed before industry can do its part. About three months will probably be necessary for each university to produce the kinds of data needed for this basic planning function. The universities were invited to volunteer, if they wished at the meeting—and a number of them did—to participate in this study which should include, according to Mr. Kent, samples representative of a broad sweep of institutions including, for example, public and private, large and small. He said that the study should result in performance objectives, experimental techniques, evaluative techniques, and a predictive model of an EDUNET.

Mr. Samuel Alexander made the point that books are becoming a small part of the resource material of the scholar and that he is often working with material that is temporary. He pointed particularly to the data used by social scientists and economists, e.g., the voluminous census records. He said that he believes these kinds of data might well be mechanized as might encyclopedias of which only small parts are used at one time. Yet, in spite of their low utility, they are important sources of data.

Mr. Alexander noted that for the decade 1946 to 1956 the universities were the shelters in which the computer industry had its foundation. Both business and government found the more sophisticated utilizations of computer technology that universities had developed were valuable tools in their respective fields. Indeed, Mr. Alexander stressed that, at this time, a close partnership of the universities, industry, government, and professional societies is essential in realizing the full potential of a computer network.

He pointed out the critical importance of standards and of conventions for common practice. Although the establishment of standards and conventions may be dull, they are important ingredients for the successful transition from a sheltered environment to a good, serviceable, economical information system. In moving toward that system, every effort must be made to avoid duplication, replication, and competition for scarce resources.

Network Functions

by J. C. R. Licklider, John W. Carr, III, and
Morris Rubinoff

While the economic and research advantages of large scale computerized information networks have been demonstrated in the private sector, academic institutions have limited their exploration of this new and developing technology to their immediate environment. And no matter how technically or economically feasible, multi-institutional systems which do not provide for the social and political realities of academia will have limited success. The creation of an entity, such as EDUCOM, that is part of, and at the same time outside of, the university systems to which it relates provides one organizational possibility. The schematic offered in this section of system predictability, standardization, and implementation—with, at the same time, inhibition but not repression on the part of the component institutions—may well suggest future development.

EDUCOM's roles in the organization and operation of an interinstitutional information network and in the support functions incidental to the network will necessarily entail relationships with the university and with many segments of society outside the university according to the various contexts in which the proposed network may be viewed.

The essential role of the EDUCOM organization and its relationships with other organizations should be largely derivable from the assumption of a central kernel network with certain general properties.

Licklider: July 8th

EDUCOM should think in terms, not of a definite, designed, blueprintable network, but of a network of networks, facilities, organizational interrelations, information resources, human resources, services, and projects. The overall network should have one part that is relatively well planned and defined, a part that can be dealt with readily in a proposal, for example, but also other parts that are not planned or defined in detail but treated in a more general way by setting forth avenues and guidelines for formal and informal interactions involving two or more participating organizations.

EDUCOM cannot construct a useful network simply by trying to meld existing networks. It can, however, foster coherence by developing and operating a central registry or directory of networks and related resources.

A basic concept of function and structure of the kernal network was described.

The initial purpose of the EDUCOM system will be to serve as a metasystem for information interconnection of various universities with one another.

Carr: July 20th

The actions of the EDUCOM system may include the following:

1. Attempts to answer questions about the presence or absence of certain types of information within the files catalogued by the EDUCOM system. Such information might include:
    a. Documents in libraries, actual or on microfilm;
    b. Reviews of documents available in review files (e.g., Chemical Abstracts, Mathematical Reviews);
    c. Names of organizations or personnel with particular capabilities in certain disciplines or combinations of disciplines, developed from the preceding file and others;
    d. Programs in computer center libraries with certifications of their previous performance and information about costs of their usage;
    e. Data banks in computer centers or other automated files with certifications of their previous usage and information about immediate or alternatively batched availability and cost of usage.
2. Actions that might be performed as the result of the above types of questions:
    a. Requests for copies of documents with the request entered automatically into the library interchange system. Appropriate feedback

SOURCE: Reprinted from Summer Study on Information Networks, University of Colorado, 1966, *EDUNET; Report* (New York: John Wiley & Sons, Inc., 1967), Chapter 5, Section 2, "Network Functions," pp. 168-176, by permission of the publisher.

would be generated upon completion of the retrieval and mailing of a copy of a document. (At a later stage in development, a copy could be sent by facsimile to the calling university.)

b. Performance of a computer program remotely at University B upon the request of a person at University A.

c. Automatic planning of audio conference calls (at a later stage video conferences) by the system. Personnel at University A would request a conference suggesting alternative times. The system would then serve as broker to arrive at a commonly agreed upon time and so inform the participants.

d. Immediate on-time, or later, retrieval of information from "open" data-banks available to all users but located in the local automatic systems of the university or consortium members.

e. The development of common automatically linked processing systems for use by geographically distant workers in a common discipline (for example, toxicology, nuclear physics, organic chemistry, clinical medicine, mathematics, engineering) that would allow the creation of growing subsystems of automatic files, automatic algorithms (computer programs), automatic retrieval systems, etc., for that particular subsystem. *The development of the facilities for such geographically distributed disciplinary structures provides one of the real opportunities for the EDUCOM system.*

f. Sending of a video tape or film by University B to University A upon request through the EDUCOM system.

Structure of the EDUCOM system. The nodes of the EDUCOM system would probably be communication centers, with files located at points, most convenient for EDUCOM members in terms of communications cost. These communications centers would contain on-line, real-time digital computers, used as communications switching devices and file searching devices. These would be large data banks, containing catalogs of information held in member files (either automatically accessible or accessible through human intervention).

Software computer systems should be available that would

1. in case of requests for information:
   a. accept on-line messages sent from individual member installations;
   b. search the data bank catalogs for information when requested or pass a request on to an appropriate member for an answer;
   c. return the information, properly screened, to the individual member line.

2. in case of requests for action:
   a. accept on-line messages sent from individual member installations;
   b. route the message to another EDUCOM node for local delivery to the receiver;
   c. set up appropriate feed-back control mechanisms so that if an answer was not received, both the sender and receiver would be "jogged."

In either case, automatic billing and accounting would be performed, with appropriate additions to standard reports.

The difference between a local EDUCOM node and a university computing center should again be emphasized so that questions of status, prestige, and control may be minimized. Since the EDUCOM system will be a service system, the *presence* of a "node" on a particular campus or locale *should not* be a prestige item. The *availability* of the EDUCOM *services,* however, should become a highly important item in the status of a university.

The number and location of EDUCOM nodes, therefore, should be based on technical considerations including:

1. The present and possibly future members,
2. The switching needs of the system,
3. The communications costs of the system,
4. The data bank requirements of the system; plus the consideration of the availability of effective personnel near the node site arrived at in technical considerations. These would be in the neighborhood of large cities or at the universities themselves.

An argument might be made that over the long range, incorporation of EDUCOM facilities with local facilities might be the best method of operation. However, the initial status of proximity to, but not possession by, a university, would appear to be politically more effective. It would also shield the EDUCOM system from local politics within the university itself.

If the EDUCOM system is to transmit the requests and to perform the actions described above, it will require staffs in both the central system planning center and the local centers which have had experience in the development of communications systems. At the same time, such staffs must know and recognize the nature of the American university and what is and is not possible in dealing with the assorted university communities.

There appear to be four distinct types of jobs that the EDUCOM system must carry out:

1. Cataloging the information on file in the various member universities and setting up an automatically retrievable machine-stored file of such information. By "information" is meant: linguistic descriptions of documents, research tools, personnel capabilities, data files, algorithms, teaching tools, etc. It will be the EDUCOM system's task to define and standardize a language and format for cataloging such information and a system for searching such a catalog. It will be the member's responsibility to provide the catalog, in machine readable and searchable form, to the EDUCOM system. Whether these catalogs shall be stored within the local EDUCOM centers or left under university control is a matter of system design. EDUCOM must provide a standardized way of receiving automatically information for updating its own files. The member must provide day-by-day information on changes in its informational structure.

2. Acting as a broker of services between various universities, including transmissions of requests for information, description of films, video tapes, documents, available computer programs, or data banks and for services (transmission by ordinary carrier of document copies or transmission by the EDUCOM system network of symbolic, facsimile, or video copies). The EDUCOM system must therefore also act as a central billing agency for these services from one organization to another. This business function of EDUCOM is important, and will require the presence of persons knowledgable about present university business procedures.

3. Acting as an automated communications system between the various individuals at the universities through

computer consoles, video displays, telephone connections, mail, and express. Therefore, a portion of the EDUCOM effort must be oriented toward construction of standard linguistics and communication structures (in general, languages) that will allow satisfactory interplay between humans, the various catalogs, and the various automatic portions of the system.

It would appear that it should be an EDUCOM responsibility to standardize on-line communications up to the interface with the members, and that the members should have the responsibility of meeting these standards through acceptance of them or through local translators into alternative local systems. Local files within member organizations need not conform to a standard, but the local organization must be able to accept EDUCOM standard queries, and the local files should be able to respond in a fashion functionally equivalent to EDUCOM standards.

4. Acting as a creator of "special-purpose disciplinary systems" with common files, common data banks, and common automatic algorithms that do not at present even exist. In this manner, researchers at various institutions would be able, through the EDUCOM system, to create interdisciplinary automated communications structures, to which EDUCOM would provide the already existing services (computer programs, file structures, languages, and transmission equipment) and at the same time would be able to incorporate completed results into the overall catalog files. The toxicology system for poison control, often described, is one example of such a function.

Special responsibilities of the EDUCOM system. Because of its nature as a repository for information on the nation's research structure, the EDUCOM system would probably be called on to perform certain special functions beyond that of central metasystem "broker" and communicator between the universities.

It could immediately serve as an agency to disseminate the results of research activities. For example:

1. A national toxicological network, in which local EDUCOM operating centers make tie-ins to the network available, could be a significant service.

2. The proposed automatic chemical documentation system might be a second candidate for inclusion in such a network.

3. The review systems of scientific communities, exemplified by *Mathematical Reviews and Computing Reviews,* are now well enough organized (but not yet automatically) so that incorporating them into the EDUCOM system might be a possibility.

4. Certain portions of the catalogs of the Defense Documentation System, now generally in the open domain, should be candidates for inclusion.

The choice of the portions of these systems to be considered as possible integral parts of an EDUCOM network is a complex one that involves economic, technical, and political questions. It would appear, however, that to become a successful undertaking a final EDUCOM system must:

1. Retain independence of the university systems to which it relates and be devoted to the classical aim of the search for knowledge as understood in the universities;

2. Nevertheless, have enough flexibility to cooperate in developments in which the community interest parallels or does not conflict with the classical university interest;

3. Not be the creature of any one group or small clique of universities, or disciplines, or special interests. This means that such a system must not be controlled by or for the computer scientists, the nuclear physicists, the biomedical community, etc., if the full effectiveness of such a system is to be achieved.

Ultimate technical goal. The ultimate goal of the EDUCOM system should be to make available answers to standard types of questions in an abbreviated form and with the shortest possible turn-around time. However, it should be recognized that the capability to do this does not exist at present in any local university information processing systems, and it will not become available without marked further planning. The EDUCOM catalogs and operations themselves should be able to achieve more nearly immediate answers than would any information interchange with the local systems. Therefore, turnaround time will vary with query, complexity, time of day, network use, etc. From the beginning, the response must be markedly better in turn-around time and overall effectiveness than is currently possible. The ultimate goal should be a conversational system with relatively short access to answers. The first systems, therefore, must be planned so that they can be easily modified to provide these later capabilities.

The structure of the network was elaborated further.

Rubinoff: July 23rd

The EDUCOM network is pictured as a central communications core surrounded by two rings of interface and terminal equipment.

At the core of the network is a system of communication channels, called the *communications system,* which serves all participants and provides for information exchange, presumably in a common standard language. Surrounding the communications system are the participating *centers,* both large and small, which interconnect with the communications system through buffer/translator equipment, called *interfaces.* Each interface is electrically connected to the communications system at a *node.* The cooperative use of data and devices at the geographically dispersed centers is the justification for the network. The communications system is simply a means for information interchange, and the interfaces are required to accommodate the many terminal devices (with their multiplicity of electrical, signal, and language characteristics) to the standardized situation of the communications system.

For our immediate purposes, then, EDUNET may be visualized as comprising three rings of equipment:

1. Terminal equipment installed at each participant's location or center. At a small center, this will include one or more remote-access (typewriter and cathode-ray tube) consoles and displays, with perhaps TV equipment for video conferencing as well. At a large center, this will include a substantially larger hardware-software computer complex with time-sharing capabilities.

2. A communications system serving all centers and providing for information interchange among centers; and

3. Interface equipment between the nodes of the communications system and the center's terminal equipment, serving a variety of purposes such as (a) TV modulation/demodulation for TV conferences among geographically dispersed groups, or (b) data buffering, language translation, message editing and formatting, and scheduling of

service (queueing of traffic under prescribed priority rules) for computer processing or data search and exchange. It is quite likely that the interface to a large computer center will itself be a small computer of the DEC-PDP8 or IBM 1130 class.

A basic premise that has been made is that the communications system can and will provide sufficient total channel capability to handle peak traffic loading. It is important to note that the EDUNET configuration is radically different from the conventional (telephone) common carrier, and the economics of the system are also radically different. The economic situation is in fact completely reversed in that the cost of communication is an order of magnitude smaller than the cost of the terminal equipments at the centers. Moreover, these reversed economics will likely hold true for the foreseeable future.

ABOUT THE AUTHORS

—J. C. R. Licklider, Consultant to Director of Research, Thomas J. Watson Research Center, International Business Machine Corporation; Ph.D., 1942, University of Rochester. His interests are in psychology and information research.

—John W. Carr, III, Chairman, Graduate Group on Computer and Information Sciences, University of Pennsylvania; Ph.D., 1951, Massachusetts Institute of Technology. His research interests are in computing machinery logic and programming theory.

—Morris Rubinoff, Professor, Moore School of Electrical Engineering, University of Pennsylvania; Ph.D., 1946, University of Toronto. His current research interests are in electronic circuit design, information retrieval, and computer logic design.